Time Out

Prague Guide

Penguin Books

PENGUIN BOOKS

Published by the Penguin Group
Penguin Books Ltd, 27 Wright's Lane, London W8 5TZ, England
Penguin Books USA Inc., 375 Hudson Street, New York, New York 10014, USA
Penguin Books Australia Ltd, Ringwood, Victoria, Australia
Penguin Books Canada Ltd, 10 Alcorn Avenue, Toronto, Ontario, Canada M4V 3B2
Penguin Books (NZ) Ltd, 182-190 Wairau Road, Auckland 10, New Zealand

Penguin Books Ltd, Registered Offices: Harmondsworth, Middlesex, England

First published 1995
10 9 8 7 6 5 4 3 2 1

Copyright © Time Out Group Ltd, 1995
All rights reserved

Colour reprographics by Argent, 32 Paul Street, London EC2A 4LB
Mono reprographics, printed and bound by William Clowes Ltd, Beccles, Suffolk NR34 9QE

Edited and designed by

Time Out Magazine Limited
Universal House
251 Tottenham Court Road
London W1P OAB
Tel: 0171 813 3000
Fax: 0171 813 6001

Editorial

Managing Editor
Peter Fiennes
Editor
Caroline Taverne
Consultant Editor
Lucy Trench

Design

Art Director
Warren Beeby
Art Editor
John Oakey
Designers
Paul Tansley, Elroy Toney
Ad Make-up
Creative Partners (Prague)
Picture Editor
Fiona Seres

Advertising

**Group Advertisement
Director**
Lesley Gill
Sales Director
Mark Phillips
**Advertisement Sales
(Prague)**
Creative Partners

Administration

Publisher
Tony Elliott
Managing Director
Mike Hardwick
Financial Director
Kevin Ellis
Marketing Director
Gillian Auld
Production Manager
Mark Lamond

Listings information checked by Resources.

Features in this guide were written and researched by:
Introduction Tom Gross. **Essential Information** MB Christie. **Getting Around** MB Christie. **Accommodation** Anna Sutton. **Prague by Season** Carole Cadwalladr. **Sightseeing** Carole Cadwalladr. **History** Paul Lewis. **Prague Today** Tom Gross. **Prague by Area** Carole Cadwalladr. **Restaurants** J Dee Hill. **Cafés, Bars & Pubs** Paul Lewis. **Shopping** Lucy Trench. **Services** MB Christie. **Art & Architecture** Lucy Trench. **Art Galleries** William Lee, Lucy Trench. **Museums** William Lee, Lucy Trench. **Literary Prague** Dana Stiffler. **Media** J Dee Hill. **Nightlife** Paul Lewis. **Film** Victoria Jones. **Music: Classical & Opera** Michael Halstead. **Music: Rock, Roots & Jazz** Gavin Stewart. **Sport & Fitness** Paolo Minoli. **Theatre & Dance** Clare Goddard. **Business** MB Christie. **Children** Lucy Trench. **Gay Prague** Jarmomir Gracka, Malcolm Griffiths. **Students** Anna Sutton. **Women's Prague** Maya Květný. **Trips Out of Town** Carole Cadwalladr, Anna Sutton. **Survival** MB Christie. **Further Reading** Lucy Trench.
The Editors would like to thank the following people for their help: Andrea Cooke, Sarah Guy, Stephen Jolly, Kei Kikuchi, Natalia Marshall, Leila McAlister, Caroline Roux.

Photography by Richard O'Rourke except for: **Kobal Collection** pages 187,188,189; **Hulton Deutsch** page 48, 62, 65, 70, 71, 72, 74, 75; **Rex** 77; **Bridgeman Art Library** page 156.

Contents

About the Guide | vi
Introduction | 1
Essential Information | 3
Getting Around | 10
Accommodation | 17
Prague by Season | 29
Sightseeing | 33

History
Key Events | 58
The Přemyslid Dynasty | 59
The Rise of Huttism | 62
The Habsburg Dynasty | 65
Nationalism & Independence | 69
The Lights Go Out | 72
From Prague Spring to Revolution | 75
Re-awakening | 78
Prague Today | 79

Prague by Area
Hradčany & Prague Castle | 86
Malá Strana | 91
Staré Město & Josefov | 95
Nové Město | 102
Further Afield | 106

Eating & Drinking
Restaurants | 112
Cafés, Bars & Pubs | 125

Shops & Services
Shopping | 134
Services | 146

Galleries & Museums
Art & Architecture | 152
Art Galleries | 158
Museums | 167

Arts & Entertainment
Literary Prague | 174
Media | 176

Nightlife | 180
Film | 187
Music: Classical & Opera | 192
Music: Rock, Folk & Jazz | 197
Sport & Fitness | 202
Theatre & Dance | 207

In Focus
Business | 214
Children | 221
Gay Prague | 225
Students | 228
Women's Prague | 231

Trips Out of Town | 235
Survival | 255

Further Reading | 263
Area Index | 264
Index | 267
Advertiser's Index | 274
Maps | 275

About the Guide

This is the first edition of the *Time Out Prague Guide*, one in series of city guides that includes London, Amsterdam, Paris, New York, Berlin, Madrid and Rome. The guide provides a complete picture of post-revolutionary Prague, from the major monuments and museums to the many new clubs, bars, restaurants and shops that have risen up in its wake. It is much more than a book for tourists and casual visitors. We also point you towards the city's more obscure and eccentric venues and tell you both what to see and what to avoid. Written and researched by people who live in the city, the guide offers an informed, insider's view: Prague as Praguers know it.

We've laboured to make the guide as useful as possible: addresses, telephone numbers, transport details, opening times, admission prices and credit card details have all been included where relevant.

CHECKED & CORRECT

All information was checked and correct at the time of writing, but please bear in mind that, especially in a city such as Prague, making a rapid transition to the free market economy, things are liable to sudden and unpredictable change. This is particularly true of clubs and bars, but also applies to museums and art galleries, a number of which have suddenly disappeared or appeared in a new guise, as collections change hands or are reorganised. Even trams are liable to unexpected alterations, when roadworks disrupt their normal routes. This state of flux is one of the things that makes Prague so exciting, but it is always wise to check opening times, dates of exhibitions, admission prices and other important details, before making a journey across town.

The prices listed throughout this guide should be used as guidelines. Prices, in shops and restaurants especially, tend to change rapidly and you will often find that there is one price for Czech customers and another for foreigners.

ADDRESSES

Prague is divided into ten city districts, arranged seemingly at random on the map. Prague 1, the central district, includes the areas that make up the compact and ancient heart of the city – Hradčany and Prague Castle, the Little Quarter (Malá Straná), the Old Town and the Jewish Quarter (Staré Město and Josefov), and the New Town (Nové Město). Most buildings have two sets of numbers: the one on the blue plaque is the street number and that on the red plaque is the registery number within the city district and can be ignored.

The following terms and abbreviations should be useful when map-reading: *most* **bridge**; *nábřeží (nábř.)* **embankment**; *náměstí (nám.)* **square**; *trh* **market**; *třída* **avenue**; *ulice (ul.)* **street**.

CREDIT CARDS

Compared to the UK or US, credit cards are not at all widely used in Prague. The following abbreviations have been used for credit cards where they are accepted: AmEx – American Express; DC – Diners Club; EC – Eurocard; JCB – Japanese credit cards; MC – Mastercard/Access; V – Visa.

TELEPHONES

The telephone system in Prague, like much else, is in a state of transition. Getting through to a venue – if it has a phone at all – can be difficult, and the chances are the person on the other end won't speak English or understand your halting Czech. Particularly when booking a restaurant, it's often easier to go along in person.

RIGHT TO REPLY

It should be stressed that the information we give is impartial. No organisation has been included in this guide because its owner or manager has advertised in our publications. We trust you will enjoy the *Time Out Prague Guide*, but if you disagree with any of our assessments, let us know. Your comments will help us update our next issue. You'll find a reader's reply card inserted into the book.

Introduction

Prague is a paradox. The past is present all around and for visitors the amount of history that has been preserved in its buildings can be almost overwhelming. But it is also a city where people live very much in the present. For Franz Kafka, as Milan Kundera points out, Prague was 'a city without memory' where 'nobody recalls anything'.

It is precisely because today's Praguers are so embroiled in history that their collective memory seems to have been put to one side. So much has happened so quickly. Who, in fast-moving present-day Prague, remembers that it was only in 1991 that the last Soviet tanks pulled out? Who now remembers the old Marxist street names? Even the memory of Czechoslovakia itself has faded into history, although it was only on 1 January 1993 that it ceased to exist and the Czech and Slovak Republics were born.

In fact, the continuity of history in Prague lies neither in the collective consciousness of today's inhabitants nor in the make-up of the city's population, but in the architecture.

The city's stunning physical beauty has not only preserved its history but has helped it once again to become a place of enjoyment, excitement and romance. The finest museum in Prague is the city itself. Mercifully untouched by wartime destruction or other disasters, it seems to float in a timewarp. Its curves and cobblestones, domes and spires, Art Nouveau frivolity and Habsburg splendour, give it a fairy-tale quality.

First-time visitors to the city are entranced by the breathtaking views and dazzled by the castle, fabulously spotlit at night. They can soak up Prague's revitalised café society, visit the jazz clubs and opera houses, bask with the buskers in the summer on Charles Bridge, and chill in the winter snow in the eerily beautiful Old Jewish Cemetery.

But Prague today isn't just a tourist destination. Visitors can witness history once again on the move, as new buildings begin to take shape and the accumulated grime of ages is cleaned off old ones.

If you are a westerner on your first visit to a former Communist state, you may not appreciate the electrifying speed with which changes have occurred. The contrast with Prague as it was before 1989 could not be greater. Today it is no longer a depressing dead-end of history but a vibrant, pulsing capital. Before, there were no private businesses or restaurants. Fresh food was reserved for the Communist Party bosses and harsh repression for anyone daring to criticise the government. It was a ghost town at night.

But Prague has recently been dubbed the 'model child of capitalism'. Eighty per cent of the economy has been transferred into private hands; business is booming; jobs outnumber jobseekers. While President Havel is better known abroad, it is Prime Minister Václav Klaus, a staunch free market conservative, who is firmly in the driving seat.

It is not just the economy that is roaring ahead. Since 1989, a massive influx of visitors and new residents has turned Prague into a cosmopolitan city once again. International influences have fused with local talent and a bohemian atmosphere has returned to Bohemia.

A word of warning, however. The iron curtain may have gone, but old habits die hard and an iron veil remains. Don't be surprised if even here, in the most successful of all former Eastern bloc states, you still encounter inefficiency, shoddy service and cheating. Over four decades of Communism has lead to a corruption of the moral code and at times it can seem as though there's little sense of what is right, only of what is do-able. So check that your bill is added correctly, your change in the shop is correct, that the taxi meter is not rigged.

But don't let any of this spoil your trip. Put it down to experiencing the heady Prague of the 1990s, for the uncomfortable aspects are easily outweighed by the intoxicating, exhilarating atmosphere. *Tom Gross*

You can get there from here.

Calling around the world is easy. Really. Just dial the AT&T access number of the country you're calling from. An AT&T Operator or English-language voice prompt will help connect you to the States and over 75 countries quickly and easily. It's that simple. With easy billing to either your AT&T Card or U.S. Local Telephone Company calling card, or by calling collect.* So when someone tells you you can't get there from here, pick up the phone and call 'em on it.

Call with AT&T.

From Czech Republic dial
00-420-00101

AT&T

*Applies only to AT&T USADirect® Se

Essential Information

All the information you need for finding your feet in Prague, from Customs' checks to getting by in Czech.

Emergencies

The following are 24-hour emergency phone numbers. You'll be lucky to get anyone who speaks English, so find a Czech person to help if you can:

Police *158*
Fire *150*
Ambulance *155*
Emergency Road Service *154*
Air Rescue Service *37 88 38*

Visas

EC nationals and citizens of the USA do not need visas for stays of up to three months, although a return ticket or proof of accommodation might be demanded, and officially they are required to declare their presence in the country to the local police station within 30 days of their arrival. Australians, Canadians, South Africans and Israelis do need visas, but these can be obtained at the airport on arrival.

After three months, all foreigners are supposed to obtain extended visas or a residence permit (*občanský průkaz*). This permit isn't easy to get (*see chapter* **Survival**), but it does entitle the holder to discounts on hotel rooms and some public

transport. The Czech police conduct periodic crackdowns on foreigners who don't have the proper papers. These operations are usually aimed at Romanians, Ukrainians, Vietnamese, Yugoslavs and other nationals that the Czechs consider to be undesirable. But there are always a few Brits and Americans that get caught in the snare.

The Czechs tend not to stamp your passport when you leave, so be sure to ask for one by saying '*razitko prosím*' if you want to show the authorities that you have left the country before the end of three months. For a list of embassies and consulates, *see chapter* **Survival**.

Customs

The customs check at the airport tends to be lax, but the customs agents who come through the trains at the Czech border are often particular in their searches. It is best to try to carry as many of your belongings with you as possible, because shipping involves dealing with customs at the post office – an event that could prove to be one of the most frustrating of your stay in this country. The allowances for importing goods are:

200 cigarettes; 100 cigars (3g each); 250g tobacco;
1 litre alcohol; 2 litres wine;
50g perfume; ¼ litre toilet water.

The import of coffee, tea and food is restricted. Currency restrictions apply only to Czech crowns. You may bring in or take out up to 5,000kč and bring in any amount of foreign currency.

Insurance

Foreign residents who contribute to the Czech national health insurance scheme are insured for Czech health services. It is a good idea to make sure that your home country's health insurance covers you in eastern and central Europe before arrival. The Czech Republic is not a member of the EC so it has no reciprocal agreements with EC countries.

If you rent a car in the Czech Republic, make sure you get a Green Card that shows you are insured outside the country. Most car rental agencies will give this to you, but if not, it can be obtained from the state insurance company Česká pojišťovna.

Central Health Insurance Office
Tyršova 7, Prague 2 (24 91 02 59). Metro I.P. Pavlova. **Open** 8am-3pm Mon; 8am-6pm Wed; 7am-3pm Tue, Thur.

Česká pojišťovna
Spálená 16, Prague 1 (24 24 11 11/24 21 21 64). Metro Národní třída/6, 18, 22, 22 tram. **Open** 9am-5pm Mon-Fri.

Opposite: *Not the opera house, but the* **Živnostenská Bank**. *See page 7.*

Money

The currency in the Czech Republic is the Czech *koruna* or crown (kč). One crown equals 100 *hellers* (haléřů), which are small light coins. There are also 1, 2, 5, 10, 20 and 50kč coins in circulation. The smallest note is 20kč, the largest 5,000kč. In 1993, after the Czech-Slovak split, the treasury introduced new Czech bank notes and coins. Sometimes tourists unknowingly accept the old – and now worthless – Czechoslovak notes. Avoid this by checking for a silver line on one side of every bank note you take.

Cash Machines

Cash machines are a new and strange beast in the Czech Republic. Locals rarely use them, so there is never a queue, but you might end up waiting ten minutes for the person in front to work out how to operate the machine. Česka Spořitelna, one of the big Czech banks, has about 100 cashpoint machines around the city from which you can withdraw cash with a bank card. Visa has machines at the airport, the Atrium Hotel (*see chapter* **Accommodation**), on Mostecká, and in many other locations. It's also possible to withdraw cash with a Visa card at the Živnostenská Banka (*see page 7*) and at bureaux de change. Mastercard (Access/Eurocard) can be used at one of the 16 Komerční bank cashpoints. Prime bank locations include the main train station (Hlavní nádraží), Na přikopě and Václavské náměstí. American Express has a machine in front of their office on Václavské náměstí 56. A word of warning, however: do not depend on cash machines as your only source of currency. If there are problems with your transaction, there aren't many people here who can help you solve them.

Banks & Bureaux de Change

In the past four years, the bureau de change business has turned into one of the most profitable enterprises in Prague. Since the Czech crown is not a hard currency, it cannot be purchased outside the Czech Republic, so anyone in the currency trading business in Prague is guaranteed a few thousand customers from the tourists who arrive each year. Even though the crown is not an internationally convertible currency, it is the strongest and most stable currency of the former Eastern Bloc. Taxis, restaurants, and shops should be paid in crowns. Prices for hotel rooms and flat rentals are often quoted in deutschmarks or dollars, but can also be paid in crowns.

The airport has bureaux de change that are open 24 hours a day and offer good rates. The exchange bureau in the main train station (Hlavní nádraží) is open from 9am to 7pm. The main business and tourist districts – Václavské náměstí,

Staroměstské náměstí and Malostranské náměstí – are all packed with exchange offices. The usual bureau rate is eight per cent commission, but it's sometimes possible to beat them down to five per cent. Most banks have bureau de change counters that charge a much lower commission – usually one to three per cent. They are generally open from 8am or 9am to 3pm or 4pm Monday to Friday, and closed at the weekend and on public holidays.

Remember to keep all receipts when you change money: you will need them if you have any crowns left at the end of your stay that you want to reconvert. You can do this at the airport or at the Komerční bank.

Komerční Banka

Na příkopě 33, Prague 1 (24 02 11 11). Metro Můstek or Náměstí Republiky. **Open** 8am-noon, 1-5pm, Mon-Fri.
The biggest bank in the country with branches everywhere.

Živnostenská Banka

Na příkopě 20, Prague 1 (24 12 11 11). Metro Můstek or Náměstí Republiky. **Open** 8am-5pm Mon-Fri.
The old trading bank that is housed in one of the most beautiful buildings in the city. Worth a visit even if you don't want to change money.

ČSOB

Na příkopě 14, Prague 1 (233 11 11). Metro Můstek or Náměstí Republiky. **Open** 7.30am-noon, 1-4pm, Mon-Fri.
The best bank to go for quick wire transfers from abroad.

Credit Cards & Eurocheques

The Czech Republic is a cash-run economy. Most locals do not understand credit cards or cheques. Shopkeepers and restaurateurs are only just starting to realise the value in accepting credit cards as payment, so never assume you will be able to pay by credit card. Eurocheques and travellers' cheques are often accepted, but not as readily as they are in the EU.

American Express

Václavské náměstí 56, Prague 1 (24 22 98 83). Metro Můstek or Muzeum. **Open** *winter* 9am-6pm Mon-Fri; 9am-noon Sat; *summer* 9am-7pm Mon-Fri; 9am-3pm Sat.

Mastercard (Access/Eurocard)

Represented at every branch of Komerční Banka (*see above*).

Visa

There is no office in Prague. Phone the UK or USA reversed charges if you have a problem with your card, or one of these emergency numbers (0044 71 9378 1111/001 410 581 3836).

Money Transfer

The easiest way to get money fast is to cash a cheque at the American Express office, who will give you dollars or the crown equivalent. You can also have money transferred from your home bank to a Czech bank. ČSOB processes transfers faster than most banks.

Tourist Information

Prague has gone a long way in the past four years towards improving its tourist facilities, but it still has a long way to go before it compares with Paris or Vienna. A good way to orient yourself is to pick up the English-language weekly newspapers, the *Prague Post* and *Prognosis* – which both have sections devoted to entertainment as well as survival hints. For a list of sightseeing tour operators, *see* chapter **Sightseeing**.

Prague Information Service (PIS)

(Pražská informační služba), Na příkopě 20, Prague 1 (26 40 22/information line 54 44 44). Metro Můstek or Náměstí Republiky. **Open** 8.30am-7pm Mon-Fri; 9am-5pm Sat, Sun.
Provides free maps of the centre of Prague as well as other useful maps and leaflets. If you want some information over the phone, try the information line list above; the information centres only deal with personal callers and will not answer phone queries.
Branches: Hlavní nádraží, Wilsonova, Prague 1; Staroměstské náměstí 22, Prague 1; Valdštejnské náměstí, Prague 1.

Holidays

Prague does not shut down completely over the holidays, but it is difficult to find an open food shop or department store. Buses, trams, and metros run on a Sunday timetable. The Communist regime and the division of Czechoslovakia left the Czech Republic with a hotchpotch of holidays. They have kept May Day and the anniversary of the founding of Czechoslovakia as official holidays, but have done away with all the parades that once accompanied these days. For a complete list of public holidays, *see* chapter **Prague by Season**.

Opening Hours

The standard opening hours for most shops are from 9am to 6pm Monday to Friday, and 9am to noon or 1pm on Saturday. Most are closed on Sunday. Shops frequently close unexpectedly for a day and put little notes on their door saying 'inventory day' or 'technical day', which can cover anything from stock-taking to the fact that the manager had a stomach ache and didn't want to work that day. Most shops stay open for lunch, though some service businesses don't. In August, many shops and theatres close for a month's holiday.

Czech Time

Czechs are clockmakers. Their love of the instruments of time has given them great respect for time, and so they are always very prompt. The Czech Republic is on the same time zone as the rest of western Europe – an hour ahead of Greenwich

Mean Time, except in summer when Daylight Saving Time pushes the clock two hours ahead. Czechs use the 24-hour clock.

The Seasons

Prague is a beautiful city, but if you visit it in January or February you may miss its beauty. Most of the residents still burn coal in the winter and by mid-winter the air can be so thick with black soot that you can't see across the river. *See chapter* **Prague by Season** for a list of seasonal events and festivities.

Spring

The best season in Prague is the spring. The city comes out of hibernation from a long, usually cold, cloudy winter into clear, bright blue days. The temperature in May is perfect for strolling outside and sleeping soundly through the night. The flowers start to bloom and people put away their winter jackets for another season.

Summer

Residents of Prague usually disappear to their summer cottages – *chatas* – in the country during the summer, leaving the city to the thousands of tourists who flock in from western Europe and the Americas. The summers can get very hot and humid but are usually pleasant and warm. The days are quite long, and it stays light until around 10pm.

Autumn

This can be the prettiest time of year – with crisp cool air and sharp blue skies – but it can also be the wettest. The days shorten quickly. By the end of October, the sun sets at around 5.30pm. September is a good month to visit the city. The streets are once again jammed with cars, the parks full of children, and the restaurants full of local business people plotting their next move.

Winter

When it snows, this city is so beautiful and white that you forget for a few minutes the dark and dingy tint that covers Prague through most of the winter. Unfortunately, the bright white snows are rarely accompanied by the clear blue skies you see in other winter wonderlands. The air pollution is usually so bad that clear skies in winter are a rare treat.

Savoir-Faire

Driving

Beware: the Czech Republic is full of inexperienced adult drivers. People who, under the old regime, relied on public transport, are now going out to buy cars in the new free market economy. Few of these new drivers with 20 year-old licences are well versed in the etiquette of driving. Be patient and be on your guard.

Street Crime

When tourists started descending on the city four years ago, the petty thieves were quick to follow. They tend to gather around the popular tourists sites – on Charles Bridge, in Malostranská náměstí and Staroměstské náměstí, the main train station and in front of the National Theatre. A common

technique is to crowd you near an exit when you get on a tram or metro, so you can't move forward into the carriage. Then, having picked your pocket, they dash out of the carriage at the next stop before you have a chance to stop them. You can significantly lower your chances of becoming a target for thieves by following the basic precautions that apply to any crowded city: carry your wallet in a front, not back, pocket; don't use large notes to pay for small items; keep a firm grip on your bag at all times.

Tipping

Czechs tend to round a bill up to the nearest round number. So, if your bill is 763kč, in a Czech restaurant it would be acceptable to leave 770kč. However at an American, Italian or French restaurant, you would be expected to leave a ten per cent tip. If you are with a large group, service is often included. Check with your waiter if you have any questions. Taxi drivers expect tips from foreigners. The rule of thumb is generally round the fare up if the driver was nice and didn't try to cheat you, but don't give him a crown extra if he was at all unpleasant (*see chapter* **Getting Around** for more on taxis).

Telephones

When the Czechs changed over to a new system of currency, they also changed most of their -

Vocabulary

Czech is a difficult language, with seven different case endings. It is always appreciated when foreigners speak Czech, but few speak it well enough to be understood. However it's important to learn a few courtesies like *prosím* meaning please, and *děkuji* meaning thank you.

For a list of Czech dishes and culinary terms, *see chapter* **Restaurants**.

Pronunciation

a – as in *up*
á – as in *father*
e – as in *let*
é – as in *air*
i, y – as in *lit*
í, ý – as in *seed*
o – as in *lot*
ó – as in *lore*
u – as in *book*
ú, ů – as in *loom*
c – as in *its*
č – as in *chin*
ď – as in *duty*
ch – as in *loch*
ň – as in *onion*
ř – as for r, but flatten the tip of the tongue making a short forceful buzz like **ž**
š – as in *shin*
ť – as in *stew*
ž – as in *pleasure*
dž as in *George*

Useful Phrases

Czech words are always stressed on the first syllable

hello/good day *dobrý den*
good evening *dobrý večer*
good night *dobrou noc*
goodbye *na shledanou*
yes *ano* (often abbreviated to *no*)
no *ne*
please *prosím*
thank you *děkuji*
excuse me *promiňte*
sorry *pardon*
help! *pomoc!*
I don't understand *nerozumím*
I do not speak Czech *nemluvím česky*
Do you speak English? *Mluvíte anglicky?*
sir *pán*
madam *paní*
open *otevřeno*
closed *zavřeno*

I would like *chtěl bych*
How much is it? *kolik to stojí?*
May I have a receipt, please *účet, prosím*
Can we pay, please *prosím, zaplatíme*
where is...? *kde je...?*
go left *doleva*
go right *doprava*
straight *rovně*
far *daleko*
near *blízko*
street *ulice*
square *náměstí*
bridge *most*
good *dobrý*
bad *špatný*
big *velký*
small *malý*

Numbers

0 *nula*	11 *jedenáct*	40 *čtyřicet*
1 *jeden*	12 *dvanáct*	50 *padesát*
2 *dva*	13 *třináct*	60 *šedesát*
3 *tři*	14 *čtrnáct*	70 *sedmdesát*
4 *čtyři*	15 *patnáct*	80 *osmdesát*
5 *pět*	16 *šestnáct*	90 *devadesát*
6 *šest*	17 *sedmnáct*	100 *sto*
7 *sedm*	18 *osmnáct*	1,000 *tisíc*
8 *osm*	19 *devatenáct*	
9 *devět*	20 *dvacet*	
10 *deset*	30 *třicet*	

Days of the Week

Monday *pondělí*; **Tuesday** *úterý*;
Wednesday *středa*; **Thursday** *čtvrtek*;
Friday *pátek*; **Saturday** *sobota*; **Sunday** *neděle*

Months & Seasons

January *leden*
February *únor*
March *březen*
April *duben*
May *květen*
June *červen*
July *červenec*
August *srpen*
September *září*
October *říjen*
November *listopad*
December *prosinec*

Spring *jaro*
Summer *léto*
Autumn *podzim*
Winter *zima*

coin-operated phone booths into card-operated ones. The cards can be bought at most newspaper stands – look for a yellow and blue sign that says 'SPT Telecom' on the window – and at any post office. The cards come in denominations of 50kč up to 300kč. If you are only making local calls, 50kč should be plenty. A local call costs 2kč for every six minutes. If you want to make international calls, buy a 300kč card or go to the main post office and place the call through the telephone operator. For more on how and where to make telephone calls, *see chapter* **Survival**.

Getting Around

How to cope with the cobbles, deal with obstreperous taxi drivers or track down night trams.

Prague's ornate main train station.

The best way to see central Prague is on foot. The oldest parts of the city were built centuries before the advent of motor vehicles, and so the narrow cobbled streets are not conducive to driving. Everyone walks – even the President and Prime Minister walk through the city (with their body guards close behind). In fact, walking is often faster than taking a car or taxi. To a newcomer, Prague is a tangle of narrow streets in which it is easy to get miserably lost. But don't worry, there are several landmarks to guide you home, like the Castle, the TV tower, the church in Vyšehrad, and the Vltava river. *See pages 277-282* for maps of Prague and a metro map; you can also buy maps of the city at any kiosk or currency exchange booth.

Prague is a large city, but its core – the centre of Staré Město, Malá Strana and the castle – is small. It takes about 20 minutes to walk from the Old Town Square (Staroměstské náměstí) to the heart of the Little Quarter (Malostranské náměstí). The two sections are connected by the Charles Bridge, the oldest bridge that crosses the Vltava river. If you are exploring areas outside the centre, public transport comes into its own.

PUBLIC TRANSPORT

The Czech Republic, like many former Communist countries, has an excellent public transport system. Using a combination of metro, tram, and bus, you can get almost anywhere you want to go in the city. The only difficulty is in working out how the systems work together. The metro, tram and bus lines are shown on most city maps, but road works often

cause unpredictable detours on the tram and bus routes, especially during the summer.

Public transport costs the same, to any of Prague's ten districts. There are no real suburbs yet and the majority of Prague's 1.5 million inhabitants live in *panálaks*, or large blocks of buildings that edge the city. The metros are crammed with passengers rushing to and from work in the early morning and mid-afternoon rush hours. If you are travelling within the central part of the city, it's fastest and most convenient to hop on a tram. If you are going to one of the outlying districts, it's best to take the metro. The trains are clean, quick and run frequently. A digital clock on each platform tells you how many minutes have lapsed since the last train. Buses and trams always have connections at metro stops.

Arriving in Prague

By Air

Prague's only airport, **Ruzyně**, is about ten kilometres from the centre of the city. There is no metro or tram stop at the airport, so you are left with three choices for getting into town: taking a taxi, an express airport bus, or a local bus. The number for airport information is 334 11 11.

Taxi

The most expensive, most comfortable and usually the quickest way to get into the centre. Special airport taxis charge about double the normal rate, which you have no choice but to pay because the city gave the fleet a monopoly. *See page 13* for details on cab etiquette. The ride should take about 20-25 minutes and cost between 300kč and 400kč for the centre of Prague. The fare will be less if you are going to Prague 6, and more if you are going to Prague 3-10. Check at the airport information kiosk for the going rate.

Express Airport Bus

Czech airlines, ČSA, runs a special airport bus between the airport and Revoluční street in the centre of town, every 30 minutes between 7am and 7.30pm. The bus is clean, quick, pleasant and cheap. It stops first at Dejvická metro station (the fare is 15kč) and then at the ČSA office on Revoluční (the fare is 30kč). If you need to continue your journey by metro, get off at Dejvická, which is the last station on line A. If you need to get to the centre of the city, take the bus all the way to Revoluční, and then take a tram or taxi to your final destination. The whole journey takes about 30-35 minutes.

Local Bus

Bus 119 is a public bus that runs from the airport to Dejvická metro station. It's the cheapest alternative but also the slowest, since the bus stops several times on the way to the metro. If you are in no hurry, it's a fine way to travel but during the rush hour the bus can get crowded with airport employees going home.

By Train

International trains arrive at two stations in Prague, Hlavní nádraží (Main Station), and Nádraží Holešovice (Holešovice Station). It's easy to get off at Holešovice station thinking that it is the main station. Check the train schedule to see whether your train stops at both, and wait to get off at the last stop, Hlavní nádraží. If your train terminates at Holešovice, you can take the metro from there into the centre of town.

The Main Station is right in the centre of town, a couple of streets from Václavské náměstí, and close to the main post office. Unfortunately, it's one of the most poorly marked stations in Europe. It has a main hall upstairs, a lower hall, and a left-luggage area just below the lower hall. Train information, taxis and the international ticket office can be found in the main hall. The lower hall has the domestic ticket office, a post office, food stalls and an exit which leads out to two trams stops – Jindřišská 200 meters straight ahead, and Hlavní nádraží 200 meters to the right. It's not a good idea to rest your weary bones in the little park outside the station – this has been nicknamed Sherwood Forest by the police because so many tourists have been pickpocketed here.

By Coach

Florenc coach station is one of the least pleasant places in Prague. Perhaps its best feature is the shiny new McDonald's which has opened a few metres away. The Kingscourt Express coach, the most popular coach running between Prague and London, picks up and drops off passengers opposite this. From here, you can catch a metro (line B or C) at Florenc metro station, or five different trams at the Florenc tram stop. There are a few hotels on Na pořičí, the main street running in front of the bus station. Although these places aren't bad, if you are travelling alone, it may be best to look in other parts of the city for somewhere to stay. The area is a notorious one for petty crime and seedy characters.

Public Transport

The Prague public transport system is one of the simplest city networks in Europe. There are no complicated travel zones or overlapping express and local trains. The network is made up of three basics – the metro, trams, and buses. There's one basic ticket for all three, which costs 6kč for a journey made anywhere within the hour. Like the Germans, the Czechs rely on the honour system.

You don't have to show your ticket to a guard or pass through a gate to enter the metro. Instead, you must stamp your ticket at a machine at the entrance to the metro, or as you board a bus or tram. Undercover guards carry out random ticket checks. If you don't have a correctly stamped ticket, you'll be fined 200kč on the spot.

Tickets

You can buy 6kč tickets at kiosks near the metro or at machines that take 1kč, 2kč, 5kč, or 10kč coins. If you don't have the right change, the guard inside the glass cage will sell you a ticket. You can also buy tickets at most newsstands.

Travel Passes

The following travel passes are available. They all allow unlimited travel on the metro, trams and buses. They can be bought at the counter marked DP at most metro stations:
One Day Pass 50kč
Two Day Pass 85kč
Three Day Pass 110kč
Four Day Pass 135kč
Five Day Pass 170kč
One Month Pass 280kč
Three Month Pass 680kč
One Year Pass 2,200kč
Ecological Pass (cannot travel on buses) 25 tickets for 115kč
Economical Pass 25 tickets for 135kč

The Metro

The metro recently celebrated its twentieth anniversary. In 1973, Prague laid down the first metro tracks with some help from the former Soviet Union. The first line in operation was the red line C, which runs north to south. In 1978, the green line A opened, running northwest to southeast. The last line, the yellow line B, was opened in 1985 and runs northeast to southwest. The initial 11 kilometres of track has grown into 40.2 kilometres today. The transit authorities expect to build another 5.3 kilometres as an extension of line B soon. They estimate that about 1.2 million people use the metro each day.

The metro is marked by signs at street level that show the colour and name of the line. Line A is the main tourist route, passing through Malostanská (for Malá Strana and the castle), Staroměstská (for the Old Town Square) and Václavské náměstí's

two stops Můstek and Muzeum. The metro runs daily from 5am until midnight. Trains run less frequently on Sundays and public holidays. The morning rush hour is roughly between 7am and 9am, the evening rush hour between 3pm and 6pm.

Czechs rules of etiquette on public transport are strictly adhered to: you must give up your seat to an older person, a child, or a disabled person. Don't crowd other passengers and be careful that your belongings don't get in the way. On a crowded train, move to the doors before your stop because people don't like making way for you at the last minute. A recorded message in Czech warns you when the doors are about to shut before a train leaves and tells you in advance the name of each stop.

Trams

Trams have long been a favourite in Prague and are certainly the easiest way of getting around if you're too tired to walk. The first route was built in 1891 between Letná and Letohradek. Originally they were painted different colours to identify their route until 1908, when numbers were introduced instead. Throughout the years of Communism all trams were painted with the same red, black and white design, but after the Velvet Revolution the transport authorities realised the trams' potential as a revenue earner, and started selling advertising space on them. Now, colourful promotions for everything from M&Ms to Macintosh computers – as well as *Penthouse* magazine – rattle through the city on the sides of trams.

There are 22 tram routes through the city and it can take months to learn their course. The most useful trams for tourists are numbers 22 and 18 which both go to Malostranské náměstí. Trams run from 5am until midnight, when night trams take over. There are special tourist trams which run in the summer with numbers in the 90s and which cost 10kč per ride. Check the maps at tram stops for their routes. The routes for regular trams are marked on most Prague maps.

Buses

The first two buses in Prague ran from Malostranské náměstí to Pohořelec in 1908, an experiment that ended a year later when it was decided that buses were not yet a feasible form of transport. In 1925 buses were introduced again, this time more successfully. Today, Prague's buses cover 1,865.4 kilometres of ground every day, most of it in the outlying districts of the city.

Most buses start their journey at metro stops outside Prague 1 and 2, and don't run through the centre of the city. Timetables are posted at bus stops. Always allow yourself plenty of time if you have to take a bus. Most buses run frequently during the rush hour and slightly less so during off-peak times, so it's not a good idea to stay in an area

that is completely dependent on bus transport. Night buses run about once an hour, between midnight and 5am.

Taxis

Taxi drivers in the city have a bad reputation for taking advantage of any foreigner who jumps in their cab. The best advice is to phone in advance for a taxi if you need one. But if you want to chance your luck on the street, here are some tips:

1. Flag down a moving taxi. Don't get one waiting at a taxi rank in the centre of town, especially not from Václavské náměsti, Staroměstské náměstí, Malostranské náměstí or from outside one of the larger hotels. The taxi ranks are controlled by tight cliques of drivers who will always overcharge you. Hotel taxis charge exorbitant rates.

2. Sit in the front with the driver. Insist he turn on the meter and that the rate (*sazba*) is on rate 1. There are four different cab rates. Rate 1 is the legal tariff of 12kč per kilometre that applies within the city limits. The others are higher rates that cabbies can charge if they have to drive through a massive snow storm or nuclear fallout. Often drivers put something in front of the meter so you can't see it – like a piece of black tape or a Christmas tree air freshener. Just peel off the tape, or move the air freshener so you can see the rate on the meter. Drivers are legally bound to display the rate, but the law is rarely enforced and it is left up to the passenger to try and enforce it. In Czech, you should

WITH US YOU WILL GROW NEW WINGS

ČSA - THE AIRLINE
WHICH PROVIDES ALL SERVICES
ON AN INTERNATIONAL LEVEL

Reservations and ticket sales:

ČSA, Revoluční 1, Praha 1
Tel.: 2480 6225, 2481 5110, 2481 5185
Fax: 2481 0426

AT HOME
IN THE SKIES

say *sazba jeden prosím*, to get the driver to switch to rate 1.

3. The driver will often argue with you, and you can't win if you don't speak Czech. He will say that rate 1 is more expensive (a lie), that you are going somewhere extraordinary, so it will cost more (a lie), or that he has a special car that you have to pay extra for (possibly true, since a ride in a Mercedes or BMW costs more than a Škoda). In answer to this, you can get out of the cab, or you can wait until you get to your destination and give the driver what you think is a reasonable fare for the journey. Even better, agree a fare in advance. If you are travelling alone to somewhere outside the centre, don't choose the latter option. Taxi drivers sometimes get violent. They kick, they hit and they have even been known to pull guns.

4. Always ask for a receipt (*účet*).

The following are numbers of reputable taxi companies. If you have a problem with one of their drivers, the company will listen to your complaints.

AAA Taxi
(34 24 10/32 24 44/312 21 12)

Mikrolux
(35 03 20/35 51 92)

Profi Taxi
(61 04 55 55)

On Foot

Walking is the best way to see Prague. Its cobbled back streets are packed with treasures, from hidden parks to odd-shaped buildings, fascinating frescos or sculptures. It is generally safe to walk through most parts of Malá Strana and the centre of Staré Město at night, but some of the seedier streets around Národní are best avoided after nightfall.

Cycling

Bicycling is a great, but dangerous, way to get around the city. You have to be a confident city cyclist to brave the pedestrian, tram and motorised traffic. The streets are often so narrow that it's difficult to squeeze a bike between a parked car and a moving car and pedestrians will yell at you if you try riding on the wide pavements. However you can ride as fast as you want through the big beautiful parks that dot the city and if you're staying in Prague for more than a few days a bike is the ideal means to escape the crowds.

Travelling at Night

The metro and regular trams and buses run until midnight. After that, night trams and buses take over. The standard 6kč tickets and passes work on all night transport. Trams usually run about every 20-30 minutes and have numbers in the 50s. Check at tram stops for their routes. Most night trams stop in front of the Kmart on Spálená and Národní, or around the corner at the junction of Lazarská and Spálená. Night buses run about once an hour.

Travel for the Disabled

Facilities for the disabled are few and far between. The Olga Havel Foundation and a few other charities have begun to lobby to improve disabled facilities, but meanwhile there are the following options:

Metro
The following metro stations have handicapped facilities: Nádraží Holešovice, Florenc, Hlavní nádraží, Pankrác, Roztyly, Chodov (line C); Karlovo náměstí (line B); Skalka (line A). Nádraží Holešovice and Hlavní nádraží have special lifts that can be operated by disabled passengers. In other stations, the disabled passenger must contact a member of staff who is qualified to operate the lift.

Trams
They usually run from Anděl to Sidliště Řepy, though at the time of writing this service was not in operation.

Buses
Those with wheelchair facilities run from Černý most to náměstí Republiky to Prague 4.

Driving

In order to drive in the Czech Republic you must have proof of international insurance (a Green Card) and an international drivers' licence. The Czech Republic is full of Sunday drivers who aren't used to having a real car to drive. Although most are safe and attentive, their indecision and herd mentality can be frustrating in city traffic. Trams represent the single largest threat to foreign drivers. Car lanes and tram tracks merge without warning and drivers need to be especially careful of tram stops, many of which are in the middle of the road. Cars are supposed to stop when a tram stops to allow passengers to cross the street.

While road signs are perfectly accurate, they tend to be poorly positioned and as a result give little warning of turns, road works, and other hazards. If you're trying to find your way out of the centre of town, it's often easiest to follow a tram route.

The police have a habit of stopping foreign cars, especially those with foreign number plates. Fines are payable on the spot and are often negotiable. After you have paid, you are usually free to drive away. Seat belts must be worn by law.

For the most part, the main roads are in good repair, but drivers should watch out for pot holes, especially around tram tracks. The main traffic in Prague flows from north to south along the river, and from east to west along the Brno motorway. The Brno motorway is the only major road in the country; all other routes – to Salzburg, Nuremberg, and Berlin – are serviced by narrow, two-lane roads.

Accommodation

Relax in Renaissance splendour, bed down in a former prison or tough it out in a campsite: Prague has accommodation to suit all tastes and pockets.

The **Grand Hotel Evropa**. See page 23.

Since the floodgates opened in 1989, tourists have been pouring into Prague in their millions to experience their share of history and drink cheap beer. Realising the potential of this seemingly infinite human commodity, a new generation of entrepreneurs have spent the past five years in a frenzy of reconstruction. Now that the dust is finally beginning to settle, there's no longer an official shortage of hotel beds in the city.

That said, it can still be hard to find a centrally located room, especially at the most popular times of year. If you're planning a visit around Christmas time or New Year, at Easter or during the month of May when Prague's musical festival is in full swing, it's worth booking several months in advance. For the summer season – from May to October – book a month ahead; in winter a couple of weeks should be plenty.

For those shopping around in the moderate, expensive or luxury categories, there's plenty of choice, ranging from cosy family-run *pensions* to modern glass constructions complete with pool and indoor tennis courts. Virtually all the hotels included in these sections are located in Prague 1, the historic centre, or Prague 2, the leafy district just east of the centre and from where all the main sights can still be reached on foot.

Budget hotels are scarce in Prague. If your funds are limited – and especially if you turn up with nowhere to stay – your best bet is to head for one of the numerous accommodation agencies that

will find you a self-contained flat or a room with a Czech family. Officially, it's illegal to lease private accommodation to tourists in central Prague, but only Čedok, the state-run and least helpful of the agencies, takes any notice of this rule, and then only because it has a vested interest in filling the city's hotels. You get to choose your own dream pad by flicking through albums of badly focused snapshots showing lush fruit bowls (that often fail to materialise) or the jazzy striped sofas that are all the rage. Prices vary according to your length of stay, the location, the number of people booking and so on. Finding somewhere cheap and charming is a matter of luck. If there's nothing available in the centre (in Prague 1 or 2) then check public transportation links before taking the keys to a *pied-à-terre* in Bratislava.

Most people in the hotel business speak at least passable and often impressively fluent English, so you should have few problems booking a room or communicating once you get there. This is not the case in the private sector, but a little improvised mime is guaranteed to endear you to your new Czech hosts.

Prices quoted in this chapter are for a single or double room with bathroom, including breakfast unless stated otherwise. They are generally quoted as a range, the exact cost depending on the season. Where only one price is quoted, this is the rate at peak times and it's worth checking if there are any seasonal discounts. As is the rule with Prague, prices are liable to fluctuate.

For longer-term accommodation *see chapters* **Students** *and* **Survival**. For a list of hotels organised by area, *see page 264* **Area Index**.

Luxury

Atrium
Pobřežní 1, Prague 8 (24 84 20 20/fax 26 81 19 73).
Metro Florenc. **Rates** *single* 3,938-5,626kč; *double* 4,365-6,247kč. **Credit** A, AmEx, DC, EC, JCB, V.
Not surprisingly, this massive, 778-roomed mirrored cube has a very large atrium – in fact the largest in the Czech Republic. Huge leather armchairs, lots of greenery and gently bubbling fountains give it an atmosphere not unlike that of an executive airline lounge. But there's lots of potential for political networking: Bill and Hilary Clinton, Nelson Mandela and the late Richard Nixon have been just a few of the Presidential Suite's bed-partners. Facilities include pool, sauna and two indoor tennis courts.

Hotel services *Babysitting. Bar. Beauty salon. Car park. Conference facilities (for up to 1,200). Gym. Laundry. Lifts. Pool. Restaurants. Tennis courts. Wheelchair access.* **Room services** *Air-conditioning. Cable TV. Hairdryer. Minibar. Radio. Room service (24-hour). Rooms for disabled. Safe. Telephone.*

Grand Hotel Bohemia Praha

Králodvorská 4, Prague 1 (232 34 17/fax 232 95 45). Metro Náměstí Republiky. **Rates** *single* 4,770-6,356kč; *double* 6,588-8,784kč. **Credit** A, AmEx, DC, EC, JCB, V.
The Bohemia has been fully renovated by the Austrian Hotels group and caters to a mainly business clientele who can rely on the efficient staff. The 78 rooms are cheerfully relaxing, and each has its own fax and trouser press in addition to the usual comforts. The extravagant gilded Boccaccio conference room is definitely the glitziest venue in town for discussing the merits of photocopiers or promoting the latest deodorant. It's close to the Powder Gate and the Estates Theatre.
Hotel services *Bar. Bureau de change. Car park. Laundry. Lifts. Restaurant. Wheelchair access.* **Room services** *Air-conditioning. Cable TV. Fax. Hairdryer. Minibar. Radio. Room service (24-hour). Rooms for disabled. Safe. Telephone.*

Palace

Panská 12, Prague 1 (240 931 11/fax 24 22 12 10). Metro Můstek. **Rates** *single* from 7,540kč; *double* from 8,900kč. **Credit** A, AmEx, DC, EC, JCB, V.
After major plastic surgery, the 125-room Palace re-opened in 1989 as the first really luxurious hotel in the city. It now rivals the Savoy for comfort and is almost as expensive, though only the Palace offers 'Lady Queen Rooms designed to please the lady traveller'. These are suitably twee with dusty pink quilted bedcovers and extra large dressing tables. Apparently the late Jackie Onassis, possibly nostalgic for the old days, preferred the Presidential Suite.
Hotel services *Babysitting. Bar. Bureau de change. Car park. Casino. Chauffeurs. Conference facilities (for up to 50). Laundry. Lifts. Restaurants. Wheelchair access.* **Room services** *Air-conditioning. Cable TV. Hairdryer. Minibar. Radio. Room service (24-hour). Rooms for disabled. Safe. Telephone.*

Prague Renaissance

V celnici 7, Prague 1 (24 81 03 96/fax 231 31 33). Metro Náměstí Republiky. **Rates** *single and double* 5,600-6,650kč. **Credit** A, AmEx, DC, EC, JCB, V.
The modern granite exterior may be uninspiring, but the 309 stylish rooms, pool, sauna, lots of gold fittings and efficient staff ensure a luxurious trouble-free stay in the heart of the city.
Hotel services *Babysitting. Bar. Bureau de change. Car park. Conference facilities (for up to 790). Laundry. Lifts. No-smoking rooms. Pool. Restaurants. Wheelchair access.* **Room services** *Air-conditioning. Cable TV. Hairdryer. Minibar. Radio. Room service. Rooms for disabled. Telephone.*

Praha

Sušická 20, Prague 6 (24 34 11 11/fax 24 31 12 18). Metro Dejvická. **Rates** *single* 4,256kč; *double* 4,704kč. **Credit** A, AmEx, DC, JCB.
This show-house of 1970s flamboyance, with its its big bulbous lights, extravagant leather upholstery and 124 rooms, used to be owned by the Communist Party and was reserved exclusively for high-ranking officials and visiting dignitaries. The advent of 1989 and all that means that ordinary mortals, albeit only those with generous expense accounts or a personal fortune, can now take a dip in the pool or sweat it out in the sauna – at one time enjoyed by the likes of Castro, Ceauşescu and Gadaffi. All the rooms have secluded balconies with excellent views of Prague.

Hotel services *Bar. Beauty salon. Bowling. Bureau de change. Car park. Conference facilities (for up to 108). Laundry. Lifts. Restaurants. Sauna. Swimming pool. Tennis courts. Volley Ball Courts.* **Room services** *Air-conditioning. Cable TV. Minibar. Radio. Room service (24-hour). Telephone.*

Savoy

Keplerova 6, Prague 1 (24 30 21 22/fax 24 30 21 28). Tram 22. **Rates** *singles and doubles* from 7,196kč. **Credit** AmEx, DC, EC, JCB, V.
Opened in May 1994, the Savoy is trying hard to outshine other contenders in the deluxe category and will probably succeed: bathrooms are pink, marble and totally luxurious, and there's a fax in each room. Up beyond the castle, the setting may not be central, but it is very picturesque. There are 61 rooms.
Hotel services *Babysitting. Bars. Beauty salon. Bureau de change. Car park. Car rental. Conference facilities. Laundry. Lifts. Non-smoking rooms. Fitness facilities (being built at the moment). Restaurants. Wheelchair access.* **Room services** *Air-conditioning. Cable TV. Fax. Hairdryer. Minibar. Radio. Refrigerator. Room service (6am-11pm). Room for disabled. Safe. Telephone.*

Reassuringly Expensive

City Hotel Morán

Na Moráni 15, Prague 2 (24 91 52 08/fax 29 75 33). Metro Karlovo náměstí. **Rates** *single* 2,900-4,800kč; *double* 3,800-5,700kč. **Credit** A, AmEx, DC, EC, V.
The exterior of this 57-roomed western-style hotel is a beautiful pale green affair with white plaster trimmings. The rooms in the same soothing colour-scheme are mercifully devoid of fuss, which is more than can be said for the lobby area, where the interior decorators' extravagances include a reception desk hung with fairy lights and billows of pink and green satin attached to the ceiling of the breakfast room.
Hotel services *Bar. Bureau de change. Car park. Laundry. Lifts. Restaurant.* **Room services** *Cable TV. Hairdryer. Minibar. Radio. Telephone.*

Kampa Stará Zbrojnice

Všehrdova 16, Prague 1, (24 51 04 09/fax 245 103 77). Metro Malostranská/22, 9 tram. **Rates** *single* 1,450-2,300kč; *double* 2,300-3,400kč. **Credit** A, AmEx, DC, EC, JCB, V.
In an excellent location down a quiet backstreet in Malá Strana, the Kampa is less than five minutes' walk from Charles Bridge and right next to its namesake, Prague's loveliest park on the edge of the Vltava river. The interior is unfortunately not so charming: restoration has left an antiseptic outlook and the 84 rooms are immaculately clean but soulless.
Hotel services *Bar. Bureau de change. Car park. Laundry. Lifts. Restaurant. Wheelchair access.* **Room services** *Radio. Telephone.*

Paříž

U Obecního domu 1, Prague 1 (24 22 21 51/fax 24 22 54 75). Metro Náměstí Republiky. **Rates** *single* from 4,480kč; *double* from 5,040kč. **Credit** AmEx, DC, EC, MC, JCB, V.
Restored to its original 1920s splendour, everything at the 100-roomed Paříž spells elegance, from the doormen clad in duck-egg blue to the mosaic portal and beautiful chandeliers hanging in the marble foyer. Such nostalgic indulgence is slightly spoilt by lackadaisical staff. Try and get a room at the back so you're not disturbed by Prague's disaffected youth who congregate at the nearby Formanka bar.
Hotel services *Bureau de change. Car park. Conference facilities (for up to 55). Laundry. Lifts. Restaurant. Wheelchair access.* **Room services** *Air-conditioning.*

Cable TV. Radio. Room service (24-hour). Room for disabled. Safe. Telephone.

Pension Páv

Křemencova 13, Prague 1 (24 91 32 86/fax 24 91 05 74). Metro Národní třída. **Rates** *singles and doubles* 3,400-3,900kč; *suite* 4,000-4,900kč. **No credit cards.**
If you haven't yet got to grips with the Czech language, the fine bronze peacock above the entrance is a handy clue to the pension's name. A small family-run establishment in a tranquil backstreet close to the National Theatre, the Páv has just eight spacious, tastefully appointed rooms.
Hotel services *Bar. Bureau de change. Car park. Restaurant.* **Room services** *Cable TV. Hairdryer. Minibar. Room service. Telephone.*

Pension U raka

Černínská 10/93, Prague 1 (35 14 53/fax 35 30 74). Tram 22. **Rates** *singles and doubles* 3,750 kč. **Credit** AmEx, EC, V.
U raka is located in Nový Svět, or New World, the inappropriately named district behind the Castle that consists of old, winding streets and from which you can hear the Loreto bells chime. Six comfortable rooms, lots of flowers, rugs and pine floors make it the sort of cosy palace Goldilocks might barge into.
Hotel services *Bar. Car park.* **Room services** *Minibar. Radio. Room service. Telephone. TV.*

Pod Věží

Mostecká 2, Prague 1 (53 37 10/fax 53 73 61). Metro Malostranská/12, 22 tram. **Rates** *single* 1,900kč; *double* 4,500kč; *apartment* 5,000kč. **Credit** AmEx, V.
Tucked behind the tower at the Mala Strána end of Charles Bridge, this hotel opened in August 1994. All 12 rooms in the sugar-pink building are gracefully decorated in sedate tones of blue and yellow. The proprietors offer a wide range of services – from nail-lengthening manicures to private secretaries – but the lack of English-speaking staff could be a problem.
Hotel services *Bar. Bureau de change. Car park. Conference facilities. Fax. Hairdresser. Laundry. Lift. Restaurant.* **Room services** *Hairdryer. Minibar. Safe. TV.*

Sidi Pension

Na Kampě 10, Prague 1 (tel/fax 53 61 35). Metro Malostranská/9, 22 tram. **Rates** *per apartment (up to 3 people)* 3,500kč. **Credit** A, AmEx, DC, JCB, V.
The Sidi pension consists of just two spacious apartments above a gay bar in Prague's most photogenic square, right next to Charles Bridge. The rooms are painted in unfortunate shades of brown, but the owner will bend over backwards to please, providing extras such as chauffeured limousines and 'ecological' cuisine in the restaurant overlooking the river.
Hotel services *Bar. Car park. Laundry. Limousine service. Restaurants.* **Room services** *Cable TV. Hairdryer. Minibar. Radio. Room service. Telephone.*

Spiritka

Atletická 115, Prague 6 (24 31 08 43/53 66 58/fax 53 64 22). Metro Anděl, then bus 191. **Rates** *single* 2,900-3,600kč; *double* 3,100-3,800kč. **Credit** A, AmEx, EC, V.
Perched high on a hill overlooking the city, the Spiritka, somewhat resembling a set from *Eldorado*, is strangely at odds with its Czech surroundings. A 15-minute drive from the centre, it's only really convenient for claustrophobic car-owners. The 26 rooms are comfortable, with slick (verging on wide-boy) black furnishings, and the large restaurant and congress room are excellent for conferences.
Hotel services *Bar. Bureau de change. Car park. Conference facilities (for up to 150). Gym. Laundry. Limousine service. Restaurant. Sauna.* **Room services** *Cable TV. Room service. Telephone.*

Hotel Paříž. *See page 19.*

U krále Karla

Úvoz 4, Prague 1 (53 88 05/fax 53 88 11). Metro Malostranská/9, 22 tram. **Rates** *single* 4,200kč; *double* 4,800kč; *apartment* 6,900kč. **Credit** A, AmEx, DC, EC, JCB, V.
Owned by the same people as U páva (*below*), U krále Karla (At King Charles') opened in the spring of 1994 and is Prague's most luxurious hotel of those in the old-fashioned mould. The solid oak furnishings and beautiful Renaissance-style ceilings lend it the feel of a country mansion. If sightseeing gets too much you can stay in, stare at the stained-glass windows and swot up on Czech history as each one portrays a notable figure from the city's past. There are 19 rooms.
Hotel services *Babysitting. Bar. Beauty salon. Bureau de change. Car park. Laundry. Lifts. Restaurant.* **Room services** *Air-conditioning. Hairdryer. Minibar. Radio. Safe. Telephone. TV.*

Ungelt

Štupartská 1, Prague 1 (24 81 13 30/fax 231 95 05). Metro Náměstí Republiky. **Rates** *single* 4,900kč; *double* 5,740kč. **Credit** AmEx, V.
Part of the very fabric of the Old Town, the Ungelt was once Prague's customs house. Local merchants coughed up the cash for its beautiful painted ceilings, but twentieth-century additions – including spangled chandeliers – have rather let the side down. Its 10 suites, each with its own kitchen, are very spacious and ideal for hyperactive children or relentless shoppers. Stairs are very steep.
Hotel services *Bureau de change. Bar. Laundry. Restaurant.* **Room services** *Cable TV. Radio. Room service. Telephone.*

U páva

U Lužického semináře 32, Prague 1 (24 51 09 22/53 22 51/fax 53 33 79). Metro Malostranská. **Rates** *single* 3,600-4,400kč; *double* 3,800-4,600kč. **Credit** A, AmEx, V.
In a serene corner of Malá Strana opposite the Vojanovy Gardens, the 11-roomed U páva is extremely comfortable, though some might find the dark oak ceilings, weighty chandeliers and heavy patterned fabrics a tad oppressive.
Hotel services *Bar. Bureau de change. Car park. Laundry. Restaurant.* **Room services** *Air-conditioning.*

Cable TV. Hairdryer. Minibar. Radio. Room service.
Telephone.

U tří pštrosů

Dražického náměstí 12, Prague 1 (24 51 07 79/fax 24 51
07 83). Metro Malostranská/9, 22 tram. **Rates** *single*
3,300kč; *double* 4,800kč. **Credit** A, AmEx, EC, V.
This beautiful Renaissance building just next to Charles
Bridge derives its name from the three ostriches painted on
its façade. Its tradition of hospitality goes back to the days
when it was the first coffee house in Bohemia; today the
Dundr family to whom it was restituted post-1989 have
created a comfortable and luxurious hotel. Many of the 18
rooms have original seventeenth-century painted ceilings
and the suites at the top have magnificent views.
Hotel services *Babysitting. Bar. Bureau de change. Car*
park. Laundry. Restaurant. **Room services** *Hairdryer.*
Radio. Room service. Telephone. TV.

Comfortable

Anna

Budečská 17, Prague 2 (25 75 39/fax 24 24 60 32).
Metro Náměstí Míru. **Rates** *single* 1,800kč; *double*
2,880kč. **No credit cards.**
This part of leafy Vinohrady is a ten-minute walk from
Wenceslas Square, which can be a bonus, especially in the
summer when the crowds in the centre can get you down. The
23 rooms (including two apartments) have bright white bathrooms, and are either coloured terracotta and black or fresh,
pale green: exceptionally tasteful for this price category.
Hotel services *Bar. Bureau de change. Car park.*
Restaurant. **Room services** *Cable TV. Radio.*

Betlem Club

Betlémské náměstí 9, Prague 1 (24 21 68 72/fax 24 21
80 54). Metro Národní třída. **Rates** *single* 1,530kč;
double 2,720kč. **No credit cards.**
Handily situated – just opposite the Bethlehem Chapel in the
heart of the Old Town – with small but comfortable rooms
(22 in all), this low-key hotel has the feel of a sleepy seaside
pension. The breakfast room is in a damp Medieval vault;
some of the rooms have a disconcerting seventies-style décor.
Hotel services *Laundry.* **Room services** *Minibar.*
Radio. Telephone. TV.

Grand Hotel Evropa

Václavské náměstí 25, Prague 1 (24 22 81 17/fax 24 22
45 44). Metro Můstek. **Rates** *single* 1,130-2,100kč; *double*
1,860-2,800kč. **No credit cards.**
Right in the centre on Wenceslas Square, this building is one
of the finest examples of Art Nouveau in the city. Unravaged
by time, it has been equally untouched by restorers. For the
languorous and romantic, who don't mind forsaking modern bathrooms for the faded *fin-de-siècle* atmosphere, the
Evropa is an exquisite place to unwind. Try and book a suite
or a double with a bathroom as these (30) rooms come complete with delicate Louis XVI furniture, silk brocade upholstery and old tiled radiators. The other 65 rooms are no-frills
teak and beige outfits.
Hotel services *Bar. Bureau de change. Café. Car park.*
Laundry. Restaurant. **Room services** *Telephone.*

Hotel 16 U sv. Kateřiny

Kateřinská 16, Prague 2 (29 53 29/fax 29 39 56). Metro
I.P. Pavlova/22, 51, 56, 57 tram. **Rates** *single* 1,600kč;
double 2,400kč. **Credit** EC, V.
St Catherine's is a charming family-run hotel in a quiet slop-
ping street near the Botanical Gardens and just a short walk

Where Clinton stays when he's in town: the
luxurious **Atrium**. *See page 17.*

from Wenceslas Square. All the 13 rooms lead off a central
covered well and some have their own terrace. Breakfast is
particularly good.
Hotel services *Bar. Bureau de change. Wheelchair*
access. **Room services** *Cable TV. Hairdryer. Minibar.*
Rooms for disabled. Telephone.

International

Koulova 15, Prague 5 (24 39 31 11/fax 24 31 06 16).
Tram 20, 25. **Rates** *single* 1,862kč; *double* 2,670kč.
Credit AmEx, DC, EC, JCB, V.
Modelled on Stalin's colossal Seven Sisters in Moscow and
adorned with Socialist Realist friezes glorifying peasant
labour, the 14-storey, 240-room International is the place to
come for a Communist nostalgia trip. Smiles and Gideon
bibles have been thrown in with privatisation, but fierce
house rules are still posted on every floor ordering you to
turn off the taps and electricity when you vacate your room
and to have a health certificate for your pet. The punishment
for offending tourists is not specified.
Hotel services *Bar. Bureau de change. Car park.*
Conference facilities. Laundry. Lifts. Restaurant. **Room**
services *Cable TV. Minibar. Radio. Telephone.*

Julian

Elišky Peškové 11, Prague 5 (53 51 37/fax 54 75 25).
Tram 6, 9, 12. **Rates** *single* 1,840kč; *double* 2,480kč.
Credit A, AmEx, DC, V.
On the edge of Smíchov, the Julian is slightly off the beaten
track, yet only ten minutes' walk from Malá Strana or the
National Theatre. The reception area, with its arched ceil-
ings, white walls and cane furniture, is discreetly elegant;
the 29 rooms are airy, though the pink sheets a little sugary.
The plush padded lift makes a delightful sighing sound as
it ascends.
Hotel services *Bar. Car park. Conference facilities.*
Lifts. Wheelchair access. **Room services** *Cable TV.*
Rooms for disabled. Safe. Telephone.

Juliš

Václavské náměstí 22, Prague 1 (24 21 70 92/fax 24 21
85 45). Metro Můstek. **Rates** *single* 1,250-2,290kč; *double*
1,800-2,990kč. **Credit** AmEx, EC, V.
The unappealing glass and concrete exterior misleadingly
disguises the fact that the 58 rooms here are large, light and
airy. The best have original 1930s furnishings, including
huge baby blue or peach double beds. Room price includes
the dubious pleasure of free entry to the hotel's disco.
Hotel services *Bar. Bureau de change. Laundry. Lifts.*
Room services *Radio. Telephone. TV.*

Koruna

Opatovická 16, Prague 1 (24 81 31 34/24 91 51 74/fax
29 24 92). Metro Národní třída. **Rates** *single* 1,500kč;
double 2,450kč; *triple* 3,350kč; *double apartments* 4,900kč.
Credit A, EC, V.
The Koruna's elegant nineteenth-century exterior is let down
by its 22 slightly dingy rooms, unchanged since the 1950s,
and with an overabundance of lace curtains and brown car-
peting. But its location just round the corner from the
National Theatre is a major advantage.
Hotel services *Lift.* **Room services** *Radio. Telephone. TV.*

Mepro

Viktora Huga 3, Prague 5 (561 81 21/fax 561 85 87).
Metro Anděl/6, 9. **Rates** *single* 1,550kč; *double* 2,420kč.
Credit A, AmEx, EC, V.
Only a ten-minute tram ride from the centre of town, but light
years away from the toy-town Old Town, the shabby streets
of Smíchov surrounding the Mepro have a lived-in charm
and seemingly remain oblivious to tourism. In keeping with
the area, the Mepro is not an elegant place, but friendly staff
and a pleasant roof terrace compensate for the mismatched
décor. There are 26 rooms.

The frescoed exterior of **U tří pštrosů**. See page 23.

Hotel services *Bar. Car park. Lifts. Restaurant.* **Room services** *Cable TV. Hairdryer. Telephone.*

Pension Dientzenhofer

Nosticova 2, Prague 1 (53 16 72/fax 245 11 11 93). Tram 12, 22. **Rates** *single 1,300-1,540kč; double 2,100-2,300kč; apartments 3,200-3,500kč.* **Credit** A, AmEx, DC, JCB, V.
This sixteenth-century building down a quiet cobbled street in Malá Strana was the birthplace of Kilián Ignaz Dientzenhofer, who, together with his father Christoph, had a hand in just about every Baroque masterpiece in the Czech Republic. All of its seven attractive pine-floored rooms and large bathrooms have been specifically adapted for the needs of wheelchair-bound travellers and there's a lovely garden at the back. Book at least a month in advance.
Hotel services *Bar. Car park. Laundry. Lift. Restaurant (open on request). Wheelchair access.* **Room services** *Cable TV. Room service (24-hour). Telephone.*

Petr

Drtinova 17, Prague 5 (54 08 44/54 05 24/fax 54 92 69). Tram 6, 9, 12. **Rates** *single 1,005-1,433 kč; double 1,490-2,130kč.* **Credit** AmEx, MC, V.
A small, new, family-run hotel nestling at the bottom of Petřín Hill and about ten minutes' walk from Malá Strana or the National Theatre. The 30 rooms are plain – which is not necessarily a bad thing – and there are beautiful light fittings throughout.
Hotel services *Bars. Bureau de change. Car park. Lifts.* **Room services** *Air-conditioning. Cable TV. Room service. Telephone.*

Sax

Jánský vršek 3, Prague 1 (53 84 22/fax 53 84 98). Metro Malostranská/12, 22 tram. **Rates** *single 1,700kč; double 2,400kč.* **No credit cards.**
Owned by Škoda Export and as competitively priced as the car, the Sax is just a minute's walk from the castle and by far the best value in this exclusive area. The interior is stylish, fitted in black and green, and there are 23 rooms. Staff are equally slick.

Hotel services *Babysitting. Bar. Currency exchange. Lift. Restaurant. Wheelchair access.* **Room services** *Hair-dryer. Air conditioning. Mini-bar. Radio. Rooms for disabled. Safe. Telephone. TV.*

Budget

Hlávkova kolej

Jenštejnská 1, Prague 2 (29 21 39/fax 29 00 98). Metro Karlovo náměstí. **Rates** *single 800kč; double 1,500kč.* **No credit cards.**
This former student hostel with 80 rooms has changed its image very little over the past few years. It retains an institutional feel, with shared bathrooms and spartan rooms, but it's well placed – just ten minutes' walk from the National Theatre.
Hotel services *Bar. Laundry. Lift. Restaurant. Wheelchair access.*

Hotel VZ Praha

Sokolská 33, Prague 2 (29 11 18/fax 24 91 44 41). Metro I.P. Pavlova. **Rates** *single 800-1,000kč; double or triple 1,200-1,500kč.* **No credit cards.**
Don't be put off by the ugly concrete exterior of this former military recreation centre; it's right next to I.P. Pavlova metro and just ten minutes' walk from Wenceslas Square. The 33 rooms (14 with bathrooms) are surprisingly light, with an only slightly unpleasant orange décor. An amusing stay is guaranteed by shambolic staff who refer to bathrooms as 'social facilities' and will entice you to try 'non-erotic massage under doctor's supervision'.
Hotel services *Snack bar.* **Room services** *Radio.*

Kafka

Cimburkova 24, Prague 3 (27 31 01/fax 27 29 84). Tram 5, 9, 26. **Rates** *single 600-900kč; double 1,000-1,300kč; breakfast 55kč.* **Credit** AmEx, V.
The Kafka offers simple comfort in 28 clean, pine-furnished rooms, and is priced accordingly. About ten minutes by tram from the main station, this part of Žižkov – with its street

urchins and countless dark beer halls – is slightly run-down but very colourful.
Hotel services *Bar. Car park.*

Pension City

Belgická 10, Prague 2 (691 13 34/tel/fax 691 09 77).
Metro Náměstí Míru. **Rates** *single 935-1,360kč; double 1,309-1,870kč.* **Credit** AmEx, DC, EC, JCB, V.
Pension City is located in the quiet residential district of Vinohrady, just a 15 minutes' stroll from Wenceslas Square. The 19 rooms, all spotlessly clean and brightly coloured, are favoured by a mainly Scandinavian clientele. Added attractions include jolly gingham tablecloths and a very fat resident cat.
Hotel services *Bureau de change. Lifts. Wheelchair access.*

Pension Větrník

U Větrníku 40, Prague 6 (351 96 22/fax 36 14 06).
Metro Hradčanská then 1, 2, 18 tram. **Rates** *single 1,800kč; double 1,900kč.* **Credit** EC.
A ten-minute tram-ride from Hradčanská metro, the Větrník is a fair way from the centre but an excellent option if you favour comfort over location. All the six rooms in this restored eighteenth-century windmill overlook a large secluded garden whose high walls block out the ugly cluster of buildings that have mushroomed in recent years. Charming owners and the use of a private tennis court are further bonuses.
Hotel services *Bar. Car park. Laundry. Restaurant.*
Room services *Cable TV. Hairdryer. Radio. Room service. Telephone.*

Pod Lipkami

Pod Lipkami 8/1520, Prague 5 (52 20 28/fax 52 20 28).
Metro Anděl, then 132, 191, 217 bus. **Rates** *single and double 1,700kč; breakfast 126kč.* **Credit** EC, V.
Out on a limb in exclusive villa-land where the newly-rich cruise in their BMWs, the Pod Lipkami is a bit of a trek if you want to stay out late, but good value if you don't mind. The 11 rooms are tastefully furnished with antiques and rugs strewn over polished parquet floors.
Hotel services *Bar. Bureau de change. Laundry. Restaurant. Terrace.* **Room services** *Cable TV. Telephone.*

U krále Jiřího

Liliova 10, Prague 1 (24 22 20 13/fax 24 22 19 83).
Metro Staroměstská. **Rates** *single 880-990kč; double 1,760-1,980kč.* **Credit** AmEx, V.
U krále Jiřího is a charming little pension tucked down a picturesque lane in the Old Town. The eight attic rooms with sloping ceilings and ancient beams are so snug you may never want to get out of bed. There's no night-porter so you need to warn the owners if you're staying out after midnight; otherwise Prague's only Irish pub, the James Joyce, is on the ground floor of the premises.
Hotel services *Babysitting. Bar. Bureau de change.*
Room services *Radio.*

Pension Unitas

Bartolomějská 9, Prague 1 (232 77 00/fax 232 77 09).
Metro Národní třída. **Rates** *single 790-920kč; double 990-1,100kč; triple 1,200-1,500kč; quadruple 1,300-1,750kč.*
Credit AmEx, EC, V.
This pension is owned by the Sisters of Mercy. You don't have to be a nun to stay here, but it helps: smoking, drinking and staying out after 1am are not allowed. The building was taken over by the Secret Police in the 1950s and you can forsake the cheery upstairs rooms for one of the ex-prison cells below. The steel doors are still in place but have been

President Havel once did time in cell P6, now the **Pension Unitas.**

painted a perky shade of pink in keeping with the new spirit of liberalism. The most popular cell is P6 whose most famous former inmate was President Havel. There are 34 rooms in total; expect to share a bathroom. **Hotel services** *Bureau de change. Car park.*

Youth Hostels

If you can't get a place in one of these hostels, then accommodation agencies – in particular RHIA and Ave (both listed below) – will probably be able to secure you a bed for the night in student accommodation. All bathrooms are shared.

Domov mládeže
Dykova 20, Prague 10 (25 06 88/fax 25 14 29). Metro Jiřiho z Poděbrad/tram 16. **Rates** 260kč.
Located in an elegant street lined with nineteenth-century mansions, this 80-bed hostel is open to all; a few rooms are used by Czech students during the week. It feels more like a village school turned into a pension than a traditional hostel. Rooms, accommodating up to five, are light and comfortable and the owners are very friendly

Hostel Sokol
Hellichova 1, Prague 10 (24 51 06 07 ext 397/fax 561 85 64). Metro Malostranská/12, 22 tram. **Rates** 180kč; *bedding* 54kč.
A hostel with an excellent location in Malá Strana with a roof terrace overlooking Petřín hill, though some may be put off by the communal showers (single sex), the no-smoking house rule and the 20kč surcharge if you come in after 12.30am. There are 85 beds in dormitories.

Libra-Q
Senovážné náměstí 21, Prague 1 (24 10 25 36/fax 24 22 15 79). Metro Mùstek or Hlavní nádraži. **Rates** *single with bathroom* 750kč, *without* 425kč; *double with bathroom* 1,100kč, *without* 700kč; *dormbed* 200kč; *breakfast not included.*
Not nearly as glamourous as its location above the Czech *Elle* offices may imply, this 24-bed hostel offers accommodation in dorms or rooms for one to four people. A central location and no curfew make it a convenient place to stay.

Slavoj-Vesico Hostel
V Náklich 1, Prague 4 (tel/fax 46 00 70). Tram 3, 17. **Rates** 170kč.
On the edge of the river and a good ten-minute walk from the end of the tramline, this is a fair trek from the centre but nevertheless extremely popular. The hostel is run and staffed by four women who dress like *Blue Peter* presenters in white leggings and cheerful polka-dot shirts, and act as super-mums to all their guests, making a point of learning their names and cooking delicious meals. There are 11 rooms with three to five beds in each.

Accommodation Agencies

The prices quoted below are a rough guide and subject to change. *See also chapter* **Survival**.

Ave
Main train station (Hlavní nádraži), Wilsonova 8, Prague 2 (24 22 35 21/fax 24 22 34 63). **Open** 6am-11pm daily. **Rates** *single* from 100kč; *double* from 300kč.
Extremely convenient if you arrive at an awkward time with no place to go, Ave can book hotels and hostels as well as organising accommodation with Czech families. Not as good a choice as some of the other agencies listed, but the office at the airport is open 24 hours a day.

Branches Ruzyně Airport, Prague 6; Holešovice Station (Nádraži Holešovice), Prague 7.

City of Prague Accommodation Service
Haštalské náměstí, Prague 1 (231 02 02/fax 24 81 06 03). Metro Staroměstská. **Open** 9am-noon, 2-6pm, daily. **Rates** *single* 850kč; *double* 1,300kč.
Pricier than average but efficient, this agency has lots of centrally located options and will pick you up from the airport or station.

Hello
Senovážné náměsti 3, Prague 1 (tel/fax 24 21 27 41). Metro Hlavní nádraži. **Open** 9am-10pm daily. **Rates** from 370-980kč per person.
Five minutes' walk from the main station and good value.

PTC
Zapova 4, Prague 5 (54 91 00/54 05 28/fax 53 37 23). Tram 4, 7, 9. **Open** 8.30am-5pm Mon-Fri. **Rates** *apartment for one in the centre* 700kč; *apartment for two* 1,400kč.
A small but flexible firm that can cater for special requests. Contact them in advance rather than on arrival in Prague.

RHIA tours
Školská 1, Prague 1 (24 91 45 14/tel/fax 29 48 43). Metro I.P. Pavlova. **Open** 10am-10pm.daily. **Rates** *single* from 450kč; *apartment for four in the centre* from 2,000kč.
Helpful, friendly, and competitively priced, RHIA also has a good range of youth hostels from 175kč a night.

Top Tour sro
Rybná 3, Prague 1 (232 10 77/fax 24 81 23 86/24 81 14 00). Metro Náměsti Republiky. **Open** 9am-8pm daily. **Rates** *single* from 400-986kč; *double* from 986-1,513kč.
There are no bargains to be found here, but very helpful staff and many satisfied clients judging by the letters on display.

Campsites

The city centre can be reached in less than half an hour by public transport from the sites listed below.

Autocamp Hájek
Trojská 377/149, Prague 7 (66 41 60 31). Metro Nádraži Holešovice then bus 112/5, 17, 25 tram. **Open** June-August. **Rates** *tent* 50-100kč; *person* 40kč; *car* 50kč.
Like most of the campsites along this road, Hájek is just someone's suburban garden. Facilities are basic – there are showers, electricity and the use of two hotplates – but the owner is very friendly. Suitable for tents and caravans.

Autocamp Trojská
Trojská 375/157, Prague 7 (66 41 60 36/fax 854 29 45). Metro Nádraži Holešovice then bus 112. **Open** mid-June-October. **Rates** *tent* 76-120kč; *person* 90kč; *car* 90kč; *bungalow* 2,210kč per person; *single in house* 325kč; *children under 6* 30kč; *children 6-15* 60kč.
Another friendly suburban garden but with the added possibility of staying in a bungalow or a room in the house. There's also a snack bar open from 8am until 10pm.

Intercamp Kotva
U Ledáren 55, Prague 4 (46 17 12/fax 46 61 10). Tram 3, 17. **Open** April-October. **Rates** *tent* 70kč; *person* 80kč; *car* 70kč; *cabin for four* 500kč.
Beautifully located on the edge of the river Vltava with views across to Barrandov hill, this is Prague's oldest campsite and probably the most attractive. Facilities include a washing machine, hotplates, bike rental, tennis courts, canoeing with the nearby watersports club and lots of pretty ducks if your tastes are more contemplative.

Prague by Season

How to celebrate revolution, the First Republic or the coming of spring – Czech style.

Few other cities undergo such a severe form of schizophrenia in the transition from the winter to the summer months as Prague. Fur hats, boots and vistas of the Charles Bridge shrouded in smog or snow give the city an undeniably melancholic air that is thrown off and forgotten as soon as spring arrives. At any time of year you're likely to encounter a music festival or a bizarre tradition.

Information

For more information on events, try the listings section of the *Prague Post* or *Prognosis*, on sale in newsstands in Wenceslas Square.

Bohemia Tickets International (BTI)
Na příkopě 16, Prague 1 (24 21 50 31). Metro Můstek or Náměstí Republiky. **Open** 9am-noon, 1-6pm, Mon-Fri; 9am-4pm Sat; 9am-3pm Sun.
Sells tickets for all the major events.
Branches: Karlova 8, Prague 1 (24 22 76 51); Salvátorská 6, Prague 1 (232 21 44/fax 24 81 03 68); Václavské náměstí 25, (24 22 72 53).

Čedok
Na příkopě 18, Prague 1 (24 19 71 11). Metro Můstek or Náměstí Republiky. **Open** 9am-6pm Mon-Fri; 9am-noon Sat.
Branches: Bílkova 6, Prague 1 (231 94 44); Pařížská 6, Prague 1 (231 43 02).

Melantrich
Václavské náměstí 38 (pasáž Rokoko), Prague 1 (24 21 50 18). Metro Muzeum or Můstek. **Open** 9am-1pm, 2-7pm, Mon-Fri; 9am-2pm Sat.
Sells tickets for the smaller events around the city.

Prague Information Service (PIS)
(Pražská informační služba), Na příkopě 20, Prague 1 (26 40 22/information line 54 44 44). Metro Můstek or Náměstí Republiky. **Open** 8.30am-7pm Mon-Fri; 9am-5pm Sat, Sun.
PIS is the official information service. Phone the information line, or drop into one of the branches.
Branches: Hlavní nádraží, Wilsonova, Prague 1; Staroměstské náměsti 22, Prague 1; Valdštejnské náměsti, Prague 1.

Public Holidays

New Year's Day (1 January); **Easter Monday**; **Labour Day** (1 May); **Day of Liberation from Fascism** (8 May); **Sts Cyril and Methodius** (5 July); **Martyrdom of Jan Hus** (6 July); **Day of the Republic** (28 October); **Christmas Eve**, Christmas Day, **Boxing Day** (24-26 December).

Spring

Spring is the season for which Prague is the most famous and it's also one of the nicest. Hippy kids take over the parks, Czech men sport improbably tight shorts and the year's festivals get under way.

Easter Monday
Public holiday.
Easter Monday is the traditional Czech excuse to indulge in a bit of good old-fashioned sado-masochism. Men with willow sticks rush around the capital laying into any women they can get their hands on. In response women give them shots of alcohol as a 'reward'. It's an ancient fertility rite which allegedly keeps the women 'fresh' for the coming year. Painted eggs – to be found on sale all over the city – are also given as presents.

Witches' Night
Date 30 April.
Witches' night (Pálení čarodějnic), is Hallowe'en and Bonfire Night rolled into one and marks the death of winter and the birth of spring. Bonfires are lit to purge the winter spirits and some more daring adherents of the custom leap over the flames. Traditionally a hag is burnt, a relic of witch hunts of former days. In these liberal times she's usually replaced by an effigy. These days the Czechs prefer to have their fires out in the country but there's usually a pyre or two to be found in the capital, for example on the top of Petřín Hill.

Labour Day
Date 1 May (public holiday).
You are now no longer in danger of being run over by a tank when walking down Wenceslas Square, but May Day is still a good excuse to throw a demonstration. The Communists, in an attempt to keep the faith alive, usually throw a rally and go in for a spot of Havel bashing, while the anarchists hold an altogether unanarchic parade.

Marlboro Rock-In
Tickets and information from Lucerna box office, Štěpánská 31, Prague 1 (24 21 20 03). Metro Můstek. **Date** May.
The Rock-In is the culmination of months of play-offs between amateur bands and the result is a fierce contest between the Good, the Bad and the terminally Ugly. Lots of twangy guitar, smoke and dirty hair.

VE Day
Date 8 May (public holiday).

The Day of Liberation from Fascism used to be 9 May, but as good Euro-citizens, the Czech government fell into line with the rest of the continent and moved it to 8 May, despite the fact that the Red Army didn't reach Prague until a day later. Flowers and wreaths are laid on Soviet monuments – for example on the place where the Soviet tank used to stand in Smichov, before it was painted pink and subsequently removed, in the Garden of Rest at Olšany Cemetery, and throughout the city.

Prague Spring Music Festival

Tickets and information from Hellichova 18, Prague 1 (24 51 04 22/53 02 93/fax 53 60 40). **Date** 12 May-2 June.
Like the revolution of the same name the Prague Spring is oversubscribed by the public and undersupported by the government, so try and book tickets well in advance. It's the biggest and the best of Prague's music festivals and begins every year on 12 May, the anniversary of Smetana's death. A ceremony at his grave in Vyšehrad is followed by a procession to the Smetana Hall and a performance of his tone poem *Má Vlast. See chapter* **Music: Classical & Opera**.

Prague International Book Fair and Writer's Festival

Information from the Prague Information Service (54 44 44), or Michael March, Avencourt Exhibitions Ltd, London (0171 266 1986/fax 0171 586 2429). **Date** May.
The big names of the Czech literary establishment get together to read extracts and hob-nob with foreign writers specially imported for the occasion. It's as good a chance as any to check out Ivan Klima's improbable hair-do and not see veteran writer Bohumil Hrabal who invariably fails to make it out of the pub in time.

May Rituals

Petřín Hill (Petřínské sady), Prague 1. Metro Malostranská/12, 22 tram. **Date** May.
As well as the chance of being pulled underneath a lilac tree and energetically snogged to keep you from being 'dry' in the coming year, May offers further romantic possibilities. Czech lovers, with the sap rising, make a pilgrimage to the statue of Karel Hynek Mácha on Petřín Hill to place flowers and engage in a spot of necking. Mácha was a nineteenth century romantic poet who spawned many myths, several bastards and an epic poem called *Máj* or *May*. It's actually a rather melancholy tale of unrequited love but nobody lets that spoil their fun.

Summer

Anybody travelling around Europe with a backpack and guitar is likely to end up in Prague at some stage or other. The streets are thronged with buskers and any peaceful outdoor drinking is always likely to be interrupted by a dubious Doors cover. As well as impromptu performances all over the city, there are also any number of small classical music festivals to choose between.

Anniversary of Kafka's Death

Olšanské hřbitovy, Vinohradská/Jana Želivského, Prague 3. Metro Flora or Želivského. **Date** 3 June.
Fans make a pilgrimage to Kafka's grave (number 137 at Olšany Cemetery in Prague 3), prayers are said in the Old-New Synagogue, and hundreds of ex-pat poets write odes to his memory.

Commemoration of parachutists who assassinated Heydrich

Kostel sv. Cyrila a Metoděj, Resslova 9, Prague 1. Metro Karlovo náměstí/4, 7, 9, 12, 16 tram. **Date** 18 June.

Summer in Wenceslas Square.

The crypt of this Baroque church was the site of one of the most poignant events of World War II in Prague, and every year a special memorial mass is held to commemorate those who died in the reprisals following Heydrich's assassination. *See chapter* **Sightseeing**.

AghaRTA Jazz Festival

Information from Prague City Council Culture Section (24 48 27 55/fax 43 03 58) or AghaRTA Jazz Centrum (22 45 58/fax26 58 34). **Date** June.
Prague has a fine tradition of jazz, although it was regarded with suspicion by both the Nazis and the Communists and so rigorously suppressed. AghaRTA is one of the city's more dynamic clubs which is keeping the flame alive. The festival is a small one, with lots of outdoor performances by top-class acts.

Dance Prague

Information from Prague City Council Culture Section (24 48 27 55/fax 43 03 58). **Date** June.
Tanec Praha, an international festival of modern dance, has proved to be one of the more successful new festivals. The word 'international' in this case is an accurate description of the participants who come from all over the world to perform in the major theatres as well as giving free exhibitions in public outdoor spaces. There's also a series of workshops, a symposium on dance theory and video demonstrations, at various venues in the city.

National Harley Davidson Rally

Information (25 55 30). Held at Strahov, Olympijská, Prague 6 (35 52 26). Tram 22/132, 143, 149 217 bus/cable-car from Újezd, then walk along Olympijská. **Date** July.
As a symbol of the West and object of desire throughout the Czech lands, Harleys have a cult following. The rally is held

in the giant Strahov Stadium, but since the number of machines in the whole country barely runs into double figures, expect to see a lot of very sad bikers. Heavy Metal and Country music is laid on and there's the chance to vote for the Rock chick of your choice in the Miss Harley Davidson contest.

Art Trek
Information (38 17 11), or from Galerie Mladých, Vodičkova 10, Prague 1 (24 21 36 18). Metro Můstek/9 tram. **Date** mid-August.
An unusual exhibition that gives you the chance to snoop around the private studios of some of the more interesting young artists all over the city.

Spiritual Music Festival
(Společnost pro duchovní hudbu), information from Prague City Council Cultural Section (24 48 27 55/fax 43 03 58). **Date** 16-28 September.
A chance to hear spiritual music, both ancient and modern, performed in some of Prague's fine selection of 630 churches while the weather is still clement enough not to make sitting in an unheated building an endurance test.

Autumn

Catch it while you can, Prague's autumn is short and very sweet.

Burčák arrives
Date late September-early October.
Burčák, the Czech equivalent of Beaujolais Nouveau, hits town in the autumn. It's a young Moravian wine, served straight from the barrel and perfect for outdoor drinking. It looks like cherryade, tastes like cherryade but has the same effect as neat vodka.

Mozart in Prague
Information from Studio Forum Praha (643 75 60). **Date** 1-31 October.
Prague has always had a special relationship with Wolfgang Amadeus and the Mozartfest is a chance to catch up on all his greatest hits in some of the loveliest venues in the city.

Festival of Best Amateur and Professional Puppet Theatre Plays
Information from Union of International Marionettists (43 84 71). **Date** October.
A festival which exploits Bohemia's long tradition of making puppets. Some of the most innovative artists in the country continue to use them, including the celebrated animator Jan Švankmajer, and there's even a faculty at the university devoted to the craft.

Anniversary of the Creation of Czechoslovakia
Date 28 October (public holiday).
The nation no longer exists but the public holiday remains. Republicans spend the day in mourning and various factions hold demonstrations on Wenceslas Square. The Communists used the holiday to commemorate the nationalisation of private property and now, amid mass privatisation, there are calls for the holiday to be moved to 28 September, the anniversary of St Wenceslas' martyrdom.

Winter

The tourists leave and the city battens down for the winter months, but there are still plenty of compensations for the sub-zero weather.

All Souls' Day
Date 2 November.
The best time of year to visit any one of the city's cemeteries. Whole families turn out to light candles, lay wreaths and say prayers for the dead. The best place to go is the enormous Olšany Cemetery (*see chapter* **Sightseeing**).

Anniversary of the Velvet Revolution
Národní and Václavské náměstí. **Date** 17 November.
The first demonstration that eventually burgeoned into the Velvet Revolution took place on 17 November 1989. There are no street parties and it has recently been revealed that the student who died in the 'masakr' didn't in fact die, but was an *agent provocateur* for the secret police. Nonetheless flowers are laid and candles are lit on the memorial on Národní (next to the passage by number 20) and in Wenceslas Square (near the statue of St Wenceslas).

St Nicholas's Eve
Around Charles Bridge, Karlovo náměstí and Staroměstské náměstí, from 4pm on. **Date** 5 December.
Grown men old enough to know better spend the evening wearing unlikely dresses, drinking large amounts of beer and terrorising small children. They parade through the streets in threesomes, dressed as St Nicholas (patron saint of children, merchants and sailors), an angel and a devil, symbolising confession, reward and punishment. Instead of a red polyester cloak, St Nicholas usually looks quite fetching in a long white vestment, with a white mitre and a gold cross. The angel hands out sweets to children who have been good, while the devil is on hand to dispense rough justice to those who haven't.

The week before Christmas
Date December.
Huge tubs of water appear in the streets filled with carp of magnificent proportions. It's the traditional Christmas dish, and while some people buy them live and store them in the bathtub, the more squeamish have the fish of their choice killed and gutted in front of a crowd of less squeamish onlookers.

New Year's Eve
Václavské náměstí and Staroměstské náměstí. **Date** 31 December.
New Year's Eve is known in these parts as St Sylvester's Day, and the streets are invariably packed with a rag-tag bunch of Euro-revellers, with much of the fun centred on Wenceslas Square and the Old Town Square.

Anniversary of Jan Palach's Death
Olšanské hřbitovy and Václavské náměstí. **Date** 19 January.
Jan Palach was the 21 year-old student who set fire to himself on 19 January 1969 in Wenceslas Square, as a protest against the Soviet invasion. His grave is awash with candles and flowers at any time of year, but many people make

Carousing in the Old Town Square on New Year's Eve.

the trip to Olšany Cemetery or the Memorial to the Victims of Communism near St Wenceslas' statue, to lay a few more.

The Ball Season
Tickets and information from Lucerna box office, Štěpánská 31, Prague 1 (24 21 20 03). Metro Můstek.
Date February.

Every self-respecting Czech knows how to waltz and fox-trot, and in February they get to road test their skills at any number of balls held throughout the month. These are attended by people of all ages in some of the most sumptuous venues across the city, including the Municipal House and the State Opera. Every taste is catered for, and you can choose between the Policeman's Ball, the MENSA Ball or the Leo Ball, organised by the porn magazine of that name. The glitziest is the Prague Opera Ball where you have the chance to rub shoulderpads with celebrities like Alain Delon and Ivana Trump.

Out of Town

Miss Czech Republic
Grand Hotel Pupp, Karlovy Vary (017 20 91 11/fax 01 72 40 32). **Date** April.

Banned under the Communists, beauty contests are now enjoying a period of unwarranted popularity and prestige. Cut-throat competition is assured as the line-up of lovelies vie not only for fame and fortune but also a Škoda Favorit.

Karlovy Vary Beer Olympiad
Karlovy Vary, information (017 20 35 69/fax 01 72 46 67). **Date** May.

From the country that produces (probably) the best beer in the world, a beer festival is the logical conclusion. While there are others, this one is sponsored by all the major Czech breweries and is attended by about 20,000 people. A chance

to take part in a 1,000-person beer relay or attempt the world record for drinking a half-litre while standing on your head (time to beat, 9.4 seconds).

International Exhibition of Military Technology
Výstaviště, Brno. Information (05 41 15 29 61/05 41 15 11 11/fax 05 41 15 58). **Date** June 1995, 1997.

The best place in Europe to check out what's new in the world of anti-personnel devices or pick up a land-to-air guided missile. There's also the chance to spot famous faces in the crowd: satisfied customers in 1994 included General Pinochet. The last two days of the five-day exhibition are open to the public.

Karlovy Vary International Film Festival
Film Festival Office (513 24 73/fax 53 05 42). **Date** July, every even year.

This genteel spa town plays host to the Czech version of Cannes. While hardly in the same league, the long-running film festival does show an interesting mix of foreign and home-grown features. *See chaper* **Film**.

Meeting of Foreign Škoda Owners
Automotoklub Heřmanův Městec, 11km SW of Pardubice (045 59 52 18/fax 045 59 57 50). **Date** July.

A highlight in the calendar of any self-respecting Škoda owner. A chance to meet fellow drivers from all over Europe, compare rust and swap new jokes.

Buchlov Festival of Folk Music
Buchlovská svíca, near Uherské Hradiště, South Moravia (06 32 32 88). **Date** end of July/beginning of August.

Folk festivals abound in Bohemia and Moravia during the summer months, but this one has a presidential endorsement. Václav Havel and his wife Olga usually show up to hear the folk-rock bands and give talks about their holidays in India.

Sightseeing

Our tour of the unmissable sights of the city: castles and cafés, Baroque extravaganzas, Cubist houses and Communist monoliths.

The inside of the **Loreto**: an outlandish piece of Baroque fantasy with a high cherub-count.

The citizens of Prague have always had an acute taste for the perverse. The city has embraced every odd-ball movement going, from alchemy to surrealism, and the list of sights is every bit as eclectic as you'd expect to find in the capital of Bohemia. Relics of medieval madness and fantastical Baroque pieces are only half the story. The twentieth century has left its own legacy of artistic outlandishness from Cubist houses to Communist monoliths.

The city, which was ringed by walls right up until the nineteenth century, easily lends itself to sightseeing on foot. And when it all gets too much, there's a wide choice of Art Nouveau cafés and Gothic wine cellars in which you can adopt the recovery position. Without a doubt Prague is at its most alluring by night and no trip to the city is complete without a late stroll through the empty cobbled back alleys, tinted a peculiar shade of orange by the ancient street lamps.

For more background on the sights listed below *see chapter* **Art & Architecture** and for more sightseeing off the beaten track, *see chapter* **Prague by Area**. *See also page 264* **Area Index**.

Hradčany

The Loreto
(Loreta)
Loretánské náměstí 7, Prague 1 (24 51 07 89/53 62 28).
Tram 22. **Open** 9am-12.15pm, 1-4.30pm, Tue-Sun.
Admission 30kč adults; 20kč children, students.
The Loreto probably ranks as the most outlandish piece of Baroque fantasy in Prague. Its attractions include a painting of a bearded lady, the skeletons of two female saints, an ecclesiastical extravagance, and the highest concentration of cherubs to be found anywhere in the city. It was built as part of a calculated plan to reconvert the masses to Catholicism after the Thirty Years War. At its heart is a small chapel called the **Santa Casa** whose history is so improbable that it quickly gained cult status. The story goes that the original Santa Casa was the home of Mary in Nazareth until, one day in 1294, some kind angels flew it over to Loreto in Italy. Two beams and a brick from the 'original' can be seen in the Prague version, as well as a crevice left on the wall by a divine thunderbolt which fell upon an unfortunate blasphemer. The shrine was a particular hit with wealthy ladies of the realm who donated the money for Baroque *maestri* Christoph and Kilián Ignaz Dientzenhofer to construct the outer courtyards and the **Church of the Nativity** (1716-23) at the back. They also sponsored the painting of St Wilgefortis, the patron saint of unhappily married women, who grew a beard as an

extreme tactic to get out of marrying a heathen (in the corner chapel to the right of the main entrance), and that of St Agatha the Unfortunate, who can be seen carrying her severed breasts upon a meat platter (in the Church of the Nativity). The famous **diamond monstrance**, designed in 1699 by Fischer von Erlach and sporting some 6,222 stones, is housed in the treasury (*see chapter* **Museums**).

Strahov Monastery

(Strahovský klášter)
Strahovské nádvoří 1, Prague 1 (24 51 03 55). Tram 8, 22/143, 149, 217 bus. **Open** 9am-noon, 12.30-5pm, Tue-Sun. **Admission** 30kč adults; 5kč children.
The Premonstratensian monks set up home here in 1140, and embarked upon their austere programme of celibacy and silent contemplation. The complex still has a quiet air of seclusion, a fragrant orchard stretching down the hill to Malá Strana and, since 1990, several cowled monks who've returned to reclaim the buildings which were nationalised by the Communists in 1948. Their services are once again held in the **Church of Our Lady** which retains its twelfth century basilica ground plan, although it was remodelled in the early seventeenth century. The cloisters house the **Museum of National Literature** (*see chapter* **Museums**) and a fine permanent exhibition of Medieval art (*see chapter* **Art Galleries**). The highlight of the complex is without a doubt the superb libraries. Within the gilded and frescoed **Theological** and **Philosophical Halls** are 130,000 volumes (there are a further 700,000 in storage) forming the most important collection in Bohemia. The comprehensive acquisition of books didn't begin until the late sixteenth century; when Joseph II effected a massive clamp-down on religious institutions in 1782, the Premonstratensians outwitted him by masquerading as an educational foundation, and their collection was swelled by the contents of the libraries from less canny monasteries. Indeed, the monks' taste ranged far beyond the standard ecclesiastical tracts, including such highlights as the oldest extant copy of *The Calendar of Minutae* or *Selected Times for Bloodletting*. Nor did they merely confine themselves to books: the 200 year-old curiosity cabinets house a collection of deep-sea monsters that any landlocked country would be proud to own.

Prague Castle

Prague Castle (Pražský hrad) looms proudly above the city. Apart from brief interludes it has been the traditional seat of the city's rulers and a symbol of their power since it was founded in the ninth century. The impressive, if somewhat sombre, collection of buildings are a grandiose reflection of the castles' past imperial inhabitants – the two monumental statues of battling Titans over the main gate set the tone as you enter. The vast complex – which includes a palace, three churches and a monastery – was added to over the centuries, and the oldest remains can be found below the crypt of St Vitus's Cathedral and in the Old Royal Palace. The grandiose façade enclosing the complex is the result of the Empress Maria Theresa's desire in the mid-eighteenth century to bring some coherence to the clumsy collection of awkward parts that the castle had become. But the fortress-like appearance of the outer grey walls is no accident: her son Joseph II attempted to turn the palace into a barracks, after which it was largely deserted by the Habsburgs altogether. Václav Havel has chosen not to live here, although he has an office in the castle. He has also been doing his best to enliven the palace, throwing

open doors kept tightly closed during the years of Communist paranoia and hiring the costume designer from the film Amadeus to remodel the guards' uniforms. The number for information on the castle (in Czech) is 33 37 33 68. For a map of the castle area and more on its buildings, *see chapter* **Prague by Area**.

The Belvedere

(Belvedér)
Pražský hrad, Královská zahrada, Prague 1. Metro Malostranská/12, 22 tram.
Seen from the town below, the Belvedere, also known as the **Royal Summer Palace**, looks uncannily like a capsized ship floating above the trees. It was built between 1538 and 1564 in a pure Italian Renaissance style incorporating delicate Ionic columns, yet it is capped by an extraordinary sheet copper roof. It was the first royal structure in Prague to be dedicated to pleasure-seeking rather than power-mongering, commissioned by Ferdinand I as a gift for his wife Anne – a loveshack one remove away from the skulduggery of life in the castle. But the long-suffering Anne never got to see 'the most beautiful piece of Renaissance architecture north of the Alps', as it's invariably dubbed in the city's tourist brochures. She drew her last breath after producing the 15th heir to the throne. The Belvedere went on to become the site of all sorts of goings on: mad King Rudolf installed his astronomers here and the Communists bricked up the windows of the upper level to prevent armed assassins getting too close to the President. Come here today to enjoy the sweetly scented Royal Gardens and a fine view of the cathedral; the art gallery formerly housed in the Belvedere is closed due to lack of funding.

Golden Lane

(Zlatá ulička)
Pražský hrad, Prague 1. Metro Malostranská/12, 22 tram.
Golden Lane is a row of oversized dolls' houses clinging to the northern castle walls and painted all the colours of the rainbow. It is undeniably photogenic and in the summer you're likely to get run over by a stampede of tourists wielding wide-angle lenses. The name is allegedly a reference to the alchemists of King Rudolf's time who were rumoured to live here. Another theory is that soldiers billetted in a nearby tower used it as a public urinal and literally made the street run with gold. In fact, the name probably dates from the seventeenth century when the city's goldsmiths worked here. Although the houses look separate, a corridor actually runs the length of their attics and used to be occupied by the sharp-shooters of the Castle Guard. Kafka lived for a time in Number 22.

Old Royal Palace

(Starý Královský palác)
Pražský hrad, Prague 1 (33 37 31 31). Metro Malostranská/12, 22 tram. **Open** 9am-4.45pm daily. **Admission** 120kč family ticket; 80kč adults; 40kč children, students, OAPs.
Six centuries of kings called the Royal Palace home and systematically built new parts over the old. In what is now the basement you can see the twelfth century remains of Prince Soběslav's residence. A dingy, uninviting chamber, it was filled in by Charles IV and Charles upon. The top floor contains the **Vladislav Hall**, built around 1500 by Benedict Reid. Its exquisitely vaulted ceiling signalled the last flowering of the Gothic, while the large, square windows are the first expressions of the Renaissance in Bohemia. In its day, its 67 metres of length easily accommodated bazaars and tournaments, and the specially designed **Rider's Steps** allowed knights to enter the hall without dismounting. Higher up again is the **Bohemian Chancellery** (*see p44* **Defenestration**).

The renovated **Estates Theatre** *continues its love affair with Mozart. See page 43.*

St Vitus's Cathedral: *it's difficult to tell where the Gothic ends and the neo-Gothic begins.*

St George's Basilica

(Bazilika sv. Jiří)
Pražský hrad, Jiřské náměstí 33, Prague 1 (33 37 31 16).
Metro Malostranská/12, 22 tram. **Open** 9am-4.45pm
daily. **Admission** 120kč family ticket; 80kč adults; 40kč
children, students, OAPs.
Behind St George's Baroque façade lies the oldest piece of
Romanesque architecture in Bohemia. Stand far enough back
from the church and you can see its two pointed towers:
Adam, the larger one on the right, stands guard over Eve on
the left. The basilica, founded by Prince Vratislav in AD921,
has been burnt down and rebuilt over the centuries. Its first
major remodelling took place 50 years after it was first
erected when a Benedictine convent was founded next door.
A major renovation in the early twentieth century swept out
most of the Baroque elements and led to the uncovering of
the original arcades, remnants of thirteenth century frescoes
and the bodies of a saint (Ludmila) and a saint-maker, the
notorious Boleslav The Cruel, who managed to turn his
brother Prince Wenceslas into a martyr by clubbing him to
death. *See chapter* **Prague by Area**; *for* **St George's
Convent**, *see chapter* **Art Galleries**.

St Vitus's Cathedral

(Katedrála sv. Vita)
Pražský hrad, Prague 1 (33 37 32 26). Metro
Malostranská/12, 22 tram. **Open** 9am-noon, 12.30-4pm,
daily. **Admission** 120kč family ticket; 80kč adults; 40kč
children, students, OAPs.
Although St Vitus's Cathedral was only completed in 1929,
exactly 1,000 years after St Wenceslas had been laid to rest
on the site, it is undoubtedly the spiritual centre of Bohemia.
It has always been a holy place: in pagan times there was a
shrine to Svantovit, Slavic god of fertility, here, and right up
until the eighteenth century young women and anxious farmers would bring offerings of wine, cakes and cocks. The cathedral's Gothic structure owes its creation to Charles IV's
lifelong love affair with Prague, but it remained unfinished
until it was adopted and completed by nineteenth century

nationalists, according to the original fourteenth century
plans of Peter Parler. The skill with which the later work was
carried out means it is difficult to tell where the Gothic ends
and the neo-Gothic begins. Its construction spanned two periods of intense nationalism and the cathedral contains treasures from both, including a stained-glass window by the Art
Nouveau master Alphonse Mucha, and some superb examples of medieval art in the **chapel of St Wenceslas**. The
chapel, which stands on the site of the original tenth century
rotunda where Prince Wenceslas was buried, was built in
1345 and has 1,345 polished amethysts, agates and jaspers
incorporated into its design. Unfortunately it is closed to the
public now – too many sweaty bodies were causing the gilded
plaster to disintegrate – but you can peer in over the railings.
Once a year, the skull of the saint is put on display, covered
with a cobweb-fine veil.

St George's Basilica.

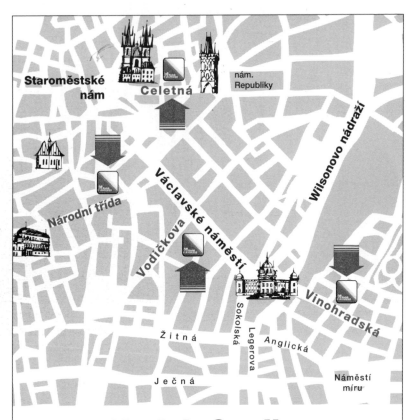

Kodak Quality
Kodak Service
Welcome to Kodak Express

Six locations in Prague to serve you:

FOTO WORLD, Celetná 3, Praha 1   FOTOGRAFIA, Vodičkova 37, Praha 1
FOTO WORLD, Národní 39, Praha 1   FOTO-HAUF, Vinohradská 6, Praha 2
FOTO WORLD, Lidická 66 Praha 5   MINILAB BERY, M. Horákové 35, Praha 7

KONTROLA KVALITY ZPRACOVÁNÍ

The dome and tower of the **Church of St Nicholas** *dominate the Malá Strana skyline.*

Spanish Hall

(Španělský sál)
*Pražský hrad, Prague 1. Metro Malostranská/12, 22
tram. Open for concerts only.*
Gaining access to the Spanish Hall has never been easy for
the general public. It was built in the seventeenth century
for court ceremonies and is connected to the former Rudolf
Gallery which housed Rudolf II's vast collection of paintings,
zoological absurdities and saints' anatomical parts. The
décor was overhauled in the nineteenth century when the
trompe-l'oeil murals were covered with white stucco, and
huge mirrors and gilded chandeliers were brought in to
transform the space into a suitable venue for the coronation
of Emperor Franz Joseph I. Franz Joseph, however, failed to
show up and it was not until the 1950s that the hall was given
a new use, as the unlikely home of the party of the proletariat. It was here that the Politburo came to discuss the success of their latest five-year plan. Today it has become the
most sumptuous concert hall in the city.

Malá Strana

Il Bambino di Praga

(Pražské Jezulátko)
*Kostel Panny Marie vítězné, Karmelitská, Prague 1 (53
07 52). Tram 12, 22. Open 8-45am-8pm daily.*
A 400 year-old wax effigy of the baby Jesus which draws pil-
grims, letters and cash from grateful and/or desperate believ-
ers the world over. The list of miracles that the Infant of
Prague is supposed to have performed is impressive and over
100 stone plaques of thanks attest to his powers. He manages entirely to eclipse his adopted home, the **Church of
Our Lady Victorious** (the first Baroque church in Prague,
built between 1611 and 1613), where the Bambino is displayed in a magnificent glass and gold case. The effigy was

brought from Spain to Prague in the seventeenth century. It
was placed under the care of the Carmelite nuns just in time
to protect them from the plague, and was later rewarded with
official miracle status by the Catholic church. A wardrobe of
over 60 outfits befits this dazzling reputation: the baby Jesus
is always magnificently turned out, and his clothes have
been changed by the Order of English Virgins at sunrise on
selected days for 200 years. While he is said to be anatomi-
cally correct, the nuns' blushes are spared by a specially
designed wax undershirt.

Church of St Nicholas

(Chrám sv. Mikuláše)
*Malostranské náměstí, Prague 1. Metro
Malostranská/12, 22 tram. Open 9am-4.45pm daily.
Admission 20kč adults; 10kč children, students.*
The immense dome and bell tower of St Nicholas, which dominate Malá Strana, are monuments to the money and effort
that the Catholic Church sank into the Counter-Reformation
in Prague. The rich façade by Christoph Dientzenhofer, completed around 1710, conceals an interior dedicated to High
Baroque at its most flamboyant. Commissioned by the Jesuits
who were living well beyond their means, it took three generations of architects (including Dientzenhofer and his son
Kilián Ignaz), several financial crises and the demolition of
much of the neighbourhood, from the presentation of the first
plans in 1653 to the church's final completion in 1755. Inside,
a *trompe-l'oeil* extravaganza created by the Austrian Johann
Lukas Kracker, covers the ceiling, seamlessly blending with
the actual structure of the church below. Frescoes portray the
life and times of St Nicholas. The saint is best known as the
Bishop of Myra and the bearer of gifts to small children, but
he is also the patron saint of municipal administration. Maybe
this is why St Nicholas's was restored by the Communists in
the 1950s when the rest of Prague's Baroque churches were
left to crumble.

Where to find a copy of Selected Times for Bloodletting *in the **Strahov Monastery**. See page 34.*

Church of St Thomas

(Kostel sv. Tomáše)
*Tomášká 8, Prague 1 (53 02 18). Metro
Malostranská/12, 22 tram.* **Open** 10-11am, 1-6pm, daily.
It's worth craning your neck to get a good look at the curvy
pink façade of St Thomas's, which is squeezed into a narrow
street. The lopsided structure is the legacy of an earlier Gothic
church built for the Order of Augustinian hermits. After the
structure was damaged by fire in 1723, Kilián Ignaz
Dientzenhofer, then at the height of his powers and popularity, was employed to give it the Baroque touch. No expense
was spared, and the newly rich burghers of Malá Strana provided enough cash for the frescoes to be completed at break-
neck speed (in only two years) and for Rubens to paint the
altar-piece *The Martyrdom of St Thomas*. They even bought
the bodies of two saints. The original altar-piece is now part
of the National Gallery's collection on show in the **Sternberg
Palace** (*see chapter* **Art Galleries**) and has been replaced
by a copy, but the skeletons of the saints dressed in period
costume are still on display. Next door are the seventeenth
century cloisters, where the monks dabbled in alchemy before
realising that transforming hops into beer was rather easier
and more lucrative than making gold out of base metals. A
door on Letenská leads to their former brewery, now the
restaurant U sv. Tomáše (At St Thomas's).

John Lennon Wall

*Velkopřevorské náměstí, Prague 1. Metro
Malostranská/12, 22 tram.*
During the 1980s a wall in Malá Strana, opposite the French
Embassy, became a place of pilgrimage for the city's hippies,
who dedicated it to John Lennon and scrawled their messages of love, peace and rock 'n' roll across it. The secret
police, spotting a dangerous subversive plot to undermine
the state, lost no time in painting over the graffiti, only to
have John's smiling face appear a few days later. This continued until 1989 when the wall was returned to the Knights
of Malta as part of a huge property package under restitution. The Knights proved to be even more po-faced than the
secret police and were poised, paint brushes in hand, when

an unlikely Beatles' fan, in the form of the French
Ambassador, came to the rescue. Claiming to enjoy the
strains of 'Give Peace a Chance' wafting through his office
window, he sparked a diplomatic incident but saved the wall.
Lennon's face is now crumbling – a victim to souvenir
hunters – but testaments to the power of love continue to be
painted here in languages from Norwegian to Serbo-Croat.

Staré Město

Astronomical Clock

(Orloj)
Staroměstské náměstí, Prague 1. Metro Staroměstská.
Open 11am-5pm Mon; 9am-5pm Tue-Sun. **Admission**
20kč adults; 10kč children.
The Orloj has been ticking, tocking and pulling in the crowds
since 1490. Every hour, on the hour, people gather to watch
wooden statuettes emerge from behind trapdoors and enact
a lurid tale of medieval morality depicting Greed, Vanity and
Death. Much more than a mere clock, the Orloj shows the
movement of the sun and moon through the 12 signs of the
zodiac as well as giving the time in three different formats:
Old Czech Time (in which the 24 hour day is reckoned around
the setting of the sun) and Babylonian Time are the two less
familiar ones. A particularly resilient Prague legend concerns
the fate of the clockmaker, Master Hanuš who was blinded
by the vainglorious burghers of the town to prevent him from
repeating his triumph elsewhere. In retaliation Hanuš thrust
his hands inside the clock and simultaneously ended his life
and (for a short time at least) that of his masterpiece.

Bethlehem Chapel

(Betlémská kaple)
*Betlémské náměstí, Prague 1. Metro Národní třída/6, 9,
18, 22 tram.* **Open** 9am-6pm daily. **Admission** 20kč
adults; 10kč children, students.
The Bethlehem Chapel, a huge, plain, barn-like structure dating from 1391, was where the proto-Protestant **Jan Hus**
delivered sermons in the Czech language to over 3,000

A Magical Experience

ORLÍK

*O*ne of the most romantic and celebrated castles in Bohemia. In 1719 it became the property of the princes of Schwarzenberg and remained so until the Communists confiscated the castle after the 1948 coup. Today lovingly owned by the Schwarzenbergs it is home to a wonderful collection of French empire furniture, paintings, unique hunting guns and rifles, the original Schwarzenberg Family library as well as many other princely treasures. The splendour and lifestyle of the family as it was at the turn of the century is here perfectly preserved.

For reservations:
tel.: ++42 362/96 181, fax: ++431 / 78 71 86

people, accusing the papacy of being, among other things, an institution of Satan. Unsurprisingly, he was hunted down and burnt at the stake in 1415. His last request before being thrown to the flames was for 'history to be kind to the Bethlehem Chapel'. In response the fanatical Jesuits bought up the site and promptly turned it into a wood shed. In the eighteenth century, German merchants moved in and built two houses within the walls. Hus's wish was finally fulfiled under the Communists who regarded him as a working-class revolutionary thwarted by the forces of imperialism and spared no expense in the extensive restoration of the chapel. Three of the original walls remain and still show the remnants of the scriptures that were painted on them in Czech to enable people to follow the service.

Café Slavia

Národní 1, Prague 1. Metro Národní třída/6, 9, 18, 22 tram.

Since the end of the nineteenth century Café Slavia has been much more than just a place to drink coffee. Generations of idlers, ne'er-do-wells and subversives have met here. Housed in the neo-Renaissance building where Smetana composed his operas *Dalibor* and *The Bartered Bride*, it was the birthplace of the Czech surrealist group, the object of a poem by the Nobel Prize-winner Jaroslav Seifert, a favourite spot for the circulation of *samizdat* literature among dissidents (and the none-too-secret policemen) and where Václav Havel wooed his wife Olga. It has been closed since 1991, when an American company won the lease and promptly shut it for 'renovation'. Two years on, with no signs of any work having been done, Václav Havel launched his first public petition since becoming President and declared that the café's continuing absence on the Prague coffee scene was 'spoiling the good relations of Czech intellectuals and American capitalists'. A guerrilla re-opening a week later by 'The Friends of the Slavia' followed by allegations of conspiracy by the American company kept the controversy alive, but at the time of writing the doors were still firmly closed.

Charles Bridge

(Karlův most)
Prague 1. Tram 17, 18.
Staré Město tower **Open** 9am-6pm daily. **Admission** 20kč adults; 10kč children.
Malá Strana tower **Open** 10am-5pm daily. **Admission** 20kč adults; 10kč children.

As well as being the oldest bridge in Prague, and an open-air sculpture gallery, the Charles Bridge is also the city's main drag for hawkers, buskers and assorted exhibitionists. After an earlier bridge had collapsed, no chances were taken with its successor. Astrologers were consulted, who decided that the new structure should be a Leo, and work began on 9 July 1357. Whether the bridge's longevity is due to its star-sign, the fact that it allegedly runs along a ley-line, or the thousands of medieval eggs that were used to bind its mortar, no one knows. But it has proved remarkably resilient to the armies which have marched over it, the saints who have been flung from it and the trams and cars which until the 1950s rattled across it. The statues, which were added in the late seventeenth century as part of an extensive advertising campaign on the part of the Catholic Church, have now mostly been replaced by copies. If you've fallen for the city (and it's hard not to), then you should seek out the gold cross located half-way across the bridge: touch it, make a wish and it's guaranteed that you will return. The very best time to come is at night when the castle is floodlit an eerie shade of green and appears to hover above your head. At the stroke of midnight the switch is thrown, and the castle disappears into the night. *See also chapter* **Prague by Area**.

Church of Our Lady before Týn

(Kostel Matky boži před Týnem)
Týnská, Štupartská, Prague 1 (232 28 01). Metro Náměstí Republiky or Staroměstská. **Open** 12.30-5.30pm

Tue, Wed; 12.30-3pm Thur, Fri; 2-6pm Sat; 12.30-5pm Sun. The twin towers of Týn topped by what look like witches' hats are one of the landmarks of the Old Town. The church dates from the same period as St Vitus's Cathedral (the late fourteenth century) but where St Vitus's was constructed to show the power of King Charles IV, Týn was a church for the people. As such it became a centre of the reforming Hussites in the fifteenth century, before being commandeered by the Jesuits in the seventeenth. They commissioned the Baroque interior which blends uncomfortably with the original Gothic structure. At the end of the southern aisle is the tombstone of **Tycho Brahe**, Rudolf II's personal astronomer, famous for his false nose-piece and his fine line in gnomic utterances. If you look closely at the red marble slab, you'll see the former while the lines above provide evidence of the latter, translating as 'Better to be than to seem to be'.

Clementinum

(Klementinum)
Křižovnické náměstí 4, Prague 1 (24 48 11 11/library 232 20 72). Metro Staroměstská/ 17, 18 tram.
Library **Open** noon-6pm Mon, Wed, Thur; 9am-3pm Tue, Fri; 9am-noon Sat.
Chapel of Mirrors **Open** for concerts only.

After the castle, the Clementinum is the largest historical complex of buildings in the city. In the twelfth and thirteenth centuries it was the Prague headquarters of the Inquisition, and when the Jesuits moved in during the sixteenth century, kicking out the Dominicans who had set up home there in the meantime, they carried on the tradition of fear, intimidation and forcible baptising of the city's Jews. They replaced the medieval church of **St Clement** with a much grander design of their own (rebuilt in 1711-15 and now used by the Greek Catholic church) and gradually constructed the building of today, which is arranged around five courtyards, demolishing several streets and 30 houses on the way. Their grandest work was the church of **St Saviour**, whose opulent but grimy façade faces the Staré Město end of the Charles Bridge, the main drag of the day, and designed to re-awaken the joys of Catholicism in the largely Protestant populace. It was built between 1600 and 1640 and was the most important Jesuit church in Bohemia. The Jesuit's main tool was education and their library, which is occasionally open to the public, is a masterpiece. It was finished in 1727, and has a magnificent *trompe-l'oeil* ceiling split into three parts, showing the three levels of knowledge, with the Dome of Wisdom occupying the central space. However the ceiling started crumbling and to prevent the whole structure from collapsing the **Chapel of Mirrors** was built next door in 1725 to bolster the walls. The interior, decorated with fake pink marble and the original mirrors, is lovely. Mozart used to play here and it is still used for chamber concerts today. At the very centre of the complex is the **Astronomical Tower**, where Kepler, who lived on nearby Karlova came to stargaze. It was used right up until the 1920s for calculating high noon: when the sun crossed a line on the wall behind a small aperture at the top, the castle would be signalled and a cannon fired.

Estates Theatre

(Stavovský divadlo)
Ovocný trh 1, Prague 1 (24 22 85 03). Metro Můstek.
Known under three different official names in its time, the Estates Theatre has always suffered from something of an identity problem, and it is currently unofficially dubbed 'The Mozart Theatre'. Unlike the gentlefolk of Vienna, Prague loved Mozart and Mozart loved Prague. During the composer's lifetime, the theatre staged a succession of his greatest operas, including the premiere of *Don Giovanni*, conducted by Wolfgang Amadeus himself. The building was paid for by Count Nostic, after whom it was named when it opened in 1783 – aimed at promoting productions of works in the German language. But by the late nineteenth century most productions were being performed in Czech, and the name was changed to the Tyl Theatre, after the dramatist J. K. Tyl. His song 'Where is my home?' was played here for

Defenestration

Prague is the home of perhaps the most perverse form of political assassination ever invented: defenestration. A pattern has emerged in which at critical times in the country's history, somebody goes through the window. Below is a hit list of the scene of the crimes.

New Town Hall

(Novoměstská radnice)
Karlovo náměstí, Prague 1. Metro Karlovo náměstí.
The site of the first defenestration is a Gothic tower on Karlovo náměstí, the largest square in the city. The present building is a fourteenth-century remnant of the original New Town Hall. It was here that in 1419 an irate mob, egged on by Jan Želivský, Hussite preacher and rabble rouser extraordinaire, gathered demanding the release of several prisoners incarcerated within the walls. Several Catholic councillors were hurled from an upstairs window and a fashion was started. It's now a popular place to get married, but Želivský is not forgotten. The revisionist historians of the 1960s recast him as a precursor of Communism and a statue of him was erected in front of the building.

Bohemian Chancellery

(Česká kancelář)
Pražský hrad, Prague 1 (33 37 31 31). Metro Malostranská/12, 22 tram. **Open** 9am-4.45pm daily. **Admission** 120kč family ticket; 80kč adults; 40kč children, OAPs.
Relations between Bohemian Protestants and the Catholic Habsburg rulers continued to deteriorate over the next 200 years and finally came to a head on 23 May 1618. A band of noblemen plotted the death of two Catholic governors appointed by Ferdinand II, marched up the steps to the castle and after a fierce struggle succeeded in throwing them and their secretary out of the window. Their fall was broken, however, by a dung heap that had collected beneath that very window. The event marked the start of the Thirty Years War which was to devastate half of Europe. The Chancellery is open to the public and you can admire the same view over the roofs of Malá Strana that the three unfortunates took in moments before their fall.

Černín Palace

(Černínský palác)
Lorentánské náměstí 5, Prague 1. Tram 22. Closed to the public.
The Černín Palace is famous for being the largest palace in Prague, but it certainly isn't the prettiest. Started in 1664, it reflects the gargantuan ambitions – and lack of vision – of its original owner Humprecht Johann Černin, the Imperial Ambassador to Venice. With its Palladian façade and Baroque dimensions, the palace towers over Hradčany. By 1851 it had become a barracks, and in World War II it was the Nazi's Prague headquarters, but after hostilities ceased the Ministry for Foreign Affairs moved back into the building. On 10 March 1948, just days after the Communist *coup d'état* had been announced, the Foreign Minister Jan Masaryk was found dead on the cobblestones outside, having taken a plunge from his office window. Whether he fell or was pushed has never been satisfactorily resolved. The son of Tomáš Masaryk, the founding father of the Czechoslovak Republic, he was the only liberal voice left in the cabinet and had raised strong objections to the Communist takeover. The comrades insisted it was suicide, but their claim would have been rather more convincing had they released the details of the autopsy.

the first time and later adopted as the Czech national anthem. A recent renovation has restored the sparkle to what is one of the finest neo-Classical buildings in the city.

Jan Hus Monument

(Pomník Jana Husa)
Staroměstské náměstí, Prague 1. Metro Staroměstská.
The reformist cleric Jan Hus was considered a heretic by the Catholics and a hero by the Protestants, but was first and foremost Czech. The massive monument to him has been an emotive symbol for nationalists ever since it was erected in 1915 – the quote on the side translates as 'Truth will Prevail'. The sculptor Ladislav Šaloun spent 15 years working on the composition, which was considered an artistic flop when it was finally unveiled on the 500th anniversary of Hus's martyrdom. By then, its fin-de-siècle flamboyancy was already regarded as old-fashioned. The monument was covered with swastikas by the Nazis, who knew a symbol when they saw one, and in black shrouds in 1968. Nowadays it's usually covered with excitable Italians who periodically get rounded up by the police and fined 100kč for sitting on the monument.

Old Town Hall

(Staroměstská radnice)
Staroměstské náměstí, Prague 1 (24 48 20 18). Metro Staroměstská. **Open** 11am-5pm Mon; 9am-5pm Tue-Sun. **Admission** 20kč adults; 10kč children.
The Old Town Hall, established in 1338, was cobbled together over the centuries out of several adjoining houses, but only a tiny portion of the original remains standing today. The present Gothic and Renaissance buildings have been carefully restored since the Nazis declared the building to be 'historische wertvoll', or of historic value, before blowing up a large chunk of it in the last days of World War II. The Old Town coat of arms, adopted by the whole city after 1784, adorns the front of the **Old Council Hall**, and the **clock tower** (*see p41* **Astronomical Clock**), built in 1364, has a viewing platform which is definitely worth the climb. The twelfth century dungeon in the basement became the headquarters of the Resistance during the Prague Uprising in 1944 when reinforcements and supplies were spirited away from the Nazis all over the Old Town via the connecting underground passages. Despite the ferocious bombing they gave the building, the Germans never penetrated the basement, although four scorched beams remain as a testament to those resistance members who fell there. On the side of the clock tower is a plaque in four languages, marked by crossed machine guns, giving thanks to the Soviet soldiers who liberated the city in 1945. There's also a pot of soil from Dukla, a pass in Slovakia where the worst battle of the Czechoslovak liberation took place, resulting in the death of 84,000 Red Army soldiers.

Old Town Square

(Staroměstské náměstí)
Prague 1. Metro Staroměstská.
In the medieval kingdom of Bohemia all roads led to the Old

Prague's answer to the Eiffel Tower, on **Petřín Hill**. *See page 56.*

*An eerie remnant of a once-thriving community: the **Old Jewish Cemetery**. See page 49.*

Town Square and it is still a place where visitors to the city converge to drink coffee, watch the clock and sing Bob Dylan songs on the steps of the **Jan Hus monument** (*see above*). It was the town's main market place and has always been at the centre of the action: criminals were executed here; martyrs were burnt at the stake; and in 1948 this is where crowds greeted the announcement of the Communist takeover. The houses are much older than they look, with Romanesque cellars and Gothic chambers hiding behind the pastel-coloured Baroque and Renaissance façades. If the effect seems somewhat toy town, especially in comparison to the crumbling structures of surrounding streets, it should come as no surprise to learn that it was the Communists who spent an unprecedented $10 million smartening up the square for the 40th anniversary of the Socialist Republic. The most controversial building on the square is the **House at the Stone Bell** on the eastern side. Its outer Baroque layer was stripped away amid much disagreement in the 1980s to reveal a Gothic tower house, now used by the National Gallery for temporary exhibitions (*see chapter* **Art Galleries**). Also worth a look is the Rococo **Golz-Kinský Palace** beside it, which took from 1755-65 to complete. *See also chapter* **Prague by Area**.

The Powder Gate

(Prašná brána)
U Prašné brány, Prague 1. Metro Náměstí Republiky.
Open 9am-5pm daily. **Admission** 20kč adults; 10kč under 6s.
The Powder Gate, or tower, is a piece of medieval flotsam, a lonely relic of the fortifications that used to ring the whole town that is now surrounded on all sides by the twentieth century. The bridge that incongruously connects it to the Art Nouveau masterpiece of Obecní dům (the Municipal House, *see below*) used to give access to the royal palace which stood on the same site during the tenth century. By the mid-fourteenth century Charles IV had founded the New Town, and the city's boundaries had changed. The Powder Gate remained mouldering until it at last gained a purpose, and a

name, when it became a store for gunpowder in 1575. This unfortunately made it a legitimate target for invading Prussian troops and it was severely damaged during the siege of 1757. It was once again left to crumble until the neo-Gothic master Josef Mocker gave it a new roof and re-decorated the sides in the 1870s. Today you can climb a precipitous staircase to the top, though the views from the astronomical clock tower (*see p41*) are better.

St Agnes's Convent

(Klášter sv. Anežky české)
U milosrdných 17, Prague 1. Metro Staroměstská or Náměstí Republiky/5, 14, 26 tram. **Open** 10am-6pm Tue-Sun. **Admission** 40kč adults; 10kč children, students, OAPs.
The convent, the oldest Gothic structure in the city, is hidden away down some of the quietest back streets of the Old Town. It has only managed to survive at all thanks to the nuns' ability to win friends and influence people. Building began in 1233 when the eponymous Agnes tapped her brother the king (Wenceslas I) for a loan and founded a Bohemian Order of Poor Clares. In the sixteenth century the nuns were ousted by their male rivals, the Dominicans, who promptly turned the convent into a brewery. After much politicking the women retrieved their property only to have their order dissolved completely in the eighteenth century by Joseph II. The cloisters became home to over 100 families and were going to be cleared as part of the same high-minded 'sanitisation' crusade that led to the destruction of the surrounding Jewish Quarter. Friends of the convent, however, gained the ear of the power-brokers in Vienna and extensive restoration work began instead. The convent is now owned by the **National Gallery** which displays its nineteenth-century Czech collection here. *See chapter* **Art Galleries**.

Charles Bridge: *favoured by buskers and assorted exhibitionists. See page 43.*

Communist Prague

Anděl Metro

Line B, Smíchov, Prague 5.

A gleaming space-age souvenir of the Soviet occupation, the whole of the metro system is a constant source of joy for Western visitors. Anděl station is worth a special mention as it still sports some fine marble murals of square-jawed Soviets thrusting forward into a bright socialist future against a backdrop of towerblocks and St Basil's Cathedral. Formerly called Moskevská, or Moscow Station, it has an enduring link with the mother country: there is an exact replica of the station in Moscow which, to this day, is called Prashskaya, or Prague Station.

Háje

Náměstí Kosmonautů, Prague 4. Metro Háje.

This high-rise housing estate of monumental tower blocks offers an authentic taste of Socialist Realism. It may not look like the worker's paradise, but the concrete monoliths are called home by one third of Prague's population. Thrown up in the sixties as a fast solution to the city's chronic housing shortage, the thin walls, overcrowded conditions and fundamental ugliness are blamed for everything, from the 75% divorce-rate to the lack of poetry in modern life. Housing developments now ring the whole city, but Háje, the last metro stop on the red Line C is as good a place as any to go to see the best of the worst. This might be an unremittingly bleak environment, but some positive legacies of the socialist way are also still in place: there's always heating and hot water, transport links are excellent and there's surprisingly little vandalism. Before the big name change of 1989, Háje used to be known as Kosmonautů, a nod in the direction of the sister state's space programme and there's still a rather humourous sculpture of two cuddly cosmonauts outside the metro. The new name means 'groves', which only adds irony to insult.

Hotel International

Koulova 15, Prague 6 (311 82 54). Metro Dejvická/20, 25 tram.

Plans were made in the 1950s to transform Prague with monumental boulevards and skyscrapers along strictly Socialist Realist lines, although happily few left the drawing board. The Hotel International is one notable exception, a solid piece of Stalinism dating from 1956 and marooned in the suburb of Dejvice. The architects, a frustrated group of rocket designers from the Institute of Military Design, preferred to remain anonymous. If you've never been to Moscow, this is what it looks like. The red star has now been tactfully removed from the top, but the façade still has decorative friezes of noble peasants wielding hammers and sickles. The bars, which used to be populated by Party officials after a hard day spent inventing production figures, have now been taken over by morose-looking mafioso types. It's still a good place to go, though, to view the marble murals and ponder upon the wisdom of combining lime-green, orange and brown.

National Memorial

(Národní památník)

U památníku, Prague 3 (627 84 52). Metro Florenc/133, 168, 207 bus. **Open** 1-5pm Tue-Fri; 10am-5pm Sat, Sun. **Admission** 10kč adults; 5kč children, students, soldiers, OAPs.

The National Memorial is one of the city's best known and least liked landmarks. Located in the eastern working class suburb of Žižkov, the massive rectangular block and

A mass rally held in April 1949.

equally enormous equestrian statue high up on Vitkov Hill can be seen from many points around the city. It was built in the Constructivist style in 1925 by Jan Zázvorka as a dignified setting for the remains of the Legionaires who fought against the Austro-Hungarian Empire in World War I and helped to gain independence. In 1953 it was refitted out by the Communist regime and was turned into a mausoleum for the heroes of the Working Class. The mummified remains of Klement Gottwald, the first Communist President, were kept here, tended by a team of scientists who (unsuccessfully) tried to prevent his body from disintegrating. In 1990 Gottwald's body was returned to his family and the mausoleum was off-limits for four years pending a change of purpose. It's now open and is one of the best-kept sightseeing secrets in the city; plans are afoot to turn it into a cultural centre but for the time being it's deserted and an English speaking guide is on hand to give you the full tour. In front of the mausoleum stands the largest equestrian sculpture in the world, more impressive, maybe, for its entry in the *Guiness Book of Records* than its overwhelming artistic merit. It portrays the one-eyed General Žižka, the scourge of fourteenth-century Catholics and the darling of the Communists who adopted him in an effort to establish genuine Bohemian credentials.

Stalin Monument

Letenské sady, Prague 1. Metro Hradčanská/12, 17 tram.

The most obvious feature of the place known as the Stalin Monument in Letná Park is that there is no longer a monument to the man. However, despite its 25-year absence, it still has a special place in the city's collective memory. The political mistiming of the monument was uncanny, barely enjoying a year's peace before Uncle Joe was denounced by Khrushchev in 1956. The monument's architects were Jiří and Vlasta Štursa and the tower block designer Otokar Švec, whose plan beat all comers because they placed two lines of workers – one Czech and one Soviet – behind the colossal figure and thus circumlocuted the problem of passers-by having to look up Stalin's bottom. Unfortunately as a result the statue gained the nickname 'tlačenice', or 'the queue', since it looked as if the comrades were heading a meat line. The hillside below is still riddled by nuclear bunkers built to protect the city's élite in the case of a rocket attack. On the massive plinth where Stalin once stood there is now a giant immobilised metronome, designed in 1991 by artist David Černý.

The **Old-New Synagogue**: *a forlorn piece of medievalism and the oldest survivor of the ghetto.*

Josefov

Klausen Synagogue

(Klauzová synagóga)
U starého hřbitova 4, Prague 1 (231 03 02). Metro Staroměstská. **Open** 9.30am-12.30pm Mon-Fri, Sun.
Admission 80kč adults; 30kč children, students.
The best view of the Klausen Synagogue is from inside the Old Jewish Cemetery. The simple façade rises behind the ancient gravestones, topped by two tablets of the decalogue engraved with a golden inscription. The exact shape of the tablets is echoed in the two semi-circular vaulted windows at the top, two larger ones lower down and in the decorative details on the balustrade. Lack of space meant the synagogue was built on the extreme edge of the ghetto on a street that had been frequented by ladies of ill-repute since the Middle Ages and was called Hámpejska, which means brothel. The building was hastily constructed on the site of the original Klausen Synagogue after the great ghetto fire of 1689 which destroyed 318 houses and 11 synagogues, and it was completed in 1694 by the same workmen who built many of Prague's Baroque churches. Inside is a permanent exhibition of Hebrew manuscripts and prints as well as other religious artefacts (*see chapter* **Museums**).

Old Jewish Cemetery

(Starý židovský hřbitov)
U Starého hřbitova, Prague 1. Metro Staroměstská.
Open 9am-4.30pm Mon-Fri, Sun.
The Old Jewish Cemetery is one of the eeriest remnants of Prague's once thriving Jewish community, which as the subject of pogroms, harassment and finally almost complete eradication under the Nazis, has now all but disappeared. While this is truly a city of the dead, its name in Hebrew is

Beth Chaim, or House of Life. Along with the Town Hall and a few synagogues, the cemetery was saved when the ghetto was razed by the city authorities in the 1890s, and today 12,000 tombstones are crammed into the cemetery, falling picturesquely on top of one another but providing a reminder of the terrible lack of space accorded the Jewish ghetto which was rigidly confined within walls until the late eighteenth century. Beneath the ground are an estimated 100,000 bodies piled up 12 deep – all Jews were buried here until 1787 when the New Jewish Cemetery was created. The most prominent tombs belong to Rabbis Maisel and Loew, and both are always covered with pebbles and messages. **Loew** is perhaps the most famous ex-inhabitant of the ghetto. A sixteenth century scholar and preacher and eventually chief rabbi of the ghetto, he was a friend of the Emperor Rudolf II, whose taste for the weird and wonderful led to an interest in the Cabbala. Loew's fabled creation was the golem – a man made from clay and brought to life by a *shem* – the unutterable name of God. **Maisel** (1528-1601) was mayor of the ghetto during the reign of Rudolf II, and died one of the wealthiest men in Europe. Decorative reliefs on the headstones symbolise the deceased's name or their occupation: a mouse, for example, represents Mr Maisel, and a pair of scissors would show that he was a tailor. For a different perspective, visit the first floor of the Museum of Decorative Arts. From here you can look down on the cemetery in peace and quiet. *See also chapters* **Prague by Area** *and* **Museums**.

Old-New Synagogue

(Staronová synagóga)
Červená 2, Prague 1. Metro Staroměstská. **Open** 9am-noon, 12.30-5pm, Mon-Thur, Sun; 9am-noon, 12.30-4pm, Fri. **Admission** 80kč adults; 30kč children, students.
The Old-New Synagogue is a rather forlorn piece of medievalism surrounded by opulent fin-de-siècle apartment

buildings on all sides, wedged as it is between the ultra-bourgeois Maiselova and Pařižská streets. The oldest survivor of the ghetto and the spiritual centre of the Jewish community for over 600 years, it's still used for services today even though it officially belongs to the state which is dragging its feet shamefully over the issue of restitution. The austere exterior walls give no clues to its peculiar Gothic interior, atmospherically lit by electric candles. An extra rib was added to the usual vaulting pattern to avoid the symbolism of the cross. Instead the décor and structure revolves around the number 12, after the 12 tribes of Israel: there are 12 windows, 12 bunches of sculpted grapes, and clusters of 12 vineleaves decorate the pillar bases. The interior was left untouched for 500 years as a reminder of the blood spilt here during the pogrom of 1389, when the men, women and children who sought sanctuary in the synagogue were slaughtered by rampaging Christians. The nineteenth century neo-Gothic crusaders, however, couldn't resist the temptation to 'restore' the original look and slapped a fresh coat of paint over the top.

Pinkas Synagogue

(Pinkasova synagóga)
Široká 3 (entrance from the Old Jewish Cemetery), Prague 1. Metro Staroměstská. **Open** 9.30am-1pm, 1.30-5.30pm, Mon-Fri, Sun. **Admission** 80kč adults; 30kč children, students.

Rabbi Pinkas – according to a contemporary chronicler a member of the clan of 'recalcitrant, sharp tongued Pinkases' – founded the synagogue in 1479 after falling out with the elders at the Old-New. The building was enlarged in 1535, and a Renaissance façade added in 1625. Its importance, however, lies not in its history or in its architecture, but in the 77,297 names painted on the inside. These list the men, women and children of Bohemia and Moravia who were dispatched to Nazi deathcamps and never returned home. The names were taken from duplicates of the transport files which the Jewish clerks secretly compiled, and cover every available wall space. The synagogue was turned into a memorial between 1950 and 1954, but when Czech-Israeli relations broke down after the Six Day War, it was closed for 21 years of 'restoration' in which time the interior decayed unseen. Now the real process of restoration is taking place and you can watch as the names are carefully repainted.

Rudolfinum

(Dům umělců)
Alšovo nábřeží 12, Prague 1 (24 89 33 52). Metro Staroměstská. **Open** 10am-5.30pm daily. **Admission** 30kč adults; 15kč OAPs, 6-15 year-olds.

Now it has been scrubbed clean of decades of Prague soot, the Rudolfinum is fit once again to fulfil its role as 'House of Artists' for which it was built (between 1876 and 1884, and named after Prince Rudolf of Habsburg). In 1918 the concert hall became home to the parliament of the new Republic. When Chamberlain returned to England from meeting Hitler in 1938 disclaiming responsibility for the 'quarrel in a faraway land between people of whom we know nothing', it was here that 250,000 of these unknown people came to take an oath and pledge themselves to the defence of the Republic. The Nazis, having little use for a parliament building, turned it back into a concert hall and called it 'The German House of Arts'. A statue of the Jewish composer Mendelssohn was ordered to be removed for obvious reasons, but the workmen, not knowing what Mendelssohn looked like, took their lessons in racial science to heart and removed the figure with the biggest nose – which turned out to be Richard Wagner. They were promptly packed off to the Front but Mendelssohn and Wagner have since been reunited.

A monument to Czech nationalism, the **National Theatre***.*

Nové Město

Church of Sts Cyril and Methodius

(Kostel sv. Cyrila a Metoděj)
Resslova 9, Prague 1 (29 55 95). Metro Karlovo náměstí/4, 7, 9, 12, 14, 16 tram. **Open** 9-11am Mon-Sat.
A Baroque church, built in the 1730s, which was restored and taken over by the Czech Orthodox Church in the 1930s. A plaque and memorial outside, which still attracts tributes and flowers today, are clues to what happened inside during World War II. In 1942 two Czech paratroopers trained in England were flown into Bohemia to carry out the assassination of Richard Heydrich, the Reichprotektor of Bohemia and Moravia and the man who gave the world the phrase 'The Final Solution'. Gabčik, Kubiš and five resistance fighters were given sanctuary in the crypt of this church after the event, until someone tipped off the Germans. In the early hours of the 18 June, 350 members of the SS and Gestapo surrounded the church and spent the night bombarding it with bullets, grenades, water cannon and smoke. The men who survived until day-break used their final bullets to shoot themselves. The incident did not end there, however. Recriminations were swift, brutal and arbitrary. Hundreds of people, many of them Jews, were rounded up in Prague and shot immediately, while five whole villages and all of their inhabitants were liquidated, the most famous being Lidice. The final body count was well over 5,000. The events brought about a turning point. Britain repudiated the Munich Agreement and Anthony Eden declared that Lidice had 'stirred the conscience of the civilised world'.

National Museum

(Národní muzeum)
Václavské náměstí 68, Prague 1 (24 23 04 85). Metro Muzeum. **Open** 10am-6pm Mon, Tue, Thur-Sun; 10am-9pm Wed. **Admission** 25kč adults; 5kč children, students, OAPs, under 6s.
The National Museum has provided Wenceslas Square with a natural focus since it was completed in 1890, despite the fact that the Communists insisted it was not on Wenceslas Square at all but on Victorious February Street. In 1989 it had its correct address restored, if not its structure, which developed several alarming cracks after the metro was tunnelled directly beneath it. It is a colossal neo-Renaissance edifice whose importance was recognised by the invading Warsaw Pact troops in 1968 when they opened fire on it. They had failed to realise that it was not in fact the parliament building – an insignificant modern structure just to the left – and the pockmarks of their mistake can still be seen in the façade today. At the heart of the building is the **Pantheon**, housing busts and statues of the great and good of Czech history. Unsurprisingly in a country that has seen its fair share of strife, the contents of the Pantheon have proved to be a controversial issue. Nationalists, Nazis, Communists and most recently Democrats, have hauled a total of 21 statues up and down the stairs from the basement over the years. The other collections housed by the museum, devoted principally to anthropology, natural history and archaeology, are rather uninspiring. *See chapter* **Museums**.

National Theatre

(Národní divadlo)
Národní 2, Prague 1 (24 91 34 37). Metro Národní třída/6, 9, 17, 18, 22 tram. **Open** *box office* 10am-6pm Mon-Fri; 10am-12.30pm, 3-6pm Sat, Sun.
Standing proudly on the banks of the Vltava, topped by a crown of gold and with sculptures of bucking stallions lining the balustrade, the National Theatre is a product and symbol of the fervour of nineteenth century Czech nationalism. It took 20 years to persuade the general public to cough up the money to begin construction, and from 1868 to 1881 to build it. Then, days before the curtain was about to go up on the first performance, it was gutted by fire in a single

1968

Olšany Cemetery

(Olšanské hřbitovy)
Vinohradská/Jana Želivského, Prague 3. Metro Flora or Želivského.
Olšany is the last resting place of two unlikely bed fellows: the first Communist president Klement Gottwald, who died after catching cold at Stalin's funeral, and the most famous anti-Communist martyr, Jan Palach. In death their fates have been strangely linked, as neither of their mortal remains has been allowed to rest in peace. Palach was originally buried here in 1969, when 800,000 people attended his funeral, but his grave became such a focus of dissent that the authorities disinterred his body and reburied it deep in the Bohemian countryside. In 1990 he was dug back up and brought back to Olšany. You can find his grave just to the right of the main entrance. Gottwald is harder to locate, hidden away in Section 5 and sharing a mass grave with various other discredited party members. In 1990 his mummified remains were ejected unceremoniously from the National Mausoleum and returned to the family. An unusual index of popular opinion is to check which grave is sporting the most floral tributes and candles.

Radio Prague Building

Vinohradská 12, Prague 2. Metro Muzeum/11 tram.
When the tanks of the Warsaw Pact rolled into town in August 1968, Prague's astonished citizens took to the streets, ripped down signposts, placed flowers in the gun barrels of the tanks and attempted to wage a war of attrition. This unremarkable building in the suburb of Vinohrady became the site of a pitched battle between the two sides as the populace attempted to safeguard the broadcasting studios of Radio Prague. Barricades were thrown up, cars were set on fire and people threw themselves in the path of armoured vehicles. For the first 14 hours of the invasion, the radio station managed to go on transmitting, marshalling the resistance and providing news of the crisis. Although the station has since moved, a plaque on the side commemorates the five people who died and the 65 who were injured.

---

night. An emotive appeal, launched immediately by the leading lights of the city's cultural institutions, raised enough money to start all over again in just six weeks. In 1883 the building finally opened with a gala performance of *Libuše*, an opera written especially for the occasion by Smetana. The city at last had a venue where plays could be performed in the native tongue rather than in German, the language of its imperial rulers.

Wenceslas Square

(Václavské náměstí)
Prague 1. Metro Můstek or Muzeum/3, 9, 14, 24 tram.
Wenceslas Square is not in the least bit square, but then its namesake 'Good King Wenceslas' was neither a king nor especially good. The square is, in fact, a wide boulevard half a mile long that is crowned by the neo-Renaissance edifice of the National Museum – the backdrop to a thousand outside broadcasts in 1989. It has always been a popular place to stage a revolution, as it can comfortably accommodate about 400,000 people. Numerologists will probably find significance in the fact that the street was founded in 1348 and played host to civil unrest in 1848, 1918, 1948, 1968 and, of course, 1989. The square was started by Charles IV who forbade any building to exceed two storeys. He would surely be horrified to see it today – a study of the best and worst of twentieth century architecture. It has become the main commercial artery and, since 1989, the vanguard of the free-market in Prague. This is where you will also find the big travel agents, McDonald's and numerous prostitutes. *See p55* **St Wenceslas' Statue,** *and p54* **Evropa Café.**

Further Afield

Troja Château

(Trojský zámek)
U trojského zámku 4, Prague 7 (84 07 61). Metro Nádraží Holešovice. **Open** 10am-5pm Tue-Sun.
Admission 40kč adults; 10kč children, students.
After winning huge tracts of land in the property lottery that followed the Thirty Years War, Count Sternberg embarked upon creating a house worthy of his ego and as a proof of his loyalty to the Habsburgs. The project was beset with numerous problems, however, and he didn't live to see it finished. Local craftsmen – card-carrying members of their guild – refused to work with the foreign architect Sternberg had employed for the job (the Burgundian Jean-Baptiste Mathey) and the plague then further disrupted the schedule. The completed villa is impressive, modelled on a Classical Italian villa and surrounded by formal gardens in the French style, interspersed with fountains and sculptures. The extravagant interior alone makes the trip here an essential one. At the core of the building is the **Grand Hall** where Godyn's stunning *trompe-l'oeil* frescoes celebrate the Habsburg dynasty. To see it you have to don huge red slippers to protect the marble floors, which have the effect of making visitors look like Smurfs. *See chapter* **Art Galleries.**

TV Tower

(Televizní vysílač)
Next to Fibichova, Prague 3. Metro Jiřího z Poděbrad.
Closed to the public.
The huge, thrusting television transmitter in Žižkov has been dubbed the 'Pražský čůrak' or 'Penis of Prague'. Seemingly modelled on a Soyuz rocket ready for blast off, it has been more of a hit with space-starved visitors than with the locals. No sooner had it been completed early in 1989 than it came under attack from nearby residents who claimed it was guilty of, among other things, jamming foreign radio waves and giving their children cancer. Although cleared on both counts, it is easy to understand the Big Brother analogies. You can take a lift up to the viewing platform, but in many ways standing at the base and looking up the 287 metres of polished steel is even more scary.

Vyšehrad

Soběslavova 1, Prague 2 (29 66 51). Metro Vyšehrad.
Open 9.30am-5.30pm daily. **Admission** 10kč.
The mythical version of Prague's history insists that Vyšehrad is the original seat of the city's rulers: it was from here that Libuše, the matriarch of the kings of Bohemia, sent out her minions to find a lusty ploughman to enable her to propagate the Přemyslid dynasty. Several teams of learned archaeologists have failed to uncover any evidence whatsoever to back this up, but it has been established that the area was a seat of power briefly in the eleventh century

Ready for take-off: Prague's unpopular **TV Tower** *in Žižkov.*

when Vladislav set up court here after falling out with his brother over land ownership. Today you will find a park situated high up on a hill with fine views over the Vltava valley and Prague itself. Further attractions include the oldest rotunda in the city (the **Church of St Martin**, which dates back to the eleventh century), some of the only remaining fortification walls, a second-rate neo-Gothic church (the **Church of Sts Peter and Paul**) and a first-rate cemetery containing most of the dead Czechs you're likely to have heard of.

Art & Design

Art Nouveau

Art Nouveau, or Secession as it was known in the Austro-Hungarian Empire, was the main architectural expression in Prague at the turn of this century. It self-consciously rejected the parade of neo-historical styles that had dominated the previous three decades and, using the new technology in steel and iron, created sensuous new shapes, heavily ornamented with flora and fauna motifs. The following buildings show the style at its most sumptuous:

Evropa Café

Václavské náměstí 25, Prague 1 (24 22 81 17). Metro Můstek. **Open** 7am-midnight daily.
The Evropa Café is the perfect place to combine coffee, cream cakes and culture, enabling you to check out exquisite Art Nouveau detailing without leaving your seat. The interior has remained untouched since its completion in 1912, and the atmosphere of down-at-heel grandeur is perfectly complemented by a down-at-heel string quartet. The café is part of the Grand Hotel Evropa, whose gold-edged façade topped by a glass globe held aloft by muscle-bound sculptures is one of the chief glories of Wenceslas Square. You're free to wander through the hotel and take in its cavernous lobbies and original fixtures and fittings.

Main Station

(Hlavní nádraží)
Wilsonova, Prague 1. Metro Hlavní nádraží.
Smelly, crumbling and inhabited by lowlifes, Hlavní nádraží (also known as Wilsonova Station) is an unlikely place to seek out the pleasures of Prague's bourgeois age. That it had been dedicated first to Emperor Franz Joseph and then to the American President Wilson gave the Communists two very good reasons to plant a high-speed bypass outside its front door, create a modern soulless extension and rechristen it Central Station. The upper levels, which have been left to rot in obscurity, are an atmospheric remnant of a bygone age. The restaurant contains some of the best Art Nouveau murals anywhere in Prague, with languorous women serving as a backdrop to the die-hard beer drinkers beneath.

Municipal House

(Obecní dům)
Náměstí Republiky 5, Prague 1. Metro Náměstí Republiky. Closed for restoration.
All the leading artists of the day were involved in the creation of Obecní dům, a masterpiece of stained glass, coloured mosaics, tiled murals and gold trimmings. Although built during the death-throes of the Austro-Hungarian Empire, the building became a symbol of the aspirations of the new republic, representing a stylistic and structural break with the *ancien régime*. It was here that the newly independent state of Czechoslovakia was signed into being in 1918, and a plaque on the side pays a now rather sad tribute to the

country which no longer exists. A major renovation costing an estimated 453kč million is underway, giving Obecní Dům the first overhaul it has had since its completion in 1912. When it re-opens, the spectacular Smetana Hall at the centre of the building will once again be used for concerts, and you'll be able to see a whole host of other civic rooms including, most splendidly of all, the Lord Mayor's Salon, which is covered with murals by Alphonse Mucha depicting the heroes of Czech history. For the time being, however, visitors will have to content themselves with peeping through the windows and examining the outside. The façade is by Osvald Polívka who also designed the exquisitely ornamented café and restaurant; the monumental mosaic called 'Homage to Prague' above the main entrance, featuring languid ladies in an altogether un-urban setting, is by K Spillar. It's off-set by Ladislav Saloun's sculptural composition entitled 'The Humiliation and Resurrection of the Nation'.

Výstaviště

U Výstaviště, Prague 7. Metro Nádraží Holešovice/5, 12, 17 tram.
Built out of curvaceous expanses of wrought iron to house the Great Exhibition of 1891, Výstaviště signalled the birth of the new architectural form in Prague. During the 1940s it became the site of various Communist congresses, but today it is principally used to house car and computer expos. It's worth dodging past the salesmen to see the interior. The industrial feeling created by the wrought-iron structure is offset by vividly stained glass and exquisite floral decorations. The best view of the exterior is from the back, where a monumental modern fountain gushes in time to popular classics. The grounds are filled with architectural oddities, an open-air cinema and a sorry-looking funfair which nevertheless pulls in crowds of Czech families at the weekends.

Cubism

No other city took Cubism to its heart as completely and energetically as Prague. Following on the heels of Picasso's and Derain's experiments in Paris, the movement enjoyed a short but vivid period of popularity from 1911 to 1920. Cubist architecture is unique to Prague and is fascinating to see.

Diamant House

(Dům Diamant)
Spálená 82/4, Prague 1. Metro Národní třída/3, 9, 14, 24 tram.
The Diamant House was designed by Emil Králíček in 1912, and takes its name from the broken up prisms that constitute the façade. The ground floor has now become a Škoda showroom and the neon strip lights that adorn it are a dubious aesthetic addition. A nice touch is the Cubist arch which shelters a piece of Baroque statuary and bridges the gap, literally and historically, between this building and the eighteenth century Church of the Holy Trinity next door.

Cubist Lamp Post

In front of kostel Panna Marie Sneznà, Jungmannovo náměstí, Prague 1. Metro Můstek.
This is not just the finest example of a Cubist lamp post you'll ever see, it is the only Cubist lamp post you'll ever see. It's a striking piece of work, designed by Emil Králíček and Matěj Blecha in 1912, and stands in front of the Church of Our Lady of the Snows on Jungmannovo Square. Four seats are incorporated into the base. The best view of it is from another important modern work, the Baťa shoe store (1927-9). Go to the third floor and see how the revolutionary glass curtain wall, used for the first time here, allows a perfect bird's eye view.

1989

'Good King' Wenceslas, the caped crusader, as seen by Josef Myslbek.

Adria Palace

(Palác Adria)

Národní 40, Prague 1 (24 22 77 75). Metro Národní třída/6, 9, 18, 22 tram.

The Adria Palace, built in 1923 for an Italian insurance company, looks like no other building in Prague. It is a perfect example of the Rondo-Cubist style developed by the pioneering designer Pavel Janák in his bid to create a distinctive twentieth century Czech architecture. This bizarre latter-day fortress was one of the few projects to get off the drawing board. The basement was until last year the home of the Laterna Magika (Magic Lantern) theatre, a form of multi-media experimental theatre invented in the 1950s. It also became a base for the Civic Forum in November 1989 after the so-called 'masakr' took place on Národní. A loose association of people, many of them signatories of Charter 77 including Václav Havel, formed themselves into Civic Forum (Občanské fórum), and became the self-appointed voice of the people. The theatre was the nerve-centre of the series of demonstrations and strikes that finally succeeded in toppling the government. Strategy was discussed on the stage against a set designed for a production of *Minotaurus*, press conferences were held in the auditorium, and from his office in a dressing room, Havel issued communiqués to the world.

Melantrich Building

Václavské náměstí 30, Prague 1. Metro Můstek.

The home of *Svobodné Slovo*, the Socialist Party's official newspaper, this is an unremarkable 1930s building topped by a Czech flag made of flashing neon bulbs. On the second floor is a long balcony that became the unlikely venue for one of the most astounding incidents of the Velvet Revolution. On 24 November, in front of a crowd of over 300,000 people, Václav Havel and Alexander Dubček stepped forward and embraced, signifying the end of 21 years of 'normalisation'. The crowd was incredulous, but within hours the entire cabinet had resigned. Foreign companies are now vying to buy up the building and redevelop it, with plans of varying unsubtlety. One involves adding a skyscraper with a helipad, which the investor declares will 'allow an American President to land on the roof and commemorate the toppling of totalitarianism'.

St Wenceslas' Statue

Václavské náměstí, Prague 1. Metro Muzeum.

Seated on his horse ready to charge down Wenceslas Square, St Wenceslas will supposedly gallop into action to save the Czechs in their hour of greatest need. Prince Wenceslas (or Václav, and not to be confused with the four kings of that name) became Bohemia's sovereign in about 921. A pious Christian at a time when most of his subjects were still pagan, he was murdered by his brother Boleslav The Cruel in 935. His legend became a national cult some 400 years later under Charles IV, and his place in posterity as a saint, national martyr and hero was thus secured. The equestrian statue took its designer, Czech sculptor Josef Václav Myslbek, 30 years to complete (in 1912). The base is flanked by the figures of four Czech patron saints, Adalbert, Procopius, Ludmila and Agnes. The caped crusader became a rallying point and information swapshop during the Velvet Revolution and a flowerbed a few metres below the statue became an unofficial memorial, covered with flowers, candles and photos, commemorating Jan Palach, the student who torched himself here in 1969 in protest at the Soviet invasion. While the posters have been scraped off the statue, the shrine remains and has been given an official name: the Memorial to the Victims of Communism.

House of the Black Madonna

(Dům U Černé matky boží)
Celetná 34, Prague 1. Metro Náměstí Republiky.
The house was the first piece of Cubist architecture to be built in Prague, but its value was neglected for many years and the interior left to decay. It stands at an angle between Celetná and Ovocný streets, a massive Cubist portal dominating the entrance. Originally built as a department store, the house had a café on the first floor, furnished in the Cubist style, which was a popular hang-out for avant-garde types in the 1920s. The Black Madonna itself is a bizarre relic from an earlier Baroque building that occupied the site, and is displayed in a cage on the outside of the building. The house has recently been bought by the Czech Museum of Fine Arts which will restore it to its former glory and use it to exhibit a permanent collection of the country's Cubist art.

Gardens & Parks

Kampa

Ostrov Kampa, Karlův most, Prague 1. Metro Malostranská/tram 12, 22.
Kampa, an island formed by the Vltava and the Čertovka, or Devil's Stream, is one of the loveliest spots in the city, as popular with love-struck hippies as with old ladies out walking their sausage dogs. The Communists proposed filling in the Čertovka to create a major road but were luckily thwarted by the forces of sanity and this 'Little Venice' with its medieval waterwheels has survived. The park was created in the nineteenth century when an egalitarian decision was made to join together the gardens of three private palaces and throw them open to the public. Come here to feed the swans, enjoy the finest view of the Charles Bridge and read some historically interesting graffiti on the river bank wall ('Let's Revolution!', 'Punk not deaf!' etc).

Paradise Garden

(Rajská zahrada)
Pražský hrad, Hradčanské náměstí. Metro Malostranská/22 tram. **Open** *April-October* 9am-5pm daily; *November-March* 9am-4pm daily.
Inside the castle and yet outside it, the Paradise Garden, which were laid out in 1562, are the oldest part of the South Gardens (Jižní zahrady) and occupy one of the best locations in the city. They provide an ideal spot for a rest from sightseeing. The inscrutable walls of the castle rise above them, and below are the red-tiled roofs of Malá Strana. This is where the victims of the second and most famous defenestration fell to earth (*see box* **Defenestration**) and for centuries was little more than a spot for the emptying of medieval chamberpots. The area was redesigned in the 1920s by the radical Slovenian architect Josip Plečnik, who was hired as official Prague Castle Architect by President Masaryk. Plečnik, who drew on a vast and various architectural vocabulary, oversaw the biggest adaptations made to the castle this century and the pyramid, oversized granite bowl and monumental staircase all bear his trademark. Changes instigated by the Communists were somewhat less sympathetic: the paths had to be re-aligned to accommodate the caterpillar tracks of the tanks which stood guard during sessions of the Political Advisory Committee of the Warsaw Pact.

Petřín Hill

(Petřínské sady)
Metro Malostranská/12, 22 tram.
Petřín Tower **Open** *1 Apr-31 Oct* 9.30am-10pm daily; *1 Nov-31 Mar* 9.30am-10pm Sat, Sun. **Admission** 20kč adults; 10kč children.
Mirror Maze **Open** 9am-5pm daily. **Admission** 20kč adults; 10kč children.
Observatory (24 51 07 09) **Open** 2-7pm Tue-Fri; 10am-noon, 2-7pm, 9-11pm Sat, Sun. **Admission** 6kč adults; 3kč children.

Petřín Hill is the largest expanse of greenery in central Prague – a favourite spot for sledging children in winter and kissing couples in summer. 'Petřín' comes from the Latin word for rock, a reference to the fact that the hill was the source for much of the city's building material. A funicular from Újezd saves your legs from the cruel ascent and at the top there's a fine collection of architectural absurdities, including a scaled-down version of the **Eiffel Tower** (rozhledna). At the time when the Parisians were still debating the aesthetic value of Eiffel's design, the Czechs decided they liked it so much they constructed their own version for the 1891 Jubilee Exhibition, out of recycled railway tracks. There's also a cast-iron mock Gothic castle complete with drawbridge and crenellations which houses a **mirror maze** (zrcadlové bludiště) and dates from the same time. At night you can peer at the stars from the 1930 **Observatory** (hvězdárna), or enjoy the view from the restaurant (Nebozízek) half-way down the hill.

Wallenstein Garden

(Valdštejnská zahrada)
Valdštejnský palác, Valdštejnské náměstí 4, Prague 1. Metro Malostranská/12, 22 tram. **Open** *May-Sept* 9am-7pm daily. **Admission** free.
The early Baroque **Wallenstein Palace** (now the Ministry of Culture), designed by the Milanese architect Andrea Spezza between 1624 and 1630, and the adjoining gardens are the legacy of the altogether larger than life General Wallenstein whose talents included trouncing the Protestants and finding not one but two rich old widows to marry. Wallenstein himself is immortalised in various friezes throughout the palace. Although short, fat and unattractive in real life, he can be seen as Mars riding to war on the ceiling of the Great Hall, and as Achilles in the Trojan War frescoes by Baccio Bianco in the stucco vault. The gardens are laid out in the formal Renaissance style, with beech hedges, fountains and a series of sculptures. The originals were by Adrian de Vries, but what you see today are copies. The De Vries versions were pillaged by rampaging Swedes in 1648 and now adorn the royal palace in Drottningholm. Open air concerts are held in the garden in summer, although there's always the risk of the peacocks installed in the original aviary misbehaving during the slow movements.

Sightseeing Tours

Čedok

Na příkopě 18, Prague 1 (24 19 71 11). Metro Můstek or Náměstí Republiky.
The state-owned company runs a comprehensive selection of tours as well as afternoon and evening excursions on the Vltava.
Branches: Bílkova 6, Prague 1 (231 94 44); Pařížská 6, Prague 1 (231 43 02).

Koala Leisure Tours

Na příkopě 12, Prague 1 (tel/fax 24 22 26 91). Metro Můstek or Náměstí Republiky.
Organises bus tours and river trips.

Martin Tour

Staroměstské náměstí (junction with Pařížská) and Náměstí Republiky (tel/fax 22 38 52). Metro Náměstí Republiky.
Pick up a bus at either of these stops for a variety of tours of the town itself; alternatively book a river cruise from them.

Wittman Tours

Uruguayská 7, Prague 2 (25 12 35/439 62 93). Metro Náměstí Míru.
Offers the best tours of Josefov (the Jewish Quarter).

History

Key Events   58
The Přemyslid Dynasty   59
The Rise of Huttism   62
The Habsburg Dynasty   65
Nationalism & Independence   69

The Lights Go Out   72
From Prague Spring to
Revolution   75
Re-awakening   78
Prague Today   79

Key Events

The Přemyslid Dynasty

c700 The Přemyslid dynasty begins
863 Cyril and Methodius bring Christianity to Bohemia
929 Good 'King' Wenceslas is killed by his brother and becomes a martyr and the Czech patron saint
973 Prague is made a Bishopric
1235 Staré Město gets a Royal Charter; Jews forced into the ghetto
1253 Otakar II becomes king and conquers half of central Europe
1257 Malá Strana receives town status
1306 Přemyslid dynasty ends with murder of Václav III

Hussites & Habsburgs

1346 Charles IV becomes Holy Roman Emperor and King of Bohemia
1348 Charles IV founds central Europe's first university in Prague
1352 Swabian architect Peter Parler begins work on St Vitus's Cathedral
1357 The first stone of the Charles Bridge is laid
1378 Charles' son Wenceslas IV becomes king
1389 3,000 Jews killed in pogrom
1403 Jan Hus, Rector of Prague University, begins preaching against church corruption
1415 Hus, having been excommunicated and declared a heretic, is burned at the stake in Constance
1419 Hussite mob throws the Mayor out of the New Town Hall window; beginning of the Hussite wars
1420s-1430s Hussites repel all attacks
1434 Moderate Hussites wipe out the radicals and the Pope agrees to allow them considerable religious freedom
1458 Czech noble George of Poděbrady becomes the 'People's king' but is soon excommunicated by the Pope
1471-1526 The Jagiellon dynasty rules in Bohemia
1526 Habsburg rule begins with Ferdinand I
1556 Ferdinand invites the Jesuits to Prague to counter fierce anti-Catholicism in Bohemia
1583 Habsburg Emperor Rudolf II moves the court to Prague, where it remains for the next two decades
1609 Astronomer Johannes Kepler publishes his *Laws of Planetary Motion*; Rudolf concedes religious rights to Bohemia's Protestants
1618 Protestants throw two Catholic councillors from a window in the castle, thus starting the Thirty Years War
1619 Frederick of the Palatinate is elected King of Bohemia

Wars, Revolutions & The Republic

1620 Protestants lose the Battle of White Mountain
1621 27 Protestant leaders are executed in the Old Town Square
1634 Bohemian born General Wallenstein, leader of Europe's Catholic armies, is stabbed in the back
1648 The Thirty Years War ends on Charles Bridge
1740 Maria Theresa becomes Empress
1743 French attack Prague
1757 Prussians attack Prague
1781 Emperor Joseph II abolishes 'useless' religious orders, including the Jesuits, and closes monasteries
1787 Mozart conducts the first performance of *Don*

Giovanni in the Estates Theatre
1835 Emperor Francis I's last words are 'change nothing'
1848 Revolutions in Europe; uprisings in Prague against Austrian troops
1891 Radical Young Czechs calling for independence sweep the Bohemian Diet elections
1893 The clearing of the Jewish ghetto begins
1914 Outbreak of World War I; Habsburgs refuse concessions on federalism and Czech soldiers desert to the allies
1918 The Czechoslovak Republic is founded. Thomáš Masaryk becomes its first President

War & Totalitarianism

1938 Chamberlain agrees to let Hitler take over the Sudetenland
1939 Hitler takes all Czechoslovakia
1942 Czech paratroopers assassinate Reichsprotektor Reinhard Heydrich. Hitler destroys villages Lidice and Ležáky and murders all their inhabitants; Jews are transported to Terezin and then to Auschwitz
1945 Prague uprising; the Red Army enters the city
1948 The Communist party assumes power under Klement Gottwald
1951 The Slánský show trials and mass purges against the regime's enemies
1968 Reformist Communist Dubček becomes First Secretary and promotes 'socialism with a human face', but the Prague Spring is crushed by Warsaw Pact troops
1969 Philosophy student Jan Palach sets fire to himself in protest and 200,000 people march to his funeral
1977 The underground movement Charter 77 is established by playwright Václav Havel to monitor human rights' abuses
1988 Soviet leader Gorbachev hints at support for a reformist government in Prague

The Velvet Revolution

1989 Student demonstrations turn into full-scale revolution and the Communist regime falls
1990 Václav Havel is elected President of Czechoslovakia
1992 Free market Thatcherite Václav Klaus becomes Prime Minister
1993 The Slovak Republic and Czech Republic become separate, independent states

The Přemyslid Dynasty

Following the soothsayings of a tribal princess, a Czech kingdom under the native Přemyslid dynasty grows into a powerful empire.

In around 400BC, a Celtic tribe called the Boii occupied the region where the Czech Republic now lies and gave it the name Bohemia. The Boii repelled attacking armies for the best part of 1,000 years; even the Romans, who described the Celts as fearless fighters who loved to feast and frolic in the forests, failed to subjugate them. But the Boii were eventually driven out by the Germanic Marcomanni and Quadi tribes who in turn were wiped out by Attila the Hun in AD451. Slavic tribes are believed to have moved into the area sometime in the seventh century. They were ruled over by arrogant Avars whose harsh regime provoked a successful Slavic rebellion.

The Slavs, who beat off Franks and Germans, were noted for their theatrical cunning. They would strike fear into the enemy by sending out soldiers dressed to look – from a distance at least – like two-headed giants. With military skills such as these the Slavs soon brought about a loosely unified, albeit short-lived, Slavic kingdom.

The Czechs had to wait until the eighth century and the founding of the Přemyslid dynasty for real independence. The skeletal historical information that is available on the dynasty's origins has been generously fleshed out by myth over the centuries. The most popular of these relates to Libuše, one of three daughters of Krok, the leader of the Čech tribe. In the absence of a male heir, Krok was succeeded by the feisty, soothsaying Libuše. But the men of the tribe, indignant at being ruled over by a woman, told her to go and find a husband.

Libuše went into a trance and sent her white horse over the hills, telling the elders of the tribe to follow it. The horse, she foretold, would find a ploughman with two spotted oxen and he would become their future leader. Her white horse seemed to know exactly where to go and the farmer, whose name was Přemysl, and who was also very good looking, was not at all surprised to see the horse.

Prague, too, is supposed to have been founded following a similar trance-induced vision. This time Libuše declared from a hilltop in Vyšehrad (now Prague 4), that 'a city whose splendour will reach to the stars' would be created nearby. Everyone then went into the woods again, this time to find a craftsman making a door sill (*práh* in Czech), for, as Libuše said, 'mighty Lords bend before a low door'. When her subjects found the craftsman, the site of the city was determined.

THE COMING OF CHRISTIANITY

From the ninth century, more concrete historical information is available. Charlemagne briefly occupied the area and a Slavic state was created in Moravia under Prince Mojmír. In 860 Mojmír's successor, Rostilav, appealed to the Pope to send him Christian apostles with a knowledge of the Slavic language to help him put an end to the worship of sun gods and the performance of fertility rites in the kingdom. His request was not answered. Three years later, however, the Byzantine Emperor sent two Greek monks, Cyril and Methodius, who had designed the script known as Cyrillic for the Slavic tongue. The Frankish and German priests objected to this initiative, declaring that it was heresy. The Pope was unperturbed at first, but following Methodius' death in 885, Slavonic liturgy was prohibited.

Rostilav's nephew Svatopluk (871-894) had sided with the Germans over the liturgical issue and with their assistance ousted his uncle. Svatopluk built an empire encompassing Moravia, Bohemia and Slovakia, eliminating many Slavic rivals in the process. But when tribes of Magyars to the south entered the fray and went into battle with Svatopluk, he found himself deprived of Slavic support. Following Svatopluk's death the Magyars grabbed a chunk of Slovakia for themselves and until the twentieth century, their presence in the area was to disrupt all attempts to unite Czechs and Slovaks.

GOOD 'KING' WENCESLAS

Over the following four centuries, Bohemia was ruled by the native Přemyslid dynasty and rode a rollercoaster which at times descended into chaos or rose to the heights of political supremacy in Central Europe. Things continued peacefully enough in the early tenth century under the humane rule of Prince Václav, or Wenceslas I (921-929). He prohibited all forms of torture, removed gallows from public places and offered to enter into personal combat with invading princes, in order to settle disputes without embroiling his subjects in full-scale war. Although Christmas carols still sing his praises today, many Czech nobles felt that Good 'King' Wenceslas had sold out to the Germans and neglected Slavic interests. The nobles chose to side with Wenceslas's brother Boleslav (the Cruel, 935-967), who clubbed his brother to death in 929. Boleslav then set upon the Germans with his armies for the next 14 years. His son and heir, Boleslav II, extended his rule at one point to Moravia and Slovakia.

Amid the ensuing ebb and flow of conquest, Bohemia was united for a while with Moravia. Prague was made a Bishopric in 973 and the process of bringing Christianity to Bohemia was soon completed. By the end of the twelfth century, however, internal bickering over succession had become so bad that, in the words of the historian Palacký, 'in the storm of ages the Czechs were about to drown as a state and a nation'. The turning-point came in 1197 when the military forces of Otakar I confronted the armies of his brother Vladislav outside Prague in a showdown for the throne. In this case, however, sibling rivalry had its limits. The night before the battle the two princes agreed a deal which made Otakar I Bohemian King and Vladislav Margrave of Moravia.

By Otakar's death in 1230 a period of peace and stability had been achieved. The prestige of the Czech monarch grew and, most significantly, his son and successor was made one of the seven electors of the Holy Roman Empire.

With Czech national prestige at new heights the natural thing to do was to look for conquests. Přemysl Otakar II (1253-1278) soon declared his interest in the Austrian throne, snatched Cheb from the Germans and won and lost Slovakia twice. For a while his empire stretched from Florence to Poland, and his economic and military power in Europe gained him the title 'King of Gold and Iron'. But Otakar was getting a little too powerful for the likes of Rudolf of Habsburg, especially when the Bohemian King challenged Rudolf for the throne of the Holy Roman Empire.

The title went to the Habsburg and in 1276 Rudolf invaded Bohemia with 100,000 troops and left his rival with only the rump of the empire – Bohemia and Moravia. Thereafter Otakar's successor, Václav II (1278-1305) was forced to look eastwards for his conquests, taking most of Poland, Hungary, Croatia and Romania. His son

Václav III was assassinated in 1306, allegedly by Habsburg agents. Since he left no heir, the Czech Přemyslid dynasty came to an abrupt end.

THE GERMANS ARRIVE

During this period the demographic nature of Prague and smaller towns in Bohemia had changed significantly. The Přemysls had encouraged German immigration and many German women had married Czech nobles. German clerics filled top positions in the Church, and German merchants gave life to the towns and introduced new urban laws and methods of administration. Prague was reorganised into three autonomous areas: Malá Strana, Hradčany and the Old Town. The Jewish community of Malá Strana was forced out to give more *lebensraum* to the Germans, and pushed into the recently constructed ghetto in the Old Town.

Successive kings drew upon the economic power of the towns to counterbalance the power of the nobles in the country. German townspeople in Prague demanded an ever greater voice in government and by the fourteenth century Czech and German nobles were at each others throats – a conflict that would underlie much of subsequent Czech history.

In 1310 John of Luxembourg, 14 year-old son of the Holy Roman Emperor, was elected King of Bohemia. The first years of his reign were marked by tussles with the Czech nobles over royal power. He was married to the second daughter of Václav II in order to give him Přemyslid credentials, but his loyalties went no further. An incurable romantic, he declared Paris to be 'the most chivalrous town in the world' and unchivalrously announced that he only wished to live there.

His interest in Prague was ephemeral and obscure. He once attempted to recreate the Knights of the Round Table by inviting all the great knights of Europe to the city. When none of them turned up he rode off across Europe with his favourite knights to fight a number of glorious foreign campaigns.

While John was successfully wheeling and dealing in the diplomatic circles of Europe, the nobles in Prague were left to do as they pleased, although John took the precaution of imprisoning his baby son, just in case they should be planning a coup. In fact, no coup was necessary. The nobles' power grew substantially and Prague gained a Town Hall and became the dominant centre of Bohemia. It was raised from a Bishopric to an Archbishopric in 1344, thus bringing it independence from the Archbishopric in Mainz.

The murder of St Wenceslas from the west door of St Vitus's Cathedral.

The Rise of Hussitism

A golden age in Prague is eclipsed by religious nationalism. Prague finds itself surrounded by enemies.

John died a noble death in a kamikaze charge against Welsh archers at the Battle of Crécy. His son Charles IV was elected Holy Roman Emperor in 1346 making his position as King of Bohemia unassailable. His support for the development of Prague had the full force of Empire behind it and ushered in a golden age for the city. Charles (1346-1378) brought to Bohemia the stability that his father John had failed to achieve. The Czechs could not have asked for more.

THE GOLDEN AGE OF CHARLES IV

Charles had been educated at the French court and learnt to speak several languages fluently, including Czech. Although in his youth he had a reputation for wild parties and very tight pants, he became a devout Christian when the Pope

Charles IV – the man who set out to make Prague the Rome of the North.

rebuked him following his coronation. He also played on the family connection, through his mother, to claim direct lineage with the Přemyslid dynasty and consequently became known as 'Father of his Country' and the 'Priest Kaiser'. Prague escaped the Black Death that ravaged Europe in 1348 and under Charles emerged as one of the most dazzling centres in Europe.

Even the most indifferent tourist today could not fail to be roused by the Gothic splendour of Charles' legacy. He brought the 23 year-old Swabian architect Peter Parler to Prague to build the Charles Bridge and to work on St Vitus's Cathedral, a Gothic masterpiece that reflected Prague's spiralling glory in Europe.

In 1348 Charles established central Europe's first university, declaring that Bohemians should 'no longer be obliged to beg for foreign alms but find a table prepared for them in their own kingdom'. By the end of his reign, the university had attracted more than 5,000 students and scholars from all over Europe. He founded the New Town which was constructed around wide streets and effectively relieved the Old Town of some of the stress created by the concentration of artisans' workshops. And he undercut the power of the nobility in 1356 by reorganising the electoral system.

Availing himself of his omnipotent position in the Holy Roman Empire, Charles declared the union of Bohemia, Moravia, Silesia and Upper Lusatia indissoluble, and through purchase and diplomacy he grafted whole chunks of Germany onto Bohemia. He abandoned claims to Italian territories but refused to accept Papal dictates north of the Alps. In 1364 he came to an understanding with the Habsburgs declaring that the succession of the Empire's territories would go to whichever royal family outlived the other. It was, in fact, the Habsburgs who benefited from the agreement.

Charles was a devout Christian. Under his rule the clergy became increasingly wealthy, owning half the land in the kingdom. But at the same time he was intensely conscious of the growing corruption in the church and often sided with the fiery preachers who condemned its excesses. These included the rabble-rousing Jan Milič of Komeříž, who had a tendency to go a little over the top. He persuaded the women in his Týn Church congregation, to discard their fine clothes and jewellery. He later stunned the crowds by declaring that their beloved Charles was really the Antichrist. He urged his followers to prepare for the imminent apocalypse, and since he preached in Czech rather than German, the anti-clerical hysteria he inspired became closely identified with Czech nationalism. It was an explosive mix.

WENCESLAS IV

The seeds of religious indignation were sown during Charles' reign but the bitter fruits were not tasted until the beginning of the fifteenth century under his incorrigible son Wenceslas IV (1378-1419). Wenceslas resided in Prague, though he preferred the street life of the Old Town to the imposing atmosphere of the royal castle, and so moved into Celetná Street. When the Archbishop of Prague ordered the burning of all of the Protestant writings of the English reformer John Wycliffe, Wenceslas, who was aware of the religious sensitivities of his subjects, forced the Archbishop to compensate the owners of the manuscripts. A champion of the common man he would go out shopping dressed in commoners' clothing, but if shopkeepers cheated him he would have them executed. Despite his notorious displays of temper such as roasting the chef who had spoilt his lunch, chroniclers of the time wrote that under his reign there was a virtual absence of crime in Prague.

Wenceslas and quiet piety had never sat easily together. At his christening he was alleged to have urinated into the holy water and he was still unable to control himself at his coronation. He was perhaps closest to God the morning after a pub crawl and is said to have spent most of his last years in a drunken stupor. The nobles were not impressed and formed a 'League of Lords' which had him imprisoned, but he escaped while in the royal bathhouse, seducing the beautiful bath attendant and persuading her to row him down the Vltava to safety.

JAN HUS

Wenceslas lacked the moral and intellectual authority to steer Bohemia through the dangerous religious waters that lay ahead. In 1403 the Rector of Prague University, Jan Hus, influenced by the reformist doctrines of John Wycliffe, took up the campaign against church corruption. The battle ground soon moved to the university where Czech supporters of Hus squabbled with the Germans. The king decreed in favour of the Czechs and the German academics left for Leipzig to found their own university. The Church establishment recognised trouble when it saw it and was quick to start a counter campaign. Hus's arguments were

declared heretical, although he was in fact a moderate compared to reformers who subsequently campaigned in his name. Nevertheless, he was persuaded by Wenceslas, under pressure from the Church, to leave Prague in 1412, allowing emotions to cool down. The Church had made a serious tactical error, however, as the obstinate preacher continued his crusade in the countryside.

In November 1414, Hus was summoned by Wenceslas' brother Sigismund, King of Hungary, to appear before the General Council at Constance. Hus went in good faith carrying a safe conduct pass granted by Sigismund. But when he arrived he was thrown in jail. The Council ordered Hus to recant his teachings and accused him of portraying himself as a fourth addition to the Holy Trinity. He challenged the Council to prove from the Scriptures that what he preached was false, but he was told that he should recant simply because his superiors had told him to do so. He refused and on his 46th birthday, 6 July 1415, Hus was burnt at the stake.

Hus embodied two vital hopes of the Czech people: reform of the established Church and independence from German dominance. It was not, therefore, surprising that he was to become a martyr. His motto 'truth wins' and the chalice, which represented lay participation in the Sacrament, became rallying symbols for his followers. The main tenets of Hussitism were contained in the famous *Four Articles of Prague*. These demanded unrestricted preaching of the word of God; communion in both kinds ('sub utraque specie' – his followers were known as Utraquists); removal of the large estates and possessions from monks and clergy; and strict punishment of sins committed by members of the church.

HUSSITISM & CZECH NATIONALISM

A few weeks after Hus's death, several hundred nobles in Bohemia sent a protest to the Council of Constance in which they declared their intention to defend Hus's name and promote his teachings. The groundswell of popular feeling soon engulfed Wenceslas IV. At first, under pressure from the Church, he suppressed the Hussites. Then on 30 July 1419 an angry Hussite crowd stormed the Town Hall protesting at the detention of prisoners who had been arrested for creating 'religious disorder'. The mob threw the Mayor and his councillors through the window to their deaths. Prague's first defenestration finally shattered hopes for peace.

Wenceslas withdrew his decrees and died in an apoplectic fit a few days later. Hussite mobs marked the occasion by rioting and setting fire to the monasteries, though with typical puritan restraint they refrained from looting. Sigismund, who had been complicit in the burning of Hus, elbowed his way onto the Bohemian throne and the moderate Utraquist nobles who were keen to find a compromise greeted him with sycophantic deference. Radical preachers however, such as Jan of Želivo, denounced Sigismund and Rome with apoplectic fury, whereupon he and the Pope called for a holy crusade against Bohemia, something usually reserved for Turks and Jews.

Prague was almost under siege but the Hussites were undaunted. The Utraquists approached Sigismund again but found him far from accommodating. They reported that the king 'stung by fury, began to agitate his limbs like a madman', swearing to destroy all heresy by fire and sword. Meanwhile the radical Hussites arrived in the city in force and, as a sign of their seriousness, burnt alive nine monks in front of the Royal Garrison.

THE HUSSITE WARS

Rome's call to arms against the heretic nation was taken up all over Europe and the Czechs soon found themselves surrounded. They were united, however, behind a powerful moral cause and had a freshness and zeal that came from being independent and free. They also had in their ranks a brilliant one-eyed Taborite General called Jan Žižka. He not only repelled the enemies from his hilltop in what is now Žižkov in Prague, but by 1432 he and his 'Warriors of God' (as the Czechs called themselves) were pillaging all the way up to the Baltic coast. Women fought and died equally alongside men.

The Hussites were united during times of greatest danger but as the tide of battle turned in their favour, old divisions re-emerged. The majority, known as Praguers, were moderate and middle-class and their leaders were based at the University of Prague. The more extreme group, known as Taborites, were based on a fortified hillside called Tabor. They banned all class divisions, shared their property and held religious services only in Czech.

Once the Pope realised that the holy war had failed, he reluctantly invited the Czechs to discuss a peace settlement. The Taborites were cynical about the Pope's overtures whereas the Praguers had never wanted to break with Rome, and viewed their Hussite allies in Tabor as a little too revolutionary. In 1434, the Prague nobles marched their army down to confront the Taborites and wiped out 13,000 of them at the Battle of Lipany. The issue of negotiations with Rome was thereby settled.

In 1436 the Pope and the Utraquists signed the Basle Compacts which recognised the Czechs as 'faithful sons of the Church', and accepted Utraquist demands for communion in both kinds. But there was no agreement on the issue of corruption in the church. The Taborites' lack of trust in Rome was to prove well founded. A Papal envoy was sent to Prague to cool things down. On his arrival he reproached the Praguers for conducting religious services that diverted from Roman practice. It was pointed out to the envoy that the Pope had agreed to this in the famous Basle Compacts.

When the envoy denied any knowledge of the Compacts, he was shown the original document as proof, whereupon he and the document disappeared. He was pursued by troops across Bohemia who found it in his suitcase.

A HOME-BORN KING

Without a strong and respected king Prague was descending into national, religious and class anarchy. The king, Ladislav of Habsburg was dependent on the advice of the local born Utraquist noble, George of Poděbrady (Jiři z Poděbrad), who allegedly advised him to drink some poisoned wine. George was formally elected to the throne in 1458. From the outset he was hemmed in by hostile opponents. He eliminated the rump of the radical Taborites. He suppressed a separatist pacifist Christian movement called the Unity of Czech Brethren which was becoming immensely popular. He also fought and defeated a confederacy of plotting nobles. He kept the reactionary Catholics at bay while trying at the same time not to antagonise Rome and resisted the incessant demands of the German population for more power. George feared another holy crusade against his country and as a diversionary tactic he tried to form a League of Christian Kings and Princes to provide mutual assistance against the menace of the Turks. The idea was pooh-poohed by princes and bishops as an impertinence against the Pope and the Holy Roman Emperor and the Pope reneged on the Basle agreement and excommunicated George.

Since the Hussite Wars the power balance in the land had altered substantially. The Church's power had been devastated and the vacuum was filled by the nobles who had seized church property and ruled mercilessly over the peasants. A hard-fought power struggle between the king and the nobles forced George to look abroad for a successor (the flagging king had failed to produce an heir despite numerous aphrodisiacs). He believed that a foreign sovereign could best keep order in Bohemia and so arranged for the Polish Jagellon dynasty to accede to the throne. Following George's death in 1471, Vladislav II became the King of Bohemia, to be followed by Ludvik in 1516.

THE INSTABILITY CONTINUES

The two Jagellon monarchs, ruling *in absentia*, failed to keep the nobles in check. In 1500 the nobles extracted a new constitution confirming their status, reducing that of the peasants to serfdom and stripping the towns of their former power. Lutheran ideas, which were close to Hussitism, seeped in from Germany and religious tensions soon flared up again. Anxious Utraquists, fearing a reproach from Rome, tried to keep the lid on these developments. They redirected all their efforts to suppressing the Unity of Czech Brethren but the Brethren simply grew in strength.

The Habsburg Dynasty

Four centuries of Habsburg rule begin; Prague becomes the centre of an empire and is then brutally subjugated.

When the second Jagellon king, Ludvík, was drowned in a river running away from the Turks at the battle of Mohác in 1526, the Estates of Bohemia elected the Austrian Habsburg Duke Ferdinand I as King of Bohemia; the dynasty was to last until 1918. Ferdinand knew how precarious his status was as a foreign Catholic monarch in a fiercely anti-Catholic country. At first he was sensitive to his new subjects, and refrained from persecuting the growing number of Lutherans. In 1546 he called upon the Estates to raise finance and an army to fight the Turks. When it transpired that he intended to use the army against Protestants in Germany, the Bohemian army refused to cross the Saxon border. The Estates, outraged at being tricked, sent a list of 57 demands to the king.

The time had come, it seemed, for Ferdinand to stop pussyfooting around. He sent troops into Prague and began a systematic suppression of all Protestant dissidents, in particular the Czech Brethren. He appointed German Catholics to key official posts and used German as the official language of the court – both actions representing a blatant violation of the constitution and the oaths that the king had taken when he came to the throne. In 1556, he invited the Jesuit Order to Bohemia. The Jesuits, who were organised on quasi military lines, spearheaded the Counter-Reformation assault. They were put in control of higher education throughout the kingdom and became tutors to the sons of leading nobles.

Ferdinand's Habsburg successors understood the importance of Bohemia. It was one of the Electors of the Holy Roman Emperor and was also extremely wealthy. Bohemia was already footing most of the bill for the disastrous war against the Turks, who were by now in possession of the Hungarian capital. Until 1618 the Habsburgs engaged in a game of religious brinkmanship with Bohemia's population, the vast majority of which was by this time Protestant.

When Maximilian II became king in 1562 he hoped to divide and rule Bohemia by supporting the conciliatory Utraquist movement (which was middle class and nominally Catholic) and suppressing the ever resilient Unity of Czech Brethren. Instead, in a series of rearguard concessions he allowed Bohemia to unhook itself from the Roman Church and gave his approval, albeit only verbally, to the adoption of the 'Confessio Bohemica' which set out the key elements of Hussite and Lutheran practices.

RUDOLFINE PRAGUE

The Estates were pleased with their gains. They duly voted through new taxes for the Turkish wars and approved Maximilian's choice of successor, Rudolf II (1576-1611). In 1583 Rudolf moved his Court from Vienna to Prague and for the first time in 200 years, Prague became the centre of an Empire. The Empire badly needed a man of action, vision and direction to deal with the Turkish invaders and the demands of Bohemia's

The eccentric, and ultimately insane, Rudolf II.

Protestants. What it got was a dour, eccentric and melancholic monarch who was engrossed in alchemy and astrology and tended to ignore everyone except Otakar his pet lion. While Europe headed inexorably towards the Thirty Years War, Prague drifted into a surreal fantasy world.

Rudolf had a staunch sense of Habsburg and Catholic destiny, but little stomach for a fight. He was more interested in developing a higher religious synthesis to heal the divisions in European Christendom than in adopting the proselytising approach of the Jesuits. In later years, in a state of semi-secluded insanity, he would issue violent threats against his Protestant nobles. But by then the Papacy had long since written him off as a liability to the Counter-Reformation.

While political life was frustrated by the emperor's political inertia, Rudolfine Prague was experiencing a dazzling confluence of artistic, scientific and mystical experimentation. Rudolf played host to scores of international artists. These included the Dutch painter Spranger, whose allegorical scenes of alchemy and astrology reflected the concerns of the Court. His compatriot Von Aachen painted portraits of nubile princesses from across Europe which were intended, vainly, to stimulate Rudolf's thoughts of marriage. Rudolf's fascination with planetary movements brought the astronomers Tycho Brahe and Johannes Kepler to his court. The latter published his *Laws of Planetary Motion* in 1609 with an effusive dedication to his patron.

Mystics and alchemists were welcomed with lodgings and a royal salary and, as news of the emperor's hospitality spread, scores of geniuses, eccentrics and fraudsters rolled into town. Those whose alchemical experiments failed to produce the quantities of gold they had promised skipped town as quickly as they had arrived. Intellectual debates raged through the city on subjects ranging from squaring the circle to the existence of ancient giants. Anyone claiming an insight into the mysteries of the universe, from foreign astrologers to rabbis from the Jewish ghetto, had the emperor's ear.

Meanwhile his political advisors were finding access to the emperor rather harder. The Spanish Ambassador did not even manage to set eyes on Rudolf for almost two years, and rumours that the emperor had topped himself became difficult to dispel. The emperor was, however, capable of sudden bursts of political activity. In 1599 he replaced several senior advisors with fierce Counter-Reformation Catholics. Their assault on Protestantism involved confiscations of property, indictments for treason and an attempt to outlaw all non-Catholic worship, save the Utraquists.

But as the Turkish armies thrust northwards, the Habsburgs relied more than ever on the military and financial support of the Protestant Estates. Protestantism may have been considered undesirable, but it was clearly thought to be preferable to Islam. An attack on Vienna was looming, and Protestant support was by no means assured. Rudolf dealt with the crisis simply by hiding away in Prague Castle and a flabbergasted coterie of Archdukes concluded that he had to go.

His brother Matthias picked up the reigns, and in 1605 concluded a peace treaty with the Hungarians and the Turks and forced Rudolf out of Hungary, Austria and Moravia. Bohemia's nobles liked the look of Matthias who in ruling Upper Austria had appeared to be more sympathetic to the demands of the Protestants. But Rudolf refused to abdicate in Bohemia or formalise religious guarantees to Bohemia's Protestants. In 1609, Rudolf gave some ground and signed the 'Letter of Majesty' codifying Protestant rights. But by then the Czechs had had enough of him. Sensing that Matthias was elbowing him out of Bohemia as well, Rudolf invited his cousin Leopold to invade. The Protestants quickly raised an army to defend Prague and called upon Matthias for assistance. Leopold hastily retreated and Rudolf was deemed incapable of governing the Czech lands. In 1611 the heirless emperor was deposed by his brother and died completely insane a few months later, the day after the death of his pet lion.

DEFENESTRATION

Despite their sweet promises to Bohemia, Matthias and his successor Ferdinand II, both strong Counter-Reformation Catholics, turned out to be rather more formidable than expected. The Bohemian Estates suddenly found themselves playing a frenzied game of threats, bluff, false promises and provocation with the new Jekyll and Hyde rulers. It would only be a matter of time before Bohemia (and Europe) would explode.

The fuse was lit in the towns of Broumov and Hrob, where Protestants had built chapels in accordance with the guarantees of the Letter of Majesty. When the Bishop of Prague ordered the destruction of one chapel and the Abbot of the Brevnov Monastery closed the other, fuming Protestants summoned an assembly of the Estates in Prague and issued a stinging rebuke to Vienna. The emperor heightened the stakes by banning the Estates from further meetings.

In Prague anger was reaching fever pitch. On 23 May 1618, the whole assembly led by Count Thurn marched to the Royal Castle. They were met by the die-hard Roman Catholic councillors of the emperor, Slavata and Martinic, whom they accused of being behind the ban. The two councillors were dragged to the window and shoved out, and their secretary was flung out after them for good measure. But Slavata and Martinic landed 50 feet below in a pile of rubbish and excrement and were saved, while the secretary landed apologetically on top of them. They ran, under a hail of shots, to a ladder at a nearby window and survived to tell an embellished tale of their heroism.

Prague's most famous defenestration was the first violent act of the Thirty Years War – and an emotive and symbolic event over which all Europe could take sides. But what actually made the crucial difference in the cold world of seventeenth century realpolitik was the election to the Bohemian throne of Frederick of the Palatinate, son of James I of England and Ireland and head of the Protestant Union of German Princes. His election tipped the balance of power between Protestant and Catholic Electors within the Holy Roman Empire, four-three in favour of the Protestants.

Ferdinand II was ready to fight it out, but unfortunately for Bohemia, the likeable young Frederick had little notion of what a battlefield looked like. While Ferdinand was preparing for war, Frederick was swimming nude in the Vltava and enjoying courtly life. The Czechs nevertheless believed that their new man would rally all the powerful Protestant princes of Europe to defend Bohemia.

THE BATTLE OF THE WHITE MOUNTAIN

By November 1620 the combined forces of the Roman Catholic League, consisting of Spain, Italy, Poland and Bavaria, were massing in support of Ferdinand. Frederick had failed to rally anyone except the Protestants of Transylvania. On 8 November 1620 the two armies faced each other at White Mountain (Bílá Hora) on the outskirts of Prague.

Many expected the Czechs to fight with the same startling bravery and military skill that their forebears the Hussites had shown. But on the second Imperial charge the Protestant infantry fled while their officers ran after them yelling at them to come back and fight. The Transylvanian Hungarians were not much better. They escaped the battle, but thousands drowned trying to ford the Vltava. Meanwhile Frederick had been happily banqueting with friends. His wife had refused to leave Prague without him, but as the catastrophe loomed she was persuaded to go. The next morning Frederick thought better of staying, too, and sneaked away to join her. As he was leaving he met an English Captain who announced that 1,600 troops from England were 12 miles away and waiting for Frederick's orders, unaware that the crucial battle had just been fought. Only Moravian mercenaries stood and fought and they were massacred to a man.

The Catholic commanders played up the religious significance of the battle; the staunchly Catholic philosopher René Descartes served as a mercenary in the Bavarian Cavalry at the time. Jesuits preached to the Imperial troops as they marched into battle. By contrast the Protestant armies were a hotchpotch of mercenaries and dis-

illusioned peasants who had been reduced to serfdom by the Czech nobles and had little interest in the system that they were defending.

On the first anniversary of the infamous defenestration a large crowd gathered in Prague's Old Town Square to witness the gruesome beheading of 27 leading Protestant nobles and scholars. The less privileged also had their tongues ripped out, hands chopped off and their heads skewered on the towers of Charles Bridge. While the Thirty Years War raged on in Europe, Ferdinand settled once and for all the Habsburg's hereditary claim to Bohemia.

HABSBURG ABSOLUTISM

Ferdinand made no bones about his plan for Bohemia when he confided that it was 'better to have no population than a population of heretics'. In the ensuing years Bohemia lost three quarters of its native nobility, along with its eminent scholars and any vestiges of national independence. The country was ravaged by the war which reduced its population from three million to 900,000. Three quarters of the land in Bohemia was seized and used to pay war expenses. All Protestant clergy and anyone refusing to abandon their faith were driven from the country or executed. Thirty thousand wealthy Protestant families had all their possessions confiscated and were sent into exile. While the depopulated towns and villages filled up with another influx of German immigrants, the peasants were forced to stay and work the land. The slightest opposition from them was suppressed ruthlessly and Jesuits swarmed into the countryside to 're-educate' them.

Ferdinand moved his court back to Vienna in 1624. In 1627 he formally cancelled all significant powers of the Bohemian Diet. He ruled virtually by royal decree, maintaining Bohemia as a separate entity only so that the Habsburgs could cast an extra vote in the election of the Holy Roman Emperor. The Czechs were taxed to the hilt and the money used to prettify Vienna and pay off war debts. The confiscated estates of the Protestant nobles were handed over to those loyal Catholics who bowed and scraped sufficiently at the court, and Catholic nobles from abroad, sensing a bonanza, swooped in to pick up some cheap assets.

THE THIRTY YEARS WAR

During the Thirty Years War, Prague was invaded by Saxon Protestants but then retaken by General Wallenstein. The Bohemian-born Wallenstein (after whom Schiller composed his drama of the same name) was born into a Protestant family in 1583, but converted to Catholicism in 1606. He rose from obscurity to become leader of the combined Imperial Catholic armies of Europe, and the greatest creditor of the Habsburg Empire. He totted up a spectacular series of victories but was hugely disliked by the emperor's Jesuit advisors who conspired to have him dismissed. Meanwhile Wallenstein, who had been negotiating with the Swedish enemy, switched sides. When he entered Bohemia in 1634, the Czech exiles suddenly pinned their hopes on a Wallenstein victory. He didn't get far. Later that year a band of Irish mercenaries burst into his Cheb residence where the great General was recovering from gout. He was gagged, stabbed and dragged down the stairs to an inglorious end. The Thirty Years War which had begun in Prague Castle petered out on Charles Bridge in 1648, as Swedish Protestants scuffled with newly Catholicised students and Jews from the ghetto.

By the mid-seventeenth century, German had replaced Czech as the official language in government circles. Czech nobles sent their sons to German schools, Charles University was renamed Charles-Ferdinand University and handed over to the Jesuits who taught in Latin. The lifeline of Czech heritage now rested with the enslaved and illiterate peasants. In 1650 at the depth of Bohemia's despair the exiled leader of the Unity of Czech Brethren Jan Comenius exhorted his people to keep hope alive, with the desperate words 'I believe that after the tempest of God's wrath shall have passed, the rule of thy country will again return unto thee, O Czech nation'.

Paradoxically this period of oppression produced some of Prague's most stunning Baroque palaces and churches. Infused with the glorification of God and Rome, the Baroque served to overwhelm and seduce Prague's population with its grandeur and beauty. The Czech writer Milan Kundera has called the Baroque explosion 'the flower of evil' and 'the fruit of oppression', but it did its job; before the century was out the vast majority of the population had reverted to Catholicism.

A BACKWATER

The eighteenth century was a dull time for Prague. Empress Maria Theresa lost Silesia to the Prussians and woke up to the fact that unless the Empire was efficiently centralised more of the same was going to happen. A new wave of Germanisation in schools and government was soon underway and the small Prague cog turned within the grand Viennese machine. Life occasionally brightened up when Mozart rolled into town to conduct a new opera, but the Czechs felt that they could do little but merely survive and wait for better times.

Maria Theresa's successor, the enlightened despot Joseph II, had little patience with the Church. He kicked out the Jesuits, closed monasteries, put the education system under state control, freed the Jews from the ghetto and vastly expanded the Empire's bureaucracy. In 1775 the peasants had been revolting and a spate of health and other reforms meant that they could now get married without their masters' permission and avoid an unnecessary beating in the process. Internal tolls were abolished and the industrial revolution was getting under way. It was all good news for the Czechs except for one thing: the reforms were taking place in the German language.

A plaque commemorates the house on Karlova where astronomer Johannes Kepler lived.

Nationalism and Independence

Czech nationhood experiences a resurrection, beginning with its dormant language and ending with a democratic nation state.

The Czech cultural landscape had lain fallow for over a century, but seemingly without plan or political motive the seeds of a rebirth were sown. A revival was gaining momentum by the end of the eighteenth century and by the nineteenth, Czechs were asserting themselves culturally with a vigour that recalled the good old Hussite days. It started with the revival of the Czech language, and ended in 1918 with political independence.

The peasants had never abandoned the Czech language, though scholars were obliged to teach and write about their history in German. By the end of the eighteenth century a number of suppressed works were published, notably Balbín's *Defence of the Czech Language* with its often-quoted rallying cry, 'Do not let us and our posterity perish.' The Bohemian Diet (Parliament) began to whisper in Czech; the Church, seeing rows of empty pews, began to preach in Czech; and Emperor Leopold II even established a chair in Czech Language at Prague's university. Once Napoleon began his shenanigans, however, it became harder for Czech leaders to claim that it was all just a harmless cultural development.

Emperor Francis I (1792-1835) feared Napoleon and everything associated with him and was taking no chances with liberal nationalist nonsense. In his will he had only two words of advice for his successor, Ferdinand V (1835-1848), 'Change nothing!'. Nevertheless the revival continued, with scholars, artists and historians setting a trailblazing pace: Jungmann reconstructed a pure Czech literary language; the historian František Palacký wrote his mammoth *History of the Czech Nation*; František Škroup composed the first Czech opera and the Czech national anthem; Prague's theatres staged new patriotic dramas; and Čelakovský had the nation singing Czech songs. Prague's dominant German population began collectively to raise an arrogant eyebrow.

THE EVENTS OF 1848

The cultural revival inevitably took a political turn. The Czechs demanded equal rights for their language in government and schools. Then in 1848, revolution once again swept through Europe. A Pan Slav Congress was held in Prague during which a conservative scholarly group led by Palacký clashed with vociferous radicals who were soon out on Prague's streets. Copycat demonstrations were multiplying throughout the Empire and they finally brought down the previously impregnable Viennese government of Prince Metternich. A shaken Emperor Ferdinand V tossed a few promises in Prague's direction to keep the radicals calm and buy time.

As with most of Europe's 1848 revolutions, there was, for many, too much talking and not enough fighting. In Prague the force of reaction came in the sinister figure of Prince Windischgrätz. He fired on a peaceful gathering in Wenceslas Square intentionally provoking a riot to give himself an excuse for wholesale suppression. Thus the new Emperor Francis Joseph (1848-1916) came to the throne on 2 December 1848 riding a tidal wave of terror. In 1849 he issued the March Constitution which declared all the Habsburg territories to be one entity ruled from the Imperial Parliament in Vienna.

AN EMBRYO NATION

The period between 1849 to 1914 was a time for tinkering with constitutions and toing and froing with promises of reform. The regime moved only as far as it was pushed and when it felt no pressure reverted to its previous position. The Czechs sat and waited for external events to provide better political conditions for change.

After taking a bashing from Bismarck in 1866, on his way to unifying Germany, the Habsburgs introduced a new Constitution which codified some basic civil rights. But it was the Hungarians who benefited by gaining internal independence. The Czech claims for independence were ignored in the new dual Austro-Hungarian structure. Francis Joseph, under pressure from the Germans and Hungarians, refused even to take a coronation oath as King of Bohemia.

The old-guard Czech deputies, led by Palacký, battled on for concessions in the Imperial Parliament. They threw in their lot with the conservative Polish and Austro-German deputies, and so won concessions on language (Charles University was re-established partly as a Czech University). But it meant accepting an electoral system in Bohemia that heavily favoured the German population. A group known as the Young Czechs attacked the Old Czechs for pursuing a 'policy of crumbs'. There was in fact little alternative, but national passions were running high and the times called for radical words if not radical deeds.

The Young Czechs adopted Jan Hus as their hero and were supported by the Realist Party leader Professor Tomáš Masaryk. Masaryk attempted to focus attention on what he felt were the moral traditions of Czech history and pointed to the Hussite and the National Revival movements as spiritual lighthouses for the nation. In the 1891 elections to the Diet, the Young Czechs swept the board.

Edvard Beneš.

The Czechs began to forge the political, social and economic infrastructure of a nation. Rapid industrialisation transformed the region with highly successful industries such as brewing, sugar production, metalworking, coal mining and textiles. A highly efficient rail network criss-crossed Bohemia and Moravia and linked it to the European economy as a whole. Industrialisation gave rise to working-class based political movements, and Catholic parties also emerged.

Culturally, the Czechs had produced composers of international standing, such as Smetana, Dvořák and Janáček, and painters such as Mucha (a major figure in the Art Nouveau movement). An indigenous literature blossomed in the form of Mácha, Neruda, Vrchlický and many others. The Czech Academy of Sciences and Arts achieved international renown. Only the political expression of nationhood remained frustrated.

WORLD WAR I

The outbreak of World War I broke the stalemate. At first they assumed that they could wring out concessions on a federal constitution in return for Czech support for the war. However, the mere mention of the 'F' word provoked repressive measures from Vienna. It would prove to be a costly policy for the Empire. The Czechs soon realised that their hopes lay in the downfall of the Empire itself and, along with millions of soldiers of other minority groups, they deserted en masse to the other side. Six divisions of Czechs were soon fighting for the allies on the Russian, Italian and French fronts while in Prague an underground society known as the Mafia carried out an incessant campaign of agitation against the regime.

Meanwhile, Masaryk and Edvard Beneš were working the allied diplomatic crowd trying to drum up support for a future independent state. They found, however, that the Habsburgs were often viewed more as misguided conspirators than as evil warmongers like the Kaiser, and that many diplomats had no wish to see the Austro-Hungarian Empire pulled apart. Europe's crown heads and aristocrats were certainly opposed to the destruction of a powerful member of their club, and many Americans were fascinated when they learned of the existence of the Czech people.

Finally, it was the United States who took the lead, granting *de jure* recognition to a provisional Czechoslovak Government under Masaryk. On 18 October 1918 Masaryk declared 'the Habsburg dynasty unworthy of leading our nation' and the provisional National Committee agreed upon a Republican constitution. But their power was only theoretical. The key to actual power lay in controlling the Empire's food supplies. Bohemia was the breadbasket of the Empire and the Habsburg generals, fearing a Soviet-style social revolution if food did not get through to the population, gave a nod and a wink to the Provisional Council.

On 28 October a National Committee member, Antonín Svehla, marched into the Corn Institute and announced that the Committee was taking over food production. Then, wishing to bring more gravitas to the occasion, he forced all the officials to take an oath of allegiance to the National Committee, which he made up as he went along. Later that day a note from the Habsburg Government acquiescing to Czechoslovak independence was sent to the American President Woodrow Wilson. The population of Prague spilled onto the streets in triumphant celebration of their new nation. Not a single shot was fired in opposition.

THE FIRST REPUBLIC

The new Republic of Czechoslovakia had a good start in life. It had suffered hardly any destruction during the war; it was highly industrialised, with generous reserves of coal and iron ore; and it had an efficient communications infrastructure and a well-trained and educated bureaucracy. Its work force was literate and politically represented. The national leadership, in particular Masaryk and Beneš, were internationally respected intellectuals and diplomats and the new nation bloomed into a liberal democracy. In the interwar years· the Republic was an oasis of democratic values set in a desert of authoritarian regimes that stretched east from Switzerland and south from Scandinavia.

Ethnic rivalry was the biggest strain on the new nation. The Pittsburgh Agreement, which had promoted the concept of a new state, referred to a hyphenated Czecho-Slovakia in recognition of the two different histories. Slovaks were predominantly agricultural people and had been ruled by Magyars not Habsburgs, and unlike the Czechs looked upon the Catholic Church as a symbol of freedom. The Slovaks resented what they felt was a patronising air from Prague, but until the late 1930s only a minority of voters backed the separatist Slovak People's Party under the pro-fascist leaders Hlinka and Tiso.

In Prague ethnic tensions were characterised more by rivalry than by jealousy. The Jews who comprised only 2.5 per cent of the population were mainly concentrated in Prague and formed a significant part of the intelligentsia. That most Jews spoke German also created some resentment on the part of the Czechs. But Jews were not a focus of hatred until the German population in Czechoslovakia began to look at them through Nazi eye glasses.

The Germans, who formed 23 per cent of the population and had their own spectrum of political parties, presented the biggest obstacle to forging a united nation. Educated, professional and relatively wealthy, they were spread throughout the Czech lands, although Prague and the Sudeten area near the German border had the greatest concentration. The Czechs were sensitive, if also a little sanctimonious, towards minority rights and permitted the German minority to run their own schools and universities.

A SUDETEN SPANNER IN THE WORKS

Only a few years earlier, however, the German language had dominated the region and the Germans were not pleased with their sudden minority status. They had lost out in the land reforms, their businesses had suffered disproportionately from the depression of the 1930s, and Sudeten savings that had foolishly been kept in Weimar Republic bank accounts had gone up in inflationary smoke. The economic and ethnic resentments found a political voice in the young German gymnastics teacher Konrad Henlein who vaulted to prominence as head of the pro-Hitler Sudeten German

Mass demonstrations in 1938 greet news of the Munich Agreement.

Fatherland Front. By 1935 the Sudeten Party was the second largest parliamentary bloc. But the sizeable Czech Communist Party was ordered by Stalin to back the liberal Edvard Beneš in the Presidential elections in order to counter the Henlein threat, and Beneš took an easy victory.

In March 1938 Henlein told Hitler 'We must always demand so much that we can never be satisfied.' In 1938 after intimidating their rivals, the Sudeten Nazis won an astonishing 91 per cent of the German vote and demanded union with Germany. It was a potent claim to which the British Prime Minister, Neville Chamberlain, was not wholly unsympathetic. For him the Sudeten crisis was a 'quarrel in a faraway country between people of whom we know nothing'. Chamberlain went to Munich with the French Premier and met Mussolini and Hitler. All parties involved in the crisis (except Czechoslovakia, which wasn't invited) agreed that Germany should take over the Sudetenland. In return Hitler guaranteed that he would make no further trouble, and to prove this he even signed his name on a piece of paper which naive Neville waved to the world promising 'peace in our time'.

The announcement was met with furious mass demonstrations in Prague. Czechoslovakia had a well-armed, well-trained army but it was in a strategically hopeless position. With Poland and Hungary also eying up border territories, Czechoslovakia found herself geographically encircled, massively outnumbered, abandoned by her allies and attempting to defend a region that did not want to be defended. Beneš capitulated. Six months later Hitler's tanks rolled over the rest of the country, with Poland snatching Těšín and Hungary grabbing parts of southern Slovakia. A Nazi puppet state was established in Slovakia (the nationalists finally getting their 'independence') and a Reich Protectorate was forced on Bohemia and Moravia.

The Lights Go Out

Squeezed between the totalitarian monsters Hitler and Stalin, the fledgling democracy is twice overwhelmed and Communists take power with an iron grip.

Except for its Jews and gypsies, Czechoslovakia survived occupation far better than most other European countries. German was made the official language of government (Hitler wanted to reduce Czech to a patois within a generation) and a National Government of Czechs was set up to follow Reich orders. Hitler had often expressed his hatred for 'Hussite Bolshevism' but he needed Czech industrial resources and skilled manpower for the war. Virtually the entire military hardware of Czechoslovakia was transferred to Germany.

NAZI OCCUPATION

Many Czechs opted to sit out the war, hope for allied victory, try to preserve their national identity and avoid suicidal acts of defiance. Hitler lost no time in demonstrating the ferocity of his revenge on those who did resist. When a student demonstration was organised, nine of its leaders were executed, 1,200 students were sent to concentration camps and all Czech universities were closed indefinitely. Reinhard Heydrich, who had just chaired the notorious Wannsee Conference at which the 'Final Solution' of the 'Jewish Question' was planned, was appointed Deputy Reichsprotektor. Aiming to wipe out any further resistance, he instituted rounds of calculated terror and executions against the intelligentsia while enticing workers and peasants to collaborate.

Beneš fled to London where he joined Jan Masaryk (son of Tomáš) to form a provisional Czechoslovak Government in exile. They were joined by thousands of Czech soldiers and airmen (such as Jan Hoch, alias Robert Maxwell) who fought alongside the British forces. Czech intelligence agents passed approximately 20,000

28 October 1939: Nazi troops occupy Wenceslas Square.

messages to London including the details of Germany's planned invasion of the Soviet Union.

LIDICE

After much thought, Beneš' approved a plan for the assassination of Reinhard Heydrich. The underground leaders in Prague doubted its effectiveness and, given the inevitability of reprisals, heavily advised against it. But they were overruled, and British-trained Czech parachutists were dropped into Bohemia; on 27 May 1942 the Reichsprotektor was assassinated.

The German reprisals were swift and terrible. The assassins were hunted down to the crypt of the Church of Sts Cyril and Methodius where all night they resisted SS fire and attempts to flush them out with fire hoses. The last two survivors used their final rounds on each other. The Germans then went on an orgy of revenge. Anyone with any connection to the paratroopers was murdered. The villages of Lidice and Lezaky were picked out at random and razed to the ground. All the adult males of the villages were murdered, the women were sent to concentration camps (in Ležáky they were shot) and the children were either 're-educated' or killed. The transportation of Jews to concentration camps was stepped up.

Acts of sabotage, such as derailing trains and demolishing bridges, continued. But the main resistance took place in the Slovak puppet state where an uprising began on 30 August 1944 and lasted four months. It was crushed by the Germans at a cost of 13,000 lives and achieved little except, perhaps, to remove the country's stain of collaboration. The Czechs' act of defiance came in the last week of the war. On 5 May 1945 an uprising took place in Prague. About 5,000 died in the four days of fighting.

LIBERATION

The US forces which had just liberated Pilsen (Plzeň) in the west of the country were only a few miles from Prague. But the allied leaders at Yalta had agreed other plans. Czechoslovakia was to be liberated by the Soviets and the US General, Eisenhower, ordered his troops to pull back. (Czech children were later taught by their Communist teachers that the American troops who had liberated Western Czechoslovakia were in fact Russian soldiers dressed up in US uniforms. They found it harder to explain why some of these 'Russians' were black.) Although Communist power was not consolidated until 1948, the country had found itself scooped up into the Soviet sphere of influence.

GENOCIDE

Over 300,000 Czechoslovaks perished in the war, the majority of whom were Jews. The Jewish population of Czechoslovakia was destroyed. Most were rounded up and sent to the Theresienstadt (Terezín) ghetto, 40 miles north of Prague. Many died there, but the remainder were transported to Auschwitz and other concentration camps. The Nazis claimed Theresienstadt was a model community living happily, but separately, from the Germans, and the Red Cross returned from its visit to tell the world that the 140,000 Jews and others interned there were safe. Shortly afterwards they were transported to their deaths.

Around 90 per cent of Prague's ancient Jewish community that had remained living in Prague were murdered. It had been one of the oldest Jewish communities in Europe, arriving at least 1,000 years earlier and possibly even before the Czechs themselves. For most of this period the community had been walled into a ghetto in the Old Town and life there was characterised by pogroms, poverty, mysticism and countless Prague legends. Between the time when they left the ghetto in the late eighteenth century and before the Nazi occupation, Jews had dominated much of Prague's cultural life. Now the rich literary culture which had produced writers such as Franz Kafka had been wiped out. Kafka's family, among most others, perished in Auschwitz. The only thing that saved some of Prague's synagogues and communal Jewish buildings from the Nazis' routine destruction was the Germans' intention to use them after the war to house 'exotic exhibits of an extinct race'.

THE COMMUNIST NOOSE TIGHTENS

Beneš' faith in liberalism had been badly knocked by the way the western powers had ditched his country. He began to look upon the ideological future of Czechoslovakia as a bridge between capitalism and communism. His foreign minister Jan Masaryk was less idealistic, stating that 'cows like to stop on a bridge and shit on it'.

Beneš needed a big power protector and believed that if he could win Stalin's trust, he could handle the hugely popular Communist party of Czechoslovakia while keeping the country independent and democratic. During the war he signed a friendship and mutual assistance treaty with the Soviet Union. To prove his earnestness to Stalin, Beneš severed co-operation with Poland at Stalin's behest and promised to cede Subcarpathia to the Soviets. Beneš, the exiled government, and the Communist party eliminated most right-of-centre parties from postwar elections and established a coalition government comprised principally of Communists and socialists friendly to the Soviet Union. When Roosevelt questioned him on his motives, Beneš allegedly signed a blank piece of paper and passed it to the US President saying, 'I am willing to sign anything that you are willing to sign with me.'

In 1945 Stalin knew that a straightforward takeover of a formerly democratic state was not politically expedient. He needed Beneš as an acceptable front in order to buy time. For all his tightrope diplomacy (he often referred to diplomacy as a 'vulgar profession'), Beneš was shuffling his country into Soviet clutches. Before he died he wrote 'my greatest mistake was that I refused to believe to the very last that even Stalin lied to me cynically'.

THE COMMUNISTS TAKE POWER

The Soviets and Czech Communists were widely regarded as war heroes and won a handsome victory in the 1946 elections. Klement Gottwald became Prime Minister of a Communist-led coalition. Beneš, still believing that Stalinist Communism could co-exist in a pluralistic democracy, remained President. The Communists made political hay while the sun shone. They set up workers militias in the factories, installed Communist loyalists in the police force and infiltrated the army and rival socialist coalition parties.

One of the first acts of the government, approved by the allies, was to expel over two and half million Germans from Bohemia. It was a popular move and, as Gottwald remarked, 'this is an extremely sharp weapon with which we can reach to the very roots of the bourgeoisie'. Thousands were executed or given life sentences, and many more were killed in a wave of self-righteous revenge. (After 1989 President Havel acknowledged that the collective nature of the expulsions had been wrong. Today, following growing pressure from Sudeten groups, the issue is worming its way back onto the political agenda.)

In 1947 Czechoslovakia was forced to turn down the American offer of Marshall Aid for the rebuilding of the economy. Stalin knew that aid came with strings and he was determined to be the only puppet master. In February 1948, with elections looming and Communist popularity rapidly declining, Gottwald sent the workers' militias onto the streets of Prague. The police occupied crucial party headquarters and offices, and the country was incapacitated by a general strike. Beneš' diplomatic skill was no match for the brutal skills of the Moscow-trained revolutionaries. With the Czech army neutralised by Communist infiltration and the Soviet army casting a long shadow over Prague, Beneš capitulated and consented to an all-Communist government. Gottwald became Czechoslovakia's first 'Working Class President'.

Shortly after the coup, Jan Masaryk dropped to his death from his office window. The Communists said it was suicide. But when his body was found, the window from his room was tightly fastened. The defenestration had a distinctly Czech flavour but the purges that followed had the stamp of Moscow knowhow. They were directed against resistance fighters, Spanish Civil War volunteers, Jews (often survivors of concentration camps) and anyone in the party hierarchy who might have posed a threat to Moscow. The most infamous trial was of Slánský, a loyal side-kick of Gottwald who had orchestrated his fair share of purges. After being showered with honours, he was arrested a few days later. In March 1951, Slánský and ten senior Communists (mostly Jews) were found guilty of being Trotskyite, Titoist, Zionist traitors in the service of US imperialists. They 'confessed' under torture, and eight of them were sentenced to death. The country had descended into a mire of fear and lunacy.

Gottwald, the first 'working class president'.

From Prague Spring to Revolution

Prague travels the long dark tunnel of Communism with hardly a glimmer of hope until a non-violent revolution sets it free.

Gottwald dutifully followed his master, Stalin, to the grave in 1953 and the paranoia that had gripped Prague took a long time to ease. By the 1960s, Communist student leaders and approved writers on the fringes of the Party hierarchy began tentatively to suggest that, possibly, Gottwald and Stalin had taken the wrong route to socialism. A trickle of criticism turned into a shower of awkward questions. On 5 January 1968 an alliance of disaffected Slovak Communists and reformists in the Party replaced Novotný with the reformist Slovak Communist, Alexander Dubček.

PRAGUE SPRING

For the next eight months, the world watched developments in Prague with passionate hope as Dubček rehabilitated political prisoners and eased and then virtually abandoned press censorship. A flood of criticism swept over the sacred cows of

Communism leaving nothing untouched. Moscow was alarmed and tried to intimidate Dubček by holding full-scale military manoeuvres in Czechoslovakia, but the reforms continued. On 27 June, 70 leading writers signed the hugely popular and widely published *Two Thousand Word Manifesto* supporting the reformist government and declaring that they would 'stand by it with weapons if need be, if it will do what we give it a mandate to do'. Suppressed literature was widely published or performed on stage, Prague was infused with the fresh air of freedom. Dubček called it 'socialism with a human face'.

The Soviet leader Leonid Brezhnev, following 'full and frank' discussions, failed to influence the Czechoslovak leader. On the night of 20 August 1968, nearly half a million Warsaw pact troops entered the country, took over the Castle and abducted Dubček and his closest supporters to Moscow. The leaders expected to be shot, but

Changing attitudes: the Soviet liberators of 1945 have become invaders.

Brezhnev needed an acceptable front for a policy of repression with a human face.

Meanwhile on the streets of Prague thousands of devastated citizens confronted the tanks, appealing to their fellow Slavs to turn back. Apparently some Russian troops, on seeing the mini Eiffel Tower on Petřín Hill, thought they had invaded Paris. Free radio stations using army transmitters continued to broadcast and newspapers went underground and encouraged Czechs to refuse any information or assistance to the occupiers. Street signs and house numbers were removed and the previously Stalinist workers' militia defended a clandestine meeting of the national Party conference.

GUSTAV HUSÁK

The resistance prevented nothing. Dubček stayed in power for eight more months and watched his collaborators being replaced by pro-Moscow ministers. In April 1969 Dubček, too, was removed in favour of Gustav Husák who was eager to push Moscow's 'normalisation'. Husák purged the Party and the whole machinery of national and local government, the army and the police, the unions, the media, every company and every other organ of the country that might have a voice in the nation's affairs. Anyone who was not for Husák was assumed to be against him. Within a very short time every aspect of Czechoslovak life was filled with Husák's mediocre yes men. A small influx of consumer goods was permitted and thus Husák was able to subdue the nation into an unquestioning apathy.

JAN PALACH

On 16 January 1969, a 21 year-old philosophy student called Jan Palach stood on the steps of the National Museum at the top of Wenceslas Square, poured a can of petrol over himself and set himself alight. He ran through the streets screaming for someone to throw a coat over him and was rushed to hospital. He died four days later. A group of his friends had agreed to burn themselves to death one by one until the restrictions were lifted. On his deathbed he begged his friends not to go through with it, though some did.

The news reader announcing his death was in tears; 200,000 people went to Wenceslas Square to place wreaths at the spot where Palach fell; and a vast procession made its way to Charles University. Crowds of mourners stretched back for two miles. His coffin was taken to the Old Town Square where 100,000 people heard the bells of Týn Church ring out and a choir sing a Hussite chorale. Palach was buried in Olšany cemetery, but the Communists, nervous about his grave becoming a focal point for unrest, disinterred his body and reburied him in an unmarked grave outside Prague.

Palach's death symbolised, with twisted irony, the extinguishing of the flame of hope. As the dissident playwright and current President, Václav

August 1968: a Czech defies the Soviet tanks.

Havel, wrote: 'People withdrew into themselves and stopped taking an interest in public affairs. An era of apathy and widespread demoralisation began, an era of grey, everyday totalitarian consumerism.'

Instead of brutal mass arrests, tortures and show trials, the Communists now bound up the nation in an endless tissue of lies and fabrications, and psychologically bludgeoned all critical thought in an Orwellian nightmare where people were rewarded for not asking awkward questions and punished for refusing to spy on their neighbours. Punishment could mean spells in prison and severe beatings, but for most it meant losing a good job and being forced into menial work. Prague possessed one of the highest proportion of window cleaners with PhDs and was probably the only city where professors became street sweepers.

CHARTER 77

There were some, however, who refused to be bowed. A diverse alternative culture emerged in which underground (*samizdat*) literature was painstakingly copied and circulated around a small group of dissidents. In December 1976 a group led by Václav Havel issued a statement demanding that the Czechoslovak authorities observe human rights obligations, and specifically those contained in the Helsinki Agreement of 1975 which the government had signed. Charter 77 became a small voice of conscience inside the country, spawning a number of smaller groups trying to defend civil liberties. In 1989 it had 1,500 signatories. But there seemed little hope for real change unless events from outside took a new turn. Then, in the mid-1980s, the unbelievable began to happen. Mikhail Gorbachev came to power in the Soviet Union and initiated his policy of *perestroika*.

THE VELVET REVOLUTION

The Soviet leader came to Prague in 1988. His spokesman was asked what he thought the difference was between the Prague Spring and Glasnost. He replied '20 years'. As usual it was change in the international environment that was required to change conditions in Czechoslovakia. In the autumn of 1989 the Berlin Wall was brought down and the Communist regimes of Eastern Europe began to falter. The Czechoslovak government, one of the most hard-line Communist regimes in Eastern Europe, seemed firmly entrenched until 17 November. When police violently broke up a demonstration on Národní commemorating the 50th anniversary of the closure of the universities by the Nazis, a rumour, picked up by Reuters news agency, said that a demonstrator had been killed. Another demonstration was called to protest against police brutality.

Two days later 200,000 people gathered in Prague to demand the resignation of the government. The police behaved with restraint and the demonstrations were broadcast on television. The government then announced that the man who had allegedly been killed on the 17th, was alive and well. Some months after the revolution it emerged that the KGB had probably been behind the rumour as part of their plan to force out the hard-line government and replace it with something more in line with Soviet *glasnost*.

That there had not been a death made little difference to the crowds which grew bigger every day.

A revolution was clearly underway. A committee of opposition groups formed themselves into the Civic Forum (Občanské fórum) and was led by Václav Havel who addressed the masses in Wenceslas Square. The next day a quarter of a million people assembled in the Square. Two days later, Dubček, who had just spoken to crowds in Bratislava, came to Prague and with Havel addressed a crowd of half a million. The government had lost control of the media, and millions more watched the scenes on their television screens. On the evening of 22 November, the Party General Secretary resigned. He was followed by the whole Politburo and then the government. It was not enough. Students from Prague raced out to factories, farms and mines to galvanise the workers into supporting a general strike for the 27th. Workers' militias had put the Communists into power in 1948; it was crucial they were persuaded not to stand by Communism in its final hour.

On 25 November three quarters of a million were on the streets as Havel and Dubček addressed them again. This time the acting Communist Prime Minister, Adamec, also appealed to the crowds, and further purges within the Communist Party ranks followed. The Party then declared that the 1968 Soviet invasion had been wrong, and promised free elections and a multi-party coalition. It was all too late. A new government of reformist Communists was proposed, but it was rejected by Civic Forum. The negotiations continued between the Communists and Civic Forum until 27 December, when a coalition of strongly reformist Communists and a majority of non-Communists – mainly from Civic Forum – took power with Havel as President. Not a single person died. Havel's co-revolutionary Rita Klímová called it the Velvet Revolution.

Václav Havel greets the crowds gathered to demand the resignation of the government.

Re-awakening

Prague sees daylight again with a philosopher President and a free-marketeering Prime Minister.

Czechoslovakia entered the last decade of the twentieth century a free country. On New Year's Day Havel spoke to the reborn nation.'For the past 40 years on this day you have heard my predecessors utter different variations on the same theme, about how our country is prospering, how many more billion tons of steel we have produced, how happy we are, how much we trust our government and what beautiful prospects lie ahead of us. I do not think that you put me into office so that I, of all people, should lie to you. Our country is not prospering. The great creative and spiritual potential of our nation is not being used to its full potential... We have become morally ill because we have become accustomed to saying one thing and thinking another... all of us have become accustomed to the totalitarian system accepting it as an unalterable fact and thereby [keeping] it running. None of us is merely a victim of it, because all of us helped to create it together.'

For months after the revolution Prague floated in a dream world. The novelty of the playwright President captured the world's imagination. His style had a bohemian flavour as he cavorted round the city, nightclubbing with Lou Reed and Mick Jagger and even tried to make Frank Zappa his cultural envoy. He drove a little scooter down the corridors of power in Prague Castle.

THE NATION SPLITS

But the serious issues of economic transformation and the relationship between Czechs and Slovaks loomed as formidable challenges. In the Summer of 1992 the right-of-centre Civic Democratic Party (ODS), led by Václav Klaus, the no-nonsense free marketeer and economic disciple of Margaret Thatcher was voted into power. Klaus's single-mindedness had its casualties. The first was the Federal Republic itself. Nationalist sentiments had grown in Slovakia but remained a fringe issue until the electoral rise of Vladimír Mečiar's Slovak separatist HZDS party. Slovaks had always resented what they had felt was a benign neglect by Prague, and Havel had never been hugely popular among them. One of his first acts as President was to abandon the arms trade. Laudable as that might seem, it took the heart out of the economy in central Slovakia where the arms industry was based. Slovaks complained that the country's economic reform was going too fast for them. Klaus, however, would not compromise on it and had an overwhelming mandate from Czech voters (though not Slovak ones) to press on. Mečiar upped his separatist threats to Prague until, with Machiavellian manoeuvring, Klaus called Mečiar's bluff and announced that he would back Slovak independence.

The two respective leaders divided up the assets of the state and the countries peacefully parted ways on 1 January 1993 without so much as a referendum. Their currencies split and within a few months the Slovak currency fell by ten per cent. Havel was elected President of the new Czech Republic, but Klaus had also out-manoeuvred him, forcing Havel into a predominantly ceremonial rather than an executive role.

Klaus indicated that he had little time for a policy of flushing out Communists from responsible positions (known as lustration). One such attempt in 1992 ended in farce after a list of 300,000 names from secret police files was published but failed to distinguish between those who had never collaborated but who the secret police thought might one day be turned, and those who had collaborated quite happily. The list included notable dissidents. Thus Communists successfully dodged the spotlight amid a blizzard of accusations and counter-accusations. A significant number of Czechs seemed to have large skeletons in their cupboards or at least a few small bones of contention and it became impossible to untangle the good from the bad. Communists remained in charge of the country's largest factories and former dissidents watched helplessly as their former interrogators and tormentors sped past in smart new sports cars.

The gap between the haves and have-nots began to widen as many citizens had properties and businesses that had been taken from them or their families by the old regime in 1948 returned to them by restitution. Life for many, often returning émigrés, was suddenly transformed as they became owners of vast castles, factories or small shops. Prague was getting a face lift as entrepreneurs began converting their new assets into gleaming shop fronts supported by a tidal wave of summer tourists that washed over the city.

While issues of lustration, corruption and racism were given low priority, the government fixed its sights on its spectacular mass privatisation programme and on the glowing beacon of the European Union.

Prague Today

Racial tensions and the discontent of its Slovak sibling take a back seat as Prague forges ahead into the free market economy.

Prague is a city of centuries' old beauty and frenetic change. Although more than five years have passed since the Velvet Revolution, the pace of change has not let up, fired on by the pro-market zeal of a shrewd and determined Prime Minister, Václav Klaus.

Although the Czech President, Václav Havel, is better known abroad, it is Klaus who has forged today's Czech political and economic realities. First, he marginalised Havel's influence. Then after the June 1992 elections he forced the Prime Minister of Slovakia, Vladimír Mečiar, into a corner. Mečiar's demand for greater autonomy had stopped short of outright independence for Slovakia, but Klaus pushed him further and proceeded to carve Czechoslovakia in two. Klaus is widely admired for his street-smart political judgement and is credited with being the guiding light

behind the Czech 'economic miracle'. He consistently receives public approval ratings of around 70 per cent.

Prague is undoubtedly booming. After 40 years of decline and stagnation, glitzy stores and state-of-the-art showrooms are opening every month. The shift to a market economy is proving more successful than anywhere else in the former Communist world. Exports and foreign investment are rising, while brokers fret and sweat on the stock market floor. While the rest of Europe grapples with high unemployment, Prague has none (in 1994 job vacancies outnumbered job-seekers by eight to one). The national unemployment rate hovers at two to three per cent, the lowest in Europe. It seems that Praguers have yet to see the downside of capitalism.

This economic success has created political

stability for the right-wing government coalition. There is little dissent, strikes are almost unheard of, and demonstrations and protests are rare.

In the 1970s and 1980s, life in Prague was drab and harsh. There were no private shops or restaurants. A western car or neon light was a rare sight. While the shop windows were full of unwanted goods, Praguers were lucky if they could find the most ordinary fresh fruit and vegetables. At the same time, the Communist Party bosses up at the castle were corrupt to the core, for example having fresh milk flown in daily from Switzerland for their private use. Anyone brave enough to question the wisdom of the hardline Communist rulers was dealt with brutally. Prague was like a beautiful city covered by a thick layer of depressing dust.

But events have moved so fast that today a few months here can seem like a decade. The old joke in Communist times was that 'You pretend to pay us and we pretend to work'. Now there is a real point to working and earning. There is the possibility of promotion, pay rises, owning an apartment and buying goods that are taken for granted elsewhere. Czechs are now free to travel abroad. They can say and write what they want. They will not be denied a university place because some distant cousin had once fallen foul of the Party.

Even so, traces of Communism prove hard to eradicate. Examples of its looking-glass logic live on and you can still find yourself paying more for travelling by slow train rather than a fast one, because you'll sit on the slow train for longer.

Yet the roots of democracy also go deep. Before 1938 Czechoslovakia was an island of freedom surrounded by authoritarian regimes and police states, which is perhaps why the Czechs today have adapted to democratic ways better than their neighbours. Former Communists are unlikely to make a come-back here as they have done in Hungary and Poland.

Besides Communism, the other important influence on Prague today is the Czech split with Slovakia in January 1993. Many feel it was thoroughly undemocratic. Between them Mečiar and Klaus received 30 per cent of the vote in the 1992 elections and neither of them had run on a separatist platform. Unable to work together, they nevertheless refused to hold a referendum on the subject, even though all opinion polls among both Czechs and Slovaks showed less than a third wanted a split.

But all this is now history. Within months of the break up, the story was a tale of two countries: of Czech prosperity and satisfaction, of Slovak loss of direction and discontent. Although they may not say so openly, most Czechs are now glad to be rid of the Slovaks and their government of former Communists, whom they believe would have crippled economic reform. Klaus called Mečiar's idea

of a 'third way' in between capitalism and Communism a 'route straight to the third world'.

Crucially too, the country has tilted westwards. Gone is the border with the old Soviet Union. The Czechs hope they are now at the front of the queue for entering west European institutions such as the EU and NATO. On the other hand, the split has reduced the size and resources of the country and only time will tell whether it was a wise move.

BLANK CHEQUES

While Praguers are becoming richer, some of them are becoming much richer. In 1993 it was rare to see a Porsche or BMW on the streets of the capital, but by 1994 Ferraris and Alfa Romeos were becoming a relatively common sight. Expensive French restaurants have opened. Czechs have started to take holidays in faraway places such as Brazil and Indonesia and smart new houses are being built for the *nouveaux riches*.

By the end of 1994, 80 per cent of the economy had been transferred into private hands, much of it given out free to citizens in the form of coupon privatisation. Some shrewd investors have seen gains of 2,000 per cent. Property has been returned to pre-Communist owners, making many of them millionaires overnight. Meanwhile many others are raking in money in the thriving black economy, whose annual profits – untaxed of course – are running in excess of 30kč billion.

As the city grows richer and 'normalises' it will inevitably lose some of its romance. Such was the cheap cost of living, the many job opportunities and the sheer beauty of the city, that in the early 1990s tens of thousands of young Americans and other westerners were lured here. Some official estimates put the numbers of tourists now visiting the city at 80 million annually. A host of entrepreneurs, students, travellers and pleasure-seekers have swarmed to the city. The Prague of the 1990s is popularly compared to the Paris of the 1920s. The lively ex-pat community teems with artists and would-be artists. English-language newspapers jump at you from the kiosks, and there is also theatre, film and radio in English. Some of the city's best restaurants, bars and clubs are run by ex-pats.

There are new as well as old problems still to be tackled in this changing city. Green clouds of smog often hang over it. Communist neglect and indifference bequeathed to Prague a great deal of industrial damage and extremely low air quality. The health of its inhabitants has suffered. So have many historic buildings, which have been left in a sad state of dilapidation. Prague has a lot to lose in this respect: unlike almost every other major city in the region it survived World War II with its buildings virtually unscathed and still contains outstanding examples of almost every type of architecture from medieval to modern.

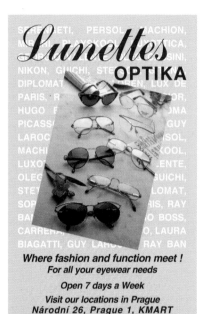

The playwright president, Václav Havel.

The accumulated grime has already been cleared off some buildings, allowing them to be seen in their original splendour. But much remains to be done. The government has passed a number of environmental regulations and will introduce 'environmental taxes', including one for drivers using the planned new Prague-Dresden highway.

Socially too, all is not as rosy as might first appear. Inefficiency, shoddy service, unrealistic expectations and corruption are still deeply rooted. Many Czechs want to pick the fruits of capitalism without doing the gardening. If Communism succeeded in one thing, it was in instilling a lack of a work ethic. It is considered crazy to hurry to an appointment, or walk up an escalator in the metro. A secretary will often stop work on the dot of 4pm even if she is halfway through typing a sentence. The taxi meters remain rigged and the city's phone system is almost surreal in its inefficiency.

To add to the list, the housing market is badly in need of reform, and despite the excellent public transport system, the city has begun to experience its first traffic jams. Students may soon have to pay 25 per cent of their fees and the withdrawal of state subsidies has struck fear into many theatres and galleries.

There has been much criticism that the Czechs have not done enough to counter money laundering and even some suggestions that the government, eager to attract hard currency into the country by any means, has encouraged it. Allegations of Mafia links have probably been exaggerated, but in 1993, realising that they were harming the country's reputation, the government responded by passing legislation to bring the Czech Republic in line with EU standards. It also agreed to let the FBI set up an office in Prague, which will be run in close collaboration with Czech intelligence agencies.

Some critics are sceptical that the Czechs have, as Klaus said, already 'crossed the Rubicon' on the road to a market economy. They argue that reforms have only been so successful because a number of difficult measures of real industrial restructuring have been postponed and the worst is still to come. (Sixty per cent of firms are estimated to be insolvent, for instance, yet there have been almost no bankruptcies or mass redundancies, since banks are reluctant to put companies into receivership.) At the same time, rents and the cost of utilities such as gas and electricity continue to be heavily subsidised. But the sceptics are in a minority.

Internationally, the Czechs continue to enjoy a high profile, thanks largely to the popularity of Václav Havel. Although the President is still personally admired for having led the 1989 revolution, his influence on public opinion and policy-making has dwindled and nowadays his speeches tend to carry more weight abroad. His relationship with the more dynamic Prime Minister, Václav Klaus, who has a large portrait of Margaret Thatcher behind his desk, is an uneasy one.

LAND GRAB

There are other problems. Central Europe is full of inherited grievances, for example. After World War II, three million ethnic Germans were expelled from Czechoslovakia and their property seized. Since 1989, the Sudeten German issue has been revived. In 1993 Sudeten pressure groups sent shivers down Czech spines, calling for the 'right to a homeland' and in 1994 mainstream German and Austrian politicians openly declared their support for these groups. So far all Czech political parties have rejected Sudeten demands, pointing out that large numbers of Sudetens participated in the burning of synagogues and worked for the Gestapo during the war. The issue remains an emotionally-charged one.

Prague's once thriving Jewish community, which at one stage made up one quarter of the city's population, now numbers under 2,000. Anti-Semitism is less of a threat than in neighbouring countries, partly because of the secular nature of Czech society (80 per cent of Czechs claim they are atheists). Indeed, at present philo-Semitism is rather trendy and there is a good deal of serious interest in the enormous contribution Jews have made to Czech culture (Kafka wrote in Prague, Einstein was professor here, Freud was born in Moravia, and many leading Czech musicians and artists were Jews). Today, a leading Czech pop group, although not Jewish, is called Shalom and its lead singer is converting to Judaism under the guidance of Prague's new rabbi, former Charter 77 signatory and political prisoner, Karel Sidon.

But anti-Semitism isn't a spent force. There has been a great deal of resistance to returning stolen property to Holocaust survivors – something which Havel said has brought shame upon the nation – and the Government only began to recti-fy this in 1994.

Racial prejudice is widespread. People here are much more willing to express racist beliefs in public than in Britain, for example. Opinion polls have shown that 62 per cent of Czechs favour the introduction of laws targeted against the country's ethnic minorities, such as Romanies (*see below*), Vietnamese and Yugoslavs. As the country gets richer, more immigrants will no doubt make their way to the Czech Republic and racial problems may well become explosive.

Finally, many Czechs think the crimes of the Communist past have not been adequately punished. Others think this is a closed chapter and the country should look to the future. But it is unlikely that there will now be any major trials – too many vested interests are at stake.

Romanies

There is a widespread failure by many in the west to appreciate that the Romany 'problem' in continental Europe is essentially a racial problem. The common stereotype in Britain and elsewhere of the 'gypsy' as a picturesque fortune-telling nomadic character out of a story book is far from reality.

The Romanies are a distinct racial or ethnic group who have preserved their own language and culture since migrating to Europe from India in the tenth century. They have lived in the Czech and Slovak lands for 600 years and 85 per cent have led a settled lifestyle for the last 350 years (the remaining nomadic tribes being forcibly settled by the Communists in 1959). Czechs talk not of 'travellers' but of 'blacks' (Romanies) and 'whites'.

In the course of Czech history (like elsewhere in the region), the Romanies have suffered persecutions second only to the Jews. In the seventeenth century, for example, their bodies were hung along the borders of Bohemia and Moravia in order to discourage others from entering. The crimes against them reached their climax when over 90 per cent of the Czech Romany population, which historians estimate numbered 6-8,000, were murdered by the Nazis in World War II.

In contrast, the wartime Fascist puppet government in Slovakia, while it ruthlessly rounded up and deported its Jews, did not kill the 200,000 Romanies resident there. After the war the Communists forcibly moved many Romanies from Slovakia to the Czech lands to replace the expelled Sudeten Germans. There are now more than 250,000 Romanies in the Czech Republic and 500,000 in Slovakia.

Their persecution continued after the war. In the 1970s and 1980s the Communists sterilised Romany women, often without their consent or knowledge, in a campaign that Václav Havel's Charter 77 group labelled as 'genocide'. Yet since becoming President, Václav Havel has remained silent on the issue and the officials and doctors responsible have not been investigated.

Since 1989 Romanies have continued to suffer racism of the most extreme kind. The simplistic way in which the Romany problem is approached by even the most liberal, educated Czechs can be striking to west European observers. Racist generalisations based upon a few isolated incidents are widely accepted without criticism – that Romanies are criminal, destroy houses, don't want to fit in, etc. Ominous statements have been made by some senior Czech officials including threats of expulsion. A local police chief in north Bohemia has remarked that people are getting 'nostalgic' for Hitler.

Romanies make easy targets. They have not been able to form an effective lobby group and they have no country to speak out on their behalf. Theirs is a history of failure to unite in an organised way around one group or leader – the nature of Romany society is to cluster around a family, a clan or a region.

However, not all has been bad since the collapse of Communism. Romanies are now free to speak their own language, publish their own newspapers and form their own cultural associations and political parties. But discrimination remains widespread. Most Romany children in Prague are routinely placed in special schools for the mentally backward, usually because they lack Czech language skills. The resulting semi-literacy is one of the causes for the appalling rate of unemployment amongst Romanies (70 per cent compared to the national average of around three per cent).

On top of all this comes the new Czech Citizenship law which has led to around 100,000 Czech Romanies being classified as Slovak citizens from July 1994 – even though two thirds were born on Czech territory and most of the rest have lived here for decades. They are now deprived of the right to vote or hold public positions and may lose social and welfare benefits and require work permits.

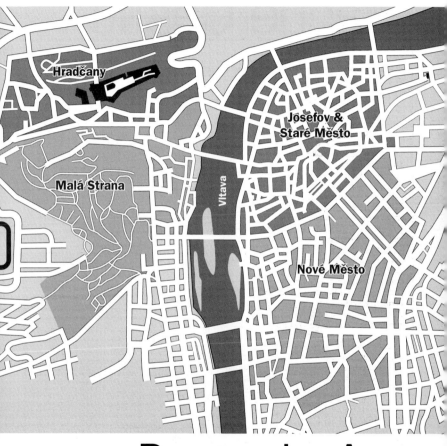

Prague by Area

Hradčany & Prague Castle	**86**
Malá Strana	**91**
Staré Město & Josefov	**95**
Nové Město	**102**
Further Afield	**106**

Hradčany & Prague Castle

Perched high above the city, Prague Castle dominates the palaces, monasteries and mansions that cluster beneath it.

Dominating Hradčany is the hrad, or castle. For over 1,000 years its silhouette has risen above the town, a symbol of the power of the city's rulers, politically and spiritually the centre of the country and still the presidential seat today. Founded in the ninth century by the Přemysl princes, it has been built, re-built and expanded over the centuries until it resembles a textbook of architectural styles from the Romanesque period to the early twentieth century.

Prague Castle

The most obvious way to enter the castle (Pražský hrad) is the same way as visiting heads of state, through the first courtyard from Hradčanské náměstí. The gateway has been dominated by Ignatz Platzer's monumental sculptures of battling Titans since 1768, and they create an impressive if not exactly welcoming entrance. This is where the changing of the guard takes place, a Havel-inspired attempt to add a bit more ceremonial pazazz to life in the castle (at noon and 3.30pm daily). To reach the second courtyard go through the **Matthias Gate** (Matyášova brána), a Baroque portal dating from 1614 topped by a German Imperial Eagle that pleased Hitler when he came to stay in 1939. The monumental stairway designed by Josip Plečnik on the left leads up to the magnificent gold and white **Spanish Hall** (Španělský sál), where the Central Committee of the Communist Party used to meet, amidst the chandeliers and mirrored walls, protected from armed assassins by a reinforced steel door (*see chapter* **Sightseeing**).

Behind the austere grey walls of the second courtyard lies a warren of opulent **state rooms** whose heyday dates from the time of Rudolf II. Rudolf's interests ranged from the arcane to the perverse; in his employ were over 200 alchemists, stationed in the Powder Tower (Prašná věž) who were engaged in attempts at brewing the Elixir of Life and transforming base metals into gold. The state rooms of the second courtyard, which are

The Titan-festooned entrance to the castle.

rarely open to the public, housed his magnificent art collection and curiosities which included a unicorn's horn and three nails from Noah's ark. Sadly, the bulk of the collection was carried off in 1648 by Swedish soldiers, although the remnants are housed in the Picture Gallery on the left hand side of the courtyard (currently closed to the public). In the middle of the courtyard is a seventeenth century Baroque fountain, and the Chapel of the Holy Rood, which was rebuilt in the neo-Baroque style in the late nineteenth century.

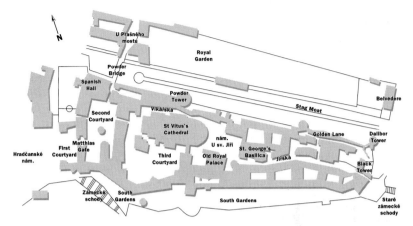

The Cathedral

The third courtyard is the oldest and most important site in the castle. It is entirely dominated by the looming towers, pinnacles and buttresses of **St Vitus's Cathedral** (katedrála sv. Víta). This was commissioned by Charles IV, Holy Roman Emperor and Bohemian king, who made Prague the centre of his empire and went about building monuments worthy of this status. In 1344 he managed to secure an archbishopric for the city and work began on the construction of a cathedral under the instructions of French architect Matthew of Arras. Inconveniently, Matthew dropped dead eight years into the project, so the German Peter Parler was called in to take up the challenge and it was he who was responsible for the 'Sondergotik' or German Late Gothic design. In pagan times Svanto vit, the god of fertility, was worshiped on this site, a clue perhaps to why St Vitus (or *svatý Vít* in Czech) – a Sicilian peasant who became a Roman legionary before being thrown to the lions – had the Cathedral dedicated to him. Although it was intended to be the court church, no Bohemian king ever got to see the finished structure and by the time the completed cathedral was inaugurated in 1929, Czechoslovakia had become a republic.

Outside, the most dominant feature is the Great Tower, a Gothic and Renaissance structure topped with a Baroque dome. Inside it hangs Sigismund, the largest bell in Bohemia weighing 15,120 kilograms. Getting Sigismund into the tower was no mean feat: according to legend it took a rope woven from the hair of the city's noblest virgins to haul it into position. Below the tower is the Gothic **Golden Portal** (Zlatá brana), decorated with a mosaic of multicoloured Venetian glass depicting the Last Judgement. On either side of the arch are sculptures of Charles IV with his wife Elizabeth of Pomerania, whose talents apparently included being able to bend a sword with her bare hands.

The door leads into the **Chapel of St Wenceslas** (Svatováclavská kaple), a beautiful painted chamber inlaid with semi-precious stones and adorned with paraphernalia from the saint's life including his armour, chain shirt and helmet. A door in the corner leads to the chamber which contains the crown jewels. A papal bull of 1346 officially protects the jewels, while popular legend unofficially prescribes death to anyone who uses them improperly. Reichprotektor Richard Heydrich was the last person to test the truthfulness of this and was assassinated within a year of placing a crown upon his head. The door of the chamber is locked with seven keys held by seven different people, after the seven seals of Revelations. The jewels seem to be safe for the time being, however, since the key held by Alexander Dubček, in his role as Chairman of Parliament, has disappeared in mysterious circumstances.

The greatest Baroque addition to the cathedral was the silver tombstone of St John of Nepomuk, the priest who was flung from Charles Bridge in 1393, after refusing to reveal the secrets of the queen's confession. The tomb, designed by Fischer von Erlach in 1733-36, is a flamboyant affair. Four fluttering angels hold up a red velvet canopy, and two tons of silver was used to create the cherubs, pedestal and statue of the saint.

The enormous nave is flooded with multicoloured light from the gallery of **stained glass windows** created at the beginning of this century. All 21 of them were sponsored by financial institutions including one (third on the right), by an insurance company whose motto 'those who sow in sorrow shall reap in joy' is incorporated into the

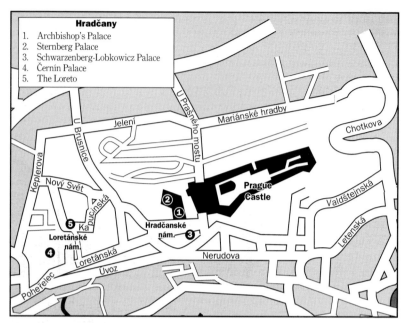

Hradčany

1. Archbishop's Palace
2. Sternberg Palace
3. Schwarzenberg-Lobkowicz Palace
4. Černín Palace
5. The Loreto

biblical allegory. The most famous is the third window on the left, in the Archbishop's Chapel, which was created by Alphonse Mucha and depicts the Christian Slavonic tribes; it was paid for, appropriately enough, by Banka Slavia.

The Third Courtyard & Beyond

After the cathedral the second most noticeable monument in the third courtyard is the 17-metre high granite obelisk, a memorial to the fallen of the First World War. Opposite the Golden Portal is the entrance to the **Old Royal Palace** (Starý královský palác) which contains three levels of royal apartments. The highlight is the Vladislav Hall. Designed by Benedickt Reid at the turn of the fifteenth century, its broad, rectangular windows – the first expression of the Renaissance in Bohemia – flood the enormous hall with sunlight, illuminating the extraordinary swooping pattern of the vault. It is here that the National Assembly elects its new President. In the basement are the remains of Prince Soběslav's Romanesque palace, and on a higher level (in the Louis Wing) is the Royal Chancellery and the window that was the exit route taken by the victims of the defenestration of 1618 (*see chapters* **History** *and* **Sightseeing**).

Skirting the cathedral on the northern side is Vikářská, where Picasso and Eluard came to drink wine in the Vikářská tavern. It leads into Jiřská náměstí, named after **St George's Basilica**

(Bazilika sv. Jiří). It's worth standing far enough back from the basilica's crumbling red and cream Baroque façade, to get a good look at the two Romanesque towers which jut out behind. The Italian craftsmen who constructed them in 1142 built a fatter male tower (Adam, on the left) standing guard over a more slender female one (Eve, on the right). Extensive renovation earlier this century stripped out the Baroque additions and restored the church to its plainer, Romanesque appearance.

In the chapel on the right of the entrance are the bones of St Ludmila, the first Czech saint, who was strangled by assassins hired by Prince Wenceslas' mother Drahomira. On the left of the main entrance is an opening built to give access for the Benedictine nuns between their convent next door (which houses part of the National Gallery's collection) and to keep to a minimum their contact with the outside world.

Going down the hill from St George's, signposts direct you to the most visited street in Prague, **Golden Lane** (Zlatá ulička). The tiny multi-coloured cottages that cling to the castle walls were thrown up by the poor in the sixteenth century out of whatever waste materials they could find. Houses used to line both sides of the street, leaving barely enough space to pass in between, but in the eighteenth century hygiene-conscious Joseph II ordered a spot of demolition. At the eastern end is the **Dalibor Tower** (Daliborka), named after its first inmate, Dalibor, who spent time here on death row and amused himself by playing the

*The miraculous **Loreto**. See page 90.*

violin. According to legend (and Smetana's opera *Dalibor*) he attracted crowds of onlookers who turned up at his execution to weep *en masse*.

Continuing down the hill takes you past another **Lobkowicz palace** (Lobkovický palác), one of several in the town. This one, finished in 1658, houses the unexciting Historical Museum. Opposite is **Burgrave House**, now the Toy Museum (for both *see chapter* **Museums**). The statue of a naked boy in the courtyard fell victim to Marxist-Leninist ideology when President Novotny decided that his genitals weren't an edifying sight for the masses and ordered them to be removed. Happily the boy and his equipment have since been re-united. The lane passes under the **Black Tower** (Černá věž) and ends at the Old Castle Steps (Staré zámecké schody) which lead to Malá Strana. Before descending, pause at the top for a **view** over the red tiled roofs and the spires and domes of the 'Little Quarter'.

An even better view can be had from the **South Gardens** (Jižní zahrady) on the ramparts below the castle walls (enter from the Bull Staircase or from outside the castle, to the right of the first courtyard). Although they date from the sixteenth century, the gardens were redesigned in the 1920s by Josip Plečnik, the Slovenian appointed to the post of Castle Architect by President Masaryk. The spiralling **Bull Staircase** leading up to the castle's third courtyard, and the huge granite bowl are his work. After their restoration is complete, it will be possible to descend to Malá Strana by the terraced slopes of the beautiful Renaissance Ledebour and Pálffy gardens.

The Belvedere & Royal Garden

Crossing over the Powder Bridge (Prašný most) back by the castle's second courtyard, you reach the **Royal Garden** (Královská zahrada), which lies on the outer side of the Stag Moat (Jelení příkop). It was laid out in the Italian style for the Emperor Ferdinand I in the 1530s and originally included a maze and a private zoo, but the area was devastated by Swedish soldiers in the seventeenth century. The **Belvedere** was itself the target of French fire in the eighteenth century, but was saved for posterity by the payment of 30 pineapples by the canny head gardener. It's a stunning Renaissance structure built by Paola della Stella between 1538-64, its strangely-shaped green copper roof supported by delicate arcades. Ferdinand commissioned its construction as a gift to his wife Anne who never lived to see it finished, though she and Ferdinand are immortalised in the reliefs adorning the façade. In front of the palace is the so-called Singing Fountain, cast in bronze by Bohemian craftsmen in the 1560s, which hums as water splashes into its basin.

On the southern side of the garden overlooking the Stag Moat is another lovely Renaissance structure, covered with elaborate black and white sgraffito and completed by Bonifác Wohlmut in 1563 to house the king's **Ball Game Court** (Míčovna). The sgrafitto has to be renewed every 20 years, although the last time this was done some decidedly anachronistic elements were added to the allegorical frieze depicting Science, the Virtues and the

Elements. Look carefully at the lovely ladies on the top of the building, and you'll see that the woman seated next to Justice (tenth along from the right), is holding a hammer and sickle.

On the same side of the garden is the mustard coloured Dientzenhofer summer house that was the presidential residence between 1948 and 1989. During this period large sections of the castle were closed to the public and huge underground shelters were built to connect the presidents' residence with the rest of the castle. No sooner were they completed than it was decided that the underground passages might help to conceal counter-revolutionary enemies and the exit shafts were blocked off with huge concrete slabs.

Hradčany

Hradčanské náměstí is perhaps the grandest square in the city, lined with imposing palaces built by the Catholic aristocracy, anxious to be close to the Habsburg court. It was nonetheless cut off from the castle and its neurotic inmates by a complicated system of moats and fortifications, which remained until the Empress Maria Theresa had a grand spring clean in the mid-eighteenth century. Along with the moat went the tiny Church of the Virgin Mary of Einsedel, which used to stand next to the castle ramp. Lovely as this was said to have been, it's hard to believe that it was lovelier than the superb **panorama** of Malá Strana, the Strahov Gardens and Petřín Hill that the demolition opened up.

Walking up the ramp, the view ahead is dominated by the **Archbishop's Palace** (Arcibiskupský palác), with a frothy Rococo façade which was added in 1763-4. Next door, slotted in between the palace and a row of former canons' houses, is the Sternberg Palace (Šternberský palác), which houses the National Gallery's collection of European Art (*see chapter* **Art Galleries**). The collection has suffered more than its fair share of tribulations since 1989. In 1991 several priceless Picassos were stolen (they have since been recovered), while more than one aggrieved owner has come forward to reclaim the family heirlooms confiscated under the Communists. Opposite is the magnificent, but heavily restored, **Schwarzenberg-Lobkowicz Palace** (Schwarzenberský palác), one of the most imposing Renaissance buildings in Prague. It was built between 1545 and 1563, the outside exquisitely decorated with 'envelope' sgraffito. It's now the Military Museum and contains as comprehensive a collection of killing instruments as you would expect from a country which gave the world the words 'pistol' and 'semtex' (*see chapter* **Museums**).

Further up Loretánská is the pub **U Červeneho vola** (the Black Ox), a simple Renaissance building with a crumbling mural on the façade. As a result of some direct action in 1991, it's one of the few places left in Hradčany where the locals can afford to drink. The regulars foiled several attempts at privatisation by forming a co-operative to run it themselves. You don't have to feel guilty about the amount you drink here – all profits go to a nearby school for the blind.

The pub looks out onto Loretánské náměstí, a split-level square built on the site of a heathen cemetery, half of which is occupied by a car park for the Ministry of Foreign Affairs based in the monolithic **Černín Palace** (Černínský palác). This is an enormous and unprepossessing structure, its long grey façade articulated by an unbroken line of 30 pillars. Commissioned in 1669 by Humprecht Černín, the Imperial ambassador to Venice, its construction ruined the family and the first people to move in were hundreds of seventeenth century squatters. In 1948, Foreign Minister Jan Masaryk took a dive from an upstairs window and was found dead on the pavement below, a few days after the Communist takeover (*see chapter* **Sightseeing**).

Dwarfed by the Černín Palace is the **Loreto**, a Baroque masterpiece and a monument to the power of the Catholic miracle-culture that swept the Czech lands after the Thirty Years War. The façade (1721), is a swirling mass of stuccoed cherubs, topped with a bell-tower. The 27 bells ring out every hour with a cacophonous melody called 'We Greet You a Thousand Times'. At the centre of the complex is the **Santa Casa**, a replica of the home of Mary in Nazareth, which was flown by angels from the Holy Land to Loreto in Italy in 1245 and spawned a copycat cult throughout Europe. This one dates from 1626-31, and with its sculptured hands rising from the altar and black-and-red colour scheme, looks more like a place to hold a black mass than a virgin's boudoir (*see chapters* **Sightseeing** *and* **Museums**).

The streets behind the Loreto are some of the prettiest and quietest in Hradčany. The quarter was built in the sixteenth century for the castle staff; now its tiny cottages are the most prized pieces of real estate in the city. Going down Kapucínská, you pass the **Domeček** or 'Little House' at number 10, once home to the notorious Fifth Department – the counter-intelligence unit of the Defence Ministry. At number 5 on nearby Černínská is **Gambra**, a quirky gallery that specialises in Surrealist art from the 1930s to the present day (*see chapter* **Art Galleries**). Its owner, animator Jan Svankmajer, lives in the house next door. At the foot of the hill is **Nový Svět** ('New World'), the street which gives its name to the whole area. Tycho Brahe, the Danish alchemist notorious for his lack of nose (which he lost in a duel) and spectacular death (of an exploding bladder), lived at number 1, appropriately called 'the Golden Griffin'. Up from Loretánské náměstí is Hradčany's last major square: Pohořelec. The passage at number 8 leads to the peaceful surroundings of the **Strahov Monastery** (Strahovský klášter, *see chapters* **Sightseeing**, **Art Galleries** *and* **Museums**).

Malá Strana

Perhaps the most charming of Prague's areas, it's difficult not to be seduced by the Baroque 'Little Quarter'.

Church of Our Lady Under the Chain.

The name Malá Strana means the 'Little Quarter' or 'Lesser Town', and this is a typically Bohemian understatement for an area which contains monumental palaces and ornate, formal gardens, as well as tiny, crumbling cottages.

It was founded by the Přemyslid Otakar II in 1287, when he invited merchants from Germany to set up shop on the land beneath the castle walls. Very little remains of this Gothic town and the present day appearance of the quarter dates from the seventeenth century. The area was transformed into a sparkling Baroque town by the wealthy Catholic aristocracy, who won huge parcels of land in the property redistribution that followed the Thirty Years War. When the fashionable followed the court to Vienna in the seventeenth century, the poor moved into the area. It has been the spiritual and actual home of poets, drunks and mystics ever since, living cheek-by-jowl with the ambassadors and diplomats who also have their residences here. Today, the character of the quarter is changing rapidly as accountancy firms, bankers and froufrou wine bars set up here.

Kampa Island

Crossing over Charles Bridge from the Staré Město side, you'll see one of the best photo-opportunities in the city: the twin towers of the bridge, framing an almost perfect view of the church of St Nicholas and the castle behind. Before continuing, however, take the flight of steps on the left, leading down to **Na Kampě**, the principal square of Kampa Island. Until 1770, it was known simply as Ostrov or Island, which understandably led to confusion with the

other islands of the Vltava; the Čertovka, or Devil's Stream, which runs around the island, went by the altogether unromantic name of The Ditch until it was cleaned up and rechristened in the nineteenth century. Kampa is an oasis of calm on even the most crowded August day, and at the southern end is one of the loveliest parks in the city. From here you have a panoramic view of the Vltava river, Charles Bridge and the National Theatre on the opposite bank.

Cross the tiny bridge on Hroznová that leads to tranquil Velkopřevorské náměstí. The French Embassy is housed in the elegant **Buquoy Palace** (Buquoyský palác), a frothy pink stucco creation dating from 1719. Staring out from the wall opposite is **John Lennon**, whose head was painted on the wall in the 1980s together with hundreds of messages, ranging from the inane to the illegible (*see chapter* **Sightseeing**).

Just around the corner is the lovely **Maltézské náměstí**. The Knights of Malta have lived here since Vladislav II offered them a refuge in Prague. Their symbol, the red cross, is all over the square, since the order (which was dissolved by the Communists), has regained great swathes of property under the restitution laws. The Baroque building on the corner was once the Museum of Musical Instruments. This has suffered more than its fair share of blows: its priceless Flemish tapestries were given to Von Ribbentrop, Hitler's Foreign Affairs adviser, its Stradivarius violins were stolen in 1990, and now a sign on the door announces that 'the museum of musical instruments is abolished'.

Although the museum has gone, the Prague Conservatoire is still at number 5, and during term-time the sound of students practising provides a soundtrack to accompany your sightseeing. The highlight of the square is the **Church of Our Lady Under the Chain** (Panna Marie pod řetězem), a strange building originally built by a military religious order to guard the Romanesque bridge across the Vltava. Two solid towers still protect the entrance, although they now contain the most unusual flats in Prague. The Hussite wars interrupted the construction of the church and it was never finished. In place of a nave is an ivy-covered courtyard which leads up to a Baroque addition (dating from 1640-50) built in the apse of the original structure. Inside, by the altar, are the chains from the original bridge that give the church its name.

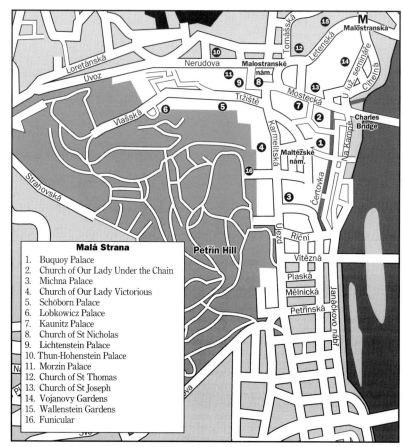

Malá Strana

1. Buquoy Palace
2. Church of Our Lady Under the Chain
3. Michna Palace
4. Church of Our Lady Victorious
5. Schöborn Palace
6. Lobkowicz Palace
7. Kaunitz Palace
8. Church of St Nicholas
9. Lichtenstein Palace
10. Thun-Hohenstein Palace
11. Morzin Palace
12. Church of St Thomas
13. Church of St Joseph
14. Vojanovy Gardens
15. Wallenstein Gardens
16. Funicular

Petřín Hill

Rising up in the west of Malá Strana is Petřín Hill (Petřínské sady), the highest, greenest and most peaceful of Prague's seven hills. The southern edge is traversed by the so-called **Hunger Wall** (Hladová zed'), an eight-metre high fortification commissioned by Charles IV to keep the starving peasants off the streets in 1362. The lazy (and fun) way up to the top of the hill is to catch the funicular from Újezd. It runs roughly every 15 minutes and stops halfway at the romantic restaurant Nebozizek.

Climb the 299 steps of the miniature **Eiffel Tower** for a spectacular view over the city. It was built in 1891 for the Jubilee Exhibition, constructed in a break-neck 31 days, and has been loved and despised in equal measure ever since. Its fiercest and most powerful opponent was Adolf

Hitler, who looked out of his guest room in the castle and made an immediate order for 'that metal contraption' to be removed. Somehow it survived, as did the mock Gothic castle, built at the same time, which houses a mirror maze (*see chapter* **Sightseeing**).

Back down at the foot of the hill, follow Újezd north and it becomes Karmelitská, which in turn leads out onto Malostranské náměstí. On the way, there are a couple of peculiar diversions. The first is the **Michna Palace** (Michnův palác, on the right-hand side of Újezd), a fine Baroque mansion built in 1640-50. It was intended to rival the Wallenstein Palace, which was itself built to rival the castle. Considering these gargantuan ambitions, it's no surprise that Francesco Caratti took Versailles as his model when it came to designing the garden wing of Michna. Today the gardens contain tennis courts, a clue to the site's present incarnation as the Sport & Physical Training Museum and headquarters of the Sokol organisation (*see chapters* **Museums** *and* **Sport & Fitness**).

Further along Karmelitská at number 9, is the **Church Our Lady Victorious** (Panna Marie Vítězná), the first Baroque church in Prague. It belongs to the Barefooted Carmelites, an order which returned to the city in 1993 and has taken charge of the church's most celebrated exhibit: Il Bambino di Praga (*see chapter* **Sightseeing**). Heading left up the hill from Karmelitská is Tržiště. The seventeenth century **Schönborn Palace** (Schönbornský palác) is at number 15, now the American Embassy. It was built by Giovanni Santini-Aichel, who, despite his name, was a third generation Praguer, and one of the descendants of Italian craftsmen who formed an ex-pat community on Vlašská just up the hill. That street now contains the German Embassy, housed in the **Lobkowicz Palace** (Lobkovický palác) at number 19. This is one of four Lobkowicz Palaces in Prague and its design (1703-1769) is based on Bernini's unrealised plans for the Louvre. You can get a glimpse of the gorgeous gardens through the gate, though sadly access to the original aviary and bear-pit is forbidden. In 1989 thousands of East Germans ignored the *Verboten* signs and scaled the high walls, setting up camp in the garden until they were granted asylum. The Lobkowicz family were major landowners in Bohemia until the nationalisation of property in 1948, and although they haven't reclaimed the palace, they have succeeded in regaining five castles, and the vinárna next door serves a good selection of wines from their estate in Mělník.

Tržiště becomes a tiny lane that winds up the hill from the American Embassy, giving access to some of the loveliest hidden alleys in Malá Strana. Washing hangs out above the streets, old ladies stare out of windows, and at number 22 is U Sebaracnicka rychta, the most traditional and insalubrious drinking establishment of the Little Quarter.

Charles Bridge to Malostranské Náměstí

The main drag between Charles Bridge and Malostranské náměsti is Mostecká ulice. It's a continuation of the Royal Route – the path taken by the Bohemian kings to their coronation – and is lined with elegant Baroque dwellings. At number 15 is the **Kaunitz Palace** (Kauniců palác). It was built in 1773 for Jan Adam Kaunitz, an advisor to Empress Maria Theresa, who sycophantically had the exterior painted her favourite colours – yellow and white. It's now the embassy of the former Yugoslavia.

At the heart of the Little Quarter is **Malostranské náměstí**. Its edges are defined by large Baroque palaces and Renaissance gabled town houses perched on top of Gothic arcades.

The formal **Wallenstein Gardens**. *See p94.*

Bang in the middle, dividing the square in two, is the **Church of St Nicholas**, a monumental late Baroque affair, whose dome and adjoining bell tower dominate the skyline of Prague's left bank. It is the largest and most ornate of the churches which the Jesuits funded in Prague and was built between 1703 and 1755. During its construction, the Society of Jesus waged a battle against the local residents who were understandably loathe to let go of the two streets, two churches and various other inconveniences which had to be demolished to make room for it. Inside, covering the dome and the vault, are 1,500 metres of frescoes which blend seamlessly with the pillars and pediments of the structure, in masterful *trompe-l'oeil* illusion. The church's ground-plan, based on three interlinking ovals, is the work of Christoph Dientzenhofer, but it was his son Kilián Ignaz who added the dome and the finishing touches.

The grim block next door at number 25 is yet another Jesuit construction, built as a college for their priests and now housing harassed-looking maths' students. More appealing is the **Lichtenstein Palace** (Lichenštejnský palác) opposite, finished in 1791. The Lichtensteins used to be major landowners in Bohemia and the alpine principality has been waging a battle to regain the palace, which was confiscated in 1918. They have been unsuccessful so far, and the palace is currently used as a concert venue (*see chapter* **Music: Classical & Opera**). Also in the square, located in the former town hall at number 21, is the club **Malostranská Beseda**, where music of a different kind is played (*see chapter* **Music: Rock, Roots & Jazz**).

Nerudova heads up from the square towards the castle, and is a fine place for deciphering the ornate signs which decorate many of Prague's houses: there's the Three Fiddles at number 12, for example, or the Devil at number 4. This practice of distinguishing houses continued up until 1770, when that relentless modernist Joseph II spoiled the fun by introducing numbers. The street is named after its famous son, the nineteenth century novelist Jan Neruda who lived at number 47, at the Two Suns (U dvou sluncu). The house has long since

You get more for your money at the **Morzin Palace**.

been turned into a pub and during the Communist period was a favourite hang-out of bad-boy rockers The Plastic People of the Population, who were major players in the events of 1989. Beer now costs a hefty 50kč a glass and the place is a joyless tourist trap. Also to be ignored is the turquoise drinking establishment at number 13 where Václav Havel, in a complete lapse of taste, took Yeltsin for a stein of beer. 'As for heads of state,' Havel is quoted as saying, 'I haven't met anyone whose eyes didn't shine when I suggested that after the official reception we should go and get a beer somewhere...'. A much better bet is U Koucura, at number 2. It's owned by a political party called The Friends of Beer. Although their manifesto is a bit vague, their ability to pull a good pint is beyond question.

The alley next door leads up to the British Embassy, at Thunovská 14, which a former ambassadorial wag christened 'Czechers'. Leading up from here are the **New Castle Steps** (Nové zámecké schody), one of the most peaceful (and least strenuous) routes up to the castle, and a star location in the film *Amadeus*.

There are more embassies back on Nerudova, the Italians occupying the **Thun-Hohenstein Palace** (Thun-Hohenštejnský palác) at number 20, built by Giovanni Santini-Aichel in 1726 and distinguished by the contorted eagles holding up the portal, the heraldic emblem of the Kolowrats for whom the palace was built. The Italians have been trumped by the Romanians, however, who inhabit the even more glorious **Morzin Palace** (Morzinský palác) opposite at number 5. Also the work of Santini-Aichel (1714) it sports two very hefty Moors, a pun on the family's name, who hold up the window ledge. Their toes have been rubbed shiny by passers-by who believe this will bring them luck.

Malostranské Náměstí to the River

Following the tram tracks from the square down towards the river brings you to the **Church of St Thomas** (sv. Tomáš), whose rich Baroque façade is easy to miss, tucked into the narrow side street of Tomášská. Based on a Gothic ground-plan, the church was rebuilt in the Baroque style by Kilián Ignaz Dientzenhofer for the Augustinian monks. The symbol of the order – a flaming heart – can be seen all over the church and adjoining cloisters (now an old people's home) and even in the hand of St Boniface, a fully dressed skeleton who occupies a glass case in the nave.

On the other side of the street is Josefská, a street which takes its name from the **Church of St Joseph** (sv. Josef), a tiny Baroque gem set back from the road and designed by Jean-Baptiste Mathey. Since 1989 it has been returned to the much-diminished Order of English Virgins, who also used to own the nearby **Vojanovy Gardens** (Vojanovy sady). This is one of the most tranquil spots in the city and the entrance is on U lužického semináře. Weeping willows, apple and walnut trees provide shade for the old people who congregate on the benches. There's a fish pond, temporary exhibitions of modern sculpture for children to clamber over, and an abandoned seventeenth century grotto.

Running parallel to U lužického semináře is Cihelná, a street named after the now derelict brick factory, which provides an opening onto the river and an almost perfect **view** of the Vltava. Back on Letenská, towards Malostranská metro station, is a door in a wall leading into the best-kept formal gardens in the city. The early seventeenth-century **Wallenstein Garden** (Valdštejnská zahrada) belonged, with the adjoining palace, to General Wallenstein, successful commander of the Catholic armies in the Thirty Years War and a formidable property speculator. The palace (now the Ministry of Culture) is enormous, and had a permanent staff of 700 servants and 1,000 horses. Unlike the Vojanovy Gardens, the formal lines of hedges and fountains don't provide a good place to lounge around, but next to the magnificent arcaded *sala terrena* at the far end is a café, where you can marvel at the artificial stalactites that the General had created on the walls, and which hid the entrance to his secret observatory (*see chapter* **Sightseeing**).

Staré Město & Josefov

Hidden passageways, forgotten courtyards, and twisting, cobbled alleys betray the medieval nature of the Old Town.

It's almost impossible not to get lost in Staré Město (the 'Old Town'), and much the best way to get a true measure of its charm is to do exactly that. Originally settled in the tenth century it has always been where the nitty-gritty of the town's business got done. While the city's rulers plotted and intrigued high up on the hill, the good merchants of the town got on with the business of making a quick buck, a skill that is re-emerging in post-Communist times as the inhabitants learn to wash the tablecloths, smile at the customers and quadruple the bill.

The Powder Gate to the Old Town Square

The Powder Gate (Prašná brána), a Gothic gateway dating from 1475 at the eastern end of Celetná, marks the boundary between the Old Town and the New and is also the start of the so-called Kralovská Česta, or Royal Route, the traditional coronation path taken by the Bohemian kings and now a popular tourist track. The first stretch runs west down Celetná, a pleasant promenade lined with freshly restored Baroque and Renaissance buildings. A more recent addition is the **House of the Black Madonna** (dům U Černé matky boži), at number 34, the first Cubist building in the city (*see chapter* **Sightseeing**).

Duck down Templová on the right, and you'll lose the crowds and be immersed in a part of the town where the pots of pastel paint have yet to penetrate and the buildings look on the verge of collapse. The **Church of St James** (sv. Jakuba) on Malá Štupartská is a typical Baroque reworking of an older, Gothic, church. It has a grand total of 21 altars, some fine frescoes and a dessicated human forearm hanging next to the door. This belonged to a jewel thief who broke into the church in the fifteenth century and tried to make off with some jewels from the statue of the Virgin. The Madonna grabbed him by the arm and kept him captive until the offending limb had to be cut off. However, its appearance – it looks like a piece of dried up salami – could be explained by the fact that the church's most prominent worshippers were members of the Butcher's Guild.

From here you can stroll through the medieval lanes behind the Church of Our Lady of Týn, Staré Město's parish church since the twelfth century (*see chapter* **Sightseeing**), and eventually come out on the Old Town Square.

The Old Town Square

For centuries Staroměstské náměstí has been the natural place for visitors to the city to gravitate. It's the only proper square in the city, closed off to traffic and awash with a cross-section of Euro youth and buskers. The grassy section behind the astronomical clock was provided by the retreating Nazi forces, who blew up the Old Town Hall on 8 May 1945 when the rest of Europe was holding street parties and celebrating the end of World War II.

The town lost most of its archives, though it gained a fine vista of the lovely **Church of St Nicholas**. Built in 1735 by Kilián Ignaz Dientzenhofer, this is an inside-out church: the exterior, with its white stucco and undulating façade, is even more ornate than the interior. An added attraction in winter is the heated seats installed to prevent your bottom freezing during organ concerts.

You can go and look at what remains of the Old Town Hall after the Nazi's handiwork, although trying to decipher the extraordinary components of the **astronomical clock** (orloj) is more rewarding. It was constructed in the fifteenth century, sometime before the new-fangled notion reached town that Prague revolves around the sun and not vice versa. Undismayed, the citizens kept their clock with its gold sunburst swinging happily around the globe. The **Old Town Hall** (Staroměstská radnice) was begun in 1338, after the councillors had spent several fruitless decades trying to persuade the king to allow them to build a suitable chamber for their affairs. John of Luxembourg finally relented, but with the bizarre proviso that all work was to be financed from the duty on wine. He obviously underestimated the

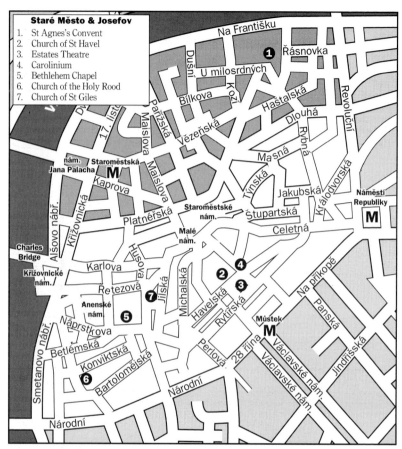

Staré Město & Josefov

1. St Agnes's Convent
2. Church of St Havel
3. Estates Theatre
4. Carolinium
5. Bethlehem Chapel
6. Church of the Holy Rood
7. Church of St Giles

high-living inhabitants of the Old Town, because within the year they had enough money to purchase the house which adjoins the present tower.

Perhaps the finest of the houses which make up what is left of the Old Town Hall is the **Minute House** (U minuty), the beautiful black and white sgraffitoed house on the corner, which dates from 1611. Franz Kafka lived here as a boy, and opposite the astronomical clock is the **Café Milena**, named after Milena Jesenská, the radical journalist who is best remembered for being Kafka's girlfriend (*see chapter* **Cafés, Bars & Pubs**).

The focal point of the square is the monument dedicated to the reformist cleric Jan Hus, designed by Ladislav Saloun and unveiled in 1915. On the orders of the Pope, Hus was burnt at the stake in 1415 for his revolutionary thinking, although the Catholic Church, over 500 years after the deed was done, has belatedly decided to appoint a commission to decide whether the punishment fitted the crime. Hus's fans are optimistic, as the quote on the side reads 'truth will prevail', words which were echoed by President Gottwald, in the 'Glorious February' of 1948. It was from the balcony of the **Goltz-Kinský Palace**, a frothy stuccoed affair which overlooks the monument, that Gottwald announced the Communist victory to jubilant crowds.

For a complete contrast to the squeaky clean façades of the square, find the **Church of St Michael** (sv. Michal), an atmospheric ruin on Michalská. You can contemplate the desolate exterior to the strains of Dvořák symphonies that float from the open windows of the music school next door. Behind the Baroque exterior is one of the oldest Romanesque basilicas in the city which neither the National Library who own it, nor the Catholic Church can afford to restore.

The Old Town Square
to Charles Bridge

The most obvious route from the Old Town Square to Charles Bridge is along **Karlova**, although twisting and curling as it does, it wouldn't be at all obvious were it not for the crowds progressing along it. It's the continuation of the Royal Route and becomes an unrelenting bottleneck in the summer when tourists and construction workers vie for supremacy of the narrow way.

To reach Karlova, walk past the Old Town Hall into **Malé náměstí** (Little Square). In the centre is a well enclosed by an ornate Renaissance grill and overlooked by the neo-Renaissance **Rott House**, built in 1890 and entirely decorated with murals of flowers and peasants by Mikoláš Aleš (it's now a hardware shop). Back on Karlova, the third twist on the way takes you past the massive, groaning giants which struggle to hold up the portal of the **Clam-Gallas Palace** (Clam-Gallasův palác) on Husova. This was designed by Fischer von Erlach and completed in 1719, and now houses the city's archives.

The vast bulk of the **Clementinum** makes up the right-hand of the last stretch of Karlova. It's the largest complex of buildings after the castle in Prague. The Jesuits, storm troopers of the Counter-Reformation, set up home here on a site which was formerly the centre of the Inquisition in Prague, and carried on the tradition of book-burning and brow beating. Inside the complex are the churches of St Clement and St Saviour as well as the Chapel of Mirrors and the buildings of the National Library (*see chapter* **Sightseeing**).

A short detour away is the **Golden Tiger** (U zlatého tygra) on Husova, the favourite watering-hole of Bohumil Hrabal, octogenarian author and Nobel Prize nominee, who has spent half his life inside a pub and the other half writing about what goes on inside pubs (*see chapter* **Cafés, Bars & Pubs**). If you fail to get a seat, go instead to the **House of the Lords of Kunštát and Poděbrady** on Řetězová. In the basement are the atmospheric remains of a Romanesque palace, and temporary exhibitions from the puppet faculty of Charles University spookily spotlit against the crumbling vaults and pillars (*see chapter* **Museums**). In the courtyard is one of the best spots for summer drinking in the Old Town.

At the foot of Karlova stands a policeman installed to prevent tourists throwing themselves in the line of the continuous stream of trams and cars which race through Knights of the Cross Square (Křižovnické náměstí). The eponymous Knights, an elderly bunch of neo-medieval crusaders, have come out of retirement and reclaimed the **Church of St Francis** (sv. František). Designed by Jean-Baptiste Mathey in the late seventeenth century, the church, which has a massive red dome and has been

*Detail on the **astronomical clock**. See p95.*

described as looking as if it has been 'gouged out of so much Dutch cheese', is unusual for Prague, not least because its altar is facing the wrong way. The gallery next door houses a job-lot of religious bric-à-brac that the Knights have extricated from various museums, and a subterranean chapel decorated with stalactites made out of dust and egg-shells, an eighteenth century fad that enjoyed unwarranted popularity in Prague.

On the western side of the square is the **Church of St Saviour** (sv. Salvátor), built between 1578 and 1602 by the Jesuits and which marks the border of the Clementinum. Opposite, guarding the entrance to Charles Bridge is the **Old Town Bridge Tower** (Staroměstská mostecká věž), a Gothic gate topped with a pointed, tiled hat. Built in 1373 along the shadow line of St Vitus's Cathedral, it was badly damaged in 1648 by marauding Swedes, but the sculptural decoration on the eastern side by Peter Parler survives. Look out for the stone knight on the left-hand side who is depicted with his hand up a lady's skirt (sadly you can no longer see the expression on her face). There's no such difficulty with the couple on the right-hand side, however, where another medieval maid is clearly enjoying having her breasts fondled. Climb the tower for a perfect birds' eye view of Prague's domes and spires, and the wayward line of Charles Bridge.

Charles Bridge

Charles Bridge (Karlův most) is the most popular place in the city to come and get your portrait painted, take photos of the castle or pick up a back-packer. The range of entertainment is always diverse, from blind folk-singers to the man who plays Beethoven concertos on wine glasses. The stone bridge was built in 1357 and has survived over 600 years of turbulent life, although a large and embarrassing chunk of it fell into the Vltava in 1890. The statues that line it were added during the seventeenth century, when Bohemia's leading sculptors, including Josef Brokof and Matthias Braun, were commissioned to create figures to inspire the masses as they went about their daily business. More mundane pieces were added in the nineteenth century by the Max brothers.

St John of Nepomuk – perhaps the most famous piece – is eighth on the right facing Malá Strana and recognisable by his doleful expression and the cartoon-like gold stars fluttering around his head. John was flung off the bridge from this very spot, after refusing to reveal the secrets of the queen's confession, and his statue – placed here in 1683 – is the bridge's earliest. He was cast in bronze and has survived better than the sandstone statues which have been badly damaged by the elements and have mostly been replaced by copies. The third statue on the right is a **crucifixion** that has a Hebrew inscription in gold. This was added in 1696 by a Jew found guilty of blaspheming in front of the statue, his punishment to pay for the inscription 'Holy, Holy, Holy, Holy Lord' to be added. Further towards Malá Strana is the Cistercian nun **St Luitgard**, made by Matthias Braun in 1710, and shown in the middle of her vision of Christ. It's considered by many, including Prince Charles, to be the finest statue on the bridge, and he has pledged the money to save her from the elements which are threatening to wipe the look of wonder off her face. She can be found fourth from the end, on the left.

Josefov

For over a millennium Jews have lived and worked in Prague, and for most of that time have inhabited a tiny portion of Staré Město. Their history – at times turbulent and frequently terrifying – can be traced through the monuments which remain in the triangle of land bounded by Pařížská, Kaprova and the Vltava. Although the cramped houses and dark alleyways of the ghetto were cleared in the late nineteenth century, the atmosphere amid the turn-of-the-century tenements which replaced them can seem eerie, not least because out of a pre-war population of around 50,000, only 1,500 Jews remain in the city today.

The first Jewish settlers preferred the land across the river, but at the time of the first crusade, in 1096, they were rounded up and enclosed in the area that is now Josefov. Surrounded by high ghetto walls, and subject to the vicissitudes of royal rulers, the Jews' first break came in 1245 when Přemysl Otakar II declared that they were royal property whose damage would be punishable by death. Encouraged by this, in around 1270 the community built the **Old-New Synagogue** (Staronová synagóga), which stands on a wedge of land between Maislova and Pařížská and is the oldest synagogue in Europe. Legend has it that the foundation stones were flown over by angels from the Holy Temple in Jerusalem under the condition (*al tnay* in Hebrew) that they should be returned on Judgement Day, hence the name *Alt-Neu* in German or Old-New in English.

The contrast between the austerity of the outside and the warm intimacy of the inside couldn't be greater. The vaulting of the twin naves is softly lit, and oak seats line the walls facing the *bema*, or platform, protected by a Gothic grille, from which the Torah has been read aloud every day for over 700 years (except during the Nazi occupation). The tall seat marked by a gold star belonged to **Rabbi Loew**, the most famous inhabitant of the ghetto whose life has become legend.

Born in 1512, Rabbi Loew was a towering figure of the Prague Renaissance, whose considerable talents included making friends with free-thinking Rudolf II, and creating a monster out of mud – the **golem**. Few versions of the story agree on how the rabbi brought the clay figure to life, but walking around the body seven times in an anti-clockwise direction, quoting the seventh chapter from the second book of Genesis, and placing a *shem* or stone tablet in his mouth, are taken to be the three key ingredients. As man-made monsters tend to, the golem ran amok when the rabbi forgot to remove the *shem*. He stormed into the Old-New Synagogue, the *shem* was removed and all that remained was a lifeless lump of clay and a staple of Prague folklore ever since. The rabbi lived to the age of 97, and a sculpture by Ladislav Šaloun to the right of the New Town Hall (in Mariánské náměstí) depicts the manner of his death. Unable to approach the scholar, who was always absorbed in study of the scriptures, Death hid in a rose which was offered to Loew by his innocent grand-daughter. The rabbi's grave is in the Old Jewish Cemetery, recognisable by the quantity of pebbles and wishes on scraps of paper that are placed upon the tomb to this day.

Next door to the Old-New Synagogue is the former **Jewish Town Hall** (Maiselova 18), dating from the 1560s, with a Rococo façade painted in various delicate shades of pink, and a Hebraic clock whose hands turn anti-clockwise. The money to build the town hall and the neighbouring High

Synagogue, was provided by Mordecai Maisel, a contemporary of Loew's and a man of inordinate wealth and discriminating taste. The Town Hall has been the centre of the Jewish community ever since.

Today the community is coming to life after 40 years of stagnation. Since 1989 it has been pressing for the restitution of Jewish property, which didn't qualify under the recent restitution laws because it was confiscated before 1948 by the Nazis. The community also wants the right to run the Jewish Museum, and it is working to improve the condition of the buildings and educate the younger generation of Jews, many of whom have grown up without knowing they are Jewish. The **High Synagague** (Vysoká synagóga), which was built at the same time as the Town Hall and is attached to it, was returned to the community early in 1994 and will eventually become a working synagogue again.

Mordecai Maisel also funded the synagogue which takes his name (Maiselova 10). Sadly, the current building is a reconstruction of the original (apparently the most splendid synagogue of them all), which burnt down in the great fire of 1689 when all 316 houses of the ghetto and 11 synagogues were destroyed. The present structure dates from 1892-1905 and is sandwiched between tenement blocks. It houses the Jewish Museum's silver collection, and the rows of Torah pointers and ceremonial crowns on display are but a fraction of the stores which the museum owns but has no space to display.

Although the origins of the **State Jewish Museum** date back to the beginning of the century, it was Hitler who was responsible for the comprehensive collections of today. He ordered the quarter to be preserved as a Museum of an Extinct Race, and the property belonging to the 153 Jewish communities of Bohemia and Moravia was sent to Prague for cataloguing and storage and remained here after the war because there was nobody to whom to return it (*see chapter* **Museums**).

The Old Jewish Cemetery

On U starého hřbitova is the Old Jewish Cemetery, a small, unruly patch of ground that contains the remains of thousands of bodies. Forbidden to enlarge their burial ground, the Jews had no choice but to bury bodies on top of each other in an estimated 12 layers, so that today crazy mounds of earth are jammed with lopsided stone tablets. This extreme overcrowding in death is a visible reminder of the overcrowding that marked the ghetto until after the revolution of 1848, when the walls were finally demolished, Jews were granted the rights of citizens and the quarter was renamed Josefov. This was in honour of enlightened despot Joseph II whose 1781 Edict of Tolerance had relaxed the rules of the ghetto: Jews were allowed

to live in other parts of town and no longer had to wear yellow garments. In 1787 further burials in the overcrowded cemetery were banned.

Burials began here in the early fifteenth century, although earlier gravestones were brought in from an abolished cemetery nearby, including that of **Avigdor Kara**. He died in 1439, and his is the oldest tombstone in the cemetery (the original has been replaced by a copy). Kara was just a boy when he witnessed the pogrom that took place during the Passover of 1389 when 3,000 people were massacred by Christians who rampaged through the quarter. One of the few survivors, he wrote an elegy of remembrance which to this day is recited on Yom Kippur every year in the Old-New Synagogue. Many of the tombstones are decorated with figures of animals and even humans, a practice which began in the free-wheeling days of the Renaissance, and is strictly forbidden by the Talmud (*see chapter* **Sightseeing**).

On the left-hand side of the entrance is the **Klausen Synagague** (Klauzová synagóga), built in 1694 and constructed by the same craftsmen who built Prague's Baroque churches. Inside, the pink marble Holy Ark could almost pass for a Catholic altar were it not for the gold inscriptions in Hebrew. Facing the synagogue is the **Ceremonial House** built in the style of a Romanesque castle at the beginning of this century. It houses an exhibition of drawings by the children interned in Terezín during World War II, the last stop of the Jewish population before being sent to the death camps in the east. The images the children drew are both shocking and poignant: the mass dormitories and stormy skies of the camp stand next to idyllic recollections of fields and flowers.

On the other side of the cemetery is the **Pinkas Synagogue**, built as the private house of the powerful Horowitz family in 1607-1625. In the courtyard, a fifteenth century ritual bath or *mikveh*, has been uncovered. The Jewish community is in the process of building a new ritual bath here, since for over 40 years the city has been without this essential part of Orthodox life. Between 1955 and 1959 the Pinkas Synagogue was a memorial to the Jews of Bohemia and Moravia who lost their lives in Nazi concentration camps; on the walls are painted the names of the 77,297 men, women and children who died in them. In 1967, after the Six Day War, the Czechoslovak government expelled the Israeli ambassador, closed the synagogue and plastered over the names – a move of appalling insensitivity that is only dwarfed by the scale of the Nazi's inhumanity conveyed by the densely written script covering every wall.

The final synagogue, the **Spanish Synagogue** (Španělská synagóga), was built just outside the boundaries of the ghetto in 1868, on Dusní. It was built for the growing number of Reform Jews, and its façade is of a rich Moorish design. Unfortunately it's closed indefinitely, and in such a state of disrepair that the whole structure is perilously close to falling down.

Despite repeated persecutions and relentless pogroms, the cultural life of the Jews has had its golden ages. One occured during the inter-war years of this century, a fruitful time which produced a large group of writers including, most famously of all, **Franz Kafka**. He was born in the neo-Baroque house on the corner of Maiselova and Kaprova, the border between the Jewish quarter and the Old Town, an opposition that prefigured the antagonism and contradictions of his life and writing. A plaque marks the spot and a small exhibition inside details his short life, spent almost entirely in and around the environs of the Old Town. After the ghetto was cleared at the turn of the century, he wrote 'living within us are still those dark corners, mysterious corridors, blind windows, dirty backyards, and noisy inns... Our hearts know nothing about the new sanitation. The unhealthy Jewish town within us is much more real than the hygienic new town around'.

The site along the banks of the Vltava wasn't incorporated into the new design of Josefov, and the grandiose buildings have their backs turned upon the old ghetto. Going down Kaprova towards the river will bring you to **náměstí Jana Palacha**, a square named after the student who set himself on fire in 1969 in protest against the Soviet invasion. Dominating the square is the **Rudolfinum** (Dům umělců) or the House of Arts, which was built in the 1880s in the popular neo-Renaissance style and entirely funded by the Czech Savings Bank to display their 'patriotic, provincial feelings'. You can see their corporate logo, the bee of thrift, in the hands of the two sphinxes with remarkably conical breasts who guard the river-front entrance. Opposite, with its back to the Old Jewish Cemetery, is the **Museum of Decorative Arts** (*see chapter* **Museums**).

Around St Agnes's Convent

Few visitors make it over to this part of the Old Town, but the streets of semi-derelict Art Nouveau tenement houses in northern Staré Město are well worth inspection, even without the attraction of **St Agnes's Convent** (Klášter sv. Anežky české). The convent (*see chapters* **Sightseeing** *and* **Art Galleries**) is the oldest example of Gothic architecture in the city. Its founder, St Agnes, was martyred a full 700 years before the Pope relented and made her a saint. Popular opinion held that miracles would accompany her canonisation, and sure enough within five days of the Vatican's announcement the Velvet Revolution had got under way.

Nearby is **Dlouhá** or Long Street, which contained no less than 13 breweries in the fourteenth century when beer-champion Charles IV forbade

Charles Bridge *statuary. See page 98.*

the export of hops. A worthy successor of its drinking heritage is **The Roxy** at number 33. It's a semi-demolished cinema that was once the headquarters of the Communist Youth Association and is now one of the city's most atmospheric bars.

Southern Staré Město

Canny German merchants were the first to settle this area. They built a church dedicated to St Havel when Charles IV generously donated some spare parts of the saint from his burgeoning relic collection. The onion domes of the existing **Church of St Havel** (on Havelská) were added later in 1722 by the Shod Carmelites (the Barefooted Carmelites settled on the other side of the river). The opposite end of Havelská is lined with slightly bowed Baroque houses precariously balanced on Gothic arcades. The merchants have at last returned, and the street now offers one of the best shopping opportunities in a city which still has much to learn about the joys of consumerism. As well as hand-made wooden toys, there are abundant piles of fruit and vegetables.

The pale green and white **Estates Theatre** (Stavovské divadlo) dominates the end of the adjacent street of Rytířská (*see chapter* **Sightseeing**). After nine years' restoration, the theatre is every bit as splendid as it was in Mozart's lifetime, when it presented the premiere of *Don Giovanni*. Opposite is the **Beriozka** restaurant, a sad reminder that this block used to be the Soviet House of Science and Culture. Fancy boutiques have taken over most of the complex, although there's a permanent exhibition of gaudy Russian paintings and some yellowing Aeroflot posters. The restaurant, however, is still satisfactorily Stalinist, and it's worth ducking into the basement to check out the Communists' ideas on colour co-ordination.

The massive oriel window overlooking the theatre belongs to the **Carolinum**, the university founded by Charles IV and named after him. Charles never made a move without first consulting the stars, and ascertained that Aries was an auspicious sign for the first university in Central Europe, which was founded on 7 April 1348. It came to grief at the hands of another Aries, Hitler, when it was badly damaged in World War II (*see* chapter **Art Galleries**).

Around Betlémské náměstí

Once the poorest quarter of the Old Town and a notorious area of cut-throats and prostitutes, this was the natural breeding ground for the radical politics of the late fourteenth century. On the north side of Bethlehem Square are the swooping twin gables of the **Bethlehem Chapel** (Betlémská kaple) built by followers of firebrand preacher Jan Hus in 1391 (*see* chapter **Sightseeing**).

Across the square is the Náprstek Museum (*see* chapter **Museums**). After making his fortune by inebriating the masses, Vojta Náprstek installed a collection of ethnological knick-knacks in the family brewery. A nineteenth century do-gooder, he didn't just spend his time hunting down shrunken heads, but also founded the first women's club in the country. The room, untouched for 100 years, can still be seen, although the peep-hole he drilled through from his office draws into question the purity of his motives.

One of the three Romanesque rotundas in the city, the **Church of the Holy Rood** (Rotunda sv. Kříže) is on nearby Konviktská. It's a tiny, charming building, dating from the early twelfth century and built entirely in the round so that the devil had no corner to hide in. Today it's dwarfed by the surrounding tenement buildings. If you don't manage to get a look inside, try the **Hostinec U rotunde** opposite. Covered with lovely sgraffito, it's as authentic a pub as you'll find in the Old Town, with cheap beer and a contingent of locals who'll try to stare you out when you walk in.

On Husova, to the north-east, is the **Church of St Giles** (sv. Jiljí), a massive Gothic structure that looks like a fortress from the outside. It was built by the Dominicans in 1340-70, an order which has recently come back to reclaim its heritage and inhabit the monastery next door. It has nothing to do with the small curiosity shop across the road, however, called **Regula Pragensis**, which sells a bizarre collection of books, jewellery, and antiques and is run by a self-styled 'secular monastic order'. Their abbot is a former pop star, they hold their services in a pub and spend their spare time combing the fields of Bohemia to find a ploughman to reclaim the Czech crown.

Parallel to Konviktská is the unnaturally quiet **Bartolomějská**. Czechs still avoid its environs – a legacy of the role it played in Communist times. Police departments line the street and most dissidents of note did time in the StB (Secret Police) cells in the former convent. The building has been

*Inside the **Clam-Gallas Palace**. See page 97.*

restored to the Sisters of Mercy and you can stay the night in the cell where Havel was sent to ponder the error of his ways (*see* chapter **Accommodation/Pension Unitas**).

To the north, and heading towards the river, you reach Anenské náměstí, the site of a former convent dedicated to St Anne. It's a lovely forgotten backwater, with a Renaissance well and allegedly the ghost of a nun, who obviously fell victim to backstabbing at the convent, and wanders around with a knife in her spine. Tucked away in the corner is the **Theatre on the Balustrade** (Divadlo na zábradlí), most famously associated with Milan Kundera and Václav Havel, though the pair are no longer on speaking terms. They fell out in the 1970s when they conducted an acrimonious correspondence on the pages of the *New York Review of Books*, Kundera expounding the view that petitions were a waste of time, and Havel accusing Kundera of being a no-good defeatist cop-out.

The river is only a few yards away and from here you have a perfect **view** across it to Kampa, with the castle high up on the hill. Turning right will take you past Novotného lávka, a cluster of buildings jutting into the river centred around a nineteenth century water tower, and back to Charles Bridge. Turn left to reach the National Theatre and the start of the New Town.

Nové Město

Playground of generations of Czechs in the last century and battleground of another generation this century, the 'New Town' has always been a barometer of Prague's changing fortunes.

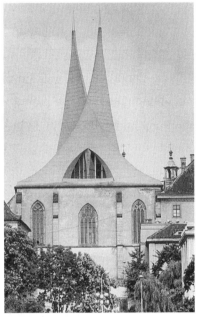

Modern spires on the ancient **Emmaus Monastery**. *See page 104.*

The 'New Town' is far from new and no longer a township. It was founded in 1348 by Charles IV, who'd had a premonition that the Old Town would be destroyed by fire and floods. Despite frequent fires and floods the Old Town is still standing, but the decision was a good one: his far-sighted urban-planning, which led to the creation of wide boulevards and broad squares, has meant the area has adapted well to the rigours of modern life.

Wenceslas Square

Václavské náměstí (*see chapter* **Sightseeing**) was laid out over 600 years ago, under the auspices of Charles IV and it has always been a good place to check out the changing fortunes of the city. This

century, Nazis, Communists, anti-Communists, and a naked Allen Ginsberg have all paraded its length. The Communists' May Day parades have been replaced by a sleazy collection of pimps and pickpockets. You'll be assailed by the smell of frying sausages and if you're a fat businessman, by any number of thin prostitutes.

The shops which used to have dull names like House of Fashion, House of Food or House of Shoes have been privatised and glamourised, though they're still more interesting for their architecture than their contents. Every architectural style of the last 150 years is represented here, from the Art Nouveau **Hotel Evropa** at number 25, to the Functionalist **Bat'a store** at number 6. Crowning the whole lot is the massive neo-Renaissance **National Museum**, an important-looking nineteenth century block that contains a disappointing collection. Next door is the ugly 1970s building that housed the **Federal Parliament** until the Czech-Slovak split in 1993. The building is due to become the new base of Radio Free Europe, which, after playing its part in the toppling of totalitarianism, is moving in to take advantage of the cheap rent. The parliament has moved to a refurbished palace on Sněmovní in Malá Strana.

Wenceslas Square to náměstí Republiky

Na příkopě runs from Wenceslas Square to náměstí Republiky along the line of what was a moat. It has been quaintly dubbed 'Prague's Wall Street' because of the concentration of banks along it, and the financial institutions range from the neo-Renaissance Živnostenská Banka at number 20 to the Art Deco Komerčni Banka at number 28.

There's usually a group of louche-looking soldiers hanging round náměstí Republiky, playing hookey from their vast crenellated barracks on the east side. They're soon to be banished to the suburbs, however, as negotiations are under way to turn their residence into yet another swanky hotel. Dominating the square is the luscious Art Nouveau **Municipal House** (Obecní dům), which stands on the border of the Old and New Towns and was built on the cusp of the nineteenth and twentieth centuries. Attached to the blackened

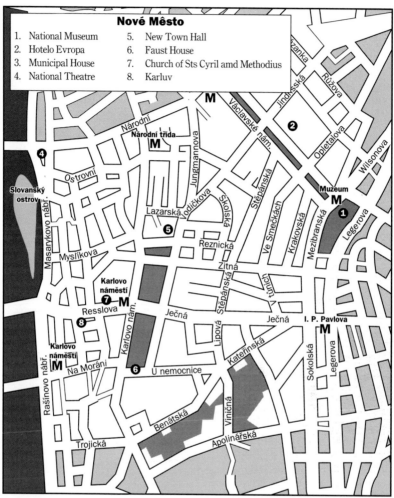

Nové Město

1. National Museum
2. Hotelo Evropa
3. Municipal House
4. National Theatre
5. New Town Hall
6. Faust House
7. Church of Sts Cyril amd Methodius
8. Karluv

Gothic Powder Tower which predates it by half a millennium, it is an extravagant combination of colour and curves, completed in 1912, and was where Czechoslovakia was signed into existence in 1918.

Just a few yards away on Revoluční, but thankfully hidden from view, is the **Kotva department store**. It was once the shopping showpiece of the Eastern Bloc, when 75,000 people a day would come from as far away as Bulgaria to snap up its fine selection of acrylic sweaters. It was built in 1971 by Swedish architects, who took the opportunity to fight the Cold War from a different front and came up with a fantastically ugly design. It

has recently been overhauled and the Communist idea of fashion replaced by the German one.

Further north, on nábřeží Ludvíka Svobody next to the river, is a monolithic structure, recognisable by a dome that glows orange at night. This is the **Ministry of Transport**, built in the 1920s and for a spell the HQ of the Central Committee of the Communist Party. It was here that on 21 August 1968 tanks arrived to escort Alexander Dubček on his way to the Kremlin where he was flown for 'fraternal discussions'.

To the south of náměstí Republiky is Hybernská, named after the Irish monks who settled here in the sixteenth century after falling foul of Elizabeth I. Their contribution to city life was to introduce the potato, an event from which Czech cuisine has never recovered. The street itself is unremarkable save for the presence of the **American Center for Culture and Trade** in the Baroque Kinský Palace, at number 7, a building which ironically used to house the Lenin Museum. At number 24 is the Café Arco, meeting place of the self-styled 'Arconauts' who included Franz Kafka and Max Brod. Few literary types stray into it now that it's a 24-hour pool hall, but across the road in the Masaryk railway station is another 24-hours spot – the Non-Stop Buffet, which serves fried cheese through the night to the cream of the city's unsavouries.

Wenceslas Square to the River

To the north-west of Wenceslas Square runs Národní třída or National Avenue, which was the playground of generations of Czechs in the last century and the battleground of another generation this century. The **National Theatre** (Národní divadlo), a grandiose affair at the far end overlooking the river, was finished in 1883 and dedicated to the idea of Czech selfhood when independence was but a twinkling in the Nationalists' eyes. A bronze memorial half way down on the south side (by number 20) pays tribute to the events of 17 November 1989, where a student demonstration sparked the beginning of the Velvet Revolution. The department store on the corner of Spálená is a barometer of the changes which have occurred since then. It used to be called 'Máj' after the most sacred date in the Communist calendar, 1 May. It now belongs to K-mart and is a source of peanut butter for the legions of Americans in town. By the memorial at number 20 is **Reduta**, the venerable jazz club where Bill Clinton tested his saxophone skills before a global audience. Further down at number 7, through an exquisite wrought iron entrance, is **Viola**, a literary hang-out which sports one of the three framed Václav Havel signatures to be found in various drinking holes around town. Next door, with a fine view across the river to the castle, is the redoubtable **Slavia**, the centre of Prague's café-life for 100 years, but currently closed due to one of the city's interminable real-estate wrangles.

The Embankment

The embankment running south (it becomes Rašínovo nábřeží) contains a fine if unremarkable collection of Art Nouveau apartment houses. At number 78 is the block containing the Havels' third-floor flat. In a deliberate break with tradition Václav Havel declined to move into the swanky Presidential quarters at the castle and stayed in his own down-at-heel tenement across the river.

*Foaming flagons at **U Fleků**.*

Now the gesture has been made, admired, and written about, he has bought an altogether more upmarket residence in Prague 6. Not that he can be blamed, however, since the plot next door is a building site where a highly controversial construction is under way: the so-called 'Ginger and Fred' building, apparently designed to look like a pair of swirling dancers.

The climax of this Art Nouveau promenade is Palackého náměstí, which is dominated by the monumental sculpture by Stanislav Sucharda of nineteenth century historian **František Palacký**, who dedicated 46 years of his life to writing a history of the Czech people. Palacký looks pretty solemn, seated on an enormous pedestal, book in hand and utterly oblivious to the bevy of beauties flying around his shoulders. Behind him rise the two modern spires of the altogether more ancient **Emmaus Monastery** or Monastery of the Slavs (klášter na Slovanech), which was founded by Charles IV, the towers added after the Baroque versions were destroyed by an Allied bomb in World War II.

The island closest to the embankment, at the bottom of Národní, is **Slovanský ostrov**. In the days before slacking was an art-form, Berlioz came here and was appalled at the 'idlers, wasters and ne'er-do-wells' who congregated on the island. With a recommendation like that it's hard to resist the outdoor café or a trip in one of the rowing boats for hire. There's also a fine statue of Božena Němcová, as seen on the back of the 500kč note. She was the Czech version of George Sands, a celebrated novelist whose private life scandalised polite society. At the southern tip is the art gallery **Mánes**, a 1930s Functionalist building incongruously attached to a medieval water tower. The left-wing intelligentsia used to gather here between the wars, as did The Union of Propertyless and Progressive students (presumably because they had no home to go to), while in 1989 Civic Forum churned out posters and leaflets from here with up-to-date information on the changing political scene. The island is also home to the newly-restored cultural centre Žofín – a large yellow building dating from the 1880s which has long been associated with the Czech cultural psyche, and hosted tea dances and concerts until just before World War II.

Around Karlovo Náměstí

There are some fine backstreets to explore, tucked away between Národní and Karlovo náměstí, as well as some major thoroughfares, but the most notable sight on the way is **U Fleků**, at Křemencova 11, the place to go if you want a genuine German drinking experience (*see chapter* **Cafés, Bars & Pubs**). **Karlovo náměstí** is an enormous expanse that used to be a cattle market and the site of Charles IV's relic fair. Once a year he would wheel out his collection of saints' skulls, toenails and underwear, the townsfolk dutifully gawped, cripples would throw down their crutches and the blind would miraculously regain their sight. These days you're most likely to come across the square in a night tram, minor miracles in their own right. Its other attractions include the **New Town Hall** (Novoměstská radnice), which dates from the fourteenth century. It was from here that several Catholic councillors were ejected from an upstairs window in 1419 and the word defenestration entered the language.

On the eastern side of the square is the splendidly restored Jesuit Church of St Ignatius (sv. Ignác), an early Baroque affair in cream, pink and orange stucco, with gold trimmings. At number 24 is the **D Club**, a pleasant enough restaurant that used to be the training ground for waiters employed by the Secret Police. The James Bonds of the catering world came to learn how to plant bugs in dissidents' soup and dish up the sauce to their eager employers. In the corner is the **Faust House** (Faustův dům), an ornate seventeenth century building that has more than a few legends attached to it. John Kelley, the earless English alchemist lived here, as apparently did the Prince of Darkness, who carried off a penniless student and secured the house a place in Prague's mythic heritage.

Half way across the square on Resslova is the Baroque **Church of Sts Cyril and Methodius**, scene of one of the most dramatic and poignant events of World War II (*see chapters* **Sightseeing** *and* **History**). Going in the opposite direction up the hill is Ječná, where **Dvořák** died at number 14; but rather than staring at the plaque on the wall, go to the museum dedicated to him nearby on Ke Karlovu. It's housed in a gorgeous Dientzenhofer-designed red and cream villa, surrounded nowadays by incongruous modern bits of concrete (*see chapter* **Museums**).

At the far end of the street is a museum of an altogether different sort. The **Police Museum**

Karlov *church: dedicated to Charlemagne.*

contains countless photos of headless torsos and some live-action videos of police thuggery in practice. Since the revolution, Brek, the stuffed wonder-dog responsible for thwarting the defection of hundreds of desperate dissidents, has been given a decent burial, but the police still have a highly dubious reputation, which the displays do nothing to dispel. If it all gets too much, you can seek sanctuary in the unusual church next door, which is dedicated to Charlemagne, Charles IV's hero and role model. The octagonal nave of **Karlov** was only completed in the sixteenth century, although the superstitious townspeople refused to go in it for years, convinced that it would collapse. The ornate gilt frescoed walls inside were restored after the building was partially destroyed in the Prussian siege of 1757, but bullets can still be seen embedded in them. From the garden there are extensive views across the Nusle valley to Vyšehrad on the other side. Close by on Vyšehradská is the Church of St John on the Rock (sv. Jan na skalce), a fine Dientzenhofer structure built in the 1730s, perched at the top of an impressive double stairway; a little further to the south are the seldom-visited **Botanical Gardens**, where the hot-houses have undoubtedly seen better days.

Further Afield

It's worth making a foray into the hinterland to see some of Prague's most interesting, and least visited, sights.

The Left Bank

Holešovice, Letná & Troja

At first glance, Holešovice is an unremarkable turn-of-the-century suburb filled with tenement buildings overlaid with a thick layer of grime from neighbouring factories. However, it contains two of the finest green spaces in the city and is rapidly throwing off its post-war torpor. New shops and bars have opened, and with the opening of the new **Gallery of Modern Art** (*see chapter* **Art Galleries**), it looks set to become one of the most lively areas in town.

At the northern end is **Stromovka**, a park laid out by Rudolf II in the sixteenth century, as a place where he could commune with nature. Rudolf's interests ranged from the eclectic to the perverse and his favoured companion at Stromovka was the English alchemist and mathematician John Dee, who got the job when he claimed to understand the language of the birds and that in which Adam conversed with Eve in Paradise.

Part of Rudolf's grand design for the gardens was a **tunnel** bringing water from the Vltava river two kilometres away and, if you don't suffer from claustrophobia, you can walk the length of it. The entrance is easy to find, on nábřeží Edvarda Beneše. Take a candle, crucifix and burly friend, as – judging from the graffiti – it's a popular place for summoning up the forces of darkness.

Next to Stromovka is **Výstaviště** ('exhibition ground'), an unusual wrought iron pavilion built to house the Grand Exhibition of 1891 and considered the first expression of Art Nouveau in the city. Come here on a summer evening to see the floodlit Křižík fountain swoop and soar in time to music, or – if you're brave – have a go on the roller-coaster, which looks as if it's held together with bits of string.

Turning off the Avenue of Dukla Heroes (Dukelských hrdinů) onto Veletržní you come to the **Veletrzni Palace** (Veletržní palác), an enormous structure that was built in the mid-1920s in the Constructivist style, to house the trade fairs when they had outgrown Výstaviště. When Le Courbusier first visited the palace he described it as 'breathtaking', although he later dismissed it as

'a very important building which after all is not refined enough to be called architecture'. It was gutted by fire in 1974 and restoration work has been slow and painful, but the inside – planned around a central atrium which rises up nine stories – is indeed breathtaking. In this light, white space the National Gallery plans to display its impressive collection of twentieth century Czech art (*see chapter* **Art Galleries**).

Close by on Janovského is one of the major centres of Prague's extensive twentysomething slacker scene, **The Globe**, an American-run bookshop and café (*see chapter* **Cafés, Bars & Pubs**). Heading down towards the river and turning right into Kostelní will lead you to the **National Technical Museum**, a Constructivist building dating from 1938-41. Apart from the coal-mine in the basement, the major crowd-puller is the atrium, packed with steam trains, aeroplanes, a hot-air balloon, innumerable cars and a flying sledge (*see chapter* **Museums**). If all that is not enough, there's an antique carousel across the road at the top of **Letná Park** (Letenské sady). This is where the biggest demonstration of 1989 took place, attended by nearly a million people. On the edge of the park, with a fine view overlooking the town, is the plinth where the statue of Stalin used to stand. It was the largest version of Uncle Joe in the world, but was judiciously blown up in 1962.

A 15-minute walk away across the river from Stromovka (or you can take the 112 bus from Nádraží Holešovice metro) is **Troja Château** (Trojský zámek). Commissioned by Count Sternberg in the 1700s and built by a French architect and Italian craftsmen, it contains some stunning *trompe-l'oeil* frescoes, fakes within fakes that completely steal the limelight from the nineteenth century paintings that are exhibited here (*see chapter* **Art Galleries**). Count Sternberg's horses were particularly fortunate, inhabiting a sumptuous stable block with marble floors and decorated with frescoes of their noble forebears. The inmates of Prague's **zoo** across the road can only curse their historical mistiming, for, despite having found a new patron in Coca Cola, their living conditions are altogether less salubrious (*see chapter* **Children**).

Opposite: *the 'breathtaking'* **Veletrzni Palace**.

Smíchov & Barrandov

Smíchov has undergone quite a few changes since the days when Mozart stayed here. Rapid industrialisation rather spoilt the ambience of the aristocracy's summer houses and the area has since been taken over by factories and factory workers. You can get an idea of what the area was once like at **Bertramka**, the house with lilac-scented gardens that belonged to František and Josefina Dušek and is now a museum devoted to their house guest, Wolfgang Amadeus Mozart (*see chapter* **Museums**).

South of Smíchov is **Barrandov**, the Czech version of Hollywood. On the cliffs below there are even huge white letters which spell out B-a-r-r-a-n-d-e, although this is actually in homage to the nineteenth century geologist after whom the quarter takes its name. Enormous studios were built here in the 1930s and the area has been the centre of the Czech film industry ever since. On the hills below the studios are some interesting modern villas and the Barrandov Terrace, a restaurant and nightclub set into the cliffs. It was designed by the uncle of Václav Havel in the Constructivist style, and now belongs to his brother Ivan. There are plans to revamp it, although at present it's a down-at-heel reminder of the glory days of the First Republic.

Dejvice & Beyond

Some of the most exclusive residences in the city are located in Prague 6, the suburbs which lie beyond the castle. The hub of the area is Vítězné náměstí, where a statue of Lenin used to stand, and leading off it is the Avenue of Yugoslav Partisans (Jugoslávských partyzánů) at the end of which you'll find the **Hotel International**. This monumental piece of Socialist Realism built in the 1950s is one of the last remaining bastions of Marxist-Leninist interior decoration in the city. On the hill above the Hotel International is the **Baba estate**, a colony of Constructivist villas built after the huge success of the 1927 Exhibition of Modern Living in Stuttgart. The houses were commissioned and inhabited by the leading figures of the Czech avantgarde, and many of them are still decorated with original fixtures and fittings.

Josip Plečnik's **Church of the Sacred Heart**.

Take bus number 131 to U Matěje and walk up Matějská to reach the estate.

On the western fringe of the city is the **Břevnov Monastery** (Markétská 28), inhabited by Benedictine monks since AD993 and modelled on 'God's perfect workshop'. The monks celebrated their millennium with an enormous spring clean, sweeping out traces of the Ministry of the Interior which for the last 40 years had used the **Basilica of St Margaret** (sv. Markéta) as a warehouse for its files on suspicious-looking foreigners. This Romanesque church was remodelled by the father and son Dientzenhofer double act in the early eighteenth century, and is one of their most successful commissions, with a single high nave and unfussy interior.

Close by, near the terminus of tram 22's meandering path through the city, a small stone pyramid marks the site of **Bilá Hora**, or White Mountain, where the battle which started the Thirty Years War in 1620 took place. Within the park is the **Star Lodge** (letohrádek Hvězda), an extraordinary product of the Renaissance mind, its angular walls and roof arranged in the pattern of a six-pointed star. It was built in the 1550s for Archduke Ferdinand of Tyrol, who when he wasn't feuding with Rudolf II over possession of the Habsburg narwhale horn, was obsessed with numerology, and the whole is conceived as an intellectual conundrum. Today it houses the rather dull Jirásek & Aleš Museum (*see chapter* **Museums**).

The Right Bank

Vyšehrad

Vyšehrad, south of Nové Město, is where all the best Prague myths were born. Libuše, the mother of Prague, fell into a trance and sent her horse out into the countryside to find her a suitable spouse. The horse returned with a strapping young ploughman called Přemysl, after whom the early Bohemian kings take their name. The historical myths were revived by the nineteenth century romantics who rebuilt the Church of Sts Peter and Paul, created a public park and established a national cemetery for the cream of Czech society. To get there, take the metro to Vyšehrad, which runs under the enormous road bridge spanning the Nusle valley. When it was built in the 1970s, the bridge was hailed as a monument to Socialism, a title that was hastily dropped with the large chunks of concrete that began to fall on passing pedestrians, and it became the most popular spot for suicides in the city. Walk past the monolithic concrete **Palace of Culture** (Palác kultury) built in 1972, and the supreme architectural expression of the years which were referred to as 'normalisation', and pass through the Baroque gateway into the park.

There's been a church on the same site at Vyšehrad since the fourteenth century, but it was apparently irrevocably damaged when Lucifer, angered by an insubordinate cleric, threw three large rocks through the roof. The granite slabs now occupy pride of place outside the Old Provost's Lodgings, but the holes are gone and the present **Church of Sts Peter and Paul** (sv. Petr a Pavel) dates from the beginning of the twentieth century. Next door is the **cemetery**, surrounded by Italianate arcades, which is the last resting place of, amongst others, Dvořák and Smetana and contains some spectacular sculpted memorials.

The edge of the park stands on a cliff overlooking the Vltava, and there's a fine **view** across the water to the castle. If you continue down the hill from Vyšehrad along Přemyslova, you'll find one of the most outstanding pieces of **Cubist architecture** in the city, a corner apartment block designed by Josef Chochol at Neklanova 30 (1911-13). He also designed the house on Libušina 3, further to the west near the river. Peep over the fence on the embankment to see the overgrown remains of some Cubist landscaping. It's opposite the railway bridge which is universally known as 'The Bridge of Intelligence', built by the intellectual élite who worked as labourers after losing their jobs during the purges of the 1950s.

Vinohrady & Žižkov

Vinohrady came into existence in what the Communist guide books call the period of Bourgeois Capitalism, and it's an area of magnificent, if crumbling, *fin de siècle* tenements. The heart of the neighbourhood is náměstí Míru, with the twin spires of the neo-Gothic **Church of St Ludmila** (sv. Ludmila) and the opulent turn-of-the-century **Vinohrady Theatre** (Divadlo na Vinohradech), home to one of the city's classiest acts, the Prague Syncopated Orchestra, who look and sound like a slice of the 1930s.

The main artery of Vinohrady, however, is Vinohradská, a little further north. It used to be called Stalinová třída, and ironically it was here that the fiercest street battles of 1968, against the Warsaw Pact troops, took place. The street heads east to náměstí Jiřího z Poděbrad, probably the most extraordinary square in the city. Art Nouveau apartment blocks line the sides, looking out onto the **Church of the Sacred Heart** (Nejsvětější Srdce Páně), one of the most inspiring pieces of modern architecture in the city, which is dominated by a huge glass clock. It was built in 1928-32 by Josip Plečnik, the pioneering Slovenian architect.

A few streets further north on Kubelíkova is the **Akropolis**, which will eventually become a theatre complex, but at the moment is a popular bar and a good place to sample absinthe, the 70 per

cent proof liqueur which drove Van Gogh to lop off his ear (*see chapter* **Restaurants**). It's next door to the infamous, space-age **TV tower** (televizní vysílač) which was completed in 1989 and still suffers from excessive unpopularity (*see chapter* **Sightseeing**).

Stretching to the east is Žižkov, which enjoys an impressive degree of notoriety because of its high quota of insalubrious pubs and large Romany population. It has always been a working class district, so it's not surprising that the post-war 'working class' presidents chose to be buried here, in the massive mausoleum on top of Vítkov Hill. Outside the **National Memorial** (Národní památník) stands the largest equestrian statue in the world, a 16.5 ton effigy of Hussite hero Jan Žižka who vanquished the combined Catholic armies and gave his name to the suburb. The corpses were ejected from the mausoleum in 1990, but it's still a fundamentally eerie place though there are plans to turn the hill into a massive leisure complex.

Further east along Vinohradská are two fine cemeteries. The first, **Olšany** (Olšanské hřbitovy), is the largest in Prague – an enormous city of the dead. Jan Palach, the student who set fire to himself in 1969, is buried here, as is the first Communist President Klement Gottwald. Since 1989 the cemetery has begun to suffer from the usual urban blights (graffiti) as well as some more unusual ones (grave-robbing). The cemetery extends on the other side of Jana Želivského, and includes a Garden of Rest, where the Red Army soldiers who died liberating Prague are buried. Their graves are marked by sculptures of crossed machine guns, and wreaths are still left by those who haven't forgotten them.

Next door is the **Jewish Cemetery** (Židovské hřbitovy), where fans of Franz Kafka come to leave stones and pay their respects at his simple grave. The cemetery is in stark contrast to the cramped quarters of the Old Jewish Cemetery in Josefov. It was founded in 1890 and only a fraction of the graveyard has been used since the decimation of the population in World War II.

To the south and east lies the wilderness of Prague 4, a postcode which to Prague residents means only one thing: **paneláks**. A panelák is the Czech word for a tower block made out of pre-fabricated concrete panels. These blocks mushroomed throughout the 1960s and 1970s as a cheap solution to the ever-present housing crisis. **Jížní Město**, or Southern Town in Prague 4, has the greatest concentration of them and houses 100,000 people. Possibly the paneláks' worst aspect is that they all look identical both outside and inside, although residents claim that even worse is the knowledge that they can't even be blown up and would have to be demolished the way they went up, panel by panel.

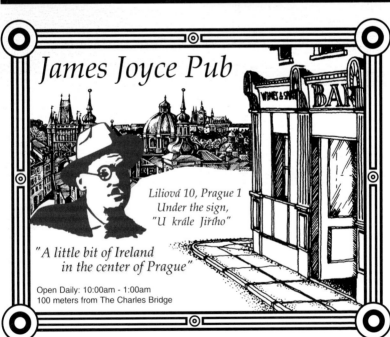

Eating & Drinking

Restaurants   **112**
Cafés, Bars & Pubs   **125**

Restaurants

The old guard offers glorious surroundings and rib-sticking food, while the ever-changing line-up of new restaurants provides added flavour.

It helps to like pork to appreciate Czech cuisine. Add pickled cabbage and bread-like *knedlíky* (dumplings) and you have the essence of Bohemian dining, which shares many characteristics with neighbouring Germany. Food is meant to be filling, rather than nutritious, and fresh vegetables are a rarity on restaurant tables even though they are now plentiful in markets.

This heavily meat- and starch-laden diet is often blamed on the years of Communism, when the ability of the state to provide 1.8 kilograms of meat per week for every individual was touted as proof of the regime's success. But a recent poll of Czech housewives revealed that only a small minority serve vegetables (not including potatoes) more than once a week to their families. Czech restaurants also tend to eschew vegetables, serving huge helpings of beef or pork with dumplings and cream sauces – all of which goes quite well with the country's famous and delicious beer.

As if force of habit were not enough, Czech law has kept a leash on new culinary developments by requiring every new dish to undergo testing by the Ministry of Health before it is offered to the public. Rather than go through this time-consuming procedure, most restaurants find it easier to offer food cooked according to the state-approved book *Recipes for Warm Meals*, which has more than outlived its function of ensuring uniform quality in government-run restaurants. There's no reason why the law can't be abolished, but for now the new democracy has more important matters to attend to than deregulating dumplings.

The arrival of innumerable foreign restaurateurs and exposure to west European culture has brought an international element to Czech dining, however. Some of the grander dining rooms don't serve Czech food, with its proletarian connotations, at all. Others have become adept at gracefully recreating traditional game dishes such as wild boar and hare. So restaurants in Prague do now offer a broader range, and you can try anything from the homeliest of pub grub to excellent international meals.

CHOOSING A RESTAURANT

Eating out is apt to be an adventure, especially given the riot of new restaurants that keep popping up – and disappearing – on every street corner. A single plot can be a restaurant, a computer shop, a travel agency and a restaurant again

U Malířů. *See page 116.*

in the space of one year, as various tenants try their hands at capitalism. Sometimes these experiments offer inedible approximations of international cuisine, while others present traditional food and hope to distinguish themselves from the hundreds of other dumpling-and-sauerkraut joints. Many restaurants have spectacular settings – romantic Gothic cellars or riverside views – that more than compensate for any deficiencies in their kitchens. And the price of eating out is markedly less than in western Europe, so that even travellers on a tight budget should be able to splash out at a fine restaurant at least once during their stay.

THE MENU

The first thing to notice about Czech menus is the two sets of entrées, one ready-to-serve (*hotová jídla*), the other cooked to order (*minutky*). The first are generally slow-cooked meats in sauces, such

The Menu

Meals (Jídel)
Snídaně breakfast; **Oběd** lunch; **Večeře** dinner.

Basics (Základní)
Chléb brown bread; **Cukr** sugar; **Drůbež** poultry; **Maslo** butter; **Maso** meat; **Ocet** vinegar; **Olej** oil; **Omačka** sauce; **Ovoce** fruit; **Pepř** pepper; **Rohlik** roll; **Ryby** fish; **Smetana** cream; **Sůl** salt; **Sýr** cheese; **Vejce** eggs; **Zeleniny** vegetables.

Appetisers (Předkremy)
Borsč Russian beet soup; **Chlebíček** open sandwich; **Hovězí vývar** beef broth; **Jazzík** tongue; **Kaviar** caviar; **Paštička** pâté; **Polévka** soup; **Sýr** cheese; **Uzený losos** smoked salmon.

Meat (Maso)
Biftek beefsteak; **Hovězí** beef; **Játra** liver; **Jehně** lamb; **Klobasa** sausage; **Králík** rabbit; **Ledvinky** kidneys; **Párek** sausage; **Slanina** bacon; **Šunka** ham; **Telecí** veal; **Vepřové** pork; **Zvěřina** game.

Poultry & Fish (Drůbež a Ryby)
Bažant pheasant; **Husa** goose; **Kachna** duck; **Kapr** carp; **Krocan** turkey; **Kuře** chicken; **Losos** salmon; **Pstruh** trout.

Main Meals (Hlavní jídel)
Gulaš goulash; **Sekana** meat loaf; **Smaženy sýr** fried cheese; **Svíčkova** beef in cream sauce; **Vepřové řizek** fried breaded pork.

Side Dishes (Přilohy)
Brambor potatoes; **Bramborák** potato pancake; **Hranolky** chips; **Kaše** mashed potatoes; **Knedlíky** dumplings; **Krokety** potato croquettes; **Rýže** rice; **Salát** salad; **Tatárska omáčka** tartar sauce; **Zelí** cabbage or sauerkraut.

Cheese (Sýr)
Balkan feta; **Eidam** hard white cheese, like Edam;
Hermelin soft, similar to brie; **Niva** blue cheese; **Pivny sýr** semi-soft cheese, flavoured with beer; **Tvaroh** soft curd cheese.

Vegetables (Zeleniny)
Česnek garlic; **Čočka** lentils; **Chřest** asparagus; **Cibule** onion; **Fazole** beans; **Žampiony** mushrooms; **Kukuřice** corn; **Květak** cauliflower; **Mrkev** carrot; **Okurka** cucumber; **Petřel** parsley; **Rajče** tomato; **Špenát** spinach; **Zelí** cabbage.

Fruit (Ovoce)
Ananas pineapple; **Borůvky** blueberries; **Broskve** peach; **Hrozny** grapes; **Hruška** pear; **Jablka** apple; **Jahody** strawberries; **Mandle** almonds; **Ořechy** peanuts; **Pomeranče** orange; **Rozinky** raisins; **Třešně** cherries.

Dessert (Moučnik)
Čokolada chocolate; **Dorte** layered cake; **Koláč** round pastry with various fillings; **Ovocné knedlíky** fruit dumplings; **Palačinka** pancake; **Slehačka** whipped cream; **Zakuska** cake; **Zmirzlina** ice-cream.

Drinks (Napoje)
Čaj tea; **Džus** juice; **Kava** coffee; **Mléko** milk; **Pivo** beer; **Sodovka** soda; **Víno** wine; **Voda** water.

Terms & Expressions
Bezmasa meatless; **Čerstvé** fresh; **Domáci** homemade; **Grilováné** grilled; **Na roštu** roasted; **Na špíž** grilled on a skewer; **Pečené** baked; **Plněné** stuffed; **Smažené** fried; **Vařené** boiled.

Do you have...? *máte...?*
I am a vegetarian *jsem vegetarián/vegetariánka (m/f)*
Can I have it without...? *můžu mít bez*
The bill, please *účet, prosím*
May I see the menu? *můžu vidět jídelní lístek?*

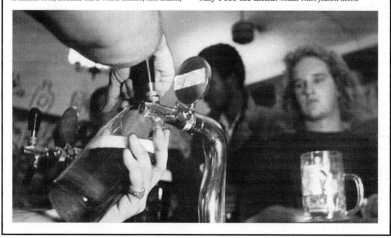

as *guláš* or *svíčková*, served with dumplings to mop up the juice. Another common practice is to list the weight of entrées in grams on the left-hand side of the menu – not to be confused with the price! The dinner entrées, *obědy*, may also be listed on the menu but are not usually available until about 4pm. Side dishes of rice or potatoes are the most commonly available accompaniments and are ordered separately. Vegetables, particularly fresh ones, are rarely seen save for the ubiquitous *obloha*, a garnish of pickled vegetables on a single lettuce leaf that finds its way into restaurants of every category.

Czech menus offer some tasty appetisers, such as Prague ham with horseradish, cheese plates and creamy soups, which complement the traditional heavy brown bread. For dessert, most places serve *palačinky*, pancakes filled with either fruit, chocolate or ice-cream (and sometimes all three).

DRINKS

Becherovka, a liqueur made to a secret recipe in the west Bohemian spa town of Karlovy Vary, is the country's favourite aperitif, usually served in a tiny, long-stemmed glass. *Fernet*, darker and more bitter, is more of an acquired taste; many people mix it with soda water and call the result 'Bavarian beer'. The most popular brand of mineral water, Mattoni, is from the same spa-water source as

U Mecenáše. *See page 117.*

Becherovka, but you can also ask for *Dobrá Voda* (Good Water, a brand name), available either carbonated or still. *Turecká* (Turkish) coffee, the most common brew, is thick stuff that will leave the unwary with a mouthful of grinds; filtered coffee is beginning to replace it but you may be asked which one you prefer.

Beer is the most important drink in the Czech Republic, as one would expect in the country that invented the pilsner brewing method. Czechs are the third largest consumers of beer in the world, aided by the fact that a half-litre mug is often cheaper than a Coke or a cup of coffee. Most restaurants are loyal to a single brand and serve it straight from the tap. Wines, mostly from southern Moravia, are equally good and destined for the world market once decisions about labelling and categorisation make large-scale export feasible. *See also chapter* **Cafés, Bars & Pubs** for more on drinking in Prague.

THE BILL

Except in high-class restaurants, the waiter will leave a little slip of white paper on your table and keep a running tab of what you order. When you are ready to pay, catch the eye of the person with the black wallet – not your waiter – and wait patiently. The system is simple and fair in theory: in practice tourists frequently get ripped off because they don't look at the bill. If the price seems a bit steep ask to see the bill and point at anything that looks suspicious. Normal charges include a few crowns for each piece of bread and a small cover charge which ought to be listed somewhere on the menu.

Somewhat nastier, but perfectly legitimate, bill-padding techniques include charging a large sum for the almonds on the table and offering hors-d'oeuvres that cost as much as the dinner. Don't eat anything that you haven't ordered unless you're prepared to pay for it.

Since the government instituted a 23 per cent value added tax (VAT), most restaurants have incorporated the increase into the prices listed on their menus. If a restaurant tries to slap a 23 per cent surcharge on top of your bill you are perfectly justified in complaining to the management, though it may not do any good, especially if you don't speak Czech.

GENERAL ADVICE

In Prague eating out is often a communal event, with strangers sharing tables (unless a table has been reserved). If an occupied table has enough spare seats to accommodate your party, politely ask *je tu volno?* (is it free?) before sitting down; similarly, don't be surprised if another diner wants to sit at your table. People wish each other *dobrou chuť* when the food arrives, but otherwise respect each others' privacy. In case conversation does ensue, *na zdraví* (cheers) is the national toast.

While the diners seem capable of getting along together, the waiters are sometimes surly to the point of savagery. Even polite waiters can be painfully slow, as anyone who has observed a waiter polish off a beer before returning to his rounds can testify. Patience and fortitude are recommended, as the locals are unlikely to appreciate any well-meaning lessons in etiquette. Fortunately service is improving as competition increases and restaurateurs realise that good service equals good business. Tipping is not mandatory; if you wish, round the bill up to the nearest 10kč, or leave a little more if the service has been excellent.

Czechs eat early (before 8pm), so it's a good idea to start scouting for somewhere to eat before your options become drastically limited. Restaurants also tend to run out of food as the day progresses. Wearing jeans or shorts is fine for all but the most top-notch establishments – there's no such thing as a dress code in a country where egalitarianism was once the state religion.

Reservations aren't necessary unless the restaurant is very smart or you wish to be assured of having a private table. If your first choice is full, don't despair: the act of wandering through the picturesque streets of the town near dusk, looking for a perfect discovery of your own, is one of the best experiences Prague has to offer.

RESTAURANT CATEGORIES

The former four-star system has been officially defunct for several years, though some restaurants continue to list themselves as belonging to a particular *skupina*, or category. Menus are posted outside in most places, enabling you to get an idea of the kind of food served and the price range. The restaurants listed below are divided by price, which in Prague doesn't necessarily relate to the quality of food or atmosphere. Because dining out is relatively inexpensive by west European standards, it is possible to have an excellent dinner in a mid-range restaurant; conversely, it is easy to pay a (relatively) high price for a mediocre meal close to a tourist slot. The average price listed below includes an appetiser and a main meal with accompanying side dish, but not a dessert or drinks.

Food can be found in any number of establishments, the most obvious of which is a *restaurace*. A *vinárna*, or wine bar, can be anything from a stand-up bar that serves only wine to a swish restaurant that takes pride in its well-stocked wine cellar. At a *pivnice*, or beer hall, the fare is bound to be plebeian: sausages, goulash with dumplings or fried cheese are typical offerings. *Bufets* and *lahůdkys*, the country's answer to fast food, are listed separately. Oddly enough, the ubiquitous *snack bar* has nothing at all to do with food; it's a place for hard drinking and slot machines.

See chapter **Cafés, Bars & Pubs** for more wine bars and beer halls in Prague; if you want to find a restaurant in a particular area, *see page 264* **Area Index**.

Top Range (500kč or more)

Au Saint Esprit
Elišky Krásnohorské 5, Prague 1 (231 00 39). Metro Staroměstská. **Lunch served** 11.30am-2pm Mon-Fri. **Dinner served** 7-10.30pm daily. **Average** 500kč. **Credit** AmEx, MC, V.
One of the most beautiful dining experiences in Prague, though by no means a typical one. The warm, modern décor of the restaurant's single room is complemented by delicate Belgian-French meals made with fresh ingredients, with fish dishes a particular strength. Diners end up lingering long after the kitchen closes, an activity which the staff graciously permit.
Booking advisable.

David
Tržiště 21, Prague 1 (53 93 25). Tram 12, 18, 22. **Lunch served** 11.30am-3pm, **dinner served** 6-11pm, daily. **Average** 700kč. **Credit** AmEx, V.
Two intimate rooms reminiscent of an old-fashioned inn are the setting for some of the best international cooking to be found in Prague. In the past, Communist Party membership was required in order to enter and sample dishes like the rosemary lamb chops. Now all you need is a good map, since David is hidden in one of the charming side streets of the Old Town. The unbelievable half-price lunch menu is probably the gourmet bargain of the century.
Booking essential.

Fakhreldine
Klimentská 48, Prague 1 (232 79 70). Metro Florenc. **Open** noon-midnight daily. **Average** 550kč. **Credit** AmEx, DC, V.
No tourist posters or folk crafts clutter the walls of this Lebanese restaurant: this chandeliered dining room is a chance to sample the exotic in elegant surroundings. The starters outnumber the main courses and one can easily make a meze out of the selection (although each small, perfectly-prepared dish is nearly as costly as a main dish). Fresh, raw lamb, Lebanese cream cheese and *sojok* (spicy Armenian sausages, grilled) are served with homemade Arabic bread. Char-grilled lamb and other types of meat form the bulk of the entrées, while a few internationally-prepared fish, veal and steak dishes round out the menu. Lebanese coffee with cardamom ends the meal.
Air-conditioning.

The Lucerna bufet – *fast food, Czech-style.*

U Malířů

(At the Painter's), Maltézské náměstí 11, Prague 1 (24 51 02 69). Tram 12, 18, 22. **Open** 11am-11pm daily. **Average** 1,000kč. **Credit** AmEx, DC, MC, V.

Prague's most expensive and authentic French restaurant is located inside a quaint sixteenth century house, with the original painted ceilings intact. The menu changes seasonally: for example, in summer escargots or pâté served with a glass of Sauterne lead on to main courses such as sea bass, lobster, lamb and pigeon. The cheeses are scrumptious. There are three fixed price menus, as well as the carte. The wine list is also fascinating, listing vintage bottles from every wine-growing region of France, although the price of one of these will double the cost of your meal. Service is formal but not oppressive.
Booking advisable.

Opera Grill

Karoliny Světlé 35, Prague 1 (26 55 08). Metro Staroměstská/9, 17, 18, 22 tram. **Dinner served** 7pm-midnight daily. **Average** 700kč. **Credit** AmEx, DC, MC, V.

After locating the plain sign you walk into a nondescript apartment building and rap on a brass knocker, to be whisked into a gorgeous little dining room as lush and sugary as the sweetest dessert. Guests sit in large, overstuffed armchairs, surrounded by voluminous draperies and statuettes, while a pianist plays in one corner. The international, nouvelle cuisine menu (on hand-lettered and handmade paper) is short but covers all the basics from beef and game when in season to pasta and seafood. There's nothing particularly Czech here, save for the beautiful Karlovy Vary porcelain figurines, but this is meant to be a cocoon-like experience.
Booking essential.

Parnas

Smetanovo nábřeží 2, Prague 1 (24 22 76 14). Tram 9, 18, 22. **Lunch served** noon-3pm, **dinner served** 5.30-11.30pm, daily. **Average** 1,000kč. **Set menu** 895kč. **Credit** AmEx, EC, MC, V.

When a nineteenth century writer dubbed Prague the Parnassus of Europe, this glitzy restaurant overlooking the Vltava was one of many catering to the socialites, artists and politicians who made up the city's burgeoning café society. Parnas and its adjoining café changed hands early this century and got the Art Deco treatment: both subsequently became immensely popular with the musicians and singers working in the National Theatre across the road. The restaurant has preserved its sumptuous interior, which includes green marble columns, walls of inlaid wood depicting the signs of the zodiac and a mosaic over the bar entitled 'The Absinthe Drinkers' which is a museum piece. The carefully-prepared international menu is one of the best in Prague, and includes some beautiful interpretations of Czech favourites (try the sautéd duck with pumpkin purée). The gracious service is impeccable. The Sunday jazz brunch – combining music with an all-you-can-eat buffet and all-you-can-drink Mimosas – draws an international business crowd.
Booking essential.

U Šuterů

Palackého 4, Prague 1 (26 10 74). Metro Národní třída or Můstek. **Lunch served** 11.30am-2.30pm, **dinner served** 6.30-11.30pm, daily. **Average** 550kč. **Credit** AmEx, EC, MC, V.

Here the cooking is done by the diners themselves on heated stones, a restaurant fad that apparently started in northern Italy. This Belgian-owned restaurant offers a variety of meat and fish, both plain and marinated, for cooking on individual stones – the flesh cooks perfectly without the aid of oil or butter. Starters might be chicken liver terrine or a warm salad of tiger prawns (there's little

for vegetarians). Wine connoisseurs will appreciate the array of French wines waiting to be uncorked beneath the Gothic arches. A classy place, despite the fact that you do all the work yourself.

V Zátiší

(In Seclusion), Liliová 1, Betlémské náměstí, Prague 1 (24 22 89 77). Metro Národní třída. **Lunch served** noon-3pm, **dinner served** 5.30-11pm, daily. **Average** 500kč. **Credit** AmEx, EC, MC, V.

A self-consciously sophisticated restaurant, located on the corner of a charming cobbled square and owned by the management of **Parnas** (*see above*). Its new rooms, furnished from the French patio furniture shop across the street, are – believe it or not – the height of elegance. Zátiši's meals feature homemade pasta, fish flown in twice weekly from Norway and a daily special that puts a deluxe spin on traditional Czech foodstuffs such as rabbit and roast duck. Beef fillet in a cognac sauce and jumbo shrimps served with roast peppers go down particularly well when one considers that it will cost half the price charged at Parnas. The jazz brunch here costs 495kč.
Booking advisable.

U Zlaté hrušky

(The Golden Pear), Nový Svět 3, Prague 1 (53 11 33). Tram 22. **Lunch served** 11.30am-3pm, **dinner served** 6.30pm-midnight, daily. **Average** 650kč. **Credit** AmEx, MC, V.

First-class service and top-notch Czech and international dishes are what you'll find here, although the game-oriented selection may not be to everyone's taste. Specialties include five kinds of tripe, game consommé and venison served with buckwheat mash. The extensive menu takes some time to read; it even includes 'suggested meals for ladies' and 'suggested meals for men'. Although the jellied goose appetiser with raw onion is gratis, it doesn't compensate for the low trick of slapping 23% VAT on top of the final bill, in addition to the 50kč a head cover charge, but for those who are prepared for these financial blows the meal will probably seem worthwhile. In summer the chef fires up the grill in the restaurant garden, and produces relatively inexpensive barbecued chicken and beef dishes.
Tables outdoors.

Moderate (200kč-500kč)

Buffalo Bill's

Vodičkova 9, Prague 1 (24 21 54 79). Metro Můstek/3, 9, 14, 24 tram. **Open** 11am-11pm daily. **Average** 350kč. **No credit cards.**

Fajitas and Margaritas have found a home in the Czech Republic, though the diners tend to be English speakers. The Tex-Mex fare is good and so is the service, performed by an eager young crew wearing American jeans and red cowboy kerchiefs. Drinks come in big, Texas-sized glasses instead of the usual juice glasses.

Cerberus

Soukenická 19, Prague 1 (231 09 85). Metro Náměstí Republiky/5, 14, 26 tram. **Open** noon-midnight daily. **Average** 250kč. **Credit** AmEx, EC, MC, V.

All white tablecloths and sparkling crystal, Cerberus offers a classy ambience without being at all fussy. The staff are congenial, a fact reflected in the invitation to 'have drinks mixed according to your own fantasy' in the bar. Whimsical desires are encouraged: if you want a rare imported liqueur, Cuban cigars or shark steak, you can find it here. The warm hors-d'oeuvres menu is devoted exclusively to a selection of pastas; cold starters include such classics as Prague ham served with a chilli sauce and horseradish. The Czech entrées are marvellous renditions of local favourites: try pork slices

One of the new breed of gourmet restaurants – U Modré kachničky. See page 119.

'forester style' with fennel, garlic, tomato and cheese, and witness to what heights a humble piece of pig flesh can be taken. The fireplace makes the basement club room particularly cosy on a cold Prague night.
Booking advisable.

U Čížků

Karlovo náměstí 34, Prague 2 (29 88 91). Metro Karlovo náměstí. **Lunch served** noon-3.30pm, **dinner served** 5-11pm, daily. **Average** 250kč. **Credit** AmEx, EC, MC, V.
Eating is a communal experience at U Čížků, from the giant ceramic soup pots to the large tables packed with German tourists. The food is the best of its kind: smoked pork, beef in creamy sauces and other hearty meat dishes served with sauerkraut and dumplings. The prices are high considering that this is the same stuff to be encountered in just about any Czech kitchen, but the portions are enormous. If you haven't come across the perfect beer cellar restaurant yet, this place, with its timbered ceilings and Gambrinus beer on tap, certainly comes close.

Elite

Korunní 1, Prague 2 (25 71 50). Metro Náměstí Míru. **Open** 11am-11pm daily. **Average** 200kč. **No credit cards.**
Pizza and pasta are served (albeit slo-o-owly) in the grand ballroom setting of a nineteenth century 'culture house'. Standard Czech dishes share the bill with salmon tagliatelle and ravioli in a cream sauce: go for the Italian. Large tables downstairs are for groups while little tables *à deux* are found upstairs along the balustrade. Elite is convenient for the occasional concerts and dances that are held in the even grander upstairs rooms, but beware of an unannounced 23% VAT on the bill. *See also chapter* **Cafés, Bars & Pubs.**

U Maltézských rytířů

(At the Knights of Malta), Prokopská 10, Prague 1 (53 63 57). Tram 12, 18, 22. **Open** 11am-11pm daily. **Average** 250kč. **Credit** AmEx, MC, V.
Atmosphere is everything in this candlelit, Gothic cellar restaurant, formerly a hospice of the Knights of Malta. Through the post-Communist process of restitution, the historic building has been returned to the family who originally owned it; they have put a few oil paintings on the bare stone walls of the basement and opened one of the best 'secret' dining establishments in town. Mrs Černíková, whose husband and two children help run the place, is guaranteed to appear at least once an evening, bang a small chime and rather theatrically narrate the house's history. The menu is limited to a few beef and pork dishes, but all of it, from the châteaubriand to the apple strudel, is wonderful. The wine list is more varied and includes some vintage Czech labels.
Booking advisable.

U Mecenáše

Malostranské náměstí 10, Prague 1 (53 38 81). Tram 12, 18, 22. **Dinner served** 5-11.30pm daily. **Average** 400kč. **Credit** AmEx, DC, MC, V.
Gasps of surprise are usually the first sounds diners make having opened the leather-embossed iron door of U Mecenáše. The rich Gothic and medieval interior is beautifully furnished: only a complete fool would choose to sit in a plastic chair on the outdoor patio, though the option exists. The Czech cuisine is beautifully prepared and presented and contains no surprises. Some dishes, such as the lobster mayonnaise, are disappointingly uncreative; others, like the beef flambé, will be appreciated both by the person who eats it and the surrounding diners. Some traditions persist from the old regime, such as charging for the nuts on the table, but the setting and food combine to make this a memorable, and entirely Czech, experience.
Booking essential. Tables outdoors.

U Modré kachničky

(The Blue Duckling), Nebovidská 6, Prague 1 (06 20 38 22). Tram 12, 18, 22. **Lunch served** noon-4.30pm, **dinner served** 6.30-11.30pm, daily. **Average** 350kč. **Credit** AmEx, DC, V.

Romantically-inclined diners will be thrilled by the 'Blue Duckling'. It's located on a hard-to-find side street within strolling distance of Charles Bridge. Although quite new, the restaurant has quickly risen to become one of the top gourmet attractions in town, due to the professional service and the exalted interpretations of Czech cuisine. The menu is strong on traditional game dishes – pheasant, boar, duck and hare – and unlike most restaurants with pretensions, it doesn't blush to pair them with dumplings and sauerkraut. But the best feature of the restaurant is the fantastic charm of its three rooms, each of which has hand-painted walls, antique furniture and plenty of wooden duck decoys as decoration. Additional entertainment is provided by endearing menu translations like 'the cooced potatoes lubricated with the butter'.

Booking advisable.

Pod Křídlem

(Under the Wing), Národní 10, Prague 1 (20 55 39). Metro Národní třída. **Average** 250kč. **Credit** AmEx, EC, MC, V.

Visitors to the British Council (next door) can't help but look enviously through the windows at this up-market establishment, with its swanky, white-on-white décor that even extends to a white baby grand piano. Excellent, uncomplicated meals of goulash, roast pork and dumplings are served on fine white china. An excellent place for a business lunch or dinner.

Red Hot and Blues

Jakubská 12, Prague 1 (231 46 39). Metro Náměstí Republiky. **Open** 11am-midnight daily. **Average** 400kč. **Credit** AmEx, MC, V.

A New Orleans-style restaurant that's the focus of a Sunday-morning brunch: fabulous French toast, beignets and Creole omelettes are made to order. During the rest of the week, RH&B proffers generous helpings of shrimp Creole, étouffée, pasta and Fat Daddy burgers. Just so you get the idea, jazz music on the stereo is reinforced by framed posters of black American jazz musicians on the wall. There's often live music in the courtyard at the weekends.

Tables outdoors.

Reykavík

Karlova 20, Prague 1 (no phone). Metro Staroměstská. **Open** 11am-11pm daily. **Average** 400kč. **Credit** AmEx, MC, V.

Fresh fish – caught in Iceland one day and cooked in Prague the next – is the main lure of this pretty, albeit slightly antiseptic place. It's on the former coronation route connecting the Old Town Square to Charles Bridge. Poached salmon with a hollandaise sauce and a rich seafood soup are among the best dishes, while chicken and hamburgers satisfy those not in the mood for fish. The pleasant atmosphere and service make this a good place to linger and watch the procession of tourists, packed like sardinky, on their way to one of the major sights.

Bookings not accepted.

Il Ritrovo

Lublaňská 11, Prague 2 (29 65 29). Metro I.P. Pavlova. **Lunch served** noon-3pm, **dinner served** 6pm-midnight, Tue-Sun. **Average** 300kč. **No credit cards.**

Twenty kinds of pasta dishes are offered here – if that's not enough choice, you can even invent your own combination. Florentine owner Antonio Salvatore boasts that all his ingredients come from Italy, and indeed the heavy white mozzarella appears to be the real thing. A large number of Italian speakers eat at Il Ritrovo, and Sig. Salvatore is usually among them in the dining room, chatting and playing unabashedly sentimental Italian songs on the old gramophone. The slow-paced service is the restaurant's only drawback.

Na Rybárně

Gorazdova 17, Prague 2 (29 97 95). Metro Karlovo náměstí/3, 17 tram. **Lunch served** noon-4pm, **dinner served** 4pm-midnight, Mon-Fri. **Average** 200kč. **Credit** AmEx, DC, EC, MC, V.

When President Václav Havel used to live around the corner he was often seen taking his meals at this modest fish restaurant. The carp and trout dishes are satisfying, though nothing to write home about, but the hearty soups are out of this world. A more formal atmosphere pervades the back room, while at the front bench seats and ocean murals are the order of the day.

Salammbo

Vyšehradská 21, Prague 2 (29 94 01). Metro Karlovo náměstí/18, 24 tram. **Lunch served** 11am-3pm Mon-Sat. **Dinner served** 6-11pm daily. **Average** 200kč. **No credit cards.**

French is spoken at this warm, family-run Tunisian restaurant. *Brik*, a traditional Tunisian dish, combines tuna, onion and a runny egg inside a giant fan-shaped pastry: the trick is to eat this hot starter without the egg running onto your plate. Bowls of warm lemon water cleanse the hands of any leftover *brik*, then dishes like couscous or grilled shrimps served with a fiery sauce appear. Tunisian and Algerian rosé wines perfectly complement the food and are a refreshing change from the Czech varieties. Colourful tiles and exotic music complete the illusion of having left Prague for Tunisia,

Red Hot and Blues – *another ex-pat joint.*

Original Budweiser Beer from Budweis

Budweiser Budvar

and should you be tempted to do so, the proprietor owns the next-door travel agency.

U Ševce Matouše

(Matthew the Cobbler), Loretanské náměstí 4, Prague 1 (53 35 97). Tram 22. **Lunch served** noon-4pm, **dinner served** 6-11pm, daily. **Average** 200kč. **No credit cards.**

Generous helpings of steak, fish and chips are served up in what was a cobbler's workshop (until recently, it was still possible to get your shoes repaired while eating lunch). Prices are reasonable given the prime location next to the Foreign Ministry and the Loreto.

Tables outdoors.

U Supa

(The Vulture), Celetná 22, Prague 1 (no phone). Metro Náměstí Republiky or Staroměstská. **Open** 11am-11pm daily. **Average** 200kč. **Credit** AmEx, DC, EC, JCB, MC.

Pork reaches its apotheosis here in the form of a whole roast pig, basted in beer and lard and carved up at the table for a mere 3,000kč. Lighter fare in the form of duck or beef, served with the ubiquitous dumplings and cabbage, is available, but a meal at The Vulture is not for the faint-hearted.

Inexpensive (under 200kč)

Akropolis

Kubelíkova 27, Prague 3 (27 21 84). Metro Jiřiho z Poděbrad. **Open** 4pm-2am Mon-Sat; 4pm-midnight Sun. **Average** 60kč. **No credit cards.**

This place is a hangout for the young, terminally hip set. The owners are members of the satirical comedy team Pražská pětka (The Prague Five), and there are plans to turn part of the building into an arts centre, with a stage, dressing rooms and other amenities. For now it's simply a restaurant, though a very strange one, with décor that looks as if surrealist Giorgio de Chirico has gone Tahitian – check out the coconut light fixtures and aquariums full of mechanical still lifes. The Czech food is inexpensive and reasonable stuff: there might be fried cheese or roast chicken with rice, but the rooms get smokier as the night progresses. It seems appropriate that this was the first restaurant in Prague to offer absinthe, a mouthwash-coloured approximation (made in Moravia) of the famous French intoxicant.

Botel Admirál

Hořejší nábřeží, Prague 5 (24 51 16 97). Metro Karlovo náměstí. **Open** 10am-midnight daily. **Average** 150kč. **No credit cards.**

Dinner on the deck of the permanently-anchored Botel Admirál is the perfect way to enjoy the Vltava river. You get a beautiful view of the nineteenth century townhouses along the riverfront, Vyšehrad castle and the occasional boatload of tourists cruising in one of the city's restaurant-cum-cruise ships. The pork and veal specialties served here are made for large appetites: most come topped with bacon, ham, melted cheese, a fried egg or some combination of the above. The menu lists not only champagne but several kinds of Spanish, German, Italian, Russian and Moravian sparklers as well. The blue and white tables are shaded during the day; at night a small (but not obnoxious) disco gets underway on deck, which now sports a lighted dance floor.

Tables outdoors.

Černý pivovar

(The Black Brewery), Karlovo náměstí 15, Prague 2 (294 45 23). Metro Karlovo náměstí. **Open** 11am-11pm daily. **Average** 100kč. **Credit** V.

The main attraction here is the giant floor-to-ceiling white glass mosaic depicting socialist stereotypes: factory workers, communal farmers and so on. Černý pivovar serves light Gambrinus beer on tap, along with pork schnitzel, stewed

beef, dumplings and other Czech standards. The food is better at U Čížků (*see above*) across the street, but this is the calmer restaurant. It shares a kitchen with the adjoining stand-up *bufet*, which offers a pared-down version of the restaurant menu along with open sandwiches and pastries to take away.

Deminka

Škrétova 1, Prague 2 (24 22 33 83). Metro I.P. Pavlova or Muzeum. **Lunch served** 11am-4pm, **dinner served** 4pm-midnight, daily. **Average** 100kč. **Credit** V.

Deminka offers cheap food amid faded grandeur. Gilt ceilings and chandeliers outdo the fish fingers and boiled potatoes, but Deminka is worth a visit to see how average Czechs dine. Excellent Czech specialities for less than 40kč are served until 4pm, when the indoor lights are suddenly turned on and a more international (and more expensive) menu is presented.

Gorgona/U Králova dvora

U Prašné brány 3, Prague 1 (232 11 83). Metro Náměstí Republiky. **Open** 10am-11pm daily. **Average** 140kč. **No credit cards.**

Gorgona seems to be trying out its new identity as a Greek restaurant, having kept both the old name and the old menu in case the new ones don't work out. This is probably not a bad idea, since the tinned dolmades and unevenly microwaved Greek desserts fail to impress (although, as Gorgona has discovered, it's hard to bungle a simple moussaka). The only reason to come here is for the excellent selection of fresh salads – or for the very good Czech dishes of smoked pork, dumplings and cabbage.

U Govindy

Na hrázi 5, Prague 8 (82 14 38). Metro Palmovka. **Open** noon-6pm Mon-Fri. **Average** 25kč. **No credit cards.**

The Czech Hare Krishna restaurant is a haven for vegetarians and offers a respite to those who feel dangerously close to a pork overdose. All the food is grown on the Krishna's organic farm outside Prague, and goes to make dishes like curried lentils, vegetable stew with homemade cheese and yoghurt fruit drinks. The place is self-service and you can take your silver tray back as often as you like for extra helpings. The only drawback is that the restaurant is a bit out of the way, although there are plans to open another more central branch with an attached *cukrárna* (sweet shop) full of delicious desserts. This place is very popular among health-conscious ex-patriates – ask any English-speaker who's lived in Prague for more than a month. Payment is by donation.

Kmotra Pizzeria

V jirchářích 12, Prague 1 (24 91 58 09). Metro Národní třída. **Open** 11am-1am daily. **Average** 90kč. **No credit cards.**

In the fierce pizza war that has erupted in Prague, Yugoslavian-owned Kmotra (The Godmother) has come out on top. Customers line up in the stairwell to get one of the coveted bench seats downstairs by the open, wood-burning pizza oven. The pizzas are enormous and the ingredients are fresh.

Booking advisable.

U Pastýřky

(The Shepherdess's), Bělehradská 15, Prague 4 (43 40 93). Tram 6, 11. **Dinner served** 6pm-1am daily. **Average** 150kč. **Credit** MC, V.

This unabashedly tourist place is a lot of fun, from the Slovakian cymbalon music to the open grill in the centre of the room where you can watch your meat being cooked by the chef. Traditional Czech dishes are augmented by some Slovak specialties such as *halušky* – a plate of doughy potato dumplings swimming in cheese and flecks of bacon. The large beer garden packs in lots of singing Germans at night.

Tables outdoors.

One of the few places in town to eat healthily is at the **Radost FX Café**.

Penguin's

Zborovská 5, Prague 5 (54 56 60). Metro Anděl/4, 7, 14, 16 tram. **Open** 11.30am-11.30pm daily. **Average** 150kč. **Credit** AmEx, EC, MC, V.

A black and white bistro that's slightly superior to most modern Czech restaurants but has a few of the usual weaknesses, including lettuce-less salads and a vegetarian menu that contains nothing that isn't tinned, pickled or processed. On the other hand, Penguin's has an interesting menu which features as many chicken dishes as beef and pork, and five kinds of rice – a welcome change from the usual side dish of boiled potatoes. The turtle soup looks perfectly alarming on the menu but is quite palatable, though a better choice might be the traditional beef broth with liver meatballs. Appetisers of stuffed tomatoes and little open sandwiches are presented on a silver tray – as is the bill, which will contain an unexpected added 23% VAT.

U Radnice

U radnice 10, Prague 1 (24 22 81 36). Metro Staroměstská. **Open** 11am-11pm daily. **Average** 125kč. **No credit cards**.

U Radnice is one of the last places in the Old Town Square where traditional food is served at prices meant for the locals instead of tourists. For lunch, tasty Czech specialties such as goulash and beef in a cream sauce are available for under 50kč. In the evening dishes like steak covered with cheese and topped with an egg are to the fore – vegetarians are probably better off avoiding this place altogether. Dark wood panelling and large tables (which are meant to be shared) create a comfortable pub atmosphere.
Tables outdoors.

Radost FX Café

Bělehradská 120, Prague 2 (25 69 98). Metro I.P. Pavlova. **Open** 11.30am-6am daily. **Average** 150kč. **No credit cards**.

Fresh vegetarian food is served in post-nuclear surroundings here. The kitchen does its best given that one or more key ingredients are apt to become suddenly unavailable; among the specialties are pizzas and salads chock-full of all the vegetables you can't get anywhere else. This is one of the few places in town to eat healthily and it's open late to serve the adjoining club. Sunday brunch is wildly popular with the English-speaking crowd: expect to wait 45 minutes for your scrambled eggs or French toast. *See also chapter* **Nightlife**.

Restaurace Jáma

(The Hollow), V jámě 5, Prague 1 (26 41 27). Metro Národní třída or Můstek. **Open** 11am-1am Mon-Fri; 1pm-1am Sat, Sun. **Average** 130kč. **Credit** AmEx, EC, MC, V.

American-owned Jáma strives to be all things to all people – and for the most part succeeds. Numerous culinary curiosities make an appearance, from California-style avocado and tuna, potato skins and Mexican food, to lasagne. The clientele is an equally eclectic mix of foreigners, nationals, white-collar professionals and travellers. The bar is particularly lively (*see chapter* **Cafés, Bars & Pubs**).

Restaurace na Vyšehradě

K rotundě 2, Prague 2 (29 40 46). Metro Vyšehrad. **Open** 10am-10pm daily. **Average** 130kč. **No credit cards**.

The pleasant, flower-filled terrace here is a suitable reward for those who have bothered to climb and explore the less touristy remains of Vyšehrad castle. Simple pork, beef and chicken dishes are served with potatoes or rice, along with a vegetable garnish that very nearly resembles a salad.
Tables outdoors.

Saté Grill

Pohořelec 3, Prague 1 (no phone). Tram 22. **Open** 12.30-10pm daily. **Average** 150kč. **No credit cards**.

The mildly-spiced pork, rice and noodle dishes served here are so tasty (and popular) that this former counter service-only Indonesian place has put out tables and chairs and become a fully-fledged restaurant. The pork satay with peanut sauce is the highlight of the short menu. Prices are unbeatable and the restaurant is just a short walk from the castle.

U Snědeného krámu

Mostecká 5, Prague 1 (53 16 13). Tram 12, 18, 22. **Open** noon-11pm. **Average** 150kč. **No credit cards.**
The menu reads like a hit parade of Czech specialties: 'drowned men' (marinated sausages), beer cheese, fried bread with goose livers, and goulash with bacon dumplings. Large wooden tables are squeezed, upstairs and down, into what looks like an antique shop, so crowded is the place with clocks, photos, bottles and musical instruments. The service can be indifferent, but the restaurant is conveniently located on the Mála Strana side of Charles Bridge.

U Vejvodů

Vejvoda 2, Prague 1 (no phone). Metro Staroměstská. **Open** 10am-11pm daily. **Average** 60kč. **No credit cards.**
Miraculously, a traditional, yet non-smoking restaurant in one of the twisting alleys off the Old Town Square. Actually, Vejvodů is divided into two, a dining room and a smokey pub where 12% Staropramen beer is available on tap. Both rooms date from the beginning of the fourteenth century and look as though they haven't seen a fresh coat of paint since. Dishes of pork, dumplings, cabbage, potatoes – the pillars of Czech cuisine – are aimed at a mostly local clientele, since tourists are usually put off by the scaffolding over the entrance. *See also chapter* **Cafés, Bars & Pubs.**

Zlatá ulička

(Golden Lane), Masná 9, Prague 1 (232 08 84). Metro Staroměstská. **Open** 11am-midnight daily. **Average** 150kč. **No credit cards.**
A tiny restaurant, run by one of Prague's many Yugoslav entrepreneurs. The menu is made up of fantastic beef and veal-based dishes that defy the bland-is-better attitude that most Czechs have towards their meat. The veal stew with mashed potatoes is a knockout, as is the *palačinka* (sweet pancake), a sinful affair which can feed two. There are upbeat comments from former diners on the wall, mournful Yugoslavian poetry on the floor, and a kitsch decoration scheme based on the Golden Lane in Prague Castle. *Tables outdoors.*

Na Zvonařce

Šafaříkova 1, Prague 2 (25 45 34). Metro I.P. Pavlova or Náměstí Míru. **Open** 10am-11pm daily. **Average** 100kč. **No credit cards.**
Despite large tables and a menu printed in four languages, this place is frequented mostly by locals who come to dance to the band on Sunday afternoons. The excellent Czech specialties are cheap, and all three kinds of *knedlíky* (regular, potato and bacon) are available. But the restaurant's best feature is its spacious, tree-filled terrace with a view over the former vineyards of Vinohrady. *Tables outdoors.*

Bufets & Lahůdkys

The stand-up *bufet* is a venerable tradition in Prague, and a convenient one for those without time for a full sit-down meal. The *bufet*, with its long counter, steaming with stewed meats, dumplings and cooked-to-death vegetables, also makes a good study for amateur anthropologists, for these are the feeding grounds of 'the typical Czech', that is, elderly pensioners, blue-uniformed labourers and office workers. The *lahůdky*, which is more like an American deli, is also good for a quick lunch or putting together a picnic. Rather than hot meals, you can get a couple of small, open sandwiches or choose from a selection of salads (usually mayonnaise-based) served with a roll. Unfortunately, both *bufet* and *lahůdky* are being squeezed out of the centre as the price of property escalates, so you may have to look around a bit to find one of these gems. Below are listed some of those centrally located *bufets* and *lahůdkys* which haven't yet fallen victim to the free market economy.

Bufet Jídelna

Štěpánska 61, Prague 1 (no phone). Metro Můstek. **Open** 8am-8.30pm Mon-Fri; 10am-4pm Sat. **Average** 30kč. **No credit cards.**
This is the real thing: a sweating table of pork, dumplings, canned spinach and *guláš* soup located inside the giant Lucerna cinema and concert hall complex off Wenceslas Square. The *bufet* packs in a colourful cast of diners, many of whom pay for their already-inexpensive food with subsidised meal tickets. Go for the experience, not for the cooking.

Catalunya

Malostranské náměstí 24, Prague 1 (no phone). Tram 12, 18, 22. **Open** 8am-9pm Mon-Sat; 1-7pm Sun. **Average** 30kč. **No credit cards.**
A traditional *lahůdky* in a clean, newly-renovated space. Open sandwiches, such as ham and potato salad, are garnished as if for a 1950's cocktail party with sliced pickles, tomatoes and egg. Other selections include salad served by the decagram, cold cuts, strudel (occasionally) and a vast array of alcoholic beverages. Grab something here on your way across Charles Bridge.

Green Bar Jonáš

Na poříčí 10, Prague 1 (no phone). Metro Náměstí Republiky. **Open** 8am-8pm Mon-Fri; 9am-3pm Sat. **Average** 30kč. **No credit cards.**
The lunch-time queue at this health-food *bufet* and *lahůdky* is long but it moves fast. The *bufet* presents some unique health food versions of Czech dishes, such as fried tofu cheese and a mayonnaise-less potato salad with enough garlic in it to keep vampires out of your path for days. The salad selection on the *lahůdky* side includes some unusual cabbage experiments and, more importantly, a fresh fruit salad.

Krone

Václavské náměstí 21, Prague 1 (no phone). Metro Můstek. **Open** 9am-8pm Mon-Sat; 10am-7pm Sun. **Average** 60kč. **No credit cards.**
Another joint *bufet/lahůdky*, on the first floor of the large department store Krone. The *lahůdky* presents the traditional array of salads: marinated beans, fluorescent purple cabbage, and potato salad studded with carrots and peas – a dollop of salad along with a roll or a bowl of soup makes a good light meal. The *bufet* offers heavier options: schnitzel, chips and mercilessly boiled vegetables. The rôtisserie-grilled chicken, priced by weight, is the best bet.

Queenz Grill

Havelská 12, Prague 1 (no phone). Metro Můstek. **Open** 9am-9pm Mon-Sat; 11am-9pm Sun. **Average** 50kč. **No credit cards.**
This Middle Eastern *bufet* is one of the best fast-food places in Prague. Among the items displayed are houmus, aubergine purée, and a selection of salads (from mild to spicy), all served with pitta bread. The *gyros* has improved dramatically since Queenz first opened and is now served in homemade flat bread with a yoghurt sauce and, on request, a dab of red chilli sauce. The lunch special – a bowl of chicken, rice and anything else the cook sees fit to put in – is usually gone by 1pm.

Cafés, Bars & Pubs

Our pick of the best watering-holes in town, from genteel tearooms and literary cafés, to cavernous beer halls and romantic wine cellars.

Finding the right place for a drink in Prague can be a sobering experience. The city offers something for almost everyone: there are sleek bars for the *nouveau riche*, elegant cafés for the nostalgic, ex-patriate holes for the hopeless and smoky beer cellars, packed rank and file with rowdy workmen. Food is almost always served in bars, though it is usually of the meat and two veg variety so reminiscent of school dinners. The customer, meanwhile, has risen in importance but still seldom comes first. If you can put up with insolent waitresses in lycra miniskirts and head waiters who routinely add imaginary drinks to your bill, boozing can be one of the great bonuses of Prague.

BEER CULTURE

The best way to get a taste of Czech culture is from the beer. It has been the national passion for over 1,000 years and there is much truth in the old Bohemian boast that the country has the best beer and the prettiest girls. You will seldom find many women, however, in a traditional Czech pub and it would seem that Czech men prefer to be seduced by the beautiful bronzed bodies and good head that is served in their local. Even the President regularly takes political cronies, such as Bill Clinton, round to his local before last orders – a time when political 'debate' in these smoke-filled pubs usually reaches an intoxicated crescendo. Not surprisingly, the country is the largest per capita consumer of beer in the world.

The most famous brands of beer are Plzeňské and Budweiser Budvar though you may want to try some of the lesser-known and sometimes better brews, such as Radegast, Velkopopovický kozel or Staropramen. Despite marketing attempts by the American brewery Anheuser Busch you should not confuse the potent Czech Budweiser Budvar with the insipid American Budweiser. Legal safeguards have prevented American Bud from flooding into most of Europe but the Americans may have the last laugh, as they look set to acquire the Czech brewery in a corporate takeover. Most beer halls or pubs serve dark beer

(*tmávé pivo*) or light beer (*světlé pivo*) and these tend to be 10 or 12 degrees (a measure of the original gravity of the brew, showing the density of malt or sugar used in it) and have an alcohol content of around four or five per cent.

CAFE SOCIETY

If none of this is your cup of tea, Prague has a great heritage as a café culture. However, its heyday before the war, when German Jewish and Czech intellectuals such as Einstein, Kafka and Siefert observed the world from their favourite cafés, has long since been extinguished. The Germans wiped out Prague's Jews, the Czechs exiled the Germans and the Communists mopped up the remains of the Czech intelligentsia. If you go to the once famous Café Arco (on Hybernská 12) in search of the ghost of Franz Kafka you may find him playing the pinball machines or shooting pool while waiting for a late-night train out of the city. Nevertheless, café culture is steadfastedly being resuscitated. Much of it is predictably and unimaginatively oriented towards tourists, though some of the best bars are run by foreigners and frequented by the ubiquitous though harmless species of young American poet that has migrated to the city.

The famous Café Slavia on Národní, hangout of former dissident writers (and the secret police who kept tabs on them), has frustratingly been closed for some years. Recently, a militant band of young American and Czech artists and caterers hit the headlines after staging a break-in, briefly forcing the café open again. Though the teapot revolutionaries have gone, it's always worth checking to see if the Slavia has re-opened (*see chapter* **Sightseeing**).

Alternatively there are a number of wine bars dotted around the city. Bohemian and Moravian wines can be refreshing but they never inspire the grandiloquence reserved for their French counterparts. Nevertheless, it's worth rinsing your palate with a glass of Frankovka or Rudlanska. Better still, become intoxicated with the national spirit, called Becherovka, a sweet, herby concoction sold in most bars which is particularly good for coughs and colds, and made to a secret formula.

If you are in the city during the summer, you may want to absorb some cool fluids, rays and a fairy-tale setting. Head for one of the clusters of garden tables adrift in the Old Town Square (Staroměstské náměstí), where you may be accompanied by the festive crashings of a Dixieland jazz band or a wily violinist weaving his way around your seat.

ETIQUETTE

Relax and absorb it all, as the city absorbs millions of tourists' foibles every year, and if you take note of a few conventions you will leave a pleasant impression with your host. For example, when you step into a crowded bar or pub, don't hover by the door waiting for a free table but ask anyone with an empty place at their table if it's free: (*je tu volno?*). Your new neighbours may not exchange a word with you all evening but when they get up to go you should smile charmingly at them as if they were old friends and say *na shledanou* (goodbye). If they order food, wish them *dobrou chut'* (bon appétit). If you want to toast your neighbour say *na zdraví* (cheers), but you will be thought considerably shifty if you don't make eye contact when the glasses clink.

When ordering, the waiter will mark a bill and leave it on your table. When you wish to pay, the waiters will understand a limp-wristed imitation of a pen scribble but it is much better to say *zaplatím* (I'll pay). A different waiter will probably appear and add up the squiggles on your bill, sometimes arriving at a suspiciously high figure. If you still want to leave a tip, round the total up to the nearest 10kč and state the higher number to the waiter, but don't be afraid to look him in the eye when the tip works out to be as little as two per cent. Not much more is expected. However, if the waiters and waitresses have smiled and not whisked your drink away before it's finished, you should perhaps let them see that such attention to detail is worth the effort and leave a little more. You will be making a greater contribution to the city than you realise. *See chapter* **Restaurants** for more places to eat in Prague, together with a menu translation.

Central

Staré Město & Josefov

Andy's Café

V kolkovně 3, Prague 1 (232 27 34). Metro Můstek. **Open** 11am-midnight daily.
A popular café crowded with a youthful clientele, and with pop art paintings covering the walls and effigies of the Simpsons leering goofily over the tables.

V Blatnici

Michalská 6, Prague 1 (22 61 69). Metro Můstek. **Open** noon-10pm Mon-Sat.
The Moravian wines from the village of Blatno won't transport you into fits of delirious pleasure but, like the regular clientele, they can be congenial and fun. The wine waiters in this cool basement will serve you with a knowing smirk that suggests that they are already several tasting hours ahead of you (a litre jug costs 100kč). Traditional Czech food of beef and pork is served for around 100kč.

Clusters of cafés in the Old Town Square: for summer drinking in idyllic surroundings.

Blatouch

Vězeňská 4, Prague 1 (232 86 43). Metro Staroměstská.
Open 11am-midnight Mon-Fri; 2pm-midnight Sat;
2-11pm Sun.
Two sisters run this gentle and reasonably priced café, a
favourite of cleancut students and professionals. Jazz and
soul music wafts through the narrow, high ceilinged room
and up the metal stairwell to the floor above, carpeted and
filled with arm chairs. The wooden floors and bookcase add
to the civilised atmosphere. To eat, there are salads and
chicken dishes, served on little plates.

Bunkr Café

*Lodecká 2, Prague 1 (231 45 71). Metro Náměstí
Republiky or Můstek.* **Open** 9am-3am daily.
The late-night bar above the once notorious nightclub has
an unobtrusive artsy and cosmopolitan atmosphere, where
you can play pinball with hairy young clubbers or chess with
introspective loners while listening to Nick Cave and Iggy
Pop. Try the cocktail concoctions or the poisonous green
75% proof absinthe at 43kč a shot, before descending to wal-
low in the puddles of beer in the club below.

Café Amadeus

*Staroměstské náměstí 18, Prague 1 (22 30 80). Metro
Staroměstská or Můstek.* **Open** 8am-10pm daily.
A first floor, high-ceilinged morning room complete with
chandeliers, overlooking the Old Town Square. There's a
wine bar and restaurant in the basement. You used to be able
to choose a cake in the café from a set of official photo portraits though now, inexplicably, there's only a picture of one
lonely chocolate cake.

Café Archa

*Na poříčí 26, Prague 1 (232 41 49). Metro Náměstí
Republiky.* **Open** 10am-11pm Mon-Fri; 11am-9pm Sat; 1-
9pm Sun.
This glass fish tank café, with long dangling lamps as bait,
seems to have hooked a young laid-back clientele with a successful combination of cheap drinks, pristine surfaces and
posters and photos from the theatre and rock worlds plastered everywhere. You can stare out at the passers-by as you
sip your drink, though they are more likely to be staring in
at you.

Café Bar Valentin

Valentinská 9, Prague 1 (26 02 94). Metro Staroměstská.
Open 10am-10pm daily.
The pleasant black and white décor, marble tables,
sparklingly clean surroundings, excellent and well priced
food and quick service all make this café a worthwhile stop
if you are between the Old Town Square and the river. The
standard Czech meat dishes (pork, beef and chicken) are prepared with particular care and at under 80kč a plateful are
good value.

Café Milena

*Staroměstské náměstí 22 (26 08 43). Metro
Staroměstská or Můstek.* **Open** 10am-10pm daily.
Milena Jesenská was one of the lovers of Franz Kafka that
he never managed to marry. The quiet, carpeted drawing
room, overseen by waiters in grey waistcoats and a classical pianist, recreates the atmosphere and the strict social propriety that was part of life at the beginning of this century.
Depending on your mood you can choose to sit in the red
room, the grey room or the sunny yellow room. The café
serves an assortment of cakes, pancakes and ice-cream
which you can eat while pondering the photographs of life
in pre-war Prague or staring out of the window at the
remarkable astrological clock.

Café Rudolfinum

*Alšovo nábřeží 12, Prague 1, (248 9 33 17). Metro
Staroměstská.* **Open** 10am-6pm daily.

*The very civilised **Blatouch**.*

A bare-walled café with pillars, panelling and a parquet floor,
reminiscent of a postgraduate student common room. It
serves cheap drinks and little cakes.

U Fleků

*Křemencova 11, Prague 1 (24 91 51 18). Metro Národní
třída.* **Open** 9am-11pm daily.
Perhaps the most famous pub in Prague, U Fleků has brewed
the city's best 13 degree dark beer on the premises for centuries. You are automatically assumed to be here for the beer
(expensive at 40kč a glass) and well-drilled waiters will keep
you supplied without waiting for your order. The courtyard
is shaded by overhanging trees and surrounded by a picturesque sgraffiti-covered wall. The hollering and thumping
of the traditional ten-piece Czech brass band goes down well
with the German tour parties who flock here and although
you have to pay an entrance fee of 15kč for all this, it's worth
it if only once. Before you leave, take a peek into the fabulous Gothic dining hall, which will probably be occupied by
another tour group.

Ganys

Národní 20, Prague 1 (29 76 65). Metro Národní třída.
Open 8am-11pm daily.
A long, lofty café which is often packed, and which somehow manages to get away with décor that combines a gar-
ish cream and turquoise colour-scheme with metallic peacock
fans. The prices are above average, but then so is the food
(there is also a restaurant in the next-door room, past the
fancy fountain). Dishes range from a prawn cocktail hors-
d'oeuvre, to vegetarian meals and steaks (around 159kč). Try
the French, American, Arab or Hangover Breakfast (from
150kč), or celebrate with a Russian one for 949kč, which
includes champagne, caviar and vodka.

The Globe. See page 132.

Hogo Fogo
Salvátorská 4, Prague 1 (231 70 23). Metro
Staroměstská. **Open** noon-midnight Mon-Thur, Sun;
noon-2am Fri, Sat.
A hangout of Prague's young innocents, tucked into a
corner off Pařížská street. The café descends down three
layers to a main room with a checked lino floor, cottage-
style furniture and low wattage lighting. The food is
cheap though nothing special (pastas, meats and salads)
and it's served by easy-going staff. You can buy one of
the paintings or pots on display or check out the corner
room market for trendy second-hand clothes and sunglasses.

H & S
Masarykovo nábřeží, Prague 1 (294 88 68). Metro
Karlovo náměstí. **Open** summer only noon-midnight
daily.
This café is situated on the raft-like extension to the wooded
island between Jiráskuv Bridge (Jiráskuv most) and
Legionaires' Bridge (Legii most) where tourist cruisers
dock, pedal boats drift and swans circle for crumbs. It
serves reasonably priced alcohol, soft drinks, ice-cream,
popcorn and prawn crackers and is a perfect spot for a hot
summer day.

In Vino Veritas
Havelská 12, Prague 1 (26 74 76). Metro Můstek. **Open**
9am-midnight daily.
A cosy wine bar which has few wines to speak of but does
have roof tiles and mock window ledges to decorate the interior and an exhausted-looking puppet on the wall. Managed
and frequented by Bosnian refugees, the place can sometimes have a melancholy air, but you can drink at tables
outside and enjoy the bustle of the ancient market in the
same street.

James Joyce
Liliová 10, Prague 1 (no phone). Metro Staroměstská.
Open 10.30am-1am Mon-Sat; noon-1am Sun.
The Hooray Henry hangout of the ex-pat crowd: Irish pride
bristles from the walls and even the Czech waitresses have
developed Irish accents. It's one of only two places in town
where you can get Guinness (the other is the Derby, see
p132), but few Czechs can afford the prices here. That is partly the purpose of this ex-pat 'oasis' but such arrogance aside,
you have to admit that the swaying hearties that come here
really know how to have a piss up. You may have a more
meaningful experience in the little cellar bar next door and
in the basement, called **U krale Jiřího**, (At King George's).
The beer is cheap and it attracts a trendy Czech clientele and
the occasional overflow from the Joyce upstairs.

John Bull Pub
Senovážná 8, Prague 1 (26 92 55). Metro Náměstí
Republiky. **Open** 11am-11pm daily.
This is not as bad as it sounds. The innocent piece of cultural diplomacy (a reproduction of Romford with prints and
memorabilia of Victorian England lining the plush, blood red
walls) gets a good reception from Czechs. It's cheap (beer
costs the equivalent of about 50p a pint), but the Czech staff
won't know what a pint is. British bitter has to compete with
Czech Pilsner and the Czech version of roast beef and
Yorkshire pudding – beef and dumplings – is served in the
back room. Not everyone's cup of tea, but it warms the cock-
les of your heart to see the foreigners enjoying something of
old Blighty.

Konírna
(The Stable), Anenská 11, Prague 1 (no phone). Metro
Staroměstská. **Open** noon-midnight Mon-Fri; 6pm-
midnight Sat, Sun.
A narrow stable bar tucked into a cobbled side street close
to Charles Bridge which serves very cheap drinks (tea, coffee, soft drinks and beer all cost under 10kč) and a variety
of fresh salads (for around 15kč). The service is quick and
friendly. Quiet scribblers frequent it during the day, while
at night the bar is usually packed with laid-back Czechs.

Konvikt Klub
Konviktská 22, Prague 1 (22 45 09). Metro
Staroměstská. **Open** 11am-1am Mon-Fri; 2pm-1am Sat;
5pm-1am Sun.
Set behind iron bars, this friendly and unpretentious pub/bar
is usually crowded with Czech and ex-pat students and
artists. The walls are decorated with violins, LPs and trum-
pets.

Lávka
(The Little Bridge), Novotného lávka 1, Prague 1 (24 21
47 97). Metro Staroměstská. **Open** 10am-5am daily.
In a perfect location by Charles Bridge, The Little Bridge
combines a theatre, nonstop bar and a garden and terrace
café during the day; but it is at its best on summer evenings
as a nightclub (see chapter **Nightlife**).

U Minuty
Staroměstské náměstí 3, Prague 1 (no phone). Metro
Staroměstská or Můstek. **Open** 10am-11pm daily.
This pricey, no-smoking Renaissance tearoom tucked into
the corner of the Old Town Square boasts 44 ways of making coffee and 60 different teas. It prides itself on its location
as a former home of Franz Kafka and the service is appropriately inhuman, in the best tradition of the author's work.

U Medvídků
(The Little Bears), Na Perštýně 7, Prague 1 (24 22 09
30). Metro Staroměstská. **Open** 11.30am-11.30pm Mon-
Sat; 11.30am-10pm Sun.
A typical beer hall, popular with tourists and locals with
glazed eyes, fixed grins and beer glasses permanently

muzzling their mouths. German tourists like to sit in the wagon at the end of the hall and dance to the 'oompah' music played by makeshift liveried musicians. You have been warned.

Reno

Uměleckoprůmyslové muzeum, ulice 17, listopadu 2, Prague 1 (24 81 13 07). Metro Staroměstská. **Open** 10.30am-10.30pm Mon-Fri; 10.30am-6pm Sat, Sun.

This modern bar in the Museum of Decorative Arts has friendly service, pleasant pictures and sculptures neatly arranged on the walls, as well as pretty mugs and teapots for sale from a glass display case. Worth popping into if you are in the area. *See chapter* **Museums**.

Sektbar Ponton

Alšovo nábřeží, Prague 1 (231 99 52). Metro Staroměstská. **Open** *Apr-Oct* noon-midnight daily.

This is another summer-time, riverside café like H & S (*see p128*), but further up river, just beyond Charles Bridge. You walk through a stone archway and across a rickety pontoon to get to it, and there are boats for hire until 8pm.

Slovansky dům

Na příkopě 22, Prague 1 (24 22 18 10). Metro Náměstí Republiky. **Open** 10.30am-11pm daily.

Before the war, this used to house the famous Café Continental which was the meeting ground for many of Prague's German-speaking intellectuals. Today it's a mere shadow of its former self, but the atmosphere still buzzes in the tree-shaded quad between May and September when the tourists are out in full and the weather's fine. It serves expensive Czech meat dishes (from 175kč) and beer (24kč).

U Vejvodů

Jilská 4, Prague 1 (24 21 05 91). Metro Staroměstská. **Open** 10am-11pm daily.

Tucked into a crumbling backstreet in the Old Town, this is one of the best Czech pubs in the city. The low Gothic doorways and ironwork hint at a proud heritage. It's popular with

tourists without being a tourist trap and is still the favourite haunt of many Czechs. To go with the beer there's hearty, homemade food. *See also chapter* **Restaurants**.

Velryba

(The Whale), Opatovická 24, Prague 1 (24 91 23 91). Metro Národní třída. **Open** 11am-2am daily.

A preciously trendy bar, but very popular with the international arty crowd, The Whale was originally favoured by Czechs who were keen to exclude foreigners, especially Americans. This is not a place to unfold your map of Prague and talk loudly about how cheap everything is. The rectangular bar, painstakingly painted with thousands of little wavey triangles, floats just below street level and from behind it the staff (with a contrived smile if necessary) serve a variety of cheap pastas, fatty meat dishes and salads. You can observe Prague's fledgling café socialites through the large concave mirror at the bar. Alternatively, wander into the pretty pastel back room and down the stairs and inspect the art gallery below.

U Zlatého tygra

(At the Golden Tiger), Husova 17, Prague 1 (24 22 90 20). Metro Staroměstská. **Open** 3-11pm daily.

Almost every seat in this rowdy, smoky pub is taken by regulars, among them the country's much loved octogenarian writer and drinker Bohumil Hrabal, numerous faded Czech heroes who only the regulars remember, and recently Bill Clinton. Get a Czech friend to take you so you won't feel out of place.

Around Václavské náměstí

Bistro Pellier

Štěpánská 57, Prague 1 (24 21 35 15). Metro Muzeum. **Open** 9am-10pm Mon-Sat.

This cheap and cheerful pitstop just off Wenceslas Square is a clean and efficient place in which to refuel on your tour with light sandwiches and snacks or a full meal. It's popular with the locals and gets crowded at lunch-time.

One of Prague's micro-breweries: **Novoměstsky pivovar.** *See page 130.*

Café Boulevard

Václavské náměstí 32, Prague 1 (24 15 23 04). Metro Můstek or Muzeum. **Open** 8am-midnight daily.
Tourists of every hue, as well as a few Czechs, meet in this steel and glass café. The prices are predictably high for such a prime location, but if you sit at a street table there is always plenty of action to watch to justify the expense.

Dobrá čajovna

(The Good Teahouse), Václavské náměstí 14, Prague 1 (24 23 14 18). Metro Můstek or Muzeum. **Open** 10am-9pm Mon-Sat; 3-9pm Sun.
A tearoom and shop which is set back from the bustle of the street, and where the owners request that customers try to understand the 'peaceful culture of the orient'. They advise you not to drink your tea near 'shouting children' or 'bickering women'. Sit at a tea chest on a low seat and choose teas from all over the world with names such as 'Memories of Kyoto' and 'Malaysian Tiger'. Then tinkle the little bell provided and one of the robed, hand clasping, waiters will come and take your order. Tea is served from a doll's house-sized teapot in a dinky little finger bowl. You should assume a serene air as you listen to the strange but calming background noises. More, similarly meditative sounds are performed live on Wednesday evenings from 9.30pm on (entrance is 50kč, which includes a cup of tea). *See also chapter* **Shopping**.

Don Manuel Vinárna

Jungmannova 25, Prague 1 (26 05 44). Metro Můstek. **Open** 11am-11pm daily.
A salubrious little restaurant bar, frequented by business lunchers and dating couples. There are avant-garde photographs by Slovak Tono Stano, cork walls, frosted glass and a porcelain leopard to decorate the place, the food is decent and the prices are reasonable. Service is with a nervous smile.

Evropa Café

Václavské náměstí 25, Prague 1 (24 22 81 17). Metro Můstek or Muzeum. **Open** 7am-midnight daily.
This enticing Art Nouveau hotel café has a certain dusty decadence about it, with its ageing prostitutes and bearded jazz trios who tinkle, scrape and puff their way through old favourites. Nowadays, most tables are filled with businessmen and backpackers and it costs 20kč to get in when the band cranks up. Service is so astonishingly appalling it will either make you laugh or cry, and the food is expensive and limited (cold cheese, ham and eggs, ham or cheese omelettes, scrambled eggs and ice-cream). However, once you've settled down at a table it's worth lingering, especially on the balcony where you can observe the subtle solicitations and the lost souls below. The bar next to the balcony stays open late.

Institut Français

Štěpánská 35, Prague 1 (24 21 40 32). Metro Muzeum. **Open** 9am-6pm Mon-Fri.
A neat and tidy café with a quiet patio in the French cultural complex, with black and white photos of Paris on the walls, cheap coffee and nice cakes. Sit here and decide for yourself whether you consider Prague to be the Paris of the 1920s.

Jáma

(The Hollow), V jámě 7, Prague 1 (26 41 27). Metro Národní třída or Můstek. **Open** 7am-1am Mon-Fri; 1pm-1am Sat, Sun.
This congenial pub and bar where pictures of Elvis Presley and Costello adorn the walls, is frequented by a young Czech crowd on the threshold of trendiness. The friendly staff serve a wide variety of good cocktails but the sandwiches and salads are puffed up with lettuce and not much else. The place gets pretty crowded at night during the week. *See also chapter* **Restaurants**.

Margaret Bar

Jungmannova 3, Prague 1 (24 21 62 32). Metro Můstek. **Open** noon-midnight daily.
Something cooler to slip into on a hot day, this narrow bar has American TV, low priced drinks and is full of Hollywood showbiz dazzle and mirrored walls.

Novoměstsky pivovar

(The New Town Brewery), Vodičkova 20, Prague 1. Metro Můstek or Muzeum. **Open** 11am-11pm Mon-Sat; noon-10pm Sun.
This labyrinthine beer hall houses Prague's other microbrewery (after U Fleků). You can see the pots and vats in full simmer as you drink the end product, the 11-degree Lezak.

One of the many waterside watering-holes.

The fifteenth century building, refurbished and re-opened in 1994 has some amusing *trompe-l'oeil* murals which come to life the more beer you consume, and there's a terrace that is popular in the summer. There is also plenty of traditional Czech food on offer, including lots of fried pork, dumplings and chips. A full meal will set you back around 150kč.

Paris-Praha
Jindřišská 7, Prague 1 (24 22 28 55). Metro Můstek or Muzeum. **Open** 8.30am-7pm Mon-Fri; 8.30am-1pm Sat.
Francophiles stranded in the city may take some solace from this café and shop that serves French cheeses, wines and bread, as well as a good Czech menu. You can contemplate your next trip to the French capital while gazing at the wall-sized photo of Paris. *See also chapter* **Shopping**.

Praha-Roma
V jámě 5 (Lucerna Passage), Prague 1 (24 16 24 75). Metro Národní třídá or Můstek. **Open** 9am-9pm Mon-Fri; 9am-7pm Sat, Sun.
Decorated with pink 1920s lampshades and pink tablecloths, this café sells a good selection of stodgy cakes. *See also chapter* **Shopping**.

Růžová čajovna
(The Pink Teahouse), Růžová 8, Prague 1 (26 27 91). Metro Můstek or Muzeum. **Open** 7.30am-9pm Mon-Fri; 11am-10pm Sat, Sun.
The Pink Teahouse provides a therapeutic atmosphere for socially challenged types. Teas from around the world are sold and the gentle background music will not upset those of a nervous disposition.

Sports Bar
Ve Smečkách 30, Prague 1 (24 19 62 55). Metro Muzeum. **Open** 11am-2am daily.
The frequent sight of clusters of sports fans watching a match from outside a TV shop window prompted some enterprising Americans to fill a gap in the Prague market. This cavernous hall has two pool tables and four screens flickering simultaneously, showing live sport as well as other highlights of Sky, including films and *The Simpsons*. The bar gets packed (and sometimes an entrance fee is charged) when there's a big final on. You can enjoy a dark beer and a burger before the game and though the food is overpriced and not that great, it's worth it if your team is playing.

Svenk Vrbovec
Václavské náměstí 10, Prague 1 (24 22 73 59). **Open** 10am-11pm Mon-Sat; 4-10pm Sun.
Surprisingly, given its location, this front-room wine bar is usually full of Czech old-timers gathered for a good gossip. It serves half a dozen Moravian wines (100kč for a litre, 15kč a glass), though the drinks list suggests there are more in the cellar.

Malá Strana

Café Bily orel
(The White Eagle Café), Malostranské náměstí 17, Prague 1 (53 17 37). Metro Malostranská. **Open** 8.30am-4am daily.
This three part bar starts on a terrace with a satisfying view of the square. Inside is an eye-catching display of Captain Marvel horror posters and a decorative fish tank. Down the steep stairs is a black leather, candle- and neon-lit Goth interior filled with loud music and pony-tailed dope-smoking Czechs. It's OK to wear your sunglasses here so long as you don't walk into one of the mirrors.

Café Colombia
U Malostranské most věže, Mostecká 3, Prague 1 (53 66 35). Metro Malostranská. **Open** 10am-midnight daily.

The closest coffee house to the Charles Bridge is pricey, cramped and dark. It's based in a part Gothic and part Renaissance building and is popular with hawkers from the bridge. The café is more bearable if you work your way through to the miniature garden patio at the back, which is filled with puce garden tables.

Café Savoy
Vítězná 5, Prague 1 (53 97 96). Metro Malostranská. **Open** 9am-midnight daily.
A nineteenth century café with a genteel Viennese atmosphere. The service is as particular as the décor, which features an elegant fountain, frosted mirrors and marble floors. The owners are particularly proud of the grand ornate ceiling, which they rescued from heartless partition under the Communists. Despite all the finery, however, the classical spirit of the place doesn't seem to have made it into this century.

Jo's Bar
Malostranské náměstí 7, Prague 1 (no phone). Metro Malostranská. **Open** 11am-2am daily.
The nerve centre of North American ex-patriate life has shown no sign of flagging since it opened a couple of years ago. The narrow bar is packed with foreign residents and backpackers, and as you squeeze your way from the terrace to the back room you'll find that Jo's is the easiest place in Prague to meet new people. Play chess, listen to loud rock, eat Mexican food, take coffee refills and double your beer intake during happy hour (6.30-7.30pm). On a bad night it can seem like an American college reunion, but if there's a reason to celebrate the punters will be dancing on the bar and showering everyone with champagne. Look out for the shrewd Canadian owner: he'll be the one with the prettiest girls, asking if they're having a good time.

Further Afield

Dejvická

Dejvická Sokolovna
Dejvická 2, Prague 6 (no phone). Metro Dejvická. **Open** 10.30am-10.30pm Mon-Sat.
If you're waiting for your laundry to be washed at Laundry Kings nearby (*see chapter* **Services**), join the idiosyncratic locals sitting on the pavement outside this Czech pub. It serves some of the cheapest beer in town.

U Tří hrochů
(At the Three Hippos), Bubenečská 12, Prague 6 (32 52 56). Metro Hradčanská. **Open** 11.30am-10pm Mon-Fri; 5pm-10pm Sat, Sun.
When you've picked up your laundry (*see above*), pop round the corner for some excellent pizza and reasonably priced drinks at this clean, air-conditioned and tiled bar that is usually full of the bright young sons and daughters of Prague's well-to-do middle classes. Three dopey looking hippos decorate the room, but you don't need to emulate them: people here are easy to engage in conversation.

Holešovice

Café Dante
Dukelských hrdinů 16, Prague 7 (87 01 93). Metro Vltavská. **Open** 8am-11pm Mon-Fri; 11am-11pm Sat, Sun.
This bright and airy café with fluorescent lamps and a big window overlooking the street is business-like during the day and more Czech than Italian in style, but it serves good cheap food (pizzas and pasta dishes for under 50kč) and the biggest portions in Prague.

Jo's Bar. *See page 131.*

The Derby
Dukelských hrdinů 20, Prague 7 (87 99 69). Metro Vltavská. **Open** 6pm-2am daily.
Another American success story – after a fashion. Somehow The Derby successfully fuses a traditional Czech pub with a trendy Camden bar and takes the best from both. It serves excellent pizzas until midnight, the beer is cheap and the music is good. Workers drop in from the local building site to enjoy a beer and the trio playing Vivaldi, but by midnight the place has usually descended into cheerful drunken raucousness.

Globe Bookstore
Janovského 14, Prague 7 (357 91 61). Metro Vltavská. **Open** 10am-midnight daily.
This late-night American-run literary café and bookshop is a hub of Prague's ex-pat literary scene, hosting regular public readings and book launches. The bookshop, furnished to look like a sitting-room, is stacked from floor to ceiling with Prague's best collection of English-language books, new and second-hand (*see also chapter* **Shopping**). The food makes a change from traditional Czech fare and includes homely favourites like peanut butter, honey and banana sandwiches and carrot cake. A wide range of caffeine-filled drinks and spirits is served, including absinthe for those writers who don't feel the need to be in possession of all their faculties. The English-speaking staff and customers bend over backwards to be nice to each other. You can read the papers, play board games or look up long words in the big dictionary in an atmosphere of middle class, twentysomething civility that refuses to be ruffled when the local drunk drops in and accuses everyone of being in the Mafia. Check the notice board for someone travelling your way or for a juggling partner.

Rhapsody
Dukelských hrdinů 46, Prague 7 (80 67 68). Metro Vltavská. **Open** 6.30pm-2am daily.
This expensive, exclusive, non-Czech speaking French bar and restaurant seems very popular with middle-aged Frenchmen wearing white slacks and navy blazers. Live music from 9pm adds to the hotel bar feel of the place. If you take a Czech date here they may be very impressed, but then again they may be disgusted.

Vinohrady

Bar Sarah
Jugoslavská 18, Prague 2 (no phone). Metro Náměstí Míru. **Open** 10am-2am daily.

If you are in the area, try this Czech local, with its black and white photos of Albert Einstein spread across the wall. The food is salty and the service friendly if sloppy, but the staff mean well and that counts for a lot in Prague.

Elite
Korunní 1, Prague 2, (25 71 50). Metro Náměstí Míru. **Open** 11am-11pm daily.
This grand, airy bar and restaurant, with its high ceilings, balcony, fake marble tables and cosy side rooms, occupies the ground floor of a Dům kultury ('culture house') in Vinohrady. It charges above average prices for average food and is popular with grannies in the afternoon. In the evening you may get swept up by a stream of nervous, overdressed teenagers going to the school prom on the first floor; it's worth following them up to take a look at the magnificent interior of the building. *See also chapter* **Restaurants**.

FX Café
Bělehradská 120, Prague 2 (25 12 10). Metro I.P. Pavlova. **Open** 11.30am-5am daily.
Prague's stylish vegetarian café, designed in the creamy décor of a Roman ruin, is run by Americans and Jugoslavs and, to judge from the attentive service and imaginative menu, this is a successful combination. It's a particularly good place to munch a brunch of French toast and egg Florentine at the weekend. The café is frequented day and night by models and trendsetters, highly unlikely film directors, a low-key gay and lesbian crowd and a smattering of ex-patriate timeservers. You can also lounge around in the seductive, air-conditioned, backroom and natter over a Margarita or a cup of Prague's best hot chocolate. There are yet more sofas to lie around on in the art gallery in the room next door. A small jazz or folk band plays on most weekday evenings and there's plenty more action in Radost nightclub downstairs (*see chapter* **Nightlife**).

Paseka
Ibsenova 1, Prague 2 (25 48 97). Metro Náměstí Míru. **Open** 11am-11pm Mon-Fri.
The pub is connected to the commercially unaware publishing house next door and attracts a heavy-drinking Czech literary and academic crowd who are far removed from the posey penseurs of some of the 'trendy' bars. The beer is cheap, the food typically Czech and the walls are scrawled with graffiti artwork. You may also stumble into the occasional book launch party.

Libeň

U Jagusky
(The Little Witch), Na žertvách 28, Prague 8. Metro Palmovka. **Open** 11am-11pm daily.
Take a trip out of the centre of town for a dose of authentic Czech beer culture. This pub, located in the industrial area of Libeň, is run for the ordinary workers who know their beer (in this case 12-degree Smíchov at 11.90kč). If you're in anydoubt, read the writing on the wall, which prays for the waiters to 'give us this day our daily jug, and forgive us our thirst' beside a mural of witches and wizards.

Smíchov

Trampsky salon na Valentince
Na Valentince 6, Prague 5 (no phone). Metro Anděl/12 tram. **Open** 11.30am-10.30pm Mon-Fri.
Close to the Smíchov train station, this log-panelled pub dwells on a Czech 'tramping' tradition which calls forth yearnings for the wild – an understandable reaction to smoky Smíchov. Traditional food like goulash is served for under 50kč and the Staropramen beer is only 8.50kč.

Shops & Services

Shopping   **134**
Services   **146**

Shopping

The advent of the free market economy has yet to make an impact on Prague's shops, which still score better on tacky appeal than consumer friendliness.

Prague is not a place for shopping therapy. You need good feet and a thick skin to seek out decent products and survive the blank looks that greet your request. The first, if not the only, Czech word many foreigners learn is *nemáme* – 'we don't have it'. This is a legacy of the Communist past, when the art of shop-keeping lay in restricting the flow of goods to a trickle. Why sell your precious stock to any Tom, Dick or Harry when you could keep it for someone important who might do you a favour?

The retail business is in a constant state of flux: small businesses are opening up daily – and closing down as fast. Foreign retailers are eyeing up prime sites; developers are beginning to build shopping malls and out-of-town shopping centres. But even though markets are expanding, there is still little worth buying in the Czech Republic for those accustomed to the variety and quality available in the west.

Among the products worth looking out for are hand-carved wooden toys (especially in the Old Town Square); crystal goods; garnets (try **Granát** in Staré Město); and cheap CDs. If you're really lucky you might hit upon something interesting in an antique shop. The *antikvariát* shops (*see below* **Old Books & Prints**) can turn up some attractive nineteenth century maps and prints, often reasonably priced. For browsers, the larger department stores have a certain tacky appeal.

The dedicated shopper will find the best hunting grounds between Wenceslas Square and Josefov, and in Malá Strana between Charles Bridge and the top of Nerudova. Opening hours are unpredictable: some shops are open all day, seven days a week; others close for lunch and pack up early on Friday. The shops listed below don't take credit cards unless stated otherwise. If all else fails, try the *Zlaté stránky* (*Yellow Pages*), or *Annonce*, the Czech exchange and mart magazine that lists everything from accommodation to PCs and ponies.

Due to open as we went to press were two new shopping centres. One in the **Koruna Palace**, on the corner of Na příkopě and Václavské náměstí, and the other – the **Pavilon Shopping Mall** – containing 65 upmarket shops, boutiques and restaurants in the indoor market (Vinohradská tržnice) on Vinohradská in Prague 2.

For a list of shops, sights, restaurants, cafés and bars in each area, *see page 264* **Area Index**.

One-stop

Bílá Labut'

Na poříčí 23, Prague 1 (24 81 13 64). Metro Náměstí Republiky/5, 14, 26 tram. **Open** 8am-7pm Mon-Fri; 8am-6pm Sat. **Credit** AmEx.

When it opened in 1937 Bílá Labut' was the height of modernity and luxury. Today it all seems a bit of a jumble, though it's a good place to buy fur hats and also boasts a newly-renovated grocery packed with imported goods.

Kmart

Národní 26, Prague 1 (24 22 79 71-9). Metro Můstek or Národní třída. **Open** 6.30am-7pm Mon-Wed; 6.30am-8pm Thur, Fri; 7am-6pm Sat; 10am-5pm Sun.

With American management Kmart is now cheerful as well as cheap. Along with a wide range of general consumer items, it offers Little Caesar's Pizza, a grocery, and various in-store services like shoe and watch repairs.

Kotva

náměstí Republiky 8, Prague 1 (24 80 11 11). Metro Náměstí Republiky/5, 14, 26 tram. **Open** *main shop* 8am-7pm Mon-Wed, Fri; 8am-8pm Thur; 8am-2pm Sat; *potraviny* 8am-9pm Mon; 6am-8pm Tue-Sat. **Credit** AmEx, EC, MC, V.

Eight out of ten for Kotva. The service is sometimes off-hand but the goods are fine. Work your way up past the glossy cosmetics, stationery, white goods, fashion, sports gear, auto accessories and end up with the fairly naff furniture and lighting. There's parking in the basement, and a travel agency, bureau de change, and shoe and watch repairs among the in-store services.

Krone

Václavské náměstí 21, Prague 1 (26 94 35/24 23 04 77). Metro Můstek. **Open** *main shop & potraviny* 8am-7pm Mon-Fri; 8am-6pm Sat; 10am-6pm Sun; *bread and cake shop* 7am-9pm Mon-Fri; 7am-8pm Sat; 9am-7pm Sun.

The best thing about Krone is the *potraviny* (grocery) in the basement. You can stagger right into the metro with your groceries.

Markets

Staré Město Market

Havelská, Prague 1. Metro Můstek. **Open** 8am-6pm Mon-Fri; 8am-1pm Sat, Sun.

Seasonal fruit and vegetables, wild mushrooms and flowers are crammed alongside wooden toys, dog food and shampoo. One stall sells that essential Czech shopping accessory: an extra-sturdy plastic shopping bag. You never need ask for a *tašku* again.

*Fresh vegetables at **Staré Město Market**: a sight to appal all true Prague restaurateurs.*

Prague Market

(Pražská tržnice), Bubenské nábřeží 1, Prague 7. Metro Vltavská. **Open** 6am-6.30pm Mon-Fri; 6am-2pm Sat.
The stalls offer mainly cheap booze and clothes, microwaves and stereo equipment. Explore the halls to find plants and DIY stuff.

Antiques

Apart from the antique shops, there are myriad junk shops, selling everything from old irons and typewriters to drawings by Mucha or Filla. The prices tend to be pitched at foreigners. For cheaper, and sometimes better, collectables, seek out the Bazar shops. These are off the beaten track but can be located through the *Zlaté stránky* (*Yellow Pages*). Prague also has some wonderful antiquarian bookshops (*see page 145* **Old Books & Prints**).

Antique

Kaprova 12, Prague 1 (tel/fax 232 90 03). Metro Staroměstská. **Open** 10am-1pm, 2-6pm, daily. **Credit** AmEx, DC, EC, JCB, MC, V.
An upmarket junk shop, with little of real class but plenty of pretty, affordable bits and pieces. Less pretty is the 1905 painting with three very dead stuffed bats pinned against an oil landscape (22,000kč).

Antiques

Josefská 1, Prague 1 (53 16 75). Metro Malostranská. **Open** 11am-6pm Mon-Fri; noon-5pm Sat, Sun. **Credit** AmEx, MC, V.
A *starožitnosti* (antique shop) that focuses on the inter-war period, with liqueur sets, chunky ceramics, Art Deco tea services and other collectables.

Bazar nábytku

Libeňský ostrov, Prague 8 (684 20 57/684 30 71). Metro Palmovka. **Open** 8am-5pm Mon-Wed; 9.30am-6pm Thur; 8am-3pm Fri.
Serious furniture seekers snap up the bargains at Libeň. Go **Branches**: Bělehradská 20, Prague 4; Moskevská 1, Prague 10.

Permits

Prague is used to seeing its cultural treasures carted off. The Swedes took their share in 1648, as did the Nazis and the Communists more recently. And now it is being despoiled again, this time by the capitalists. The growing trade in antiques, legal and illegal, has alarmed the authorities so much that new legislation was passed in 1994 requiring export permits for a whole range of objects, including glass and graphics over 50 years old. Heavy fines and confiscations are promised to those who break the law. The high-class antique shops now provide export permits; others don't. If you want to hang onto your purchases make sure you get the relevant papers before leaving the country.

PAVILON *fashion with taste*

La Perla • Christian Dior • Lancôme • Nike • Donna Privata • Gianfranco Ferre • Yves Saint Laurent • Sergio Tacchini • Nina Ricci • Timberland • Q+Q • Weekender • Jeffrey Rogers • Elisa Landri • Benetton Sport Systems • Prince • KangaROOS • Ivano Boni • Cotton Club • News Fashion • Parker • Levi's • Adidas • Ruta Baga • Pentel • Chagal • Jelly Flynn • Donati • Fausto • Mod Eckan • Sembol • Elizabeth Arden • Denver • Crowana • Raymond Weil • Pollini • Roberti Rattan • Lacoste • Citizen • Staedler • Timex • Pelican Maurice Lacroix • Confiserie Walter Heindl Wien • Bailo • Labod • Mustang • Sketchers • Ray-Ban • Beti Cassuci • Unique Collection • Steilmann Group •

Browse in airconditioned art nouveau splendour, through more than 60 shops and food emporia, seven days a week from 9.30 am until 9.30 pm. Pavilon Vinohradská tržnice, Vinohradská street no. 50, Prague 1.

PAVILON
VINOHRADSKÁ TRŽNICE

It will take your breath away.

Jan Huněk Starožitnosti
Pařižká 1, Prague 1 (23 23 604). Metro Staroměstská.
Open 10am-6pm daily. **Credit** AmEx, DC, MC, V.
A shop to die for, with exquisite Czech glass of all periods, from the eighteenth century to the 1930s. At 140,000kč for an Art Nouveau vase by Loetz or Leonora these are collectors' pieces.

Military Antiquities
Charvátova 11, Prague 1 (24 22 74 34). Metro Národní třída. **Open** 10am-6pm Mon-Sat.
Everything for playing soldiers, from lead figurines to guns, swords and uniforms, plus copies of *Mein Kampf* for background reading.

Rudolf Špičák
Ostrovní 26, Prague 1 (29 79 19). Metro Národní třída. **Open** 10am-7pm Mon-Fri; 10am-3pm Sat.
A great junk shop in a damp basement. Among the old telephones, dress suits and model ships you might spot a Secession cabinet.

Vladimír Kůrka Starožitnosti
Panská 1, Prague 1 (26 14 25). Metro Můstek. **Open** 10am-6pm Mon-Fri; 10am-2pm Sat.
The best things here are the textiles: gorgeously elaborate Moravian folk costumes, embroidered bedspreads and tablecloths.

Bookshops & Newsagents

Bohemian Ventures
náměstí Jana Palacha 2, Prague 1 (231 95 16). Metro Staroměstská. **Open** 9am-5pm Mon-Fri. **Credit** AmEx, DC, JCB, V.
English-language books with an Eng. Lit. slant – hardly surprising since it is located within the university. Also a good stock of reference, current affairs and history books.

Cizojazyčné knihkupectví
Na příkopě 27, Prague 1 (26 28 37). Metro Můstek. **Open** 9am-7pm Mon-Fri; 9am-6pm Sat; 10am-5pm Sun. **Credit** AmEx, DC, MC, V.
As its name implies, this shop specialises in foreign-language books. Apart from the usual fiction, dictionaries and Prague guides, there are some useful oddities: guides to fly-fishing and elementary statistics, or copies of *Domus*.

Globe Bookstore
Janovského 14, Prague 7 (357 91 61). Metro Vltavská/1, 8, 17 tram. **Open** 10am-midnight daily. **Credit** AmEx, V.
A literary café with quality journals and bulging bookshelves. The new books are mainly Central European in focus, the second-hand ones (mostly American) range from high-brow tomes to airport trash (*see chapter* **Cafés, Bars & Pubs**).

U knihomola
Mánesova 79, Prague 2 (627 77 70/fax 627 77 69). Metro Jiřího z Poděbrad. **Open** 9am-1am Mon-Sat; 11am-6pm Sun. **Credit** AmEx, V.
The biggest and best foreign-language bookshop in Prague. It claims to sell books in 80 languages but wisely concentrates on English, French, German and Czech. The art and fiction sections are outstanding.

PNS Noviny - časopisy
Na příkopě 22, Prague 1 (24 21 13 85). Metro Můstek. **Open** 7.30am-6pm Mon-Fri; 8am-1pm Sat.
A newsagent which eschews foreign languages but caters, in Czech, for all tastes, from pedagogy and architecture to nature studies and porn.

Children

An invasion of Barbie dolls and Polly Pockets has hit Prague. But traditional Czech toys are holding their ground well. The Old Town Square stalls have all the old favourites – puppets, puzzles and pull-a-longs – while **Kotva** (*under* **Onestop**) has tin tractors and steam rollers, as well as some fabulous painted wooden zoos and farms. At around 1,200kč complete down to the last rabbit hutch, piglet and jolly peasant, these will become heirlooms.

Albatros
Na Perštýně 1, Prague 1 (24 22 12 00). Metro Národní třída. **Open** 9.30am-6pm Mon-Fri; 9.30am-noon Sat.
Cut-out books (from 15kč), which range from quite manageable dinosaurs to a mind-boggling *Cutty Sark*.

Akvaristika
Eliášova 41, Prague 6 (312 24 36). Metro Hradčanská. **Open** 10am-6pm Mon-Fri.
Cheer up ex-patriated offspring with a hamster, fish or baby rat (15kč). For the dog, dried food and beauty requisites.

Creation Stummer
Jungmannova 18, Prague 1 (24 22 86 68). Metro Národní třída. **Open** 9am-6pm Mon-Fri; 9am-noon Sat.
An Austrian 'baby boutique' with its own brand. Most of the stock is for babies and toddlers and the range peters out at around five years.

Dětský dům
Na příkopě 15, Prague 1 (24 21 60 73). Metro Můstek. **Open** 8.30am-7pm Mon-Fri; 9am-4pm Sat. **Credit** V.
The Formica shelving, leatherette chairs and hostile assistants are dire, but don't let this put you off – the Dětsky dům is excellent for cheap clothes and shoes, especially winter wellies and clumpy suede ankle boots. *Shipping.*

Obchod loutkami
Nerudova 47, Prague 1 (53 00 65). Metro Malostranská/12, 22 tram. **Open** 9.30am-8pm daily. **Credit** AmEx, MC, V.
Huge, grotesque trolls and witches leer over a pantheon of fairy story characters in stick, string or finger form. The big puppets are very expensive, the smaller ones are pricey but well-made.

Cosmetics & Perfumes

Christian Dior
Pařížská 7, Prague 1 (232 62 29/232 73 82). Metro Staroměstská. **Open** 10am-6pm Mon-Fri; 9am-noon Sat. **Credit** AmEx, DC, JCB, MC, V.

Elizabeth Arden
Rybná 2, Prague 1 (232 54 71). Metro Náměstí Republiky/5, 14, 26 tram. **Open** 10am-7pm Mon-Fri; 10am-2pm Sat. **Credit** AmEx, MC, V.

Nina Ricci
Pařížská 4, Prague 1 (24 81 09 05). Metro Staroměstská. **Open** 10am-6pm Mon-Fri. **Credit** AmEx, V.

Perfumerie Lancôme
Jungmannovo náměstí 20, Prague 1 (24 21 71 89). Metro Můstek. **Open** 10am-6pm Mon-Fri; 9am-1pm Sat. **Credit** AmEx, MC, V.

Fashion

Adam

Na příkopě 18, Prague 1 (26 15 23). Metro Můstek.
Open 9am-7pm Mon-Fri; 9am-1pm Sat. **Credit** AmEx,
MC, V.
The business-like clothes for men and women include Italian
suits, a good range of shirts and discreet underwear. A tailor-
made suit costs 9,000kč excluding fabric.

Ano Ano

Panská 9, Prague 1 (24 21 04 92). Metro Můstek. **Open**
8am-6pm Mon-Fri; 8am-1pm Sat. **Credit** AmEx, EC, JCB,
V.
Smart, expensive German clothes for ladies who lunch. Hugo
Boss suits for their husbands.

A+G Flora

*Štěpánská 61 (Lucerna Passage), Prague 1 (24 21 15
14). Metro Můstek.* **Open** 9am-5pm Mon-Fri. **Credit**
AmEx, DC, EC, JCB, V.
One-off designer clothes for women, including knitwear and
hand-painted silks, at prices that are steep by local standards
but a snip for foreigners (7,990kč for a wool coat, 2,290kč for
a linen jacket). The colours are fashionably drab, but you can
have a linen outfit copied in something brighter.

Branches: Přemyslovská 29, Prague 3 (27 17 16);
Rytířská 31, Prague 1 (24 23 06 14).

Art & Fashion Gallery

*Maiselova 21, Prague 1 (tel/fax 231 95 29). Metro
Staroměstská.* **Open** 10am-7pm daily. **Credit** AmEx,
MC, V.
One-off Czech design with the emphasis on hand-decorated
silk. Prices range from 1,200kč for a scarf to 7,800kč for a
heavy, beautifully draped kimono jacket.

Camomilla

Panská 1, Prague 1 (26 14 14). Metro Můstek.
Open 9am-6pm Mon-Fri; 9am-1pm Sat. **Credit**
AmEx, MC, V.
Nothing exciting here, simply pretty, wearable clothes for
women, made in Greece and therefore cheap.

Model Praha

Václavské náměstí 8, Prague 1 (26 11 26). **Open** 9am-
7pm Mon-Fri; 10am-3pm Sat. **Credit** AmEx, EC, MC, V.
Defy the central European winter in a black felt bowler
(570kč), then save your skin in a straw sun hat (490kč). One-
off designs can be made with your own materials.
Branches: Maiselova 60/3, Prague 1 (232 35 89);
Mikulandská 2, Prague 1 (20 24 84); Vodičkova 14,
Prague 1 (236 73 13).

The Glamour Factor

In 1994 it seemed that the return of glamour and
fashion to Prague was complete with the launch
of not one but three locally produced editions of
international fashion/lifestyle magazines: *Elle*
(the very first women's glossy to be published
in a former Eastern Bloc country), *Cosmopolitan*
and *Max*.

In rapidly changing Czech society many
women are using fashion to help them forge a new
identity. After 40 drab years of Communism, they
have had enough of dumplings and dowdiness,
blue overalls, and magazines filled only with knitting patterns, recipes and child-rearing tips. The
new self-aware Czech woman has been quick to
regain her sense of style, dressing for pleasure and
in tune with what's going on in the world.

In fact Prague had a developed fashion industry before World War II. Pre-Communist Czech
tailoring matched that of Paris, and British man-
ufacturers even came here to learn Czech techniques for producing tweed. Fashion magazines
such as *Elegantni Praha* and firms such as
Rosenbaum and Bat'a helped to forge a particular Prague style.

Under Communism, however, there was no
room for 'bourgeois fashion'. Factories mass
produced workers' clothing that lacked all signs
of a personal touch and Czechs were forced to
apply their own needles to add variety to their
wardrobe. The 1980s saw the tentative beginnings of a revived fashion industry, but

materials and fabrics were hard to come by and
creative expression suppressed. Designers ran
severe risks if they produced a T-shirt with a
logo or slogan on it.

After the 1989 revolution, everyone rushed to
buy the most basic items of western fashion,
such as jeans and T-shirts, previously only
available on the black market. Since then the
fashion industry has begun to develop. The
huge international success of Czech models,
including Paulina Pořízková (Estée Lauder),
Daniela Peštová (Pepsi Cola, L'Oréal) and Eva
Herzigová (Wonderbra), has been a source of
inspiration. The younger generation has been
quick to latch on to the latest trends, and MTV,
western magazines and the flood of tourists
have brought a new flavour to the city.

However, there is still little available in the
shops to tempt the discerning shopper from
abroad. Imported clothes are expensive and
although a number of innovative Czech designers
have emerged since the revolution, they are not yet
able to compete with their western counterparts.

Street fashion remains tacky, and men's fashion indescribable. Whereas much of women's
fashion is imported, men's tends to be locally
made. Shiny jackets are the order of the day, ill-
fitting, badly made and badly worn. Couple this
with white socks and metal tie pins, take a look
at the shoes, and you know you are in eastern
Europe.

Modes Robes
Benediktská 5, Prague 1 (232 24 61). Metro Náměstí Republiky/5, 14, 26 tram. **Open** 10am-7pm Mon-Fri; 10am-4pm Sat.
The frocks, droopy but not grungey, are disappointing but you can dig out interesting oddities at this women's clothes shop. The hats and jewellery are fun, and good value too at 480kč for a fringed felt trilby or a dangling, richly beaded necklace.

Nostalgie
Jilská 22, Prague 1 (236 65 89/tel/fax 26 62 56). Metro Můstek. **Open** 10am-4pm Tue-Sun. **Credit** AmEx, JCB, MC, V.
A hunting ground for fashion freaks. Here you can find anything from a pin-striped trouser suit to a deconstructed, crushed, frayed, splodgy linen dress. These are all one-off or short-run items from leading Czech designers. Look out for Marie Eder eveningwear (1,700kč for a satin tunic with bead fringes) and the deconstructions by Marcela Simečková (3,000kč for a dress and cropped jacket). The menswear includes bulky jackets (3,648kč) and interesting ties.

Tess Design
Na Perštýně 10, Prague 1 (tel/fax 26 56 24). Metro Staroměstská. **Open** 10am-6pm Mon-Fri.
Fancy gear from Amsterdam, very skimpy, black and sequinned. Corsets cost 500kč, little dresses 4,450kč.

Jewellery & Accessories

Granát
Dlouhá 30, Prague 1 (231 56 12). Metro Náměstí Republiky/5, 14, 26 tram. **Open** 9am-5pm Mon-Fri; 10am-1pm Sat. **Credit** AmEx, MC, V.
Czech garnets, which are found in a small area in the Vltava basin south of Prague, are considered to be the finest in the world. They have been used since the Middle Ages for jewellery and embroidery, but took off as an industry in the nineteenth century. Since then garnet jewellery has been a perennial favourite with traditionally minded Czechs. After the Communist takeover its production was confined to the Granát co-operative in Turnov, whose wares are displayed in this shop.

L. Mádr
Prokopská 3, Prague 1 (no phone). Metro Malostranská/tram 12, 22. **Open** 10am-6pm Mon-Fri.
A jewellery shop and workshop from which you can commission designs from the very best young artists. Their work is subtle and sophisticated, but not highly priced: around 2,000kč for a silver pendant.

Optika Jan Tietz
Prokopská 3, Prague 1 (tel/fax 42 01 92). Metro Malostranská/tram 12, 22. **Open** 10am-7pm Mon, Wed, Fri; 10am-8pm Tue; 10am-9pm Thur; noon-6pm Sat. **Credit** AmEx, DC, JCB, MC.
An optician with class. Besides the designer glasses, Mr Tietz also sells and repairs antique specs. He has a great sideline too: sumptuous silk waistcoats (2,500kč) and hand-made white shirts in loose, slightly arty styles (1,600kč).

Royal Bijou
Na příkopě 12, Prague 1 (24 21 05 59). Metro Můstek. **Open** 9.30am-7pm daily. **Credit** MC, V.
The showcase of Czech costume jewellery. This began in the nineteenth century as a spin-off from the glass industry, when factories in Jablonec nad Nisou in North Bohemia began to make glass gemstones that rivalled the real thing. It developed into an innovative and hugely successful business which even managed to flourish in the Communist period, with the USSR taking the lion's share. Prices range from 49kč to 2,290kč.

Lingerie

Celestýn
Dlouhá 20, Prague 1 (232 48 77). Metro Náměstí Republiky/5, 14, 26 tram. **Open** 10am-7pm Mon-Fri. **Credit** AmEx, DC, MC, V.
Heavily scented and sun-tanned ladies preside over French perfumes, Oleg Cassini swimwear, Triumph, Gossard and Perélè lingerie.

Palmers
Královodvorská 7, Prague 1 (231 69 15). Metro Náměstí Republiky/5, 14, 26 tram. **Open** 9am-6pm Mon-Fri; 10am-1pm Sat. **Credit** AE, DC, MC, V.
An Austrian company selling its own brand as well as swimwear.

Shoes & Leather Goods

If you need to get a pair of shoes repaired, *see chapter* **Services.**

Baťa
Václavské náměstí 6, Prague 1 (24 21 81 33). Metro Můstek. **Open** 8.30am-7pm Mon-Fri; 9am-4pm Sat. **Credit** AmEx, EC, MC, V.
The Baťa family, whose shoe-making operation was one of the world's first multinationals, saw trouble coming in 1938 and wisely moved their headquarters to Batawa in Canada. The rump of the parent company was nationalised by the Communists ten years later. Now Tomáš Bať a is back in the driving seat and has refurbished the original 1928 flagship store. The display of Baťa shoes, alongside British, German and Italian imports, is seductive, but the service less so. A request for a style in your size invariably draws a scornful *'nemáme'*.
Branches: Jindřišská 20, Prague 1 (26 86 22/24 23 02 54); Moskevská 27, Prague 10 (72 31 13).

Belt
Pařížská 10, Prague 1 (231 51 82). Metro Staroměstská. **Open** 9.30am-7pm Mon-Fri; 9am-5pm Sat, Sun. **Credit** AmEx, DC, JCB, MC, V.
Beautiful leatherware for Japanese tourists and other big spenders. The labels include Joop!, Adpel, Picard and Giorgio Armani. A neat little red handbag will set you back a neat little 12,320kč.

Ko>ená galanterie
Karlova 12, Prague 1 (no phone). Metro Staroměstská. **Open** 10am-6pm daily. **Credit** AmEx, DC, JCB, MC, V.
Around 90% of the leather goods sold here are made in the Czech Republic. They are well styled, apart from some naff buckles, and reasonably priced (2,000kč for a briefcase and 2,500kč-5,500kč for an overnight bag).
Branch: Vodičková 36, Prague 1 (no phone).

Leiser
U Prašné brány 1, Prague 1 (231 47 00). Metro Náměstí Republiky/5, 14, 26 tram. **Open** 9.30am-6pm Mon-Fri; 9.30am-2pm Sat. **Credit** AmEx, DC, EC, JCB, MC, V.
Here you can avoid the *'nemáme'* syndrome by searching along the racks yourself. The children's department does proper shoe fittings.

Pavo Obuv
Celetná 27, Prague 1 (232 50 71). Metro Náměstí Republiky/5, 14, 26 tram. **Open** 9am-7pm Mon-Fri; 9am-3pm Sat. **Credit** AmEx, DC, MC, V.
This hidden-away shoe shop is worth seeking out for its Spanish 'Camper' range: soft women's moccasins and lace-ups, in bi-coloured suede or subtly funky styles, cost around 1,240kč. There's also a good selection of Czech-made Doc Martens (875kč) and men's suede lace-ups (730kč).

Flowers

Ateliér Kavka
Elišky Krásnohorské 3, Prague 1 (232 08 47). Metro Staroměstská. **Open** 9am-6pm daily. **Credit** AmEx, V.
Unlike those in most flower shops, the arrangements here are graceful and modern. Equally good dried flowers are available too, from 150kč for a small bunch to 3,500kč for an imposing urn-full.
Deliveries.

Flora Ton
ulice 28 října 11, Prague 1 (24 21 47 76). Metro Můstek. **Open** 8am-6pm Mon-Fri; 9am-1pm Sat.
A pleasantly damp and crowded shop where the flowers and indoor plants are in peak condition.

Zahradnické centrum
Střešovická 47, Prague 6 (tel/fax 36 10 32). Metro Hradčanská then 1, 18 tram. **Open** 8am-6pm Mon-Fri; 8am-noon Sat.
A well-stocked and professional garden centre with garden furniture, indoor and outdoor plants, pots and planters.

Food & Drink

Food shopping in Prague has improved out of all recognition. Just a few years ago people would jump off a tram to join a queue for potatoes. Now, even the local grocer might sell exotica such as mangoes, pitta bread and olive oil; while street markets stock seasonal delights like cherries and green walnuts (*see above* **One-stop**). Western-style supermarkets are still few and far between, but most everyday shopping can be done in the local grocer or *potraviny*. Take a carrier bag, or mutter *tašku, prosím,* ('a bag, please') at the check-out. Return any empty bottles to the counter marked *láhvi.*

Supermarkets

Billa
Vysočanská 20, Prague 9 (858 63 33-5). Metro Strašnická. **Open** 8am-8pm Mon-Sat; 8am-2pm Sun.
A vast Austrian supermarket much frequented by ex-pat mums. The vegetables are indifferent but the meat is good.
Branch: Senova 2232, Prague 4 (793 34 66).

Delvita
Křejpského 1752, Prague 4 (791 01 13). Metro Chodov. **Open** 7am-7pm Mon-Sat.
This well-stocked Belgian chain has good vegetables, meat and wine, but poor bread and no fish. There are ten branches: check the *Yellow Pages* (*Zlaté stránky*) for your nearest.

Specialist

Casa Pascual
Národní 27, Prague 1 (24 22 05 29). Metro Národní třída. **Open** 8am-7pm Mon-Fri; 8am-1pm Sat.
A good greengrocer, not in the same league as Fruits de France (*below*), but a lot cheaper.

Country Life
Melantrichova 15, Prague 1 (24 21 33 66). Metro Můstek. **Open** 9.30am-6.30pm Mon-Thur; 10am-3pm Fri.
A Seventh Day Adventist enterprise selling a small but useful selection of grains, dried fruit and seaweed. Their bread – substantial, tasty and moist – makes a welcome change

from the local rye loaf.
Branch: Jungmannova 1, Prague 1 (24 19 17 39).

Dobrá čajovná
Václavské náměstí 14, Prague 1 (24 23 14 80). Metro Můstek. **Open** 10am-9pm Mon-Sat; 3-9pm Sun.
More of a shrine than a tea shop, this sells a daunting array of oriental teas which can be sampled in the dark, womb-like café. It also stocks all you need for a tea ceremony: tiny tea pots and cups, joss sticks and Japanese tea whisks.

Fruits de France
Jindřišská 9, Prague 1 (24 22 03 04). Metro Můstek. **Open** 9.30am-6.30pm Mon-Wed, Fri; 11.30am-6.30pm Thur; 9.30am-1pm Sat.
Opened by an astute Frenchwoman in November 1991 when Prague was a gastronomic desert, Fruits de France is still an oasis of mouth-watering fruit, vegetables, cheese, chocolate, oil and wine. Deliveries from France arrive on Thursdays, but storage is good and everything remains in excellent condition. Such luxury does not come cheap: a block of mozzarella could set you back 185kč.

Gartnerova
Václavské náměstí 34, Prague 1 (24 22 74 39). Metro Můstek. **Open** 7.30am-7pm Mon-Fri; 8am-6pm Sat; 10am-4pm Sun.
A mind-blowing, nose-tingling selection of Czech and Hungarian sausages, hams, brawns and smoked meats is sold here. Great for picnics or barbecues.

Gyma
V jámě 3 (Lucerna Passage), Prague 1 (no phone). Metro Národní třída or Můstek. **Open** 10am-6pm Mon-Fri.
Unusual spices can be hard to come by in Prague, but this shop – hardly more than a stall – sells a full range, as well as vinegars, mustards and sauces. Devotees of Indian food will be pleased to find coriander and cumin in large jars.

Obchod loutkami. See *page 137.*

Street hawking in the Old Town: it's no fun unless you haggle.

J & J Mašek

Karmelitská 30, Prague 1 (53 98 70). Metro Malostranská. **Open** 8am-6pm Mon-Fri; 8am-noon Sat.
Prague's most famous delicatessen renowned for its game, 'real' chicken, caviar and smoked fish.

Leonidas

Karlovo náměstí 32, Prague 2 (29 94 91). Metro Karlovo náměstí. **Open** 10am-6pm Mon-Fri.
World-famous and utterly delicious Belgian chocolates at stratospheric prices.

Maso

Spálená 57, Prague 1 (29 01 89). Metro Národní třída.
Open 7am-6pm Tue, Wed, Fri; 7am-7pm Thur; 7am-noon Sat.
A butcher's that includes specialties such as burgers, barbecue meat and home-made sausages. On a good day they have osso bucco.

Moby Dick

Strossmayerovo náměstí 11, Prague 7 (87 81 27). Metro Vltavská. **Open** 9.30am-6pm Mon-Fri; 9.30am-4pm Sat.
This is a fishmonger mainly for the trade, hence its scanty display. Delivery is on Tuesday and Friday and virtually anything that lives in water can be ordered.

Paris-Praha

Jindřišská 7, Prague 1 (24 22 28 55). Metro Můstek. **Open** 8.30am-7pm Mon-Fri; 8.30am-1pm Sat. **Credit** JCB, MC, V.
As well as having top-quality French champagnes, cognacs and Bordeaux, this café also sells a few delicious pastries. Get here early before they are snapped up by French shoppers on their way to Fruits de France.

Praha-Roma

V jámě 5 (Lucerna Passage), Prague 1 (24 16 24 75). Metro Národní třída or Můstek. **Open** 9am-9pm Mon-Fri; 9am-7pm Sat, Sun.
A café with an excellent range of pâtisserie. Open fruit tarts or cakes blanketed in chocolate can be taken home whole.

Wine

Most Czech wine is cheap and pleasant but hardly exciting. Adventurous drinkers must go either to **Fruits de France** (*see above*) or **Dionýsos** (*below*) to seek out the best vintages. For French and other foreign wines, **Paris-Praha** (*above*) is also worth a visit.

Blatnice

Michalská 4, Prague 1 (no phone). Metro Můstek. **Open** 10am-10pm Mon-Fri.
This is where to buy Moravian wine for every-day drinking. It costs 40kč-42kč per litre and comes in plastic bottles straight from the barrel.

Dionýsos

Botičská 10, Prague 2 (tel/fax 29 53 42). Metro Karlovo náměstí/18, 24 tram. **Open** 10am-6pm Mon-Fri.
A classy wine merchant patronised by the Prague élite, Dionýsos has a respectable range of foreign wines but specialises in top-quality local production, including older vintages. The staff, who know and love their wines, will guide you through the shelves.
Delivery. Phone and fax orders. Storage.

Gifts

Český národní podnik

Husova 12, Prague 1 (24 21 08 86). Metro Staroměstská. **Open** 10am-6.30pm daily. **Credit** AmEx, MC, V.
A chain of shops selling touristy but pleasant folk art, including straw nativities (780kč), a vast range of painted Easter eggs and beribbonned willow twigs for whacking girls at Easter (*see chapter* **Prague by Season**). The various branches have different specialties: Jilská does textiles, Nerudova toys.

SERVING THE WORLD SINCE 1894

BAŤA STORES IN PRAGUE

VÁCLAVSKÉ NÁMĚSTÍ 6, PRAHA 1
JINDŘIŠSKÁ 20, PRAHA 1
NÁMĚSTÍ BRATŘÍ SYNKŮ, PRAHA 4
FRANTIŠKA KŘÍŽKA 11, PRAHA 7
MOSKEVSKÁ 27, PRAHA 10

SOME SELECTED STORES IN CITIES OUTSIDE OF PRAGUE

BRNO, OSTRAVA, OLOMOUC, ZLÍN,
ČESKÉ BUDĚJOVICE, ÚSTÍ N. LABEM,
MOST, KARLOVY VARY, LIBEREC, ZNOJMO, PLZEŇ,
MARIÁNSKÉ LÁZNĚ, KLATOVY, STRAKONICE,
HRADEC KRÁLOVÉ

Branches: Jilská 7 and 22, Prague 1 (26 01 70); Karlova 12 and 26, Prague 1 (no phone); Melantrichova 17, Prague 1 (26 03 85); Mostecká 17, Prague 1 (53 12 65); Nerudova 21 and 31, Prague 1 (24 51 09 52/6); Zlatá ulička 16, Prague 1 (33 37 22 92).

Galerie Špička
V pevnosti 9b, Prague 2 (733 94 65). Metro Vyšehrad.
Open 10am-6pm daily.
Among a brooding collection of African masks and some imposing folk cupboards lie pile after pile of earthenware plates and bowls (from 300kč). In sophisticated but rustic styles, with abstract or faintly Picasso-like decoration, they are the work of a French sculptor-turned-potter. Although usually open all day, the shop's opening times do vary.

Museum Shop
Jiřská 6, Prague 1 (33 37 32 55). Metro Malostranská.
Open 10am-6pm daily. **Credit** AmEx, JCB, V.
A British initiative to sell tasteful souvenirs drawn from the state art collections. The display of stationery, jewellery, ties and glass would not look out of place in London or New York, but the designs are distinctive.

Spartaklub
U Sparty 2, Prague 7 (37 09 53/37 12 03). Metro Hradčanská. **Open** 8am-noon, 1pm-4pm, Mon-Thur; 8am-noon Fri.
Fans can stock up on the local team's scarves, shorts and T-shirts.

Glass & China

Glass shops have sprung up everywhere in Prague, and one of the depressing legacies of Communism is that most of them sell exactly the same stuff. The ones listed below are less run-of-the-mill.

Karlovarský porcelán
Pařížká 2, Prague 1 (tel/fax 24 81 10 23). Metro Staroměstská. **Open** 10am-7pm Mon-Fri; 10am-1pm, 2-6pm, Sat; 10am-2pm Sun. **Credit** AmEx, DC, JCB, MC, V.
A mind-blowing display of kitsch porcelain, much of it from the spa town of Karlovy Vary. At one end of the spectrum lie the boudoir-pink rococo tea services, at the other, some quite palatable white and gold dinner sets.
Shipping.

Květa salon
Jindřišská 2, Prague 1 (24 22 46 10). Metro Můstek.
Open 6am-9pm Mon-Fri; 8am-3pm Sat, Sun. **Credit** AmEx, DC, JCB, V.
In an oddly Czech arrangement, these premises combine a hairdressing salon and a glass showroom. The glass is colourful, witty and reasonably priced. It's unmistakably the work of the Bohemia Art Glass factory, an outfit set up in 1992 to break the stranglehold of tradition with a dose of Post-Modernism.

Lustry
Jungmannova 27, Prague 1 (tel/fax 26 23 94). Metro Můstek. **Open** 10am-6pm Mon-Fri; 9am-5pm Sat; 10am-3pm Sun. **Credit** AmEx, DC, JCB, MC, V.
Lustry emerged from the 'rationalisation' of the chandelier factories in Kamenický Šenov, an industry which got off to a good start in the early eighteenth century with orders from Louis XIV and has been lighting up palaces ever since. Lead crystal ranges from 7,800kč to 35,000kč. Around 9,000kč will get you a Murano monstrosity or a watered-down Post-Modern *objet*.
Shipping.

Glass

Glass-making in Czechoslovakia dates back to the thirteenth century when craftsmen started blowing glass in monastery workshops. Through the centuries it went from strength to strength until in 1936 it produced ten per cent of the world's glass. Materially, it owed its success to the vast beech forests of North Bohemia, which supplied the potash for the mix and heat for the kilns, and to plentiful supplies of quartz. Commercially it scored through the glass workers' extraordinary technical skill and innate ability to identify and then supersede fashionable European trends.

This great tradition was brought to a rapid standstill after World War II, when the Sudeten Germans, who possessed much of the technical and commercial know-how, were expelled and the industry was nationalised. However, all was not lost. A few dedicated glass artists, working in ateliers alongside the factories, escaped the scrutiny of the cultural gauleiters and developed a Studio Glass movement which took the glass world by storm in the late 1950s. Now the factories are being privatised and modernised, while designers are revamping the products. Given the history of Czech glass making, they are likely to succeed. For a potted history of Czech glassmaking and a list of shops, museums and producers, buy *A Guide to Czech and Slovak Glass* by Diane E. Foulds from **Moser** (*see under* **Glass & China**) or a large bookshop.

Moser

Na příkopě 12, Prague 1 (24 21 12 93-4). Metro Můstek. **Open** 9am-7pm Mon-Fri; 9am-2pm Sat. **Credit** AmEx, DC, JCB, MC, V.

Moser glass, made in Karlovy Vary since 1857, claims to be the 'King of Glass' and the 'Glass of Kings'. The secret, lead-free formula produces a crystal of great brilliance and durability, which, hand-engraved and gilded, has been bought by monarchs, maharajahs and movie stars. Naturally, it is very, very expensive, but you could content yourself with a tiny ashtray at 530kč.
Delivery. Shipping.

Sklo-svítidla

Kozí 9, Prague 1 (232 23 65). Metro Náměstí Republiky/5, 14, 26 tram. **Open** 10am-6pm daily. **Credit** AmEx, JCB, MC, V.

A good range of plain, modestly priced glassware, including jugs of every size and shape.

Household

Baumax-x

Hall 22, Pražská tržnice, Bubenské nábřeži, Prague 7 (66 71 06 15). Metro Vltavská. **Open** 8.30am-6pm Mon-Fri; 8am-12.30pm Sat. **Credit** EC.

A must for homemakers: tools, wood, paint, sanitary ware, hardware, camping gear, gardening stuff, outdoor furniture, paddling pools and garden gnomes.

Ikea

Budějovická 1667-Krč 64, Prague 4 (61 21 28 95-9). Metro Budějovická. **Open** 9am-7pm Mon-Fri; 9am-4pm Sat.

Only one thing distinguishes this Ikea from its worldwide sister-stores: it doesn't take credit cards. So for those essential but boring household purchases, take wads of cash.

KDS Sedlčany

Národní 43, Prague 1 (26 53 03). Metro Můstek. **Open** 9am-6pm Mon-Fri; 9am-1pm Sat.

Stainless steel Czech knives in every size and shape. For a modest outlay (522kč for a massive kitchen chopper) you can buy presents for foodie friends.

Krásná jizba

Národní 36, Prague 1 (26 56 83/24 21 43 02). Metro Můstek. **Open** 9am-6.30pm Mon-Fri; 10am-3pm Sat. **Credit** AmEx, V.

Czech-made furniture, ceramics, textiles and toys in modernised 'folk' styles. The bare pine, clean lines and natural colours are redolent of Scandinavian design of the 1970s or even 1950s, but the prices are reasonable and the textiles quite zingy.

Ligne Roset

Ječná 15, Prague 2 (29 43 67/tel/fax 29 84 77). Metro Karlovo náměstí. **Open** 10am-6.30pm Mon-Fri; 10am-2pm Sat.

An upmarket and therefore expensive French furniture chain, Ligne Roset is enjoying a surprising success with the Czech *nouveaux riches*.

Le Patio

Václavské náměstí 53, Prague 1 (24 21 48 42). Metro Muzeum. **Open** 10am-7pm Mon-Sat; 11am-7pm Sun. **Credit** AmEx, DC, JCB, V.

The Belgian owner has craftily married local iron-working skills with the latest western design fad. Wrought-iron constructions from candleholders (1,095kč) to bird cages (7,500kč) crowd her shops, set off by the odd bunch of paper flowers or sculptural wooden bowl.

Branches: Liliova 6, Prague 1 (24 21 07 96); U radnice 12, Prague 1 (24 48 31 44).

Potten & Pannen

Vodičkova 2, Prague 1 (24 91 21 73). Metro Národní třída. **Open** noon-6pm Mon; 9am-6pm Tue-Fri; 9am-4pm Sat. **Credit** AmEx, DC, V.

The last word in German cookware – grinders, choppers, graters and squeezers as well as shining pots and pans. P&P also sells Calphalm aluminium saucepans from the USA and Emile Henry oven-to-tableware.

Rendl

třída 5 května 31, Prague 4 (43 12 65). Metro Pražského povstání. **Open** 10am-6pm Mon-Fri.

A newish Czech design company that makes smooth, modern lights at astonishingly good prices. The shop also sells the Italian big names: Artemide, Arte Luce and Flos.

Leisure

Stationery & Art Materials

The ubiquitous *papírnictví* shops sell everything from envelopes to toilet paper. If you can't find what you want in one, try **Kotva** (*under* **One-stop**) or one of those listed below.

*The latest styles at **Nostalgie**. See page 139.*

Loco Plus

Palackého 10, Prague 1 (tel/fax 26 27 69). Metro Národní třída or Můstek. **Open** 8am-6.30pm Mon-Fri; 9am-noon Sat.

Masses of good, cheap, local stationery and no overpriced imports.

McPaper & Co.

Vršovická 70, Prague 10 (67 31 06 06). Tram 4, 7, 22, 24. **Open** 9am-6pm Mon-Fri; 9am-noon Sat.

Glossy German Berlitz products, including sketch pads, wrapping paper, jiffy bags and tableware.

Branch: Dukelských hrdinů 39, Prague 7 (37 38 03).

Zebra Atelier

Vítězná 18, Prague 1 (no phone). Tram 6, 9, 22. **Open** 10am-6pm Mon-Fri.

A truly specialist art shop, crammed with stretchers, easels, canvasses, paints, chalks and brushes. The papers are disappointing, but they do include a heavily watermarked sheet that has been hand-made in Velké Losiny since 1596.

Photography

Jan Pazdera

Vodičkova 30, Prague 1 (26 06 83). Metro Národní třída. **Open** 9am-6pm Mon-Fri.

A shop specialising in processing and equipment for professionals as well as old cameras.

Music

Karel Schuss

Národní 25 (in the passage), Prague 1 (no phone). Metro Národní třída. **Open** 11am-7.30pm Mon-Sat. **Credit** AmEx, DC, MC, V.

A collectors' paradise with hundreds of used CDs, and LPs from the 1950s onwards. It includes jazz, blues, country, folk, Czech pop/rock and a pricey stack of Live Rarities.

Maximum Underground

Dlouhá 36, Prague 1 (no telephone). Metro Náměstí Republiky/5, 14, 26 tram. **Open** 10am-7pm Mon-Fri; 11am-5pm Sun.

The first and last resort for alternative music fans. Stock includes underground Czech labels as well as exclusive new releases from foreign distributors (Big Cat, City Slang, Wax Trax).

Memphis Melody

Václavské náměstí 17 (in the passage), Prague 1 (24 22 90 03). Metro Můstek. **Open** 9am-8pm Mon-Wed, Fri, Sat; 9am-9pm Thur; noon-7pm Sun. **Credit** AmEx, MC, V.

Rock, pop, country and jazz, including independent labels and Czech releases.

Popron

Jungmannova 30, Prague 1 (24 21 19 82). Metro Národní třída or Můstek. **Open** 9.30am-7pm Mon-Sat; 10am-6pm Sun. **Credit** MC, V.

A noisy bustling shop with a large selection of pop, rock and classical music as well as rock videos.

Listening facilities.

Studio Matouš

Kinských palác, Staroměstské náměstí 12, Prague 1 (231 10 39). Metro Staroměstská or Náměstí Republiky. **Open** 10.30am-6pm daily. **Credit** AmEx, MC, V.

The best bet for classical CDs, with a lot of opera and a connoisseur's selection of Czech music.

Branch: Lobkovický palác, Jiřská 3, Prague 1.

Listening facilities.

Sport

Brymová

Staroměstské náměstí 8, Prague 1 (tel/fax 231 07 73). Metro Staroměstská or Náměstí Republiky. **Open** 9am-6pm Mon-Fri; 10am-2pm Sat. **Credit** AmEx, MC.

Off-duty security guards drool over a horrifying collection of arms. Are they going to buy the neat little Luger pistol for 14,500kč or the toy machine-gun plus sound effects for 395kč? Probably the only useful thing in the shop is the pepper spray.

Druchema – U Petra

Dlouhá 3, Prague 1 (231 75 30). Metro Staroměstská or Náměstí Republiky. **Open** 9am-6pm Mon-Thur; 9am-5pm Fri; 9am-1pm Sat.

Stockists of good quality Czech and German fishing gear. Fly-fishers will find all their favourite imitations here – with English names.

Kastner Öhler – sportovní dům

Václavské náměstí 66, Prague 1 (24 21 51 45). Metro Muzeum. **Open** 10am-7pm Mon-Fri; 10am-2pm Sat.

Recommended for ski clothing and equipment. Otherwise, try Kotva or Kmart (*under* **One-stop**).

Tico Trek

Jilská 8, Prague 1 (23 27 384/24 22 59 29). Metro Můstek. **Open** 9am-7pm Mon-Fri; 8am-3pm Sat. **Credit** AmEx, DC, JCB, MC, V.

Authorised dealers offering American Trek bikes 30% cheaper than in the USA. Prices range from 30,000kč for a basic competition bike to 100,000kč for a top mountain or track model.

Old Books & Prints

Prague's second-hand bookshops, which also sell prints, maps and graphics, are known as *antikvariáts*.

Antikvariát Galerie Můstek

ulice 28 října 13, Prague 1 (26 80 58). Metro Můstek. **Open** 10am-6pm Mon-Fri; 10am-2pm Sat. **Credit** AmEx, MC, V.

A discriminating *antikvariát* with fine antiquarian books (nineteenth century natural history especially) and a steady stream of key works on Czech art.

Antikvariát Karel Křenek

Celetná 31, Prague 1 (232 29 19). Metro Náměstí Republiky/5, 14, 26 tram. **Open** 10am-noon, 2-6pm, Mon-Fri; 10am-2pm Sat. **Credit** AmEx, DC, MC, V.

The nineteenth and twentieth century graphic work is excellent and not outrageously priced here. If you're skint, go for the book plates, little gems at 150kč upwards; if adventurous, ask for the erotica.

Antikvariát U Karlova mostu

Karlova 2, Prague 1 (242 29 205). Metro Staroměstská. **Open** 10am-6pm Mon-Fri; 11am-4pm Sat. **Credit** AmEx, DC, EC, JCB, MC, V.

A prestigious shop selling antiquarian books, maps and prints. For the fogey in your life buy the eighteenth century view of the Vladislav Hall (10,000kč), with periwigged dignitaries attending Maria Teresa's coronation.

Kiwi

Jungmannova 23, Prague 1 (26 12 82). Metro Národní třída or Můstek. **Open** 9am-6pm Mon-Fri; 9am-2pm Sat.

A global stock of maps and guide books (including Michelin) for local and more exotic travel.

Services

Where to have your clothes or car washed, your shoes mended, hire a ball gown or a tent.

Costume hire for the reluctant bride at **Ladana**. See page 147.

The Czech Republic is only just beginning to adjust to the idea of a free market economy, and it may be another generation before it becomes a true service economy. The Communist regime was driven by subsidies and full employment, not efficiency. Workers in shops, restaurants, and businesses received the same pay regardless of whether they had customers or not, so they had very little incentive to work hard and please clients. This indifferent attitude is inbred in most adults in the Czech Republic and it is proving very difficult to exorcise it. Words like *nemůžu* (I can't), *bohužel* (unfortunately), *nemáme* (we don't have it), and *obsazeno* (busy, or full), are some of those most frequently used in the Czech language.

Not surprisingly, business service companies in Prague are predominantly owned by foreigners. Most of the employees of these establishments are young Czechs who have quickly adopted the attitude that 'the customer is always right'. Domestic service companies, like laundries and shoe repair shops, are usually Czech-owned. While these companies have come a long way in the past four years, they do not yet rival their western neighbours in the quality of their service. Dealing with this lack of quality service is one of the challenges of living in Prague. Word spreads quickly about any establishment that provides consistently good service.

Clothes & Accessories

Costume Hire

There are some great costumes to be found in Prague, should you suddenly find yourself invited to a fancy dress party. Look through the antique shops and rummage through the markets, or try one of the hire outlets listed below. There are also some wonderful hat shops to add spice to any costume (*see chapter* **Shopping**).

AB Barrandov
Křiženeckého náměstí 322, Prague 5 (59 04 40). Metro Anděl. **Open** 7am-2.30pm Mon-Fri.
Barrandov is the Hollywood of Prague. You can rent costumes from the studios' huge wardrobe department for very little money. Be sure to take your green residency card, if you have one, or your passport.

Ladana
Opatovická 20, Prague 1 (269 71 34). Metro Národní třída. **Open** 9am-6pm Mon, Wed, Thur.
A small costume shop that has some amusing dresses, period costumes and masks. Ladana's greatest advantage is its central location, just near Národni. Take your green residency card or passport as proof of identity.

Formal Dress Rental

During the winter ball season, the Czechs get to practice their dancing skills at any number of balls, that range from the student to the celebrity-filled (*see chapter* **Prague by Season**). School children and students go to dancing school in the autumn to prepare for these important gala events. If you've left your glad rags at home, try one of the formal dress shops listed below.

Gabriela
Sokolovská 239, Prague 9 (683 70 04). Metro Florenc.
Phone for an appointment.

Gloria
Slovenská 19, Prague 2 (25 40 86). Metro Náměstí Míru. **Open** 4-7pm Mon; 3-7pm Tue, Wed.

Romantik
Karoliny Světlé 23, Prague 1 (27 54 89). Metro Malostranská. Phone for an appointment.

Studio Chic
Žitná 40, Prague 2 (24 22 24 98). Metro Muzeum. **Open** 8am-6pm Mon-Sat.

Catching up on the news at **Laundry Kings**.

Dry Cleaners & Laundries

Dry cleaning in Prague is still far from perfect. If you have a particularly delicate item of clothing, you might want to wait until you get home before you surrender it to be cleaned. The laundry services are fine, however, though you should count your clothes when you get them back, since as in all laundries, items sometimes go astray.

Affordable Luxuries
Sarajevská 14, Prague 2 (37 53 79). **Open** 9am-6pm Mon-Fri.
Operates a pick up and delivery service only, for dry cleaning and laundry.

Laundry Kings
Dejvická 16, Prague 6 (312 37 43). Metro Dejvická. **Open** 6am-10pm Mon-Fri; 8am-10pm Sat, Sun.
A launderette that does service washes and also doubles as an ex-pat meeting place and information point.

Laundryland
Londýnská 71, Prague 2 (25 11 24). Metro Náměstí Míru/22, 26 tram. **Open** 8am-10pm daily.
Does dry cleaning as well as laundry.

Rapid Service
Dejvická 30, Prague 6 (no phone). Metro Dejvická. **Open** 6am-7pm Mon-Fri; 8am-noon Sat.
A reliable dry cleaner.
Branch: Francouzská 15, Prague 2 (no phone).

General Services
All Purpose Rentals

Check with the individual shops about the kind of deposit necessary on rented goods.

A-Landa
Šumavská 33, Prague 2 (253 99 82). Metro Náměstí Míru. **Open** 10am-1pm, 2-6pm, Mon-Fri.
You can hire sports equipment from here, including skiing paraphernalia for the winter and camping equipment for the summer.
Branch: Terronská 57, Prague 6 (311 93 50).

Půjčovna jídelnich servis
Petrohradská 19, Prague 10 (72 33 16). Metro Jiřího z Poděbrad then 124, 139 or 213 bus. Phone for an appointment.
Cutlery and crockery rental.

Shoe Repairs

There are shoe repair booths in the major department stores, Kmart, Baťa, and Kotva (*see chapter* **Shopping**); or you can try one of the outlets listed below. The Czechs have a strong tradition of shoemaking. They are good craftsmen and can usually carry out repairs for a fraction of the price the work would cost elsewhere.

Austria Miniservis

Spálená 37, Prague 1 (24 91 08 22). Metro Národní třída. **Open** 9am-5pm Mon-Fri.

Jan Ondráček

Navrátilova 12, Prague 1 (29 66 53). Metro Muzeum or Můstek. **Open** 8am-6pm Mon-Fri.

Nicol-Opravna obuvi

Italská 20, Prague 2 (25 01 76). Metro I.P. Pavlova. **Open** 9am-6pm Mon-Thur; 9am-4pm Fri.

Photo Developing

There are so many tourists in Prague that photography developing shops have mushroomed to meet their picture-snapping demand. Below is a short list of shops where you can have your holiday pictures developed, but there are dozens more around the Old Town Square and in Malostranské náměsti. Most are open until 7pm or 8pm in the summer.

Fotocentrum

Na příkopě 24, Prague 1 (24 21 37 19). Metro Můstek or Náměstí Republiky. **Open** 7.30am-noon, 12.30-6pm, Mon-Fri. **Branch**: Opletalova 32, Prague 1 (24 22 55 31).

Fotoplus

Na příkopě 17, Prague 1 (24 21 31 21). Metro Můstek or Náměstí Republiky. **Open** 9am-7.30pm Mon-Fri; 10am-7pm Sat, Sun. **Credit** AmEx, MC, V.
Does one hour developing.

Kodak

Národní 39, Prague 1 (no phone). Metro Národní třída. **Open** 8am-7pm daily. **Credit** V.
Does one hour developing.
Branches: Celetná 3, Prague 1; Vodičkova 37, Prague 1.

Made Photo service

Karlovo náměstí 16, Prague 2 (29 10 66). Metro Karlovo náměstí. **Open** 8.30am-7.30pm Mon-Fri; 8.30-11am Sat. **Credit** V.

Hair & Beauty

All the big international hotels have hair salons (*see chapter* **Accommodation**). Below is a list of some of the more reliable ones in the city. Think twice about having your hair coloured in any of them – you could end up with a very strange shade. The salons all also have manicure services. *See also chapter* **Women's Prague**.

Hair & Cosmetic Salon

(Kadeřnický a kosmetický salon), Masarykovo nábřeží 4, Prague 2 (29 62 09). Metro Národní třída. **Open** 8am-8pm Mon-Fri; 11am-6pm Sat.

Hair-Line International

Vyskočilova 2, Prague 4 (42 17 33). Metro Budějovická. **Open** 10am-7pm Mon, Sat, Sun; 7.30am-7pm Tue, Fri; 7.30am-8pm Wed, Thur.

Šarm

Jindřišská 2, Prague 1 (24 22 46 10). Metro Můstek or
Muzeum. **Open** 9am-4pm Mon-Sat.
Šarm is a chain with 17 branches, 10 of which are in Prague
1 and Prague 2. Check the *Zlaté stránky (Yellow Pages)* or
enquire here for your nearest branch.

Feasts & Flowers

Flower Delivery

Flower delivery is a relatively new concept in
Prague. The shop listed below delivers in Prague
or abroad, but you can't always guarantee that
your floral tribute will get to the right person at
the right time. You can also try using one of the
courier services or a taxi to deliver flowers (*see
chapters* **Business** *and* **Getting Around**). *See
chapter* **Shopping** for more florists.

Floraservis

*Bubenské nábřeží 9, Prague 7 (80 56 35). Metro
Vltavská.* **Open** 8am-6pm Mon-Fri; 8am-1pm Sat.

Food & Drink

Most of the food available for home delivery in
Prague is pizza. As an alternative, you can always
try and persuade your favourite restaurant to prepare something, put it in a taxi, and bring it to your
doorstep.

Affordable Luxuries

Sarajevská 14, Prague 2 (25 78 64). **Open** 9am-6pm
Mon-Fri.
Place your order by telephone and this company will arrange

for dinner to be prepared and delivered to your door at a time
specified by you. There are a few basic menus to chose from,
which you can tailor to meet your needs.

Chicago's Famous Pizza

(316 61 44/316 61 35). **Open** 9am-9.30pm daily.
The first western-style pizza place to open in Prague. Pizzas
(for delivery only) have the thick Chicago crust.

Pizza Hut

*Králodvorská 5, Prague 1 (232 78 70). Metro Náměstí
Republiky.* **Open** 11am-11pm daily.
This branch serves the same deep-pan pizzas found at Pizza
Huts all over the world.

Pizza Taxi

*Karlovo náměstí 28, Prague 2 (29 07 06). Metro Karlovo
náměstí.* **Open** 11am-11pm daily.
Thin crusted individual pizzas and pasta dishes can be
delivered to your door.

U Cedru

Na hutích 13, Prague 6 (312 29 74). Metro Dejvická.
Open noon-3.30pm, 5-10pm, daily.
For a welcome change from pizza, order in some Lebanese
food. The best dishes here are the appetizers – humus,
tabouli, yoghurt with garlic, fatoush and other falafel. Orders
are delivered to your door.

Video & Cassette Rental

Video to Go

*Vítězné náměstí 10, Prague 6 (312 40 96). Metro
Dejvická.* **Open** 10am-8pm daily. **Membership** 500kč
per year. **Credit** V.
Started by the wife of an American executive a few years
ago, Video to Go has been very successful. It is the only shop
that stocks English-language videos in the original version,
in both European and American television formats.

Bicycle Rental

Many bike shops have blossomed in Prague in the past couple of years, although not all of them offer bicycle rentals (*see chapter* **Sport & Fitness** for details). During the summer, there's also usually a canny Czech who sets up a dozen bicycles in Staroměstské náměstí and rents them out on a first come, first served basis. Some travel agencies offer mountain bike trips. Check the classified sections of *Prognosis* and the *Prague Post* as well as the bulletin boards at **Radost** (*see chapter* **Nightlife**), **Laundry Kings** (*see page 147*), and the **Globe Bookstore** (*see chapter* **Cafés, Bars & Pubs**) for bike trips in the summer.

Car Hire

It's easier to rent a car than a bicycle in Prague, but it can be very expensive. Sometimes the car is cheaper if you have a Czech residency permit. Always bring your drivers' licence, passport and credit card with you. The car rental agency should provide you with a green insurance card that permits you to drive the car across the border. Below is a list of the biggest car hire firms. However most of them charge west European prices; it's usually worth looking in the *Zlaté stránky (Yellow Pages)* for a list of local firms who are likely to charge cheaper, Czech prices.

Avis

Elišky Krásnohorské 9, Prague 1 (231 55 15). Metro Staroměstská. **Open** 7am-6pm Mon-Fri; 8am-2pm Sat; 8am-1pm Sun. **Credit** AmEx, MC, V.

Budget

Hotel Inter-Continental, náměstí Curieových, Prague 1 (231 95 95). Metro Staroměstská. **Open** 8am-8pm daily. **Credit** AmEx, MC, V.

Europcar/National Car Rental

Pařížská 28, Prague 1 (24 81 0 515). Metro Staroměstská. **Open** 8am-8pm daily. **Credit** AmEx, MC, V.

Hertz

Karlovo náměstí 28, Prague 2 (29 62 37). Metro Karlovo náměstí. **Open** 8am-8pm daily. **Credit** AmEx, MC, V.

Rent A Car

Opletalova 33, Prague 1 (24 22 98 48). Metro Muzeum. **Open** 8am-8pm daily. **Credit** AmEx, MC, V.

Car Washes

BP Filling Station

K Barrandovu, Prague 5 (628 11 33). **Open** 24 hours daily.

Car Service

Přístavní 27, Prague 7 (80 01 97). **Open** 8am-5pm Mon-Fri; 9am-2pm Sat.

Segár

Václavské náměstí 18, Prague 2 (29 00 27). **Open** 7am-6pm daily.

Galleries & Museums

Art & Architecture   **152**
Art Galleries   **158**
Museums   **167**

Art &
Architecture

Untangling the history and politics behind Prague's buildings and paintings.

In recent years the art and architecture of Bohemia has been hidden from view behind the iron curtain that dropped across Europe in the 1950s. Now it is being unveiled as one of Europe's most innovative cultures. Prague stands at the crossroads of Europe: its art and architecture has benefited from outside influences while managing to maintain its Czech identity.

Roughly speaking, Prague's art and architecture enjoyed four moments of glory: the mid-fourteenth century, when Charles IV set out to make Prague the Rome of the North; the reign of Rudolf II from 1575 to 1611, when Prague attracted artists across Europe; the High Baroque period of the late seventeenth to mid-eighteenth century when architecture, sculpture and painting were pressed into the service of Catholic indoctrination; and the early years of the twentieth century, when the First Republic was one of the crucibles of Modernism.

(To find the buildings listed below, *see page 264* **Area Index**.)

The Remains of Romanesque

The first patrons of the arts were the successive members of the **Přemyslid dynasty**, who in their efforts to establish Christianity built stone buildings and religious foundations. They employed the Romanesque style, which had originated in Germany and France in the tenth century and took as its model the great stone-vaulted, round-arched buildings of early Christian Rome. Today little survives from the Romanesque period. Most of the churches have been destroyed in wars or rebuilding programmes; the wall paintings have flaked away; and the manuscripts are hidden in libraries.

What to see: **Hradčany** St George's Basilica; **Staré Město** House of the Lords of Kunštát and Poděbrady; **further afield** Church of St Martin, Vyšehrad.

The Golden Age

Around 1230 the Gothic style arrived from France. It opened up buildings, using pointed arches,

ribbed vaults and flying buttresses to give a sense of lightness and verticality. The first Gothic constructions – St Agnes's Convent and the Old-New Synagogue – followed the restrained Cistercian model, but by the mid-fourteenth century, when Charles IV embarked on his cathedral, High Gothic was in full swing in France. The king's first architect, Matthew of Arras, followed the standard French cathedral plan. When he died in 1352 his place was taken by a German, **Peter Parler**, a far more innovative designer whose flowing window tracery, flying ribs and complicated vaulting patterns set the trend for the next 150 years.

During the reign of **Charles IV** (1346-78) Prague became the artistic centre of Northern Europe. The king had spent his youth in France and Italy and his cosmopolitan outlook, enhanced by the foreign artists attracted to his court, gave rise to the first great period of Czech art. Charles founded the New Town in 1348 and embellished his capital with a plethora of *grands projets*. Outside Prague he built the castle of Karlštejn (*see chapter* **Trips Out of Town**), whose inner sanctum, the Chapel of the Holy Rood, can rightly claim to be one of the most extraordinary creations of the Gothic period.

In painting Byzantine traditions lingered among the latest artistic trends from France and Italy. Artists aimed for a degree of realism, and portraiture – an entirely new concept in medieval Europe – became part of the royal agenda. At the end of the century painters rejected these innovations and turned instead to a decorative, somewhat old-fashioned approach known appropriately as the **Beautiful Style**.

What to see: **Hradčany** St George's Convent (gallery), St Vitus's Cathedral; **Staré Město** Charles Bridge, Judith Tower, St Agnes's Convent; **Josefov** Old-New Synagogue; **Nové Město** Karlov; **out of town** Karlštejn.

A Gothic Swansong

All this came to a rapid end with the outbreak of the Hussite wars in 1419. Eventually, after decades of destruction and instability, Vladislav Jagiellon took up the throne in 1471. His position was not entirely secure and in a time-honoured ploy he used the propaganda of architecture to prop it up. To reinforce a link with his great predecessor Charles IV, he restored the Castle as the royal seat and brought in a German architect, **Benedict Ried**, to fortify it.

Ried was one of the last outstanding Gothic architects, whose Vladislav Hall of 1493 was technically so daring that it collapsed during construction. The Hall is both the swansong of the Gothic period and the harbinger of the Renaissance. Its rectilinear windows framed by pilasters mark the first appearance in Central Europe of the new classicism that had been developing in Italy since the 1420s. This arrived via Hungary, for in 1490 Vladislav inherited the throne of Hungary from Matthias Corvinus, and with it a hotbed of advanced Humanist thought.

Painting at this period was nothing special. The only major artist was the obscure **Master of the Litoměřice Altarpiece**, whose work also marks the transition from the Gothic to the Renaissance sensibility. In sculpture the Gothic style was still dominant, in the ornate vegetal stone carving of **Matěj Rejsek** and the emotionally overwrought compositions of the wood carvers.

What to see: **Hradčany** Prague Castle (the Old Royal Palace, especially the Vladislav Hall and the Louis Wing), the Dalibor Tower, the White Tower, St George's Convent (gallery); **Staré Město** Astronomical Clock.

Imperial Patronage

The first Habsburg king, Ferdinand I (1526-64), went one step further than Vladislav. He blatantly used full-blown Renaissance imagery to establish his dynasty, linking his role as Holy Roman Emperor to the Roman emperors of antiquity. The most complete expression of this policy is the Belvedere or Summer Palace of 1537-63, the first fully Renaissance building north of the Alps (England had nothing similar until 1616). The initial design, based on fashionable Italian pattern books, was by **Paolo della Stella**. The building was finished off by **Bonifaz Wohlmut**, a learned Rhineland architect who combined advanced Italian ideas with a quirky Gothicism.

The court patronage was undoubtedly important for it gave Prague a handful of Renaissance masterpieces that were unequalled in any other northern European city. But by this period patronage was not confined to the court. The devastating fire that swept Malá Strana in 1541 opened the way for nobles and wealthy burghers to develop their own version of the Renaissance. Despite the example set by the court, and despite the fact that many of the architects were from the Como region

of Italy, the result was thoroughly northern. Renaissance detailing was grafted onto the local Gothic tradition of high gables, arcaded courtyards and irregular floor plans.

Many of the buildings were decorated with classical or religious themes in **sgraffito** work, a technique in which the outer layer of plaster was scratched away to reveal the darker render below.

The reign of **Rudolf II** (1575-1611) may have been a disaster politically, but artistically it was a triumph. The Emperor's guiding passion was to discover the hidden mysteries that would unify and elucidate the whole of creation. To this end he employed astronomers, alchemists, botanists – and artists. By now the calm and assurance of the Renaissance had been superseded by **Mannerism**, which deliberately set out to flout the rules of classicism and baffle the spectator with bizarre compositions and obscure allegory. The Emperor was a passionate collector and an enlightened patron. He loved Mannerism, allowing **Archimboldo** to develop a line in visual punning that was later admired by the Surrealists, but also encouraged more far-reaching visual exploration. The Flemish artist **Roelandt Savery** was packed off to the Alps to study the natural landscape.

What to see: **Hradčany** Ball Game Court (Belvedere Gardens), Belvedere (Summer Palace), St George's Convent (gallery), Schwarzenburg Palace, Strahov Gallery; **Staré Město** house 'U minuty'; **Nové Město** Emmaus Monastery (Vyšehradská, Prague 5); **further afield** Star Lodge.

Art & Faith

Rudolf lost his throne; his collections were removed to Vienna or plundered by the Swedes (a loss that still rankles in Prague); Bohemia was razed by the Thirty Years War. When the country began to rebuild itself in the late seventeenth century, a new style emerged to bolster the *arriviste* nobility and browbeat the populace into Catholicism. This was the **Baroque**, the art of persuasion. In a gamut of illusionistic trickery, architecture, sculpture and painting were woven into an indivisible whole, a form of virtual reality in which the humble spectator was able to participate directly in the Divine Mystery.

Despite a brave attempt by a French architect, **Jean-Baptiste Mathey**, to introduce the more sober, classical forms of French Baroque, it was the Italian High Baroque that appealed to Bohemian tastes. An Italian building mafia had dominated Prague since the early seventeenth century (among its members was Francesco Caratti, the creator of that 'tasteless mass of stone' the Černín Palace). The style it practised was a heavy and unsubtle form of Mannerism, in which huge pilasters topped by grimacing heads marched along interminably long façades.

A first inkling of the radical developments that had been taking place in Italy appeared in 1679 when the Turinese architect **Guarino Guarini** designed a church for Malá Strana. Guarini was a mathematician and philosopher, who created elaborate vaulting schemes and immensely complicated plans composed of intersecting stars and ovals. The church was never built, but Guarini's ideas were enthusiastically taken up by **Christoph Dientzenhofer**, a German architect recently arrived in Prague.

The work of Christoph Dientzenhofer and his son **Kilián Ignaz** crystallised the Bohemian Baroque style. In their masterpiece, the church of St Nicholas in Malá Strana of 1703-52 (*see chapters* **Sightseeing** *and* **By Area**), one can see the full Dientzenhofer repertory – the swelling concave and convex curves, the dynamic, gouged out spaces, the soaring vaults – that they repeated in countless variations in other churches.

The other leading Bohemian architect was **Giovanni Santini-Aichel**, who practised a perfectly respectable Baroque style as well as his own weird neo-Gothic. Only the former can be seen in Prague, in palaces in Malá Strana. The Gothic was requested by ecclesiastical patrons, who wished to rebuild their premises in a style that evoked the true faith of the Middle Ages, before the advent of the troublesome Hussites. In it, Santini combined the intersecting geometric plans of Guarini, with intricate, but entirely fake, Gothic vaulting patterns. Symbolism played a part too: his famous pilgrimage complex at Žd'ár nad Sázavou, near Brno, is composed around a pointed shape that commemorates the undecayed tongue of St John Nepomuk.

In its assault on the hearts and minds of Czechs, the **Counter-Reformation** required the appropriate paintings and statuary. Here again the Italian Baroque provided a model, for a dramatic yet realistic style that would grab the spectator. In painting, the instigator of the Baroque was **Karel Škréta**, who spent his youth in Rome; its leading, though greatly over-valued, exponent, **Petr Brandl**; its genius **Jan Kupecký**, who as a Protestant worked in exile all his life. Ceiling painting, an essential tool of illusionism, burst on the scene at Troja and made a glorious exit in the Philosophical Hall at Strahov.

A rash of sculpture appeared all over Bohemia in churches, palaces and urban squares; Marian columns, giving praise to the Virgin for her intervention in the plague, were put up in every self-respecting town. The greatest artists in this vast production were **Ferdinand Maximilián Brokof**, the son of a Slovak sculptor who had expediently converted to Catholicism while working on the statue of St John Nepomuk on Charles Bridge, and **Mathias Bernard Braun**, whose agitated, emotionally charged figures have been compared to a lava flow.

The Bohemian Baroque peaked between 1710 and 1730, during the reign of Charles VI, who encouraged the nobility in extravagant display and the Church in its proselyting zeal. The canonisation of St John Nepomuk in 1729 marked the apogee of the Czech Counter-Reformation. In sculpture it heralded a change towards a more accessible, but crudely theatrical manner. This can be best seen in Karlov church, where painted wooden spectators lean from the balconies to watch the stilled action of a Passion play.

As the century progressed the fervour abated. The Baroque metamorphosed gradually into the **Rococo**, a more decorative, intimate style, and was then extinguished altogether by the reforms of Joseph II in the 1770s and 1780s. By expelling the Jesuits and dissolving the monasteries, the Emperor deprived artists of both patronage and subject matter. This, combined with the general impoverishment of the country and the nobles' preference for life in Vienna, opened yet another chasm in Czech cultural history.

Building perforce continued. **Neo-classicism**, a rational style based on antique models, was considered appropriate for public architecture, while **Romanticism** ran riot in garden follies in the shape of Greek temples and Chinese pavilions. Painting and sculpture languished, despite the efforts of concerned Czech aristocrats who in 1796 founded a Society of Patriotic Friends of the Arts in Bohemia.

See: **Hradčany** Černin Palace, the Loreto, St George's Convent (gallery), Strahov Monastery (libraries and gallery); **Malá Strana** St Nicholas, Wallenstein Palace; **Staré Město** Charles Bridge, Clam-Gallas Palace, the Clementinum, Estates Theatre, Goltz-Kinský Palace, St Nicholas; **Nové Město** Karlov, Villa Amerika (Dvořák Museum); **further afield** the Lapidarium, Troja Château; **out of town** Veltrussy.

A Nationalist Revival

Rescue came 50 years later in a new source of patronage – the prosperous mid-nineteenth century bourgeoisie – and a new philosophy – Czech nationalism. Artists portrayed Czech history, myth, landscape, rural life and even the Czech physiognomy. Their great collective effort was the decoration of the National Theatre from 1868-81, an enterprise that so absorbed the painters, sculptors and architects of the time that they became known as the **National Theatre Generation**.

The National Theatre was designed in a neo-Renaissance style, which for no obvious reason was considered suitable for cultural venues. This was a historicist period. The neo-Gothic style was also rampant, with the Cathedral underway again and **Joseph Mocker** busy reinventing Gothic monuments. A 'neo-Czech Renaissance' was contrived, decorated with fancy gables, sgraffito work and wall paintings of suitably patriotic themes.

What to see: **Staré Město** St Agnes's Convent (gallery); **Josefov** the Rudolfinum; **Nové Město** National Museum, National Theatre, the Živnostenská bank (Na příkopě 20).

Opening the Windows to Europe

By the 1890s Prague had become an artistic backwater. Impressionism and its successor Post-Impressionism had passed by virtually unnoticed as artists continued to concentrate on the realistic depiction of nationalist and folk themes. Frustrated by this stagnation, an avant-garde minority turned to Paris, where they found art and poetry swirling in a torrent of emotion. The *fin-de-siècle* mood was one of introspection, mysticism, anxiety and even fear. **Karel Hlaváček**, whose work expresses a traumatic experience of sexuality, claimed 'I love Fear. With fear, I mortify my body and revive my soul'. Other artists were less extreme and found release for their inner feelings through **Symbolism** and **Primitivism**.

A series of exhibitions in the 1900s swept Prague into the European mainstream. Of these, the Rodin show of 1902 ended the hegemony of the neo-Renaissance nationalist sculptor **Josef Myslbek**, while the Munch show of 1905 unleashed the searing emotion of **Expressionism**. Even **Cubism**, which at that time was barely understood in Paris, found a ready response in Prague when it was first shown in 1907. A whole school of Cubist painters

Petr Brandl's Tobias Restoring the Sight of his Father *in* **St George's Convent**.

quickly emerged, including orthodox followers like Emil Filla, and others such as Bohumil Kubišta who tried to fuse the French Cubist vision with the prevailing Central European *angst*. This approach was also taken by **Otto Gutfreund** (unquestionably the greatest twentieth century Czech sculptor) in a series of bronzes that combine an intense spirituality with Cubist notions of space and form (many are now in the Gallery of Modern Art).

Such was the interest in Cubism that it was even adopted by architects – a unique experiment that, perhaps wisely, was not repeated anywhere else in Europe. A heated debate was now taking place in architecture. Historicism had been discredited and its successor, Art Nouveau, had been written off as purely decorative. The way forward was generally believed to lie in rationalism, which would take into account only form, function and construction. The Cubist architects, a small but vociferous group, believed this to be a sterile approach which denied man's need for spiritual expression.

What to see: **Nové Město** Municipal House; **further afield** Bílek Villa, Gallery of Modern Art; for more on Art Nouveau and Cubism, *see* **Art & Design** *in chapter* **Sightseeing**.

Art & Politics

This debate was interrupted by World War I. When the dust settled, artists found themselves working for and in a new state. They took their

Mucha & Kupka

It is an unfortunate irony that the best-known Czech artists earned their reputation abroad. Apart from Kupecky, the Baroque portrait painter, there was **Alfonse Mucha**, the populariser of the Art Nouveau style, and **František Kupka**, an avant-garde pioneer working in Paris who beat Malevich to the post with the first abstract paintings in 1911-13.

Mucha owes his fame to the posters he designed for Sarah Bernhardt in the 1890s. His commercial work (which was highly lucrative) epitomises the Art Nouveau delight in swirling lines, intricate decoration and bare-bosomed females. There was, however, a darker side to his psyche, which dwelt on Slavic nationalism and metaphysical notions of spirit and matter. This can be seen (or will be, when it re-opens) in his murals of 1910-11 for the Lord Mayor's room in the **Municipal House** (Obecní dům).

role seriously, believing that art had an important part to play in the young democracy.

Two schools of thought developed. The first was determined to find a truly national form of expression, one that was fresh, decorative and ethnically correct. In sculpture Gutfreund came up with **Objective Realism** which dignified the role of working people. In architecture a solution was found in **Rondo-Cubism**, in which Slavism was proclaimed by bright colours and massive curved forms. A more subtle approach can be seen in the work of **Josip Plečnik**, the Slovenian architect favoured by President Masaryk. Its classical, early Christian and Slav imagery underlined the high moral purpose of Masaryk's Republic.

The second group, which soon ousted the first, was internationalist. Prague was once again at the crossroads of Europe and artists worked in close contact with the avant-garde in France, Germany, Holland and Russia. Like their counterparts abroad, they were enthralled by modern life, by technology and social change. 'Revolution in art and life' was the cry. They sought to break down the hierarchy of the arts – photography, film and typography were as valid as painting – and to create new art forms that were more appropriate to the age. In this they totally succeeded. **Modernism** became the lingua franca of the First Republic.

The leading light of this avant-garde was **Karel Teige**, a painter turned graphic artist and theorist, who was always able to articulate the mood of the moment. In the early days this was decidedly optimistic. **Devětsil**, the movement which Teige founded in 1920, set out to celebrate the poetry of modern life. To this end it coined the 'picture poem', an assembly of images and words that delicately evoked sensations of travel and popular culture.

In the late 1920s the mood hardened. The Wall Street Crash sparked off an economic depression, to which artists responded by throwing themselves into the service of socialism. **Functionalism**, in architecture and design, was seen as the obvious style for a proletarian society. However, it soon became painfully obvious that Stalinist Russia – the model for such a society – had no time for a free-thinking avant-garde. Artists, including Teige, took refuge in **Surrealism**, through which they explored the uncomfortable, even threatening, workings of the subconscious.

What to see: **Hradčany** Plečnik's work at the Castle (Bull Staircase, South Gardens, entrance to Spanish Hall); **Staré Město** Galerie Pallas (*see chapter* **Art Galleries**); **Nové Město** Adria Palace (Národní 36), Alfa arcade (Václavské náměstí 28), Hotel Juliš (Václavské náměstí 22), the Legiobank (Na poříčí 24), the Lindt building (Václavské náměstí 4), the Baťa building (Václavské náměstí 6); **further afield** Church of the Sacred Heart

Giuseppe Archimboldo's Mannerist Portrait of Adam. *See page 153.*

(náměstí Jiřího z Poděbrad), the Muller house (Nad hradním vodojemen 14), Gallery of Modern Art; Baba housing development (Dejvice).

Hibernation

The early years of Communism were tough. Modern art from Impressionism onwards was decried as bourgeois and **Socialist Realism** was prescribed instead. Blandly historicist architectural schemes and stirring portrayals of the workers' struggle became the daily fare. By the 1960s this was totally discredited and artists had considerable freedom. The abstract art from this period, which combines a firm grasp of structure with a typically Czech spirituality, is very fine. In the 1970s and 1980s a guarded approach was necessary. Artists toed the line in public and veiled their private criticism in metaphor and allusion.

What to see: **Nové Město** Kmart department store, National Theatre extension; **further afield** Gallery of Modern Art; *see also* **Communist Prague** *in chapter* **Sightseeing**.

A New Dawn?

Since the Velvet Revolution there has been a surge in creative activity in Prague. During the Communist period artists were largely cut off from the outside world. The 'isms' – conceptualism, postmodernism – that have shaped western art never took root and instead Czech artists evolved a more individual voice – personal, nostalgic, romantic. Their main problem now is to maintain the Czech identity that is so precious while gaining recognition on the international stage.

In architecture, Communism left a depressing legacy of mediocrity. Creative thought was stifled and even the best architects found it virtually impossible to execute a good building with shoddy materials. But the Velvet Revolution has brought a new tyranny – that of the market place.

Western developers have piled into Prague and property prices are among the highest in Europe. Despite the feverish activity, however, results are slow to emerge. The lack of empty sites, problems with ownership and the difficulty of obtaining finance and planning permission are putting the brakes on development. Although a handful of foreign architects are working in Prague, the future lies with the Czechs. The best architects are highly sophisticated. They tend to shun western fads and instead are proud of their own cultural heritage. It is too early to identify any trends in new Czech architecture, but the signs are promising.

What to see: **Nové Město** British Council interior by Jestico+Whiles (Národní 10), 'Ginger and Fred' building by Frank O. Gehry and Vlado Milunič (Rašínovo nábřeží 80), office building by ADNS (Římská 15).

Art Galleries

Despite shortage of funds and the thorny issue of restitution, Prague's galleries and exhibition spaces still manage some splendid displays.

Antonín Střížek's work on show at the **Galerie MXM**. *See page 164.*

This chapter covers the city's major art collections and displays, as well as the principal exhibition spaces and commercial galleries. The Prague art scene is still in a state of post-revolutionary flux, with galleries opening, closing or being re-organised in response to restitution, lack of space, or lack of funds. One major upheaval involves the National Gallery's collection of nineteenth and twentieth century Czech sculpture, previously housed in the Zbraslav Monastery, which will be displayed in the new Gallery of Modern Art (*see below*) due to open imminently as we went to press. Prague Castle Picture Gallery has fallen victim to lack of funds and will remain closed until they are found, and the Belvedere (Royal Summer Palace) exhibition space shares the same fate. Howeve,r the Czech Museum of Fine Arts is about to open a new exhibition space in the restored House of the

Black Madonna (Dům U černé Matky boží). *See page 56* for more details.

THE NATIONAL GALLERY
The National Gallery is an umbrella organisation that displays its collections and holds temporary exhibitions in various locations across the city. Recently its image has been slightly dented by the acrimonious issue of restitution. Many important works confiscated under the Communist regime are being returned to their original owners, but some art lovers fear that they might be neglected or even sold abroad. However, the more public-spirited owners are co-operating with the Gallery and are happy to loan their paintings (thereby avoiding hefty bills for insurance).

INFORMATION
For the most up-to-date information on cultural events in Prague, including exhibitions in galleries and museums, consult the listings pages of the *Prague Post*, or *Culture in Prague*, the white listings booklet available from most newsstands in and around Wenceslas Square. Alternatively, try one of the English-speaking staff at the **Prague Information Service**, *Na příkopě 20 (54 44 44)*.

Most galleries and museums are closed on Mondays and in August, but it's always best to check that one hasn't suddenly 'temporarily' closed before setting out for a far-flung foray.

See chapter **Art & Architecture** for more background information on Prague's artists, buildings and paintings.

National Gallery

Gallery of Modern Art
(Galerie moderního umění), Veletržní palác, Veletržní 45, Prague 7 (24 30 10 15). Metro Vltavská. **Open** 10am-6pm Tue-Sun. **Admission** 40kč adults; 20kč students, OAPs; free under 6s.

At time of writing, this gallery was due to open sometime in 1995. It will display the National Gallery's collection of Czech twentieth century art, including painting, sculpture (formerly displayed in the Zbraslav Monastery), architecture, film and the performing arts. The Trade Fair Building (Veletržní palác) is a vast Constructivist masterpiece designed in 1924-8 by Oldřich Tyl and Josef Fuchs. The decision to use it as an art gallery was made in 1978 and has been fiercely criticised ever since. Nevertheless, the gallery will be a sensation, revealing to locals and foreigners alike the immense vitality of Czech modern art – a culture that has been under wraps for too long.

Detail from the Votive Panel of Jan Očko of Vlašim *in* St George's Convent.

St Agnes's Convent

(Klášter sv. Anežky české), U milosrdných 17, Prague 1 (24 81 06 28). Metro Náměstí Republiky/5, 14, 26 tram. **Open** 10am-6pm Tue-Sun. **Admission** 40kč adults; 20kč children, students, OAPs; free under 6s.

Taking up where St Agnes's Convent stops (*see below*), the gallery of St Agnes displays nineteenth century Czech art. It kicks off with the founders of nationalist painting: Antonín Machek, who specialised in portraits of Czech intellectuals, and Antonín Mánes, who did romanticised views of Czech landscape and monuments. His son, Josef Mánes, was one of the dominant figures of the mid-nineteenth century; he experimented in styles and subject matter but was most admired for his depictions of Czech legend and country life. History painting, which popularised heroic events in newly discovered Czech history, became a dominant theme. It was carried out most convincingly by Jaroslav Čermák and Mikuláš Aleš, most laughably by František Ženíšek. (The last two were both members of the so-called National Theatre Generation of the 1870s.)

Realism was the main concern of the nineteenth century. Impressionism, which erupted in Paris in the 1870s, was virtually ignored in Prague, even though artists had been going to France from the middle of the century. It is not until the final gallery, in the deeply atmospheric night views of Prague by Jakub Schikaneder, that one can find any sign of a new vision.

St George's Convent

(Klášter sv. Jiří), Jiřské náměstí 33, Prague 1 (24 51 06 95). Metro Malostranská/12, 22 tram. **Open** 10am-6pm Tue-Sun. **Admission** 60kč family ticket; 40kč adults; 20kč children, students, OAPs; free under 6s.

This gallery houses Bohemian painting and sculpture from the early Middle Ages to around 1800. Its glory is the early section, filled with the lyricism and humanity of Czech medieval art. During the reign of Charles IV (1348-78) Prague was in the forefront of European artistic development. The bronze statue of St George and the Dragon, for example, is so advanced, so Renaissance in spirit, that scholars are still arguing over its date. One innovation was portraiture, an example of which can be seen in the *Votive Panel of Jan Očko of Vlašim*, where the emperor and archbishop Očko are painted with compelling realism. The panels by Master Theodoric – just a few of the many hundred executed for the Chapel of the Holy Rood at Karlštejn – show a similar interest in realism (*see chapter* **Trips Out of Town**).

The outstanding artist of the end of the fourteenth century was the Master of Třeboň. His many-panelled altarpiece that includes the *Resurrection of Christ* shows a change in mood, in which realism has been replaced by an atmosphere of mystery and miracle. Another of his paintings, the *Madonna of Roudnice*, is an example of the so-called Beautiful Style that prevailed until the outbreak of the Hussite wars. The following rooms show how the Gothic style remained popular in Bohemia right up to the sixteenth century. They end with an extraordinary wood carving by the Monogrammist IP in which the skeletal, half-decomposed figure of Death is brushed aside by the Risen Christ. The frog gnawing at Death's entrails symbolises Vanity.

The galleries upstairs begin with a handful of paintings that survive from the collections of Rudolf II (1575-1608). They include masterpieces by the Antwerp painter Bartholomaeus Spranger, whose sophisticated colours, elegant eroticism and obscure themes are typically Mannerist; and landscapes by Roelandt Savery that show the growing interest in the natural world.

The next rooms are devoted to Baroque art, starting with Karel Škréta, the founder of Baroque painting in Bohemia. He spent his youth as a Protestant exile in Rome but returned to Prague in 1638, a convert ready to serve the Counter-Reformation. He was a down-to-earth painter, in contrast to Michael-Leopold Willmann and Jan Kryštof Liška whose work was feverishly religious. A distinct characteristic of Baroque art was the way in which painting and sculpture borrowed from each other. This can be seen in the following rooms, where the paintings of Petr Brandl, the most acclaimed artist of the early eighteenth century, are displayed beside the sculpture of Mathias Bernard Braun, the finest sculptor. The other great sculptor of the period was Ferdinand Maximilián Brokof, the creator of the swaggering Moors that once guarded the château of Count Morzini.

At the end of the eighteenth century the arts went into decline. The work of Norbert Grund is interesting not for its style, which is an uninspired version of French Rococo, but for its subject matter. His small studies of artists' studios give a rare glimpse of the craftsman's daily grind.

Sternberg Palace

(Šternberský palác), Hradčanské náměstí 15, Prague 1 (24 51 05 94). Metro Malostranská/22 tram. **Open** 10am-6pm Tue-Sun. **Admission** 40kč adults; 20kč children, students, OAPs; free under 6s.

The Sternberg Gallery was founded in the 1790s by the Society of Patriotic Friends of the Arts in Bohemia, a group of enlightened aristocrats determined to rouse Prague from its provincial stupor. Now it houses the National Gallery's European Old Masters. It's not a large or well balanced collection but it does include some outstanding paintings, including the *Haymaking* landscape by Pieter Bruegel, a brilliant portrait by Frans Hals and Dürer's *Feast of the Rosary*. This much damaged and restored panel was so prized by Rudolf II that he had it carried over the Alps from Venice upright and wrapped in carpets.

The earlier paintings in the collection were acquired

Sklo **Bohemia**
Světlá nad Sázavou

The Finest Crystal in Prague

Na Příkopě 17, Prague 1

Dürer's Feast of the Rosary *in the* **Sternberg Palace**. *See page 159.*

through random gifts and purchases, but the twentieth century galleries benefitted from the systematic approach of Vincenc Kramář, the Gallery's director during the First Republic. He was an extraordinarily perceptive critic and one of the first people in or outside Paris to recognise the importance of Picasso. His Parisian spending sprees in 1925, 1934 and 1935 gave the Czech public a superb collection of French contemporary art. The corner devoted to Picasso and Braque – small, select and instructive – is a perfect introduction to Cubism.

Other Collections

Bílek Villa

(Bílkova vila), Mickiewiczowa 1, Prague 6 (34 26 03). Metro Hradčanská/22 tram. **Open** *15 May-15 Oct* 10am-noon, 1pm-6pm, Tue-Sun. **Admission** 20kč adults; 5kč children, students, OAPs.

This must be the only museum in the world designed in the form of a wheatfield. It was built in 1911-12 by the mystic sculptor František Bílek as his studio and home, and still contains much of his work. Bílek went to Paris in his youth to study as a painter but finding he was half colour-blind turned to sculpture and illustration instead. Repelled by the decadence of modern life, he embarked on a spiritual quest to uncover a universal cosmic truth that would unite the visible and invisible world. The wheatfield, representing spiritual fertility and the harvest of creative work, was only one of the many symbols he dwelt on. Light was an emanation of creative energy, trees were associated with Man and the continual cycle of birth and decay. This is strong stuff, and the work it inspired ranges from the sublime to the sickening.

Lapidarium

Výstaviště, Holešovice, Prague 5 (37 31 98). Metro Nádraží Holešovice then 5, 12, 37 tram. **Open** noon-6pm Tue-Fri; 10am-6pm Sat, Sun. **Admission** 20kč adults; 10kč children, students, OAPs.

Officially the Lapidarium is the last resting place of sculptures

that have been rescued from demolished buildings or taken in from the weather. Unofficially, it's also a testimony to the city's recent swings in fortune. The collection includes the Marian column from the Old Town Square that was put up in 1648 in gratitude for the defence of Prague from the Protestant Swedes; a fine equestrian statue of Emperor Francis II, one of the least attractive Habsburgs who was responsible for the country's atrophy in the first half of the nineteenth century; and a magnificent bronze group of the Austrian marshal, Josef Radecký. All these were torn down in 1918: Communist monuments that have suffered a similar fate are not yet on view. This handsome, well-modernised gallery also includes the original Baroque masterpieces from the Charles Bridge and copies of Peter Parler's famous heads. Tantalisingly out of view in St Vitus' cathedral, these date from the late fourteenth century and are among the first European portraits. Parler was rightly proud of his achievements and included himself in the exalted company of kings, queens, bishops and clergy.

Strahov Gallery

(Strahovský klášter), Strahovské nádvoří 1/132, Prague 1 (24 51 03 55). Tram 22. **Open** 9-11.45am, 1-4.45pm, Tue-Sun. **Admission** 30kč adults; 10kč children, students, OAPs.

The Strahov paintings, sculpture and metalwork form one of the most important monastic collections in Central Europe. It was seized by the State – like all other church property – in the early 1950s and has now been restituted to its rightful owner. Strahov's gain has been the National Gallery's loss, for the collection includes paintings such as the fourteenth-century Strahov *Madonna* and Spranger's *Resurrection of Christ* that not so long ago took pride of place down at the Castle.

Troja Château

(Trojský zámek), U trojského zámku 4, Prague 7 (84 07 61). Metro Nádraží Holešovice then bus 112. **Open** 10am-5pm Tue-Sat. **Admission** 40kč adults; 10kč children, students, OAPs.

Troja was built around 1700 by Count Sternberg. As a native

Eva Švankmajerová at the **Gambra-Surrealisticka Galerie**. *See page 165.*

Czech nobleman he was understandably anxious to prove his loyalty to the Habsburg emperor and, literally, moved mountains to do so. The hillside had to be dug out to align the villa with the royal hunting park of Stromovka and the distant spires of the cathedral; the French architect, Jean-Baptiste Mathey, had to be defended against the Italian building mafia; sculptors had to be imported from Dresden and painters from Flanders. The result is a paean to the Habsburg dynasty. On the massive **external staircase** (by Johann Georg Heerman and his nephew Paul) gods hurl the rebellious giants into a dank grotto. In the **Grand Hall** (by Abraham and Isaac Godyn) the virtuous Habsburgs enjoy a well-earned victory over the infidel Turks. This, a fascinating though slightly ludicrous example of illusionistic painting, is the main attraction of Troja. An insensitive restoration programme has destroyed the atmosphere of the villa, and the installation of a small collection of nineteenth-century Czech painting does nothing to redeem it.

Exhibition Spaces

Temporary exhibition spaces come and go in Prague, but the main organising bodies are the National Gallery, the Office of the President of the Republic (the Castle) and the Gallery of the City of Prague. Mainstream exhibitions organised by them tend to be small and select, rather than blockbusters.

Locally-curated exhibitions are frequently devoted to the current Czech re-appraisal of their artistic heritage. Recent exhibitions, for example, have covered the avant-garde inter-war years, Karel Teige, Stalinist architecture, paintings of the

post-war period, and restituted artworks and historic buildings. An important exhibition covering art at the time of Rudolf II is planned for the future.

Carolinum
(Výstavní síň Karolinum), Železná 9, Prague 1 (24 49 16 14). Metro Můstek. **Open** *Nov-Mar* 10.30am-7pm daily; *Apr-Oct* 10.30am 8pm daily. **Admission** *gallery* free; *exhibitions* 10kč.
The vaulted ground floor of the Carolinum makes an excellent gallery space. International travelling exhibitions find their way here as well as shows by Czech artists. One of the galleries run by the Czech Museum of Fine Arts (*see below*), it's definitely worth checking out.

Czech Museum of Fine Arts
(České muzeum výtarných umění), Husova 21, Prague 1 (24 22 20 68). Metro Národní třída/9, 18, 22 tram. **Open** 10am-noon, 1-6pm, daily. **Admission** 15kč adults; 10kč children, students, OAPs.
This organisation, based in an elegant Baroque town house close to Charles Bridge, mostly exhibits twentieth century Czech art, but also organises international exhibitions and retrospectives of foriegn artists (recent ones have featured Henry Moore, Peter Blake and the pop artist Erró). *See above* **Carolinum**.

Galerie Hollar
Smetanovo nábřeží 6, Prague 1 (24 81 08 04). Metro Národní třída/6, 9, 17, 18, 22 tram. **Open** 10am-1pm, 2-6pm, Tue-Sun.
The gallery of the Union of Czech Graphic Artists is located on the ground floor of the University's Faculty of Sociology. The building faces the river but is rather swamped by traffic noise from the busy embankment. As well as monthly exhibitions – normally of Czech or Slovak artists – there are large racks of prints to browse through or buy.

Galerie Jaroslav Fragnera
Betlémské náměstí, Prague 1 (242 28 30 41). Metro Národní třída. **Open** 10am-6pm Tue-Sun.
Recently re-opened after extensive renovation, this beautiful Gothic building in the Bethlehem Chapel's quadrangle, is the gallery of the Society of Czech Architects. Shows focusing on both foreign and local architects are held in the main exhibition hall, while the commercial exhibition space on the ground floor displays work by top firms from the international building industry.

Galerie Rudolfinum
Alšovo nábřeží 12, Prague 1 (24 89 32 55). Metro Staroměstská/17 tram. **Open** 10am-6pm Tue-Sun.
A series of grand rooms in the newly refurbished nineteenth century concert building, used as an exhibition space under the auspices of the Ministery of Culture.

House at the Stone Bell
(Dům U Kamenného zvonu), Staroměstské náměstí 13, Prague 1 (24 81 00 36/231 02 72). Metro Staroměstská. **Open** 10am-6pm Tue-Sun.
A Gothic sandstone building on the east side of the Old Town Square which was opened to the public after extensive renovation in 1986. Inside, a gorgeous Baroque courtyard is surrounded by three floors of exhibition rooms, some still with their original vaulting. Concerts are also held here.

Imperial Stables
(Cisařská konírna), Pražský hrad (second courtyard), Prague 1 (33 37 33 68). Metro Malostranská/22, 31 tram. **Open** 10am-6pm Tue-Sun.
Rudolf II would probably be pleased to find that his stables are now an art gallery. The exhibitions are always well curated and beautifully displayed.

Contemporary Czech artists show at the **Výstavní síň Mánes**. *See page 166.*

Kinský Palace

(Palác Kinských), Staroměstské náměstí 12, Prague 1 (24 81 07 58). Metro Staroměstská. **Open** 10am-6pm Tue-Sun.

The exhibition rooms are nondescript but they hold interesting shows drawn from the National Gallery's collection of prints and drawings.

Municipal Library

(Městská knihovna), Mariánské náměstí 1, Prague 1 (232 28 83). Metro Staroměstská. **Open** 10am-6pm Tue-Sun.

Carefully converted, combining modern and classical details, these large well-lit rooms easily rival the National Gallery's spaces.

Wheelchair access.

Prague Castle Riding School

(Jízdárna pražského hradu), U Pražného mostu 55, Prague 1 (33 37 32 32). Metro Malostranská/22 tram. **Open** 10am-6pm Tue-Sun.

This and the Wallenstein Riding School (*below*) are the National Gallery's principal venues for major exhibitions. The Castle Riding School was built in 1694 to designs by Jean-Baptiste Mathey and restored by Pavel Janák after World War II. Its bookstall is a good source of current and remaindered catalogues on Czech art.

Wallenstein Riding School

(Valdštejnská jízdárna), Valdštejnská 3, Prague 1 (53 68 14). Metro Malostranská/12, 22 tram. **Open** 10am-6pm Tue-Sun.

See **Prague Castle Riding School** *above.* It forms part of the Wallenstein Palace, completed by the over-ambitious general in 1630 (*see chapter* **Sightseeing**).

Commercial Galleries

Prague could hardly be described as the centre of the international art market, but the commercial scene is alive and kicking and can be viewed at a host of small galleries throughout the city. Artists to watch out for include: Václav Stratil, Viktor Pivovarov, Jiří David, František Skála and Petr Nikl.

Exhibitions vary in quality and very few spaces show consistently good work. However, the Galerie Pallas has a collection of Czech Cubist and Surrealist art that rivals that of the National Gallery and galleries Behémot, MXM and Ruce are the places to see the leading edge of Czech art. Potential buyers interested in contemporary Czech art should start there. Other galleries are well worth exploring if only to sample the undoubtedly unique character of Czech contemporary art.

Hradčany & Malá Strana

Galerie MXM

Nosticova 6, Prague 1 (53 15 64). Metro Malostranská/12, 18, 22. **Open** noon-7pm Tue-Sun.

Conceived in 1990 as a private gallery that would represent Czech artists, this small vaulted space, hidden in the heart of Malá Strana, is the oldest private gallery in Prague and one of the most influential. Only Czech artists are shown here and the gallery has built up a stable of 17 artists from all generations. Exhibitions are consistently good and recent ones have included works by Martin Mainer, Petr Nikl and Jiří David.

Wheelchair access.

Galerie Rob Van Den Doel

Jánský vršek 15, Prague 1 (533 92 71). Tram 12, 22. **Open** 10am-5pm Wed-Sun.

Van Den Doel is a Dutch glass artist who has been exhibiting the work of Czech glass-makers in the Hague for many years. His gallery in Malá Strana is one of the few in the city that specialises in this medium and he has a formidable collection of artists on display. Past displays have included the work of Jan Frydrych, Václav Cigler and Eva Fišrová. If you haven't seen the melted glass works of Čermák or Frydrych's polished gems before, then a visit to this gallery is a must.

Gambra-Surrealisticka Galerie

Černínská 5, Prague 1 (no phone). Metro Hradčanská/1, 8, 18, 25, 26 tram.
Tucked away in a cottage in a beautiful street in Hradčany, is a gallery whose unprepossessing exterior hides one of the most interesting exhibitions in the city. It's the gallery of the Czech Surrealist Movement and part-owned by the cult hero of animated filmmaking, Jan Švankmajer. Švankmajer has always said that his films are only a small part of his work as a Surrealist: it's possible to see the other side here, where some of his lithographs and ceramics are on show. The gallery's emphasis is on group work however, and as much importance is given to the other members of the movement, both classic and contemporary, such as Medek, Karel Baron and Švankmajer's wife, Eva.

Staré Město & Josefov

Betlémská Galerie

Betlémské náměstí, Prague 1 (53 42 55). Metro Národní třída/6, 9, 18, 22 tram. **Open** *during exhibitions* 10am-6pm.
A new gallery housed beneath the Bethlehem Chapel which opened with a display of therapeutic art. Its best feature is its situation – the large, low-ceilinged hall is interrupted by the vestiges of the church's ancient foundations. Entry is down a spiral staircase leading off the Chapel's east courtyard.

Galerie Behémot

Elišky Krásnohorské 6, Prague 1 (231 78 29). Metro Staroměstská/17, 18 tram. **Open** 10am-6pm daily.
Karel Babiček, the owner of this gallery in Josefov, considers the conditions between viewer and art to be as important as the original creative act and encourages exhibiting artists to work with the gallery space itself. His preference for installations means the gallery has some of the most interesting and dynamic shows in Prague. Focusing mostly on young Czech and Slovak artists, the gallery shows the work of artists such as Vladimír Kokolia. Because of the non-commerical nature of installations, the gallery relies on sponsorship to keep going, although they do sell to companies and collectors. If you're interested in buying something, there's a large selection of (transportable) work upstairs which can be viewed on request.

Galerie Jednorožec s harfou

Průchozí 4, Prague 1 (24 23 08 01). Metro Národní třída. **Open** 11am-9pm Mon-Fri; noon-9pm Sat, Sun.
The 'Unicorn With a Harp' gallery shows the work of mentally and physically handicapped artists. It's a quiet space and has a tiny café which is a peaceful respite from the bustle of nearby Národní.
Wheelchair access.

Galerie Pallas

Náprstkova 10, Prague 1 (24 23 07 95). Metro Staroměstská. **Open** 10am-6pm Mon-Sat.
Undoubtedly one of the best private galleries in Prague, both for the quality of the works on display and for its interior. Georg Pallanich has a collection of Czech art that stretches from the 1890s to the 1990s and his collection of Cubist and Surrealist works rivals that of the National Gallery. You can see work by the Surrealists Josef Šima and Toyen and the Cubists Emil Filla, Václav Špála and Bohumil Kubišta. The gallery is deceptively large and well worth taking time to browse through.

Galerie Peithner-Lichtenfels

Michalská 12, Prague 1 (24 22 76 80). Metro Můstek. **Open** 10am-7pm daily.
A small gallery in the Old Town with a permanent collection of nineteenth and twentieth century Czech art, including artists like Beneš, Kolář and Kokoschka, shown in conjunction with five or six temporary exhibitions a year. Poor lighting makes the space seem cluttered.

Staronová Galerie

Maiselova 15, Prague 1 (232 10 49). Metro Staroměstská. **Open** 10am-6pm daily.
Opened in 1991 by František Lukaš, one of the last surviving members of the Terezin concentration camp, this gallery exploits its position in Josefov, only showing work with a Jewish theme. A well-lit solo gallery at the back puts on regular exhibitions by contemporary Czech artists.
Wheelchair access.

Středoeuropská Galerie a nakladadelství

(Central European Gallery and Publishing House), Husova 10 & 21, Prague 1 (24 22 20 68). Metro Národni třída/9, 18, 22 tram. **Open** 10am-6pm daily.
Divided into a graphics gallery (Husova 10) and an oil gallery (Husova 21) the Central European Gallery shows both Czech and international art, aiming to focus on periods which are under-represented elsewhere. The gallery stocks a large selection of their own literature and posters.

Nové Město

Galerie Böhm

Anglická 1 (entry on Legerova), Prague 2 (236 20 16). Metro I.P. Pavlova/4, 6, 11, 16, 22 tram. **Open** 2-6pm Tue-Fri; 10am-3pm Sat, Sun.
The other quality gallery devoted entirely to Czech glassmakers (*see p164* **Rob Van Den Doel**). The emphasis here is on painted glass, objects and installations. The impressive stable of artists includes Vladimír Kopecký and Jaroslav Matouš. Though slightly off the beaten track, the gallery is well worth the trek.

Galerie Mladých

Vodičkova 10, Prague 1 (24 21 36 18). Metro Můstek/9 tram. **Open** 10am-1pm, 2-6pm, Tue-Sun.
The name translates as 'gallery of youth', although the term at this artists' co-operative is extended to include anyone under the age of 35. The Gothic vaults and Baroque figurines of the three first floor rooms contrast with the art on display. Work can be bought direct from the artists (talk to the director).

Galerie Petra Brandla

Na slupi 17, Prague 2 (29 81 29). Metro Vyšehrad/7, 8 24 tram. **Open** noon-6pm Mon; 10am-6pm Tue-Fri.
This is the gallery to visit if you're feeling flush and want to buy classic art. It displays hitherto unknown masterpieces aquired from private collections in the Czech Republic. It owns a large selection of both Czech and European paintings including works by Kokoschka, as well as Dutch and French masters.

Galerie Ruce

V jirchářích 6 (first floor), Prague 1 (29 37 60). Metro Národní třída. **Open** 1-7pm daily.
A gallery that aims to promote the work of Czech *émigrés* and ex-dissidents. Jaroslav Krbůšek, a partner in the gallery, previously ran the dissident gallery Opatov before the Velvet Revolution. Exhibitions here are solo, with names like Jan Knap, Vladimir Škoda, Vladimir Stratil and Adreana Simatová being shown.

Invest in some classic Czech photography from the **Pražský dům fotografie.**

Galerie Vltavín

Masarykovo nábřeži 36, Prague 1 (24 91 45 40). Metro Národní třída/6, 9, 17, 18, 22 tram. **Open** *Apr-Oct 10am-noon, 1-7pm, daily; Nov-Mar 1-7pm daily.*
Overlooking the Vltava and close to the National Theatre, the Vltavín has become a popular venue for Czech artists, despite its small size. Focusing mainly on contemporary work by the older generation, exhibitions can be more low-key than elsewhere.
Wheelchair access.

Czech Union of Fine Arts

Exhibitions organised by the Union are always by contemporary Czech artists; the quality of the work varies enormously, but entry is cheap (or free) and the galleries are usually worth a visit. Works can be purchased direct from the artists; this can usually be arranged through the individual galleries.

Výstavní síň Mánes

Masarykovo nábřeži 250, Prague 1 (29 55 77). Metro Národní třída/17, 21 tram. **Admission** 10kč adults; 5kč children, students, OAPs.
The largest and most important of the galleries, and a beautiful piece of Functionalist architectiure as well (built by Otakar Novotný in 1930). There are usually three or four exhibitions on at the same time, ranging from international travelling exhibits to those of classic and contemporary Czech artists. The home of the Mánes Graphics Artist Society, today it's a shadow of the vibrant centre it used to be, but the Cubist ceiling frescoes on the lower ground floor are still unmissable.

Galerie Václava Špály

Národní 30, Prague 1 (24 21 30 00). Metro Národní

třída/6, 9, 18, 22 tram. **Open** 10am-1pm, 2-6pm, daily.
Much larger than it seems from busy Národní, this gallery has three floors of exhibition space. Originally a bookshop, it has been going for 40 years in its present incarnation. Recent shows have included works by František Skalá and Michal Ranný.

Nóvá síň

Voršilská 3, Prague 1 (29 20 46). Metro Národní třída. **Open** 10am-1pm, 2-6pm, daily.
A single bright clean room tucked away in a building close to Národni. The excellent lighting makes it a great place to view art by Czech artists like Rotislav Novak and Jan Pištěk.
Wheelchair access.

Photography Galleries

Dobrá Galerie

Kostečná 5, Prague 1 (23 21 70 02). Metro Staroměstská/17 tram. **Open** 2-6pm daily.
Alternating monthly exhibitions of contemporary international photographers like Teflik Ataman and V Karášek, with retrospectives, this gallery has a lively program of shows. Owner Rifo Dobrá has an extensive collection of classic Czech photographs including work by Josef Sudek, Jan Saudek and František Drtikol. Contemporary prints begin at 4,000kč.
Wheelchair access.

Pražský dům fotografie

Husova 23, Prague 1 (24 23 20 22/24 23 21 11). Metro Národní třída/9, 18, 22 tram. **Open** 11am-6pm daily.
A reputation for high quality exhibitions has made this gallery one of the most popular in Prague. It shows work by both Czech and foreign photographers, contemporary and period, and is well worth a visit. Contemporary prints start at 2,000kč, while classic works by photographers like Jan Sandek cost between 20,000kč and 30,000kč.

Museums

Prague's miscellaneous museums – from the musical to the military.

Though perhaps not on the same scale as many other European capitals, Prague's collection of museums is rich and varied. As with its galleries, revolution and restitution have taken their toll, and some collections either remain homeless (for example the splendid collection of the Museum of Musical Instruments) or have disappeared altogether (the Museum of National Security and Interior Ministry, for obvious reasons). However, many museums, freed from state control and pressed into action by the need to be commercial, are making a determined effort to make their collections more accessible to the public.

For national collections of paintings and sculpture and a note on opening hours and listings, *see* chapter **Art Galleries**.

Decorative Arts

Loreto Treasury

(Loretánská klenotnice), Loretánské náměstí 7, Prague 1 (24 51 07 89/53 62 28). Metro Malostranská/22 tram. **Open** 9am-12.15pm, 1-4.30pm, Tue-Sun. **Admission** 30kč adults; 20kč children, students, OAPs.

Home of the famous diamond monstrance, or 'Prague Sun', designed in 1699 by Fischer von Erlach and crafted by Viennese court jewellers, who encrusted it with some 6,222 diamonds. The treasury was founded in 1636, and despite being plundered several times to finance military campaigns against the Turks and Napoleon, it still contains an impressive collection of liturgical treasures, including a Gothic chalice dating from 1510 and several other magnificent Baroque monstrances, donated by Bohemian nobles keen to display their dedication to the Counter-Reformation. *See also* chapter **Sightseeing**.

Museum of Decorative Arts

(Uměleckoprůmyslové muzeum), ulice 17 listopadu 2, Prague 1 (24 81 12 41). Metro Staroměstská. **Open** 10am-6pm Tue-Sun. **Admission** 30kč adults; 15kč students, OAPs; 5kč 10-15 year-olds; free under 10s.

With typical nineteenth century philanthropy, this museum was founded in 1885 to display fine examples of decorative art for educational purposes. Unfortunately much of its contents are now in store and the galleries occupy only a single floor. This could be seen as a virtue rather than a disappointment: in a limited space the visitor can enjoy a tour through the major European decorative styles without succumbing to physical and mental exhaustion. Apart from furniture (which includes magnificent pieces made in Rudolf II's court workshop), there are excellent displays of glass and ceramics. Bohemian glassmakers were highly inventive and managed to perfect techniques such as engraving, facet-cutting and ruby-glass manufacture that their competitors found hard to rival. Bruce Chatwin fans will be intrigued by the Meissen porcelain. His novella *Utz* describes a Jewish collector in nearby Široká street who

The Loreto.

smashes the beloved Meissen that has been requisitioned by the Party hacks in the Museum.

History

Historical Museum

Lobkovický palác, Jiřská 1, Prague 1 (53 73 06). Metro Malostranská/22 tram. **Open** 9am-4.30pm Tue-Sun. **Admission** 30kč.

The wing of the National Museum in the early Baroque Lobkowicz Palace houses a permanent exhibition enticingly called Monuments of the Nation's Past. Part of the sgraffiti-covered façade of the original Renaissance building can be seen in the courtyard, but the palace itself was rebuilt in the late seventeenth century by the Catholic Lobkowicz family. The imposing banqueting hall, with frescoes by Fabián Harovník, is used for concerts and recitals. The museum covers the history of Bohemia and Moravia from the Celts to the revolution of 1848, but despite the high quality of the exhibits, the English language texts blandly fail to capture the tensions of Czech history. However, the display includes some beautiful examples of Czech craftsmanship, jewellery

and furniture, as well as copies of the Czech coronation jewels, and for these alone the museum is worth a visit.

House of the Lords of Kunštát and Poděbrady

(Dům pánů z Kunštátu a Poděbrad), Řetězová 3, Prague 1 (no phone). Metro Staroměstská. **Open** *May-Sept* 10am-6pm Tue-Sun. **Admission** 10kč.

This house is one of the few accessible examples of Romanesque architecture in Prague. It was begun in 1250, originally built as a walled-in farmstead, but like its neighbours in the Old Town was partially buried in the flood-protection scheme of the late thirteenth century, which reduced the vaulted ground floor to a cellar. By the mid-fifteenth century it was quite palatial, a suitably grand dwelling for George of Poděbrady, who set out from here for his election as King. The upper storeys were later greatly altered. Now it houses a modern art display and an interesting little exhibition in honour of George of Poděbrady whose well-meaning scheme for international co-operation is hailed as a forerunner of the League of Nations.

Komenský Pedagogical Museum

(Pedagogické muzeum J.A. Komenského), Valdštejnský palác, Valdštejnské náměstí 4, Prague 1 (513 24 54). Metro Malostranská/tram 12, 22. **Open** 10am-noon, 1-5pm, Tue-Sun. **Admission** 6kč adults; 3kč children.

Jan Ámos Komenský (Comenius), Czech philosopher and Protestant pedagogue, was one of the first men to identify the struggle for peace and understanding with the need for a sound education system, and he's now a national hero. The museum traces his tragic life (1592-1670) and although exhibits are in Czech, if you're lucky the woman at the ticket office will provide an enthusiastic tour in English. The museum is housed in part of the Ministry of Culture.

Museum of the City of Prague

(Muzeum hlavního města Prahy), Na poříčí 52, Prague 8 (24 22 31 79). Metro Florenc/3, 5, 24 tram. **Open** 10am-6pm Tue-Sun. **Admission** 10kč adults; 5kč children, students, OAPs.

Antonín Langweil spent 11 years building a paper model of Prague (he died in 1837). It's now the museum's prize exhibit and has unsurprisingly earned itself an international reputation. Also on show here is Josef Mánes' original calendar painting for the astronomical clock in the Old Town Square (the original was removed for safe-keeping and replaced with a copy). The rest of the museum's permanent collection covers the history of the city, from its foundation in the ninth century to the battle of Bílá Hora in 1620. The display is surprisingly small given the size of the building in which it's housed, but the two rooms do provide an excellent comparative view of Gothic and Renaissance arts and crafts. Temporary exhibitions are housed on the second floor.

Vyšehrad Museum

Soběslavova 1, Prague 2 (29 66 51). Metro Vyšehrad/17 tram. **Open** 9.30am-5.30pm daily. **Admission** 5kč adults; 3kč children; 15kč day pass to all exhibitions.

The rocky outcrop of Vyšehrad, rising above the right bank of the Vltava, has played an important role in the history of Prague since the first ancient Slav fortifications were built here in the tenth century. Today, as well as a pleasant park offering superb views over the river, it's a vast archeological monument where layers of history, from the Romanesque to the Baroque, have been uncovered and left on view for visitors. The monuments of the ancient citadel are co-ordinated by a small museum (near the Romanesque rotunda, the Church of St Martin) which contains reconstructions of the Gothic and Baroque fortress. A visit to the museum before a tour of the area provides a useful background to the

The Old Jewish Cemetery. *See page 170.*

citadel's history and archaeology. There's also a small exhibition of Prague and Vyšehrad fortifications housed in the Cihelná brána (Brick Gate) on the north side of the citadel.

Natural History & Ethnography

Náprstek Museum

(Náprstkovo muzeum), Betlémské náměstí 1, Prague 1 (24 21 45 37). Metro Můstek. **Open** 9am-noon, 12.45-5.30pm, Tue-Sun. **Admission** 20kč adults; 10kč students and soldiers; free under 6s.

Vojta Náprstek was a nineteenth century nationalist whose twin passions were modern technology and primitive cultures. The gadgets he collected are now in the National Technical Museum (*see p172*), while the ethnographic bits and bobs that he acquired from Czech travellers are housed in an extension to his own house, an ungainly building which smells strongly of disinfectant. The displays, which are excellently arranged and full of interest, concentrate on the Americas, Australasia and the Pacific Islands. The museum also stages temporary exhibitions from its own collection and that of its sister museum at Liběchov château, Mělník.

National Museum

(Národní muzeum), Václavské náměstí 68, Prague 1 (24 23 04 85). Metro Muzeum. **Open** 10am-6pm Mon, Tue, Thur, Fri-Sun; 10am-9pm Wed. **Admission** 50kč adults; 35kč 6-15 year-olds, students, OAPs.

The city's grandest museum and its biggest disappointment. The vast building dominates the top of Wenceslas Square, its neo-Renaissance flamboyance promising an interior bursting with delights. Instead it is filled with roomfuls of dusty fossils and minerals, and more cabinets of stuffed animals than would seem possible. However the museum is worth visiting for its splendid architecture. It was designed by Joseph Schulz (who collaborated on the National Theatre) and finished in 1890, a proud symbol of the Czech nationalist revival. The figures of Bohemia, flanked by Vltava, Elbe, Moravia and Silesia decorate the façade, while the interior contains murals by František Ženíšek and Václav Brožik depicting key events in Czech history, including Libuše summoning Přemysl to rule over the Czechs and Charles IV founding the university of Prague in 1348.

State Jewish Museum

The museum was founded in 1906 to preserve the historical monuments of the former Jewish ghetto, at the time when the surrounding area was under reconstruction. Today the collection is housed in five different Josefov buildings and is one of the most popular in Prague. The headquarters of the museum (Státní židovské muzeum v Praže), is at *Jáchymova 3, Prague 1 (24 81 00 99/02 32 18 14). See also chapter* **Prague by Area: Josefov.**

Ceremonial Hall

U starého hřbitova, Prague 1 (24 81 00 99/02 32 18 14). Metro Staroměstská. **Open** 9am-4.30pm Mon-Fri, Sun. **Admission** 80kč adults; 30kč children, students, OAPs.

Turreted and arched, the Romanesque details of this building next door to the Klausen Synagogue make it appear as old as the gravestones in the cemetery. However it was built in 1906 for the Prague Burial Society, though only used by them for 20 years. Since 1978 it has housed a collection of art produced by victims of the Terezín concentration camp (both adults and children), presented in an emotional and upsetting exhibition. It documents all aspects of ghetto life – food queues, dormitories, transportation – with a compelling intensity.

High Synagogue

(Vysoká synagóga), Červená 4, Prague 1 (231 81 61).
Metro Staroměstská. Closed for restoration.
The High Synagogue houses the museum's valuable collection of textiles, which dates back to the sixteenth century. Restored to the Jewish community in 1994, the builting is currently under restoration and will eventually become a working synagogue again.

Klausen Synagogue

(Klauzová synagóga), U starého hřbitova 4, Prague 1
(231 03 02). Metro Staroměstská. **Open** 9.30am-12.30pm Mon-Fri, Sun. **Admission** 80kč adults; 30kč children, students, OAPs.
Adjacent to the Ceremonial Hall, this early Renaissance synagogue contains an eloquent exhibition on Jewish ceremonies and their relevance to Jewish life. Display cases house artefacts collected from the ghetto's 1,000-year history, used in rituals ranging from birth and circumcision through to death and the preparation of the body for burial.

Maisel Synagogue

(Maiselova synagóga), Maiselova 10, Prague 1 (24 81 00
99/02 32 18 14). Metro Staroměstská. **Open** 9am-6pm Mon-Fri, Sun. **Admission** 80kč adults; 30kč children.
The synagogue was burnt down in the ghetto fire of 1689 and only restored to its present state at the beginning of this century. Today it contains the museum's silver collection – mostly religious ornaments used for dressing the Torah scrolls, but also including some exquisite eighteenth and nineteenth century spice holders.

Old Jewish Cemetery

(Starý židovský hřbitov), U starého hřbitova 3, Prague 1.
Metro Staroměstská. **Open** 9am-4.30pm Mon-Fri, Sun.
Shaded by trees, the jumbled cemetery and its multitude of gravestones eerily conjures up echoes of the fifteenth century when it was founded. There are an estimated 12,000 graves crammed into the tiny plot, the bodies buried 12 layers deep in some cases. The black headstones are the oldest, carved from fifteen century sandstone; the white ones, of marble, date from the sixteenth and seventeenth centuries. Hours can

be spent deciphering the symbols carved over them. *See also chapters* **Sightseeing** *and* **Prague by Area.**

Pinkas Synagogue

(Pinkasova synagóga), Široká 3 (entrance from U starého
hřbitova), Prague 1. Metro Staroměstská. **Open** 9.30am-1pm, 1.30-5.30pm, Mon-Fri, Sun. **Admission** 80kč adults; 30kč children, students.
The Pinkas Synagogue, which dates back to the late fifteenth century, houses the museum's Holocaust memorial. In the 1950s the names of the 77,297 Czech Jews who died in the Holocaust were first inscribed on its walls. The building fell into disrepair in the 1970s and it is only since the revolution of 1989 that the museum has been able to start the long task of restoring the monument. *See also chapters* **Sightseeing** *and* **Prague by Area.**

Literature

Jirásek & Aleš Museum

Letohrádek hvězda, Obora hvězda, Prague 6 (36 79 38).
Metro Hradčanská, then 11, 2, 18 tram. **Open** 10am-5pm Tue-Sun. **Admission** 10kč adults; 5kč children, students, OAPs.
Star Lodge, the former star-shaped hunting lodge near the site of the Battle of the White Mountain (Bílá Hora) is now a rather dull museum dedicated to the Czech nationalist writer Alois Jirásek (1851-1930) and painter and illustrator Mikoláš Aleš (1852-1913). The museum also contains an exhibition on the battle.

Museum of National Literature

(Památník národního písemnictví), Strahovské nádvoří 1,
Prague 1 (24 51 11 37). Tram 8, 22/143, 149, 217 bus.
Open 9am-4.30pm Tue-Sun. **Admission** 15kč adults; 5kč children, students, OAPs.
The library of the Strahov Monastery has collected nearly 130,000 books over the past 800 years and most of them are housed in two reading halls. Neither is open to the general public, but you can peer through the doorways (go before 10.30am to beat the crowds). In the **Philosophical Hall** the

Langweil's labour of love at the **Museum of the City of Prague.** *See page 169.*

The National Technical Museum – *a lot more fun than it sounds. See page 172.*

books are arranged on gold-plated and beautifully carved walnut shelves, to accommodate which the ceiling had to be dismantled and rebuilt. In celebration, the monks commissioned Franz A. Maulbertsch in 1794 to cover it with a monumental fresco entitled *The Struggle of Mankind to Know Real Wisdom*. The smaller, more intimate **Theological Hall** is older, dating from 1691, with a stuccoed ceiling and fine collection of antique globes and spheres. The comprehensive acquisition of books by the monastery didn't begin in earnest until the late sixteenth century under the auspices of one Abbot Crispin Fuck, though the collection really came into its own when it received the libraries of hundreds of Bohemian monasteries which were closed down by Joseph II in 1782. Their taste ranged far beyond the standard ecclesiastical tracts, including books which were on the Vatican's Index and choice secular works such as the oldest extant copy of *The Calendar of Minutae*, or *Selected Times for Bloodletting*. Nor did they merely confine themselves to books: the 200 year-old curiosity cabinets house a bizarre collection of deep-sea monsters. The museum also mounts excellent exhibitions.

Military

Aeronautical & Cosmonautical Exhibition

Letecké muzeum, Mladoboleslavská, Prague 9 (82 47 09). Metro Českomoravská, then bus 185 or 259 to Kbely. **Open** *May-Oct* 10am-6pm Tue-Sun. **Admission** 15kč. Though it's a bit of an excursion to get to Kbely airport, if you are interested in glimpsing the other side of the Cold War a visit here is essential. The geometrical display of aeroplanes is a spectacle in itself. The huge collection of military and civil aircraft ranges from World War I biplanes to a McDonnell Phantom and more Migs than you can shake a stick at. There's a small cosmonautical section, with displays of space suits and segments of rockets, but it's the collection of Russian tanks – including a mobile tactical missile from the 1970s – that is the show-stopper. Very threatening. At

the time of writing, two of the halls were shut due to lack of funding, so the biplanes and the Spitfires weren't on view. *Wheelchair access.*

Military Museum

(Vojenské muzeum), Schwarzenberský palác, Hradčanské náměstí 2, Prague 1 (53 64 88). Metro Malostranská/22 tram. **Open** 10am-6pm Tue-Sun. **Admission** 20kč adults; 10kč children, students, OAPs; free Tuesdays. Czech military campaigns, from thirteenth century battles against marauding Mongols and Tartars, up to the end of World War I, are charted alongside advancing military technologies at this museum housed in a Renaissance palace. An array of blood-thirsty weapons accompanies every exhibit and there's a collection of scale models to please the heart of anyone who ever owned a set of toy soldiers. The façade of the splendid Schwarzenberg Palace – begun in 1545 and built for the Lobkowicz family – is a tour de force of sgraffito diamond-pointed rustication.

Museum of the Resistance & the History of the Army

(Muzeum odboje a dějin armády), U památníku 2, Prague 3 (24 72 23 42). Metro Florenc/107, 133 bus. **Open** *May-Oct* 10am-6pm Tue-Sun; *Nov-Mar* 9am-5pm Tue-Sun. **Admission** 12kč adults; 5kč children, students, OAPs; free Tuesdays.
A museum which covers the history of the Czech army during World Wars I and II, including a fascinating section on the troops parachuted into the country during the Nazi occupation. Still under extension, the collection looks unfinished and the displays, though well illustrated, are directed more towards Czech speakers than foreigners.

Music & Musicians

Dvořák Museum

(Muzeum Antonína Dvořáka), Villa Amerika, Ke Karlovu 20, Prague 2 (29 82 14). Metro I.P. Pavlova.

Open 10am-5pm Tue-Fri; 10am-noon, 1-5pm, Sat, Sun. **Admission** 20kč adults; 10kč children, students, OAPs.
It's hard to believe that this splendid Baroque summer house was used as a cattle market during the last century. But the red and ochre villa, built by Kilian Ignaz Dientzenhofer in 1720 for Count Jan Václav Michna (it was originally known as the Michna Pavilion), has been restored to its former glory. The same care has been taken with the lay-out of the exhibition inside. Opened in the spring of 1991 by the Dvořák Society, the small museum is filled with that organisation's enthusiasm. The ground floor displays cover the composer's life, with memorabilia, photographs and even the gown he wore to receive an honourary doctorate from Cambridge University on display. Upstairs is a recital hall decorated with the restored eighteenth century frescoes by Jan Ferdinand Schor. Staff at the museum are helpful and an English language translation of the exhibition is available at the ticket desk. The house is also known as the Villa Amerika, after a local pub.

Mozart Museum

Bertramka, Mozartova 169, Prague 5 (54 38 93). Metro Anděl. **Open** 9.30-6pm Tue-Sun. **Admission** 50kč adults; 30kč children, students, OAPs.
Mozart stayed at Bertramka several times during visits to Prague, as a guest of the villa's owners, composer František Dušek and his wife Josefina. He was here in 1787 while working on *Don Giovanni*, composing the overture at Bertramka the night before its première in what is now the Estates Theatre. The house and grounds have been restored to their eighteenth century glory (the building was badly damaged by fire in 1871), and though the collection of memorabilia it contains is somewhat slim (much of it with only the most tenuous of connections to the composer), the museum is very popular with tour parties in the summer. The best time to come here and appreciate the villa's greatest asset – its tranquillity – is mid-morning or late in the afternoon. In the summer recitals are held on the terrace; tickets start at 150kč.

Smetana Museum

(Muzeum Bedřicha Smetany), Novotného lávka 1 (726 53 71). Metro Staroměstská. Closed to the public.
Situated on a small peninsular by the Vltava next to Charles Bridge, the museum devoted to the hero of Czech music is housed in a converted neo-Renaissance water tower. It contains a collection of musical memorabilia – letters, scores and photographs – and there is a statue of the composer on the embankment outside. At time of writing, the museum was closed 'indefinitely' with no concrete plans for the future.

Science & Technology

City Transport Museum

(Muzeum MHD Střešovice), Patockova 4, Prague 6 (312 33 49). Tram 1, 8, 18. **Open** *Apr-Oct* 9am-5pm Sat, Sun and Bank Holidays. **Admission** 14kč adults; 10kč children, students, OAPs.
Filled with a mesmerising collection of big shiny engines, and very popular with children and their fathers, the Transport Museum contains nearly every model of tram and trolley bus that ever ran the streets of Prague, polished and oiled to perfection. The museum is only open at the weekends; after a tour you can take a trip on a special tram that runs from the depot to the city centre and back.
Wheelchair access.

National Technical Museum

(Národní technické muzeum), Kostelní 42, Prague 7 (37 36 51). Metro Malostranská/5, 12, 17, 24, 26 tram. **Open** 9am-5pm Tue-Sun. **Admission** 20kč adults; 5kč children, students, OAPs.

One of the few museums in Prague to use interactive displays and so bring its collections to life. The museum traces the development of technology and science within the Czech Republic and among the highlights are the Transport Hall and the coal mine in the basement. The hall, filled with steam trains, racing cars and the obligatory set of biplanes suspended from the ceiling, forms a sharp contrast to the claustrophobic mine where all manner of sinister coal-cutting tools are displayed in tunnels. Guided tours of the mine leave from the ticket office and are available in English. There's also an extensive photography and cinematography section, as well as a collection of rare and fascinating astronomical instruments.

Specialist

Police Museum

(Muzeum policie ČR), Ke Karlovu 1, Prague 2 (29 52 09). Metro I.P. Pavlova. **Open** 10am-5pm Tue-Sun. **Admission** 10kč adults; 5kč children, students, OAPs.
A former convent attached to the Karlov church is the incongruous home of Prague's grim chamber of horrors, the Police Museum. The extensive criminology section is accompanied by accounts (in Czech) of murder mysteries illustrated with photographs, weapons and photo-fits. Kids love it, though be warned that some of the photographs are explicit. The final room contains an arsenal of home-made weaponry that James Bond would be proud of: sword sticks, home-made pistols, pen guns, and even a converted lighter.

Postage Stamp Museum

(Poštovní muzeum), Nové mlýny 2, Prague 1 (231 20 60). Metro Náměstí Republiky. **Open** 9am-5pm Tue-Sun. **Admission** 15kč adults; 5kč children, students, OAPs.
Although philately may not be everyone's cup of tea, this is one of the most enjoyable museums in Prague – a cross between a Baroque villa and a second-hand bookshop. The villa was built in 1678, originally the home of millers. The postage stamp collection can be found on the ground floor, containing stamps of the Czech Republic and Slovakia dating from 1918 to 1992, and European stamps from 1840. But it's the first floor, with its nineteenth century frescoes and library, that gives the museum its unique character. It's now a gallery which displays contemporary Czech graphic art which has played a role in the design of Czech stamps.
Wheelchair access to ground floor.

Sport & Physical Training Museum

(Tyršovo muzeum tělezné výchovy a sportu), Michnův palác, Újezd 40, Prague 1 (53 21 93). Metro Malostranská/12, 22, 57 tram. **Open** 9am-5pm Tue-Sat; 10am-5pm Sun. **Admission** 7kč.
A rather dull museum that hasn't managed to lay the ghost of its socialist past. Photographs and documents illustrating the history of Czech sport are displayed alongside an assortment of dumb bells, bicycles, sledges and busts of long dead wrestlers. For more on the Michna Palace, *see chapter* **Prague by Area: Malá Strana.**

Toy Museum

(Muzeum hraček), Jiřská 4, Prague 1 (33 37 22 94/33 37 22 95). Metro Malostranská. **Open** 9.30am-5.30pm Tue-Sun. **Admission** 40kč adults; 15kč children, students, OAPs.
Part of Czech émigré Ivan Steiger's large toy collection, the museum relies heavily on the reputation of its German counterpart to draw the punters in. A random collection of toys ranging from Barbie to Victorian dolls, teddy bears and train sets, are grouped together in lifeless glass cabinets with no description or explanation. Good for a rainy day, perhaps, but don't get too excited.

Arts & Entertainment

Literary Prague	**174**	Music: Classical & Opera	**192**
Media	**176**	Music: Rock, Folk & Jazz	**197**
Nightlife	**180**	Sport & Fitness	**202**
Film	**187**	Theatre & Dance	**207**

Literary Prague

A run-down on Prague's literary scene, past and present.

For people who speak a language that was formalised less than 200 years ago, the Czechs have produced a remarkable volume of world class literature. After the Thirty Years War and the devastation of Bohemia, German had replaced Czech as the language of the educated classes and it wasn't until the rise of Czech nationalism in the nineteenth century, that formal written language guidelines were set and a linguistic revival saw the beginnings of modern Czech literature.

One of the first people writing this century to significantly abuse these guidelines was **Jaroslav Hašek**, author of and prototype for *The Good Soldier Švejk*. Hašek, an alcoholic amateur dog breeder, womanised his way through the Austro-Hungarian empire and ended up serving during the Great War. His alter ego, Švejk, enjoys a series of wartime misadventures, including a dog-breeding fraud, sleeping with his superior's mistress, and triumphing over the forces of evil (elitism) through sheer cheerfulness and (seeming) deference to authority. Hašek wasn't so lucky: the ultimate Bohemian eventually drank himself to death in 1923.

A more 'respectable' writer, who emerged during the interwar period, was **Karel Čapek**, a talented journalist, novelist and playwright, and close friend of President Masaryk. Čapek is considered by most Czechs to be the leading literary figure of the ill-fated First Republic. He is best known for giving international currency to the Czech word 'robot', from his play *R.U.R.* ('Rossum's Universal Robots'), which when it was published in 1921 was translated into a dozen languages and was performed on stages all over the world.

While Hašek boozed his way around Europe and Čapek wrote political speeches, **Franz Kafka** lived a more anonymous life in the Bohemian capital. Kafka, who found Prague considerably less charming than most visitors will do today, was a member of Prague's large and vibrant German-speaking Jewish community. In novels like *The Trial* and *The Castle*, he defined alienation and depression for later generations of black turtle-neck-wearing literary types, and the theme of the individual inexplicably caught up in a nightmareish situation beyond his control – that recurs throughout his works – took on significant meaning during the Stalinist years, during which Kafka's works were banned. Today, as consumerism sweeps the city, his face and name are

*Goatee night at **Beefstew**. See page 175.*

emblazoned on countless T-shirts and coffee mugs for sale in the centre of town.

Kafka's circle of German-Jewish writers also included **Franz Werfel** and Kafka's friend and benefactor **Max Brod**, who wrote fine books himself but will mainly be remembered as the man who brought Kafka's writing to the attention of the world. Kafka died in 1924, and the Final Solution effectively destroyed his community two decades later; nearly all of Prague's Jewish community ended their days in Auschwitz or Terezín. Among the chroniclers of this period, who wrote about their experiences during the Occupation, were **Arnošt Lustig** and **Jiří Weil**.

When Communism came to Czechoslovakia in 1948, Czechs didn't stop writing, but were suddenly held more accountable for their projects. Many challenged the Party and were banished to *samizdat* existence, rotten day jobs or exile. Sexuality, the only unregulated form of social expression, became a central theme in many Czech novels during this period.

This applies to the works of **Milan Kundera**. The most widely-read Czech author outside his native land, though by no means as popular with his compatriots, Kundera was closely involved with the Czech New Wave film-makers (*see chapter* **Film**) and originally taught at FAMU film school. *The Unbearable Lightness of Being* is perhaps his best-known work. His portrayals of the crueller sides of love are hard to take, but whether or not you agree with the sexual commentary, his earlier novels like *The Joke* and *The Book of Laughter and Forgetting* succeed in depicting the absurdity and bureaucracy of Stalinism.

Václav Havel, the playwright president, doesn't

have the free time to write that he did when he was in prison during his dissident days. But there's still plenty of Havel to dig into, beginning with his 1963 absurdist play, *The Garden Party*, and leading up to *Letters to Olga* (1988), written to his wife while he was in prison in the 1970s. For an insight into Havel the man, however, try reading *Disturbing the Peace* (1990), in which he talks about his privileged childhood as well as events leading up to the 1968 invasion.

Bohumil Hrabal, who recently celebrated his 80th birthday in his favourite pub, The Golden Tiger, was another New Wave figure and is adored by the Czechs. In his tragicomic and idiosyncratic masterpieces *Closely Observed Trains* and *I Served the King of England*, Hrabal lovingly captures the smaller details of life and transforms them into the only things that really matter.

Ivan Klíma is famous for his bittersweet novels, among them *My First Loves* (1986) and *Love and Garbage* (1990), in which he explores that favourite Czech pastime, the love affair. To Klíma's protagonists, love is the one thing beyond the control of the Party. Unfortunately, it's usually also beyond the control of his protagonists.

The works of the dissident publisher Josef Škvorecký, the first of which appeared in the 1950s, and which include *The Swell Season, Talkin' Moscow Blues* and *The Miracle Game*, are among the most popular among Czechs, and were largely banned during the Communist years; also worth investigating are the works of scientist-poet **Miroslav Holub** (*The Vanishing Lung Syndrome* and *The Dimension of the Present Moment*).

Many western critics have expressed their disappointment with the work of their former dissident darlings since 1989, complaining that these new works are less valid than those written under the Communist regime, that Czechs are no longer engaged in major political or moral struggles and are therefore lacking in inspiration. This may be a hasty judgement. Czech writers have moved beyond the Velvet Revolution, but critics seem reluctant to follow. However, Ivan Klíma, writing recently in *Granta* has added his voice to the debate, arguing that the triumph of the market-place has been culture's loss, as the public embraces the most banal forms of consumerism (which, where literature is concerned, includes a lot of foreign trash) with open arms.

There is a new generation of Czech writers who have established a local following but have yet to make an international impact. **Jachym Topol** is one of the few of the new breed whose work has been translated into other languages. He is beginning to earn a reputation as a fine poet, and his work has also been set to music by his brother's legendary rock band, the now defunct *Psi vojaci* (Dog Soldiers).

Eva Hauserova and **Carola Biedermann** are both well-known in the Czech Republic for their mainstream sci-fi writing. However they have recently caused a stir with a selection of harrowing short stories and essays, in which they express their dissatisfaction with their lot in the traditional and feminist-fearing Czech Republic.

A major American publishing house recently published **Eva Pekarkova**'s *Truck Stop Rainbows*, a politically incorrect tale of roadside prostitution on the E50 highway between Plzeň and the German border. Since the mid-1980s Pekarkova has been driving a cab in New York. Another member of the new breed, **Michael Ajvaz**, writes magical stories and poetry which take the reader on surreal tours of Prague, where sharks leap out from belfries and characters from nightmares materialise in local coffee houses.

Lukas Tomin writes experimental novels that are almost poetry-like. Tomin, who grew up abroad and speaks several languages, takes up where Kafka and his cronies left off, choosing to write in German. English translations of *The Doll* and *Ashtrays* are available in bookshops around Prague, published by the Twisted Spoon Press.

Apart from selected works by Topol and Pekarkova, none of this new generation of writers has been published in the west yet. Your best bet for finding translations of their work is to look in one of the many English-language literary magazines, which have flourished recently and which feature both Czech writers in translation and works by native English-speakers. *Yazzyk* features some of the better-known unknowns along with striking graphics and photographs from Czech artists. The bilingual *one eye open* concentrates on feminist issues, and *Trafika*, a stylish literary quarterly, has a wide range of contributors, including some big names. *See chapter* **Media** for more on the Czech and English-language press in Prague.

Receiving a disturbing amount of attention from the American media circus, Prague's ex-patriate writers spend their time attending poetry readings, shielding their eyes from the glare of camera crews, and occasionally writing some interesting fiction. Though the scene can sometimes seem like a giant in-joke, it's worth paying a visit to the weekly poetry reading, Beefstew, where the crowd is young and amazingly tolerant, and dutifully applauds the series of songs and extracts from novels-in-progress sometimes read straight from the lap-top. For a selected reading list, *see page 263*.

Beefstew
Radost, Bělehradská 120, Prague 2 (25 12 10). Metro I.P. Pavlova. **Open** 9pm-5am daily.
The open mike poetry night is on Sundays at 8pm. *See also chapter* **Nightlife**.

Globe Bookstore
Janovského 14, Prague 7 (357 91 61). Metro Vltavská/1, 5, 8, 12, 25, 26 tram. **Open** 10am-midnight daily.
The American-run bookshop and café hosts occasional readings, book launches and other literary events. Check the shop's noticeboard for more details.

Media

After freedom of the press came the burgeoning tabloid industry, a rash of English-language publications and a battle for TV supremacy.

A rich diversity of interests and intellectual opinion is evident in Prague's numerous newspapers, many of which were formerly opposition papers to the Communist government. From the esteemed columns of *Lidové noviny* to the titillating pages of *NEI* (*National Erotic Initiative*) *Report*, published by the brother of famous smut-art photographer Jan Saudek, Czechs regard freedom of the press as sacred. Tabloid journalism has made an easy entry into this tolerant market; foreign-owned *Blesk*, featuring photos of topless women and suicides, became the capital's top-selling daily within a few months of its first issue.

A more worrying threat to the mainstream press may not be competition from the tabloids but diktats from their new owners. Foreign news chains have entered the market like cherrypickers on a summer outing, harvesting the newspapers with the greatest readership and assimilating them: the Czech Republic – unlike many west European countries – doesn't limit foreign ownership of the media. Ringier of Switzerland, which published *Blesk* as its first Czech venture, now owns the investigative weekly *Respekt* and the former dissident newspaper *Lidové noviny*, causing purists to worry that the *Blesk* style will be applied to both serious papers. Fidelis Schlée, a multimillionaire publishing magnate who once boasted of being the last Czech publisher, recently made a deal with Ringier to shut down his 49 year-old competitor paper, in exchange for the right to produce a TV guide for the Ringier chain.

Newspapers

Blesk
This sensationalist daily, full of crime and celebrities, is the number-one selling newspaper in Prague. Always controversial, the paper has sparked debates about the propriety of paying taxi drivers to tip off reporters, as well as about the sensitivity of publishing a frame-by-frame photo record of a suicide's jump off a bridge. The acquisitive tactics of the paper's Swiss owners are almost as controversial as the paper itself.

Český deník, Denní Telegraf
Both are well-read, conservative dailies.

Dobrý večerník
Formed by disenchanted employees of Fidelis Schlée's *Večerník Praha* during a massive defection, *Dobrý večer*

('Good Evening') had to augment its name a bit when the embittered Schlée had it copyrighted first.

Expres
This daily tabloid takes a modified *Blesk* approach to the news; its circulation is rapidly increasing.

Hospodářské noviny
The city's most respected source of business information is published daily, and includes the most widely-followed index (HN/Wood) to the Prague stock exchange.

Katolický týdeník
The weekly Catholic newspaper boasts a circulation of 70,000 despite opinion polls showing that four out of five Czechs consider themselves atheists or agnostics.

Lidové noviny
This intellectual daily, formerly a dissident paper, features influential front-page editorials. It's now owned by the Ringier chain.

Mladá fronta Dnes
The former youth newspaper is now the voice of conservatism

and boasts the highest circulation in the country after *Blesk*. It gives well-balanced coverage of both local, regional and international news.

Práce

The Czech Trade Union daily presents strongly slanted coverage of local and regional affairs.

Respekt

The pony-tailed editor of this probing weekly has been called a 'Thatcher hippie', a term that highlights the country's strange role reversal in which 'conservative' means 'pro-socialist', while 'radical' (and 'youth' and 'counterculture') means 'pro-capitalism'. Its gung-ho reporting in essay style seeks to expose corruption at all levels, but especially among former members of the Communist Party.

Rudé pravo

'Red Truth' is the former official newspaper of the Communist Party. After the revolution it quickly re-organised itself into a respectable, left-leaning daily that now has the third largest readership after *Blesk* and *Mladá fronta Dnes*. Some virulent anti-communists publish a weekly with the satirical title *Rudé kravo* ('Red Cow').

Sport

The daily sports sheet covers all the sports news from abroad as well as the triumphs and failures of Prague's beloved Sparta football team.

Svobodné Slovo

A left-of-centre daily.

Večerník Praha

A 'lite' evening paper, featuring mostly upbeat news articles and pieces of trivia. It's owned by successful Czech entrepreneur Fidelis Schlée.

ZN noviny

The wide circulation of this agricultural daily proves that there is still power in the countryside.

Magazines

Babylon

Music, celebrity interviews and soft sex sell this student publication.

Ekonom

The weekly business magazine contains strong business and economic features as well as a one-page language guide for businessmen learning English.

Mladý svět

World news and investigative reporting of local affairs and culture. Great pictures.

Reflex

A popular weekly magazine with investigative claims, it has a soft spot for 'investigating' things like houses of prostitution with tantalisingly blurred photographs.

Týdeník Květy

A popular illustrated weekly full of crossword puzzles, short stories and pictures of the (British) royal family.

Vlasta

This extremely popular women's magazine is devoted to traditional home arts such as knitting, cooking and gardening.

100&1 Zahraniční zajímavost

This monthly digest of foreign magazine articles was once the only source of world news at a time when other media were tightly censored. It still has a dedicated readership.

Foreign Papers & Magazines

Central European Business Weekly

A British-owned financial pink sheet that strives to cover the entire region through correspondents spread out from Warsaw to southern Bulgaria. It runs pared-down charts of the region's nascent stock markets as well as occasional arts and general interest features. A weekly column chronicles the (drunken) escapades of a permanently anonymous staff reporter.

La Tribune de Prague

This super-slick, bi-monthly and bi-lingual magazine (in English and in French) is aimed at an elusive reader: the French businessman who wants to invest in the Czech Republic. Articles on the economy, industrial sectors and legislation get spiced up with items on where to mingle with the hoi polloi in Prague and how to rent a castle for your next board meeting (typically French concerns). At 250kč a pop, it's not the most widely-read source of business information.

The Prague Post

Former *Prognosis* staffers started up this English-language weekly, which quickly rose to surpass the other in terms of circulation (now around 13,000). It usually follows the Czech press in the news, but occasionally breaks new ground, particularly in its relentless coverage of the country's infamous arms industry. Several pages of business news are complemented by complete stock exchange listings and a weekly ranking of companies in various industries. The pull-out 'Night & Day' section features entertainment listings, restaurant reviews and a column by white-haired editor-in-chief Alan Levy, who takes the blame for formulating the 'Prague is the Paris-in-the-twenties of the nineties' cliché.

Prognosis Weekly

The first English-language newspaper to emerge following the Velvet Revolution is a real writers' paper, with longer, magazine-style features on everything from Bosnian war refugees to an editor's touching encounter with a Czech housewife posing as an actress in a local club. *Prognosis* also offers comprehensive arts and entertainment listings and a visitors' guide with a different thematic walking tour each week. A recent injection of capital by a Swiss investor has allowed the paper to be published weekly, instead of every other week, so that it now competes head to head with *The Prague Post* for readership. In the transition to a weekly, *Prognosis* also dispensed with some of the student-style features that occasionally gave it the feel of a college newspaper and began running housing classifieds in conjunction with the Czech classifieds paper *Annonce*.

Listings Magazines

Annonce

This thrice-weekly classifieds paper is the most eagerly sought-after source of affordable housing in Prague, although to make any use of it it's necessary to get the paper the moment it begins being distributed (around 5.30am) with a bleary-eyed Czech in tow to help translate and make phone calls. Nothing but incredibly expensive flats with rents payable in Deutschmarks is left by 10am. It comes out on Mondays, Wednesdays and Fridays.

Přehled

A comprehensive, monthly culture listings with sections on clubs, concerts, cinema, galleries, formal dances and children's events. No advertising.

Program

This weekly culture guide also contains a TV schedule and a three-page, English language section featuring condensed entertainment listings and often bizarre commentary by resident foreigners.

Satelit

A satellite and cable TV weekly which contains listings as well as celebrity interviews.

Televize Týdenik

This weekly TV and radio listings guide also contains English, Spanish and German 'TV' language lessons.

Cultural Papers & Magazines

Czech

Analagon

Perhaps the only surrealist publication in the world to receive state funding, Analagon features erudite, often jargon-filled, essays on strange topics such as 'The Language Traditions of Hermeticism', automatic writing and spiritualism. Published quarterly in both Czech and French, the international language of surrealism.

Labyrint Revue

A monthly magazine that features reviews of films, music, gallery shows and literature; it also contains an exhaustive list of books newly published in Czech.

Literarni noviny

This weekly newspaper tends to haunt the paper racks of cafés where chain-smoking is the main activity. It has essays, interviews and short poems, as well as novel excerpts.

Revolver Revue

The most respected of the Czech literary publications, this thick quarterly presents new works by the country's most well-known authors in addition to lesser-known works by pet favourites such as Kafka.

Vokno

The magazine for the new generation of cyberpunk hippies; *Vokno* is dedicated to alternative culture, music and social issues.

English

Publishing has become a second career for many foreigners living in Prague, to judge from the number of English-language publications that have surfaced recently. Some of these lend credence to the myth of a flourishing foreign artist's colony here; others are obviously just an alternative to spending Prague's long and dreary winter in the pub for their writers.

gristle floss

Prague's first English-language 'zine is a xeroxed collection of cartoons, collages, poetry and coupons. It's published monthly, subject to the editors' possible relocation to another global youth hotspot.

one eye open

This bilingual and infrequently published magazine is devoted to writings about women and feminism, though contributors are not exclusively female. While foreigners tend to criticise Czech women for their lack of interest in feminist issues, American editor Debbie DuBois has gathered essays and stories from local women that prove the contrary.

Trafika

This international literary quarterly could be published anywhere, though it is, in fact, published by one of the owners

Radio Metropolis. *See page 179.*

of the Globe Bookstore in an office adjoining that favourite ex-patriate hangout. Contributors have included Joyce Carol Oates, Don DeLillo and Czech writer Miroslav Holub.

Yazzyk

The first English-language literary magazine published after the revolution seems to have lost some momentum and now appears only infrequently. When it does, it presents stories in translation from a variety of Central European contributors according to the issue's theme ('Magic, Mystery and Madness' for example).

Television

The spring of 1994 saw the launch of Nova, the post-communist world's first private, national TV station. Viewers were treated to a live broadcast from Nova's black-tie VIP celebration, complete with dancing girls and fireworks, at the National Museum. They were also treated to a bombardment of well-produced commercials the like of which had never been seen on the two state-owned channels, where advertising is limited to just two per cent of broadcast time and is shown in block segments once or twice a day.

Owned by a foreign investor group which includes the former US ambassador to Hungary, Nova is providing some serious competition to underfunded and overstaffed Czech Television, which operates channels ČT1 and ČT2. The competition between the two companies has reached epic proportions, with Czech Television substituting ingenuity for what it lacks in financial resources. The night of Nova's premiere, Czech Television, audience-savvy for the first time in its history, broadcast *The Godfather Part II*, having shown Part I the previous Friday night. When Nova acquired the rights to broadcast live football matches of every first and second-league team in the Czech Republic, ČT camera crews perched on buildings outside the stadium with telefoto lenses in order to replay 45-minute long 'highlights' of the games later in the evening – a move that spurred Nova to pursue legal action. Then Nova announced a new show called *Gumaci* (or 'The Rubberheads'), a political satire using life-size rubber puppets, at which point Czech Television accused Nova of 'stealing' the idea and pre-empting their own show (although at the time the state company didn't have a single puppet to its name).

ČT1

Owned by government-run Česka Televize, this station has dismal offerings (nature shows and live classical broadcasts) augmented by feature films occasionally shown in English with Czech subtitles.

ČT2

The same as ČT1, although there's some talk about privatising this station in the same manner as the former ČT3 (now Nova). BBC news is presented every weekday morning at 7.25am.

Nova

Morning chat shows, western feature films, live football and a sophisticated newscast are some of the offerings from the nation's only private, nationally-broadcast TV station. A popular show is 'Vox Populi', an edited series of clips taken from video booths in Prague and Brno; people hop in and say whatever is on their mind.

Premiéra

An Italian-owned private station that broadcasts only in Prague, it hasn't delivered on its original promise of innovative and locally-produced programming. Dubbed Italian serials fill up the time between long broadcasts of America's NBC Superchannel news.

Kabel Plus

A cable station that offers occasionally-interesting programming, it has announced plans to launch a children's-only channel soon.

Radio

The radio, by contrast to television, has seen over a dozen private stations spring up to compete with publicly-owned Praha and Radiožurnal. Foreigners compare listening to Czech radio to visiting a graveyard of the west's greatest hits. In fact, the number of indistinguishable, classic rock formatted stations in Prague has led some to predict a consolidation of the industry in the near future.

BBC (101.0 FM)
The World Service

Country Radio (89.5 FM)
A truly bizarre phenomenon is the Czech passion for, and identification with, the American Old West, made manifest in the popularity of 'country balls' and the recent construction of a Wild West village in the Moravian capital of Brno. Country Radio, featuring a full range of bluegrass, folk and country & western, is Prague's number one private station with an estimated 12.4% of the listening market.

Evropa 2 (89.5 FM)
Music ranging from sixties' classics to contemporary hits.

Praha (639 KHz AM; 100.7/92.6 FM)
One of two public, national stations owned by Czech Radio (Česke rozhlas), it has the largest listening audience in the country, with about 2.6 million tuning in daily to its general interest and current affairs programs. Part of its popularlity is due to the fact that under Communism, every new, government-built flat came equipped with a cheap radio that played this as its only station. President Havel gives a live address every Sunday evening.

Radio BONTON (99.7 FM)
Owned by the BONTON musical conglomerate, which also has its own record label and music shops, this station plays more original Czech pop than others with the same light rock formula. Not surprisingly, its own artists are represented heavily.

Radio Golem (90.3 FM)
The station where you're most likely to pick up something from the era between the thirties and the fifties, Golem also broadcasts talk shows, sitcoms, and religious programmes. Owned by Evropa 2.

Radio Kiss (98.0 FM)
Owned by Irish media mogul Dennis O'Brian, Kiss is one of the most interesting – and visible – stations in town, not least on account of the 'Kiss Patrol', a fleet of black jeeps painted with the radio's logo and driven around in formation by young, good-looking (and often female) drivers. The station plays formulaic, classic pop hits. Though it's a market leader, some Czechs dislike it because the broadcast is so heavily-scripted it reminds them of Communist days.

Radio Metropolis (106.2 FM)
All-English news, community service announcements, traffic reports, talk shows and DJs who love the sound of their own voices, conspire to edge out the station's designated format of adult-oriented rock. The Voice of America broadcasts overnight.

Radio 1 (91.9 FM)
This indie music station, which formerly broadcast from a room adjoining the Bunkr night club, has a cult following in Prague. The eclectic selection ranges from grind-core to sacred music, and the English-language weekly *Prognosis* hosts its own music show at 11.25am on weekdays.

Radiožurnal (94.6 FM)
Strong news-oriented station similar to Praha, the only other national station.

RFE (Radio Free Europe, 1287 KHz AM)
US-funded news, commentary and community service announcements are broadcast from the station's new European headquarters in Prague's former parliament building.

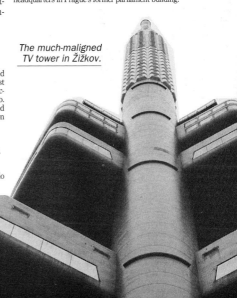

The much-maligned TV tower in Žižkov.

Nightlife

Where to find the all-night revellers in a city where most people are tucked up in bed by 11pm.

*Saturday night fever at the mother of Prague discos, **Music Park**. See page 185.*

It's not every night that President Havel goes clubbing with Lou Reed and finds a local Czech band singing Velvet Underground songs, and then for the rock poet to join them on stage. Or for a senior government minister to give an impromptu Jerry Lee Lewis impression on the piano. But after the 1989 revolution, Prague's night scene changed completely. Underground rock and jazz clubs blasted into the open and an Anglo-American invasion of Generation Xers brought soul, house, techno, reggae and dance music to the city. Historic buildings became nightclubs and went wild for months, until the neighbours complained or the momentum moved on.

The crazy days are over and today too many half-empty clubs vie for too few restless revellers, while DJs, with one eye on the tourist market, play the same safe chart hits and techno beats every night. You'll be lucky, for example, to hear some acid jazz or get to do the Lambada. But it's always worth checking the English-language papers, the *Prague Post* and *Prognosis* for new listings, since

the club scene, like much else in Prague, is in a constant state of flux. *See chapter* **Music: Rock, Roots & Jazz** for details of where to find the best live gigs.

Only the most popular or the most desperate clubs will deny you a look before paying (say *můžu se podívat?* – may I have a look?) and although bouncers may occasionally object to track suits, trainers or ripped jeans, they don't discriminate against people with no dress sense at all. Clubs are cheap, too, with entry ranging from free to around 50kč, depending on whether there's a live band playing.

Clubs usually close around 5am and if you can stomach it, you could join other drunken, starving nightclubbers afterwards in the grimy, twilighted world of the non-stop restaurant. Although these can be excellent, the staff may occasionally be asleep and in the more hostile places you might get into a tug of war over a cooked chicken that you grabbed after the owner snatched your money.

If things come to blows, there are a number of

all night chemists listed below, where you can get bandages or some aspirin for that hangover. Ring a bell to wake up the staff and gesticulate your needs through the little window.

Clubs

Malá Strana

Borat

Újezd 18, Prague 1 (53 83 62). Tram 6, 9, 22, 42. **Open** 2pm-5am daily.

This grimy, graffiti-covered three storey squat with sweaty walls, is one of the friendliest venues in town. A pre-revolution underground rock club, Borat has kept its generous optimism and does so even when the most atrocious rock band is playing. You can easily engage Borat's creative, doped and drunken clientele in meaningful conversation in the dimly glowing top-floor room, which is plastered with rock posters and is from where very cheap drink is dispensed.

Café Rubín

Malostranské náměstí 9, Prague 1 (no phone). Metro Malostranská/12, 22 tram.

One of several theatre café/nightclubs, set in a vaulted Gothic cellar and frequented by street musicians and amateur actors full of goodwill to all struggling performers. The theatre behind the curtain hosts many excellent local and touring English-language productions. The music and the very cheap bar keep going till the early hours.

Malostranská Beseda

Malostranské náměstí 21, Prague 1 (53 90 24). Metro Malostranská/12, 22 tram. **Open** 7pm-1am daily.

A spacious two-room jazz café that looks as if someone has opened up their grand living room and rushed in some wooden tables and chairs for the guests. The jazz, blues and rock are almost always excellent, but the poor acoustics make the listening better from the street. *See also chapter* **Music: Rock, Roots & Jazz.**

Staré Město & Josefov

Bílý koníček

(The White Horse), Staroměstské náměstí 20, Prague 1 (no phone). Metro Staroměstská or Náměstí Republiky. **Open** 5pm-4am daily.

This former hangout of the Communist youth has repackaged itself with a vengeance, and now urges customers to experience its twelfth century cellar disco. What you'll really experience, down the very steep and narrow steps, is a nerd-filled interior lit by coloured disco lights where standard, but sometimes great, hits are played. However, if you're out on the pull it's as good a place as any, and there are plenty of tourists with similar romantic ambitions, though you may find the choice limited to excitable Swedish teenagers.

Classic Club

Pařížská 4, Prague 1 (no phone). Metro Staroměstská. **Open** 8pm-5am daily.

The entrance hall of this theatre bar is decorated with luminous art; the theatre itself hosts a black light show and occasional jazz performances. A disco in the school-like assembly hall usually follows performances but it's not the main attraction and most of the young live minds stay in the bar.

Lávka

(The Little Bridge), Novotného lávka 1, Prague 1 (24 21 47 97). Metro Staroměstská. **Open** 10am-5am daily.

In the warm evenings under a starlit sky and a mesmerising postcard view of Charles Bridge, Lávka's riverside disco garden complex is the smart place to be. Older Czechs and foreign residents mix with eager young tourists in search of that perfect romantic moment. You can boogie on the terrace to an unchanging formula of old popular hits or jostle on the desperately awkward dancefloor in the basement. The narrow non-stop bar stays open after the club closes.

Legenda

Křížovnická 12, Prague 1 (232 20 40). Metro Staroměstská/15, 17, 54 tram. **Open** 8pm-5am daily.

Another rock club full of empty promise and empty menace, with guns, baseball bats, motorbikes, skulls and rock videos decorating the walls. Despite the death metal screams, the lack of dedicated rockers means that cheerful backpackers have to fill in and try to look as deranged as they can until the rock 'n' roll comes on. Loners in denim and leather with their foreheads sunk on the bar give the club a 1950s American alienated youth feel, but they're not half as confused as the DJ downstairs when he's looking at all the funny buttons he's meant to press to get the music going.

Nové Město

AghaRTA Jazz Centrum

Krakovská 5, Prague 1 (24 21 29 14). Metro Muzeum/4, 6, 16, 22 tram. **Open** 4pm-1am Mon-Fri; 7pm-1am Sat, Sun.

This is a cozy little jazz club and music shop which attracts some old hands and plenty of impressive raw young talent. Although popular with tourists, this is still a place for jazz enthusiasts. Just be careful what you say to the person sitting next to you; she may look like a bag lady but she could be the star billing of the evening. *See also chapter* **Music: Rock, Roots & Jazz.**

Jostling for space at **Lávka.**

Discos on Wenceslas Square

If you're happy to run the seedy gauntlet of Wenceslas Square, below we've listed the best and the worst you can expect (metro Muzeum or Můstek/3, 9, 14, 17, 24 tram).

Alfa
Number 28. **Open** 10pm-late daily.
Techno hell or heaven depending on your point of view, in a steamy race track layout.

Astra
Number 2. **Open** 10.30pm-4am daily.
The balcony looks good from the outside but the club is filled with Euro schoolkids at their first disco abroad, plus a handful of hostesses.

Hotel Zlatá husa
Number 7. **Open** 8pm-2.30am daily.
Full of tourists, businessmen, gangs of their girlie groupies,

pricey drinks and, unbelievably, one of the best DJs in Prague playing great reggae, plus classic 1970s soul and rock.

Jizera
Number 48. **Open** 11pm-5am daily.
The intimidating hangout of over-eager gypsy gals. Good food, though.

Quality Club
Number 21. **Open** 9pm-4am daily.
There's an attractive sixth floor view of Wenceslas Square from the Quality, which is full of young tourists dancing to MTV hits. Maybe a place to find your one-night stand.

Rokoko Club
Number 38. **Open** 9.30pm-5am daily.
Mainly full of students and squares who look as if they've arrived at the wrong place but can't be bothered to move on.

Barclub
Hybernská 10, Prague 1 (no phone). Metro Náměstí Republiky/5, 14, 26 tram. **Open** 9pm-5am daily.
The best, well the only, reggae club in town is a magnet for Prague's African community. Set in a dim, plush but run-down room, it is appropriately laid-back, with excellent reggae and soul and plenty of things to smoke.

Beastiarium
Karlovo náměstí 31, Prague 2 (no phone). Metro Karlovo náměstí/4, 6, 16, 22 tram. **Open** 11.30am-4am daily.
Usually filled with an unpretentious and unadventurous Czech crowd who enjoy the contrived horror décor of beastly masks and ghouls, the Beastiarium is particularly popular with office parties. Dancing can be fun if the music is right: don't expect too much and you may have a good time. At the time of writing the club was about to change hands, so things may change.

Bunkr
Lodecká 2, Prague 1 (231 45 35). Metro Náměstí Republiky or Můstek. **Open** 8pm-6am daily.
A steel and concrete bunker which was Prague's first post-revolution rock club and which the neighbours have been trying to close down ever since. It sometimes looks as though the nuclear explosion has already happened and you've walked into a post holocaust *Blade Runner* world, with vast numbers of devastated zombies sweating and swaying to rock, house, and rock 'n' roll, or clinging for dear life to the very long bar. *See also chapter* **Music: Rock, Roots & Jazz**.

Kamyk
Moored by Švermův Bridge, Prague 1 (no phone). Metro Náměstí Republiky. **Open** *summer* 10pm-4am daily.
From a distance Kamyk looks like a refugee boat with hundreds of stragglers huddled on the decks, but close up, the mostly young, trendy Czech crowd seems happy and boisterous. There are two bars below deck and one on deck serving warm beer. Most importantly, the boat is moored, which makes for the best sort of boat party since you can leave whenever you want.

Reduta
Národní 20, Prague 1 (24 91 22 46). Metro Národní třída. **Open** 9pm-2am Mon-Sat.

Every club has its moment of glory and Reduta trumped all the competition when Bill Clinton dropped by with his sax and a few hundred friends from the CIA) for a jamming session before negotiating Europe's new security arrangements. Reduta has been dining off the occasion ever since, but it still attracts big local names who get whoops and whistles from the crowd. It's a plush, intimate and typically dim lit venue, and during the break you can hobnob with the stars in the bar. *See also chapter* **Music: Rock, Roots & Jazz**.

Rock Cafe
Národní 20, Prague 1 (249 44 14). Metro Národní třída. **Open** 8pm-3am daily.
The live bands here are often excellent (*see chapter* **Music: Rock, Roots & Jazz**) but the venue is usually full of foreign school parties. However the Rock Café is worth a visit for the trendy late-night café downstairs and the clothes shop next to the dance floor, though you'd be better off slipping into the Reduta jazz club next door (*above*) or the Riviéra club upstairs (*see chapter* **Gay Prague**).

Roxy
Dlouhá 33, Prague 1 (no phone). Metro Náměstí Republiky/5, 14, 17, 26 tram. **Open** 9pm-4am Thur-Sat.
This cool, concrete underground amphitheatre is an art-house club that experiments with films, exhibitions and music. Full of Japanese lanterns, Persian rugs, a multitude of levels and ledges and an eerie excitement even if only the bar area is full, it also has a tearoom with floor cushions that's open till midnight. A venue that seems set to take off.

Studio Gag
Národní 25, Prague 1 (no phone). Metro Národní třída or Můstek/6, 9, 18, 22, 51, 57, 58 tram. **Open** 5pm-midnight daily.
This red-hot psychedelic club, decorated with Anglophile props – British bobby dummies, Sgt Pepper posters and a red telephone box – used to be more of a bar and club, but has recently reverted to its original purpose as a theatre and venue for top jazz and blues performers. It's popular with Czech students who are prone to spontaneous fits of dancing. The multi-coloured piano regularly gets commandeered by 'life and soul of the party' types.

Shake a leg at **Radost**. *See page 186.*

Uzi

Legerova 44, Prague 2 (24 91 32 01). Metro I.P.
Pavlova/4, 11, 16, 22, 31, 32 tram. **Open** 7pm-3am
daily.
The outsized Uzi machine gun hanging over the entrance
says it all. There are bikers without bikes, skinheads dancing to Bryan Adams, Confederate flags, frustrated fantasies,
a tattoo studio upstairs (open from 2pm to 8pm), but some
of the decent law-abiding citizens who come here are worth
meeting.

Further Afield

African Safari Club

Zborovská 54, Prague 5 (no phone). Metro Anděl/6, 9, 22
tram. **Open** 7pm-5am daily.
A completely inauthentic African experience, with zebra-
and leopard-skin décor and out of date music. It's popular with Czech couples fantasising about going on safari.
Go for the food and to get away from other tourists and
foreigners.

Alterna Komotovka

Seifertova 3, Prague 3 (no phone). Metro Flora/5, 9, 26
tram. **Open** 3pm-5am daily.
An easy-going rock club and disco in a narrow cavern with
poor acoustics. It fills up with ponytail types when a band
is playing but is hopelessly empty on disco-only nights. *See*
also chapter **Music: Rock, Roots & Jazz**.

Jam

Štefánikova 44, Prague 5 (no phone). Metro Anděl/6, 9,
12, 59 tram. **Open** 10pm-4am daily.
The best new club in Prague, located in a dimly glowing cellar, serves up a mix of acid jazz and funky soul, excellent
food and cheap drinks. British DJs playing their own trea-
sured record collections are interrupted by impromptu jamming sessions and live performances by local heroes. Sadly,
the club is often empty.

Jorco

Budějovická 17, Prague 4 (42 41 81). Metro Budějovická.
Open 3pm-6am daily.
For some incognito exploration of a shiny suburban disco,
get here before 9.30pm – it'll be packed by 10pm. Don't lose
your drinks card or you'll have to pay through the nose when
you want to leave. Get a cheap drink from the little bar and
check out the dance floor, the jealously-guarded pool tables
and the video games. The lack of English spoken here will
only be part of your communication problems. If it's all a little too much, there will still be time to head back into town
and go elsewhere.

Labyrint

Štefánikova 57, Prague 5 (24 51 17 37). Metro Anděl/6,
9, 12. **Open** 6pm-late Mon-Sat.
A similar set up to Café Rubin (*see p181*), set in a huge barn-
like building. The club is sometimes a rock and jazz venue,
sometimes a theatre and sometimes both, full of unpretentious and easy-going people. Look out for the innovative
'Inside Out' productions during the summer. *See also chap-*
ter **Theatre & Dance**.

Music Park

Francouzská 4, Prague 2 (691 17 68). Metro Náměstí
Míru/16, 22 tram. **Open** 9.30pm-7am Tue-Sun.
Love it or hate it, you can't deny that the mother of all Prague
discos is where to get some Saturday Night Fever. The illu-
minated dance floor, space-age lighting system, red pillars
and mirrors, half a dozen bars and restaurant are all designed
in Costa del Sol style to create the greatest happiness for the
greatest number. 'Megastar' DJs whip up crowds of sweet
suburban 16 year-olds, Balkan mafioso types and west
European entrepreneurs into an excitable handclapping frenzy, all to the poundings of safe Euro chart hits. On Thursdays
it's Ladies' Night and the former lighting operator Abdul
croons along karaoke-style, but if you hit the Park on 'theme'
nights (perhaps Cowboy or Caribbean night) the confetti flies,
the alcohol flows and entertainers hop and juggle their way
through a hilarious routine. Get pissed and party!

Mr Pizza
Revoluční 16, Prague 1. Metro Náměstí Republiky. **Open** 24 hours daily.
Near Barclub and Kamyk, this is the best non-stop, serving good pizzas and a standard menu of Czech dishes. Despite well-meaning prints of Kandinsky and Klee, the décor is just too bright for the early hours.

Rebecca
Olšanské náměstí 8, Prague 3. Metro Flora/26, 58 tram. **Open** 24 hours daily.
This non-stop in Žižkov has a popular following amongst clubbers, who make the trek from miles around to sit in the narrow, hideously purple setting and eat reasonably stale food.

Snack Bar Agnes
Hybernská 1, Prague 1. Metro Náměstí Republiky. **Open** 9am-6am daily.
Opposite Barclub, this small, clean two-floor restaurant is always crowded and serves decent, though occasionally stale, food day and night. Service is polite, no matter what time of night it is.

Non-stop Shops

If all you want to do is stock up on some provisions to see you through until morning, these non-stop grocery stores should do the trick. Be wary of following street placards directing you to a non-stop. You can march for miles on an empty stomach and find that the address advertised is all boarded up.

Radost
Bělehradská 120, Prague 2 (25 12 10). Metro I.P. Pavlova. **Open** 9pm-5am daily.
Below the **FX Café** (*see chapter* **Cafés, Bars & Pubs**), Radost used to be *the* glamourous hot-spot in Prague, but it is now struggling to recreate those heady days. It's still the best dressed and most creative venue in the city, with walls covered in triangles, twirls and dots set aglow by dangly, twisted halogen lights. You can slink away to the brainwashing, zebra-striped psychedelic side room, or surrender to the disarming arm chairs and sofas and observe the clusters of hopeful foreign men lining the bar and the drifting regulars in search of vague acquaintances. Screens all around the club flicker in subliminal silence while determined dancers shake and gyrate to house and techno on the sunken dancefloor beneath an omniscient video eye. Specials include 1970s classics (Tuesday nights), African music (occasional Thursday nights), poetry readings (8pm Sundays) and a film night (7pm Mondays).

Elephant
Vodičkova 18, Prague 1. Metro Muzeum or Můstek. **Open** 24 hours Mon-Sat.
A small supermarket with two armed guards outside to ensure that there are no fights over the last litre of milk.

Potraviny non-stop
Michalská 19, Prague 1. Metro Můstek. **Open** 24 hours daily.
Open all hours, this resembles a village grocery.

Kolonial Vega
Štěpánská 30, Prague 1. Metro Muzeum. **Open** 24 hours daily.
A small shop where the worn-out assistants will serve you through a window, so your order better be simple and your sign-language effective.

Non-stop Pharmacies

Below is a list of the addresses of chemists (*lékárny*) that should be open 24 hours a day. For a further list *see chapter* **Survival**.

Na příkopě 7, Prague 1 (24 21 02 30). Metro Můstek or Náměstí Republiky.

Koněvova 210, Prague 3 (644 18 95). Metro Florenc/9, 16 tram/133 bus.

Antala Staška 80, Prague 4 (42 44 87). Metro Budějovická.

Tererova 1356, Prague 4 (791 63 89). Metro Háje/221, 213, 224, 260 bus.

Non-Stops

Bar Ve Zdi
Seifertova 19, Prague 3. Metro Flora. **Open** 9am-4am daily.
Opposite Alterna Komotovka, this glass-fronted café serves lots of cheap food to craggy cabbies.

U Havrana
Hálkova 6, Prague 2. Metro I.P. Pavlova. **Open** 24 hours Mon-Sat.
Near Radost, Uzi, Music Park and AghaRTA, this place is clean, serves good food and has attentive service (if you get the right waitress). When conversation becomes too much, there's a TV to distract you.

Film

We chart the turbulent history of Czech cinema – from its avant-garde origins to its recent rebirth after four decades of censorship.

The avant-garde eroticism of *Extáze* placed Czech film on the international stage in 1933. Gustav Machatý's film raised eyebrows the world over with the first appearance in a feature film of a naked woman – the young Slovak actress Hedy Lamarr. Czech cinema has since had more than its fair share of setbacks: the Nazi occupation; Socialist Realism under Stalin; the censorship of the late 1950s and the clampdown after the 1968 invasion. But there were happier intervals, too. The 1960s saw the flowering of the Czech New Wave, and the Velvet Revolution has unleashed 40 years of stifled expression, paving the way for a new generation, ready to guide Czech cinema onto the crest of the next wave.

AVANT-GARDE TO NATIONALISATION

The state provision of funding – and recognition of the importance of the film industry – coincided with the opening of the Barrandov Film Studios financed by President Havel's great uncle, in 1933. At the same time entrepreneur Tomáš Baťa opened the Zlín Film Studios in Moravia, designed to produce advertising for his shoe empire. These two soon became the focus for much experimental and animated film-making.

The Nazis commandeered Barrandov during World War II, and although domestic production wasn't completely halted, the war marked the first of several serious breaks in the continuity of the young industry. Fortunately Hitler viewed the studio as a useful propaganda base and it remained undamaged. In fact, the Nazi-funded expansion of Barrandov left it with healthy prospects as one of the only fully-functioning, undamaged studios left in postwar Europe.

Immediately after the war President Beneš announced that film was to be nationalised and at the same time the Prague Film Academy (FAMU) was founded and began its internationally recognised programme of practical film education. Training students in the fields of directing, production, editing, cinematography, documentary and animation, it was to become the base of the film-makers of the Czech New Wave.

SOCIALIST REALISM AND CENSORSHIP

Lenin had decreed in the early days of the revolution that 'film is the most important art'. But under

Hedy Lamarr breaking new ground in Extáze.

Stalin, the idealistic visions for the film form were replaced by the ideological **Socialist Realism** – the Happy Worker film, in which the only conflict was between 'good and better'. Socialist it may have been, Realist it certainly was not. Characters were two-dimensional – worker goodies versus capitalist baddies – in endless well-intentioned yarns of bricklaying and tractors.

In the battle against the censors which was fought throughout the Communist years, films which didn't follow this formula were frowned upon. Alfréd Radok's *The Long Journey* (1949), filmed chiefly in the Terezín concentration camp, managed to slip past the censors, but was met with an icy reception by the Party. Censorship generally occurred at the point of distribution rather than at the point of production, so that films were made and simply not seen or only given a desultory distribution. Unlike their Polish or Hungarian counterparts, Czech films of this period were rarely overtly political. But it was their avoidance of politics that made them dangerous. If they didn't speak for or against the system, then what exactly were they saying? The film archive safes all over Eastern and Central Europe began to fill up with films which are only now gaining public recognition.

It wasn't until after Khruschev had denounced the cult of Stalin in 1956, and the film partnerships of Ján Kádar with Elmar Klos and writer Jan

A scene from the 1966 Oscar-winning Shop on Main Street.

Procházka with director Karel Kachyň had emerged, that the first stage of the Czech New Wave began to redress the balance of Socialist Realism. Film-makers began to fill the huge gap in personal experience left out of Communist films.

THE NEW WAVE
The Film Academy enjoyed a modicum of freedom during the 1950s and 1960s (thanks to Socialist Realism, film was not a popular field of study). Left to their own devices, students like Miloš Forman began working in what he described as the FAMU 'ghetto', untouched by the outside world, able to express their own opinions, experiment and watch a range of films not available to the general public. World War II and the occupation was the starting point for several films of this period. In 1966 Ján Kádár and Elmar Klos made the Oscar-winning *Shop on Main Street* which was about the Nazi puppet state in Slovakia. *Sunshine in a Net* by Štefan Uher and *Closely Observed Trains* (also an Oscar winner and based on the novel by Bohumil Hrabal), by Jiří Menzel, focussed on the fear wrought by the occupation. For the first time, Czech audiences were able to witness the personalised conflicts and human dilemmas of their contemporary society.

The New Wave was characterised by its diversity of styles and vital and innovative attitude towards cinematography. Its film-makers were concerned, not with heroes and their dramatic gestures, but with the often darkly humourous failures and triumphs of average people. In Jaromil Jireš's film *The Joke* (1969) based on a Milan

Kundera story (he was one head of screenwriting at FAMU), the sinister repercussions of a joke at the Party's expense are played out. The film, which was banned soon after its release, is typical of the New Wave, and shows its concern with the existential concepts of manipulation, permanent anxiety, loneliness and the inability to communicate – a personal microcosm of society's macrocosm.

When two young girls eat their way through a dull summer in Věra Chytilová's *Daisies* (1966), there is an irreverent surrealism which is also present in the animated films of Jan Švankmajer and which demonstrates the increasing freedom of expression that flowered in the 1960s. It didn't last long.

PRAGUE SPRING TO VELVET REVOLUTION
The figure eight recurs at crucial points in Czech history: in the formation of Czechoslovakia in 1918; in the arrival of Communism in 1948; and in the invasion by Warsaw Pact troops in 1968 which brought a definitive end to the Prague Spring and to Czech New Wave cinema. The reins were severely tightened, and the turgid ideology of Socialist Realism resurfaced. Public interest in film diminished.

Many directors left the country, including such leading figures as Miloš Forman, Ivan Passer and Jaromír Jireš. To continue working in Czechoslovakia, film-makers were obliged to self-criticise, which was tantamount to welcoming the 'friendly help' of the invaders. None of them did. Some directors – like Věra Chytilová – didn't make another film for years. Jiří Menzel, too famous to be silenced after his 1968 Oscar, found sanctuary in adapting Bohumil Hrabal's work for the screen. Even so, several of his films were banned, including the 1969 film *Larks on a String*, which wasn't released until 1989 when it won the Golden Bear at the Berlin Film Festival, 20 years after it was made. During this period, Zdeněk Svěrák made some good comedies in which somewhere beyond the tenth layer of meaning could be detected the mildest of critiques. Meanwhile, those who emigrated were struggling, with the exception of Miloš Forman, whose films *One Flew Over the Cuckoo's Nest* and *Amadeus* brought him deserved acclaim.

THE NEXT WAVE

The 1989 revolution spawned a multitude of documentaries and opened the floodgates holding back all the censored films of the previous four decades. Czech television screened them, the cinemas showed them, and today there are regular retrospectives in Prague's cinemas.

Directors like Menzel, Chytilová and Jireš returned from exile to teach at FAMU, though Menzel has since left. Their films since the revolution have been disappointing – mild comedies and historical romps which have attracted healthy audiences but failed to impress critics. Jan Svěrák (Zdeněk's son) is the most successful of the new directors, with an Oscar nomination for best foreign film for *Elementary School* (1992). Švankmajer continues his surrealist animation with *Faust*, and Drahomíra Vihanová, after years of struggling to make feature films has completed *The Fortress* in the tradition of the Czech New Wave, with some post-revolutionary hindsight.

Foreign film crews have been flocking to the newly privatised Barrandov studios (*Amadeus,* the Indiana Jones films, *The Trial, Underground,* and *Immortal Beloved* were all made there), and with massive reductions in state funding for film, it is hoped that this international collaboration will feed back into domestic production. You are bound to see one film crew or another shooting in the Old Town during your stay, usually recognisable by the number of Nazi uniforms adorning the cast. As for cinemas, most of Prague's 30 or so are still open, showing a predictable fare of Hollywood movies, which are popular, but viewed with a healthy disdain for the most part. With the growing popularity of FAMU (which now runs a year-long course for foreigners in English) and the rapidly increasing number of production companies working in film, advertising and television, the industry is looking pretty healthy.

Screening Information

Most of Prague's cinemas are situated around Václavské náměsti. Each has a large blue and white poster displayed somewhere in the foyer, called the *Program pražských kin* (Programme of Prague Cinemas). This is the most reliable source of information for what's showing where and at what time. It's written in Czech, but don't be put off, since it's quite straightforward to follow. English-language films are usually listed in Czech and English. The Programme runs from Thursday to Wednesday across the city and a typical listing goes like this:

Cinema name, address, phone number
Screening times (usually 11am, 3pm, 5.30pm and 8pm); days of the week are abbreviated: **pon** (*pondělí*) Monday; **út** (*úterý*) Tuesday; **stř** (*středa*) Wednesday; **čtv** (*čtvrtek*) Thursday; **pá** (*pátek*) Friday; **so** (*sobota*) Saturday; **ne** (*neděle*) Sunday. (*jen* /*pouze* only; *mimo* except; *hod* hour)

Film title, country of origin, length of run in weeks (*týden*)
At the end of this row will be a symbol: a square = film dubbed in Czech; a star = for those over 15 years of age only; a circle = those over 18 only; a triangle = suitable for children under 12.

Buying a Ticket

There is often a sign up at the box office (*pokladna*) saying whether a film is subtitled or dubbed. Tickets range from 30kč to 40kč, and one crown from every ticket sold goes to the Czech Cinematographers Fund. In certain cinemas tickets are half price on Mondays. When you buy your ticket you will be expected to say where you want to sit. There should be a plan so you can point, otherwise you'll be seated at random (*řada* means row; *sedadlo* seat; *přízemí* stalls; *lože* box; *balkón* balcony).

Smoking isn't allowed in cinemas except in the *kinokavárnas* (cinema coffeehouses) and at open-air cinemas. Ironically, you'll be able to see all those old cattle-steering Marlboro ads from the 1970s which have been banned everywhere else but provide great amusement in Prague cinemas.

Jiří Menzel's Closely Observed Trains.

During the winter you may get hassled by an old lady tugging at your coat sleeve; she wants you to check your coat into the cloakroom (*šatna*). Don't argue: she'll win.

For further information about what's on at the cinema, check the English-language press, the *Prague Post* (out on Wednesdays) and *Prognosis* (out on Thursdays). *Program*, the Czech cultural guide, has full cinema listings and an English section at the beginning (*see chapter* **Media** for more details).

Unusual Cinemas

Lucerna
Vodičkova 36, Prague 1 (242 11 69-72). Metro Můstek.
The Lucerna is by far the grandest of Prague's cinemas. Part of the Havel empire, it is the showcase cinema for sister distribution company Lucerna Film's new releases. Annoyingly, the box office only opens 15 minutes before a performance begins which, combined with the very punctual projectionist, means that there are usually a lot of bobbing heads across the subtitles for the first 10 minutes of a film. The foyer to the cinema has a bar which has recently been adorned with some pretty gruesome flashing coloured lights, but it still retains most of its wonderful faded glory and you can hear the muted sounds of the film from it.

Cinema Coffeehouses

There are a few *kinokavárnas* left in Prague – café-like rooms with a screen, a bar, a bit of chatter and a generally relaxed atmosphere. Screenings are usually at 11am, 1.30pm and 4.30pm.

DIF Centrum
Václavské náměstí 43, Prague 1 (24 22 88 14). Metro Můstek.

Mišmaš
Veletržní 61, Prague 7 (37 92 78). Metro Vltavská/1, 8, 25, 26 tram.

Open-air Cinemas

Prague has two outdoor cinemas, both at Výstaviště in Prague 7 (*see chapter* **Sightseeing**). They usually show popular recent releases. Performances (in the summer only) start when it gets dark, which can be at any time between 9pm and 10pm.

kino Fulda, kino Julda
U Výstaviště, Prague 7 (872 91 11). Metro Nádraží Holešovice/5, 12, 17 tram.

Repertory

Although films that aren't mainstream are still not widely available, with a little effort you can see a variety of international films in Prague. The most comprehensive film club is that of the National Film Archive (Ponrepo). Essentially the Film Archive exists to record and preserve film history. The archivists were able to see all films produced

The **Lucerna** *complex.*

under the Communist regime as, for some inexplicable reason, there was a projector in the censored film's safe. The Archive now has quite a job on its hands screening all the films that were banned during those years, but the films are gradually beginning to emerge from obscurity.

Dlabačov Film Club
(filmový klub Dlabačov), Hotel Pyramida, Bělohorská 24, Prague 6 (311 32 41). Tram 8, 22, 31. **Annual membership** 20kč.
Out in Prague 6, in the rather ugly Pyramid Hotel, you'll find the Dlabačov Film Club. It tends to show re-runs of recent successes which are marginally out of the mainstream. *Easy Rider* has been a Czech cult film since the Velvet Revolution and it's shown at least once a month here.

Film Academy
(Městská knihovna), Mariánské náměstí 1, Prague 1 (24 48 11 11). Metro Staroměstská.
On Mondays in term time at 5pm, the Film Academy screens films at the Old Town Library which are open to the public and free. You'll have to take pot luck or ask a student to find out what's on, as the films are only announced on the morning of the screening. Get tickets in advance from the box office or Melantrich (*see chapter* **Prague by Season**).

Goethe Institute
Masarykovo nábřeží 32, Prague 1 (24 91 57 25). Tram 17.
The Goethe Institute screens German films in the original version and although the screening room is very small, if you're a Fassbinder fan that shouldn't put you off.

Institut Français
Štěpánská 35, Prague 1 (24 21 40 32). Metro Můstek.

It is always worth having a look at the film programme here as the Institute has a free cinema which regularly shows French films and also has a good café and gallery on the ground floor.

National Film Archive/Ponrepo

(Český filmový archív/Ponrepo), Národní 40, Prague 1 (24 22 71 37). Metro Můstek or Národní třída. **Annual membership** 120kč adults; 60kč students.
Membership entitles you to see two films a day.

Prague Film Club

(Pražský filmový klub), Václavské náměstí 17, Prague 1 (26 20 35). Metro Můstek. **Annual membership** 25kč.
The Kino Praha on Wenceslas Square also runs a film club in its second cinema. The Prague Film Club is open to the public, although there are some members-only screenings. The repertory concentrates on the better-known classics from the National Film Archive and it is here that you can also come to gaze appreciatively at Fellini or Truffaut films.

Festivals & Special Events

Prague doesn't yet have its own film festival, but in the last few years it has hosted a number of different film events (although it is not always certain that these will continue with any regularity).

FAMU Film Festival

Smetanovo nábřeží 2, Prague 1 (24 22 94 68/fax 232 80 80). Tram 17.
The annual Film Academy Festival of Student Films takes place in April over one weekend. This is an opportunity to see what film students from all years have been up to and it usually coincides with the beginning of the warm weather and light evenings, so spirits are always high. For one-off film events or festivals it is worth paying a visit to FAMU. Check the noticeboards for posters with details of forthcoming events, or enquire at the foreigners' department (3F), where the staff speak English.

Karlovy Vary International Film Festival

The biennial Karlovy Vary International Film Festival takes place in the beautiful spa town in west Bohemia in July. Before the revolution in 1989 most of the visitors were more interested in taking the waters than watching the films. However, in 1990 the film festival hosted a special retrospective of works previously banned in Czechoslovakia and since then the profile of the festival has been rising steadily.

There are regular buses from Prague to Karlovy Vary (Karlsbad) that leave from Florenc coach station. When you arrive, register for the festival at reception at the Hotel Thermal in the centre of town. Everyone must have an identity card to get into the building. Then go to the booking office with your programme and order your film tickets. Cheap accommodation is available at the student college at Drahovice at very reasonable rates (from 40kč to 170kč a night), but it is a good idea to call in at the festival office in Prague and book somewhere to stay before you go (*see chapter* **Trips Out of Town** for some suggestions and more information about the town).

English translation is available for all of the films shown at the festival, either as subtitles or simultaneous translation over headphones. In the evenings, you can lounge around by the elevated pool at the Hotel Thermal or mull over the day's screenings while having a massage at one of the spas.

Festival Office

Ministry of Culture, Valdštejnský palác, Valdštejnská 12, Prague 1 (513 24 73). Metro Malostranská/12, 22 tram.

Festival Reception

Hotel Thermal, nábřeží Jana Palacha, Karlovy Vary (01 72 64 65/244 51/282 83).

Kolej Drahovice

Stará Kýsbelská, Karlovy Vary (01 72 86 71).

Animation

After World War II the Czech puppet theatre tradition found its way into film in the careful hands of Jiří Trnka, whose delightful animated tales were amongst the first to appeal to both children and adults. Films such as *The Czech Year* (1947) established Trnka as a world leader in the field of animation. So novel was his work that Stephen Bosustow and UPA, fighting Walt Disney's exploitative dictatorship in Hollywood, declared him to be the first real opposition to Disney's aesthetic.

The Zlín Film Studios generated innovative mixed media animation from directors Hermína Týrlová and Karel Zeman, but it was Jan Švankmajer who re-invented the medium with his bizarre compositions of claymation, mixed with animated humans and objects. Švankmajer refers to himself as a surrealist first and last. Perhaps this is what enabled him to evade the censors with films like *Garden* (1967) and *Dimensions of a Dialogue* (1982), which revealed both the author's fascination with irrationality and his macabre sense of the absurdity of reason.

He has always stood somewhat at a distance from the rest of the industry, and though active during the New Wave he was never really associated with it. Švankmajer's features *Alice* (1987) and *Faust* (1994) as well as his short films, especially *The End of Stalinism in Bohemia* (which uses propaganda materials, sculptures and portraits of Communist leaders to evoke a nightmarish world of mechanical activity with no purpose), established Švankmajer's international reputation as a pioneer in his field and answered his own call during the revolution for 'more imagination please'.

Music: Classical & Opera

You don't have to like Mozart to enjoy classical music in Prague, but it helps.

The Czechs are very proud of their musical tradition – and rightly so. Although the Big Four – Smetana, Dvořák, Janáček and Martinů – are firmly established throughout the world, there are many composers, particularly from the Baroque and Classical periods, who have remained largely unknown outside the Czech Republic. Prague has always been one of the musical capitals of Europe, and it now boasts three theatres where opera is regularly performed, three major orchestras and countless smaller ensemble groups, ranging from early music to contemporary. Whatever your tastes, you are sure to find something that appeals.

Long before the premiere of *Don Giovanni* in Prague in 1787 (the one landmark in Czech musical history that everyone seems to know), the city and Bohemia as a whole had produced numerous composers whose influence extended far beyond the boundaries of Bohemia. The many chamber concerts held in churches and palaces throughout the city provide a good introduction to the works of Zelenka, Mysliveček, Benda, Černohorský and Brixi – to name only a handful. Furthermore, as a result of recent research largely forbidden under the Communist regime, a good deal of new material has been unearthed from the archives of monasteries, abbeys and nunneries, as well as the National Museum, and is being given an airing for the first time in over 100 years.

Although Mozart-mania doesn't quite reach the level of kitsch found in Salzburg, it's hard to get away from any reference to him. Prague, unlike Vienna, gave *The Marriage of Figaro* a rapturous reception, and commissioned not only *Don Giovanni* (dedicated to 'the good people of Prague'), but also *La Clemenza di Tito*, written for the coronation of Emperor Leopold II as King of Bohemia. And then there is, of course, the 'Prague Symphony'. Practically every second chamber concert will include a work by the great Wolfgang Amadeus, who has seemingly been accorded the status of an honorary Czech.

The other great musical heroes are Smetana and Dvořák. The growth of Nationalism in the latter half of the nineteenth century produced an emphasis on Bohemian musical folk traditions (though Smetana and Dvořák actually used folk music very rarely in their melodies). It was Smetana who was the guiding force behind the establishment of the National Theatre, which opened in 1881 with the premiere of *Libuše*, his 'solemn festival tableau' dealing with the mythical foundation of the Czech nation. Regarded as 'the father of Bohemian music' (which seems a little unfair on his Baroque and Classical predecessors), Smetana's status as the pre-eminent Czech composer remains undisputed and he is followed a close second by Dvořák.

Owing to the inherent conservatism of the average Czech music-lover, the two giants of Czech twentieth century music, Janáček and Martinů, aren't so well represented. Unlike in Britain and America, they are still regarded as 'difficult' composers; though this may well be a legacy of the Communist era. For various historical reasons, it took a long time for Janáček's reputation to be established in Prague. He was far more widely accepted in Brno, the capital of his native Moravia. As for Martinů, his many years of self-imposed exile made him for a long time persona non grata. It's only in recent years that he has been granted a genuine place in the Czech musical pantheon.

There are other Czech composers worth discovering: Josef Suk, Dvořák's son-in-law – a late romantic who is only really recognised in the west for the *Asrael* symphony; Fibich, a contemporary of Smetana and Dvořák; and quite a few contemporary composers, with Petr Eben at their head, who are only now finding their own voice after many years of censorship and the dictates of socialist realism.

Principal Orchestras

There are three main orchestras resident in Prague. The oldest and most venerable is the world-renowned **Czech Philharmonic**, which

Musica Antica Kolín at the Prague Spring Festival in 1994.

performs regularly in the Rudolfinum. Recently, veteran conductor Václav Neumann was succeeded by German maestro Gerd Albrecht – the first non-Czech to hold the post of musical director of the orchestra. Albrecht manages to get music-making of a high quality out of the orchestra, which concentrates on the standard Classical and Romantic repertoire as well as the stalwarts of Czech music.

The **Prague Symphony Orchestra** is at present undergoing something of a transformation. The musical director, Martin Turnovský has resigned and so far no successor has been found. Instead the orchestra will have three guest conductors: Turnovský himself, former director Jiří Bělohlávek, and the current director of the Royal Liverpool Philharmonic Orchestra, Libor Pešek. As if this weren't enough, their main venue, the Smetana Hall in the Municipal House, is closed for much-needed repairs. Despite all this, the orchestra has great plans for the future. Rather than seeing itself as a rival to the Czech Philharmonic, it intends to be an equal alternative, concentrating on twentieth century music and venturing into a non-European repertoire.

The **Prague Radio Symphony Orchestra** doesn't have the kudos of the other two and is sometimes regarded as their poor relation. Nevertheless it frequently turns out creditable performances which compare well with those of its more famous rivals.

Principal Concert Halls

Rudolfinum

Alšovo nábřeží 12, Prague 1 (24 89 33 52). Metro Staroměstská/17 tram.
One of the most beautiful concert venues in Europe. Built in neo-Renaissance style at the end of the nineteenth century, it has two halls, the Dvořák Hall for orchestral works and major recitals, and the Suk Hall for chamber, instrumental and solo vocal music. Opinions are divided about the acoustics of the Dvořák Hall, but the grandeur of the interior of the building as a whole – plus the invariably high standard of the concerts themselves – make an evening here worthwhile. *See chapter* **Sightseeing**.

The Smetana Hall

(Smetanova síň Obecního domu), Obecní dům, Náměstí Republiky 5, Prague 1. Metro Náměstí Republiky. Closed for restoration.
A stunning example of Czech Art Nouveau, unfortunately closed for restoration until some time in 1996. *See* **Municipal House** *in chapter* **Sightseeing**.

Other Venues

The number of venues for chamber music and instrumental recitals is legion. Practically every church and palace offers a variety of concerts almost all year round. Programming is mainly from the Baroque and Classical repertoire, in keeping with the style of the buildings. The emphasis is on Czech music and the concerts are a good way of hearing the works of eighteenth century composers

who are still relatively unknown abroad. The quality of performance is variable but is usually good. Some of the best venues are listed below.

Bertramka

Mozartova 169, Prague 5 (54 38 93). Metro Anděl/4, 7, 9 tram.
The house where Mozart stayed when he came to Prague is now a museum devoted to him, and has regular concerts. Practically all of them, inevitably, include at least one work by the great Austrian composer.

Chapel of Mirrors

Zrcadlová síň, Klementinum, Křižovnické náměstí, Prague 1 (24 48 11 11). Metro Staroměstská.
A pink marble chapel in the vast Clementinum complex built by the Jesuits. *See chapter* **Sightseeing**.

Church of St Nicholas

(Chrám sv. Mikuláše), Malostranské náměstí, Prague 1. Metro Malostranská/12, 22 tram.
The most celebrated church in Prague apart from St Vitus's Cathedral, with a stunning Baroque interior. There are regular choral concerts and organ recitals. *See chapter* **Sightseeing**.

Church of St Nicholas

(Kostel sv. Mikuláše), Staroměstské náměstí, Prague 1. Metro Staroměstská.
Regular organ, instrumental and vocal recitals are held here, with the emphasis on Baroque music.

House at the Stone Bell

(Dům U Kamenného zvonu), Staroměstské náměstí 13, Prague 1 (24 81 00 36). Metro Staroměstská.
One of the oldest buildings in Prague, situated on the Old Town Square, where concerts of contemporary music as well as more staple fare.

Church of St Simon and St Jude

(Kostel sv. Šimona a Judy), Dušní, Prague 1. Metro Staroměstská.
Recently renovated, this is set to become one of the major venues for chamber music in the city. The Prague Symphony Orchestra, which also promotes selected ensembles, is responsible for the programming.

Basilica of St Jakub

(Bazilika sv. Jakuba), Malá Štupartská, Prague 1. Metro Náměstí Republiky.
Another prime example of Czech Baroque architecture, and with excellent acoustics. In addition to performances of large-scale sacred choral works, music accompanying the celebration of mass (usually at 10am) is a regular feature on Sunday mornings.

Lobkowicz Palace

(Lobkovický palác), Jiřská 1, Prague 1 (53 73 06). Metro Malostranská/22 tram.
Concerts are held in the imposing banqueting hall, with frescoes by Fabián Harovnik.

Lichtenstein Palace

(Lichtenštejnský palác), Malostranské náměstí 13, Prague 1. Metro Malostranská/12, 22 tram.
Regular concerts are given in the Gallery and in the Martinů Hall.

Nostic Palace

(Nostický palác), Maltézské náměstí 1, Prague 1 (24 51 12 85). Metro Malostranská/12, 22 tram.
The palace of the man who paid for the Estates Theatre. Concerts are of a high standard and a glass of champagne is included in the price of the ticket.

The Rudolfinum. *See page 194.*

St Agnes's Convent

(Klášter sv. Anežky české), U milosrdných 17, Prague 1 (24 81 06 28/tickets 24 21 50 18 or 24 91 59 43). Metro Staroměstská or Náměstí Republiky/5, 14, 26 tram.
Opinions on the acoustics vary, but the high standard of chamber music – usually from the Classical, Romantic and twentieth century repertoire, with an emphasis on Smetana, Dvořák and Janáček – makes this venue worth a visit.

Opera

There are three major venues for opera in Prague: the National Theatre, the State Opera and the Estates Theatre. Tickets can cost anything from 390kč to 1,500kč. For theatre productions at the National Theatre and the Estates Theatre *see* chapter **Theatre & Dance.**

Estates Theatre

(Stavovské divadlo), Ovocný trh 1, Prague 1 (26 77 97/24 21 50 01). Metro Můstek. **Open** box office 10am-6pm Mon-Fri; 10am-12.30pm, 3-6pm, Sat, Sun.
This is a shrine for Mozart-lovers, and is where *Don Giovanni* and *La Clemenza di Tito* were first performed. The theatre was built by Count Nostic in 1784 and its beautiful dark blue and gold auditorium has recently been renovated. It began life as the Prague home of Italian opera, but in 1807 became the German opera with Carl Maria von Weber as its musical director (1813-17). Today most of the programming is given over to theatre but there are regular performances of Mozart – including, of course, *Don Giovanni.*

National Theatre

(Národní divadlo), Národní 2, Prague 1 (24 91 34 37). Metro Národní třída/6, 9, 18, 17, 22 tram. **Open** box office 10am-6pm Mon-Fri; 10am-12.30pm, 3-6pm, Sat, Sun.
Smetana was a guiding light behind the establishment of the National Theatre, a symbol of Czech Nationalism which finally opened in 1883 with a performance of his opera *Libuše.* In keeping with tradition, the theatre today tends to concentrate on Czech opera, the core of the repertoire being works by Smetana and Dvořák (including lesser known works such as Dvořák's *The Devil and Kate* and Smetana's *The Kiss*), together with some Janáček. Operas by non-Czech composers are also performed. *See* chapter **Sightseeing.**

State Opera

Smetanovo divadlo, Legerova 75, Prague 1 (24 22 76 93). Metro Muzeum. **Open** box office 10am-5.30pm Mon-Fri; 10am-noon, 1-5.30pm, Sat, Sun.
The State Opera (then called the German Theatre) opened in 1887. Music directors and regular conductors included Seidl, Mahler, Zemlinský, Klemperer and Szell, and up until World War II the theatre was regarded as one of the finest German opera houses outside Germany. After the war it changed its name to the Smetana Theatre and became the second house of the National Theatre. Today it's a separate organisation and presents operas from the standard Italian repertoire (Donizetti, Rossini, Verdi, Puccini) with an occasional excursion into German and French opera. Standards of production and musical execution vary – the orchestral playing can be ragged – but on a good night the State Opera will provide a memorable evening. It has the reputation of being a springboard for young singers from former eastern European countries on their way to careers in the more lucrative west.

Festivals

The major musical event in the calendar is the Prague Spring Festival which runs from May to June. Since the Velvet Revolution it has a much stronger international flavour and ranks with the Edinburgh Festival or the Proms in its ability to attract first class performers from all over the world. Traditionally the festival opens with Smetana's patriotic cycle of symphonic poems, *Má Vlast* (My Country), and concludes with Beethoven's Ninth Symphony. Many of the major events sell out quite quickly and it's best to obtain tickets from the Prague Spring Festival box office (*see page 196* **Ticket Agencies**), rather than from agencies which add a hefty mark-up.

Other regular summer festivals outside Prague are held in the spa towns of western Bohemia, at Karlovy Vary and Mariánské Lázně (*see chapter* **Trips Out of Town**).

Buying Tickets

The best way of obtaining tickets is via the relevant box office. Although there are numerous ticket agencies (the principal ones are listed below), they tend to raise their prices to foreigners. As elsewhere, tickets touts are to be avoided unless you're absolutely desperate. Prices for concerts vary and some (in the smaller churches) are free, but the cost is usually between 250kč and 350kč; in some cases the price includes a glass of champagne.

Information about forthcoming events tends to be haphazard. It's frequently worth trying to get a ticket at the relevant venue an hour before the beginning of a performance, even if you've been told it is sold out. This is more true of concerts than of opera. Prague, like most cities in central Europe, has a tradition of subscription evenings and so you may find that certain occasions are rather difficult to get into.

Ticket Agencies

Bohemia Ticket International (BTI)
Na příkopě 16, Prague 1 (24 21 50 31). Metro Můstek or Náměstí Republiky. **Open** 9am-noon, 1-6pm, Mon-Fri; 9am-4pm Sat; 9am-3pm Sun.
Tickets for the opera, orchestral and chamber concerts.
Branches: Karlova 8, Prague 1 (24 22 76 51/24 22 90 78); Salvátorská 6, Prague 1 (24 22 78 32).

Čedok
Na příkopě 18, Prague 1 (24 81 18 70). Metro Můstek or Náměstí Republiky. **Open** 9am-5pm Mon-Fri; 9am-1pm Sat.
Tickets for assorted events as well as some concerts.
Branch: Bilkova 6, Prague 1 (231 05 70); Pařížská 6, Prague 1 (231 25 81).

Divertimento
Pařížská 13, Prague 1 (232 40 60). Metro Staroměstská. **Open** 10am-6pm Mon-Fri; noon-5pm Sat, Sun.

Laterna Magika
Národní 4, Prague 1 (24 91 41 29). **Open** 10am-8pm Mon-Fri.

Lucerna
Štěpánská 61, Prague 1 (24 21 20 03). Metro Muzeum or Národní třída/3, 9, 14, 24 tram. **Open** 9am-4.30pm Mon-Fri.

Melantrich
Václavské náměstí 38, (pasáž Rokoko), Prague 1 (24 21 50 18). Metro Muzeum or Můstek. **Open** 10am-6pm Mon-Fri.

Prague Information Service (PIS)
Na příkopě 20, Prague 1 (26 40 22/information line 54 44 44). Metro Můstek or Náměstí Republiky. **Open** 8.30am-7pm Mon-Fri; 9am-5pm Sat, Sun.

Prague Spring Festival Box Office
Hellichova 18, Prague 1 (24 51 04 22/53 02 93/53 34 74/fax 53 60 40). Metro Malostranská/12, 22 tram.

Pragokonzert
Nostický palác, Maltézské náměstí 1, Prague 1 (24 51 12 85/53 60 62). Metro Malostranská/12, 22 tram.
Concert promoters, based in the Nostic Palace, who organise chamber music concerts as well as major gala events such as the 1994 Domingo concert.

Tiketpro
Rytířská 31, Prague 1 (telephone booking 24 23 21 10/fax 24 23 20 21). Metro Můstek or Staroměstská.
Offers advance booking for most concerts and other events.

Wolff Travel Agency
Na příkopě 24, Prague 1 (24 21 37 18/24 22 80 99). Metro Můstek or Náměstí Republiky.
Tickets for the opera and chamber concerts.

Other Musical Attractions

Three composers have museums dedicated to their life and work, and it should come as no surprise that they are Mozart, Smetana and Dvořák. *See chapter* **Museums** for more details.

National Marionette Theatre
(Národní divadlo marionet), Žatecká 1, Prague 1 (232 34 29/232 25 36). Metro Staroměstská.
If you don't manage to catch *Don Giovanni* at the Estates

Theatre, there is always the National Marionette Theatre which gives regular performances of the opera in the summer months. Tickets (from 390kč) should be bought an hour before the performance.

The Original Music Theatre Prague
Kounický palác, Panská 7, Prague 1. Metro Můstek or Náměstí Republiky.
Box office *Kartouzká 4, Prague 5 (54 68 06/reservations 70 47 24). Metro Anděl/6, 9 tram.*
An organisation that presents regular evenings of music and drama in episodes from the lives of Mozart, Dvořák and Johann Strauss. Though not everybody's cup of tea, this is kitsch of a fairly high standard.

Vyšehrad Cemetery
(Vyšehradský hřbitov), Soběslavova 1, Prague 2 (29 66 51). Metro Vyšehrad. **Open** 9.30am-5.30pm daily.
Admission 10kč.
For those who wish to pay their respects, both Dvořák and Smetana are buried in the Vyšehrad cemetery along with many other leading citizens.

Buying CDs

On the whole CDs are extremely cheap compared with the UK and western Europe, prices usually ranging from 150kč to 480kč. Home-grown labels such as Supraphon form the cheaper end of the market, while the more expensive CDs tend to be imports of major labels such as Deutsche Gramophon, Decca, Philips and RCA. The British-based label Chandos has its own subsidiary company in the Czech Republic. CDs can be purchased just about anywhere in the city centre, either from music shops or street stalls. They can also be bought at the box office in some concert halls and theatres and in the musical museums (*see chapter* **Museums**). We list some of the larger outlets below.

Albatros
Havelská 20, Prague 1 (24 22 93 22). Metro Můstek. **Open** *summer* 10am-6pm Mon-Fri; 10am-4pm Sat; *winter* 10am-6pm Mon-Fri; 10am-2pm Sat.
Branch: Na Perštýně 1, Prague 1 (24 22 93 22).

Alstar
Václavské náměstí 15, Prague 1 (24 22 40 76). Metro Můstek. **Open** 9am-7.30pm Mon-Fri; 9am-6pm Sat; 10am-6pm Sun.

Musical Classical
Celetná 18, Prague 1 (no phone). Metro Náměstí Republiky or Můstek. **Open** 10am-7pm daily.

Supraphon
Jungmannova 20, Prague 1 (26 33 83). Metro Můstek. **Open** 9am-7pm Mon-Fri; 9am-1pm Sat.

Trio Music Shop
Karlova 23, Prague 1 (24 21 08 91). Metro Staroměstská. **Open** 10am-7pm Mon-Fri; 10am-6pm Sat.

Music: Rock, Roots & Jazz

There are gigs galore but a shortage of good venues in Prague's rock-versus-techno music scene.

Prague is a city with a lot of bands, but not many venues. While groups working the international circuit can charge (and expect to receive) huge sums, local bands have no such luck. Over the last five years, the explosion in the number of groups vying for attention, and the lack of diversity between them, has meant that prices have had to remain static if a band is to have a chance of pulling in the punters. Also, gigs are rarely the sole reason for going to a club; most of them are open until six or seven in the morning, with the band leaving the stage at around 11pm, when a DJ takes over. In the centre of town, most of the clubs with music pumping out of them are simply discos. The places there that do hold gigs, like the Bunkr or the Borát, usually double as discos, with only outlying suburban clubs, usually ex-*kulturní domy* (culture houses) such as the Delta, opening specifically for a band and then closing before midnight.

The result is that there are plenty of gigs to choose from every night, but if you want to avoid going to the same places in the centre of town all the time, you're going to need a map and a sense of adventure. Many of the more distant venues are situated slap in the middle of huge housing estates, full of monolithic *paneláks* (prefab apartment blocks), and little else.

THE SCENE

The music scene itself is divided quite sharply between the old and the new, rock versus techno, foreign against Czech, plus a few unclassifiables. Most of the old 'underground' bands, like Garáž or Půlnoc still enjoy a certain reputation, although they were hardly barnstorming revolutionaries; the authorities frowned on them simply because decadent rock music wasn't what good socialists should be listening to. For most younger bands, mindless heavy rock/metal has become the main influence, although some, like the Sebastians or Shalom, think a bit harder before setting finger to fretboard. The latter are a decidedly strange group, at present converting to Judaism and singing about the joys of the process.

Stranger still are the oddities that have sprung up on the scene and do much to enrich it. The

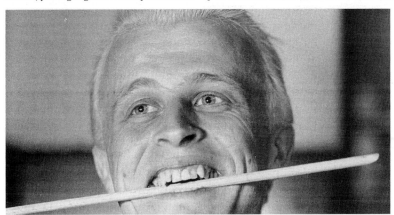

A gig too far for the lead singer of Šum Svistů.

PRAGUE IS THE CITY OF CULTURE

TOP THEATRE TICKETS - YOUR PARTNER
FOR THE BEST OF PRAGUE CULTURE

OPERA MOZART
NATIONAL MARIONETTE THEATRE
FRANZ KAFKA THEATER
BAROQUE THEATRE
THEATRE FESTIVAL
MOZART OPEN ETC.

TICKETS AND ADVANCE BOOKING:

TEL/FAX +02 - 2322536, 2324189, 2323429

Latino/North African-influenced Šum Svistů are a joy, and are one of the few Czech bands who can induce the locals to stand up and dance (it's not unusual for everyone to remain seated on the floor at a gig, creating a predictable dampener on the atmosphere). Trad reggae and ska are passably played by The Hypnotix and Sto Zvířat, while Zuby Nehty are an all-woman band (the only one), whose jazz-punk fusion leaves you tapping your feet and scratching your head. The few groups that have eschewed guitars for samplers – Vanessa, Teknofactory and Datwerk being the biggest names – play uncompromising, brutal industrial techno, taking their cue from Ministry and Front 242 rather than from more dance-oriented exponents.

Increasingly, Prague is being included on the international tour circuit. Small European and American bands (but surprisingly few British ones) have long known they can get an audience here, and the predominance of heavy rock has meant that the city's sports stadiums are often hosts to bands such as Guns 'n' Roses, Aerosmith and Pink Floyd. However, ticket prices for these gigs are expensive, and some of the agencies have sorely overestimated how much the Czechs are willing to pay, leaving them with poor gates and small audiences.

As for festivals, new ones seem to be on every time you open the paper, but they rarely last from one year to the next. Most of them are heavy rock extravaganzas, with the honourable exception of the Drop-In Festival – an evening at the Lucerna complex which occurs annually in late March or early April. Ostensibly a fundraiser and awareness-heightener for a young people's drug rehabilitation clinic, it is in fact a huge 'Legalise it!' benefit, the posters and hall being heavily decked with pictures and representations of marijuana plants. Just about every Czech band who is anybody plays this gig, and it works out as a very

cheap crash course on who's in and who's out on the local scene.

Tickets & Information

Billposting laws seem to be non-existent in Prague, and every available space is plastered with club listings and concert posters, so information is easy to come by. Details of concerts can also be found in either of the two English-language newspapers, the *Prague Post* and *Prognosis*, and in *Program*, the Czech weekly listings guide which has an English section. Tickets for small gigs can be bought on the door (it's rare for anyone to sell out), or in advance, either at the venue or at Melantrich, the ticket office in the Lucerna complex (*see chapter* **Prague by Season** for details). It costs between 40kč and 50kč to see local bands, small foreign bands might cost as much as 100kč, while medium- and large-sized international acts charge between 300kč and 500kč for tickets (usually with a 50kč booking fee on top).

Alterna Komotovka

Seifertova 3, Prague 3 (no phone). Metro Flora/26 tram. **Open** 3pm-5am daily; concerts start 9.30pm. **Admission** 30kč-60kč.
AK is one of the newer clubs in the city. It's just far enough from the centre to discourage casual tourists, but close enough to make it worth your while if you want to escape the huge crowds at more central clubs. Occupying a basement, it has a dark, gloomy atmosphere, lightened by the management's choice of dance-oriented bands. The space is long but not very roomy, so it can be a bit claustrophobic, and when the place is full the walls are slick with moisture. The dancefloor is tiny, which means that people often start dancing in, around, and occasionally on, the tables. Surprisingly, vegetarian food is served.

Belmondo Revival Club

Bubenská 1, Prague 7 (791 48 54). Metro Vltavská. **Open** concerts start 8pm. **Admission** 40kč.
As the name suggests, Belmondo regularly plays host to Beatles, Doors and Stones 'revival' bands. The club also manages to bring in occasional mid-sized foreign bands and some of the big name Czech bands. Sometimes there are discos after the band, but this is one of the few genuine concert halls in town. It boasts three bars, all of which serve cheap draft beer, and a couple of pool tables. Although a little bit out of the centre, it's easy enough to find, right beside Vltavská metro station.

Borát

Újezd 18, Prague 1 (53 83 62). Metro Malostranská/12, 22 tram. **Open** 1pm-5am Mon-Fri; 8pm-5pm Sat, Sun. **Admission** 30kč.
Probably the oldest 'alternative' club in Prague, Borát actually pre-dates the revolution. Having survived Communism, it now ekes out a precarious existence sandwiched between expensive restaurants and a hotel, none of which is happy with their down-at-heel neighbour. Each night it comes under musical assault by bands that even most Czechs have never heard of. Cheap draft beer is served in what looks like a cave downstairs, while on the ground floor there's a dingy café offering more expensive cans. Very loud everywhere, it can feel like a squatters' house party that people have been unable to escape.

Bunkr

Lodecká 2, Prague 1 (231 45 35). Metro Náměstí Republiky or Můstek. **Open** 8pm-6am daily. **Admission** 40kč-100kč.

Bunkr is the underground club that everyone knows and it's featured in any media piece on 'young people in Prague'. The first club to open after the revolution, it pulls in the alternative/rock crowd plus tourists. Fairly well-known American indie bands play here along with the best of the locals. If you've read anything about it, you'll know it has the longest bar in Prague, but that doesn't make it any easier to get a (relatively overpriced) drink. As morning approaches it can take on the atmosphere of a party in a spaceship gone adrift. The neighbours hate it, but the management have so far resisted all efforts to have it shut down. A piece of Prague youth culture history, such as it is.

Delta

Vlastina 887, Prague 6 (301 72 08). Metro Dejvická/119, 218 bus. **Open** concerts start 7.30pm. **Admission** from 40kč.

Far out, in more ways than one. The club is situated on the edge of Prague, on the way to the airport. From the outside, it looks totally nondescript; inside, however, is a large, quite classy theatre space. Here you can see concerts by the more avant-garde members of the local scene, most notably Iva Bittová, a reclusive Laurie Anderson type. The drinks are extremely cheap, and everything is over in time to catch a bus back to more familiar surroundings.

Junior Club na Chmelnici

Koněvova 219, Prague 3 (82 85 98). Metro Florenc/9, 16 tram/133 bus. **Open** concerts begin 7.30pm. **Admission** 30kč-40kč.

This was the indie club of days gone by and it still retains a thoroughly uncommercial feel. A lot of Czech bands will forever include it in their tour itinerary, as it's the place most of them first got exposure. It seems way out of the centre of

town, but it's easily reached by tram. It's the discerning Czech indie-kid's preferred venue, as prices are low and the surroundings unpretentious.

Lucerna

Vodičkova 36, Prague 1 (242 11 69-72). Metro Národní třída or Můstek. **Open** concerts start 8pm. **Admission** 100kč-400kč.

Part of the huge Lucerna complex built by, among others, President Havel's grandfather and now part-owned by the man himself. A classy, turn-of-the-century ballroom, it's just about the only mid-to-large sized venue in the centre of town. While it doesn't stage even a quarter of the gigs that the smaller venues do, the ones it does put on are of a high standard and worth the higher price. A favourite of touring indie bands, in the past year the Lucerna has hosted Nick Cave, Sugar, the Cocteau Twins and Primal Scream, as well as the *tančírny* (dance parties) of local calypso lords Šum Svistů.

Malostranská Beseda

Malostranské náměstí 21, Prague 1 (53 90 24). Metro Malostranská/12, 22 tram. **Open** 7pm-1am daily; concerts start 7.30pm. **Admission** 30kč-50kč.

Situated in the centre of one of the most beautiful areas of Prague, this club has managed to retain a rough and ready atmosphere and a relaxed attitude. Drinks are cheap and one of the local bands playing a Czech variety of ska, swing or rock 'n' roll is usually on hand to get the place going, although you could just as easily find yourself sitting among folkies listening attentively to one of the many local heroes. The regular monthly shows by the Original Prague Syncopated Orchestra – a musical time capsule that refuses to take itself too seriously – should not be missed. There's a CD shop on the premises, too.

Prosek

Jablonecká 322, Prague 9 (88 94 42). Metro Palmovka, then 156, 158, 159, 201 bus. **Open** 5-11pm Tue-Sun; concerts start 8pm. **Admission** 25kč-50kč.

Young but not techno – local band The Angry Pigs.

Only seasoned adventurers make it this far – like the Delta, Prosek is right in the middle of an enormous and depressing housing estate, and requires you to take the metro to Palmovka followed by a bus to the Liberecká stop; after that you're on your own. Essentially a grown-up youth club with a bar, it normally hosts some of the heaviest of local rock bands. The trip's not worth the bother unless you want to absorb the vibes of a true Czech rock club and enjoy the dubious honour of knowing that you are, without a doubt, the only foreigner there.

Rock Café
Národní 20, Prague 1 (249 44 14). Metro Národní třída.
Open 10pm-3am Mon-Fri; noon-3am Sat, Sun.
Admission 25kč-50kč.
Too cheap to pay for the franchise fee which would let them put 'Hard' in front of the name, this is nonetheless a cool space with a café down below, and a deceptively small concert space above. The Robert Crumb murals on the walls heighten the sensation that the Rock is trying hard to be a hip American joint, and the DJs are nothing short of appalling. A favoured place for many local rock bands to hold their CD launch parties, Rock Café also gets unknown foreign bands trying to flog their latest self-produced records. The bar staff can be unhelpful to those who haven't mastered the art of ordering a beer in Czech.

Jazz

Prague has a fine jazz tradition, and boasts a number of internationally known names. Surprisingly, however, only a handful of clubs have opened or remained open over the last five years. The town's reputation for jazz is better known to visitors than to many locals, and in most of the clubs there's usually a heavy preponderance of tourists. It could be that familiarity has bred if not contempt, then at least indifference; the same names crop up month after month, as they do the (limited) rounds of the clubs.

Visit a few clubs and the sense of *déjà vu* is heightened by the fact that the scene is constantly shifting and changing, with musicians being members of perhaps two or three different groups, pumping out trad, free form or fusion, depending on the character of the ensemble. For visitors, this can be exciting; for residents, it removes any sense of urgency over deciding when to go and see a particular group or musician; they know that if they don't go on one night, they can always go the next, or the following week, or month, and little will have changed. The high prices charged by some of the clubs don't help much either. Apart from the clubs listed below, some hotels, most notably the Praha and Paříž, occasionally host jazz nights in their (expensive) bars (*see chapter* **Accommodation** for their addresses).

AghaRTA Jazz Centrum
Krakovská 5, Prague 1 (24 21 29 14). Metro Muzeum.
Open 4pm-1am Mon-Fri; 7pm-1am Sat, Sun; concerts start 9pm. **Admission** 60kč.
Situated just off Wenceslas Square, this, along with Reduta, is one of the two top spots for local jazz groups. AJC is the cheaper and less publicised of the two and the clientele is a

fairly even mix of Czechs and foreigners. Cosy and intimate, the club has trouble finding the space to host large bands, but is perfect for sitting back and enjoying the virtuoso performances of someone like Jiří Stivin, an extraordinary flautist. Come early, as the place fills up fast and can get steamy on hot evenings. Like Reduta, there's a CD shop in the same building that is open until late, and which stocks a wide selection of local and international jazz at reasonable prices.

Highlander – Blue Note
Národní 28, Prague 1 (24 21 35 55). Metro Národní třída. **Open** noon-2am daily; concerts start 9pm.
Admission 60kč.
Recently opened, this club doubles as a restaurant. The décor is odd – it looks a little like the Hawaiian medieval dungeon in Monty Python's *The Meaning of Life*; it certainly gives you plenty to look at. Situated in Prague's 'Jazz Quarter' (four of the five clubs featured here are situated either on just off Národní), it resides under the Lucerna building. Large and spacious, it has several snugs for those who wish to avoid the full sound effects; otherwise the club's layout makes conversation extremely difficult when a concert is in progress. The food is better than average and the beer comes on tap, though it's more expensive than in a pub.

Metropolitan Jazz Club
Jungmannova 14, Prague 1 (24 21 60 25). Metro Můstek. **Open** 11am-1am Mon-Fri; 5pm-1am Sat, Sun; concerts start 9pm. **Admission** 25kč.
In a basement, like all the jazz clubs, the Metropolitan is hidden away down a side passage and often missed by the crowds who flock to the larger and better known clubs. It's a small place with a regular clientele and an easy-going atmosphere. The music is rarely challenging, the owner preferring a staple diet of swing, ragtime and blues. The resident house trio fills about a third of the slots, the rest being taken up by various 'Dixie' and 'Old Timer' groups. The décor is unassuming and for tall people the low tables are a bit of a squeeze, but the layout offers little corners for romantics and the music is rarely too loud to drown conversation. It also has a pretty extensive menu of cold dishes.

Reduta
Národní 20, Prague 1 (24 91 22 46). Metro Národní třída. **Open** 9pm-2am Mon-Sat; concerts start 9.30pm. **Admission** 80kč.
The best-known of jazz clubs, and the owner knows it. Both cover charge and drinks are the most expensive in town; the latter rival west European prices. But this is where the big Czech names and out-of-towners play – including Bill Clinton, who famously blew a sax here the last time he was in town. CDs and photos of this memorable occasion are on sale in the foyer. The concert area is well laid out, with tables strewn haphazardly around the floor, and the lighting low and intimate. The acoustics are not, however, and when some of the more avant-garde bands play you may feel the need to repair to the bar, a small, mirrored place that has a ceiling made of beer crates. Not a place for budget travellers.

Viola
Národní 7, Prague 1 (24 22 08 44). Metro Národní třída. **Open** 24 hours daily; concerts start 8.30pm and 11.30pm Sat. **Admission** 45kč.
Viola used to be quite a good space, combining a restaurant with a small patio bar and a theatre-cum-concert hall. The food is still reasonable, but you can now only hear jazz on Saturday nights, while the rest of the time bland radio pop is pumped out of the sound system. While Highlander shows the way forward for places like these, with good food and music at reasonable prices, Viola is a definite throwback to the bad old days. Surly waiters claim there's no drinks menu and then charge the earth – a small bottle of beer costs 50kč. The bands sometimes appeal, but you can catch them in more sympathetic surroundings. One to avoid.

Sport & Fitness

For the fitness fanatic or keen spectator, Prague offers plenty of sporting chances.

Prague's 1.5 million population is surprisingly well-served with sports facilities. This is mostly for historical reasons. The Sokol movement – founded in 1862 and devoted to the revival of the Czech nation through the education of the body and spirit – advocated daily fitness routines and the Communist regime provided subsidies to ensure national excellence in all sports, leaving a legacy of huge arenas and high levels of public participation. Prior to 1989, joining one of the numerous sports clubs was seen as the best way of socialising and relaxing away from watchful eyes. However, many of the city's sports facilities are now badly in need of refurbishment and renovation.

The largest sports complex in Prague is **Strahov**, which has four stadia built in the 1930s. The main arena, which accommodates up to 200,000 people, was used by the Sokol movement for its rallies, held every sixth year. It then became the natural venue for the massive synchronised gymnastic display, the *Spartakíadon*, staged

every five years by the Communists. These days it's used for the occasional rock concert or exhibition polo match and will soon be converted into two exhibition halls. The other main arena, **Stadión Sparta**, is the home of the Czech Football Association and is used for all national games (*see below* **Football**).

Strahov

Olympijská, Prague 6 (35 52 26/35 30 95). Tram 22/132, 143, 149 217 bus/cable-car from Újezd, then walk along Olympijská.
The mezi-stadion houses the office of the Federation of Czech Sports Associations (35 44 41).

Spectator Sports

Football

The toughest challenge facing Czech football is not the influx of expensive foreign players, but the need to prevent the best of the home-grown talent from fleeing to the wealthier clubs of Europe at the

Germany falls foul of Sparta – the league champions.

first sign of a fat cheque book. Some have already left, notably Škuhravý to Genoa, Moklosko to West Ham, Nemeček to Toulouse and Kubík to Nuremburg. Strong performances in European football are the best way of raising much needed hard currency, but equally are the best showcase for Czech players – a double-edged sword for the clubs. The crowds can be painfully quiet at times and managers have been known to resort to the public address system in an effort to stir up support for their team. Cries of 'go for it boys' and 'fight boys, fight' leave you wishing for some Kop-style singing. The league teams take an eight week break during the worst of the winter (January to March), and the season closes in June with the Czech-Moravian Cup Final.

Slavia Praha
Stadión SK Slavia Praha, Vršovice, Prague 10 (731 22 19). Tram 4, 7, 22, 24. **Admission** 20kč-35kč.
SK Slavia finished as runners-up to Sparta in 1993/94, which qualified them for the 1995 UEFA Cup.

Sparta Praha
Stadión Sparta, U Sparty 2, Letná, Prague 7 (38 16 91). Metro Hradčanská/8, 25, 26 tram. **Admission** *European games* 150kč; *league games* 30kč.
Like all great teams Sparta plays in red and its domination of the league is total. Few remember the last time that it didn't finish at the top. As champions, the team has had a season ticket to the European football championships and matches against the giants of the French, Italian, Spanish and German leagues are a great night out.

Viktoria Žižkov
Stadión TJ Viktoria Žižkov, Seifertova, Prague 3 (272 27 75/27 94 10). Tram 5, 9, 26. **Admission** *European games* 130kč; *league games* 20kč-40kč.
The smallest of the first division teams plays in Europe for the first time in 1995 as the 1993/94 Czech-Moravian Cup winner.

Horse Racing

The Velká Pardubická is the longest steeple-chase in the world. It's held every autumn in Pardubice, a small pretty town in the Bohemian flatlands, and attracts crowds of spectators for what is traditionally a great day at the races. In 1992, the race was disrupted by anti-blood sports demonstrators, protesting about the past number of horse fatalities. As a result, the sponsors, Martell, got cold feet and pulled out. Then, in 1993, only one horse finished the race. However, the Czech Jockey Club has fought back. Newly forged links with Doncaster racecourse have already brought changes to the infamous 'Taxis' fence and the introduction of stringent entry criteria for horses, in the hope that the race will start to attract more international entries.

Chuchle
Radotínská 69, Prague 5 (54 30 91/fax 53 66 10). Metro Anděl, then 129, 172, 241, 244 bus. **Admission** 20kč.
Flat race meetings are held here at 2pm throughout the summer, as well as trotting races on a cinder track.

Dostihový spolek a.s.
Pražská 70, Pardubice (04 03 00 96/fax 04 03 47 01). Metro Florenc then bus from the terminal. **Admission** *Saturday races (ten times a year)* 30kč; *Velká Pardubická* 150kč-1,800kč.
Race meetings from May throughout the summer months culminate in the Velká Pardubická on the second Sunday of October. Pardubice is 110kms east of Prague.

Ice Hockey

National fervour runs high when the Czech team plays, as there is an enduring hope that one day they will be world champions. The team suffered badly when Czechoslovakia split into two republics and it was all the Czechs could do to finish just above the Slovaks in the 1994 Winter Olympics and World Championships. As with football, the best players are lost to the professional ranks abroad, notably Canada and the USA, while the league teams have had to cope with a loss of state funding and diminishing crowds.

HC Sparta Praha
Sportovní hala Sparta Praha, Korunovační, Prague 7 (872 74 43). Tram 5, 12, 17. **Admission** 30kč.
This large indoor arena in Holešovice bears a striking resemblance to the one at Wembley, both architecturally and acoustically. It's the home venue of Sparta, and is also used as a concert and exhibition hall. Unlike its footballing namesake, Sparta does not dominate the ice hockey league, which is always closely contested.

Slavia Praha

Stadión SK Slavia Praha, Vršovice, Prague 10 (73 31 91). Tram 4, 7, 22, 24. **Admission** 30kč.
Slavia was promoted at the end of the 1993/4 season, making it the only other Prague team in the first division.

Activities

Cycling

The first bike messengers have been sighted on Prague's cobbled streets, a sure sign that western advertising agencies have set up shop and the copy deadline was yesterday. There are signposted cycle routes, but the traffic, cobbles and tram tracks make city cycling a nightmare. Things are better at weekends when the streets are deserted, but for sheer enjoyment put your bike on a train (there's a small charge) and head into the splendid Moravian or Bohemian countryside for the day or weekend. It's easy and cheap to hire a mountain bike from the numerous specialist shops that have recently opened. Serious cyclists can contact the **Czech Cycling Association** (*see below*) for details of cyclocross and touring races – increasingly popular events that are now bringing in large crowds.

Czech Cycling Federation

(Český svaz cyklistiky), Nad Třebešínem 111, Prague 10 (781 91 17).

Landa

Šumavksá 33, Prague 2 (253 99 82). Metro Náměstí Míru/11, 16 tram. **Open** 9am-1pm, 2-6pm, Mon-Fri.
You can hire mountain bikes from this general sports hire shop for 160kč a day. For four days or more the rate drops to 120kč a day. The deposit is 4,000kč.

Fishing

Czech Fishing Association

(Český rybářský svaz), Nad Olšinami 31, Prague 10 (78 11 75 13/fax 78 11 17 54).
This is where to purchase the relevant licences for fishing in the Czech Republic. The association can advise you on the best areas in which to catch carp, pike, trout and eel. Licences can also be bought at tackle shops.

Golf

Along with mountain bike riding, golf is probably the fastest growing sport in the Czech Republic. It is far from new to the country – the course at Mariánské Lázně is approaching its centenary year – but Prague is poorly served when it comes to courses. However, new developments should mean an increase in quality and choice. Always book tee times at weekends, and bring a handicap certificate or membership card.

Karlštejn

30km SW of Prague (office 795 39 44/golf course 031 19 47 17). **Green fee** 800kč-1,000kč.
A new 18-hole course opened here in July 1994 and includes a shop selling golf equipment. The fourteenth century

Bohemian castle forms a spectacular backdrop to many of the holes, but the town itself is a sleepy place. *See chapter* **Trips Out of Town.**

Karlovy Vary

130km W of Prague (017 322 40 11). **Green fee** 700kč.
An excellent 18-hole course set out in undulating wooded valleys, Karlovy Vary was the venue of the first Czech Open in 1937 which was won by Henry Cotton. Definitely worth a day trip. *See chapter* **Trips Out of Town.**

Mariánské Lázně

140km W of Prague (01 65 43 00). **Green fee** 1,000kč.
This 18-hole course was opened by Edward VII in 1905. The layout has changed little since then, although the course has been beefed up in the last two years to attract PGA tour events.

Poděbrady

45km E of Prague (tel/fax 03 24 34 83). **Green fee** 300kč Mon-Fri; 400kč Sat, Sun; 4,000kč annual membership.
This is a demanding nine-hole course on the tree-lined banks of the river Elbe, that seems as attractive to mosquitoes as it is to golfers.

Strahov

Olympijská, Prague 6 (35 52 26/35 30 95). Tram 22/132, 143, 149 217 bus/cable-car from Újezd, then walk along Olympijská. **Price** 50kč per bucket of balls.
This indoor driving range was opened by the Karlštejn Club in 1993. Practice on synthetic tees and a putting green in the depths of the main stadium. Clubs can also be hired.

TJ Golf Praha

Motol, Prague 5 (644 38 28). Tram 4, 7, 9. **Green fee** 500kč.
A nine-hole course and driving range on a hill top. The course can get very dry in the summer months, so be prepared for the occasional erratic bounce.

Health & Fitness

Few of the numerous gyms that have opened lately will match up to the expectations of visitors to Prague. Fitness centres often have equipment designed for heavy domestic use which is constantly out of order, or simply do not have enough machines to cope with demand. You will rarely find anyone who can draw up a personal fitness routine or advise you on the correct use of machinery, and too many of the gyms are packed with people posing in stretch Lycra, drinking protein and energy supplements.

A number of Prague's hotels have facilities which are available to non-guests. If you like to work out in the lap of luxury, try one of those listed below.

Cardiofitness

Hotel Axa, Na poříčí 40, Prague 1 (232 66 56, 232 39 67). Metro Florenc or Náměstí Republiky. **Open** 8am-10pm Mon-Fri; 9am-4pm Sat, Sun. **Admission** 30kč.
This is possibly the largest and best-equipped gym in Prague, and it's in a prime central location. Unfortunately it doesn't offer any fitness classes.

Club Hotel Praha

Průhonice 400, Průhonice (643 04 45). Metro Opatov then 227 bus. **Admission** *fitness centre and pool* 120kč 150 min.
This purpose-built hotel is 15km down the main Brno

motorway (E50, E55, D1). It offers the widest range of sports facilities in and around Prague, including six indoor and four outdoor tennis courts, two squash courts, badminton, table tennis, two lanes of ten-pin bowling and a fitness centre. There's also a small circular swimming pool in which young children should be well supervised, since it has a strong counter-current. Yearly membership is available.

Fit Club Classic
Vladivostocká 1460/2, Prague 10 (67 31 04 84). Tram 4, 7, 22, 24. **Open** 8-10am Mon-Fri; 9am-4pm Sat, Sun. **Admission** from 30kč.
Part of the SK Slavia complex, this small but well-equipped gym has staff on hand for guidance and runs a full programme of aerobic and body-shaping classes.

Fit Studio Pohořelec
Diskařská 1, Prague 1 (35 34 88). Tram 22. **Open** 9am-10pm Mon-Fri; 9am-2pm Sat. **Admission** 35kč day ticket; 500kč annual membership.
Fit Studio is situated just beyond Strahov Monastery. It has an excellent gym which is used by the Czech gymnastic squad for training and proper instruction is also provided. There's a range of aerobic classes (high, low and step) in the evenings, some of which are taken by an American instructress. If you take out club membership, you qualify for a 10% discount on classes, which start at 35kč.

Hotel Atrium
Pobřežní 1, Prague 8 (24 84 20 13). Metro Florenc. **Open** 7am-10pm daily. **Admission** 100kč-350kč day ticket; 5,000kč monthly membership; 50,000kč annual membership.
Membership gives you unlimited use of the well-equipped gym, small pool and sauna, weekly use of the small indoor tennis courts and a monthly massage. Even non-member swimmers at the Atrium are given white towelling robes, a range of toiletries and can lounge around on the sun-chairs all day.

Hotel Forum
Kongresová 1, Prague 4 (61 19 13 26). Metro Vyšehrad. **Open** 7am-11pm daily. **Admission** *activities* from 180kč-300kč per hour; *membership* 12,000kč 6 monthly; 21,000kč annual.
The Forum offers a gym with a view on the top floor of the building – you can look down over the city as you work out. The squash court doubles as the aerobics studio, so check class times. Gym entrance also includes use of the small pool and the sauna.

Jogging

Joggers, Prague is not for you. During the summer, the tree-lined trails in Stromovka Park are enjoyable jogging ground; otherwise, don't do it. From October to May, the high levels of airborne pollution mean that jogging is more likely to injure than improve your health.

Stromovka Park
Bubeneč, Prague 7. Metro Nádraží Holešovice then 5, 17, 12 tram.

Riding

Lišnice
30km SW of Prague (030 59 27 85). **Rates** 300kč per hour.
Jitka Breyerova runs a small, friendly stable with four horses. She is happy to take beginners, but prefers them to start with two-hour lessons for quicker progress. The

surrounding countryside offers many peaceful trails. It's best to book at weekends.

Tělovýchovná jednota
Na Císařské ledce 76, Žižka, Prague 7 (37 53 61/87 84 76). **Rates** 300kč per hour.
Situated on Císařský Ostrov, this large riding stable has good facilities, with a dressage ring and a show-jumping arena. It's not suitable for the complete beginner as there are no structured classes, although all riders are accompanied. For a 200kč supplement you can ride on trails in Stromovka Park, a far more enjoyable setting.

Squash

For hotels with squash courts, *see page 204* **Health & Fitness**.

Esguo Club
Strahov 1230, Prague 6 (35 70 93). Metro Dejvická then 132, 143, 149, 219 bus. **Rates** 100kč-250kč per hour.
A newly-opened club hidden behind the police car pound in the Strahov complex. There are three glass-backed courts, and a club league for the very keen. At weekends it can be hard to get a court, as the sport is proving to be immensely popular with Czech yuppies.

Skating

In January and February, when the reservoirs at Hostivař and Šarká freeze over, wrap up warmly and head for some great outdoor skating under blue skies. Vendors lining the banks hire out skates and sell *párky* (hot dogs), beer, coffee and grog. Otherwise, head for one of the *Zimní stadia* (ice rinks) in town, which open from October to April. They all have skates for hire which cost from 10kč an hour.

SK Slavia
Stadión SK Slavia Praha, Vršovice, Prague 10 (73 31 91). Tram 4, 7, 22, 24.

Smichov
Bellušova 1277, Prague 5 (54 05 91). Metro Anděl.

Sportovní hala
Výstaviště, Prague 7 (37 11 41). Tram 5, 12, 17.

Vokovice
Za lány 1, Prague 6 (36 27 57). Metro Dejvická, then 26 tram.

Swimming

Ask ten Praguers which are the best pools in Prague and you will end up with 20 different answers. Unfortunately, many of Prague's public pools have been tagged with a 'dirty water' label that is hard to shake off. Until the public authorities employ a convincing quality control system, word of mouth remains the best form of information. The pools (*koupaliště*) listed below are those most commonly recommended. Many of the indoor pools close for maintenance during the summer months, but the outdoor pools will be open, and you can swim in the various reservoirs around Prague.

For more hotels with swimming pools *see page 204* **Health & Fitness**.

Areál Strahov Stadión

Olympijská, Prague 6 (35 52 26/35 30 95). Tram 22/132, 143, 149 217 bus/cable-car from Újezd, then walk along Olympijská. **Open** 6am-8pm Mon, Thur, Fri; 6am-5pm Tue; 6am-5pm, 7-8pm Wed; 8am-2pm Sat. **Closed** July and August. **Admission** 25kč.
An indoor pool.

Divoká Šárka

Šárka, Prague 6. Tram 26, then short walk through a rocky valley. **Open** 9am-7pm daily. **Admission** 10kč.
Follow the other swimmers, or the red and white striped trail up the valley to find this outdoor pool. It's only open in the summer months (June to September) and is a firm favourite with Czechs. The setting is idyllic and the lawned sunbathing area gets more crowded than the pool.

Džbán Reservoir

(vodni nádriž Džbán), Vokovice, Prague 6. Tram 26. **Open** May-Sept 9am-dusk daily. **Admission** 10kč
A large reservoir with a naturist beach, it's close to the tram stop and very popular.

Hostivař Reservoir

(vodni nádriž Hostivař), Prague 10. Metro Háje, then bus 165, 170, 212, 213/tram 22, 26 then short walk through forest. **Open** 10am-7pm daily. **Admission** 10kč.
Hostivař is larger and deeper than Džbán and has more activities on offer, including rowing, wind surfing, tennis, volleyball and a water slide. It also has a naturist beach.

Hotel Axa

Na poříčí 40, Prague 1 (232 66 56/232 39 67). Metro Florenc or Náměstí Republiky. **Open** to public 5-10pm Mon-Fri; 9am-6pm Sat; 9am-8pm Sun. **Admission** 25kč.
At 25 metres, this is the largest of the hotel pools. Sauna and massage are also available.

Poseidon Club-Hloubětín

Nademlejnská, Prague 9 (86 29 70). Tram 3, 8. **Open** 6am-10pm Mon-Fri; 10am-6pm Sat, Sun. **Admission** 20kč.
Afternoon lessons for children and families are available here. It's an indoor pool, a little way out of the centre of town.

Pyramida Hotel

Bělohorská 24, Prague 6 (311 32 41). Tram 8, 22. **Open** 9am-10pm Mon-Fri; 10am-10pm Sat, Sun. **Admission** 30kč per hour.
The modern Pyramida Hotel, situated just above Hradčany, has a small (12-metre) pool with a sun-lounge area. It's a good place to take children.

SK Slavia

Stadión SK Slavia Praha, Vršovice, Prague 10 (73 31 91). Tram 4, 7, 22, 24. **Open** *indoor* September-April 6am-8.45pm Mon-Fri; 9am-7pm Sat, Sun; *outdoor* May-August 6am-7.45pm Mon-Fri; 9am-6.45pm Sat, Sun. **Admission** *indoor*15kč adults, 9kč children; *outdoor* 30kč adults, 15kč children.
The Swiss 'Pool Actif' system ensures water cleanliness here.

Tennis

After Budweiser and Pilsner Urquell, the country's most famous exports are its tennis stars. It started with Drobný and Kodeš, continued with Lendl and Navrátilová, and now a whole generation of younger players dominates the world game. The Škoda Czech Open may not be in Courier's or Sampras's

playing diary, but the games are well attended by this tennis-playing nation. There are surprisingly few public courts in Prague, but fortunately most private clubs hire theirs out at off-peak times.

For hotels with tennis courts, *see page 204* **Health & Fitness**.

Czech Tennis Federation

Štvanice ostrov, Prague 7 (232 46 01). Metro Florenc. **Open** 10am-3pm daily. **Rates** 200kč per hour.
The Škoda Czech Open (ATP tour) is held in the first week of August. Otherwise, there are six outdoor courts available for hire. Booking is essential.

Fit Studio Pohořelec

Diskařská 1, Prague 1 (35 34 88). Tram 22. **Open** 9am-10pm Mon-Fri; 9am-2pm Sat. **Rates** 110kč per 50 mins.
This fitness club has three outdoor courts that can be booked.

TCVŠ Praha

Nad Hlinikem, Prague 5 (52 41 20). Tram 4, 7, 9. **Open** 10am-3pm daily. **Rates** 100kč per hour.
Following the sign to the sports camp from Plzeňská takes you to this private club, situated on a wooded hillside in front of the Hotel Golf. Courts are hired out to the public at off-peak times.

TJ Vyšehrad

Pevnostni 6, Prague 4 (42 75 78). Metro Vyšehrad. **Rates** 120kč per hour.
A private club tucked under the castle walls. You can use the courts when they are not in use by members (phone to check).

The Great Outdoors

The Czech Republic has some spectacular scenery and the best way to see it is on foot. Within the environs of Prague, and in the countryside beyond, there are well-marked, coloured trails. These are shown in the Soubor Turistických map series, which is available in most bookshops.

For the more energetic, orienteering is a popular pastime and the Czechs are one of the leading nations in this sport. For the experienced orienteer, the **Czech Orienteering Association** can put you in contact with a local club that organises events throughout the spring and autumn. Climbers may find the lack of high mountains a disappointment, but the **Český ráj** region (*see chapter* **Trips Out of Town**), 100km north-east of Prague, is littered with sandstone outcrops, while **Srbsko**, which is 60km west of Prague, has limestone cliffs that offer rock climbers a good day's challenge. You must stick to the pegged routes and no metal protection is allowed, only knotted strings.

When the snow falls, head for the **Krkonoše mountains** north of Prague. Skiing is predominantly of the cross-country variety, but the two main resorts, **Harrachov** and **Spindlerův Mlýn**, are installing more chair-lifts for downhill skiers. Expect to pay around 240kč for a day pass.

Czech Orienteering Association

(Česká asociace orientačního běhu) Strahov, Prague 6 (35 46 79).

Theatre & Dance

The great Czech theatrical tradition lives on, and Prague can provide live entertainment to rival any European capital.

Prague's **National Theatre.** *See page 210.*

Theatre has long been a vital part of Prague's rich cultural life and has been a key medium for keeping national identity and the Czech language alive throughout the centuries. It played a major role in the nineteenth century National Revival and was both a mouthpiece and a victim of twentieth century political unrest. Contemporary Czech theatre, like the country itself, is in a state of flux. Though it is no longer beleaguered by political oppression, it is now at the mercy of market forces.

What you are likely to see on the Prague stage today might look slightly old-fashioned, but performances will invariably be accomplished. English-language and bi-lingual productions abound, and equally accessible to the visitor are the puppet, mime and mixed performance shows which flourish here, in which actions speak louder than words.

THEATRE AND POLITICS

Czech-language theatre played an important political role in the period between the Battle of the White Mountain (1620) and the end of the eighteenth century. During this time Habsburg domination meant that Prague's cultural and intellectual life was conducted in German. But productions in Czech continued to be performed in the countryside by puppeteers and travelling players, who went from town to town and so preserved Czech theatrical traditions.

This long period of provincial exile left a definite stamp on Czech theatre. Impressive puppet techniques were developed, as was the style that combines several different performance forms in a single production. Some of the most original and respected theatrical groups today are those that continue these traditions. One of the best known is the **Drak Theatre**, an avant-garde puppet theatre that uses both puppets and live actors.

The period between the Soviet invasion in 1968 and the Velvet Revolution of 1989 also had a dramatic impact on Czech theatre. Many survivors of the left-wing theatre groups of the inter-war years had begun to stage productions after 1945, this time supporting the ideology of the current regime. After the Soviet invasion, however, directors and actors were either banned from their profession entirely, or encouraged to leave the city and work in regional theatres. Many of these professionals have now returned to prominent positions in Prague, but the most radical work is still being produced outside the capital: the seat of the Czech theatrical avant-garde is Brno and Drak Theatre's headquarters are in Hradec Králové.

Meanwhile in Prague itself, some groups resorted to using comedy as a subtle version of protest. Without directly challenging the regime or establishing an overtly 'political' agenda, they relied instead on irony, black humour and satire. The group designated the Prague Five – the **Sklep Theatre**, and two of the smaller city theatres, the **Theatre na zábradlí** and **Studio Ypsilon**, date from this time.

Many members of the theatrical community, like Václav Havel, whose political activities meant they could only work underground in dissident theatres, have now moved back into public life. Ivan Ramyk, another former prominent dissident, is now head of the National Theatre.

Since the Velvet Revolution, market forces have come into play and – as in other areas of the arts – the decrease in government funding has led to a

MAGIC THEATRE
of BAROQUE WORLD
**ORIGINAL BAROQUE
STAGE TECHNOLOGY!**

Advertising one of the National Marionette Theatre's long-running productions.

growing reliance on sponsorship and marketing. Although there are currently no commercial West End or Broadway style theatres in Prague, there could be very soon.

THEATRE-GOING TODAY

Apart from the shows that are only aimed at tourists, tickets rarely cost more than 100kč. Praguers take theatre-going seriously and many go once if not twice a month; if you show up casually dressed, you'll certainly stand out and get snide looks from the usher in all but the smallest studio theatres.

The city has nearly 40 different theatres and it's almost impossible to walk down the street without being handed a flyer for some performance or other. The theatres all run on a repertory system, so plays are performed only two or three times each month. While a production will usually stay in repertory for several years, the limited number of performances means that actors can pursue a variety of projects and you

will rarely see a production that has become stale with over-performance.

Practical Information

Tickets can be bought – usually on the day of performance – from individual box offices or from one of the ticket agencies listed below (*see chapter* **Music: Classical & Opera** for more). Some theatres cater for the disabled, but it is best to check with individual venues about wheelchair access and other provisions. For the most up-to-date round-up of current shows, consult the listings pages of *Prognosis* and the *Prague Post*, or the English-language version of the monthly Czech listings booklet *Culture in Prague* (*Kultura v Praze*).

American Express

Václavské náměstí 56, Prague 1 (24 22 98 83). Metro Můstek. **Open** *summer* 9am-7pm Mon-Fri; 9am-3pm Sat; *winter* 9am-6pm Mon-Fri; 9am-noon Sat.
Branch: Hybernská 38, Prague 1 (24 03 23 07).

Prague Information Service (PIS)

(Pražská informační služba), Na příkopě 20, Prague 1 (26 40 22/information line 54 44 44). Metro Můstek or Náměstí Republiky. **Open** 8.30am-7pm Mon-Fri; 9am-5pm Sat, Sun.
Branches: Hlavní nádraží, Wilsonova, Prague 1; Staroměstské náměstí 22, Prague 1; Valdštejnské náměsti, Prague 1.

Major Theatres

Estates Theatre

(Stavovské divadlo),Ovocný trh 1, Prague 1 (26 77 97/24 21 50 01/box office 24 22 85 03). Metro Můstek. **Open** box office 10am-6pm Mon-Fri; 10am-12.30pm, 3-6pm, Sat, Sun.
The neo-Classical Estates Theatre pulls in Mozart fans, as it has done since *Don Giovanni* had its premiere here. Simultaneous translation headsets are available for all performances, except on opening nights. The theatrical repertoire is of both classical and contemporary drama, including Shakespeare, Ibsen, Miller and Ionesco.

Image Theatre

(Divadlo Image), Pařížská 4, Prague 1(232 91 91/231 44 48/fax 74 43 93). Metro Staroměstská/17, 18 tram. **Open** box office 1-8pm daily.
Situated just off the Old Town Square, the Image is a magnet for tourists thanks to its popular bar as well as its productions. These tend to be non-verbal or performed in foreign languages and are based on 'Black Light' theatre and pantomime.

Kolowrat Theatre

(Divadlo Kolowrat), Ovocný trh 6, Prague 1 (24 21 50 01). Metro Můstek. **Open** box office 10am-6pm Mon-Fri; 10am-noon, 3-6pm, Sat, Sun.
The Kolowrat Palace was restored to its Baroque glory in 1991, together with the studio theatre in its attic. Plays are put on here by the drama company of the National Theatre and are often more interesting (and esoteric) than those which grace the Estates Theatre's stage, opposite. Be prepared to bake – the heat certainly rises in this enclosed space.

Magic Lantern

Nová scéna, Národní 4, Prague 1 (24 91 41 29). Metro Národní třída. **Open** *box office* 10am-6pm Mon-Fri; 3-6pm Sat, Sun.
Palác kultury, 5. května 65, Prague 4 (61 17 27 11). Metro Vyšehrad. Box office as above.
The Laterna magika caused a storm when it hit the world stage at the 1958 Brussels Expo, and the company is still regarded as the godfather of progressive, radical theatre. Its performances combine theatre, film, dance, and mime, and still make for a good night out, although tickets tend to be pricey and the shows are no longer really at the cutting edge. The company moves between the Nová scéna – the controversial glass 'new stage' extension next to the National Theatre designed by Karel Prager in 1983 – and the Palace of Culture.

Music Theatre in Karlín

(Hudební divadlo v Karlíně), Křižíkova 10, Prague 8 (24 22 75 14/box office 24 21 07 10/24 21 27 76). Metro Florenc/8, 24 tram. **Open** *box office* 10am-1pm, 2-6pm, Mon-Sat.
The Music Theatre puts on popular musical shows from classical operettas to *Westside Story*. Its small stage in the basement – the Karlínek – is also used for light musical performances and studio productions.

National Theatre

(Národní divadlo), Národní 2, Prague 1 (24 91 34 37). Metro Národní třída/6, 9, 18, 17, 22 tram. **Open** *box office* 10am-6pm Mon-Fri; 10am-12.30pm, 3-6pm, Sat, Sun.
The National Theatre combines stunning neo-Renaissance architecture with a repertoire of predictable classics by the likes of Molière, Shaw, and Čapek – the Czech playwright who wrote *R.U.R* and coined the word robot. It's also the place to see opera and ballet (*see p211* **Dance** *and chapter* **Music: Classical & Opera**).

Ta Fantastika

Karlova 8, Prague 1 (24 22 90 78). Metro Staroměstská/17, 18 tram. **Open** *box office* 1-9pm daily.
Ta Fantastika's many performances for foreigners are based on 'Black Theatre', where black-clad actors holding props move almost invisibly across the stage. Their work comprises dance, movement, music and mime, and the imaginative pieces often have no dialogue – so there's no language problem.

Off the Beaten Track

Archa Theatre

(Divadlo Archa), Na poříčí 26, Prague 1 (232 62 32/box office 232 88 00). Metro Náměstí Republiky or Florenc/3, 24 tram. **Open** *box office* 10am-6pm Mon-Fri.
One of the first Czech theatres to abandon the repertory format and present a wide variety of international dance, theatre, music and multi-media shows. The newly built theatre incorporates two elegant performance spaces, a gallery and a coffee bar.

Celetná Theatre

(Divadlo v Celetné), Celetná 17, Prague 1 (25 13 11). Metro Náměstí Republiky/5, 14, 26 tram. **Open** *box office* one hour before performance.
This studio theatre forms part of the Theatre Institute of Prague. It's a base for independent Czech groups and visiting companies who often perform in English. During the summer there are six performances a week for tourists, in English or German, including puppet opera. The theatre is also the home of *Divadlo Franze Kafky* – a performance based on the life of one of Prague's most famous sons.

Dramatic Club

(Činoherní klub), Ve smečkách 26, Prague 1 (24 21 68 12). Metro Muzeum. **Open** *box office* 10am-6pm Mon-Fri.
Founded by the great director Jan Kačer and considered to be one of the best theatres in Prague, the Dramatic Club boasts gifted actors and a wide, if literary, repertoire. Expect to see works by Havel, Hrabal, Frayn and Orton (in Czech), directed by the notable Jiří Menzel, among others.

Labyrinth

(Labyrint), Štefánikova 57, Prague 5 (24 51 17 37). Tram 6, 9, 12. **Open** *box office* 10am-7pm Mon-Sat.
The attractive basement studio theatre here tends to have more interesting and progressive programming than the main auditorium, and the bar's better, too. A production worth looking out for is *Dada Opera* of which some performances are in English. In the summer the studio becomes a music venue and an open house for British theatre companies.

Rococo Drama Studio

(Rokoko činoherní studio), Václavské náměstí 38, Prague 1 (24 21 71 13). Metro Můstek/6, 8, 22, 18 tram. **Open** *box office* 10am-1pm, 2-7pm, daily.
The Rococo recently re-established itself as a 'progressive company on the edge between experimental and classical', according to its own publicity. Centrally located on Wenceslas Square, it's a commercial theatre that appeals to a tourist market, and has a bar that stays open all day.

Studio Ypsilon

Spálená 16, Prague 1 (29 22 55). Metro Národní třída/6, 9, 18, 22 tram. **Open** *box office* 1-6pm Mon-Thur; 10am-noon, 1-5pm, Fri.
Founded in 1963-64, Studio Ypsilon brings together a variety of genres including drama, music, movement and the visual arts. Before 1989 it was an oasis of artistic freedom and has exerted a marked influence on the general development of Czech theatre. It's considered by many to be the best drama company in town, and tickets sell out a long time in advance. Performances (in Czech) include witty and clever adaptations of *Othello, Mozart in Prague,* Woody Allen's *God* and Kafka's *Amerika.*

Theatre on the Balustrade

(Divadlo na zábradlí), Anenské náměstí 5, Prague 1 (24 22 19 33). Metro Staroměstská/17, 18 tram. **Open** *box office* 2-7.30pm Mon-Fri; two hours before performance, Sat, Sun; *café* 11am-11pm Mon-Fri; noon-11pm Sat, Sun.
A born-again theatre for the new era. It was a famous venue in the 1960s: Havel worked as a stage hand here and it was where his first plays were performed. It's now run by gifted young directors and managers, and offers a diverse and stimulating repertoire, often of Czech translations of foreign plays. There's also a lively café where actors hang out.

Puppet Theatre

Prague is perhaps the marionette capital of the world. An evening at one of the theatres listed below will give you an idea of what it's all about. For the National Marionette Theatre, *see chapter* **Music: Classical & Opera.**

Minor Theatre

(Divadlo Minor), Senovážné náměstí 28, Prague 1 (24 21 43 04). Metro Náměstí Republiky/3, 9, 14, 24 tram. **Open** *box office* one hour before performance.
Before 1989, the Minor was the national puppet theatre. Since then it has begun to produce a combination of puppet and live drama.

Spejbl and Hurvínek Theatre

(Divadlo Špejbla a Hurvínka), Dejvická 38, Prague 6 (25 15 74). Metro Hradčanská. **Open** *box office* 3-6pm Mon-Fri; 1-5pm Sat.

The puppet characters Spejbl and Hurvínk were created by Josef Skupa in the 1930s. Performances here are made up of comic sketches involving the duo.

English-language Theatre

Since 1989 a number of English-language companies, both amateur and professional, have sprung up in the city, although none has a fixed venue yet. Consult *Prognosis*, the *Prague Post* or *Culture in Prague* for details of their venues.

Artists for Prague

This veteran group is highly thought of among the business community. They tend to tackle large, ambitious productions, including popular musicals.

Black Box

One of the longest running and most prolific of the English-language companies. Their work has included familiar names like Sam Shepard and Alan Bennett.

Inside Out

Although they perform in English, Inside Out often collaborate with Czech directors. Their focus is international, concentrating on works not previously translated into or regularly performed in English.

Misery Makes Company

A successful combination of Czech and English-speaking professionals. Productions are of a high standard with work by both known and unknown Czech and international dramatists. A company to look out for.

Small and Dangerous

The first to produce entirely new, original pieces. Their programming is eclectic and their professional productions are enjoyed by both Czechs and visitors.

Festivals

The 1995 Prague Quadrennial

The next Prague Quadrennial will take place in June and July 1995. It is a huge international exhibition of stage and costume design, backed by UNESCO and held every four years, in which over 35 countries compete for the Golden Trigue. The 1995 event will be staged at Výstaviště (*see chapter* **Sightseeing**).

Dance

Anyone expecting Prague to be a centre for modern dance will be disappointed. During the 1930s, Prague was visited by many 'modern' dance troupes, and the movement began to gain popularity, but World War II and the subsequent regime stifled any further development. Since that time, classical ballet – along traditional Russian lines – has been the thing, and it has been hard to convince the dance establishment, especially the Dance Conservatory, otherwise. However, there are changes afoot.

Every year the cultural organisation **Dance Prague** (Tanec Praha) organises an international dance and movement festival that usually takes place during the summer. The festival's aim is to establish contact with foreign artists and stimulate more wide-spread public interest in modern dance, as well as to motivate Czech choreographers to develop their own styles. The policy seems to be working: certainly among young dancers there is a growing desire to break away from traditional forms and take a more expressive approach. At present Tanec is also in the process of founding an independent studio space to serve as a workshop and permanent venue. Meanwhile, Tanec Praha and visiting troupes from Europe and America tend to perform at the **Theatre Below Palmovka**, which also supports young choreographers and dancers. Czech names to watch out for include Barbara Kryslová, František Kreuzmann and the Monika Rebcová Dance Company. Occasionally, international or Czech performances can be seen at the **Labyrinth** (*see above* **Off the Beaten Track**).

A venue not to be missed is the impressive **Archa Theatre** (*see above* **Off the Beaten Track**), which has a strong commitment to dance and was opened in June 1994 by the famous Japanese Buto dancer, Min Tanaka. If there's dance to be found anywhere in the city, it's sure to be here.

If you're after the classics, then check the programmes at the **National Theatre**, its modern extension the **Nová scéna**, the **Estates Theatre** (*see p209* **Major Theatres**), and the **State Opera** (*see chapter* **Music: Classical & Opera**). The National Ballet, Prague's foremost dance company, performs at all of these venues. Apart from the old favourites, you might catch a Czech rendition of the 'Psycho' story, *Malý Pan Friedemann/Psycho* or *Some Like It Hot*.

Theatre Below Palmovka

(Dividlo Pod Palmovkou), Zenklova 34, Prague 8 (822 14 14). Metro Palmovka.

Dance Prague

(Tanec Praha), Pod Vyšehradem 20/69, Prague 4 (tel/fax 43 03 58).

In Focus

Business	**214**
Children	**221**
Gay Prague	**225**
Students	**228**
Women's Prague	**231**

Business

Boomtown Prague is a rollercoaster ride – we help you to negotiate it safely.

When the *Wall Street Journal* asked one young American if she would call Prague the 'The Paris of the 1990s', she laughed and answered 'I haven`t seen a lot of aspiring Ernest Hemingways here, but I have seen a lot of aspiring Donald Trumps'. And it's true – Prague is a city of opportunities, of entrepreneurial energy and of amateur professionals; it is a city where there's a sense that anything is possible.

The reasons for this atmosphere are various. The Czech Republic has the most stable economic and political situation of the former Eastern Bloc. It has the lowest inflation rate, the lowest per capita national debt, and the most stable currency. Trade is booming: foreign investment topped $1.8 billion in June 1994, and over 27,000 large and small business had been privatised between 1991 and 1994.

Unlike Hungary, Poland and Slovakia, the Czech Republic's economic policies have not been strangled by political in-fighting. Prime Minister Václav Klaus – the man credited with the Czech 'economic miracle' – is a strong proponent of mass privatisation and a Thatcherite monetarist. His pro-reform Civic Democratic party has a 53 per cent majority in parliament. The split with Slovakia engineered by Klaus in January 1993 has helped quicken the pace of the Czech Republic's move towards integration into the European Union. It seems that the Czech Republic has yet to experience the downside of capitalism.

The market has grown much more sophisticated over the past few years. Gone are the days when marketing consisted of stopping at the only salad bar in Prague to show off your new product. There are now dozens of advertising firms, hundreds of lawyers and accountants, and seemingly thousands of consultants based here. Competition is alive and well. But the market is far from saturated. The service sector, capital markets, and communications are in their fledgling stages and there are hundreds of niches that have not been filled. Prague continues to act as a magnet for local and foreign entrepreneurs: it is one of the few places left in Europe that is experiencing quick growth.

Agencies & Information

There are many organisations which offer advice on different aspects of setting up a business in Prague. If you are completely unfamiliar with the city it is best to get some background information and guidance before hiring lawyers, consultants and accountants. Unless otherwise stated, the organisations listed below are open for enquiries during business hours (9am-5pm).

British Embassy Commercial Section
Jungmannova 30, Prague 1 (24 51 04 39).
A division of the Embassy that can provide useful contacts for those wanting to set up a business with those already established. Advice is also available on reciprocal trade agreements, tax treaties and other issues.

Canadian Chamber of Commerce
Celetná 19, Prague 1 (232 12 47).
There are strong ties between the Czech and Slovak Republics and Canada because so many Czechs escaped to Canada during World War II and during the Communist era. The chamber has information about the activities of its members and can tell you about tax and trade treaties in effect between the two countries.

Commercial and Cultural Center of Quebec
Salvátorská 10, Prague 1 (24 81 18 32).
The group supports Quebec-based companies in Prague and promotes Quebec in the Czech Republic.

CzechInvest
Politických vězňů 20, Prague 1 (24 22 15 40/24 06 24 46).
A Czech government body that encourages investment in the Czech Republic. Helpful background material is available, and staff can suggest Czech contacts in the field you are interested in.

Economic Chamber of the Czech Republic
Argentinská 36, Prague 7 (66 79 11 11).
This group, the equivalent of a Chamber of Commerce, has some background information on Czech industrial sectors, Czech companies and economic trends. The staff don't necessarily speak English, so if you don't speak the language it would be wise to bring a Czech speaker with you.

The Fleet Sheet
PO Box 67, Prague 3 (24 10 25 15/fax 24 10 25 16).
A one-page brief in English of the main stories in the daily Czech newspapers. The page can be faxed every morning or every afternoon. Give them a ring or send a fax for delivery details and prices.

Irish Trade Board
Na strži 63, Motokov Building, Prague 4 (61 21 11 68).
A small group devoted to encouraging Irish trade and investment in the region. They hold information on Irish companies in the Czech Republic and existing trade and tax agreements between the two countries.

Resources
Spalená 15, Prague 1 (29 67 18).
An useful directory of contacts for anyone doing business in Prague. The book, which is updated every three months, lists

Kiss FM generated massive publicity with its in-your-face patrol.

the names, addresses and direct phone numbers of government officials, diplomats, managers of foreign businesses, banks, accountants, lawyers, journalists, justices and more. It is sold at most major hotels and at the Resources office. Phone for more details.

South African Embassy

Ruská 65, Prague 10 (67 31 11 14).
The Embassy opened its doors after the Velvet Revolution. The trade consul will provide details on any agreements and trade links that exist between the two countries.

Trade Links

PO Box 131, Opletalova 4, Prague 1 (24 21 06 92/24 21 08 97).
This organisation provides English translations of Czech laws. Phone them for a list of publications and prices.

US Embassy Foreign Commercial Service

Hybernská 7a, Prague 1 (24 51 08 47).
The commercial service has played a key role in encouraging Americans to invest in the Czech Republic. It has a decent library and can notify you of a host of different business services available. The Gold Key Service provides interested American investors with interpreters, computers, and telephones for a few days to set up meetings with perspective Czech partners. The service is only open to Americans. Call the commercial service for details and prices.

Banking

Anyone can open a bank account in Prague, but some banks require a minimum amount of money before they are willing to handle a customer's account. If you are opening a company account, you will need the company's founding papers, your own identification, and a minimum

amount of money that is dependent upon the legal type of company you are. Most banks now have some English-language speakers. When deciding where to open a company account, consider the bank's opening hours, banking fees, the speed of banking transfers and the usual length of its queues. Some of the Czech banks have very long queues.

Česká spořitelna

Na příkopě 29, Prague 1 (26 36 96).
One of the larger banks in town. Its great advantage is the dozens of cash machines it has around the country.

ČSOB

Na příkopě 14, Prague 1 (233 11 11).
Has a reputation for wiring transfers from abroad quicker than any other Czech bank, so a good place for an account if your business involves a lot of foreign exchange transactions.

Investiční a poštovní banka

Senovážné náměstí 32, Prague 1 (24 07 11 11).
This bank broke new ground by offering cheque books to customers. Unfortunately, the cheque clearing system is not yet a smooth operation in the Czech Republic.

Komerčni banka

Na příkopě 33, Prague 1 (24 02 11 11).
The largest of the Czech banks. Komerčni offers a host of different services, including cash machines and 85 branch offices (useful if your business is spread throughout the Republic).

Živnostenská banka

Na příkopě 20, Prague 1 (24 12 11 11).
Architecturally, the most beautiful of the Czech banks, Živno is known for having excellent staff, long opening hours and low banking fees.

Price Waterhouse's *swanky new offices.*

Stock Exchange

Prague Stock Exchange
Burza Praha, Na můstku 3, Prague 1 (24 49 31 01).
The Czech Stock Exchange is still in its infancy. It recently increased its trading from twice a week to five days a week, but only a few dozen firms are currently actively traded on the exchange, though over 900 are registered public companies. The end of the second wave of large-scale privatisation in 1994 increased interest in Czech stocks.

Business Services

Accountants & Consultants

Arthur Andersen
Husova 5, Prague 1 (24 40 13 00).

Coopers & Lybrand
Karlovo náměstí 17, Prague 1 (29 78 00).

Deloitte & Touche
Týnská 12, Prague 1 (24 81 14 56).

Ernst & Young
Vinohradská 184, Prague 3 (67 13 30 10).

KPMG Peat Marwick
Jindřišská 20, Prague 1 (24 22 28 02).
Consultancy work only, no accounting.

KPMG Reviconsult
Jana Masaryka 12, Prague 2 (691 01 94).

Price Waterhouse
Římská 15, Prague 1 (24 40 83 33).
Also publishes a useful booklet on doing business in Prague. Phone for details.

Recruitment Agencies

Finding good employees can be a challenge in Prague where unemployment is almost non-existent. Below is a short list of some recruiting firms. If you want to find out about competitive salaries, contact Coopers & Lybrand (*above*) and ask for their wage survey. *See also below* **Looking for a Job.**

Helmut Neumann International
Národní 10, Prague 1 (24 95 15 30).

Manpower Praha
Valentinská 7, Prague 1 (232 27 93).

Personnel Select
Milady Horákové 139, Prague 6 (32 12 69).

Start Agency
Národní 43, Prague 1 (24 22 88 86).

Exhibitions & Trade Fairs

Areall
Veveří 8, 602 00 Brno (05 41 21 82 93).
Trade fair management.

BVV Brno
Výstaviště 1, PO Box 491, 660 91 Brno (05 41 15 11 11).
The biggest trade fair grounds in the country.

Palac kultury
5 května 65, Prague 4 (61 17 22 63).
An important exhibition centre that hosts most of the larger trade fairs in Prague. The Prague Book Fair, Sports Fair and Computer Fair are among some of the larger fairs held at this site. Many companies host large conferences at the Palace, too.

Výstaviště Praha
U Výstaviště, Prague 7 (872 91 11).
The biggest trade fair grounds in Prague.

Výstaviště u Hybernů
náměstí Republiky 4, Prague 1 (37 87 43).

Interpreting & Translating Agencies

Artlingua
Myslíkova 6, Prague 2 (29 55 97).

Babel Service
Palác kultury, 5 května 65, Prague 4 (61 21 51 07).

Kahlen Servis
Havelkova 22, Prague 3 (24 21 68 26).

Precision Translations
Šlejnická 9, Prague 6 (311 49 86).

Presto
Masná 21, Prague 1 (231 68 86).
Specialists in technical, economic and legal translations.

Union of Translators and Interpreters
Senovážné náměstí 23, Prague 1 (24 14 25 17).
The Union has a list of over 600 interpreters and translators.
It will provide you with the range of prices you can expect
to pay for translation, in line with the legal rates.

Market Research

AISA
Lešanská 2a, Prague 4 (24 24 55 21).

Opinion Window
U Nikolajky 23, Prague 5 (54 62 03).

Nielsen Prag
Havelkova 22, Prague 3 (24 22 41 81).
All the above three market research companies conduct polls
and focus groups.

Resources
Spalená 15, Prague 1 (29 67 18).
Customised lists can be created for companies looking at a
specific target.

Estate Agents

Finding office space in Prague is a trial even
though there are dozens of estate agencies. Most
charge a success fee of between one or two months'
rent, so the agents tend not to show cheap properties. Make sure you rent a space with adequate
phone lines in a building that isn't due for repairs.
If you move into a building undergoing reconstruction, work will be impossible. If parking is
important, look for a building outside the con-
gested centre of the city.

AHI
Malé náměstí 13, Prague 1 (24 21 03 45).

Healey & Baker
Jindřišská 20, Prague 1 (24 22 28 02).

King & Co
Haštalská 16, Prague 1 (232 81 01).

The Benetton tram shows the company's usual restraint.

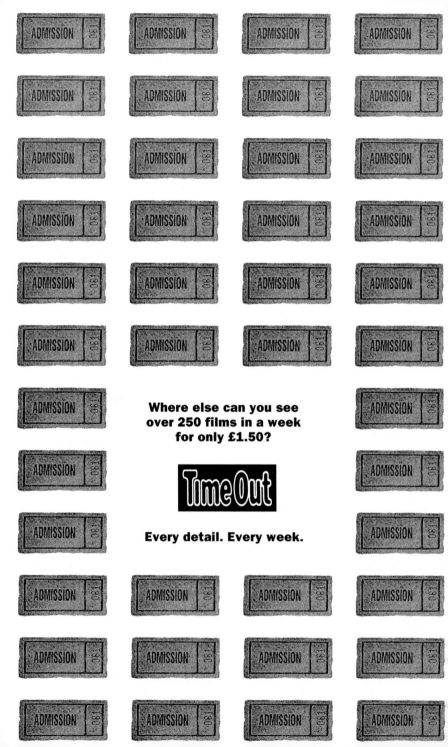

Lexxus, People and Places
Janáčkovo nábřeží 33, Prague 5 (53 35 26).

Law Firms

There are dozens of international law firms in Prague. For a local lawyer, consult the Czech Chamber of Commercial Lawyers. Below is a list of the major British law firms with offices in Prague.

Czech Chamber of Commercial Lawyers
Senovážné náměstí 23, Prague 1 (24 14 24 57).
The Chamber has a list of registered lawyers and attempts to keep track of the English-speaking ones.

Allen & Overy
Jindřišská 34, Prague 1 (24 21 36 50).

Denton Hall Burgin & Warrens
Opletalova 36, Prague 1 (24 22 61 38).

Lovell, White & Durrant
U Prašné brány 3, Prague 1 (24 81 16 72).

McKenna & Co
Husova 5, Prague 1 (24 24 85 18).

Office Services

For more information and inspiration, consult the local *Yellow Pages (Zlaté stránky).*

Furniture

Domus Schuster
Jungmannova 5, Prague 1 (24 21 57 06). Metro Můstek. **Open** 9am-7pm Mon-Fri.

Febru Praha
Francouzská 4, Prague 2 (691 14 79). Metro Náměstí Míru. **Open** 9am-6pm Mon-Fri.

Ikea
Budějovická 1667-Krč 64, Prague 4 (61 21 28 95-9). Metro Budějovická. **Open** 9am-7pm Mon-Fri; 9am-4pm Sat; 10am-4pm Sun.

Scandinavisk Industries Praha
Jungmannova 31, Prague 1 (24 23 11 85). Metro Můstek. **Open** 8am-6pm Mon-Fri.

Office Hire

City of Prague Canadian Centre
Celetná 19, Prague 1 (232 1705/231 3232). Metro Můstek. **Open** 8am-5pm Mon-Fri.
The Centre provides office space, a temporary business address and secretarial back-up.

Chronos
Václavské náměstí 66, Prague 1 (24 22 66 12). Metro Muzeum or Můstek. **Open** 8am-6pm Mon-Fri.
On offer are telephone services, office space, a temporary business address, secretarial work and photocopiers.

Pedus Office
Žitná 52, Prague 2 (24 21 45 80). Metro Muzeum or I.P. Pavlova. **Open** 9am-5pm Mon-Fri.
The office provides business and secretarial services, as well as conference rooms.

Satellite Office
Olbrachtova 3, Prague 4 (61 21 48 53). Metro Budějovická. **Open** 8am-6pm Mon-Thur; 8am-5pm Fri.
Options include a temporary business address, a telephone, fax services, secretarial services, photocopiers, and a taxi pick-up service.

Computer Leasing

All the companies listed below also sell and install computers.

Auroton Computer
Žitná 49, Prague 2 (24 22 15 09). Metro Muzeum or I.P. Pavlova. **Open** 9am-5pm Mon-Fri.

BCD
Žitná 28, Prague 2 (24 22 32 78). Metro Muzeum or I.P. Pavlova. **Open** 9am-6pm Mon-Fri.

Elko Elektronic-Computer
Jinonická 80, Prague 5 (52 31 64). Metro Jinonice or Radlická. **Open** 9am-5pm Mon-Fri.

Happycomp
Kouřimská 9, Prague 3 (73 32 35). Metro Želivského. **Open** phone for an appointment.

MacSource
Krkonošská 2, Prague 2 (627 22 24). Metro Jiřího z Poděbrad. **Open** 9am-5pm Mon-Fri.

SysComput
Jeremiášova 870, Prague 5 (529 43 49). Bus 184, 225.

Photocopying

Copia
Senovážné náměstí 23, Prague 1 (24 14 21 20/24 14 21 27 96). Metro Hlavní Nádraží or Můstek/3, 9, 14, 24 tram. **Open** 7am-7pm Mon-Fri; 9am-1pm Sat.

Copy General
Senovážné náměstí 26, Prague 1 (2423 0020). Metro Hlavní Nádraží or Můstek/3, 9, 14, 24 tram. **Open** 24 hours daily.

Rank Xerox
Štěpánská 36, Prague 1 (24 21 57 16). Metro Můstek. **Open** 8am-6pm Mon-Fri.

Reprostudio
Školská 34, Prague 1 (26 67 98). Metro Můstek. **Open** 8am-8pm Mon-Fri; 10am-5pm Sat, Sun.

Express Mail Services

The normal postal service is slow and erratic, so if you need to be sure, use one of the following services. *See page 258* for more information.

American Rainbow
Nikoly Tesly 10/1095, Prague 6 (311 92 39). Metro Dejvická. **Open** 8am-5.30pm Mon-Fri.

DHL
Na poříčí 4, Prague 1 (35 42 42). Metro Náměstí Republiky/3, 24 tram. **Open** 7am-7pm Mon-Fri; 8am-3pm Sat.

UPS
Komunardů 39, Prague 7 (66 71 21 33). Metro Vltavská/1, 2, 12, 14, 25 tram. **Open** 7.30am-5pm Mon-Fri.

Výstaviště: *the biggest trade fair grounds in Prague. See page 217.*

Courier Services

Express Parcel Service
Pod lysinami 9, Prague 4 (402 20 70). Metro Smíchovské nádraží. **Open** 8am-7pm Mon-Fri.

Messenger Service
Na čihadle 51, Prague 6 (311 63 98). Metro Dejvická. **Open** 8am-7pm Mon-Fri.

Mobile Phones & Paging Systems

Eurotel Praha
IBC Building, Pobřežní 3, Prague 8 (67 01 11 11). Metro Florenc or Křižíkova. **Open** phone for an appointment.

Radiokontakt Operator
Skokanská 1, Prague 6 (341 00 41). Bus 191. **Open** phone for an appointment.

Looking for a Job

Prague can be an employee's dreamland. If you speak English and Czech and have some office skills it isn't hard to find a job. But if you don't speak any Czech, don't expect to be welcomed into the Prague working world with open arms. As the market becomes more mature, foreign companies are turning to a local rather than an ex-pat work-force. Locals are cheaper to hire and more likely to take a long-term view of their job. Despite these strictures, there are still plenty of opportunities in Prague for those who learn quickly and have the patience to look for them.

If you are a recent graduate with little experience, the best way to start is by teaching English. There are plenty of positions available, especially for those with TEFL (Teaching English as a Foreign Language) or ESL (English as a Second Language) training. For those with a long-term view, the best way to start is by teaching in one of the small villages outside Prague where the locals need native speakers and where you can become completely familiar with the Czech lifestyle before finding a long-term job in Prague. There are several exchange programmes listed below that can help you find a teaching position or a volunteer position in a Czech company.

The best place to look for a short-term job is by consulting the pages of the *Prague Post, Prognosis*, the Resources directory, the weekly advertising paper *Annonce* and by doing the rounds of the recruitment agencies (*see above*). In Prague you can expect to be given a lot of responsibility and very little compensation by west European standards. Businesses are expanding so quickly that a lowly receptionist can easily be promoted to an account manager in less than a year. Foreigners hired in Prague are required to pay the same 47 per cent wage tax (which includes social, health, and income tax) as Czechs, unless they make special arrangements with their employer. You will also need to get a work permit (*see chapter* **Survival**) before taking a permanent job. *See chapter* **Students** for details of courses to study in Prague.

AIESEC ČR
(International Association of Students of Economics and Business), Senovážná náměstí 2, Prague 1 (24 22 43 37/fax 24 21 86 85).
Contact the President, Radovan Nezrala, for more information.

AISE
(American Intercultural Student Exchange), Radnické schody 5, Prague 1 (53 92 38/fax 55 11 11).
An exchange programme designed for those aged between 15 and 18. Contact Jaromir Cigler for more details.

ASSE
(International Student Exchange Program), Francouzská 23, Prague 2 (25 05 42/fax 25 72 79).

Fulbright Commission
Táboritská 23, Prague 3 (27 71 55/27 55 83/fax 27 42 08).

IAESTE ČR
(International Association for the Exchange of Students for Technical Experience), Technická 5, Prague 6 (332 33 30/tel/fax 24 35 33 30).

Students for Central/Eastern Europe
U Michelského lesa 366, Prague 4 (49 66 93/fax 49 66 19).
Contact Scott Douglas for more information.

Children

All the information you need to keep the little blighters amused and entertained.

A couple of Prague Zoo's residents. See page 223.

Prague doesn't have so many or such glamourous attractions for children as Paris or London, but it is a lot easier to cope with. Everything is very cheap (if you are a foreigner), the city is small, the public transport works. There is an old-fashioned quality to life, which will escape children reared on Disney and Nintendo but may appeal to their parents. This is best seen at Christmas, which is not yet the consumer orgy that it is in west Europe or America. Christmas Day itself is a low-key affair. The excitement is concentrated on St Nicholas's Eve (5 December), when fearsome devils send tremors down children's spines and benign angels cheer them up again with sweets. *See chapter* **Prague by Season**.

THE FAMILY

The very rapid changes that have taken place since 1989 have impinged on the family – for better and for worse. Women have more choice to stay at home or pursue a career. There is less pressure on them to marry early. (Scare stories used to suggest that women could only have healthy children between the ages of 20 and 25. This, along with the housing shortage and general lack of freedom, encouraged very young marriages.) Contraception has improved, and the abortion rate, which in 1989 was 1:1, is falling rapidly. On the other hand, the financial pressures are mounting. State subsidies are being withdrawn from nursery and kindergarten education, and husbands and partners are working long hours to earn a decent wage.

Even so, some things never change: namely grandmothers. Families are generally small, with one or two children. Grandmothers are generally young. They take a very strong – some would say too strong – interest in their progeny and are usually happy to shoulder the burden of childminding.

School gets off to a leisurely start at kindergarten (mateřská škola), and begins in earnest at six or seven in the základní škola. Between 11 and 15 children are streamed into gymnasia, followed by university, or into specialised secondary schools for studying building, hotel management, etc (sometimes also followed by tertiary education), or into vocational schools, for catering, nursing, shop work, and so on. The education is rigorous and old-fashioned, very good at imparting knowledge and discipline, less good at encouraging creative thought. But overall the system works, and Czechs regard the new private schools with some suspicion.

Practicalities

Transport

Children up to ten years old travel free on public transport. Those aged between ten and 16 travel half price (3kč), as do adults accompanying children up to three years old. Children under 12 are forbidden to travel in the front of a car. Seat belts are not obligatory in the back.

Legalities

Young people can vote and buy cigarettes or alcohol at 18. The age of consent is 15.

Baby Requirements

Disposable nappies and baby food are widely available.

Childminding & Home Help

The large hotels usually have a babysitting service. Otherwise try one of the agencies below.

Affordable Luxuries

Sarajevská 14, Prague 2 (37 53 79).
Babysitting, cleaning, grocery shopping.

Agentura Martina

P.O. Box 12, Prague 9 (85 91 14 27).
Babysitting, care for the elderly, housework and cleaning for 35kč per hour.

Babysitting

Vondroušova 11194, Prague 6 (301 17 64-5/302 11 30).
Petra Tajovská will supply English-speaking babysitters for 49kč per hour.

Sightseeing

Children have a limited appetite for sightseeing, but don't despair: there are plenty of modest sights that don't require much stamina. Start with a trip to the astronomical clock in the Old Town Square. Then wear them out with a goat-like ascent of the nearby tower (*see chapter* **Sightseeing**). A trip up Petřín Hill on the funicular is another dead cert. Then, when they go on strike, retreat to the river, where you can row or cruise while admiring the picture-postcard views. When you are really stuck go on a tram ride. Trams have an unaccountable fascination for small children, and at weekends you can treat them to a special trip on the historic tram.

On rainy days there are the museums. The following are particularly suited to children: the National Technical Museum, the Toy Museum, the Náprstek Museum, the Police Museum, the City Transport Museum and the Military Museums (*see*

chapter **Museums**). St Agnes's Convent has a children's art room which can be used by the public at any time (*see chapter* **Art Galleries**).

Historic tram

(Information 312 33 49). From Malostranská to Výstaviště, via the National Theatre and Wenceslas Square. **Times** *April-Oct* 12.10am-8pm Sat, Sun, Bank Holidays. **Fare** 10kč adults; 5kč children.

Petřín Hill

(Petřínské sady), Prague 1. Metro Malostranská/12, 22 tram then funicular from Újezd. **Open** 9.15am-10.45pm daily.
This is a terrific outing for children. They love the funicular and are enchanted by the Mirror Maze. There is also a playground at the top of the hill (exit the wall by the Tower and turn right) and the possibility of finding some scrawny ponies giving rides. In the winter you can witness, or even join, some hair-raising tobogganing (*see chapter* **Sightseeing** for opening times).

Towers

Children love romping up ancient towers, particularly when there's a good view from the top. The towers on Charles Bridge, the Astronomical Clock Tower and the Powder Gate are all open daily between 9am and 7pm to be scaled. *See chapter* **Sightseeing**.

Trips Out of Town

Easy. In a car or a rackety train you can get your kids out into the countryside in under an hour. Local maps will help you to find walking, picnicking and paddling spots. There are castles everywhere. Křivoklát (with torture instruments) and Kokořín are particularly good for children. Karlštejn isn't: there are too many coaches and not enough dungeons. Older children might like walking in the Český ráj. For more details, *see chapter* **Trips Out of Town**.

Parks & Entertainment

There are many beautiful parks in Prague. Vyšehrad, Stromovka and Hvězda Park are good for strolling and triking. The top end of the Šárka valley is big enough and wild enough for cyclists to let off steam without any danger from traffic.

Divoká Šárka, *Vokovice, Prague 6. Tram 26.*
Obora Hvězda, *Liboc, Prague 6. Metro Malostranská then 22 tram/tram 1, 2, 18.*
Stromovka, *Bubeneč, Prague 7. Metro Nádraží Holešovice then 5, 12, 17 tram.*
Vyšehrad, *Prague 2. Metro Vyšehrad.*

Playgrounds

Prague's playgrounds are disappointing. Most are old and broken down, and are viewed by nervous foreign mothers as far from safe. There are a few exceptions, including those listed below, which are worth visiting if you are in the area. (Children should be well supervised at Slovanský ostrov, where the concrete construction is irresistible but dangerous.)

Puppet shows always go down a treat, and there's no language barrier.

Židovské pece, *Malešická, Prague 3. Tram 9, 16, 19.*
Riegrovy sady, *Rajská zahrada, Prague 2. Metro Jiřího z Poděbrad then 11 tram.*
Slovanský ostrov, *Nové Město, Prague 1. Tram 22.*

Funfair

Výstaviště

U Výstaviště, Prague 7 (37 22 04/37 10 43). Metro Nádraží Holešovice/5, 12, 17 tram.
Funfair & playground (Lunar Park) **Open** 2-10pm Tue-Fri; 10am-10pm Sat, Sun.
Children's indoor play area (Dětský svět) **Open** 2-6pm Tue-Fri; 11am-6pm Sat, Sun.
Panorama **Open** 2-5.30pm Tue-Fri; 10am-5.30pm Sat, Sun.
A funfair which is as noisy and tacky as you could find anywhere – and it doesn't even have any great rides. But it is dead cheap (5-15kč a go) and boasts a carousel at the entrance with King Kong rearing over Chinese dragon boats. The funfair itself and the playground are behind the exhibition building, so don't linger with King Kong. In the spring there's a special fair, the Matějská pouť, which starts on 24 Feb, St Matthew's Day, and runs for a month. Bloodthirsty children will also enjoy the panorama of the epic Hussite defeat at the Battle of Lipany.

Zoo

Zoologická zahrada v Praze

U Trojského zámku 3, Prague 7 (66 41 04 80). Metro Nádraží Holešovice, then 112 bus, or walk through Stromovka park and across Císařský ostrov. **Open** summer 9am-7pm daily; winter 9am-4pm daily.
Admission 20kč adults; 15kč children, students; free under 6s.
The zoo was built in 1931 and isn't in great shape. But despite the shortage of cash the animals are quite well cared for and there is a successful breeding programme. The 1994 generation included a Turkmenian wild ass, a Przewalski horse and triplet Siberian tigers. The safety precautions are such that children can stroke the rhino's back. Using the zoo as a bribe, you could also take in the adjacent **Troja Château** (*see chapters* **Sightseeing** *and* **Art Galleries**). Even the bolshiest child might be amused by the Grand Salon.

Shows & Television

For children's shows and films, check out the listing magazines, *Kultura v Praze*, *Přehled* and *Program*, as well as the *Prague Post*. Keep an eye open for visiting circuses and sporadic performances of *Broučci*, a favourite children's ballet based on the story of a firefly who marries and has ten babies. Older kids can be taken to concerts or *Cinderella*, where you will find impeccably-behaved Czech children in shiny shoes and party dresses.

Children's films are shown all over the city (foreign ones are dubbed). Children's TV – often enjoyable, despite the language barrier – appears briefly in the evening and on Saturday and Sunday mornings at 8am. If you get desperate, hire a video (*see chapter* **Services**).

Minor Theatre

(Divadlo Minor), Senovážné náměstí 28, Prague 1 (24 21 43 04). Metro Náměstí Republiky.

Divadlo na Starém Městě

Dlouhá 39, Staré Město, Prague 1 (231 16 40/231 17 39/231 48 33). Metro Náměstí Republiky.
The children's theatre at these two venues is very lively but rather inaccessible to non-Czech speakers. With the use of a dictionary, try to find a performance of a known fairy tale: *Kocour v botách* (Puss in Boots) or *Kráska a zvíře* (Beauty and the Beast) for example.

Spejbl and Hurvínek Theatre

(Divadlo Spejbla a Hurvínka), Dejvická 38, Prague 6 (25 15 74). Metro Hradčanská.
The home of the well-loved puppet duo Spejbl and Hurvínek.

Sport

There are plenty of opportunities for children to go skiing, skating and swimming (*see chapter*

Sport & Fitness). The skating rinks sometimes have special hours for children.

Hucul Club
Zmrzlík 3, Řeporyjská, Prague 5 (52 83 13). Metro Nové Butovice then 230, 249, 256 bus. **Children's lessons** Sat, Sun. **Fees** 150kč per hour. **Membership** 450kč per year (lessons free).
Czech horses tend to be very large and pretty wild. This is one of the few stables that has mounts suitable for children.

Koupaliště Tichá Šárka
Šárecké údolí, Prague 6 (312 10 88). Metro Dejvická, then 161, 254 bus. **Open** *1 June-30 Sept* 10am-6pm daily. **Admission** 15kč adults; 5kč children under 10.
A charming outdoor swimming area, quiet and shaded, with two pools fed by clean spring water. The smaller one is for paddling, the larger one shallow enough for young children to stand in.

Eating Out

The dire service that still prevails in some restaurants can test a saint's patience, let alone a hungry child's. You may prefer to play safe by going to McDonald's or a pizza joint (*see chapter* **Services** for some takeaway and home-delivery options). If you are travelling out of town, consider taking a picnic. With ice-creams, don't be seduced by the ubiquitous Algida umbrellas. Czech ice-cream, which is often hidden at the back of the store, is just as good and a fraction of the price.

McDonald's
Václavské náměstí 9, Prague 1 (24 22 67 08). Metro Můstek. **Open** 8am-11pm daily.
Branches: Anděl, Prague 5; Florenc, Prague 8; Mostecká 21, Prague 1; Vodičkova 15, Prague 1.

Health

It is not advisable to drink the Prague water, which is loaded with nitrates and other undesirables. Atmospheric pollution is also a problem. On some winter days the radio warns parents to keep young children indoors. If you are planning to live in Prague, look for accommodation on the outskirts or on the hills of Prague 5 and Prague 6. *See also chapter* **Survival** for more information on obtaining medical treatment.

Na Homolce Hospital
Nemocnice na Homolce, Roentgenova 2, Prague 5 (52 92 20 17). Tram 4, 7, 9/167 bus. **Open** 24 hours daily.
The hospital has a **paediatric department** (52 92 20 33) with English-speaking doctors. It's open 8am-4pm daily. There is also a 24-hour emergency service (52 92 20 43) that will make home visits if necessary. The International Women's Club (*see chapter* **Women**) also supplies a list of foreign-language speaking doctors from which Prague residents can pick and choose.

Health Care Unlimited
Nemocnice na Homolce, Room D120, Roentgenova 2, Prague 5 (52 92 20 17). Tram 4, 7, 9/167 bus. **Open** 24 hours daily.
A comprehensive health service which will make emergency visits and can refer you to specialists in any area. The staff includes a trained midwife who runs pre- and ante-natal classes.

Injections

If you are living in Prague, or planning to travel around the countryside, it's advisable to be vaccinated against tick-born encephalitis, which is endemic throughout eastern Europe. The ticks are prevalent in wooded areas and in some parts of the country they carry the encephalitis virus. The hospital Na Homolce (*see above*) will provide the vaccine – a course of three injections.

The ticks start very tiny, smaller than a pin-head, and must be removed intact. A great deal of local lore is attached to this. One approach is to smother them in soap or vaseline and then use tweezers to twist them off anticlockwise. If you are too squeamish for this, try a drop of superglue. After a bit it usually separates from the skin and the tick can be pulled away whole. Disinfect the area thoroughly. Occasionally the bite causes an infection, with a red mark around the spot and a fever. This should be treated immediately with antibiotics.

Playgroups & Schools

The International Women's Club (*see chapter* **Women's Prague**) runs informal playgroups. A few ex-pat children go to local kindergartens. The education is fine in a creative, free-and-easy way, but the language can be a problem. Otherwise try the English-speaking schools below; families who are, or aspire to be, bi-lingual could try the German and French schools.

British International Day School
Belgická 25, Prague 2 (25 68 59/fax 25 00 73). **Age** 3-12.
British curriculum and staff and branches in Prague 2, 4 and 6.

English College in Prague
Jožky Jaburkové 139, Prague 9 (tel/fax 66 31 09 45). **Age** 13-18.
A private school with Prince Charles, President Havel and others as sponsors, which operates within the Czech education system. It provides a British education with International Baccalaureate exams.

International School of Prague
Mylnerovka 2, Prague 6 (tel/fax 24 31 02 23). **Age** 4-18.
Not exactly international: American.

Riverside School
Roztocká 9, Prague 6 (32 27 69). **Age** 3-16.
An English school set up by an enterprising group of parents.

Deutsche Schule Prag
Skuteckého 1384, Prague 6 (301 17 25/fax 301 17 03). **Age** 6-18.

Ecole Française de Prague
Postal address: *Štěpánská 35, P.O. Box 850, Nové Město, Prague 1.* School premises: *Krupkovo náměstí, Prague 6 (32 28 72/fax 24 22 87 01).* **Age** 3-18.

Gay Prague

Though gay life in Prague is apparently low-key, there's still plenty going on behind the scenes.

The Czechs are proud of their long tradition of tolerance and democracy, and it may actually be true that Czech homosexuals have fared better over the years than many of their west European counterparts. Even in darker periods of history, the state has often been too busy with political or religious repression to concern itself with sexual orientation. In the 1960s, Czechoslovakia was the first socialist state to decriminalise homosexuality. Now there is one age of consent (15) common to everyone.

Official positions and public attitudes have continued to look encouraging since 1989: legal registration of same sex partnerships may be on the cards, open hostility and queer bashing are almost unknown (skinheads are more interested in ethnic issues) and even the President's wife likes to patronise a restaurant run by two gays.

Despite all this, Prague is no San Francisco. Gay life is still mostly under wraps. The same polls which suggest liberal attitudes also reveal low levels of public awareness. Openly gay public figures have almost no impact on public life, even in artistic circles. Modesty and discretion are highly valued by Czechs and, since society appears to pose little threat, the homosexual community, undemanding and relatively content, seems to reciprocate by politely avoiding confrontation. Czech society is so firmly rooted in the home and in family life that the 'four per cent' easily pass unnoticed. Gay men and lesbians take care to keep their personal lives private and, despite the efforts of groups such as SOHO (*see below* **Organisations**), political activity remains pretty low-key.

Behind the scenes, however, gay life is still quite rich and relatively unrepressed, with a high proportion of the activity centred on Prague. Those who aren't themselves fully absorbed in partnership and domesticity can pursue a reasonably healthy demand for social activity while everyone else is safely tucked away at home and blissfully unaware.

Even in the capital, the gay scene, like most other aspects of society, is still heavily male-dominated. For more on the lesbian scene, *see chapter* **Women's Prague**.

The dance floor at the **Mercury Club***: Prague is no San Francisco. See page 226.*

Health & Safety

Gay or straight, pick-pocketing and theft are probably the biggest threats to visitors in Prague. Still, should your sightseeing interests take you to cruising spots such as Letná Park (Letenské Sady in Prague 6), you should be prepared for the same risks as anywhere else.

Prague is no haven from AIDS. Though official statistics are low and awareness is pretty high, *SOHO* magazine warns that levels of safety in practice do not necessarily correspond. So, however things may look, don't expect sex to be safer here than anywhere else. Condoms (*preservativy*) are readily available at all the main clubs, from chemists and some metro stations.

See also chapter **Survival** for more on obtaining medical treatment in Prague.

HIV Tests
Hygenická stanice, Dittrichova 17, Prague 2. Metro Karlovo náměstí. **Open** 8am-noon Mon-Fri.

Helplines

HIV Helpline
(14 21 09 56). **Open** 6-10pm Tue.

AIDS Helpline
(29 17 73). **Open** 1-4pm Mon-Fri.

Radio Metropolis
(27 27 71/27 28 18)
For information about HIV testing.

Emergency Health Care
Freephone 155 or (51 71 11/ 52 60 40)
A helpline that deals with general medical enquiries. English and German is spoken.

Out & About

Ironically, the post-Communist property restitutions have seen off several legendary gay night spots and the scene hasn't yet recovered. Attempts to recreate the much-lamented and peculiarly Czech atmosphere of these places (a uniquely successful balance between cosy and sleazy) have come to little. Many post-revolutionary clubs have already fallen prey to a volatile commercial situation or the fickleness of the new community. One or two establishments have opened as gay clubs only to 'straighten out' soon after. The clubs and bars listed here are those which have managed to cling on for a while and look likely to survive for a bit longer. It's always best to double-check new establishments you hear about, unless you want to trail over to the other side of town only to find yourself amongst a busload of German pensioners.

Most bars and clubs give you a tab on entry which you settle when you leave. Losing it could be costly. Entry to nightclubs usually costs between 20kč and 30kč.

Bars & Pubs

U Dubu
Záhřebská 14, Prague 2 (691 08 80). Metro I.P. Pavlova or Náměstí Míru. **Open** 5pm-midnight Tue-Sun.
At first sight just like any other Czech beer pub, serving plates of *gulaš* and *knedlíky* and with glasses of frothing beer landing unbidden in front of the mature regulars. The total, rather than virtual, absence of female clientele is the main give-away. A good place to meet people – the atmosphere can sometimes even be called lively.

Pavlač
Slezská 134, Prague 3 (no phone). Metro Flora. **Open** *summer* noon-10pm daily.
Whatever must the neighbours think! Someone's backyard has been festooned with voluminous undies that do little to camouflage this tiny day-time off-shoot of the Mercury Club (*see below*). Wittily decorated and very friendly, Pavlač offers a fairly limited selection of drinks and food (barbecued on a converted dustbin), but it's still a great place to start off a summer evening (it's closed in the winter). Check that it's open with Mercury at the weekends in case all the staff are off at one of the extra-mural Adam/Mercury activities.

Sam
Čajkovského 34, Prague 3 (no phone). Metro Jiřího z Poděbrad. **Open** 3pm-midnight Tue-Sat.
Sam declares itself to be a 'Lederklub' and 'Here for the boys'. Boys you'll probably find, but you may need to bring your own leather – sightings of home-grown leather queens are mythically rare.

Clubs & Discos

Drake's
Petřínská 5, Prague 1 (no phone). Tram 6, 9, 12. **Open** 24 hours daily.
A 24-hour gay complex and up-front 'really big cruise facility', Drake's offers plenty of opportunities: shopping, cruising, relaxing, drinking, live strip shows and private video cabins. You either love it or loath it. It's a bit pricey unless you think you're going to want to slip in and out on a day pass.

Mercury Club
Kolínská 11, Prague 3 (67 31 06 03). Metro Flora. **Open** 9.30pm-6am daily.
Its not hard to see why Mercury is just a touch too camp for some tastes. Mercurians may not be divine messengers but plenty of them seem to have wings. Mirrors encourage show-offs on the dance-floor and poseurs around the bar. As if that weren't enough, foam spurts from the ceiling as things hot up on the floor. But the staff and a varied and unpredictable clientele create a friendly atmosphere. The club is popular with lesbians – phone for an update on club nights.

Riviéra
Národní 20, Prague 1 (24 91 22 49). Metro Národní třída. **Open** *bar* 11.30am-9pm, *club* 9pm-5am, daily.
Its central position is probably the main factor in the popularity of Prague's biggest and busiest gay club. The décor is a blend of the drab (the entrance lounge and video bar), Prague-style glitz (the disco and main bar area), the incongruous (the fish tank) and the dark (the dark room). Take a look around and you'll see that it's not only the fish who've seen it all before. Singalong standards pack the intimate dance-floor, the DJ's occasional techno indulgences usually manage to clear it. The clientele is of a mixed age group but predominantly male. Unless you're pursuing specific goals, the neutral atmosphere can wear thin after a few visits here, but the club is a good introduction to Prague's gay night-life.

to switch to sweat and steam as disco business moved nearer the centre of town. It's a fairly up-market, clean and salubrious milieu for a variety of activities.

Inkognito

Střelničná 1969, Prague 8 (85 66 16). Tram 14, 17, 24, 25. **Open** *3pm-midnight Mon, Tue; 1pm-midnight Thur, Fri; noon-midnight Sat, Sun.*

Its a fair old hike from the centre, but Czech sauna aficionados remain devotees of Inkognito. Partitioning and videos contribute the free and easy atmosphere.

Gay penzion David

Has a small sauna open to non-residents (*see above* **Accommodation**).

Organisations

SOHO

(25 78 91).

A large umbrella organisation for lesbian and gay groups in the Czech and Slovak republics. Publishes the monthly *SOHO Revue* (*see below*).

Men-Klub Lambda

Rubensova 2180, Prague 10.

A gay organisation that meets on alternate Thursdays at the Mercury Club (*see p226*).

Logos

U školské zahrady 1, Prague 8 (66 41 01 45). Tram 14, 17, 24, 25.

An ecumenical gay men and lesbian Christian association which meets on the first Sunday of every month. It's an active and friendly group. Contact Father Storek for information.

Publications

The clubs and bars are the best place to pick up gay publications, which are both informative and entertaining.

SOHO Revue

A fairly serious monthly magazine which lists activities and contact addresses around the country. There's a useful English-language summary and personal ads for foreigners.

GAY Service

A free monthly bulletin of commercial activities in the Czech and Slovak Republics. Check the listings carefully before setting out – many don't specify the city. Look for the Prague telephone code (02) before you find yourself searching for a Bratislava club.

Information

Gay Information Center (GIC)

Krakovská 3, Prague 1 (tel/fax 26 44 08). Metro Muzeum. **Open** *summer 2pm-2am daily.*

For information about accommodation, guided tours, erotica, legal and commercial services, this is a useful helpline.

Adam/Mercury

Mercury Club, Kolínská 11, Prague 2 (67 31 06 03). Metro Flora.

Sorts out the fun activities: monthly *parník* (river-boat) parties as well as tram parties, zoo trips and football matches. Check the information display at Mercury, which also has information about lesbian activities.

U střelce

Střelecký ostrov, Prague 1 (no phone). Tram 6, 9, 18, 22. **Open** *9pm-6am Mon-Sat.*

Try a bit of local colour on a Friday or Saturday night. Lady Pitchfork and her famous troupe of 'artistes' have been offering much the same cabaret in a variety of locations (check where before you go) for as long as anyone can remember. Thankfully there seems little chance of it ever losing its 'freshness'. Devoted (or hardened) regulars, male and female, add sparkle of their own to the proceedings. It's a good chance to catch up on the 1960s – Czech style – and to marvel once more at favourite divas. Arrive well before 11pm to get a seat. If you stay long enough you could strike lucky – on the Tombola.

Tom's Bar

Pernerova 4, Prague 8 (732 11 70). Metro Florenc. **Open** *bar 6pm-5am daily; disco 10pm-4am daily.*

A popular men-only bar and disco. The ground floor looks much like any other no-nonsense Czech restaurant and serves reasonable food. The cellar houses a dance-floor (mostly used for display purposes), a video room and a cavernous dark area. There are occasional live shows. The mixed-age crowd often thins out around midnight as people move on into the centre of town.

Accommodation

Gay penzion David

Holubova 5, Prague 5 (tel/fax 54 98 20). Metro Anděl/231 bus. **Rates** *single* 1,200kč; *double* 1,800kč.

Gay visitors (male and female) will find this suburban villa a good base for unwinding. The well equipped, clean rooms are good value. Advanced booking is essential. There's also a sauna (*see below*) and delightful terrace restaurant that's open to non-residents and is possibly the best gay kitchen in town.

Gay Information Center (GIC)

GIC (*see below* **Information**) can fix up private accommodation. Prices vary according to the location and amenities.

Adam/Mercury

Adam (*see below* **Information**) may also be able to provide accommodation. Mercury plans to open its own pension soon – phone for details.

Saunas

David Club

Sokolovská 77, Prague 8 (23 17 8 82). Metro Křižíkova. **Open** *5pm-3am daily.*

What used to be Prague's only gay night-spot wisely decided

Students

Surviving on a shoe-string as a student in Prague: where to study, where to stay and where to hang out.

Since the Velvet Revolution in 1989 there have been some major upheavals in the Czech education system. The political change has meant that many courses previously based on Marxist-Leninist ideology have had to be entirely restructured; there has been a decrease in the number of students studying the formerly promoted fields of agriculture and engineering and an increase in the numbers studying humanities and sciences. In contrast to the tight central control imposed on universities by the Communist government, individual faculties now function as semi-autonomous units setting their own student quotas and entrance requirements.

Bookshop, café and hang-out. See page 230.

As in Britain, only a small percentage of the population goes on to further education, as there is rigorous competition for a limited number of places. The minimum requirement is the *maturita* or school-leaving certificate which enables students to apply to individual university faculties which then have their own selection procedures, usually involving both an entrance exam and interviews.

Foreigners can enrol on degree courses at Czech universities provided they fill in lots of forms, part with an appropriate sum of money and – hardest of all – master the finer points of the Czech language. But even if you're not up to this last challenge there are a number of other options. Since 1989, many faculties have set up summer, semester or year-long courses taught in English, in an effort to promote educational exchange and replenish their coffers.

The courses listed here are all aimed at foreigners. For further information on other courses in Prague and the Czech Republic, try contacting one of the organisations listed below or the British Council (*see page 229*).

International Relations Office

Univerzita Karlova Rektorát, Ovocný trh 3-5, Prague 1, (24 49 13 10/fax 24 22 94 87).

The J. William Fulbright Commission

Central European University, Táboritská 23, Prague 3, (27 71 55/fax 27 42 08).
The Central European University (*see p229* **Other Courses**) is a good place for non-Czech speakers to find out more about further studies in the Czech Republic and central and eastern Europe generally.

Charles University

Charles University (Univerzita Karlova), which was founded in 1348 by Emperor Charles IV, is the largest university in the Czech Republic and the oldest in central Europe. Its heart is the Carolinum, an unspectacular building on Ovocný trh near the Estates Theatre, which houses the central administration offices. If you come here looking for an admissions' office and glossy prospectus you'll be disappointed, however; each of the university's 16 faculties is a mysterious world unto itself and you need to contact the Dean or International Relations' Office of the faculty concerned for information on courses and admissions procedures.

FAMU

Smetanovo nábřeží 2, Prague 1, (24 22 91 76/fax 24 23 02 85).

Famous alumni of the Film, TV and Photography School include Oscar-winning directors Věra Chytilová and Miloš Forman. To embark on a BA or MA a working knowledge of Czech is necessary, but FAMU also runs several courses in English, including an intensive one-year course in various fields of film and TV production; a two-year BA in photography, and several summer workshops.

Institute of Language and Professional Training

(Ústav jazykové a odborné přípravy), Univerzita Karlova, Jindřišská 29, Prague 1 (24 23 00 27/fax 24 22 94 97). Fees $380 6-week course; $8 per hour, private lessons. This institute runs one year courses in the Czech language to prepare students who want to embark on degree courses at Czech universities.

Summer School of Czech Studies

SF Servis s.r.o., Filozofická fakulta, Univerzita Karlova, náměstí Jana Palacha 2, Prague 1, (24 81 11 26 ext 297/fax 781 56 93). Fees $440.

Runs annual four-week summer courses, with language lessons in the morning and lectures on Czech culture in the afternoon. The course covers various levels, with no former knowledge of Czech necessary.

Summer School of Slavonic Studies

Filozofická fakulta, Univerzita Karlova, náměstí Jana Palacha 2, Prague 1 (tel/fax 231 96 45). Fees $380.

A one month summer course designed for professors, lecturers and advanced students in Slavonic studies.

Other Courses

Central European University

Táboritská 23, Prague 3, (27 48 21/27 49 13).
The CEU, with twin bases in Prague and Budapest, was set up in 1990 by George Soroš, the multimillionaire philanthropist famous for his share dealings on Black Wednesday and for showering millions on post-Communist countries. The University was founded, in the words of Soroš, to 'educate a new élite that would be inured to the pitfalls of both Communism and nationalism'. The CEU offers up to 500 scholarships a year to students from 22 former Communist countries to enable them to follow one year MA courses in Art History, Economics, European Studies, Sociology, Environmental Studies, Legal Studies, Medieval Studies, History or Political Sciences. Students from outside the region are required to pay academic fees of $8,000, though a limited number of scholarships is also available for them.

Vysoká Škola Ekonomická

Senovážné náměstí 2, Prague 1 (235 19 29/fax 235 45 61). Fees $1,800 per semester.
The University of Economics runs a one or two semester Central and East European Studies programme in English, open to both undergraduate and graduate students. For further details apply to the European Studies office at the above address.

Language Courses

There are numerous schools offering Czech language classes. If you prefer a more informal approach place a notice on one of the boards at the Charles University Philosophy Faculty (*see page 228* **Summer School of Czech Studies**).

Many students are happy to offer Czech conversation in exchange for English conversation, though intensive group courses are always the best. While Czech is the obvious language to learn, Prague also offers good value courses in other languages.

Angličtina Expres

Pasáž Světozor-galerie, Vodičkova 39, Prague 1 (25 68 33). Fees 3,000kč four weeks ((7½ hrs a week).
As the name suggests this school was initially set up to teach English to Czech people, but with an increasing number of ex-pats living in the city, educating foreigners has become equally, if not more, profitable.
Branch: Záhřebská 32, Prague 2 (25 68 33).

Berlitz

Na poříčí 12, Prague 1 (24 87 20 52).
This well established school runs courses in a number of languages including, of course, Czech, but prices are more expensive than most. A one month course with three lessons a week in a class will set you back about 2,000kč.
Branch: Konviktská 18, Prague 1 (232 44 73).

Goethe Institute

Masarykovo nábřeží 32, Prague 1 (24 91 57 25).
Learning the finer points of the German language will set you back between 2,500kč per semester with four lessons a week, and 5,000kč with 12 lessons a week.

Institut Français

Štěpánská 35, Prague 1 (24 21 40 32/fax 24 22 87 01).
The French have naturally built the most stylish cultural embassy in town. This state-of-the-art complex includes a well stocked library, a café and a cinema. French lessons taught by chic natives will cost you 1,700kč for 72 hours.

Jazyková Škola

Národní 20, Prague 1 (24 91 41 14). Fees 3,965kč one year (4 hrs a week); 2,035kč five months (4 hrs a week). The state language school offers a wide range of reasonably priced language courses including Czech for foreigners.

Libraries

For a full list of Prague's libraries ask at the National Library or look in the *Zlaté stránky (Yellow Pages)* under *knihovny*. Admission rules vary; generally you don't need to register to use the reading rooms but you do in order to borrow books, and for this you'll need your passport and sometimes a document stating that you are a student or researcher and where. Most libraries have restricted opening hours or close altogether in July and August.

American Center for Culture and Commerce

Hybernská 7, Prague 1 (24 23 10 85). Metro Náměstí Republiky. Open 11am-5pm Mon, Tue, Thur; noon-5pm Wed; 11am-3pm Fri.
The American equivalent of the British Council. A good place to read *Rolling Stone* or flick through hefty reference volumes if the security guards will let you in.

British Council

Národní 10, Prague 1 (24 91 21 79/fax 24 91 38 39). Metro Národní třída. Open 9am-4pm Mon-Fri. Closed July, Aug.
The light and airy upper floor reading room of the British

Council is the best place to come and catch up on home news: it has a good selection of British dailies and magazines. There's also a library providing materials for English language teachers.

Central European University
Táboritská 23, Prague 3, (27 97 31/fax 27 41 12). Metro Flora. **Open** 9am-11pm Mon-Fri; 1pm-8pm Sat, Sun.
Only students and staff at the CEU are allowed to borrow books from this library but all are welcome to use it for reference purposes. It has the biggest selection of books in English and has helpful English-speaking staff.

National Library
Národní knihovna v Praze (Klementinum), Křížovnické náměstí 4, Prague 1 (24 22 94 00-04/24 22 97 80). Metro Staroměstská. **Open** 8am-7pm Mon-Sat.
This is the country's central library, where you should have access to everything printed in the Czech Republic, as well as a good English-language section. Books can't be taken out and you need to bring your passport to become a reader.

Museum of Decorative Arts
(Uměleckoprůmyslové muzeum), ulice 17, listopadu 2, Prague 1 (232 00 51). Metro Staroměstská. **Open** noon-6pm Mon; 10am-6pm Tue-Fri.
The large reading room overlooking the Rudolfinum and a popular café downstairs makes this one of the more enjoyable places to pretend to bury your nose in a book.

Bookshops

There are no really large academic bookshops in Prague but the following count among the better stocked ones:

Bohemian Ventures
náměstí Jana Palacha 2, Prague 1 (231 95 16). Metro Staroměstská. **Open** 9am-5pm Mon-Fri.
A bookshop inside the Philosophy Faculty building of Charles University.

Globe Bookstore
Janovského 14, Prague 7 (357 91 61). Metro Vltavská/1, 8, 17 tram. **Open** 10am-midnight daily. **Credit** AmEx, V.
Home to a good selection of new and second-hand books in English and a not so good selection of aspiring poets and novelists. *See chapter* **Cafés, Bars & Pubs**.

Knihkupectví Academia
Václavské náměstí 34, Prague 1 (24 22 35 11). Metro Muzeum or Můstek. **Open** 9am-6pm Mon-Fri; 10am-4pm Sat.

Knihkupectví Fišer
Kaprova 10, Prague 1 (232 07 33). Metro Staroměstská. **Open** 9am-6pm Mon-Fri; 10am-3pm Sat.

City Life

Prague student life is far removed from that of most British and American campus universities. Most students live at home and there's no central student union building. There isn't even a student quarter in Prague, as faculties are dispersed around the city. Instead, students can be found almost everywhere, in all the obvious haunts ranging from cheap cafés to trendy nightspots.

Accommodation

Compared to other European capitals, rent in Prague is fairly low and most young foreign residents get away with paying between 2,500kč and 4,500kč each for a shared flat. But finding your dream pad is not easy, as demand outstrips supply. The best way to go about flat-hunting is by posting a notice in the Philosophy Faculty of **Charles University** (*see page 228* **Summer School of Czech Studies**), at the **Globe Bookstore** (*see above* **Bookshops**) and at **Laundry Kings** where the ex-pats do their washing (Dejvická 16, Prague 6). You can also check the classifieds in the English-language paper *Prognosis* which are translated from the Czech tabloid *Annonce*, the main outlet for accommodation ads.

If you are registered at a Czech institute of higher education you are entitled to a room in a *kolej* or student hostel. These are dotted around the city, the greatest concentration being an ugly complex of 1960s highrises in Strahov, next to the giant stadium. However, while Czech students coming from outside the city receive generous subsidies, foreigners have to pay the inflated price of 5,500kč a month, which is hardly a bargain considering you usually have to share a room.

While you're looking for a flat, the cheapest places to stay are youth hostels, though it's also worth consulting accommodation agencies which can sometimes negotiate long-term rental deals, especially out of season (*see chapter* **Accommodation**).

Cheap Food

Finding a cheap place to eat in Prague is not difficult once you leave the most hard-beaten tourist trails, but for the very best value head to one of the student cafeterias or *mensas*. All of them serve up a choice of 'nutritional' (read filling) if uninspired Czech dishes priced at 8.20kč for Czech students and 25kč for their visitors. To cut down on wastage, meal tickets must be bought a day in advance from the counter near the entrance (the best time to avoid queues is between 1pm and 2pm). The largest *mensa* is at Opletalova 38, Prague 1, but if you're desperately seeking greens head to the more health-conscious medical students' local at Albertov 3, Prague 2.

Student Travel

CKM
Czech Youth Travel Agency, Žitná 12, Prague 2 (24 91 57 67/fax 235 12 97). Metro Karlovo náměstí. **Open** 9am-noon, 1pm, 5pm Mon-Fri.
This is the place to come for cheap flights, railway tickets, coach tickets and the occasional discount package holiday. ISIC cards are issued at the branch on Jindřišská. **Branch**: Jindřišská 28, Prague 1 (26 86 23).

Women's Prague

Practical information, from helplines to hairdressers, taxis to tattooing, in the city where 'feminism' is an unknown word.

Compared with their western counterparts, women in the Czech Republic have less freedom of choice and equality. Although they now have more choice whether to work or stay at home (under Communism unmarried women were obliged to work) economic pressures mean that many women find themselves in the position of having to work and be paid less than their male counterparts, while carrying the main burden of childcare and housework, which is seen as their responsibility.

Czech society is deeply patriarchal and the Czech male remains for the most part unreconstructed. Although there are now women deputies in parliament, women's issues are never a priority. Feminism is largely regarded as just another ideology, and several decades of Communism has encouraged a deep Czech suspicion of any 'isms'.

HARASSMENT

Although street crime in Prague is on the increase, by comparison with London or New York it remains pretty low. However the same precautions that apply to any other major city are sensible here. Women on their own should avoid the area around Wenceslas Square late at night or early in the morning, since this is one of the main areas for the city's burgeoning population of prostitutes and pimps. Other areas to be avoided include that around the main station (Hlavní nádraží in Nové Město, around Florenc bus station and Uhelný trh in Staré Město. If you get to the point where you feel like screaming, *pomoc!* (pómots) means help!

The majority of **taxi drivers** are inclined to rip their customers off in general and female ones in particular: if you need to get a taxi late at night, try AAA Taxi (34 24 10/32 24 44) or Profit Taxi (61 04 55 55); *see also chapter* **Getting Around**. For more practical information *see chapter* **Survival**; for information on the family and children, *see chapter* **Children**.

Accommodation

Although there isn't a women's hostel or hotel in Prague, we'd recommend the **Slavoj-Vesico**

Hostel to women travellers on a budget. It's run by women and is particularly safe and welcoming. *See chapter* **Accommodation: Youth Hostels**.

Books, Magazines & Archives

The last couple of years has seen the arrival of several women's magazines produced by the expatriate community in Prague. *One eye open (Jedním okem)* is a bilingual publication of essays, poems and fiction by, and about, women. *Yazzyk* is an English-language literary magazine still in its infancy, which devoted one of its issues to the thorny topic of feminism. *Bread & Butter* is a compilation of essays translated from the Czech, by feminists and sociologists writing on women in the post-Communist Czech Republic. It's available from the Center for Gender Studies. The other publications can be bought at the Globe Bookstore.

Center for Gender Studies

Legerova 39, Prague 2 (no phone). Metro Muzeum or I.P. Pavlova.
Postal address: Klimentská 17, Prague 1 (tel/fax 232 71 06). **Open** 10am-2pm Mon, Thur.
Jiřina Šiklová started up the Center in 1991 in her own flat. It offers a small but comprehensive English-language lending library of books, magazines and articles covering all topics relating to women, as well as a selection of Czech publications. It also publishes a quarterly bulletin in English.

Globe Bookstore

Janovského 14, Prague 7 (357 91 61). Metro Vltavská/1, 5, 8, 12, 14, 17, 25, 26 tram . **Open** 10am-midnight daily.
This popular English-language bookshop has a tiny women's section (two shelves) and a laid-back café.

Cafés, Bars & Restaurants

The following are unthreatening places to go if you are on your own, or with other women and don't want to get hassled. For more cafés and restaurants, *see chapters* **Restaurants** *and* **Cafés, Bars & Pubs**.

Bar Bar

Všehrdova 17, Prague 1 (no phone). Tram 9, 12, 18, 22. **Open** 11am-midnight Mon-Fri; noon-midnight Sat, Sun.

Crepes and large fresh salads are on offer at this restaurant tucked away in Malá Strana.

Bistro Café Pelier
Štěpánská 59, Prague 1 (24 21 35 15). Metro Můstek. **Open** *9am-10pm Mon-Fri.*
A cheap and cheerful café that's packed at lunch-time and popular with women.

Galérie Jednorožec s harfou
Průchozí 4, Prague 1 (24 23 08 01). Metro Národní třída. **Open** *11am-9pm Mon-Fri; noon-9pm Sat, Sun.*
Czech university students come here to drink endless cups of tea and coffee.

Greenbar Jonáš
Na poříčí 10, Prague 1 (no phone). Metro Náměstí Republiky. **Open** *9am-9pm Mon-Sat.*
There's just one window table here, but it's a good place to buy salads to eat standing up or to take away, and it also sells fresh wholegrain bread and sandwiches.

Hogo-Fogo
Salvátorská 32, Prague 1 (231 70 23). Metro Staroměstská. **Open** *10am-midnight daily.*
A funky café and second-hand shop in one. The place has a distinctive black-and-white checked floor and serves a mixed Czech/vegetarian menu which even runs to soya goulash.

Kavárna Archa
Na poříčí 26, Prague 1 (232 41 49). Metro Náměstí Republiky. **Open** *10am-11pm Mon-Fri; 11am-9pm Sun.*
A brand new coffee house that's especially clean and bright.

Podolí *swimming pool. See page 233.*

Literární Kavárna
Betlemské náměstí, Prague 1 (no phone). Metro Národní třída. **Open** *11am-10pm daily.*
If you crave real peace and quiet, or maybe a table for two, this sweet little café is the place to go.

Rubín
Malostranské náměstí 9 (tel/fax 53 50 15). Metro Malostranská. **Open** *6pm-1am daily.*
This basement theatre café is often filled with people reading books or waiting for the nightly 7pm performance to begin. Drink prices are very reasonable for the area.

Theatre on the Balustrade
(Divadlo na zábradlí), Anenské náměstí 5, Prague 1 (24 22 19 33). Metro Staroměstská/17, 18 tram. **Open** *café 11am-11pm Mon-Fri; noon-11pm Sat, Sun.*
This theatre near Charles Bridge contains a small bar and café with long shared tables which serves an assortment of salads. It's frequented by musicians and actors.

Health

Bulovka Hospital
Budínova 2, Prague 8 (66 08 32 39/66 08 32 68). Tram 12, 14.
The Meda Clinic is favoured by British and American women living in Prague. It's a privately-run clinic housed within a state hospital. The gynaecologists speak English. Contraception and HIV testing are available.

Podolí Hospital
Podolské nábřeží 157, Prague 4 (61 21 45 18). Metro Karlovo náměstí then 3, 17, 21 tram.
The Podoli Hospital has two obstetricians/gynaecologists who speak English and treat foreign women: Dr Figarová and Dr Hulvert.

Dr Kateřina Bittmanová
Mánesova 64, Prague 2 (627 19 51). Metro Jiřího z Poděbrad/11 tram.
Dr Bittmanová, who worked in Israel for 23 years, speaks fluent English. She runs a private practice and is on call 24 hours a day. Her fee for a general examination is 700kč.

Natur Centrum
Dukelských hrdinů 17, Prague 7 (37 37 91). Tram 12, 14, 17, 26.
Prague's holistic healing centre offers alternative treatments and also has a sauna.

Pharmacies

There are *lékárný* all over Prague: the sign to look for is a red snake wound around a cross on a white background. Pharmacists rarely speak English, so look up your symptoms, and take a dictionary with you when you go.

U Zlatého Iva
Vinohradská 65, Prague 3 (no phone). Metro Jiřího z Poděbrad/10, 11, 16 tram. **Open** *10am-5pm Tue-Sat.*
A well-stocked chemist that will also order goods on request.

Help & Information

Nonie Valentine
Široká 9, Prague 1 (tel/fax 231 14 95). Metro Staroměstská. **Open** *phone for an appointment.*

The Center for Gender Studies. *See page 231.*

American Nonie Valentine is a licensed therapist who specialises in holistic psychotherapy. Fees are on a sliding scale.

Rape Crisis Helpline

White Circle of Safety (43 88 33). **Open** 5-8pm Tue.
This helpline works as a rape crisis line one evening a week; the rest of the time it deals with marital and adolescent problems. The staff don't always speak English, however.

Recreation

Podolí

Podolská 34, Prague 4 (43 91 51). Tram 3, 17, 21. **Open** 6am-9.45pm Mon-Fri. **Admission** 15kč an hour; 30kč a day.
A swimming centre which is popular with families and single women. There are two Olympic-sized swimming pools (one indoor, and a heated one outside) and an incredibly long waterslide. The women's section has sauna, massage and steam bath facilities. Also available are aerobics classes, a weights room and a general beauty salon for haircuts, manicures, pedicures and leg-waxing.

Shops & Services

Shops

Country Life

Melantrichova 15, Prague 1 (24 21 33 66). Metro
Můstek. **Open** 9.30am-6.30pm Mon-Thur; 10am-3pm Fri.
Run by Seventh Day Adventists, Country Life sells a selection of health food, vitamins and prepared vegetarian food, as well as delicious bread. The branch on Jungmannova sells natural beauty aids.
Branch: Jungmannova 1, Prague 1 (24 19 17 39).

Kmart

Národní 26, Prague 1 (242 27 97 19). Metro Národní
třída. **Open** 6.30am-7pm Mon-Wed; 6.30am-8pm Thur, Fri; 7am-6pm Sat; 10am-5pm Sun.
An American-managed department store with a large range of stock, including western beauty and health products and a huge display of tampons and towels.

Natural Potraviny

Novomlýnská 2, Prague 1 (231 41 49). Metro Náměstí
Republiky. **Open** 8am-6pm Mon-Fri.
A tiny chemist, but with a comprehensive stock and the advantage of an English-speaking owner.

Hairdressers

Hair Cutting School

Navrátilova 8, Prague 1 (24 21 62 42). Metro Karlovo
náměstí. **Open** 9am-noon Mon-Fri.
If you bring along a photograph of your preferred style, the students here will do their best to copy it, usually successfully. A cut costs about 30kč.

Salon Marie

Politických vězňů 21, Prague 1 (24 21 99 59). Metro

Můstek. **Open** 7am-7pm Mon-Fri; 9am-2pm Sat.
This is where Czech movie stars get their hair done.

Tattooing

Ladislav
'Mororai', Libeňský most, Prague 8 (no phone). Tram 1, 12, 14.
Ladislav, a San Franciscan/Czech, offers hygienic, artistic tattoos at incredibly reasonable prices.

Women's Groups

The Center for Gender Studies (*see above* **Books, Magazines & Archives**) runs a twice-monthly discussion group.

International Women's Club of Prague
PO Box 357, 111 21 Prague 1. **Membership** 500kč a year.
This is a group of about 600 women mostly made up of professionals and executives' wives. A hospitality meeting for newcomers is held on the second Tuesday of each month from 10-11.45am at the Savoy Café, Vítězná 5, Prague 5. Regular meetings take place several times a month, and the group also organises cultural events and theatre outings. It has no real headquarters; contact the American Embassy's Cultural and Commercial Section (24 21 98 44/24 21 98 46) for the most recent contact for the group.

Lesbian Prague

Before the Velvet Revolution, any kind of lesbian organisation was illegal, although for a short time during the Prague Spring of 1968, and also for a few months in 1983, lesbians were allowed to place personal ads in newspapers. Unsurprisingly, this means that gay women are a fairly invisible group, and lesbian relationships are conducted with a great deal of discretion. Things are, of course, changing rapidly and you'll now find plenty of personal ads in *Annonce*, the thrice-weekly classifieds paper, although they're still most likely to be asking for 'straight-acting' or 'discreet' potential partners. It looks as if it will be a while before a real lesbian scene emerges. And since this is a place where women are generally expected to go out in the company of men, when it comes to the prospect of a women-only bar opening up, don't hold your breath.

Although some newsagents carry *Soho Revue*, the monthly magazine that lists activities and contact addresses around the country, the clubs and bars are the best place to pick up gay publications (*see also chapter* **Gay Prague**).

Bars, Clubs & Restaurants

Bar Incognito
Prokopova 18, Prague 3 (27 01 53). Metro Florenc, then 133 bus. **Open** 11pm-8am daily.

A tiny lesbian bar with a DJ and disco lights. Call ahead to reserve one of the four tables.

Black Point
Štěpánská 32, Prague 1 (24 21 70 44). Metro Muzeum. **Open** *winter* 11am-2am daily; *summer* 2pm-2am daily.
This gay-owned, modern restaurant is a breath of fresh air in Prague. The interior is high-tech, spacious and clean, and the food is light and elegant. There are even some outdoor tables.

Mercury Club
Kolínská 11, Prague 3 (67 31 06 03). Metro Flora. **Open** 9.30pm-6am daily.
The Mercury hosts a Lesbian-Klub Lambda-run lesbian night every second and fourth Wednesday. It has a sophisticated atmosphere, great bartenders, a DJ, and a minuscule dance floor, plus lots of cosy nooks and tables.

Riviéra
Národní 20, Prague 1 (24 91 22 49). Metro Národní třída. **Open** *bar* 11.30am-9pm, *club* 9pm-5am, daily. **Admission** *club* 25kč (incl. one drink).
The Riviéra is a large, centrally located lesbian and gay bar by day and club by night. There are quiet conversation areas as well as a techno-filled steel dance floor.

Tropic
Jeruzalémská 13, Prague 1 (no phone). Metro Náměstí Republiky. **Open** 11am-1am daily.
The waiters are friendly, the drinks fairly priced and the cocktails and décor exotic at this mixed straight, lesbian/gay café near the main post office.

U střelce
Střelecký ostrov, Prague 1 (no phone). Tram 6, 9, 18, 22. **Open** 9pm-6am Mon-Sat.
A gay and lesbian bar on an island just off Legii Bridge.

Help & Information

Gay Information Center (GIC)
Krakovská 3, Prague 1 (tel/fax 26 44 08). Metro Muzeum. **Open** *summer* 2pm-2am daily.
A useful helpline that will provide information on anything from guided tours to health matters.

Lambda
Zborovská 22, Prague 5 (54 91 27). Metro Anděl.
The original gay and lesbian organisation has two branches, Lesbian-Klub Lambda and Men-Klub Lambda. The former holds regular meetings (in Czech) on Wednesdays at the Mercury Club (*see above*).

Lesbian Gay Bi Coffee Clatsch
This group holds weekly meetings in English, usually on Mondays at 7pm. Check at the Globe Bookstore (*see above* **Books, Magazines & Archives**) for the location, which changes regularly.

Promluv
V olšinách 50, Prague 10 (78 17 15 8).
This radical sub-group of Lesbian-Klub Lambda publishes a lesbian magazine in Czech and, at time of writing, was trying to set up a centre for lesbians, bi-sexuals and feminists.

Logos
U školské zahrady 1, Prague 8 (66 41 01 45). Tram 14, 17, 24, 25.
An ecumenical gay and lesbian Christian association which meets the first Sunday of every month at 4pm. It's an active and friendly group.

Trips Out of Town

Trips Out of Town

Leave the bustle of Prague for the glories of the countryside, packed with fairy-tale castles, splendid spa towns and macabre religious relics.

Getting Out of Town

By Bus

Most intercity bus services depart from Florenc bus station in Prague 8 (by the metro stop of the same name). Bus services are more frequent in the morning and it's worth checking the return times before you leave, as often the last bus back leaves before 6pm. The bus information line (in Czech) is on (22 14 45) and operates between 6am and 6pm, Monday to Friday. A few buses leave from Nádraží Holešovice across the river in Prague 7. Most destinations are covered by the state bus company ČSAD, although a number of private services have been set up offering competitive prices and times. One of the largest of these is **Čebus** *Za Poříčskou bránou, Prague 8 (24 81 16 76)*.

By Train

Trains often follow more scenic routes than buses, but they cover less ground and they usually take longer. There are four main railway stations in Prague but no fixed pattern as to which destinations they serve. Hlavní nádraží is the main station and the principal departure point for international services, although some domestic services also leave from there. Timetables can be obtained at the state railways (ČSD) information office at that station (236 44 41/26 49 30). Nádraží Holešovice is also principally used for international services. Masarykovo nádraží serves most destinations in northern and eastern Bohemia. Domestic routes to the south and west leave from Smíchovské nádraží. Travel is priced by the kilometre and is still absurdly cheap by British standards.

Hlavní nádraží
Wilsonova, Prague 1. Metro Hlavní nádraží.

Masarykovo nádraží
Hybernská, Prague 1. Metro Náměstí Republiky.

Nádraží Holešovice
Arnoštovská, Prague 7. Metro Nádraží Holešovice.

Smíchovské nádraží
Nádražní ulice, Prague 5. Metro Smíchovské nádraží.

By Road

The one-way system, the intimidating trams and the inconsistent signposting can make leaving the city tricky. Before you set off, find the route number you need and the name of the nearest big city. Following the bus or tram routes is a useful way of navigating out of Prague, but don't attempt a journey without a good map. There are very few motorways in the Czech Republic, although more are planned for the future, and you'll mostly be confined to A roads.

Petrol stations (some marked by a big sign saying *benzína*) are thin on the ground, so if you see one it's a good idea to fill up. Petrol comes in two grades, super and special; the latter is recommended for most west European cars. Unleaded is called *natural* and diesel is *diesel* or *nafta*. The maximum speed limit is 60kph in built up areas and 90kph elsewhere. On the motorways you can cruise at up to 110kph. If you have an accident call the **Emergency Road Service** (154). *See chapter* **Getting Around** *for more on driving and chapter* **Survival** *for petrol stations in Prague.*

Heading North

Mělník

Lying in the heart of fertile grape-growing country, Mělník is a sleepy little town just 33km north of Prague with a fine castle, a bizarre ossuary and spectacular views over the surrounding countryside. It's also the home of **Ludmila wine**, the beverage its producers claim gave Mozart the creative energy he needed to write *Don Giovanni*.

The main sights are concentrated near the **castle**, a lovely building that was rebuilt during the sixteenth and seventeenth centuries and occupies a prime position on a steep escarpment overlooking the confluence of the Vltava and Labe rivers. Although a settlement has existed here since the tenth century, it was Charles IV who introduced vines to the region from his lands in Burgundy in the fourteenth century, and he established a palace for the Bohemian queens. Up until the end of the fifteenth century, this was where the royal ladies of the court would come when they needed a break from Prague. Under the recent restitution laws, the castle has been returned to the Lobkowicz family, who were one of the most powerful aristocratic clans in Bohemia before they were driven into exile by the Communists. The family has now returned to reclaim their birthright and have smartened the place up considerably. You can take a tour around the castle's interior, and even better, one round the wine cellars, where a lesson in viticulture is followed by a chance to sample the end product.

Opposite the castle is the church of **Sts Peter and Paul** (sv. Petr a Pavel), a late Gothic structure with a 60-metre high tower that was topped with an onion-shaped cupola in the sixteenth century. For a magnificently weird experience, pay a visit to the **ossuary** in the church's crypt. Pass through red velvet curtains and descend to the basement, where skulls and bones are piled up to the ceiling. Two speakers precariously balanced on top of a stack of femurs broadcast a breathless English commentary delivered in a Hammer House of Horror style, accompanied by liberal doses of Bach organ music.

The site was established as a burial place for plague victims in the sixteenth century and sealed off for the next few hundred years. However in 1914, a social anthropology professor from Charles University cracked open the vault and shipped in his students to lend their artistic talents to arranging the 15,000 skeletons he found piled up there. The end result includes 'Look death!' written in Latin in skulls and a cage displaying the remains of people with spectacular physical deformities.

The main square below the castle, náměstí Míru, is lined with typically Bohemian Renaissance and Baroque buildings. The fountain dates from considerably later, and is decorated with square-jawed peasant women picking grapes. Leave the square, passing the sunshine yellow *lékárna* (pharmacy) and turn right onto U Tanku, where, as the name suggests, there's a tank. It's a Russian model that entered the town in 1945 and never left, being turned instead into a monument of thanks to the liberating Soviet soldiers. After the role of Russian tanks in the later events of 1968, Prague has since got rid of its own tank memorial, but the Mělník tank – for the time being at least – still proudly sports its red star.

Getting There
By bus: buses leave from stand 18 at Prague's Florenc station, at roughly half-hourly intervals. The trip takes under an hour.
By car: head north out of the city via Holešovice and follow signs to Neratovice and Veltrusy, then Mělník on Route 9.

Where to Stay
Pension Bomi *Mladoboleslavská 2265, Mělník (tel/fax 0206 62 25 88)*. **Rates** *single room with breakfast* 700kč; *double room with breakfast* 1,000kč.

Where to Eat
Restaurace Stará škola *(0206 622 853)*. The restaurant is just behind the Church of Sts Peter and Paul and the terrace has a stunning view over the surrounding countryside. There are currently two restaurants inside the castle with two more due to open. The **vinárna** is the swankiest: the crockery is embossed with the Lobkowicz insignia, the vaulted walls are painted peach and it's one of the best places to splash out on an expensive meal in Bohemia.

The Castle
Svatováclavská 19 (tourist information 0206 62 21 25). **Open** *summer* 10am-6pm daily; *winter* 10am-4pm daily; closed Jan, Feb.
Tours of the castle last 40 minutes and cost 50kč. Tours of the cellars (including wine tasting) take 30 minutes and cost 60kč. Last tours start at 5.30pm. You can ring and reserve a place to make sure that you get a tour in the right language.

The Ossuary (kostnice)
English language tours at 10.30am, 1pm, 3pm, 5pm.
Admission 30kč adults, 15kč children.

Kokořín

Perched on a rocky promontory and surrounded by tall fir trees and eerie sandstone rock formations, **Kokořín castle** looks like the archetypal abode of a distressed medieval damsel. The origins of the castle are uncertain; it may have been the site of the ancient Slav encampment of Canburg, where Charlemagne's knights were forced into retreat in 805, during a failed campaign to convert the Slavs to Christianity. The earliest parts of the existing structure date back to the thirteenth century but the castle's present Gothic appearance is largely the work of Jan Špaček, the last owner of the castle, who carried out enthusiastic, though not very historically sensitive, renovation at the beginning of this century. The guided tour of the interior is not of great interest since none of the furnishings are original and many have little to do with the castle's history. The views from the top of the tower are more appealing. Beyond the woods – the former hiding ground of robbers and anti-Fascist partisans – fields stretch away into the distance.

Getting There
Kokořín can be visited en route to Český ráj *(see p240)* or in conjunction with Mělník.
By bus: there's a local service from Mělník.
By car: 12km north of Mělník, the turning is just south of the town.

The Castle

(0206 69 50 64). At the time of writing, the castle was about to change hands. Check with the Prague Information Service (*see p29*) for details of the new opening times.

Terezín

Terezín, originally known as Theresienstadt, was purpose-built as a fortress town in 1780 on the orders of Emperor Joseph II, to protect his empire from Prussian invaders. However its notoriety dates from this century: in 1941 the whole town became a holding camp for Jews before they were sent on to the death camps further east.

The atmosphere of the **town** today is still distinctly eerie, accentuated by soulless streets laid out to a grid pattern. The Nazis expelled the native population and unsurprisingly few of them chose to return after the war. In the town itself the Ghetto Museum is the most important site, although you can also visit the cemetery and crematorium located beyond the disused railway tracks, which were constructed by the prisoners themselves and used to speed their departure to Auschwitz.

The **Ghetto Museum**, which was only established in 1991, is the best place to start a tour of the area. Documentary films are shown in several languages and you can request the ones you'd like to see. Without a doubt the creepiest is the one

The entrance to the prison at **Terezín**.

which contains clips from the Nazi propaganda film *A Town Presented to the Jews by the Nazis*. The film was part of the sophisticated Nazi strategy to hoodwink the world. Red Cross officials visited the camp twice, and saw specially rehearsed gymnastic performances, a children's playground and new street signs with names instead of numbers. The impression was successfully conveyed of a self-governing Jewish community with a flourishing cultural life. To complete the illusion, the Nazis established the Terezín Family Camp in Auschwitz, where the inmates were kept in special conditions for long enough to write a postcard home before being sent to the gas chambers.

On the ground floor of the museum is a harrowing collection of artwork produced by the prisoners, many of them children, while upstairs is a well laid-out exhibition documenting the Nazi occupation of Bohemia and Moravia. Decrees of discriminating measures taken against Jews are detailed – including the certificate that a customer in a pet shop intending to buy a canary had to sign, promising that the pet would not be exposed to any Jewish people – as well as more gruesome facts. Out of 140,000 men, women and children who passed through Terezín, 87,000 left on transports to the death camps in the east (mainly Auschwitz) and only 3,000 returned alive; 34,000 people died within the ghetto of Terezín itself.

THE SMALL FORTRESS

Just a 15-minute walk back down the road from Prague brings you to the Small Fortress (Malá pevnost) which was built at the same time as the larger town fortress. The high, red brick walls which surround it made it an opportune site for the Gestapo to establish a prison here in 1940. Until it was liberated in 1945, 32,000 political prisoners passed through it, and about 2,500 of them died within its walls.

The first thing you see on approaching the Small Fortress is the **National Cemetery** where some 10,000 Nazi victims are buried. Most of their graves are marked by numbers rather than names and are interspersed with hundreds of red roses. In the middle stands a giant wooden cross – an insensitive memorial considering the tiny percentage of non-Jews who lost their lives here.

The whole fortress is now a museum and a free map (available from the ticket office) enables you to explore the network of courtyards, cells and exhibitions. To the left of the main entrance is an arch which still displays the infamous Nazi slogan *Arbeit Macht Frei* (Work brings freedom). Walking through the arch brings you to the main prison courtyards, lined with mass cells which housed over 250 inmates at any one time, and 20 tiny windowless solitary confinement cells. On the wall of Number 1 is a plaque commemorating an earlier inmate, Gavrilo Princip, who was sent here

The Great Outdoors

Ever since nineteenth century Romantic poets headed for the hills and extolled the virtues of beautiful Bohemia, rural fantasies have been fashionable among Czechs. Fears of pollution, the overcrowded modern flats, and in Communist times the inaccessibility of foreign holidays, has meant that the mass exodus from Prague on Friday nights has become a tradition. The vast majority of the population has at least one relative with a *chata* – an all-encompassing term for a country cottage that can range from a one-room wooden shack to a substantial rural villa. Travelling through the Czech countryside, you're sure to see them, usually in clusters on the banks of rivers or on the slopes of mountains. Vegetable plots are assiduously cultivated and the weekends are often a frenzy of berry-picking, jam-making and gherkin pickling in preparation for the (previously) poor supply of fresh produce during the winter months.

In addition, hiking in summer and skiing in winter enjoy tremendous levels of popularity.

This interest in the outdoor life has also led to the development of a curious Czech sub-culture: trampers. It's a peculiar phenomenon, particularly popular (although by no means exclusively) with adolescent boys, whereby groups of city folk dress up in camouflage fatigues and tramp through the countryside, sleeping under the stars. You can't fail to spot them, attired as they are with paramilitary accoutrements, hunting knives and serious boots. Their role models are the pioneers of the American frontier, their taste in music is usually folk or country and western, and large amounts of beer are often part of the package.

The best way to enjoy a sojourn in a *chata* is to make a Czech friend. Failing that, they can be booked through **Čedok** but only several months in advance. Contact the London branch at *49 Southwark Street, London SE1 1RU (0171 378 6009)*. They are also advertised privately in the Czech classifieds paper *Annonce* and occasionally in the *Prague Post*.

The sandstone pinnacles of **Český ráj**. *See page 240.*

in 1918 after taking a pot-shot at Archduke Franz Ferdinand. The plaque, a present from the Yugoslav ambassador, commemorates him as a national hero.

Continuing past the hospital, a long dank tunnel takes you out to the Gestapo's execution ground where prisoners were variously shot or hanged. The former SS Commander's house is now a museum with displays detailing the appalling physical condition of the inmates, as well as a chronological overview of the Nazi occupation. There's also one of the few references you'll find in the Czech Republic to the fact that in 1945 Terezín became a holding camp for 3 million Sudeten Germans, before their mass expulsion later that year.

Getting There

By bus: buses go from Florenc station about once an hour, starting at 7.50am. The last one leaves at 2.50pm.
By car: join Route 8 or the E55 at Holešovice.

Where to Stay

Hotel Helena *Žreletická 12, Litoměřice (0416 51 79).* **Rates** *double* 400kč incl breakfast.

Where to Eat

Light meals and snacks can be had in the former guards' canteen just inside the entrance to the Small Fortress. In the town itself the best bet is **Restaurace u Hojtašů** *Komenského 152, Terezín (0416 922 03).*

The Ghetto Museum

Komenského 411/55 Terezín (0416 92 25 76/7/fax 0416 922 45). **Open** *Oct 1-Mar 31* 9am-4.30pm daily; *April* 9am-5.30pm daily; *May 1-Sept 30* 9am-6.30pm daily.
Admission *Ghetto Museum and Small Fortress* 80kč adults; 40kč children, students, OAPs.

The Small Fortress

Open *Oct 1-Mar 31* 8am-4.30pm daily; *April* 8am-5.30pm daily; *May 1-Sept 30* 8am-6.30pm daily.
Admission 50kč adults; 25kč children, students, OAPs. The guided tour costs 150kč.

Wittman Tours

Uruguayská 7, Prague 2 (25 12 35/439 62 93). Metro Náměstí Míru.
Organised tours depart from Prague and cost 550kč for adults, 450kč for students and 300kč for children.

Further North

Český ráj

Český ráj literally means 'Czech Paradise' and this protected **national park** is a peaceful haven of densely forested hills, giant rock formations and ruined castles in the otherwise industrial and polluted north-east of Bohemia. For many Czechs, donning walking boots and venturing into the great outdoors comes close to paradise *(see page 239* **The Great Outdoors***)*. Praguers flock here at weekends for activities ranging from gentle hiking to scaling the huge sandstone rocks. Though

the area is accessible by road, the best way to explore it is on foot; even reluctant amateurs can cross the region in two days. The neighbouring towns of **Jičín** and **Turnov** provide a good base from which to begin your exploration.

The greatest concentration of protruding rocks is to be found around **Hrubá skála**: follow any of the marked footpaths from the village and you'll soon find yourself surrounded by these pock-marked giants covered in human spiders.

Supreme among the ruined castles in the area is **Trosky** (the name means 'ruins'). Its two towers, built on absurdly inaccessible basalt outcrops, form the most prominent silhouette in the region. The taller, thinner rock goes by the name of Panna (Maiden), while the smaller one is Bába (Grandmother). In the fourteenth century, Čeněk of Vartemberk undertook a monumental feat of medieval architecture by building a tower on each promontory, with a series of interconnecting ramparts joining the two peaks together. The towers still remained virtually impenetrable, though, as they could only be reached by an ingenious wooden structure that could be dismantled in times of siege, leaving invaders with the choice of scaling the impossibly steep rocks or, more likely, beating a hasty retreat. In the nineteenth century Trosky became a favourite haunt of Romantic poets, painters and patriots. Now you can climb to the base of the tower on Panna for outstanding views of the surrounding countryside.

Getting There

By bus: one bus a day goes to Malá skála from Holešovice bus station in Prague. It's roughly a two-hour ride.
By train: a local train goes from Jičín to Turnov, or there are trains to Turnov from Prague's Hlavní nádraží.
By car: about 90km from Prague; follow signs to Mladá Boleslav and join the E65 or Route 10 which continues all the way to Turnov. Jičín lies 23km south-west of Turnov. Hrubá skála and Trosky are both just off the Turnov-Jičín road.
On foot: the obvious and most popular way of exploring the region. The best map is the *Český ráj poděbradsko* which can be bought at any decent bookshop in Prague and from kiosks or gift shops at the main sights.

Where to Stay

Hotel Štekl *Hrubá skála (0436 91 62 84).* **Rates** *single* 250kč; *double* 390kč incl. breakfast. Resembles an alpine resthouse, and has views over the surrounding valleys; rooms are old-fashioned. **Hotel Zámek** inside Hrubá skála castle *(0436 91 62 81)* has fantastic views and ivy-covered turret rooms (from 92kč for a single room, 184kč for a double, depending on the season). **Camping** is the other option; there are several campsites but most people just pitch their tent unofficially on an appealing plot of land.

Where to Eat

There are no sizeable towns within the national reserve area, but close to each of the main tourist sights there are places offering filling, if uninspiring, Czech fare. There are also restaurants in the hotels mentioned above. In Jičín **U Zlatý anděl** (The Golden Angel) on the main square serves good pub-style food, but the best option by far is to stock up with supplies en route and picnic in any number of locations within the national park.

Climbing

From 1 April until 31 October certified climbers can scale the sandstone pinnacles in the region.

Trosky Castle

Open *April, Oct* 9am-4pm Sat, Sun, public holidays; *May-Aug* 8am-5pm Tue-Sun; *Sept* 9am-5pm Tue-Sun.

Heading West

Křivoklát

The approach to Křivoklát is almost more satisfying than the tour of the castle itself. The road winds along the banks of the Berounka river, passing cornfields and meadows, and up a densely forested hill before the **castle** (perched on a high natural promontory) appears before you. It bristles with Gothic towers and, surrounded by pine woods where Good King Wenceslas once hunted, it looks just like a fairy tale castle.

It's actually a hotchpotch of different buildings and styles added over the centuries. The Přemyslid King Otakar II established the castle in 1110 – his other notable work being the establishment of Malá Strana in Prague. The biggest building projects here took place under the auspices of the Polish King Vladislav Jagiellon (1471-1516) whose trade-mark W insignia can be seen all over the castle.

The barley-sugar pillars and vaulted ceiling of the **chapel** are the work of Vladislav's architect and wood carver, Hans Spiess. The nineteenth century pews are decorated with carved dragons, armadillos and other reptilian horrors, while the fine Gothic altarpiece includes an elaborate polychrome statue of Christ surrounded by sweet-looking angels holding medieval instruments of torture in their hands. A much more varied selection of instruments of torture is to be found in the **dungeon**, which the official guide saves until last and relishes demonstrating. The unrestored chamber contains some magnificently unpleasant pain-inflicting devices, including a fully operational rack, two cages, a thumb screw, the so-called Rosary of Shame (an attractive necklace made out of lead weights) and the Iron Virgin, a body box lined with pointed prongs.

The castle's most impressive feature is the enormous Round Tower which dwarfs the other buildings. It dates from 1280 and was a prison up until the sixteenth century, when the Habsburgs came to power, lost interest in the place and eventually sold it to the Wallenstein family in 1685. Prisoners were lowered in through the small hole in the ceiling and left there to rot. A door on the lower level, cut through the ten-foot thick walls, allows rather easier access today.

Getting There

By bus: buses leave from Dejvická metro station – go to the stands opposite the Diplomat Hotel, Evropská 15, Prague 6.

Downtown **Karlovy Vary**. *See page 242.*

Spas

The west Bohemian spa towns of Karlovy Vary, Mariánské Lázně and Františkovy Lázně (previously known by their German names of Karlsbad, Marienbad and Franzensbad) enjoyed their heyday in the nineteenth century when tuberculosis, gout, and unrequited love were all the rage. The beau monde sat out the winter on the promenade in Nice and when the carnival celebrations were over and the spring sun threatened to ruin their complexions they relocated to the verdant hills of Bohemia. Each spa had its own specialities but treatment followed the same basic pattern: patients were required to sip a prescribed amount of water at a prescribed time of day from a prescribed spring, to undertake mud baths and enjoy a strenuous social life.

The popularity of these aristocratic playgrounds gradually waned with the demise of the Habsburg and Russian empires. Under Communism the spa doors were thrown open to the proletariat, but since 1989 they've lost 30 per cent of their domestic market and are once again trying to attract foreign hypochondriacs. Contemporary spa medicine offers a whole range of cures ranging from radioactive treatment for impotence to more mundane mud baths for improved circulation, as well as, of course, the opportunity for some major pampering in splendid surroundings.

For more information about spas in the Czech Republic and what they can do for you contact **Balnea** *Široká 6, Prague 1 (232 44 45/fax 232 43 01).*

By train: trains leave from Smíchovské nádraží, with a change at Beroun.
By car: this is much the best way to get to Křivoklát and means the excursion can be combined with a trip to Karlovy Vary. To travel on the most picturesque route, take the E50 out of Prague, turn off at junction 14 and follow the Berounka valley.

Where to Stay & Eat
Hotel U Dvořáků *Rostoky 225, Křivoklát (0313 983 55).* **Rates** *double room* 240kč; *double room with bathroom* 300kč.

The Castle
Information (0313 981 20). **Open** *Mar, April, Oct-Dec* 9am-4pm, *May, Sept* 9am-5pm, *June-Aug* 9am-6pm, Tue-Sun. Guided tours are compulsory (last tour one hour before closing) and English-language versions are much less frequent than Czech or German ones. If neither language is your forte you can take a translated script and muddle through, wondering what the jokes were.

Karlovy Vary

With its grand hotels, elaborate colonnades and turn-of-the-century mansions, Karlovy Vary is the oldest and most prestigious of the south-west Bohemian spa towns. It's as popular with daytrippers who come to experience its faded *fin de siècle* charm as it is with those who come to take the waters.

Karlovy Vary began its ascent to fame in 1358 when one of Charles IV's hunting hounds leapt off a steep crag in hot pursuit of a more nimble stag: the unfortunate dog fell to the ground injuring its paw but made a miraculous recovery as it limped through a pool of hot bubbly water. Experts were summoned to test the waters and declared them to be beneficial for all kinds of ills and from that moment Karlovy Vary's fate was

sealed; its reputation spread across Europe and over the ensuing centuries it attracted various illustrious visitors, ranging from Peter the Great to Karl Marx.

The most obvious point to begin a sightseeing tour of Karlovy Vary is at the **Hotel Thermal**, a hideous 1970s monstrosity that you can't fail to see as you step off the bus from Prague. Beyond this eyesore you enter the spa zone, where a number of signposts remind you that smoking, rollerskating, wearing dirty clothes and various other activities considered detrimental to health, are strictly prohibited. The genteel promenades lined with elegant mansions follow the curves of the meandering river Teplá all the way to the **Grand Hotel Pupp**, a spectacularly opulent hotel at the southern edge of the town. All 12 of Karlovy Vary's springs are located along this route. Though few visitors these days come for the full therapeutic cure, a visit to a spa town is not complete without sampling the waters; all are warm, taste equally foul and should be slurped through the spout of a specially designed porcelain cup.

The grandest place to have a tipple is along the neo-renaissance **Mühlbrunnen Colonnade** designed by Joseph Zítek, architect of the National Theatre in Prague. There's often an orchestra playing here; in the grand old days doctors did the conducting and patients quaffed the medicinal waters in time to the music. To counteract the salty taste of the waters you're supposed to nibble on another local delicacy, the sugary sweet *oplatky* wafer. If these don't do the trick, head to the nearest bar to sample Karlovy Vary's thirteenth spring, Becherovka, a strong liqueur and the country's most popular 'medicine'.

The most powerful spring is the **Vřídlo**, or geyser, housed in a giant glass shell where you will also find **Kur-Info**, the tourist office. Looking out across the river through the glass panes you can glimpse the twin towers of **St Mary Magdalene** (sv. Marie Magdaléna), a beautiful Baroque church built by Kilián Ignaz Dientzenhofer between 1732 and 1736. From the Vřídlo the steep road that ascends past the Hotel Pushkin leads to the Russian Orthodox church of **Sts Peter and Paul** (sv. Petr a Pavel); en route you'll pass a statue of **Karl Marx**, possibly the last one left in the Czech Republic. Continuing along the promenade, lovers of Art Nouveau should look out for the **Živnostenská Banka**. Built by Felix Zawoski between 1897 and 1900, it has wrought iron balconies and turquoise and gold mosaics decorating its façade, the ensemble surmounted by a crown of gold.

If you want a treatment but don't want to book a full cure, head to Lázně or Bath 1 just opposite the Grand Hotel Pupp; this glorious late nineteenth century establishment (built for Emperor Franz Josef) runs an out-patient service by day and turns into a casino at night. And when the oppressive atmosphere of the promenades gets too much, escape to the hills: there's a **funicular** behind the Grand Hotel Pupp as well as several footpaths that lead to romantic observatories with refreshingly detached views of the town below. There's also a pool filled with warm spring water above the Hotel Thermal.

Getting There

By bus: from Florenc buses run more or less hourly but set off early as the last bus back leaves at 6pm.
By car: 130km from Prague. Follow signs from the centre to the E48 or Route 6; for a scenic approach turn off the road about 5km before Karlovy Vary when you see a sign on your left to the Hotel Pupp and the Hotel Dvořák.

Where to Stay

The larger hotels offer a full range of therapeutic treatments, though the prices quoted here are for bed and breakfast only. **Grand Hotel Pupp** *Mírové náměstí, Karlovy Vary (017 20 91 11/fax 017 240 32)*. **Rates** *single with bath* 2,550kč; *double with bath* 3,600kč. This is the grandest hotel in town. Lots of special events are staged here including the Miss Czech Republic competition in early spring *(see chapter* **Prague by Season***)*. Cheaper alternatives are the **Elefant Pension** *Stará Louka 30, Karlovy Vary (017 12 34 06)*, or the **Youth Hostel** *Zámecký vrch 43, Karlovy Vary (017 234 74)*.

Where to Eat

Elefant Café *Stará Louka 30, Karlovy Vary (017 12 34 06)*. Offers delicious cream cakes and good views of the promenade.
Grand Hotel Pupp Restaurant *Mírové náměstí, Karlovy Vary (017 20 91 11)*. A main course costs about 300kč; the faded grand décor includes frescoed ceilings and lush pink velvet curtains.
Karel IV Zámecká restaurace *Zámecký vrch Karlovy Vary (017 272 55)*. An extensive menu includes turtle soup, snails, wild boar and dishes prepared on the 'lava-fired grill'. The building itself dates from the seventeenth century and was erected on the site of Charles IV's hunting lodge. The interior is cosy, and there are glorious views from the outdoor terrace.
Embassy Restaurant *Nová louka 21, Karlovy Vary (017 230 49/fax 017 231 46)*. A cosy wood-panelled interior and excellent service. A meal will cost about 400kč a head.

Kur-Info (Tourist Information)

Vřídelní kolonáda, Karlovy Vary (017 240 97/fax 017 246 67). Located in the big glass complex built around the main spring. Staff are helpful. Karlovy Vary hosts a number of arts festivals, including the biennial international film festival held in July (of even years) and a number of classical music festivals *(see chapters* **Prague by Season** *and* **Film***)*.

Heading South

Karlštejn

Half a million visitors come to Karlštejn every year, making it the most popular tourist destination in the Czech Republic after Prague. This has its disadvantages – it's a one-street town, and so copes with the masses less well than the capital. In summertime the steep ascent to the castle is lined with kitsch souvenir stalls that hide an otherwise attractive village. But in the winter when the Bohemian countryside is covered in snow, Charles IV's favourite hideaway recovers its charms and makes an easily accessible and worthwhile day trip from Prague. In addition, there are lots of opportunities for gentle hiking and picnics in the surrounding Berounka valley.

The **castle** was begun in 1348 by the French architect Matthew of Arras to house the Bohemian crown jewels and Charles IV's personal collection of relics; its structure was designed as a spiritual ascent with the emperor's living quarters in the lower parts and the **Chapel of the Holy Rood** (where the valuables were kept) at the very top of the great tower.

The highlight of the tour should be the Chapel, where no expense was spared to create a suitably opulent home for the Holy Roman Emperor's treasures; stars made of Venetian glass are embedded in the gilt ceiling and the walls are encrusted with over 2,000 semi-precious stones and covered with paintings by the fourteenth century Bohemian painter, Master Theodoric. Sadly, this jewel has been closed since 1980 as too many tourists, exhausted from the steep ascent, had panted excessive amounts of damaging moisture over it; no decision has been made as to when – if at all – it will be open to the public again.

Knowing that you are being deprived of the highlight makes the present tour a slight disappointment – all you see are the more mundane and heavily restored parts of the castle. Apart from the

Going for a Dip

If you've seen your fill of castles and need a break from the city streets, these are the nicest (and cleanest) places to take a plunge.

Slapy Dam

The long narrow lake created by the enormous Slapy dam is a popular weekend spot with Praguers. Surrounded by the hills of the Vltava valley it's a picturesque place to go for a swim and to watch the motor boats that cruise up and down the waters.

Getting There

By bus: about an hour's ride from Prague, buses leave from Na Knížeci bus terminal (Anděl metro). From the village of Slapy you can walk to the water or catch a local bus.
By car: 30km south of Prague. Head out of Prague through Smíchov and join Route 4, then turn off to Slapy at Zbraslav.

Malá Ameriká

Malá Ameriká (Little America) is so called because of its resemblance to the grand canyon, although it's not quite on the same scale. It's really a flooded stone quarry but the absurdly turquoise waters make it the most scenic place to go for a dip in the vicinity of Prague. The only disadvantage is that it is only accessible by car.

Getting There

By car: about 25km south of Prague. Follow signs to Plzeň to join the E50, leave the motorway at exit 10 and follow signs to Karlštejn. The path leading down to the gorge is about 7km before Karlštejn – the only clue as to the exact spot is the number of cars parked along an unremarkable stretch of country road.

Koněpruské Jeskyně

The largest caves in Bohemia have some interesting stalagmites and stalactites, but the tour is long and the caves very dank for those who do not share the guide's passion for speleology.

Getting There

By car: From Karlštejn follow signs to Koněpruské jeskyně. The caves are about 10km to the south-west. **Open** *April-Sept* 8am-4pm daily. **Admission** 20kč.

---

magnificent views, the remaining highlights are the **Church of the Virgin Mary**, which has 338 angels painted on the ceiling, and the adjoining **Chapel of St Catherine**, which you can peer into but not actually enter. The chapel was Charles' own private one and is richly decorated with stained glass windows and walls encrusted with semi-precious stones.

Getting There

By train: trains leave Prague's Smíchovské nádraží for Karlštejn about every hour. The trip takes roughly 40 minutes, runs through the beautiful Berounka valley, as well as through Řevnice, Martina Navratilova's home town. It's a 20-minute walk from the station up to the castle.
By car: 30km south of Prague; follow signs to Plzeň to get on to the E50 or Route 5, then leave the motorway at exit 10 and follow signs to Karlštejn.

Where to Eat

There are plenty of eating possibilities lining the road to the castle. The best are **Restaurace U Janů** *(0311 942 10)*. Cosy atmosphere, antlers hanging from the ceiling and a nice terrace garden. **Restaurant Koruna** *(0311 944 65)*. Gingham table cloths, good food and a solid quota of old men sitting around and drinking beer to prove it's not just for the tourists.

The Castle

(0311 942 11). **Open** *March, April, Oct-Dec* 9am-noon, 1-4pm, Tue-Sun; *May-Sept* 8am-noon, 1-6pm, Tue-Sun. **Admission** 90kč adults; 45kč children, students, OAPs. Last tour one hour before closing; tours available in English.

Bicycle and Canoe Tours

Central European Adventures *(232 88 79/fax 25 14 28)*. A Prague-based company that arranges organised tours taking in Karlštejn and the surrounding countryside.

Further South

Ceské Budějovice

České Budějovice is the regional capital of south Bohemia and although it's surrounded by some smoky suburbs, the old centre retains its original medieval town plan. It was founded in 1265 by Otakar II and its main square, which bears his name (náměstí Přemysla Otakara II) is enormous. Its monumental proportions are exaggerated by the small number of tourists and the tiny Shetland ponies that will no doubt appeal to visiting children.

There are some attractive crumbling streets in the town, but if you're combining the trip with Český Krumlov (a mere 22 kilometres away) you'll have already been spoilt in such matters. Beer is the town's reason for existence today, and it's also the best excuse for a visit. Since 1894, when bottle-fermented beer really took off, the **Budvar brewery** has been producing the legendary lager; it has given rise to many imitations – including the cheekily-named American Budweiser – but no equals. The brewery has only recently opened to the public, in reponse to the tours operated by its biggest rival, Pilsner Urquell in Plzeň. It's worth taking the longer tour, as the extra half hour is devoted to a comprehensive sampling of the product.

České Budějovice is at the centre of the **south Bohemian lakeland**, and it's a good starting point to explore the UNESCO-protected region. It has some 270 ponds, created in the sixteenth century and used ever since for breeding carp, the national Christmas dish. These days most of the fish are exported to Germany, where they can be sold for three times the Czech market price, but at least visitors are left with plenty of opportunities for a scenic swim. The best stopping-off place along the way is **Třeboň**, a tiny Renaissance town. It boasts a miniature, but nonetheless stunning, square and an interesting château where there's a series of tranquil courtyards, decorated with sgraffitoed façades and connected by ornate archways.

Getting There
By bus: buses leave from Florenc bus station and take about four hours.
By car: leave the city on the E60 towards Brno and then take the E55 to České Budějovice, passing through Tábor.

Where to Stay
The Tourist Information Office (*below*) can book a pension for around 250kč a night, although a better selection is available in nearby Český Krumlov.

Where to Eat
Restaurace Masné krámy *Krajinská 29, České Budějovice (038 326 52)*. The long, thin room looks rather like a train carriage and has cosy alcoves leading off it. It's the most popular place in town to down the mighty Budvar.
Pivnice U Šrejka *ulice Karla IV 100 (no phone)*. A cavernous beer hall with clean white walls and an unprecedented no-smoking area. It serves Samson beer, a lesser-known local brew that (judging from the packed tables) has many fans among the locals.

Tourist Information
náměstí Přemysla Otakara II 2 (038 594 80/fax 038 592 91). **Open** 9am-6pm Mon-Sat.

Brewery Tours
Budvar Pivovar *Pražská třída, České Budějovice (038 770 52 01)*. **Open** 8.30am-4pm Mon-Thur; 8.30am-noon Fri. There are two different tours; the first lasts one hour and costs 95kč, the second lasts an hour and a half, involves sampling the product and costs 155kč.

Červená Lhota

The tiny, dusty pink Renaissance castle of Červená Lhota – on an island in the middle of a lake and accessible by a narrow stone bridge – is one of the most romantic sights in the Czech Republic. In the late eighteenth century it was the home of the composer Karel Ditters von Dittersdorf; more recently it was used as the film set for *Goldilocks*, a popular

Czech film. There is very little to see inside but on a fine day it's a beautiful spot to spend an afternoon, rowing on the waters.

Getting There
The castle is best visited as part of a trip to Telč, Jindřichův Hradec, or České Budějovice.
By car: 18km from Jindřichův Hradec, halfway between the villages of Dírná and Deštná.
By bus: on Saturday there is a direct service from Florenc leaving at 6.45am, 7.15am, and 12.15pm; these buses continue to Jindřichův Hradec.

Where to Eat
There is a restaurant and hotel just next to the castle but it was for sale at the time of writing, so its future is unclear.

The Castle
Open *summer* 9am-noon, 1-5pm Tue-Thur, Sat, Sun; *winter* 9am-noon, 1-4pm Sat, Sun, public holidays. **Admission** 5kč-35kč.

Český Krumlov

In 1992 Český Krumlov's outstanding beauty was recognised by the outside world when UNESCO declared the tiny south Bohemian town to be second in importance only to Venice on the World Heritage list. The castle and fantastical pink Renaissance tower rise high above the town, which is idyllically positioned on a double loop of the Vltava river. It's almost impossible not to be impressed and charmed. The streets are a labyrinth of tiny cobbled alleyways and almost every building is an architectural gem, the crumbling Renaissance façades and overhanging balconies made even more attractive by flower-filled window-boxes and lines of washing strung across the passageways.

THE CASTLE
The castle, and in particular the tower, dominates the town. It's one of the most extensive complexes in central Europe, consisting of 40 buildings spread through five courtyards, gradually added over the course of six centuries. Founded before 1250, the castle's heyday began when the Rožmberk family adopted it as their seat in 1302, and as their riches and influence increased with each successive generation, it was gradually transformed into the Renaissance palace that still exists today. Craftsmen and artists flocked to the town to work on the extensive building schemes, creating a cosmopolitan community; the Rožmberks, enlightened humanists and generous patrons, endowed the town with a vigour and vitality unmatched in the region. The castle was sold in 1602 and, after various owners, was inherited by the Schwarzenberg family in 1715 with whom it remained until 1947.

*Home of the Budvar brewery, **České Budějovice**. See page 245.*

Český Krumlov, *second only to Venice on the World Heritage List.*

The **tower**, the castle's most obvious feature, dates from the thirteenth century and was transformed into a whimsical Renaissance affair in 1591. It's painted pink and yellow, covered with murals, and topped with marble busts and gold trimmings. Walk up to the **arcaded gallery** and there's a bird's eye view of the steeply-pitched red tiled roofs below.

You can wander through the five interconnecting courtyards, all of which are covered with ornate Renaissance murals, the last of which is reached via the **Plášťový Bridge** (Plášťový most). This is a spectacular five-tiered affair which rises at an angle between two steep escarpments, although you can only get a true sense of its unique structure from the ground. For the best view descend to the **Jelení Gardens** (Jelení zahrada) and look upwards. If you want to see the inside, you have to go with a guide through the warren-like enclosure; highlights of the tour include the Eggenberg coach, a gilded carriage built in 1638 to convey presents to the Pope. The Mirror and Masquerade Halls are triumphs of the art of stucco and *trompe-l'oeil* painting, while the Baroque Theatre is a uniquely preserved monument complete with original auditorium, stage scenery, lighting and costumes. It has been closed for extensive refurbishment since 1966, but it's worth checking to see whether it has re-opened.

THE TOWN

The best way to see Český Krumlov is to indulge in some aimless wandering. It's difficult to pick out certain parts of the town as being more picturesque than others, as it's all so delightful. The streets aren't merely tourist showpieces – it's still a working town whose residents are employed in mining, beer-making or at the nearby paper-mills. Before World War II, the town was predominantly German-speaking, but as a part of the Sudetenland, it was annexed by Hitler in 1938, and in 1945 the majority of the region's 3 million German-speaking inhabitants were expelled and the town's centuries-old bi-cultural life came to an abrupt end.

Český Krumlov originally developed as two separate settlements on either side of the river, one (called Latrán) around the castle, the other on a gentle slope between the two bends of the Vltava. Although the two were united in 1555, the main street on the castle side is still called Latrán and winds its way from the charming, painted Budějovická Gate and over to the wooden Lazebnický Bridge on the other side. Take the street called Na novém městě or New Town (the name refers to alterations carried out seven centuries ago) and you'll end up at the **Eggenberg Brewery**, which moved here from its original Renaissance house on the main square in 1945.

Although tours of the brewery are not officially encouraged, they have been known to happen. If you're unlucky, console yourself in the rollicking *pivnice* next door. Follow the river path back and you'll see the entrances to the medieval graphite mines that run underneath the town and are still worked today.

Crossing Lazebnický Bridge will bring you up to Svornosti náměstí, the **main square**. It's a small, intimate space by Bohemian standards, dominated by the Old Town Hall built in the Renaissance style in the sixteenth century and stamped with emblems of various noble families and, since 1992, the UNESCO insignia. Close by on Horní, is the **Church of St Vitus**, the long slender tower of which is visible from all parts of the town. It was finished in 1439 and the Baroque ornamentation that was added inside at a later date is somewhat at odds with the clean, vertical lines of the nave.

Finally, you shouldn't miss the **Egon Schiele Cultural Centre**, just west of the main square on Široká. Český Krumlov was the home town of the artist's mother and he spent some time here before 1918. In 1993 his former studios were adapted into an exhibition space, showing 80 of his works that the founders have somehow managed to procure on permanent loan from private American collectors.

Getting There

By bus: buses leave from Florenc bus station. The trip takes about four hours, with a change at České Budějovice.
By train: the trip from Hlavní nádraží takes five hours and also includes a change at České Budějovice.
By car: the fastest and easiest way to get to the town. There are two possible routes: either leave Prague on the Brno motorway (E60) and then take the E55 past Tábor and České Budějovice and then follow signs to Český Krumlov; or go via Písek leaving Prague on Route 4, in the direction of Strakonice.

Where to Eat

Krumlovská U kalacha *Latrán 13, Český Krumlov (no phone).* Very good no-nonsense *pivnice* (beer hall) with a terrace overlooking the river.
Hospoda Na louzi *Kajovská 66, Český Krumlov (0337 54 95).* A rust-coloured crumbling façade, original 1930s fittings inside.

Where to Stay

Finding a room in Český Krumlov is not a problem. Dozens of tiny cottages offer *zimmer frei* (rooms for rent). Some of the best are located on Parkán, a tranquil terrace with abundant flowers that looks onto the river. Options for a double room, include **Pension U Vltavy** *Parkán 107 (0337 43 96)* and **U dvou Marií** *Parkán 104 (0337 52 28).*

Tourist Information

Zámek 57, Český Krumlov (tel/fax 0337 48 06). Staff can book canoe and boat tours down the fast flowing Vltava. Trips range from a one-hour jaunt to an eight-hour expedition.

The Castle

(tel/fax 0337 20 75). **Open** *April, Oct* 9am-noon, 1-4pm, Tue-Sun; *May-Aug* 8am-noon, 1-5pm, Tue-Sun; *Sept* 9am-

noon, 1-5pm, Tue-Sun. **Admission** 60kč adults; 40kč children. The last ticket is sold one hour before closing time. The only way to see the castle is to take an hour-long tour. The tower is open from 9am-6pm Tue-Sun.

Egon Schiele Cultural Centre

Široká 70-72, Český Krumlov (0337 42 32/fax 0337 28 20). **Open** 10am-6pm daily.

South-West Moravia

Telč

The tiny town of Telč, with its immaculately preserved Renaissance buildings still partly enclosed by medieval fortifications and surrounded by lakes, undoubtedly deserves its place on UNESCO's World and Natural Heritage list. The large rhomboid **central square** dates back to the fourteenth century but its present appearance – a delicate colonnade runs down three of its sides which are lined with absurdly photogenic gabled houses – was determined in the sixteenth century during Zachariaš of Hradec's period of administration. A trip to Genova and a fortuitous marriage to Katerina of Wallenstein gave this Renaissance man the inspiration and means to reconstruct the town following a devastating fire in 1530. Each of the pastel-hued buildings has a different façade adorned with frescoes, sgraffito or later Baroque and Rococo sculptures.

The narrower end of the square is dominated by the onion-domed bell towers of the seventeenth century Jesuit **church** on one side and the Renaissance **château** opposite. In 1552 Zachariaš of Hradec decided to turn this fourteenth century family seat into his principal residence; at his invitation the Italian architect Baldassare Maggi arrived in town with a troupe of master masons and stuccodores and set to work transforming the Gothic fort into the Italianate palace you can see today. The coffered ceilings of the Golden Hall and of the Blue Hall, and the monochrome *trompe-l'oeil* decorations that cover every inch of plaster in the Treasury, count among the finest Renaissance interior decorations in central Europe. In the Marble Hall is some fantastic armour for both knight and steed, while the African Hall contains a motley collection of hunting trophies including a stuffed rhino and a very large elephant's ear.

The castle also houses a permanent exhibition of works by the Moravian artist Jan Zrzavý (1890-1977), and a small municipal museum which contains an unusual nineteenth century mechanical nativity crib which the custodian will willingly activate for you. After you've exhausted the interior possibilities, relax in the peaceful gardens which stretch down to the lake.

*The Renaissance dolls' houses of **Telč**, each with a different façade.*

Getting There

By bus: buses leave every day from Florenc bus station at 6.05am and 11.45am Mon-Fri; 6.05am and 8.30am Sat; 6.05am and 10.30am Sun. The journey takes just under four hours.

By car: 150kms from Prague. Head out of Prague across the Nusle bridge and onto the Brno motorway which you leave at exit 112 following signs to Jihlava; then follow signs to Telč along Route 19 and then Route 406.

Where to Eat

Šenk pod věží *Palackého 116, Telč (066 96 28 89).* There are various choices, but this is the most charming. It serves good Czech fare, has friendly staff and a terrace outside.

Where to Stay

Pension Privát Nika *45 náměstí Zachariáše z Hradce, Telč (066 96 21 04).* **Rates** 350kč per person per night. Comfortable and good value. **Hotel Pod Kaštaní** *Štepnická 409 (066 721 30 42).* **Rates** *double* 660kč.

Tourist information

náměstí Zachariáše z Hradce, Telč (066 96 22 33). **Open** 8am-6pm Mon-Fri; 10am-6pm Sat, Sun. Staff can book accommodation, plus fishing, horse riding and hunting expeditions.

The Castle

Open *April-Oct* 9am-noon, 1-4pm, *May-Aug* 9am-noon, 1-5pm, Thur-Sun. **Admission** *castle & gallerie* 35kč adults.
Tours of the castle are conducted in Czech but you can pick up a detailed English text at the ticket counter.

Galerie Jana Zrzavého

Open *April-Oct* 9am-noon, 1pm-4pm daily; *Nov-March* 9am-1pm Sat.

Slavonice

Few places with a mere 2,000 inhabitants can boast such wonderful Renaissance architecture as Slavonice. Located in the south-western tip of Moravia just three kilometres from the Austrian border, the town was off bounds to visitors during the Communist years and still retains the atmosphere of a village lost in a time-warp. The peeling sgraffitoed façades of the houses are testimony to its heyday in the sixteenth century when it thrived as an important trading post for merchants on the Vienna-Prague stagecoach route. However, its prosperity was shortlived; decline set in early with extensive destruction during the Thirty Years War and the eventual relocation of the trade route. Until World War II the inhabitants were mainly Austrian, but they were forced to leave in 1945 under the mass expulsion of the German-speaking population. The town was gradually repopulated by Czechs.

The town consists of little more than two adjoining squares. The lower one and larger of the two, contains the **Municipal Museum** (which documents the history of Slavonice's architecture, open daily between 8am-6pm), the sixteenth century parish **Church of the Virgin Mary**, and Slavonice's most original architectural feature: diamond vaulting. Step into the local police station or the *cukrárna* (sweetshop) to gawp at this geometric wonder that preempts Cubism by some 400 years.

The most famous building on the upper square is the **Besídka snack bar and gallery**, owned and run by members of the former dissident Prague-based theatre group Sklep. They bought the building in 1989, and decided to put the long-neglected Slavonice back on the map by opening an arty café that would function as a base for summer workshops. A little further up from the Besídka, the friendly Italian owner of Number 85 will show you the sixteenth century prayer room on the first floor of his house. A complete cycle of biblical frescoes is preserved in what was once a

Kutná Hora's **Cathedral of St Barbara**, *built by miners and dedicated to their patron saint.*

secret Protestant chapel. Look out for the crocodile wearing a papal tiara, one of the more unusual expressions of anti-papal sentiment and, in the final fresco, the pathetic 'beast' that looks like a depressed cartoon character with a sagging bosom and bulbous eyes.

All the streets branching off the main square lead almost immediately into the countryside. There are lots of good picnic spots around the dilapidated village of Mariz which lay in no-man's land until 1989.

Getting There

By bus: catch a bus to Dačice (famous for giving the sugar cube to the world); from there you can get a local bus or train to Slavonice.
By train: local trains leave every hour from Telč.
By car: from Telč follow signs to Dačice, and then to Slavonice. The journey takes about half an hour.

Where to Stay

Hotel Arkada *on the lower square, Slavonice (0332 935 25/6/fax 0332 935 27)*. **Rates** *double room* 1,500kč. The best room in town; friendly staff and comfortable lodgings. **Besídka** *on the upper square, Slavonice (0332 932 93)*. **Rates** 50kč. Dormitory-style accommodation above the café of the same name. **Estec** *opposite the Besídka*. **Rates** *double room* 600kč. A few rooms to let in a private home, very spacious but no private bathroom. Ask at the Besídka for more information.

Where to Eat

Besídka *on the upper square, Slavonice (0332 932 93)*. By far the most interesting place to eat and drink in Slavonice, it serves cheap and tasty Czech food and excellent coffee.

Summer Workshops

Multilingual classes on sculpture, drawing, painting, theatre, music and photography are held annually in July. For more information contact Jan Boháč at the *Besídka, Slavonice (0332 932 92)* or in Prague *(46 44 79/643 42 33)*.

Heading East

Kutná Hora

Kutná Hora's short-lived wealth but lasting fame began with the discovery of silver ore here in the late thirteenth century. A boom town was born, the silver rush financing the construction of a sparkling new Gothic town, even after the Bohemian kings had siphoned off a lion's share of the profits. For 250 years the town was second in importance only to Prague.

A testimony to its former riches and the town's greatest landmark is the **Cathedral of St Barbara** (sv. Barbora). A magnificent building, the exterior outclasses even St Vitus' Cathedral in Prague and both buildings owe their construction to Peter Parler's workshop. Work was started on St Barbara's in 1388 but was interrupted by the Hussite wars. Benedict Ried took over in 1512 and undertook the construction of the nave, giving it his distinctive flower-patterned vaulting. Remarkably, the money for the entire construction came not out of the royal coffers, but from the miners' pockets, and the church is a monument to their hazardous profession. Their spiritual welfare was protected by St Barbara, their patron saint, and the ceiling is decorated with the emblems of the guilds, guardians of their worldly interests. Numerous other interior details dignify their labours, most notably the Miner's Chapel, where recent renovation has uncovered late Gothic frescoes depicting miners with wheel-barrows and pick-axes. The silver minters also sponsored a chapel and it is similarly homely, the paintings showing the craftsmen perched on three-legged stools hammering out coins.

If you want to get some idea of life in a medieval mine, head downhill from the cathedral to the **Hrádek** on Barborská, where an exhibition on mining, housed in a late Gothic fort, prepares you for a trip into the tunnels themselves.

Continuing towards the centre of the town you'll come to the site of the former royal mint. Tiny cell-like workshops line the walls of the **Vlašský dvůr** (Italian Court) – thus named because Italian artisans were drafted in to hammer out the silver Prague groschens (*pražské groše*) in the fifteenth century, in the days when Bohemia could boast a hard currency that was used throughout Europe. Today the architecture is a mix of Gothic and neo-Gothic and the inside houses a collection of rare coins.

Above the Court looms the 80-metre high tower of St Jacob's (sv. Jakub), a Gothic church dating from 1330. Climb the tower for the best view in town, taking in a broad sweep of the verdant Vrchlice valley and the dizzying towers of St Barbara.

The rest of the town is pleasant to wander through. There are quiet side streets lined with some interesting Renaissance houses, and although the main square (Palackého náměstí) is not overly exciting, it's where most of the bars and restaurants are to be found. It's also worth making your way to the Plague column on Šultyskovo náměstí. These monuments are typical features of many Bohemian towns: this one dates from 1713, when the survivors of the plague had good reason to count their blessings, although it's unclear if the bulbous forms on which the cherubs are perched are stylistic representations of clouds or graphic representations of bubonic swellings.

Getting There

By bus: buses leave from outside Želivského metro at 8.25am, 12.30pm, Mon-Fri; 8.25am, 12.30pm, 12.45pm Sat; 8.25am,12.45pm Sun. From Florenc bus station they leave at noon, 1pm, 1.40pm daily.
By train: trains run from Hlavní nádraží, and take 50 minutes. Between 9am and 10am there are several trains, but very few later in the day.
By car: the fastest route is to head out through Žižkov and follow signs to Kolín to get on to Route 12; the scenic way is on Route 333 via Říčany, further south.

Where to Stay

See **Tourist Information** *below.*

Where to Eat

U Morového sloupu *Šultysovo náměstí, Kutná Hora (0327 38 10).* The main decorative feature of the interior is a wall covered in visiting cards – not as good as the Renaissance frescoes and sculptures of reclining dames which adorn the façade, but the traditional Czech food is good and reasonably priced.
Harmonia *U Jakuba, Husova-Vysokostelská 104, Kutná Hora (0327 22 75).* If the weather is fine there's a beautiful terrace overlooking a picturesque lane, and the menu's relatively extensive.
Restaurace U Hvairu *Šultyskovo náměstí, Kutná Hora (no phone).* A smoky vaulted room and small outdoor courtyard serving Gambrinus beer and the usual Czech dishes. It's open long hours – 10am-10pm daily.

Tourist Information

Vlašský dvůr, Havlíčkovo náměstí (0327 28 73). **Open** 9am-5pm daily
Staff can book accommodation in private houses.

The Museum of Mining

(Muzeum a středověké důlní dílo), Barborská 28, Kutná Hora (0327 20 08/21 59). **Open** 9am-noon, 1-5pm, Tue-Sun. **Admission** 30kč.
A guided tour is compulsory. As places are limited and often reserved by tour groups, it's worth booking in advance.

Sedlec

No trip to Kutná Hora is complete without a visit to Sedlec and its famous bone chapel. This is the last resting place of an estimated 40,000 bodies that haven't been allowed to rest in peace, but instead have been used as ornate and macabre decoration.

The **Cistercian Abbey** was founded in Sedlec in 1142. Today, the remaining church – an eighteenth century structure rebuilt by Giovanni Santini-Aichel after the fourteenth century version was gutted by fire – is in a permanent state of restoration, and the role of the adjoining monastic buildings could hardly be more secular (they're occupied by the largest tobacco factory in central Europe). But while the monks were still in control, they built the **ossuary**, a few hundred yards north of the church on Zámecká. From the outside, as a result of some nineteenth century remodelling, this chapel looks like a stray chunk that has fallen off St Barbara's Cathedral. In the late thirteenth century Abbot Jindřich returned from a trip to Jerusalem with a pot of soil he had swiped from the holy grave. As a result, the abbey quickly gained a name throughout central and northern Europe and corpses from Poland, Bavaria and even Belgium came flooding in. The plague of 1318 contributed some 30,000 bodies and the crypt was close to bursting point when the Schwarzenberg family acquired it in 1784.

A rudimentary arrangement of bones had already been carried out by a half-blind monk in the sixteenth century, but the Schwarzenbergs had altogether grander designs and hired a local woodcarver in 1870 to fashion the creative display seen today. The result is truly remarkable: every single part of the human body has been utilised and skulls, femurs, tibias and pelvises are combined in ornate patterns. From the ceiling hangs a skeletal chandelier, the centrepiece shaped from human skulls. There are urns made of thigh bones, several monstrances, an anchor and even the coat of arms of the Schwarzenberg family, all made out of bones.

Getting There

By bus: take bus no. 1 or 4 from Kutná Hora.
By car: 3km East out of Kutná Hora on the Kolin road.

Where to Stay

Hotel U Ruze *Zámecká 52, Sedlec, Kutná Hora (0327 74115).*

The Ossuary (kostnice)

Open *summer* 8am-noon, 1-5pm, Tue-Sun; *winter* 9am-noon, 1-6pm, Tue-Sun; otherwise the key may be collected from the vegetable shop at Zámecá 127.

Kuks

Although little is left of the magnificent Baroque spa town that once stood on the banks of the Labe, few people fail to be charmed by the strange and melancholy atmosphere of the surviving ruins and nearby Betlém woods.

The large palace that stands imposingly over the village of Kuks is in fact a church, flanked on either side by what used to be the hospital building. Kuks' greatest treasures are the **sculptures** that line the terraces in front of both wings. These are the work of leading eighteenth century sculptor Matthias Braun, famous in Prague for his sculpture of St Luitgard on Charles Bridge (*see chapter* **Prague by Area: Staré Město**). To the right as you face the building stands the *Angel of Woeful Death* and the 12 *Vices*. Each has a prop or suitably exaggerated appearance: Envy eating her own tongue, Gluttony represented by a Bacchanalian gourmet with a sturdy pig at her side, and Laziness leaning on a donkey. To the left the 12 *Virtues* (Chastity is covered by a veil, Generosity carries a cornucopia), led by the *Angel of Blissful Death,* stand somewhat more demurely. The statues are copies, the originals having been moved to the **museum** which also houses an extremely well preserved Baroque apothecary.

Although impressive, the town you see today is only a fraction of Anton Šporck's original conception. After discovering a mineral spring on his estate in the early eighteenth century, this enlightened patron of Baroque art employed the leading architects and sculptors of the day to create a spa town that would rival Karlovy Vary in elegance and match Versailles in grandeur. The extravagant

complex was spread out on both banks of the Labe and linked by a giant staircase. On the left bank stood a palace, a library, fountains and, most importantly of all, the baths, as well as a racetrack surrounded by statues of dwarves. The right bank was reserved for the hospital and church.

Only 50 years after it was built, disaster struck when the Labe burst its banks in 1748, washing away most of the structures on the left bank and destroying the spring itself. Kuks' days as a spa were over and the remaining buildings have been slowly decaying ever since.

Continue up river for about three kilometres to the **Betlém (Bethlehem) woods**, which are signposted from the village. Here you can see some of Braun's most powerful masterpieces, a series of anchorites and penitents carved out of the rock face. This outdoor sculpture gallery is one of the more strange and wonderful Baroque follies in Europe. From the car-park, head down the path into the woods; after about five minutes' walk you'll come across the first sculpture. The crouching figure is the hermit Garinus, one of many obscure figures whom the eclectic Šporck commissioned Braun to sculpt. According to a tenth century myth, the Egyptian Garinus spent ten years and ten days crawling on all fours with his eyes cast down as a self-inflicted penance for raping and killing a young girl entrusted to his care. She was then miraculously found unharmed in a well and Garinus, as depicted in this sculpture, was once again able to gaze towards the heavens. The two statues nearby are of St John the Baptist and another crouching hermit, Onufrius, an early Christian Egyptian of whom little is known. Further on Mary Magdalene lies close to a relief of the nativity, from which the woods derive their name. The final sculpture is of Jacob's Well, with the damaged figures of Christ and the woman from Samaria sitting on its sides.

Getting There

By bus: about 40 minutes from Hradec Králové.
By car: 112km from Prague; follow signs to Poděbrady to get onto the E67 and continue on this road all the way to Jaroměř. From there take Route 299 towards Dvůr Králové, and after 6km you will arrive at the village of Kuks. Kuks is close to the Český ráj area; if you are coming from Jičín, take the E442 to Hořice and then Route 300 to Dvůr Králové and from there head south on Route 29 to Kuks.

Where to Stay

There is bed and breakfast accommodation next to the château *(0437 67 80).*

Where to Eat

There's an 'authentic' goulash, fried cheese, and more importantly, beer-serving local in Kuks, just opposite the stairs leading up to the château.

The Château

(0437 47 61). **Open** *April, Oct* 9am-noon, 1-4pm, Sat, Sun; *May-Sept* 9am-noon, 1-6pm, Tue-Sun. Last guided tour is one hour before closing time.

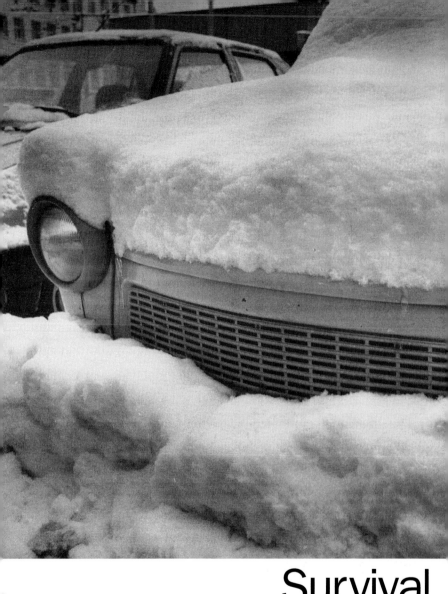

Survival

Survival

All the tips you need for short- or long-term survival in the Czech capital: finding a flat, getting a work permit or simply using the phones.

There is a disproportionately large number of dogs in Prague and no law that stops them fouling the pavement, so beware. Dogs that are small enough to fit into a bag can be taken on public transport free of charge.

Vets

Mudr. Olga Dvořáková
Liliová 17, Prague 1 (26 75 92). Metro Staroměstská.
Open 9am-8pm daily.

Veterinární klinika
Jinonická 78, Prague 5 (52 25 32). Bus 130, 149. **Open** 8am-8pm Mon-Fri; 1-6pm Sat, Sun.

Bureaucracy

Establishing Residency

Becoming a resident of the Czech Republic will test your patience to the point where you wonder why you want to stay in the country in the first place. The process is fraught with difficulties. Be patient and persistent and finally your little green card will appear. Once you've got the card, it also entitles you to a few privileges, such as discounts on hotel rooms and some forms of transport.

There are two primary obstacles to obtaining a green card – your landlord and your work place. The chances are that your landlord is like the thousands of others who rent flats on the black market. This means that he or she does not have official permission to rent an apartment from the state (which still owns the majority of residential buildings in Prague), is not paying tax on your rent, and is therefore not likely to want to write a letter declaring that you live in his or her flat. If you need a green card, tell your landlord you must have a notarised letter stating that you live there before you sign the rental agreement. The other problem is a classic Catch-22. In order to get a residency permit, you have to show you have a job; to get a job, officially you have to show you have a work permit; to get a work permit, you have to have a residency permit. The usual way of breaking this cycle is by taking a job without the proper papers and then filling out the official paperwork later.

Office for Registering as a Foreign Resident
Olšanská 2, Prague 3 (27 27 30/27 95 43). Metro Flora/26 tram/136 bus. **Open** 7.30am-2pm Mon, Tue, Thur; 7.30am-5pm Wed; 7.30am-noon Fri.
To register, you need to bring the following with you: three passport pictures, a 1,000kč stamp, your passport, a notarised letter from your landlord showing you have a place to live, and a registration card from the employment office or proof from a Czech school showing that you are enrolled as a student. Arrive early to secure a place in the queue, and take a good book as you'll be in it some time.

Work Permits

The Czech Republic is not a member of the EU, so Europeans as well as nationals of other countries are supposed to obtain permission to work in the country. Applications for work permits are made at the same office as residency applications.

In the Czech Republic, as elsewhere, the policy is that Czech residents should get offered new jobs first. So, your employer has to show proof that your position was advertised at the Employment Office for at least 21 days, and that no one else could fill the employment requirements. Your employer must have a copy of your passport, a letter authorising him to act for you, and a copy of your diploma or other educational qualifications.

Student Permits

It is fairly simple to get permission to study in the Czech Republic. You need a letter from the Czech educational body where you plan to study, together with the other bits and pieces needed for registering as a foreign resident (*see page 256*).

Communications
Telephone

The telephone system has undergone some cosmetic changes in the past few years, but the residents of Prague are still waiting for the age of high-tech communications to dawn in eastern Europe. Over 60,000 phones in Prague 1 and Prague 2 are now on a digital system, which means the phones can read a tone and pulse sound, and connections with foreign countries are better.

It takes literally years to get a phone line installed, unless you know the right people in the right places and can pay them handsomely for sneaking a line your way. This means that businesses are forever scrambling for new phone lines, and are often forced to move premises if they need additional phone lines. Property prices are directly related to how many phone lines are linked to an office space. Many apartments have no phone lines at all – only rent one with a phone line installed and working. Make sure that the line is a state one and not a party line or switchboard service. If a landlord promises that a phone will be installed next week, don't believe him, no matter how nice, sincere and convincing he may sound.

The telephone system is still based on old switchboxes, so that a call shoots around the city like a pinball hitting the pins and can miss its ultimate target completely. Sometimes the switchboxes in certain districts, especially in Prague 2 and 5, become so clogged that you simply can't dial these areas. At other times, the number you dial has no relation to the number you reach. Call waiting, voice mail, answering services, recorded messages and itemised billing are all things of the future and no one, not even SPT Telecom, the state telephone monopoly, knows when these events will happen. At the time of writing, the Czech government was deciding how to privatise SPT.

Emergencies

For a list of 24-hour emergency numbers (police, fire and ambulance) *see chapter* **Essential Information**.

Emergency Repairs

There are a few 24-hour emergency repair services dealing with locks, heating, water or gas. Sometimes the quickest way to get something fixed is to phone your landlord or neighbour who will probably have handy friends who can repair things quickly – the Czech Republic is a country of engineers, who are always tinkering with their cars or washing machines. If you fail to find a helpful neighbour, try one of the services listed below (you'll need to have a Czech-speaker in tow).

Electricity
(24 91 51 51)

Gas
(24 22 74 62)

Locksmith
(858 63 48)

Water
(67 31 05 43)

Phone Numbers

There are between three and eight digits in Czech numbers. The eight-digit numbers are generally digital ones. Be patient when dialling: it can take between three and five tries before you get through to the number you're trying to reach. Unfortunately SPT Telecom doesn't have a service that notifies callers that the number they are trying has been digitalised and therefore changed.

Public Phone Booths

Most of the phone booths use phone cards. The cards come in 50kč denominations up to 300kč. Calls cost about 2kč for six minutes locally, so a 50kč card is adequate if you plan to make calls only in Prague. Buy a 200kč or 300kč card if you want to make long-distance calls. The cards are sold at most newsstands and all branches of the post office.

International Calls

To make an international call from Prague, dial 00, followed by the appropriate country code, area code (omitting 0 for the UK) and number. You can make an international call from any of the card phones in Prague. The best time to do so is outside business hours.

Size conversion chart for clothes

Women's clothes									
British	8	10	12	14	16	•	•	•	•
American	6	8	10	12	14	•	•	•	•
French	36	38	40	42	44	•	•	•	•
Italian	36	38	40	42	44	•	•	•	•
Women's shoes									
British	8	10	12	14	16	•	•	•	•
American	6	8	10	12	14	•	•	•	•
Continental	36	38	40	42	44	•	•	•	•
Men's suits/overcoats									
British	38	40	42	44	46	•	•	•	•
American	38	40	42	44	46	•	•	•	•
Continental	48	50/2	54	56	58/60	•	•	•	•
Men's shirts									
British	14	14.5	15	15.5	16	16.5	17	•	•
American	14	14.5	15	15.5	16	16.5	17	•	•
Continental	35	36/7	38	39/40	41	42/3	44	•	•
Men's shoes									
British	8	9	10	11	12	•	•	•	•
American	9	10	11	12	13	•	•	•	•
Continental	42	43	44	45	46	•	•	•	•
Children's shoes									
British	7	8	9	10	11	12	13	1	2
American	7.5	8.5	9.5	10.5	11.5	12.5	13.5	1.5	2.5
Continental	24	25.5	27	28	29	30	32	33	34

Children's clothes

In all countries, size descriptions vary from make to make, but are usually done by age

International dialling codes

Australia 61; **Canada** 1; **Ireland** 353; **New Zealand** 64; **United Kingdom** 44; **United States** 1.

Operator Services

Directory Information (in Czech) Prague (120); Czech Republic (121)
Information about international and national dialling codes (0149)
Information about telecommunication services (0139)
AT&T international operator:
USA Direct (004 200 0101)
Canada Direct (004 200 0151)
United Kingdom Direct (004 200 4401)
MCI Call USA (004 200 0112)

Post

The Czech Republic has beautiful stamps that can be bought from the post office, newsagents or a tabák. Unfortunately, these colourful stamps don't always ensure your mail gets to its final destination very fast, if at all. There are dozens of small post offices dotted around the city. If you choose to go to the main post office (*see below*), expect some confusion. Clerks can send you on a wild goose chase just to get a stamp. Packages, letters, express letters or registered letters are all dealt with at different windows. Be patient, take a deep breath and you'll make it through the experience. Letters cost 8kč to send within Europe and 11kč to North America. Packages must be securely wrapped in brown paper and string or sealed in a padded envelope.

Main Post Office

(Hlavní pošta), Jindřišská 14, Prague 1 (24 22 88 56/24 22 90 51/fax 232 08 78/232 09 78). Metro Můstek or Náměstí Republiky. **Open** 24 hours daily.
Come here to pick up Poste Restante letters, buy special stamps and send (or receive) faxes. You can send documents in Europe by two-day express mail through *EMS expresní pošta*, but the service is not as reliable as the private express delivery companies (*see chapter* **Business**). This is not to be confused with express mail, which is a priority mail service that is only useful inside the Czech Republic. To pick up Poste Restante mail, you'll need your passport and some small change.

If you receive a package in the mail that the post office has been unable to deliver, you'll get a slip of paper notifying you that it is waiting and must be picked up by a certain date. This slip will tell you where and when to collect your package. If you owe some duty on a package, phone the post office to find out how much you owe and when the customs window is open. These packages will either be at the main post office or the Customs post office on Plzeňská in Prague 5. Be careful about having valuable items sent to you by mail, since packages quite frequently go missing.

Disabled Access

The Olga Havel Foundation, a group started by President Havel's wife in 1990, seeks to improve the living conditions of disabled people in the Czech Republic. Currently, life is very difficult for anyone who is wheelchair bound. Few of the old buildings are equipped with lifts that can accommodate wheelchairs. Some of the pavements have ramps, but the majority do not. Public transport has extremely limited access (*see chapter* **Getting Around**). For information on the situation for disabled people in the Czech Republic, contact the Olga Havel Foundation, *PO Box 240, 111 21 Prague 1 (24 21 73 31)*.

Discount Travel

All the major airlines are trying to expand their business in the Czech Republic and as a result there are some bargain package deals to be found. Check the local newspapers or ask at the different airline offices to find out about them. Those airlines that have had promotional package trips in the past include KLM, Turkish Airways, SAS, and Alitalia. The airlines also offer special prices for those under 25 years old.

ČKM

Žitná 12, Prague 2 (24 21 79 54/29 12 40). Metro Muzeum. **Open** 9am-noon, 1-5pm, Mon-Fri.
The former youth travel arm of Čedok, the state travel company, ČKM offers discount travel tickets for students and those under 25. Phone or call at their office for details. You can also purchase an International Student Identity Card here (you need a passport photo and proof of enrolment at a school or college).

GEOS

In Vltavská metro station, Prague 7 (80 05 21). **Open** 9am-6pm Mon-Fri.
Offers discount bus tickets to Paris, Munich, Rome, Frankfurt and other major European cities.
Branch: Letohradská 58, Prague 7 (37 94 81).

Kingscourt

Antala staška 60, Prague 4 (49 92 56/61 21 16 68). Metro Budějovická. **Open** 8am-6pm Mon-Fri; 9am-1pm Sat.
The cheapest and most popular bus line between London and Prague.

Tom's Travel Service

Ostrovní 7, Prague 1 (29 39 72/29 06 96/fax 29 18 66). Metro Národní třída. **Open** 9am-10pm daily. **Credit** AmEx, DC, EC, MC, V.
A friendly and efficient agency with an assortment of hotels, pensions and furnished apartments on its books. The multilingual staff will provide discounts on advance reservations and free transfers to or from the airport or train stations, as well as last-minute accommodation.

Driving

Driving in the centre of town in the middle of a working day is not recommended. Not only do you have to negotiate the pedestrian and tram traffic,

you also have to find somewhere to park. *See chapter* **Getting Around** for alternative modes of transport. However here are some points to bear in mind if you insist on driving around Prague:

By law, seat belts must be worn at all times.
Keep copies of your driving licence, Green Card, and vehicle registration at all times.
Don't leave valuables in your car.
At night, watch out for traffic lights flashing yellow: at an intersection there's usually a point when all the lights flash yellow at once and no one has a clear right of way.
If you're driving a large car stay away from the narrow cobbled streets. Cars have been known to get stuck trying to navigate around parked vehicles on these roads.
A lot of the major two-lane roads take right-angled turns. If you are uncertain about which direction to take at a junction, look out for the sign before it and follow the thickest line on it.
Watch out for trams, which always have right of way, and be particularly careful at tram stops.
If you park illegally, your car is likely to be clamped or towed away.

Breakdown Service

Getting a Škoda fixed is easy, but getting a foreign car repaired can be costly, especially if the parts have to be sent for. If you are involved in an accident, you must leave your car at the scene of the accident until the police arrive to write a report (which is why after every fender bender the traffic is always jammed for several streets in Prague).

Emergency Road Service (154)
AAA (37 37 47)
Autodopravna Škoda (75 41 73)
Euro A Car Transport (43 95 14)
Help Servis Praha (311 18 45)

Parking

The Czech police have recently started clamping illegally parked cars with what's popularly known as the 'Denver Boot'. It costs a minimum of 300kč and a fair amount of time and trouble to unclamp the car. The police leave a note on your windscreen stating the time they clamped the car and where to go to get it unlocked.

Being clamped is preferable to being towed away, which the police have been known to do while a car is in gear, stripping it of its transmission and other internal organs. If your car is missing, call the **Emergency Road Service** (154) or the police (158) and report where your car was last seen. They usually tow your car to the nearest car pound and it costs a minimum of 300kč to get it out.

Twenty-four hour car parks are the safest place to park your car. Many hotels have garages or reserved parking spaces available for rent. Below is a list of the car parks in central Prague.

Družstvo

Hlavní nádraží, Prague 1 (24 22 63 91).

Helios Parking Centrum
U divadla 77, Prague 1 (24 21 07 75).

PGS
Vinohradská 28, Prague 2 (25 24 19).

Petrol

Petrol costs a bit less in the Czech Republic than it does in some other European countries. Unleaded fuel is called *natural*, leaded is called *special*, and diesel is *diesel* or *nafta*. Most petrol stations are self-service. The stations on the motorway are usually open 24 hours a day, or else they close at 1am and re-open at 5am or 6am. BP, Agip, and Shell all have glistening new stations in the city.

Agip
K sídlišti, Prague 4 (42 31 33). **Open** 6am-8pm daily.
Branches: Ruská, Prague 10; Liberecká, Prague 8.

BP
K Barrandovu, Prague 5 (381 07 54). **Open** 24 hours daily.

Shell
Jeremenkova, Prague 5 (529 42 47). **Open** 24 hours daily.

Embassies

Embassies and consulates are closed on Czech holidays and on their national holidays. It's always best to phone in advance to check when they are open. The commercial service which handles business affairs is often in a completely different location from the embassy; *see chapter* **Business** for a list of these.

American Embassy
Tržiště 15, Prague 1 (24 51 08 47). Metro Malostranská/12, 22 tram.

Australian High Commission
Estonska 3/5, Saska kepa, Warsaw, Poland (48 2 617 60 81.

British Embassy
Thunovská 14, Prague 1 (24 51 04 39). Metro Malostranská/12, 22 tram.

Canadian High Commission
Mickiewiczova 6, Prague 6 (24 31 11 08). Metro Hradčanská.

Health

You should obtain private health insurance to cover you in eastern Europe. The UK and 30 other countries have reciprocal agreements with the Czech Republic but only for first aid and emergency treatment. However, should you need treatment, you might have a hard time getting the papers through the Czech health authorities. The medical facilities in Prague range from excellent to below par. Though many of the well-trained doctors speak English, they do not have access to the sophisticated diagnostic equipment that western Europeans take for granted. In an emergency, remain calm and insist on choosing a doctor and a hospital where you feel comfortable and well tended.

Call the **Ambulance Service** (155) for any medical emergency.

Medical Treatment

AIDS Clinic
Fakultní nemocnice Bulovka, Budinova 2, Prague 8 (66 08 26 28). Metro Nádraží Holešovice then tram 12, 14, 24/102, 144, 152, 175 bus. **Open** 24 hours daily.

Children's Hospital
Fakultní nemocnice Motol, V úralu 84, Prague 5 (52 95 11 11). Tram 8, 9/167, 174, 179, 180 bus. **Open** 24 hours daily.
There are several children's hospitals in the city; this one is equipped to handle the largest range of ailments.

Dental Emergencies
Vladislavova 22, Prague 1 (24 22 76 63). Metro Národní třída. **Open** 7pm-7am Mon-Thur; 24 hours Fri-Sun.

Emergency Medical Aid
Karlovo náměstí 32, Prague 2 (24 91 48 24). Metro Karlovo náměstí. **Open** 24 hours daily.
Often a first stop for foreigners. Come here if your ailment isn't too serious – if you need some antibiotics, for example.

First Medical Clinic
Vyšehradská 22, Prague 2 (29 22 86). Metro Karlovo náměstí/8, 24 tram. **Open** 7am-7pm Mon-Fri.

A private clinic where the doctors and nurses speak English. Seek their advice if you do not have anything drastically wrong, but go to one of the hospitals if you need serious attention.

Health Care Unlimited
Nemocnice na Homolce, Room D120 Roentgenova 2, Prague 5 (52 92 20 17). Tram 4, 7, 9/167 bus. **Open** 24 hours daily.
The woman who runs this private advisory service is a nurse from the United States who aims to help outsiders through the intricacies of the Czech health system. The service gives advice on where to find good treatment for various injuries and illnesses. You do have to pay for the service, but it is worth it if you are staying in Prague for a long time.

Orthopedics
Fakultní nemocnice Bulovka, Budinova 2, Prague 8 (66 31 15 06). Metro Nádraží Holešovice then tram 12, 14, 24/102, 144, 152, 175 bus. **Open** 24 hours daily.
The best place for the treatment of broken bones.

Polyclinic for Foreigners
Nemocnice na Homolce, Roentgenova 2, Prague 5 (52 92 21 46). Tram 4, 7, 9/167 bus. **Open** 4pm-8am Mon-Fri; 24-hours Sat, Sun.
The first stop for many foreigners who need hospital treatment. The clinic isn't always equipped to treat your ailment, but the staff know the health system well enough to advise you about where to go to get the treatment you need.

AIDS

AIDS is still considered a foreigners' disease in the Czech Republic. As a result there aren't many facilities for treatment in Prague. The **Stop AIDS helpline** (29 17 73) can give you advice on where to get an HIV test and recommend doctors who treat AIDS, but the volunteers manning the phones don't always speak English.

Addiction/Alcoholism

There are meetings of Alcoholics Anonymous every week in Prague for English speakers. Consult the classifieds section of the *Prague Post* and *Prognosis* for the time, place and date of the next meeting.

Alternative Medicine

Czech Acupuncture Society
Mudr. F. Pára (37 59 95). Phone for an appointment.

Centre for Homeopathic Education
Mudr. Miloš Rýc, Vlkova 40, Prague 3 (27 33 38). Phone for an appointment.

Monáda
(Centre for Complete Rehabilitation and Natural Cure Methods), Hotel Sandra, Bardounova 2140, Prague 4 (79 40 01). Phone for an appointment.

Pharmacies

Pharmacies (*lékárny*) open after hours on a rotating basis, so there will always be at least one open late in your area of Prague. None of them has a home delivery service, but you can arrange for a messenger or a cab to pick up your medication and bring it to you. There are hundreds of pharmacies in Prague. Below is a list of some of the most central and those that are open long hours.

Lékárna
Pod Marjánkou 12, Prague 6 (35 26 41). Metro Hradčanská then 1, 8, 18, 25, 26 tram. **Open** 24 hours daily.

Lékárna Opletalova
Opletalova 30, Prague 1 (24 22 07 03). Metro Muzeum or Můstek. **Open** 8am-6pm Mon-Fri.

Lékárna U anděla
Štefánikova 6, Prague 5 (24 51 11 21/53 70 39). Metro Anděl/6, 9, 12 tram. **Open** 24 hours daily.

Lékárna U zlatého lva
Vinohradská 65, Prague 2 (25 98 44). Metro Náměstí Míru or Muzeum. **Open** 8am-6pm Mon-Fri.

Help & Advice

There are few help or SOS-lines in Prague and none exclusively in English. The best way to find English-speaking support groups is to look through the classifieds section of *Prognosis* or the *Prague Post* and to read the notice boards at ex-pat hangouts like **Radost** (*see chapter* **Nightlife**), **The Globe Bookstore** (*see chapter* **Cafés, Bars & Pubs**), and **Laundry Kings** (*see chapter* **Services**).

Renting a Flat

Apartment space is tight in Prague. Before you begin your search, you should be aware of a few of the realities of life for the local population. Under the old regime, there was a 20-year waiting list for flats in the centre of town, and at least a ten-year wait in the outlying districts. As a result of this divorced couples often had to keep living together after the divorce; newlyweds had to live with one set of parents; and families fought over who would get granny's flat decades before her death.

It's not surprising, then, that the average Czech finds foreigners' demands for luxuries like a fully equipped kitchen, a washing machine, telephone and parking to be incomprehensible. It should be enough just to have a private place of your own. This difference in expectations can cause a lot of problems when looking at flats. You state your conditions – a small building, unfurnished, with a telephone, near a metro station in Prague 6 – and you get dragged out to a 20-story grey building filled with earth tone furniture, no phone, and the only public transport nearby is a bus. The landlord or estate agent will tell you that it is the only flat available in your price range. This is not entirely true. There are nice flats available, but you have to be patient, lucky and persistent to find one.

Legal Rights

Despite restitution, which has begun to restore property to those who owned it before nationalisation

Flat-space is scarce in Prague, and you might well end up with a view like this.

after 1948, the majority of residential apartments in Prague are still state-owned. This means that people often find themselves renting a black market apartment. To meet the increasing demand, families rent out their flats to foreigners, charging ten times or more the legal rent of 1,000kč a month, and do not pay taxes on that income or declare your presence in the flat to the state authorities. Not surprisingly in this situation, you have no legal rights if there's any trouble with the landlord. Any lease you sign will not be legally binding. If you want to live in Prague, you should find a privately-owned building and sign a legally-binding lease that can protect you from being evicted at the whim of your landlord.

Landlord-tenant rights have not been legally defined in the new free market economy. The best way to deal with landlord troubles is by employing negotiation and patience. Novice landlords do not understand privacy and tenant rights. Some regard tenants as visitors and won't be happy if you want to rearrange their furniture. Find out what a landlord expects of you before you sign a lease.

Flat Hunting

There is no consistency in rent prices for foreigners. The price you pay (generally in dollars or deutschmarks) depends on who you are negotiating with, the security of the lease, and how rich the landlord thinks you are. An American executive with a generous housing allowance may pay $2,500 per month for an apartment in the Old Town Square, while an English-language teacher

may live in the same size flat in the same building for $400 per month.

There are five basic ways to find a flat in Prague:

1. Word of Mouth

The most effective and the most elusive way of finding a flat. Hang out at the ex-pat bars and restaurants – Jo's Bar, the Sports Bar, the Globe, the Derby (*see chapter* **Cafés, Bars & Pubs**), Red Hot & Blues (*see chapter* **Restaurants**), Radost (*see chapter* **Nightlife**) – and tell people you're looking for a flat. You might be lucky and run into someone who is leaving town soon or someone who needs a flatmate.

2. Advertising

Get a Czech-speaker to help you look through the apartment rental section of *Annonce*, which comes out three times a week on Monday, Wednesday and Friday. You could also place an ad in it. Also look through the classifieds section of *Prognosis* and the *Prague Post*, both of which occasionally list flats available.

3. Bulletin Boards

There are bulletin boards at Radost, Laundry Kings (*see chapter* **Services**), and the Globe which frequently have notices up about flats available for rent.

4. Targeting an Area

If you want to live in a particular area of the city, consider putting a 'looking for an apartment' notice up in the buildings in that area. Like a mail shot, this technique can either be very successful, or it can bear no results at all.

5. Estate Agents

Like the property market itself, agents are very inconsistent. They usually charge a success fee of between one and two months' rent for finding you somewhere to live. This means that they tend to show more expensive flats. Most good agents will not bother with any apartment that costs less than $500 a month. If you are not constricted by a tight budget, getting an agent can be the most painless way to find a flat (*see chapter* **Business** for a list of estate agents).

Further Reading

History & Dissent

Most of the useful sources are out of print or very obscure. They must be tracked down through libraries and second-hand book dealers.

Brogan, Patrick: *Eastern Europe: The Real End of World War II?* (Bloomsbury,1990). Clear, concise political history of Soviet satelites under Communism.

Crampton, RJ: *Eastern Europe in the Twentieth Century* (Routledge, 1994). Though dealing also with other eastern European countries, this is a useful introduction to the history of Czechoslovakia. Excellent, up-to-date bibliography.

Evans, RJW: *Rudolf II and His World* (OUP, 1973).

Garton Ash, Timothy: *We the People: The Revolution of 1989 Witnessed in Warsaw, Budapest, Berlin and Prague* (Granta, 1990).

Havel, Václav: *Open Letters* (Faber, 1991). A good introduction to Havel's thought that includes his famous letter 'Dear Dr Hušak'.

Havel, Václav: *Disturbing the Peace* (Faber, 1991).

Karl, Frederick R: *Franz Kafka. Representative Man* (Ticknor and Fields, 1991).

Margolius Kovaly, Heda: *Prague Farewell* (Gollancz, 1988). A heart-stopping account of the Nazi occupation and Stalinist terror.

Lützow, Count Francis: *The Story of Prague* (JM Dent, 1907). Choice anecdotes and insights written in a slightly affected tone, finishing in the nineteenth century.

Renner, Hans: *A History of Czechoslovakia Since 1945* (Routledge, 1989).

Ripellino, Angelo: *Magic Prague* (The Macmillan Press, 1994). A masterly fusion of history, travelogue, fiction and autobiography.

Seton-Watson, RW: *A History of the Czechs and the Slovaks* (Hutchinson, 1943).

Shawcross, William: *Dubček* (Weidenfeld and Nicholson, 1970).

Young, Edgar: *Czechoslovakia* (Royal Navy, 1938). Plenty of basic facts, though the analysis is unchallenging.

Art & Architecture

As with the books on history, information is hard to find. The best source is the *Dictionary of Art* (Macmillan, 1995) which has articles on every aspect of Czech art with good bibliographies. This encyclopedic reference work is only available in major libraries.

Anděl, Jaroslav and others: *Czech Modernism 1900-1945* (Museum of Fine Arts, Houston, 1989).

Margolius, Ivan: *Prague: A Guide to Twentieth-Century Architecture* (Artemis, 1994). Small, succinct and portable.

Petrová, Sylva, and Olivié, Jean-Luc: *Bohemian Glass* (Flammarion, 1990).

Slapeta, Vladimir, and Peichl, Gustav: *Czech Functionalism 1918-1938* (Architectural Association, 1987).

Smejkal, František and Svacha, Rostislav: *Devětsil: Czech Avant-Garde Art, Architecture and Design of the 1920s and 1930s* (Museum of Modern Art, Oxford, 1990).

Literature

Some Czech fiction can be found in good British bookshops. Otherwise head for the major English bookstores in Prague (*see chapters* **Shopping** *and* **Students**). For a discussion of Czech writing and comments on individual authors, *see chapter* **Literary Prague**. The editions given here are the most recent paperback ones.

Čapek, Karel: *War with the Newts* (Allen and Unwin, 1986; Catbird Press 1990).

Čapek, Karel: *Towards the Radical Centre: Karel Čapek Reader* (Catbird Press, 1990). Includes his famous play 'R.U.R'.

Chatwin, Bruce: *Utz* (Picador, 1988). An exquisite and mysterious novalla about a Jewish collector of Meissen porcelain.

Hašek, Jaroslav: *The Good Soldier Švejk* (Penguin, 1990).

Holub, Miroslav: *The Dimension of the Present Moment* (Faber, 1990).

Holub, Miroslav: *The Vanishing Lung Syndrome* (Faber, 1990).

Hrabal, Bohumil: *Too Loud a Solitude* (Abacus, 1993).

Hrabal, Bohumil: *I Served the King of England* (Abacus, 1990).

Hrabal, Bohumil: *Closely Observed Trains* (Abacus, 1990).

Hrabal, Bohumil: *The Little Town Where Time Stood Still* (Abacus, 1993).

Kafka, Franz: *The Complete Novels* (Minerva, 1992).

Klíma, Ivan: *My First Loves* (Penguin, 1989).

Klíma, Ivan: *A Summer Affair* (Penguin, 1990).

Klíma, Ivan: *Love and Garbage* (Penguin, 1991).

Kundera: Milan: *The Joke* (Penguin, 1984).

Kundera: Milan: *The Unbearable Lightness of Being* (Faber, 1985).

Lustig, Arnošt: *Darkness Casts No Shadow* (Quartet, 1989). Life in a concentration camp, by one of the great recorders of the Holocaust.

Lustig, Arnošt: *Diamonds of the Night* (Quartet, 1989).

Lustig, Arnošt: *Night and Hope* (Quartet, 1989).

Lustig, Arnošt: *A Prayer for Katerina Horovitzová* (Quartet, 1990)

Neruda, Jan: *Prague Tales* (Chatto and Windus, 1993). Neruda was one of the first great Czech writers. His record of daily life in Malá Strana is a classic.

Petiška, Eduard: *A Treasury of Tales from the Kingdom of Bohemia* (Martin, Prague 1994).

Škvorecký, Josef: *Talkin' Moscow Blues* (Faber, 1988).

Škvorecký, Josef: *The Miracle Game* (Faber, 1991).

Vaculík, Ludvík: *A Cup of Coffee with my Interrogator* (Readers International, 1987).

Weil, Jiří: *Life with a Star* (Fontana, 1990). A crushing fictionalised account of Weil's life in hiding during the Occupation.

Weil, Jiří: *Mendelsson is on the Roof* (Flamingo, 1992).

Area Index

Basilica, p37; St Vitus's Cathedral, p37; Spanish Hall, p39; Paradise Garden, p56; Strahov Monastery, p34.

Malá Strana

ACCOMMODATION: Hostel Sokol, p28; Kampa Stará Zbrojnice, p19; Pension Dientzenhofer, p25; Pod Věží, p21; Sax, p25; Sidi Pension, p21; U krále Karla, p21; U páva, p21; U tří pštrosů, p23.

CAFES, BARS & PUBS: Bar Bar, p232; Café Bily orel, p131; Café Colombia, p131; Café Savoy, p131; Jo's Bar, p131; Rubin, p232.

MUSEUMS & GALLERIES: Komenský Pedagogical Museum, p169; Sport & Physical Training Museum, p172; Wallenstein Riding School, p164.

RESTAURANTS: Catalunya, p124; U Malířů, p115; U Maltézských rytířů, p117; U Mecenáše, p117; U Modré kachničky, p119; U Snědeného krámu, p124.

SHOPPING: *antiques* Antiques, p135; *children* Obchod loutkami, p137; *jewellery & accessories* L. Mádr, p139; Optika Jan Tietz, p139; J & J Mašek, p141; *leisure* Zebra Atelier, p145.

SIGHTSEEING: Il Bambino di Praga, p39; Church of St Nicholas, p39; Church of St Thomas, p41; John Lennon Wall, p41; Kampa, p56; Petřín Hill, p56; Wallenstein Garden, p56.

Staré Město & Josefov

ACCOMMODATION: Betlem Club, p23; U krále Jiřího, p27; Ungelt, p21.

CAFES, BARS & PUBS: Andy's Café, p126; Blatouch, p127; Bunkr Café, p127; Café Amadeus, p127; Café Archa, p127; Café Bar Valentin, p127; Café Milena, p127; Café Rudolfinum, p127; Ganys, p127; Hogo Fogo, p128; H & S, p128; In Vino Veritas, p128; James Joyce, p128; John Bull Pub, p128; Kavárna Archa, p232; Konirna, p128; Konvikt Klub, p128; Lávka, p128; Literární Kavárna, p232; Reno, p129; Sektbar Ponton, p129; Slovansky dům, p129; Theatre on the Balustrade, p232; U Fleků, p127; U Minuty, p128; U Medvídků, p128; U

See chapter **Prague by Area** for maps and information on each area.

Hradčany & Prague Castle

ACCOMMODATION: Savoy, p19; Pension U raka, p21.

MUSEUMS & GALLERIES: Historical Museum, p167; Imperial Stables, p163; Loreto Treasury, p167; Military Museum, p171; Museum of National Literature, p170; Prague Castle Riding School, p164; St George's Convent, p159; Sternberg Palace, p159; Strahov Gallery, p161; Toy Museum, p172.

RESTAURANTS: Saté Grill, p123; U Ševce Matouše, p121; U Zlaté hrušky, p116.

SHOPPING: *gifts* Museum Shop, p143.

SIGHTSEEING: Černín Palace, p44; The Loreto, p33; *Prague Castle* The Belvedere, p34; Bohemian Chancellery, p44; Golden Lane, p34; Old Royal Palace, p34; St George's

Vejvodů, p129; Velryba, p129; U Zlatého tygra, p129; V Blatnici, p126.

MUSEUMS & GALLERIES: Carolinum, p163; Czech Museum of Fine Arts, p163; Galerie Hollar, p163; Galerie Jaroslav Fragnera, p163; Galerie Rudolfinum, p163; House at the Stone Bell, p163; House of the Lords of Kinský Palace, p164; Kunštat and Poděbrady, p169; Municipal Library, p164; Museum of Decorative Arts, p167; Náprstek Museum, p169; St Agnes's Convent, p159; Smetana Museum, p172; State Jewish Museum, pp169-170.

RESTAURANTS: Au Saint Esprit, p115; David, p115; Green Bar Jonáš, p124; Gorgona/U Králova dvora, p121; Opera Grill, p115; Parnas, p116; Queenz Grill, p124; Red Hot and Blues, p119; Reykavik, p119; U Radnice, p123; U Supa, p121; U Vejvodů, p124; Zlatá ulička, p124; V Zátiší, p116.

SHOPPING: *markets* Staré Město Market, p134; *antiques* Antique, p135; Jan Huněk Starožitnosti, p137; *bookshops & newsagents* Bohemian Ventures, p137, p230; Knihkupectví Fišer, p230; *children* Albatros, p137; *cosmetics & perfumes* Christian Dior, p137; Nina Ricci, p137; *fashion* Art & Fashion Gallery, p138; Modes Robes, p139; Tess Design, p139; *jewellery & accessories* Granát, p139; *lingerie* Celestýn, p139; Palmers, p139; *shoes & leather goods* Belt, p139; Kožená galanterie, p139; Leiser, p139; Pavo Obuv, p139; *flowers* Ateliér Kavka, p140; *gifts* Český národní podnik, 141; *china & glass* Karlovarský porcelán, p143; Sklo-svitidla, p144; *leisure* Maximum Underground, p145; Studio Matouš, p145; Brymová, p145; Druchema – U Petra, p145; *old books & prints* Antikvariát Karel Křenek, p145; Antikvariát U Karlova mostu, p145.

SIGHTSEEING: Astronomical Clock, p41; Bethlehem Chapel, p41; Café Slavia, p43; Charles Bridge, p43; Church of Our Lady before Týn, p43; Clementinum, p43; Estates Theatre, p43; House of the Black Madonna, p56; Jan Hus Monument, p44; Klausen Synagogue, p49; Municipal House, p54; Old Jewish Cemetery, p49; Old-New Synagogue, p49; Old Town Hall, p44; Old Town Square, p44; Pinkas Synagogue, p51; The Powder Gate, p46; Rudolfinum, p51; St Agnes's Convent, p46.

Nové Město

ACCOMMODATION: City Hotel Moráň, p19; Grand Hotel Bohemia Praha, p19; Grand Hotel Evropa, p23; Hlávkova kolej, p25; Hotel 16 U sv.

Kateřiny, p23; Juliš, p23; Koruna, p23; Hotel VZ Praha, p25; Libra-Q, p28; Palace p19; Prague Renaissance, p19; Pařiž, p19; Pension Páv, p21; Pension Unitas, p27.

CAFES, BARS & PUBS: Bistro Pellier, p129; Café Boulevard, p130; Dobrá čajovna, p130; Don Manuel Vinárna, p130; Evropa Café, p130; Institut Français, p130; Jáma, p130; Margaret Bar, p130; Novoměstsky pivovar, p130; Paris-Praha, p131; Praha-Roma, p131; Růžová čajovna, p131; Sports Bar, p131; Svenk Vrbovec, p131.

MUSEUMS & GALLERIES: Dvořák Museum, p171; Museum of the City of Prague, p169; National Museum, p169; Police Museum, p172; Postage Stamp Museum, p172.

RESTAURANTS: Botel Admirál, p121; Bufet Jídelna, p124; Buffalo Bill's, p116; Černý pivovar, p121; Cerberus, p116; Deminka, p121; Kmotra Pizzeria, p121; Krone, p124; Na Rybárně, p119; Pod Křídlem, p119; McDonald's, p224; Restaurace Jáma, p123; Salammbo, p119; U Čižků, p117; U Šuterů, p116.

SHOPPING: *one-stop* Koruna Palace, p134; Bílá Labuť, p134; Kmart, p134; Kotva, p134; Krone, p134; *antiques* Military Antiquities, p137; Rudolf Špičák, p137; Vladimir Kůrka Starožitnosti, p137; *bookshops & newsagents* Cizojazyčné knihkupectví, p137; Knihkupectví Academia, p230; PNS Noviny – časopisy, p137; *children* Creation Stummer, p137; Dětský dům, p137; *cosmetics & perfume* Elizabeth Arden, p137; A+G Flora, p138; Perfumerie Lancôme, p137; *fashion* Adam, p138; Ano Ano, p138; Camomilla, p138; Model Praha, p138; Nostalgie, p138; *jewellery & accessories* Royal Bijou, p139; *shoes & leather goods* Baťa, p140; *flowers* Flora Ton, p140; *food & drink* Casa Pascual, p140; Country Life, p140; Dobrá čajovná, p140; Fruits of France, p140; Gartnerova, p140; Gyma, p140; Leonidas, p141; Maso, p141; Paris-Praha, p141; Praha-Roma, p141; Blatnice, p141; Dionýsos, p141; *china & glass* Květa salon, p143; Lustry, p143; Moser, p144; *household* KDS Sedlčany, p144; Krásná jizba, p144; Ligne Roset, p144; Le Patio, p144; Potten & Pannen, p144; *leisure* Loco Plus, p145; Jan Pazdera, p145; Karel Schuss, p145; Memphis Melody, p145; Popron, p145; Kastner Öhler – sportovní dům, p145; Tico Trek, p145; *old books & prints* Antikvariát Galerie Můstek, p145; Kiwi, p145.

SIGHTSEEING: Adria Palace, p55; Church of Sts Cyril and Methodius, p51; Cubist Lamp Post, p54; Diamant House, p54; Evropa Café, p54;

Melantrich Building, p55; National Museum, p51; National Theatre, p51; New Town Hall, p44; Radio Prague Building, p52; St Wenceslas' Statue, p55; Wenceslas Square, p52.

Further Afield

ACCOMMODATION: Anna, p23; Atrium, p17; Autocamp Hájek, p28; Autocamp Trojská, p28; Domov mládeže, p28; Gay penzion David, 227; International, p19; Julian, p23; Kafka, p25; Mepro, p23; Pension City, p27; Pension Větrník, p27; Petr, p25; Pod Lipkami, p27; Praha, p19; Spiritka, p21; Slavoj-Vesico Hostel, p28.

CAFES, BARS & PUBS: Bar Sarah, p132; Bar Incognito, p234; Black Point, p234; Café Dante, p131; Dejvická Sokolovna, p131; The Derby, p132; Elite, p132; Globe Bookstore, p132, p175, p229; Paseka, p132; Pavlač, p226; Radost FX Café, p132; Rhapsody, p132; Sam, p226; Trampsky salon na Valentince, p132; U Dubu, p226; U Jagusky, p132; U Tří hrochů, p131.

MUSEUMS & GALLERIES: Aeronautical & Cosmonautical Exhibition, p171; Bilek Villa, p161; City Transport Museum, p172; Gallery of Modern Art, p158; Jirásek & Aleš Museum, p170; Lapidarium, p161; Mozart Museum, p172; Museum of the Resistance & the History of the Army, p171; National Technical Museum, p172; Troja Château, p161; Vyšehrad Museum, p169.

RESTAURANTS: Akropolis, p121; Elite, p117; Fakhreldine, p115; Na Zvonařce, p124; Penguin's, p123; Radost FX Café, p132; Restaurace na Vyšehradě, p123; Il Ritrovo, p119; U Govindy, p121; U Pastýřky, p121.

SHOPPING: *one-stop* Pavilon Shopping Mall, p134; *markets* Prague Market, p135; *antiques* Bazar nábytku, p135; *bookshops & newsagents* Globe Bookstore, p137; U knihomola, p137; *children* Akvaristika, p137; *flowers* Zahradnické centrum, p140; *food & drink* Billa, p140; Delvita, p140; Moby Dick, p141; *gifts* Galerie Spička, p143; Spartaklub, p143; *household* Baumax-x, p144; Ikea, p144; Rendl, p144; *leisure* McPaper & Co, p145.

SIGHTSEEING: Anděl Metro, p48; Háje, p48; Hotel International, p48; Main Station, p54; National Memorial, p48; Olšany Cemetery, p48; Stalin Monument, p48; Troja Château, p52; TV Tower, p52; Vyšehrad, p52; Výstaviště, p54; Zoologická zahrada v Praze, p223.

Index

Accommodation pp17-28, p230
accommodation agencies p28
for women p231
gay p227
renting a flat pp261-262
flat hunting p262
Accountants & consultants p216
Adria Palace (Palác Adria) p55, p157
Alfa Arcade p157
AIDS p261
Air pollution p8
Airport *see* **Ruzyně airport**
Aleš, Mikoláš p97, p159, p170
Alternative medicine p261
Ambulance service p260
American Center for Culture and Commerce p104, p229
American Express p7, p209
Anděl Metro p48
Animals p256
Animation p191
Anniversaries *see* **Festivals & events**
Antiques pp135-137
permits p135
old books & prints p145
Archbishop's Palace

(Arcbiskupský palác) p90
Art *see also* **Art Nouveau, Cubism, Surrealism**
art & architecture pp152-157
art galleries pp158-166
art materials pp144-145
Art Trek p31
exhibition spaces pp163-164
commercial galleries pp164-166
Art Nouveau p23, p33, p54, p70, p100, p102, p104, p106, p109, p155, p243
Živnostenská Banka p4, p5, p7, (in Karlovy Vary) p243
Astronomical Clock (Orloj) p41, p44, p95, p153
Astronomical Tower p43
Atrium Hotel p5, p17, p23, p205

Babysitting p222
Baba estate p107
Ball Game Court p89, p153
Ball Season p32
Banking p215
Il Bambino di Praga (Pražské Jezulátko) p39, p93
Bars pp125-132
gay bars & pubs p226
for women p231-232

Baťa building p54, p102, p157, p139
Baťa, Tomáš p139, p187
Barrandov p107
Barrandov Film Studios p107, p187, p189
Basilica of St Jakub (Bazilika sv. Jakuba) p194
Basilica of St Margaret (sv. Markéta) p108
Bazilika sv. Jiří *see* **St George's Basilica**
BBC World Service p179
Beautiful Style p152, p159
Beefstew p175
Beer p114, p125
Karlovy Vary Beer Olympiad p32
Belvedér *see* **Belvedere**
Belvedere (Belvedér) p34, pp89-90, p153, p158
Beneš, Edvard p70, p71, pp72-74
Bertramka *see* **Mozart Museum**
Bethlehem Chapel (Betlémská kaple) p41, p101
Betlémská kaple *see* **Bethlehem Chapel**
Bílá Hora p108
Bílek Villa p155, p161
Black Tower (Černá věž) p89
Bohemian Chancellery (Česká kancelář) p34, p44 *see also*

Defenestration
Boleslav The Cruel p34, p55, p60
Bookshops p137, p145, p230
Botanical gardens p105
Brahe, Tycho p43, p90
Brandl, Petr p154, p155, p159
British Council p157, p229
**British Embassy Commerical
Section** p214
Braun, Matthias p98, 154, p254
Břevnov Monastery p108
Brod, Max p104, p174
Brokof, Ferdinand Maximilián
p154, p159
Bufets & Lahůdkys p124
Bunkr p183, p200
Buquoy Palace p91
Bureaucracy pp256-257
  residency permits p256
  work permits pp256-257
  student permits p257
Buses p13
  night buses p13, p15
Business pp214-220
  banking p215
  business agencies p214
  business services pp216-219
  looking for a job p220
  office services pp219-220
  stock exchange p216

Café Arco p104, p125
Cafés pp125-132
  for women pp231-232
Café Slavia p43, p125
Campsites p28
**Canadian Chamber of
Commerce** p214
Čapek, Karel p174
Car hire p150
Carolinum p100, p163
Čedok p17, p29, p56, p196, p239
Cemeteries
  Jewish Cemetery p109
  Old Jewish Cemetery (Starý
  židovský hřbitov) p49, p98, p99, p170
  Olšany Cemetery (Olšanské
  hřbitovy) p52, p109
  Vyšehrad Cemetery p30, p54, p109,
  p196
**Central European Business
Weekly** p177
Central European University
p229, p230
Ceramics p167
Ceremonial House p99
**Černín Palace (Černínský
palác)** p44, p90, p153, p154
Černínský palác *see* **Černín
Palace**
Černý, David p48
Čertovka *see* **Devil's Stream**
Červená Lhota p246
Česká kancelář *see* **Bohemian
Chancellery**
České Budějovice p245, p246
Český Krumlov p245, p246, p249
Český ráj p206, p239, p240
Chapel of Mirrors p43, p194
Chapel of St Wenceslas p37, p87
Charles IV pp62-63, p87, p92, p100,
p102, p104, p105, p152, p154, p159,

p169, p228, p237, p242, p243
Charles Bridge (Karlův most)
p8, p43, p46, p62, p68, p93, p98, p152
Charles University pp228-229
Charter 77 p55, pp76-77, p83
Chatas p8, p239
Chemists *see* **Pharmacies**
Childminding p222
Children pp221-224
  shops for p137
China & glass pp143-144
Chrám sv. Mikuláše *see* **Church
of St Nicholas**
Christmas Day p221
Church of the Holy Rood p101
Church of the Nativity p33, p34
Church of Our Lady p34
**Church of Our Lady before Týn
(Kostel Matky boží před
Týnem)** p43
**Church of Our Lady Under the
Chain** p91
Church of Our Lady Victorious
p39, p93
Church of the Sacred Heart
p109, p157
**Church of Sts Cyril and
Methodius (Kostel sv. Cyrila a
Metoděj)** p51, p105
Church of St Francis p97
Church of St Giles p101
Church of St Havel p100
Church of St James p95
Church of St Joseph p94
Church of St Michael p96
Church of St Martin p54, p152
**Church of St Nicholas (Chrám
sv. Mikuláše)** p39, p93, p154, p194
**Church of St Nicholas, Staré
Město (Kostel sv. Mikuláše)**
p95, p154
Church of Sts Peter and Paul
p54, p108, p109
Church of St Saviour p97
Church of St Simon and St Jude
p194
**Church of St Thomas (Kostel
sv. Tomáše)** p41, p94
Cinema pp187-191
  animation p191
  cinema coffeehouses p190
  festivals p191
  open-air cinemas p190
  repertory p190
City Transport Museum p172
Civic Forum p55, p77, p104
Clam-Gallas Palace p97, p154
Clementinum (Klementinum)
p43, p97, p154, p194
Clinton, Bill p17, p104, p125, p129,
p183
Clubs pp180-186
  gay clubs & discos pp226-227
  rock, roots & jazz pp199-201
Coach station, Florenc p11
Communications pp257-258
Communist Prague p23, p48,
pp73-78, p81, p86, p90, p96, p101,
p103, p107, p171, p192 *see also*
defenestration
  Beriozka restaurant p100
  Labour Day p29
  theatre p207
  trams p13

Computer leasing p219
Coronation jewels p169
Cosmetics & perfumes p137
Costume hire p146
Counter-Reformation p154
Courier services p220
Crime p8
  women & harassment p231
Cubism pp54-56, p109, p155, p157,
p161, p165
  Cubist Lamp Post p54
  House of the Black Madonna p56,
  p95, p158
Customs p5
  allowances p5
Cycling p15, p150, p204
Czech cuisine p11
  drink p114
  the menu p113
Czech history pp58-78
  key events p58
  Military history p171
  Museums pp167-170
  Prague today p79
Czech language p68, p69, p207
Czech literature pp174-175
  cultural papers p178
  museums pp170-171
Czech Museum of Fine Arts
p163
Czech Philharmonic p192
Czech time pp7-8
Czech Union of Fine Arts p165

Dalibor Tower (Daliborka) p88,
p153
Dance p211
  Ball Season p32
  Dance Prague p30, p211
Defenestration p44, p56, p63,
pp66-67, p74, p88, p90, p105
Dejvice p107
Devil's Stream p91
Diamant House (Dům Diamant)
p54
Dientzenhofer, Christoph p25,
p33, p39, p93, p108, p154
Dientzenhofer, Kilián Ignaz p25,
p33, p39, p41, p93, p94, p95, p108,
p154, p172, p243
Disabled
  access p259
  transport for p15
Discos p183 *see also* **clubs**
  gay discos pp226-227
Driving p8, p15, pp259-260
  breakdown service p259
  car hire p150
  emergency road service p259
  parking pp259-260
  petrol p260
Dry cleaners & laundries p147
Dubček, Alexander p55, pp75-77,
p87, p103
Dům Diamant *see* **Diamant
House**
Dům U Černé matky boží *see*
House of the Black Madonna
Dům umělců *see* **Rudolfinum**
Dvořák, Antonín p70, p105, p109,
pp171-172, p192, p195, p196
Dvořák Hall p194

Drop-In Festival p199
Easter Monday p29
Festival of Best Amateur and
Professional Puppet Theatre Plays
p31
International Exhibition of Military
Technology p32
Karlovy Vary Beer Olympiad p32
Karlovy Vary International Film
Festival p32, p191
Labour Day p29
Marlboro Rock-in p29
May Rituals p30
Meeting of Foreign Škoda Owners
p32
Miss Czech Republic p32
Mozart in Prague p31
National Harley Davidson rally
pp30-31
New Year's Eve p31
Prague by Season pp29-32
Prague International Book Fair and
Writer's Festival p30
Prague Spring Music Festival p30,
p195
public holidays p29
rock, roots & jazz p199
Spiritual Music Festival p31
St Nicholas' Eve p31
VE Day pp29-30
Witches' night p29
Film pp187-191
courses p229
for children p223
Karlovy Vary Film Festival p32,
p191
First Republic pp70-71
Fishing p204
Flat-hunting pp261-262
estate agents p217
Florenc coach station p11
Flowers p140, p149
Food & drink pp112-115
shopping pp140-141
home delivery p149
Football p202
Forman, Miloš p188
**Františkovy Lázně
(Franzensbad)** p242
Funfair p222
Further education p228

Dvořák Museum p105, p154, p171
Dvořák Society p172

Education p221, p224
English-language courses pp228-
229
English-language film p189
**English-language newspapers
and magazines** p81, pp177-178
English-language schools p224
English-language theatre p211
Embassies p260
French Embassy p41
British Embassy Commerical
Section p214
Emergencies p3, p257
breakdown service p259
emergency phone numbers p3
emergency repairs p257
emergency road service p259
**Emmaus Monastery (klášter Na
Slovanech)** p104, p153
Erlach, Fischer von p34, p87, p97
Estate agents p217, p262
**Estates Theatre (Stavovské
divadlo)** p34, p43, p100, p154, p195,
p210, p211
Etiquette pp114-115, p126, p209
Evropa (Hotel & Café) p17, p23,

p54, p130
Express Airport Bus p10

FAMU (Prague Film Academy)
p187, p190, p229
Fashion pp138-139
size conversion chart p258
Faust House p105
Ferdinand I p34, p65, p89
Ferdinand II p44, pp66-67
Festivals & events
the 1995 Prague Quadrennial p211
AghaRTA Jazz Festival p30
All Souls' Day p31
Anniversary of the Creation of
Czechoslovakia p31
Anniversary of Jan Palach's Death
pp31-32
Anniversary of Kafka's Death p30
Anniversary of the Velvet
Revolution p31
Art Trek p31
ball season p32
Buchlov Festival of Folk Music p32
Burčák arrives p31
classical music p195
Commemoration of parachutists
who assassinated Heydrich p30
Dance Prague p30, p211

Galerie Rudolfinum p163
Galleries pp158-166
commercial galleries pp164-166
exhibition spaces pp163-164
photography galleries p166
Gallery of Modern Art p106,
p155, p158
Gallery Pallas p157
Gambra-Surrealisticka Galerie
p90, p165
Gardens & parks p56, p89, p94,
p105
Letná Park p106, p226
Paradise Garden (Rajská zahrada)
p56
Stromovka Park p106, p205
Wallenstein Garden (Valdštejnská
zahrada) p56, p94
Gay pp225-227
accommodation p227

bar & pubs 226
clubs & discos pp226-227
health & safety p226
helplines p226
information p227
organisations p227
publications p227
saunas p227
Gifts pp141-143
Ginger & Fred building p104, p157
Glass p143-144, p167
Globe Bookstore & Café p106, p128, p132, p137, p175, p230, p231, p262
Goethe Institute p190, p229
Golden Lane (Zlatá ulička) p34, p88
Golden Portal (Zlatá brana) p87
Golden Tiger (U Zlatého tygra) p97, p129, p175
golem p98
Golf p204
Goltz-Kinský Palace p46, p96, p154
The Good Soldier Švejk p174
Gottwald, Klement p48, p52, p74, p75, p96, p109
gristle floss p178

Habsburg Dynasty pp65-68
Hairdressers p148
Háje p48
Hašek, Jaroslav p174
Havel, Václav p27, p28, p32, p34, p43, p55, p74, p76, pp77-78, p79, p83, p86, p94, p101, p104, p107, p119, p174, p180, p207, p263
Health p224, pp260-261
Czech health services p5
gay health & safety p226
medical treatment pp260-261
women's health p232
Help & advice p232, p261
gay helplines p226
gay information/organisations p227
lesbian help & information p234
rape crisis helpline p233
Heydrich, Richard (Reinhard) p30, p51, p72, p73, p87
High Synagogue p99, p170
Historical Museum p89, p167
Historic tram p222
History Museums pp167-170
Hlavní nádraží (Main Station) p10, p11, p54, p236
Holešovice p106
Holidays, national p7, p29
Holub, Miroslav p175
Horse riding p224, p205
Horse racing p203
Hospitals p224
Hotel International p48, p107
Hotels *see* **Accommodation**
House at the Stone Bell p46, p163, p194
House of the Black Madonna (Dům U Černé matky boží) p56, p95, p158
House of the Lords of Kunštát and Poděbrady p97, p152, p169
Hrabal, Bohumil p30, p97, p129,

p175, p188
Hradčany pp33-39, pp86-90
map p88
Hrubá skála p240
Hunger Wall p92
Hus, Jan p41, p44, p63, p70, p96, p101
Husák, Gustav p76
Hussitism pp62-64

Ice hockey p203
Injections p224
Institut Français p130, p190, p229
Insurance p5
car insurance p5, p15, p150
health insurance p5
International Hotel p23

Jan Hus Monument (Pomník Jana Husa) p44, p46
Jazz p201
AghaRTA Jazz Festival p30
clubs p201
Jazz AghaRTA Jazz Centrum p181
Jesenská, Milena p96, p127
Jewish Cemetery p109
Jewish history p60, p68, p71, pp72-74, p83, pp98-100, pp169-170, p174
Jewish Town Hall p98
Jirásek & Aleš Museum p108, p170
Jireš, Jaromil p188
Job-seeking p220, p216
John Lennon Wall p41, p91
Josefov pp49-51, pp98-100, pp169-170
map p96
Joseph II p34, p46, p68, p88, p93, p99, p154, p171, p238
Judith Tower p152

Kádár, Ján p188
Kafka, Franz p30, p34, p73, p96, p100, p104, p109, p125, p127, p174, p263
Anniversary of Kafka's Death p30
Kampa Island p56, p91
Kara, Avigdor p99
Karlov p105, p152, p154
Karlovy Vary (Karlsbad) p195, p204, p242
Beer Olympiad p32
International Film Festival p32, p191
Karlštejn p152, p204, p222, p243
Chapel of the Holy Rood p152, p159, p243
Karlův most *see* **Charles Bridge**
Katedrála sv. Vita *see* **St Vitus's Cathedral**
Kaunitz Palace p93
Kepler, Johannes p43, p68
Kindergartens p221
Kiss Patrol p179, p215
Klášter Na Slovanech *see* **Emmaus Monastery**
Klášter sv. Anežky české *see* **St Agnes's Convent**

Klaus, Václav, p78, p79, p81, p83, p214
Klausen Synagogue (Klauzová synagóga) p49, p99, p170
Klauzová synagóga *see* **Klausen Synagogue**
Klementinum *see* **Clementinum**
Klíma, Ivan p30, p175, p263
Klos, Elmar p188
Knights of Malta p41, p91, p117
Kokořín, p222, p237
Komenský Pedagogical Museum p169
Komerční Banka p7, p102, p215
Koněpruské Jeskyně p245
Koruna Palace p134
Kostel Matky boží před Týnem *see* **Church of Our Lady before Týn**
Kostel sv. Cyrila a Metoděj *see* **Church of Sts Cyril and Methodius**
Kostel sv. Mikuláše *see* **Church of St Nicholas**
Kostel sv. Tomáše *see* **Church of St Thomas**
Kuks p254
Kundera, Milan p68, p101, p174, p188, p263
Kupka, František p155
Kutná Hora p252
Křivoklát, p222, p241

Labour Day p29
Lahůdkys *see* **Bufets & Lahůdkys**
Lamarr, Hedy p187
Language courses p229
Langweil, Antonín p169
Lapidarium p154, p161
Laundry Kings p131, p147, p262
Lawyers p219
Leather goods p139
Legiobank p157
Lesbians p234
Letná p106
Letná Park p106, p226
Libraries pp229-230
Philosophical Hall p34, p170
Theological Hall p34, p171
US Embassy Foreign Commercial Service p215
Lichtenstein Palace p93, p194
Lindt building p157
Lingerie p139
Listings Magazines p177
Literary Museums pp170-171
Lobkowicz Palace p89, p93, p167, p194 *see also* **Historical Museum**
Loew, Rabbi p49, p98
Loreto (Loreta) p33, p90, p154, p167
Loreta *see* **Loreto**
Lucerna p190, p196, p200
Lustig, Arnošt p174

Mácha, Karel Hynek p30, p70
Magazines p177
Magic Lantern Theatre p55, p210
Main Station *see* **Hlavní nádraží**

Maisel Synagogue p170
Malá Amerika p245
Malá Strana pp39-41, pp91-94
map p92
Malá Strana tower p43
Malostranská náměstí p8
Mánes, Josef p159, p169
Maria Theresa, Empress p34,
p68, p90
Mariánská Lázně (Marianbad)
p195, p204, p242
Markets pp134-135
The Martyrdom of St Thomas
p41
Masaryk, Jan p44, pp72-74, p90
Masaryk Tomáš p70, p71, p157
Mathey, Jean-Baptiste p52, p94,
p153, p163
Matthias Gate (Matyášova
brána) p86
McDonald's p52, p224
Mečiar, Vladimir p78, p79, p81
Media p81, pp176-179
Medical treatment pp260-261
Melantrich Building p55
Mělník p169, p236
Mensas p230
Menzel, Jiří p188
Metro pp11-13
etiquette p13
Michna Palace p92
Michna Pavilion *see* Dvořák
Museum
Military Museum p171
Minute House p96
Mirror Maze p56, p222
Mocker, Josef p46, p154
Money pp5-7
American Express p7
banks & bureaux de change pp5-7,
p215
cash machines p5
credit cards & eurocheques p7
Komerční Banka p7, p215
money transfer p7
wire transfers p7
Živnostenská Banka p4, p5, p7,
p215
Monstrance, diamond p34, p167
Mozart, Wolfgang Amadeus p31,
p43, p68, p107, p172, p192, p194
premiere of *Don Giovanni* p43,
p172, p192, p195, p236
Mozart Museum p107, p172, p194
Mozart Theatre *see* Stavovské
divadlo
Mucha, Alphonse p37, p54, p70,
p88, p155
Munich Agreement p71
Municipal House (Obecní dům)
p30, p32, p54, p102, p155
Museums pp167-172
Museum of the City of Prague
p169
Museum of Decorative Arts
p100, p129, p167, p230
Museum of the Resistance &
History of the Army p171
Museum of National Literature
p34, p170
Music
AghaRTA Jazz Festival p30
Buchlov Festival of Folk Music p32
buying CDs p196

Drop-In Festival p199
Marlboro Rock-In p31
Music Museums pp171-172
Mozart in Prague p31
Principal Orchestras pp192-194
Prague Spring Music Festival p30,
p195
shops p145
Spiritual Music Festival p31
Music: Classical & Opera pp192-
196
Music Museums pp171-172
Music: Rock, Roots & Jazz p197

Náprstek Museum p101, p169
Národní divadlo *see* National
Theatre
Národní muzeum *see* National
Museum
Národní památník *see* National
Memorial
National Film Archive/Ponrepo
p191
National Gallery p158
National Library p230
National Marionette Theatre
p210
National Memorial (Národní
památník) p48, p109
National Museum (Národní
muzeum) p51, p102, p169
National Revival p70, p154, p192,
p207
National Technical Museum
p106, p172
National Theatre (Národní
divadlo) p51, p104, p154, p157,
p195, p210, p211
Němcová, Božena p104
Neruda, Jan p93
Newsagents p137
Newspapers pp176-177
New Town Hall (Novoměstská
radnice) p44, p105
New Wave Cinema p188
New World *see* Nový Svět
New Year's Eve p31
Nightlife pp180-186
Nostic Palace p194
Nové Město pp51-52, pp102-105
map p103
Novoměstská radnice *see* New
Town Hall p44
Nový Svět (New World) p21, p90

Obecní dům *see* Municipal
House
Observatory p56
Office for Registering as a
Foreign Resident p256
Office services pp219-220
Old Council Hall p44
Old Jewish Cemetery (Starý
židovský hřbitov) p46, p49, p98,
pp99-100, p170
Old-New Synagogue (Staronová
synagóga) p49, p98, p152
Old Royal Palace (Starý
Královský palác) p34, p88
Old Town Bridge Tower

(Staroměstská mosteká věž)
p97
Old Town Hall (Staroměstská
radnice) p44, p95
Old Town Square
(Staroměstské náměstí) p8, p32,
p44, pp95-97
Olga Havel Foundation p15, p259
Olšanské hřbitovy *see* Olšany
Cemetery
Olšany Cemetery (Olšanské
hřbitovy) p30, p52, p109
one eye open p175, p178
Opening hours p7
Opera p195
Orchestras pp192-194
Orienteering p206
Orloj *see* Astronomical Clock

Painted eggs p29
Palác Adria (Adria Palace) p55
Palác kultury *see* Palace of
Culture
Palace of Culture (Palác
kultury) p108, p216
Palach, Jan p31, p52, p55, p76,
p100, p109
Palacký, František p104
Panálaks p10, p109
Pantheon p51
Paradise Garden (Rajská
zahrada) p56
Parking p259
Parler, Peter p37, p62, p87, p97,
p152, p161, p252
Pavilion Shopping Mall p134
Pekarkova, Eva p175
Pension Unitas pp27-28
Petřín Hill (Petřínské sady) p29,
p30, p44, p56, p76, p222
Eiffel Tower p44, p56, p92
Petřínské sady *see* Petřín Hill
Petrol p260
Pharmacies p232, p261
late-night p186
Philosophical Hall p34, p170
Photocopying p219
Photography
courses p229
developing p148
shops p145
Pinkasova synagóga see Pinkas
Synagogue
Pinkas Synagogue (Pinkasova
synagóga) p51, p99, p170
Platzer, Ignatz p86
Playgrounds p222
Playgroups p224
Plečnik, Josip p56, p86, p89, p109,
p157
Plzeň p246
Poetry readings p175
Police p15
Police Museum p105, p172
Pomník Jana Husa *see* Jan Hus
Monument
Postage Stamp Museum p172
Post p219, p258
main post office p258
Powder Gate (Prašná brána)
p46, p95
Prague Castle (Pražský hrad)

pp34-39, pp86-90, p153
  map p87
Prague Castle Picture Gallery
p158
Prague Five (Pražská pětka)
p121, p207
**Prague Information Service
(PIS)** p7, p29, p158, p196, p209
**Prague International Book Fair
and Writer's Festival** p30
Prague Post p7, p29, p150, p158,
p177, p180, p209, p211, p220, p262
Prague Quadrennial (1995)
p211
**Prague Radio Symphony
Orchestra** p194
Prague Spring p17, p52, pp75-76
Prague Spring Music Festival
p30, p195
Prague Symphony Orchestra
p194
Prague Uprising 1944 p44
Prašná brána *see* **Powder Gate**
Pražské Jezulátko *see* **Il
Bambino di Praga**
Pražský hrad *see* **Prague Castle**
Přemyslid dynasty pp59-60, p108,
p241, p152
  Libuše p52, p59, p108
Prognosis Weekly p7, p29, p150,
p158, p177, p180, p209, p211, p220,
p262
Public transport p10, pp11-13
  tickets p11
  travel passes p11
Pubs pp125-132
Puppets p31, p137, p140, p196,
p207, p209, pp210-211

Racism p84
Radio p179
Radio Free Europe p102, p179
Radio Prague Building p52
Radost p185, p186, p262
Rajská zahrada *see* **Paradise
Garden**
Recruitment agencies p216
Reduta p104, p183, p201
Reid, Benedickt p34, p88, p153
Residency permit p3, p256
Resources p214, p217, p220
Restaurants pp112-124, p224, p230
  the menu p113
  for women p231-232
Restitution p78, p117, p261
Revolution & resistance
  1968 p51, p52, pp75-76
  1989 p55, p78
  World War I p70
  World War II p30, p44, p51, pp72-
  74, p81, p83, p171
Rider's Steps p34
Romanies p84, p109
Rott House p97
Royal Summer Palace *see*
Belvedere
Rubens p41
Rudolf II p34, p39, p49, pp65-66,
p86, p98, p106, p108, p152, p153,
p159
Rudolfinum (Dům umělců) p51,
p100, p194, p195

Ruzyně airport p10

S

**St Agnes's Convent (Klášter sv.
Anežky české)** p46, p100, p152,
p155, p159, p195
St Clement p43
**St George's Basilica (Bazilika
sv. Jiří)** p37, p88, p152
St George's Convent p152, p153,
p154, p159
St John of Nepomuk p87, p98,
p154
St Luitgard p98
St Nicholas's Eve p31, p221
St Saviour p43
**St Vitus's Cathedral (Katedrála
sv. Vita)** p37, p62, pp87-88, p152
St Wenceslas p31, p37, p46,
pp59-60
  murder p37
St Wenceslas' Statue p31, p55
Santini-Aichel, Giovanni p93,
p94, p154, p253
Saloun, Ladislav p44, p54, p96,
p98
Santa Casa p33, p90 *see also*
Loreto
Saunas
  gay p227
Schiele, Egon p250
Schools p224
Schönborn Palace p93
Schulz, Joseph p169
Schwarzenberg Palace p90, p153,
p171
**Science and technology
museums** p172
Seasons 8
Sedlec p253
Services pp146-150
  all purpose rentals p147
  costume hire p146
  dry cleaners & laundries p147
  flower delivery p149
  food & drink p149
  formal dress rental p147
  hair & beauty p148
  photo developing p148
  shoe repairs p148
Sgraffito p89, p90, p96, p101, p153
Shoes p139
  shoe repairs p148
Shopping pp134-145, pp233-234 *see
also* **Area Index** p264
  antiques pp135-137
  bookshops & newsagents p137,
  p231
  children p137
  cosmetics & perfumes p137
  fashion pp138-139
  flowers p140, p149
  food & drink pp140-141
  gifts pp141-143
  glass & china pp143-144
  household p144
  leisure p144-145
  markets pp134-135
  non-stop p186
  old books & prints p145
  one-stop p134
  size conversion chart p258
  transport p150

Video & casette rental p149
Sightseeing pp33-56
Size conversion chart p258
Skating p205
Škoda p32
Slapy Dam p245
Slavonic studies p229
Slavonice p251
Slovakia p59, p71, p79
Slovak independence p78
Smetana, Bedřich p30, p43, p52,
p70, p89, p109, p172, p192, p195,
p196
Smetana Museum p172
Smetana Hall *see* **Obecní dům**
Smíchov p108
Socialist Realism p48, p157, p187
Sokol movement p202
Soroš, George p229
South Gardens *see* **Paradise
Garden**
Španělský sál *see* **Spanish Hall**
Spanish Hall (Španělský sál)
p39, p86
Spas p242
Spiritual Music Festival p31
Sport & Fitness pp202-206
**Sport & Physical Training
Museum** p172
Squash p205
Stalin p23, pp73-74, p75, p106
  Stalin Monument p48
Stalin Monument p48
**Star Lodge (Letohrádek
hvězda)** p108, p153, p170 *see also*
Jirásek & Aleš Museum
Staré Město pp41-46, pp95-101
  map p96
Staré Město tower p43
Staroměstské náměstí *see* **Old
Town Square**
Staroměstská radnice *see* **Old
Town Hall**
Starý Královský palác *see* **Old
Royal Palace**
Starý židovský hřbitov *see* **Old
Jewish Cemetery**
State Jewish Museum p99, p169
State Opera p32, p195, p211
Stationery pp144-145
Stavovské divadlo *see* **Estates
Theatre**
Sternberg Palace p90, p159, p161
Stock exchange p216
**Strahov Monastery (Strahovský
klášter)** p34, p90, p154, p170
Strahov Gallery p153, p161
Strahov Stadium p31, p202, p204,
p206
Strahovský klášter *see* **Strahov
Monastery**
Stromovka Park p106, p205
Students & study pp228-230
  teaching English p220
  student permits p257
Sudeten Germans p71, p74, p83,
p143, p240, p249, p251
Supermarkets p140
Surrealism p157, p165, p178
Survival pp256-262
Švankmajer, Jan p165, p191
Svobodné Slovo p55
Swimming pools p224, p232
  going for a dip p245

Synagogues
High Synagogue (Vysoká
synagóga) p99, p170
Klausen Synagogue (Klauzová
synagóga) p49, p99, p170
Maisel Synagogue (Maiselova
synagóga) p99, 170
Old-New Synagogue (Staronová
synagóga) p49, p98, p152
Pinkas Synagogue (Pinkasova
synagóga) p51, p99, p170
Spanish Synagogue pp99-100

Taxis p10, pp13-15
taxi companies p15
Teige, Karel p157, p163
Telč p250, p251
Telephones pp8-9, pp257-258
international calls p257
international dialling codes p258
operator services p258
phone numbers p257
phone cards p257
public phone booths p257
Television p178
for children p223
Televizní vysílač *see* **TV Tower**
Tennis p206
Terezín (Theresienstadt) p238
concentration camp p73, p99, p169,
p187
Theatre pp207-211
English-language theatre p211
festival p211
major theatres pp209-210
puppet theatre pp210-211
ticket sales p209
Theological Hall p34, p171
Theresienstadt *see* **Terezín**
Thirty Years War p33, p44, p52,
pp67-68, p153
Three Ostriches (U tří pštrosů)
p23, p25
Tickets
buying p195, p199, p209
ticket agencies p196, p209
Tipping p8, p115, p126
Tomín, Lukas p175
Topol, Jachym p175
Tourist information p7,
Prague Information Service (PIS) p7,
p29, p158, p196
Tours p56
Town Hall Clock *see*
Astronomical Clock
Toy Museum p89, p172
Trafika p175, p178
Trade Fair Building p106, p158
Trams p13
night trams p15
Transport pp10-15
air pp10-11
coach p11, p236
car hire p150
car insurance p5
car washes p150
cycling p15, p150
driving p8, p15, p236
for the disabled p15
getting around pp10-15
petrol stations p236
public transport p10, pp11-13

taxis pp13-15
tickets & travel passes p11
train p11, p236
walking p15
Translating agencies p217
Travel agency p230
Travel, discount p259
Travel passes p11
Třebon p246
U tří pštrosů *see* **The Three
Ostriches**
Trnka, Jiří p191
Troja p106
Troja Château (Trojský zámek)
p52, p106, p154, p161
Trojský zámek *see* **Troja
Château**
Trosky p240, p241
TV Tower (Televizní vysílač)
p52, p109, p179

Universities pp228-229
U Fleků p127
U Minuty p153
**US Embassy Foreign
Commerical Service**, p215
U Zlatého tygra *see* **The Golden
Tiger**

Vaccinations p224
Václavské náměstí *see*
Wenceslas Square
VE Day pp29-30
Vegetarians, restaurants for
Buffalo Bill's p116
Elite p117
Fakhredline p115
FX Café p123, p132
U Govindy p121
Kmotra Pizzeria p121
Queenz Grill p124
Red Hot and Blues p119
Il Ritrovo p119
Veletržní palác *see* **Trade Fair
Building**
Veltrussy p154
Velvet Revolution p13, p31, p55,
p77, p79, p100, p104, p157
film p189
Villa Amerika *see* **Dvořák
Museum**
Visas p3
Video & casette rental p149
Views
of church of St Nicholas and castle
p91
from Eiffel Tower p92
over Malá Strana p89, p90
over Prague and the Vltava valley
p54
river p91, p94, p101, p109, p121
over vineyards of Vinohrady
towards Vyšehrad from Karlov
p105
Vinohrady p109
Vladislav Hall p34, p88, p153
Vocabulary p9
Vojanovy Gardens p94
Vyšehrad p52, p59, pp108-109, p169

Vyšehrad Cemetery p30, p54,
p109, p196
Vyšehrad Museum p169
Výstaviště p54, p106, p217
Výstaviště funfair p223

Walking
in Prague p15
the great outdoors p206
**Wallenstein Garden
(Valdštenjnská zahrada)** p56,
p94
Wallenstein, General pp67-68,
p94
Wallenstein Palace p56, p154
Weil, Jiří p174, p263
Wenceslas IV p63
**Wenceslas Square (Václavské
náměstí)** p23, p29, p30, p31, p52,
p76, pp102-104
St Wenceslas' Statue p55
Wilsonova Station *see* **Hlavní
nádraží**
Wine p141
Burčák arrives p31
Wittman Tours p56
Women pp231-234 *see also*
Lesbians
accommodation p231
books, magazines & archives p231
cafés, bars & restaurants p231
harassment p231
health p232
women's groups p234
World War I p70
World War II p44, pp72-74, p81,
p83, p86, p95, p171, p249
Work
recruitment agencies p216
looking for a job p220

Yazzyk p175, p178
Youth Hostels p28

Zbraslav Monastery p158
Želivský, Jan p44
Živnostenská Banka p4, p5, p7,
p102, p215
Žižka, General p48, p64, p109
Žižkov p109
Zlatá ulička *see* **Golden Lane**
Zoo p106, p223

Prague Guide

Advertiser's Index

Please refer to the relevant sections for addresses/telephone numbers

American Express	**IFC**

Essential Information

AT&T	**Page 2**
Galerie Pallas	**Page 6**
Charles Bridge Bookstore & Gallery	**Page 6**

Getting Around

American Rainbow	**Page 12**
Hertz Rentex	**Page 12**
Prague International Ltd	**Page 12**
Czechoslovak Airlines	**Page 14**

Accommodation

Hotel Atrium Praha	**Page 16**
Hotel Panorama	**Page 18**
Hotel Forum Praha	**Page 18**
Rhapsody Piano Bar & Restaurant	**Page 18**
Galerie Peithner & Lichtenfels	**Page 20**
Hotel Hoffmeister	**Page 20**
AVE Travel Agency	**Page 24**
Pension Diezenthofer	**Page 24**
Tour Tip Viviane	**Page 24**
Ivan Číla Travel Agency	**Page 24**
Tom's Apartments & Residences	**Page 26**
Kingscourt Express	**Page 26**

Sightseeing

ČEDOK	**Page 36**
Kodak	**Page 38**
Budget Union rent-a-car Ltd	**Page 40**
Exact Change	**Page 40**
Spa Hotel Bristol	**Page 40**
Orlík Castle	**Page 42**

Prague Today

Kotva Department Store	**Page 80**
Lunettes Optika	**Page 82**
Ivana Follová	**Page 82**
Český Porcelán a.s.	**Page 82**

Eating & Drinking

The Globe	**Page 110**

James Joyce Pub	**Page 110**
Opera Grill	**Page 118**
Restaurant Na Rybárně	**Page 118**
Fakhreldine Lebanese Restaurant	**Page 118**
Budweiser Budvar Brewery	**Page 120**
Karlovarská Becherovka a.s.	**Page 122**

Shops & Services

Pavilon Shopping Mall	**Page 136**
Bat'a	**Page 142**
Sklo Bohemia a.s.	**Page 160**
Bohemia Crystal Skloexport a.s.	**Page 162**

Nightlife

Buffalo Bill's Restaurant	**Page 182**
Casino ČSFR	**Page 182**
Derby Restaurant & Bar	**Page 182**
Radost FX	**Page 182**
Casino VIP	**Page 184**

Music

Top Theatre Tickets	**Page 198**

Theatre

The Black Light Theatre of Prague	**Page 208**
Bohemia Ticket International	**Page 208**
Laterna Magika	**Page 208**

In Focus

Bílá Labut' Department Store	**Page 212**
Mappin & Webb	**Page 212**

Trips Out of Town

Antik Mignon	**Page 244**
Hotel Victoria	**Page 244**
Bohemia Euroexpress	**Page 248**
K-Mart Department Store	**IBC**

TimeOut Maps

Time Out City Guides

The essential guides to the world's most exciting cities

Amsterdam**Berlin**London
MadridNewYork**Paris**
PragueRome

Available from February 1996
Budapest & San Francisco

Prague Metro

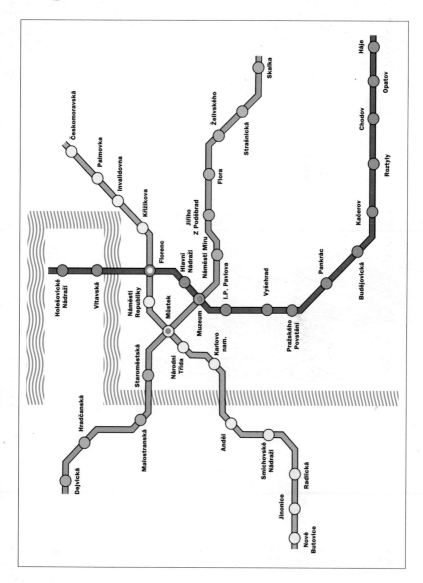

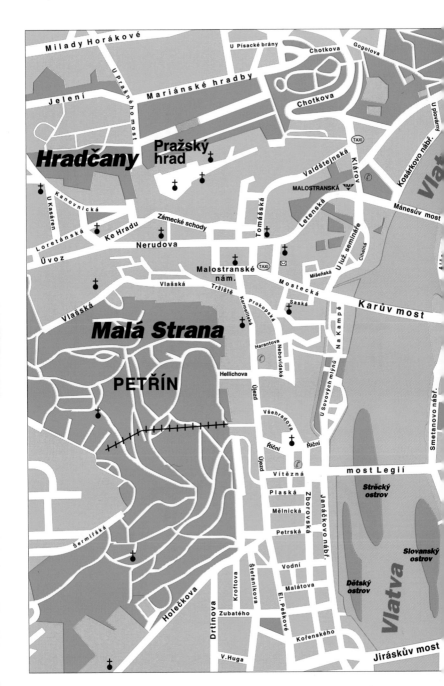

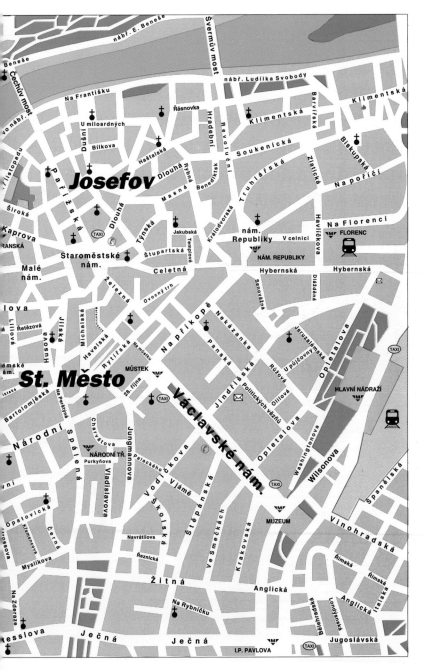

Czech Republic

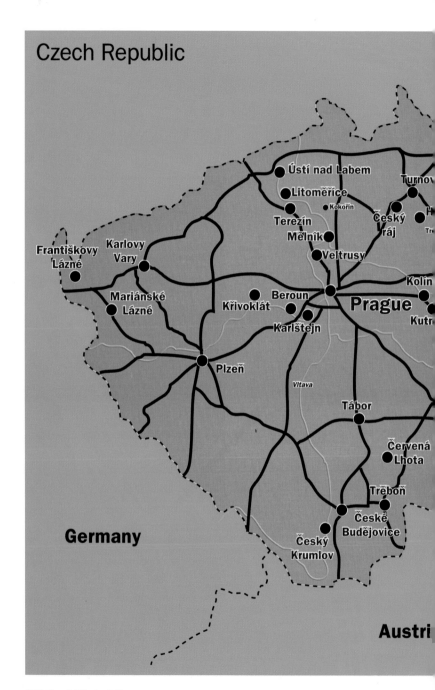

Ústí nad Labem

Litoměřice

Terezín

Kokořín

Český ráj

Turnov

Mělník

Veltrusy

Františkovy Lázně

Karlovy Vary

Kolín

Mariánské Lázné

Křivoklát

Beroun

Prague

Kutr

Karlštejn

Plzeň

Vltava

Tábor

Červená Lhota

Třeboň

Germany

Český Budějovice

Český Krumlov

Austri

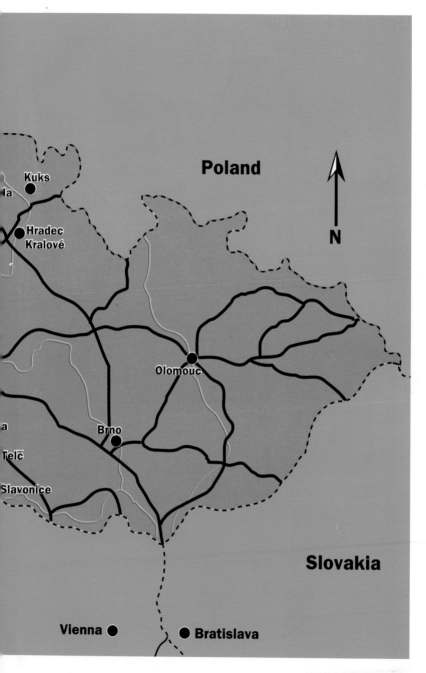

Poland

Kuks

Ha

Hradec
Kralové

Olomouc

a

Brno

Telč

Slavonice

Slovakia

Vienna ●   ● Bratislava

Greater Prague

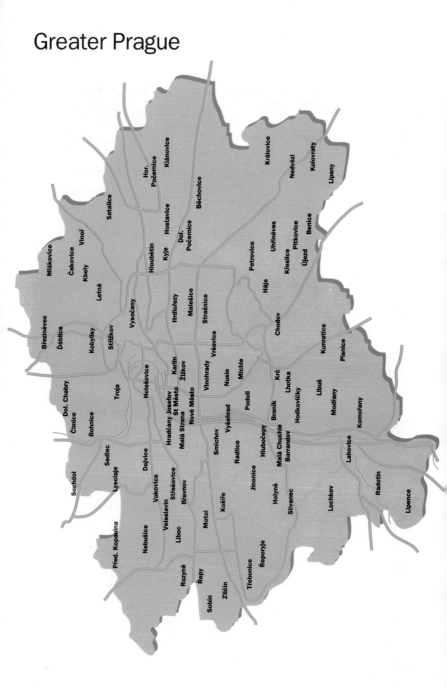